HENRY BROUGHAM AND HIS WORLD:

A BIOGRAPHY

FROM A GREAT ADMIRER OF WILLIAM JEFFERSON CLINTON

who believes that English-speaking people should recognise that the efforts by counsel Charles Ruff, David Kendall, Alan Dershowitz, and others to save his Presidency have followed in the footsteps of Henry Brougham, the great English barrister, who prevented Lord Melville, the Royal Navy's Treasurer, an office held on good behavior, from being removed from office by the House of Lords in 1806 during the last great British impeachment trial after he had been impeached by the Whig Opposition in the House of Commons because of alleged misuse of government funds in the prosecution of the war against Emperor Napoleon.

HENRY BROUGHAM AND HIS WORLD:

A BIOGRAPHY

by

TROWBRIDGE H. FORD, Ph.D.

Published by
Barry Rose, Chichester
West Sussex, England

ISBN 1 872328 40 7

Jacket photograph from the painting of Brougham, 1825
by Sir Thomas Lawrence

Published by
Barry Rose Law Publishers Limited
Chichester, England

Printed by Hobbs the Printers of Southampton

TABLE OF CONTENTS

CASES CITED

INTRODUCTION

A biography of Henry Brougham seems to require no introduction. This nineteenth-century British politician, whose life spanned the gap between the uncertainties of the American Revolution and the stability of Queen Victoria's reign, has long been seen as a worthy object of study. Walter Bagehot, for example, wrote a sketch of Brougham as a reformer even before he died. A decade later, Lord Campbell ended his studies of the Lord Chancellor with a controversial portrayal of Brougham on the Woolsack. Brougham added to debate and analysis by writing a most self-serving, three-volume autobiography during his last days. Over the next half-century, there were all kinds of essays, memoirs, and collections of letters which added lustre to his reputation. J.B. Atlay tried to undo Campbell's mischief by writing a longer, more detached study of Brougham as Lord Chancellor. R.H.M.B. Atkinson and G.A. Jackson published two volumes of his correspondence with people like James Loch, and an explanatory volume as to their meaning and significance under the title of *Brougham and His Early Friends.*

It was not until 1927 that the first professional treatment of one aspect of Brougham's career was published by Professor Arthur Aspinall, *Lord Brougham and the Whig Party.* By this time, historians like Sir William Holdsworth were apparently getting such a firm grip on Brougham's career as a politician and reformer that more traditional works on the former Lord Chancellor, especially those by G.T. Garratt and Mrs Hawes, were seen as fanciful and superficial respectively. It was in this complex, fragmented setting that Professor Chester W. New, the authority on Lord Durham of the Reform Bill, tried to write a definitive two-volume biography of Brougham. In 1961, shortly after New's death, the first volume appeared under the title of *The Life of Henry Brougham to 1830*, published by Clarendon Press. While New's research and notes were passed along to another historian to complete the biography, the second volume has not appeared during the past two decades. Except for Brougham's short tenure of the Woolsack, New, it seems, gave us the essentials of his career. In 1985, Robert Stewart filled this gap in his *Henry Brougham, 1778-1868: His Public Career*, and it seemed we need worry ourselves no more about this most maverick of Whig politicians.

The trouble with Stewart's and New's treatments of Brougham is that they fail to appreciate the consequences of a piecemeal approach to a most important figure, while historiographical tastes were changing. The implicit Whig interpretation of history in many of the early descriptions of Brougham's career is in need of revision. Everything that Brougham did was not necessarily great, and some important figures suffered unfairly from the proportions and significance that early commentators gave his work. For example, Professor Clive was quite right to try to determine the contributions of others, especially Francis Jeffrey, in the creation and running of the *Edinburgh Review*,[1] something that the earlier mentioned work by Atkinson and Jackson neglected. But the great danger of revisions is that the opinions and interpretations of an earlier age will be judged as totally without merit. With most of the serious treatments of Brougham, there is far too much of the unwarranted assumption that Brougham hardly accounted for much. Current historians would do well to remember the caveat by which Aspinall prefaced his work:

> The present volume is not intended as a biography of Brougham, and many events in his life that would have to be dealt with in such a volume have not been touched upon at all. An attempt has been made to sketch his career as a statesman, with special reference to the history of that political party with which he was most closely connected during his

1. See John Clive, *Scotch Reviewers* (Faber, London, 1957).

public life.[2]

In reading Holdsworth's criticism of Brougham's approach to reform, and behaviour as a politician, one should recall his general evaluation of the man as a law reformer: "Of the Whigs the man who did most to forward its progress all through this period was Henry Brougham, who, as we have seen, had been quick to see the opportunities for the reformer which the peace gave."[3] Too many historians, it seems, when considering Brougham, have mistaken the narrow clarifications and qualifications for the sum and substance of what he did and why.

In fairness to current views, it must be said that the most common approach, the so-called Tory historiography, encourages such distortions. This approach is more interested in the governments which actually reformed Britain than in the process, the actions, aims and outcomes, which made it happen. As historians have tried to keep pace with the developing social sciences for professional reasons,[4] they have adopted a more realistic attitude towards their discipline which tends to result in partial, piecemeal considerations of people like Brougham. Based upon the assumption that there is more to politics than meets the eye, and that the coming of democracy results in more pluralistic decision-making for the state, the scope and method of this approach emphasizes private papers and government documents - ie, the activities of a wider circle of participants - for understanding how the current state of affairs developed. Unlike Whig historiography which stressed how superior persons provided for a predetermined future, the current one assumes that many people, many sources of special interests and concerns, made things turn out the way they are. As private papers were

---

2. Arthur Aspinall, *Lord Brougham and the Whig Party* (Archon, Hamden, CT, reprinted 1972), p.vii.
3. Sir William Holdsworth, *A History of English Law* (Methuen. London, 1952, 14 vols.), vol.XIII, pp.194-5.
4. For s superficial explanation of why this happened, see Trowbridge H. Ford, "Towards a Better Relation between History and Political Science," *Government & Opposition*, vol.VII, no.2, pp.207-28.

opened to professional historians, and government ones were made available to places like the Public Record Office, Brougham (like Judge Jeffreys, another inflated figure of Whig historiography) was reduced to his apparent proper dimensions, something that Bagehot predicted might happen when he wrote his sketch of Brougham.[5] As the aristocratic world of the eighteenth century, with its hierarchical, traditional political order, gave way to a more egalitarian, horizontal society, it was assumed figures of traditional description like Brougham would be reduced to their proper role, and the new evidence seemed to corroborate the theory.

Relying upon private evidence and official documents to explain the affairs of a relatively open society, to clarify more precisely exactly who did what, when, and why, may help provide a worse analysis than the original descriptions. While letters and diaries, for example, may shed light on motives and personalities, they never can be more informative and reliable about public affairs than sources like *Hansard's Parliamentary Debates*, the law reports, the periodical press and daily newspapers. A letter in *The Times*, for example, will almost invariably count for more as to what happened, and why, than a private letter that one political figure wrote to another. Public affairs are by definition public matters. Official correspondence about public affairs is rarely comprehensive and self-generated, and hardly constitutes authoritative evidence. To stress private and routine sources is to mistake the peripheral and predictable for persuasive evidence. After all, letters are almost invariably practical efforts, intended to influence individual behaviour and thought through a mixture of evidence, description, and analysis. To put it simply, how often has anyone put his actual thoughts, real ends, and actual behaviour in personal letters?

The task of explaining Brougham's life requires an explanation of the political process and change from the Napoleonic War to the Crimean War in terms of the actions of the people who really made them happen rather than the rationalizations, omissions,

---

5. Walter Bagehot, "Lord Brougham and His Circle," in R.H. Hutton, ed., *Biographical Studies* (Silver Library, London, 1895), p.64.

and deceptions of interested subjects, responsible politicians, and harried officials. In addition, to be fair to Brougham, a broad consideration of his activities as a barrister and Judge must be included, most relevant concerns when an aristocratic society with a Common Law tradition is being democratized and reformed. Brougham was the most important actor of the period, and to use standard approaches in his case is to engage in over-theorizing - to mistake often what Brougham did for the activity of others. In determining what he did, however, the biographer must sift every shred of evidence in a comprehensive, weighted fashion regarding the individuals, institutions, and interests which comprised Henry Brougham and his world. If this is properly done, we shall finally have a satisfactory life of the period's most important politician.

BIBLIOGRAPHY

Every aspect of Victorian political development has aroused controversy, and a full, academic justification of the approach used in this biography would have required a totally different manuscript. Many of the statements in this book represent judgments between interpretations vastly different in scope and method, and all I can do at this point is to indicate where I started, how I progressed, and leave the outcome for the reader to determine. This biography attempts to re-establish the validity of political history and the men who made it without the Whiggish overtones which marred original efforts. While it has taken advantage of what Marxist and Tory historians have had to say about nineteenth century British politics, the biography has been intended to correct mistakes and fill in the gaps of writers working in the tradition of Macaulay and Trevelyan.

For criticism of traditional approaches, see Herbert Butterfield, *The Whig Interpretation of History* (London, 1931) and *Man on his Past* (Boston, 1955). The classic general survey of a social approach to the period is provided by G. Kitson Clark, *The Making of Victorian England* (London, 1962). Its justification appears in his *The Critical Historian* (New York, 1967). For a more detailed treatment of British development in the age of revolution, see Asa Briggs, *The Age of Improvement* (London, 1959). The greatest treatment in the Marxist tradition is E.P. Thompson, *The Making of the English Working Class* (New York, 1964). The best Tory studies of the period are Norman Gash, *Mr Secretary Peel* (Cambridge, Mass., 1961), *Politics in the Age of Peel* (London, 1953) and the biography of Lord Liverpool. The basis of these studies can be found in George Kitson Clark, *Peel and the Conservative Party* (London, 1929). The best traditional explanation of this development is to be found in the many volumes by Sir William Holdsworth, *A History of English Law.*

The best study of Henry Brougham is still Arthur Aspinall, *Lord Brougham and the Whig Party* (Manchester, 1927) both for what it says and ignores about the subject. The best biography is Chester W. New, *The Life of Henry Brougham to 1830* (Clarendon, 1961). While published in the same year as the first volume of Gash's biography of Peel, indicating the rivalry between the two politicians, the fact that it was never completed after New died, even though his papers were given to another historian, says much about nineteenth century British historiography. The belated biography by Robert Stewart, *Henry Brougham: His Public Career, 1778-1868* (London, 1985) is little more than a rehash of New with additional chapters about Brougham as Lord Chancellor, and his peregrinations, as Thomas Greville predicted, as a political Ishmael. Earlier biographies by G.T. Garratt, *Lord Brougham* (London, 1935), and Frances Hawes, *Henry Brougham* (London, 1957) add a few details to the established portrayal of the one-time Chancellor.

With Brougham reduced to a fatally flawed politician, perhaps of congenital origin, few articles, outside of my own, have been devoted to his activities. There is E.G. Collieu, "Lord Brougham and the Conservative Party," in the volume H.R. Trevor-Roper edited, *Essays in British History* (New York, 1964). My articles relating to this volume are: "Brougham as a Barrister: Courtroom Dilemmas of a Notorious Radical," in Albert Kiralfy, Michele Slatter and Roger Virgoe (eds.), *Custom, Courts & Counsel: Selected Papers of the 6th British Legal History Conference* (London, 1985); "English Criminal Law Reform during and after the Napoleonic Wars," *The Anglo-American Law Review*, vol.7 (Sept. 1978): pp.243-70; "English Criminal Law Reform from Peterloo to Peel," *Durham University Journal*, vol.LXXVI (June 1984): pp.205-16; "Henry Brougham and the Reform of Private Bill Legislation," *Parliaments, Estates and Representation*, vol.4 (Dec.1984): pp.169-86; "Lord Brougham among his Critics," *The Legal History Review*, vol.XLIX (Dec.1981): pp.389-410; "Political Coverage in *The Times*: the role of Barnes and Brougham," *Bulletin of the Institute of Historical Research*, vol.LIX (May 1986): pp.91-107; "Peterloo: The

Legal Background," *Durham University Journal*, vol.LXXIV (June 1982): pp.211-25; "The Constitutional Association: Private Prosecutions in Reaction to Peterloo," *The Journal of Legal History*, vol.7 (Dec.1986): pp.293-314; "The Making of the Reform Act: A New Look at the Role of the Whigs," vol.I, pp.201-19, *The Consortium on Revolutionary Europe Proceedings, 1989* (2 vols., Athens, Ga., 1990); and "Towards a Better Relation between History and Political Science," *Government and Opposition*, vol.7 (Spring 1972): pp.207-28. Of course, there are still Walter Bagehot's famous articles on Peel and Brougham which can be found in the volume Norman St John Stevas edited, *Walter Bagehot* (Bloomington, 1959). There is also A.W. Wallace's address, "Life and Character of Lord Brougham," which was presented before the Virginia State Bar Association (Richmond, Virg., 1911).

Biographies of Brougham's contemporaries are understandably even less helpful in throwing light on his career, and only a few are of any help. There is the Sidmouth biography by Philip Ziegler: *Addington* (London, 1965). Lord David Cecil has some interesting things to say about Lord Brougham in his biography, *Melbourne* (London, 1955). Then Kenneth Bourne, in characteristic fashion, has followed his case-study of one of Brougham's peccadilloes, *The Blackmailing of the Chancellor* (London, 1975), with the first volume of a more acceptable subject, *Palmerston: The Early Years, 1784-1841* (London, 1982). There is no new biography of the former Lord Chief Justice, only Sir Joseph Arnould, *Memoirs of Thomas, First Lord Denman* (3 vols., London, 1873). Lord Campbell's studies of the Lord Chancellors and Lord Chief Justices can also be helpful. In keeping with the institutional concerns of Tory historiography, there has been a new biography of another Whig Prime Minister, John Prest's *Lord John Russell* (Columbia, S.C., 1972), which says some interesting things about Brougham's influence, pro and con, upon a one-time colleague. Finally, there is Chester New's earlier biography, the research of which led him to see the merits of Brougham, *Lord Durham* (Oxford, 1926).

There are many published works which relate to Brougham's family, upbringing, education and early thoughts. As with all aspects of his life, one should first consult his autobiography, *The Life and Times of Henry Brougham* (3 vols., New York, 1871). For some details about Penrith, Brougham and Brougham Hall, see Joseph Nicolson and Richard Burn, *The History and Antiquities of the Counties of Westmorland and Cumberland* (2 vols., London, 1772). There is a good survey of the teaching of Brougham's great uncle in the volume edited by Alfred Howard, *The Beauties of Robertson* (London, 1834). For what Edinburgh was like when Brougham was a student and legal examiner during the 1790s, see D.B. Horn, *A Short History of the University of Edinburgh, 1556-1889* (Edinburgh, 1967). Lord Cockburn's works give some additional insights into Brougham's life. For what Brougham and his friends were thinking and doing at the time, see the volumes of correspondence edited by R.H.M.B. Atkinson and G.A. Jackson, *Brougham and His Early Friends* (3 vols., London, 1908). Regarding the history of Edinburgh's most important club, see the *History of the Speculative Society from its Institution in 1764* (Edinburgh, 1845) and *The History of the Speculative Society, 1764-1904* (Edinburgh, 1905). For a partial accounting of Brougham's role in the creation and operation of the *Edinburgh Review*, consult John Clive, *Scotch Reviewers: The Edinburgh Review, 1802-1815* (London, 1957). For the basis of its omissions, see the section on the authorship of the *Review's* articles in *The Wellesley Index*.

In recreating Brougham's life in London, there are a few reliable sources. For official details about his legal career, see *The Records of the Honourable Society of Lincoln's Inn* (5 vols., London, 1902). For Brougham's legal arguments in various courts, see the following volumes: *The English Reports*, vols.III, IV and V: House of Lords (London, 1901); *The English Reports*, vol.XII: The Privy Council (London, 1901); P. Dow, *Reports of Cases upon Appeals and Writs of Error in the House of Lords* (2 vols., London, 1814); John Campbell, *Reports of Cases Determined at Nisi Prius* (4 vols., London, 1811); and the annual volumes of the *Law Journal*, 1823-1828. For more details about cases and more mundane matters, consult the *Annual Register* and the volumes of the *Gentleman's Magazine*.

There are reports of Brougham's speeches in the Commons in *Cobbett's Parliamentary Debates* and *Hansard's Parliamentary*

Debates. Dolby's Political Register is also helpful. Then, of course, there are the Commons' official reports and records relating to him. For especially important efforts in this regard, see Brougham's own *Speeches of Henry Brougham* (4 vols., Edinburgh, 1838), and his *Letters and Speeches on Various Subjects* (2 vols., Phila. 1840). Of the pamphlets that he is known to have written, a practice which would become significant in the latter half of his life, note should be taken of "The Country without a Government ..." (London, 1830), and "The Result of the General Election" (London, 1830).

Brougham's most important writings during the first half of his life appeared in the *Edinburgh Review* and *The Times*. Again, this biography claims that Brougham wrote more for them, especially Barnes's newspaper, than he is given credit for. In reading Derek Hudson, *Thomas Barnes of The Times* (Cambridge, 1943); *The History of The Times: 'The Thunderer' in the Making, 1785-1841* (London, 1935); and Stephen Koss, *The Rise and Fall of the Political Press in Britain: the Nineteenth Century* (London, 1981), one might conclude that Brougham's working for *The Times* is most unlikely; yet, a reading of H.R. Fox Bourne's earlier volumes, *English Newspapers: Chapters in the History of Journalism* (2 vols., London, 1887) and *The Times* itself seems to indicate otherwise. The coverage and editorial stance of the newspaper from 1811 until after passage of the Reform Bills, except for two short periods, represented such a match between the interests of Barnes and Brougham that they just had to be working together. Otherwise, Daniel Maclise's sketch of Brougham, in wig and gown, dashing off a column for *The Times* just before deadline, simply makes no sense. Also, see, of course, A. Aspinall, *Politics and the Press* (London, 1949).

While it is conventional for biographers to cite first the private papers of the person in question when making up the bibliography, it is often a myth as to the conduct of the research, and certainly would be so in this case. When the Brougham Papers at University College Library, London were finally consulted, they turned out to be a great disappointment. None of the expected letters to people like Barnes and Denman have survived. Until Brougham became Chancellor and employed the services of Denis Le Marchant, he preserved few of the letters he wrote and received, and most of them have already been noted, except the ones from Jeremy Bentham. Brougham's Papers only become important when he was raised to the Woolsack, as will be seen in the second volume of this biography.

CHAPTER ONE

THE MAKING OF A MODERN COLUMBUS

Henry Peter Brougham was born in Edinburgh on September 19, 1778, the first born of the marriage between Henry Brougham Sr to Miss Eleanor Syme, a niece of one of Scotland's most famous historians, Professor William Robertson. The Broughams were an old gentry family from Westmorland who could trace their hold upon Brougham Hall, the family manor, back to the days of Henry II. Odard de Burgham had been saved from his treason in surrendering Appleby Castle to the King of Scotland during Henry's troubled reign by being permitted to retain the property on which the family seat was situated, Brougham Castle. Brougham Hall was constructed in the style of the times, and it was only during the reign of Queen Elizabeth that the hall and the family adopted the modern spelling, pronounced "Broom". It was about this time that the Broughams started embellishing their rather modest background, adopting a coat of arms of "... Gules, a chevron between three luces argent."[1] It was in the same spirit that the latest Brougham, when he was struggling during his last years to give his family most exalted origins, claimed "... descent from the ancient and noble house of Vaux in Normandy ..."[2]

The Broughams were much like the land they so long inhabited: tough, uncultivated creatures who were often prone

---

1. Joseph Nicolson and Richard Burn, *The History and Antiquities of the Counties of Westmorland and Cumberland* (Strachan, London, 1777, 2 vols.), vol.1, p.397.
2. Arthus Aspinall, *Lord Brougham and the Whig Party* (Archon, Hamden, CT, 1972, reprinted), p.1.

to fits of excess. Westmorland has always been the most inaccessible of England's counties, fit, until recently, for little more than sheep and enterprising holiday-makers. Its barren, mountainous, uncultivated moorland, noted originally for its helm-wind from the peaks to the north-east, has had such a pervasive effect upon its inhabitants that it has even perverted the etymology of the county's name. Westmorland, it seems, was originally named after part of the domain of Marius, King of the Britons, but the people concluded that it came from the character of the land. The helms were clouds which appeared over the tops of the nearby mountains. "This helm is not dispersed or blown away by the wind," explained the county's historians, "but continues in its station; although a violent roaring hurricane comes tumbling down the mountain, ready to tear up all before it."[3]

Brougham Hall was not the only building of note within the parish which went along Westmorland's border with Cumberland. This rough territory had not only been traversed by rivers like the Eamont, Lowther, and Eden but also by marauding Romans, Saxons, and Scots. Brougham Hall, like most manors in the county, had been built originally in the style of a small fortress to protect its inhabitants from the invaders to the north. It was only in the eighteenth century that Brougham Hall was made into a respectable country house. Nearby Brougham Castle, from which the Brougham family had long been estranged, was a Norman building, but only its ruins remained. In typical fashion, family tradition claimed that there was once a secret passage between the Hall and the Castle which was barricaded during some restoration.[4] Evidence of either a genealogical or physical kind connecting the Broughams to ancient aristocrats is, however, hard to come by. Actually, the parish's best architectural remains are ecclesiastical, as Brougham's account of the merry mourners at his grandfather's funeral relates. The grandfather, Samuel Brougham, had travelled

3. *Op. cit.*, pp.8-9.
4. *Op. cit.*, p.1.

to London to become an attorney and had been so successful that he became attorney to the Duke of Norfolk. At his funeral, his mourners, it seems, had become so tipsy drinking the health of people like the family physician that the body had slipped off the hearse on the way to the burial into the River Eamont, smashing to pieces the outer coffin. The cortege had been on route to Ninekirks, the common name for the parish church of St Ninian.[5] The church could trace its origins back to Saxon times, and had been rebuilt by Lady Anne Clifford of the Castle in 1660 to mark the Stuart restoration to the throne. Westmorland identified with Scottish Protestantism. Near to St Ninian's was the chapel of St Wilfred de Burgham, known for its interesting screen and stalls.[6]

The best things about Westmorland, as far as the Broughams like Samuel were concerned, were the eight turnpike roads that served the county. They led to such potentially rewarding places as Edinburgh, Durham, and the metropolis in London. While the Broughams, like most people from the Border counties, were quick to defend their rights and privileges, they were not slow to recognize the advantages of other jurisdictions. If the family's recent fortunes represented an area trend, Professor Edward Hughes could have expanded his generalizations to include Westmorland: "Certainly in Northumberland and Durham that period saw liquidation, in varying degree, of scores of ancient families, lesser gentry and freeholders, and the rise out of the ashes of vast new agglomerations of landed estates."[7] The Broughams could actually only trace their hold on Brougham Hall back to Samuel's uncle John, a Cumberland gentleman, who bought it from James Bird. In two generations, the Broughams had undergone a rapid reduction, and could hardly be confident of the role that they were playing in this phoenix-like process.

---

5. Henry Brougham, *The Life and Times of Henry Lord Brougham* (Harper, New York, 1871, 3 vols.), vol.1, pp.18-19.
6. *Treasures of Britain* (Automobile Ass., London, 1972, 2nd edn.), p.104.
7. Edward Hughes, "The Professions in the Eighteenth Century," in Daniel A. Baugh, ed., *Aristocratic Government and Society in Eighteenth Century England* (Watts, N.Y., 1975), p.187.

Samuel Brougham had been one of many children, and took the lead for the City of London in its disputes with the Commons over John Wilkes. But Samuel was only survived by his son Henry. Much had happened in Westmorland of a negative nature since its magistrates had tried to reassure Richard Cromwell thus: "Our lot is fallen very far remote from the great scene of public affairs which makes us lagg in ye reare, yet we trust to strive to an equality with ye forwardest in our affections and faithfulness ... nor, shall we willingly give place to any in this."[8] Henry's father had reached maturity before there was any real evidence of improvement, especially in the county's political stability. The Broughams, like Samuel's wife, could not bring themselves to consider the Stuarts pretenders, and the "rising of '45" had led people with similar sentiments to the scaffold at Carlisle. "Until the last quarter of the eighteenth century," Hughes wrote, "the region remained remote and comparatively little known. The discovery of the Lakes - there were regattas on Derwentwater in Lord North's time - altered all that."[9]

The Broughams, however, were not persuaded by this and, consequently, Henry Sr., also prepared for a career in London. Like his brother Charles, he attended Eton College, perhaps with the intention of becoming a barrister, where he had the Duke of Buccleuch fag for him. North Countrymen were known for their legal eminence, although the law was an expensive career to get started in. Lord Hardwicke, the Lord Chancellor, had read law in the chambers of Serjeant Salkeld, a famous Northumbrian instructor. Other North Country youths had been attracted to the chambers of Charles Saunderson. The models for such training had been Lord Chancellor Talbot, the son of a Bishop of Durham, and John Ord, a Newcastle attorney who became the Chief Baron of the Scottish Exchequer in 1755. This trend would culminate in the judicial attainment of the Scott brothers, Lords Eldon and Stowell, sons of a Newcastle coal factor. Hughes explained the

---

8. Quoted from Edward Hughes, *North Country Life* (Oxford Univ. Press, London, 1965), p.1.
9. *Ibid.*, p.26.

process thus:

> This northern galaxy, I submit, was no legal comet. Thanks to coal and its attendant problems - thanks also, possibly, to the survival of Palatinate jurisdiction at Durham - the region had long presented unique opportunities to lawyers.[10]

In fact, opposition to the region in legal advancement had led Lord Lovat to express concern over the future Lord Mansfield's chances in the Common Law courts: "I wish that his being born in the North may not hinder him from preferment that his merit and learning deserve."[11] Brougham's father was dissuaded from joining the Bar for far more immediate reasons. He apparently did not have the quick, lively, and distinguishing mind required for the law. Anyway, he developed a taste for literature.[12] After the usual grand tour of Europe and assorted travels, he settled down at Brougham Hall to enjoy the life of the country landowner. As necessity and convenience dictated, he soon fell in love with his cousin, the rich Mary Whelpdale. "Her father's estate, to which she was sole heiress, was close to Brougham, so that the alliance was all that could be wished."[13] Unfortunately, the future Mrs Brougham died on the eve of her wedding, spoiling Henry's plans for a renewed gentry life in Westmorland. When he could no longer afford trips to the Continent to try to attenuate his sorrow and rage over this misfortune, he decided to follow Lord Buchan's advice, and settle in Edinburgh. Buchan, David Stuart Erskine, was the eldest brother of Thomas Erskine, the future Lord Chancellor, who had just set his life on an admirable course by a chance meeting with Captain Baillie at a friend's table in London. Baillie, the suspended Lieutenant-Governor of Greenwich Hospital, hired the impoverished Erskine as his counsel in the libel action that Lord

---

10. Hughes, *op. cit.*, p.189.
11. *Ibid.* Quoted from Yorke's *Life of Hardwicke*, p.53.
12. G.T. Garratt, *Lord Brougham* (Macmillan, London, 1935), p.4.
13. Brougham, *op. cit.*, vol.1, p.16.

Sandwich, First Lord of the Admiralty, had brought against him.[14] Erskine's eldest brother, noted for his egotism, promised Henry Brougham similar opportunities in Edinburgh.

Lord Buchan did not disappoint Brougham. Through him, he met William Robertson, the Principal of Edinburgh University. Robertson was a living legend who dominated the life of one of Europe's leading cities. Thanks to the abolition of the regent system in 1708, the University experienced unprecedented improvement during the eighteenth century. Robertson, an accomplished historian, had been elected Principal in 1762. "The 30 years during which William Robertson presided over the University perhaps represent the highest point in its history."[15] Robertson had written a *History of Scotland*, and studies of Columbus, Mary Queen of Scots, and Charles V. "The popularity of his published works," D.B. Horn wrote, "spread the fame of the University beyond Europe into America and Asia."[16] Robertson's reputation had been increased by what was known about him as a conscientious Christian and a university administrator. "During his principalship, Robertson continued to preach on Sundays in one of the Edinburgh churches and as a historian he sometimes attributed the course of events to divine providence."[17] As Principal, Robertson totally dominated town and gown affairs. While the Town Council deferred to him on all questions relating to the University, "his colleagues of the Senatus followed his lead so implicitly that no divisions are recorded at any of the meetings over which he presided as principal."[18] Edward Topham wrote in 1776, in his *Letters from Edinburgh*, that Robertson was institutionalizing through its professors "... an example of civility and good manners as of morality and virtue ... Though all of them are men of letters, and

---

14. Sir William Holdsworth, *A History of English Law* (Methuen, London, 1952, 14 vols.), vol.XIII, pp.581-4.
15. D.B. Horn, *A Short History of the University of Edinburgh, 1556-1889* (Univ. of Edin. Press, Edin., 1967), p.76.
16. *Ibid.*, p.76.
17. *Ibid.*, p.78.
18. *Ibid.*, p.76.

skilled in the sciences they profess, they are not less acquainted with the world, and with polite behaviour, than with polite literature."[19]

At the Principal's house, Henry Brougham met Robertson's widowed sister, Mrs Syme, and her daughter Eleanor. She was a beautiful and accomplished woman in the prime of life. He soon arranged to rent a flat at Mrs Syme's house, looking out on Candlemaker Row and to marry the daughter. She had only agreed on the understanding that they would live permanently in Edinburgh. The marriage was solemnized by Robertson himself. Henry Jr, in typical fashion that detracted from masculine influences in his life for apparent feminine ones, said this about Robertson's sister:

> Remarkable for beauty, but far more for a masculine intellect and clear understanding, she instilled into me from my cradle the strongest desire for information, and the first principles of that persevering energy in the pursuit of every kind of knowledge which, more than any natural talents I may possess, has enabled me to stick to, and to accomplish, how far successfully it is not for me to say, every task I ever undertook.[20]

As he could not do justice to the direction that Samuel Brougham had given his life, preferring to contend that his paternal grandmother Mary had given him insight as to how to deal with political turmoil,[21] Brougham could not acknowledge just what the Principal had meant to his life. Male company came easily to the young Brougham, but not the recognition of its contributions, influences, and debts.

Brougham illustrated these tendencies when he recounted his educational development. He would have us believe that Mrs Syme, wife of the minister for Alloa, gave him the direction and

---

19. Quoted from *ibid.*, p.66.
20. Brougham, *op. cit.*, vol.1, p.20.
21. *Ibid.*, pp.15-19.

insight at the house where he was born on St Andrew's Square that stood him in such good stead at Mr Stalker's Academy and Luke Fraser's class at the Edinburgh High School. According to Brougham, it was because of her sustained effort that he had the obstinacy and temerity to correct Mr Fraser during a Latin class when he had been wrong, for which he received the customary cruel punishment. Henry Cockburn, a schoolmate, could not bring himself to moderate the terror of Fraser's classes, during which he was daily flogged, when he wrote his memoirs years later. Once this wrong had been recognized by Fraser himself, Brougham became the idol of his classmates. Actually, it was during Robertson's visits to St Andrew's Square and Brougham Hall that young Henry came to respect everything that he had said and done. Brougham was really thinking about his grand-uncle's role in his life when he attributed this to Dr Alexander Adam, the High School's rector:

> His great learning, his able and useful works, and his irreproachable character, as well as his untiring diligence and exemplary patience in the discharge of his duties, commanded the respect of all, and endeared him to those who had the inestimable benefit of his instruction. He had the faculty of exciting both an ardent love of the subjects he taught and a spirit of inquiry into all that related to them.[22]

This was a typical distortion by Brougham, intended to deceive others as to who he really was, and how he became that way. Henry was constantly trying to mystify people he had no respect for. While he wanted to play a joke on his deceased aristocratic friends about his family's "noble" origins, he was reluctant to take credit for its radicalism. The duplicity of this attribution was graphically illustrated when Brougham hardly made further mention of Dr Adam's role, except as a substitute for the

---

22. *Ibid.*, p.21.

Principal's.[23]

Brougham compounded the omission by discussing his own kinsman only as a grammarian and preacher. Yet from Robertson's history books, Brougham learned, especially when he was confined to bed with the fever during 1789, to appreciate the role of climate, character, and condition in human existence. "In every part of the earth where man exists," Robertson wrote, "the power of climate operates, with decisive influence, upon his condition and character."[24] Rude nations towards the earth's poles felt the adverse effects of climate more, and took steps to mitigate its consequences. "But the improvident savage is affected by every circumstance peculiar to his situation. He takes no precaution either to mitigate it or to improve it."[25] Institutions like clans and the law tended to make life easier in harsher climes. In Scotland, for example, the clans provided an improvement over the feudal system, Robertson said, by making chiefs both leaders and friends. In general, the feudal system suffered from a lack of balance in its institutions. Princes and ministers had long used standing armies to subvert feudal society. Civil law, especially that based upon Roman law, was the greatest institution of civilized society. "Men, as soon as they were acquainted with fixed and general laws, perceived the advantage of them," Robertson wrote, "and became impatient to ascertain the principles and forms by which Judges should regulate their decisions."[26] In discussing the civilizing role of institutions, the Scottish historian excepted everything Roman Catholic, eg, clergy, cardinals, and canon law.

In explaining Scotland's condition, Robertson blamed the character of her leaders. Outside of Knox, she had no one to compare with Charles V or Queen Elizabeth. James IV threw

---

23. *N.B.* what Brougham said about the "beauties" of Adam: "But in no particular was his instruction more valuable than in opening the mind to the contemplation of characters, ancient and modern, and drawing from them the conclusions in favour of political virtue of every kind." (*Ibid.*, p.40).
24. Alfred Howard, ed., *The Beauties of Robertson* (T. Davison, London, 1834), p.58.
25. *Ibid.*, p.59.
26. *Ibid.*, p.35.

away everything he sought over the rash battle at Flodden. James V suffered the fate of all infant princes - "... his education had been neglected."[27] About the Regent, the Earl of Arran, Robertson said that he was "... the perpetual slave of his own fears, and, by consequence, the perpetual tool of those who found their advantage in practising upon them."[28] Robertson saved his harshest characterizations for the Lord Chancellor, Lord Arran:

> ... a man educated as a soldier of fortune, ignorant of the law, and a contemner of justice, appointed to preside in parliament, in the privy council, in the court of session, and intrusted with the supreme disposal of the property of his fellow-subjects.[29]

Political motives made Cardinal Beaton support superstition, and to oppose reform. With such leadership, assassination became common practice, almost condoned by public sentiment. "The vices of another age astonish and shock us; the vices of our own become familiar, and excite little horror,"[30] Robertson wrote with much effect for the young Brougham.Robertson's discussions of international organization and affairs had an even greater impact on Henry's political ideas. About the origin of the main concept of world affairs Robertson wrote: "The maxim of preserving a balance of power is founded so much upon obvious reasoning, and the situation of Europe rendered it so necessary, that it soon became a matter of chief attention of all wise politicians."[31] As individuals could benefit by travelling to other regions and countries to see how people lived, so could representatives of higher levels of organization, like confederations and states. "It was not possible for the Crusaders to travel through so many countries, and to behold their various customs and institutions, without acquiring information and improvement."[32] In public

---

27. *Ibid.*, p.104.
28. *Ibid.*, p.21.
29. *Ibid.*, p.22.
30. *Ibid.*, p.28.
31. *Ibid.*, p.29.
32. *Ibid.*, p.61.

affairs, the ideal kind of leader was Charles V, who, unlike Henry VIII and Francis I, "... had the appearance of a consistent system, in which all the parts were arranged."[33] It was while Robertson was discussing Charles's disastrous expedition against Algiers that he elaborated upon what the true leader needed:

> During this dreadful series of calamities, the emperor discovered great qualities, many of which a long-continued flow of prosperity had scarcely afforded him an opportunity of displaying. He appeared conspicuous for firmness, and constancy of spirit, for magnanimity, for firmness, humanity, and compassion. He endured as great hardships as the meanest soldier; he exposed his own person whenever danger threatened; he encouraged the desponding, visited the sick and wounded; and animated all by his words and example.[34]

In appreciating Charles's role, Robertson relied upon the experience of other leaders. Bayard, for example, "... was always called, in times of real danger, to the post of greatest difficulty and importance."[35] Cortes, on the other hand, was so ill-suited for a career at law, wasting his years at Salamanca by a life of sport, martial arts, and dissipation, "... that his father was glad to comply with his inclination, and send him abroad as an adventurer in arms."[36] Erasmus, Robertson wrote for Henry's benefit, was a failure:

> The natural timidity of his temper; his want of that strength of mind which alone can prompt a man to assume the character of a reformer; his excessive deference for persons in high stations; his dread of losing pensions and other emoluments which their liberality had conferred upon him; his extreme love of peace, and hopes of reforming abuses gradually, and by gentle methods; all concurred in

---

33. *Ibid.*, p.41.
34. *Ibid.*, p.6.
35. *Ibid.*, pp.29-30.
36. *Ibid.*, p.73.

> determining him not only to repress and to moderate the zeal with which he had once been animated against the errors of the church, but to assume the character of a mediator between Luther and his opponents.[37]

By way of apology, he added this about the insurrection of the Anabaptists: "When the human mind is roused by grand objects, and agitated by strong passions, its operations acquire such force, that they are apt to become irregular and extravagant."[38]

The culmination of Robertson's lectures on political leadership was his discussion of the character of Columbus. He was the professional who had so combined human information and abilities as to become a true leader of men:

> He possessed a thorough knowledge of mankind, an insinuating address, a patient perseverance in executing any plan, the perfect government of his own passions, and the talent of acquiring an ascendant over those of other men.[39]

About Columbus's approach, Robertson wrote: "... he attended to the motion of the tides and currents, watched the flights of birds, the appearance of fishes, of seaweeds, and of everything that floated on the waves, and entered every occurrence, with a minute exactness, in a journal which he kept."[40] The explorer's greatest challenge was managing the crew, a typical body of men, prone to alarm, and quick, but irrational, action. For instance, Columbus, when the compass failed, "... invented a reason for this appearance, which, though it did not satisfy himself, seemed so plausible to them, that it dispelled their fears, or silenced their murmurs."[41] He, after hiding the real progress of the voyage, converted the sighting of seaweed into the belief that land was near at hand. When despair returned, and the men started

---

37. *Ibid.*, p.102.
38. *Ibid.*, p.7.
39. *Ibid.*, p.63.
40. *Ibid.*
41. *Ibid.*, p.64.

organizing his overthrow, Columbus feigned to be unaware of what was going on. Despite his own concern and anxiety, Columbus acted as if everything was in order, like a satisfied man confident of success. Robertson explained:

> Sometimes he employed all the arts of insinuation, to soothe his men. Sometimes he endeavoured to work upon their ambition or avarice, by magnificent descriptions of fame and wealth which they were about to acquire. On other occasions, he assumed a tone of authority, and threatened them with vengeance from their sovereign, if, by their dastardly behaviour, they should defeat this noble effort to promote the glory of God, and to exalt the Spanish name above that of every other nation.[42]

Finally, Columbus had to resort to bold prediction about sighting land to stave off a mutiny, an act of faith which paid off so handsomely not only for himself but also for the nations of Europe. As for the natives, Robertson said that they, "... simple and undiscerning, had no foresight of the calamities and desolation which were approaching their country."[43]

Young Brougham, in reading Robertson's thoughts about politics, international affairs, and political leadership, found, consciously or unconsciously, the comprehensive role model for success not only in school but also in real life. When Brougham returned to the High School after his long illness, he moved to the head of his class and the school and was named *dux*. Francis Horner, his lifelong friend, and future associate at the *Edinburgh Review*, gained the same distinction the following year. Brougham's other classmates included Cockburn, the biographer Lord Jeffrey, the Lord Advocate, and John Murray, a future Lord Advocate. John Campbell, in his life of the Lord Chancellor, has recounted what a distant relative of Brougham's said about the budding High School leader:

---

42. *Ibid.*, p.67.
43. *Ibid.*, p.72.

> The first time I was introduced to him he was about 12 years old and was on one of the bridges of Edinburgh, with a huge quarto under his arm which proved to be a work of Laplace in the original. I wondered what sort of lad this must be who not only studied mathematics for pleasure, but through the reading of a foreign tongue.[44]

Robertson's influence, his ability to lecture, was also seen in the young Brougham's organizing the Juvenile Literary Society. In this debating society, with which Horner was also associated, Brougham was able to develop a style and manner of speaking about the wisdom of the modern age which was to stand him in such good stead at the Speculative Society. At the former's sessions, they debated such questions as the existence of innate ideas, the value of empires, the scope of trial by jury, the value of the East India Company, and Aristotle's contribution to modern science.[45] Brougham left Edinburgh in August 1791 for Brougham Hall upon graduating from the High School.

While Henry was prepared to go to the University (the Principal had entered it when he was only 12) Brougham's father was afraid apparently that the bubbling adventurer would get into trouble. Edinburgh was being racked by controversy surrounding the French Revolution, and the completion of Robertson's New College. The cornerstone of the long-needed new buildings had been laid in November 1789 with so much hope and anticipation that even the High School had been given the day off to attend the festivities. Events in France seemed to justify the predictions that Robertson had made the previous year upon the centenary of the Glorious Revolution. "It was of singular and striking interest," Brougham wrote in his memoirs, "from the extreme earnestness, the youthful fervour, with which it was delivered ... I well remember his referring to the events then passing on the Continent as the forerunners of far greater

---

44. Quotes from Chester New, *Henry Brougham to 1830* (Clarendon Press, Oxford, 1961), p.5.
45. *Ibid.*, pp.4-5.

ones which he saw casting their shadows before."[46]

When events took an unexpected ugly turn, leaving not only France but the rest of the Continent in turmoil, Brougham's father had to be worried about what Robertson's enemies might do with his leading protg. Henry Dundas, the Crown's manager of Scottish affairs, used the contentious debate and constant agitation about established institutions and ways to postpone the completion of the New College during the Principal's lifetime. About Dundas's role, New has written that he "... ruled the country with a smiling face and an iron hand, and delivered it bound and gagged to successive governments at every mock election."[47] Prospects for the young Henry, whose debating powers were so great that Robertson himself had once mistaken them for classroom achievement,[48] were far more ominous. In 1792, while the French Revolution was intensifying with the overthrow of the monarchy, the adolescent Brougham was organizing and leading a debating society. At the University, Henry was bound to take the lead in the life of its student clubs, as Robertson had done, and recommended to others. "It would be difficult," Horn wrote, "to overestimate the importance of these students societies in the life of the eighteenth century university."[49] Dundas might see to it, with the help of the conservative Professor David Hume, that Henry paid a high price for his ultra-liberal views and actions. Consequently, his father arranged for a cooling-off period at Brougham to try to re-direct his character, interests, and inclinations. Even Francis Jeffrey, an earlier, radical graduate of the High School, sought the safe confines of Oxford while reaction was sweeping Edinburgh.

In Westmorland, Henry developed, thanks to activities by his tutor, Mr Mitchell, and his father, the interest in Greek and Latin that he himself attributed to Dr Adam's influence. Actually, interest in Greek and mathematics had been prescribed at the High School. When Adam had been reduced by the Dundases

---

46. Brougham, *op. cit.*, vol.1, p.30.
47. New, *op. cit.*, p.10.
48. Brougham, *op. cit.*, vol.1, pp.22-23.
49. Horn, *op. cit.*, p.91.

to a most prosaic explication of Latin texts at the High School by the crimes of the French mobs, Brougham was receiving similar instruction at Brougham Hall at the hands of Dr Mitchell. This exercise, at the recommendation of the Principal's son, Lord Robertson, soon expanded into translating the History of Florus, a bit of busy work for the frustrated scholar. As Brougham sarcastically wrote in a letter to Robertson, he selected Florus over Livy neither because of style, familiarity, nor personal preference. "As he writes in a very peculiar style, so I thought that by a literal translation his elegance would be lost."[50] The result was a work on the beauties of Florus, rather than one on the beauties of Robertson, something that he was more inclined to do. When Brougham was not confined to this "holiday task", he wrote English essays for his father on subjects like the folly of a life of wisdom. Its hero, Memnon, was partially blinded, bankrupted, nearly seduced, and threatened with the loss of the other eye because of his dispassionate approach to life. If this remedy did not prove worse than the problem for young Henry, there were all the siblings to contend with at Brougham Hall. The Broughams had had four sons and one daughter during the 17 years after Henry was born. While in Edinburgh, he had to deal with peers like Horner, Jeffrey, Cockburn, James Loch, and Murray. In Westmorland, he was constantly confronted by the needs and wants of his younger brothers.

When Brougham entered Edinburgh University in October 1792, he continued the course of study that Dr Mitchell had initiated at Brougham Hall. Jeffrey had tested the troubled waters of the city by returning without incident the previous summer. Moreover, the Jacobins had dried up all favourable opinion of the Revolution. Brougham took the widest course of study, concentrating upon the mathematics classes taught by Professor John Playfair. "He was at all times accessible to his pupils for explaining things left short in the class, and removing doubts and difficulties that occurred in their reading at home."[51] The rest

50. Letter to Robertson, January 15, 1792: quoted in Brougham, *op. cit.*, vol.1, p.25.
51. *Ibid.*, pp.56-57.

of Edinburgh's professors had adopted a most formal lecturing style, out of choice or fear, in order to avoid debate over controversial points and issues. Dugald Stewart, for instance, chose this approach in his lectures on philosophy to reduce the possibilities of offending the powers-that-be over his liberal sentiments, while David Hume was free to give vent to his conservative proclivities with impunity in his course on Scots Law. Cockburn noted the change in Hume's class since Jeffrey's sojourn to Oxford thus: "The political sensitiveness of the day at one time obtruded itself rather violently into this hall of philosophical orators ..."[52] With Tory stalwarts like Hume unmuzzled, Jeffrey contented himself with a most prudential preparation for a career at law, and a most traditional role in the life of student societies. Before the Speculative Society, which Jeffrey joined in December 1792, he restricted himself to challenging traditional authorities and teachers with papers on nobility, effects of discovering America, authenticity of Ossian's poems, metrical harmony, and character of commercial nations. It was little wonder that once the reaction to the French Revolution passed, Jeffrey deprecated these efforts, especially the one on the value of nobility.

For Jeffrey, however, the darkest days of the 1790s were when Robert Morehead, a first offender, whose mother dreamed that he one day would become Lord Chancellor,[53] was banished for 14 years for sedition. About the sentence of transportation, Lord Cockburn wrote:

> At that period it implied a frightful voyage of many months, great wretchedness in the new colony, an almost complete extinction of all communication with home and such difficulty on returning that a man transported was considered as a man never to be seen again.[54]

---

52. Lord Cockburn's Works: *Life of Francis Jeffrey* (Black, Edinburgh, 1872, 2 vols.), vol.1, p.51.
53. *Ibid.*, p.55.
54. *Ibid.*, *Memorials of His Time*, vol.2, p.88.

The atmosphere reduced Jeffrey to writing: "Indeed I hate this place more and more, and in January as well as in June."[55] Cockburn was not guilty of overstatement when he wrote: "Never, since our own Revolution, was there a period when public life was so exasperated by hatred, or the charities of private life were so soured by political aversion."[56] The culmination of the repressive process was when Henry Erskine, Thomas's younger brother, was deprived of the Deanship of the Faculty of Advocates for presiding over a public meeting petitioning an end to the war. Jeffrey, like attorneys George Cranstoun and Thomas Thomsom, stayed away because of political pressure when the disgraceful act took place, and, consequently, Erskine only received 38 supporting votes from the Faculty. "He envied the 38," Cockburn wrote in Jeffrey's biography, "and always thought less of himself from his not having been one of them."[57]

With such mature Whig stalwarts muzzled, Brougham could only afford to do the same. With Cranstoun yielding in the crucial vote to the Duke of Buccleuch, the same one who had fagged for Henry's father at Eton, the extraordinary character of political affairs had to be recognized. Truth, justice, and right were suspended for the duration of the war, and Whigs who failed to take note would do so at their peril. Brougham, consequently, expanded his field of mystification to mathematics, and his highjinks took on a more collective character. What he had done of a classical character to confound his tutors was now diverted to confuse the least politically inclined professionals, the mathematicians. Brougham used his acquaintance with the binomial theorem to persuade Playfair that he was a research genius, recognition that led him to investigate a most abstract field, flexional calculus. Playfair once noted that Brougham's interest in the subject was inversely proportional to his distance from the professor.[58] When Brougham scored a bull's eye when

---

55. *Ibid.*, vol.1, p.60.
56. *Ibid.*, p.71.
57. *Ibid.*, p.91.
58. Brougham, *op. cit.*, vol.1, p.58.

the artillery corps volunteers were having target practice in anticipation of a French invasion, Playfair was reduced to say: "You see how we mathematicians carry the day."[59] Brougham was so persuaded of his scientific acumen that he prepared a paper for the Berlin Academy of Sciences suggesting that a projectile was deflected out of its vertical plane by its rotary motion, and its condensing "the air".[60] To determine the effects of a projectile's rotation, a bullet was then fired through a series of screens, leading to the conclusion that its direction was changed by hitting them. Brougham continued his mathematical inquiries by writing a paper on prisms, and performed some experiments in optics, discovering incidentally, he claimed, the science of photography.

While interpreters of Brougham have increasingly made light of these efforts, thanks to the evaluation that Lord Campbell gave them in his biography of the Lord Chancellors, they were unduly appreciated by his contemporaries, increasing even further his suspicion that the world was largely humbug. The Royal Society published Brougham's two papers on optics, and the one on prisms. Campbell generalized about Brougham's failure to say anything either new or true thus:

> By seeking distinction in almost every department of genius, he has failed to establish a great name in any. He accomplished nothing as a statesman; he cannot be said to have extended the bounds of human knowledge by philosophical discovery; his writings, although displaying marvellous fertility, are already falling into neglect; his speeches, which when delivered nearly set the world on fire, when perused in print cause disappointment and weariness; and he must chiefly be remembered by the professional and party struggles in which he was engaged, and by the juridical improvements which he assisted to introduce.[61]

---

59. Quoted from *ibid.*
60. *Ibid.*
61. John Lord Campbell, *Lives of the Lord Chancellors* (Murray, London, 1869, 8 vols.), vol.VIII, p.215.

As far as Brougham's scientific writings during college were concerned, he was closer to the mark when he told Lord Campbell that they were "... extravagances for the purpose of amusing himself and astonishing his contemporaries."[62] He failed to mention, however, that he had been reduced to this role by the reaction to the French Revolution.

It was the reaction to the correspondence between the Corresponding Society and the United Irishmen that forced Brougham out of his non-political, scientific world. While Jeffrey could join the Speculative Society, and discuss prosaic topics as the kingdom experienced its darkest days, Brougham did not have the patience and character to take such risks. When Edinburgh's medical students had rioted in April 1794 because of the playing of *The Royal Martyr* at the Royal Theatre, Tories like Hume were on the lookout for Whigs like Brougham joining the fray: "Not only had they applauded republican sentiments: they had attempted to prevent the singing of the national anthem and, after a struggle, had been forcibly expelled from the theatre by the Tory spectators, with Sir Walter Scott well to the fore."[63] In fact, the repression was so oppressive and excessive, (one was expected to be most traditional in one's dress, toast the King endlessly, and join the Gentlemen Volunteers), that it backfired. The ravings of such people who so hated liberty drove out traditional conservatives like Henry Cockburn. Conservative reaction to the war on the Continent, and rebellion in Ireland gave the Whigs a new lease on life. The culmination of the process was when the Ministry used an address by the Society to the United Irishmen to justify oppression of political societies as part of revolutionary France's expansionist designs.

Brougham was now studying for the examinations to the Scottish Bar. When he was not making mischief with associates like Sandrie Finlay, Jack Gordon, and Frank Drummond, activity increasing in frequency because serious academic disputation had been suspended for the war's duration, he was reading Scots and

---

62. *Ibid.*, p.229.
63. Horn, *op. cit.*, p.40.

Roman Law. Francis Horner allayed James Loch's suspicion that Brougham was all play, and no work:

> But you are mistaken if you suppose he has nothing to do, unless you call it nothing to study Voet and the Corpus Juris four or five hours a day. This I should never have expected, if I had not known from observation of some years standing, that Brougham has a mind capable of any exertion that he chooses to put it to.[64]

The political climate of Edinburgh was so bad, however, with its growing paranoia and suppression, that Brougham could not continuously apply himself to his studies. Even debauching excursions, as we learn from James Ferguson, could not erase from participants' minds the terrible conditions under which they struggled.[65]

In this desperate situation, Brougham decided to take on Scotland's Tory establishment. Given the risks of such a course, one can only suspect, in light of subsequent events, that he did it with some assurances and assistance from Dundas, who was no reactionary. Brougham joined the Speculative Society in 1797, deciding to make a political association out of the leading pillar of Scottish society. Sir Walter Scott had joined the Society in 1790, and had used its sessions to attack everything that Brougham held dear, for example the waste of the aristocracy, the barbarity of the slave trade, and the value of the balance of power. Scott had been able, through strength of character, during its sessions to legitimize to a high degree the repression that the kingdom was experiencing: "His constant good temper softened the asperities of debates; which his multifarious lore, and the quaint humour with which he enlivened its display, made him more a favourite as a speaker than some whose powers of rhetoric were

---

64. Horner's letter to Loch, dated August 25, 1798: quoted from R.H.M.B. Atkinson and G.A. Jackson, eds., *Brougham and His Early Friends: Letters to James Loch, 1798-1809* (privately printed, London, 1908, 3 vols.), vol.1, pp.41-42.
65. Letter to Loch, dated October 15, 1798: *ibid.*, p.45.

far above his."[66] Scott, during his membership, held all the Society's various offices. Just when the Whigs were withdrawing from Parliament at Westminster because of the Ministry's comprehensive repression,[67] a new generation of Scottish Whigs was entering the Society to try to bring Scotland under the suspended Constitution. Henry Petty, the future Lord Lansdowne, Murray, Charles Kinnaird, and James Moncreiff joined it, along with Brougham, Cockburn and Horner. "From 1797 to 1805 is perhaps the most brilliant period in the Society's history."[68]

The Speculative Society, founded in 1764, had been drawn into politics, despite its rules, because of the French Revolution. The rules were suspended to discuss the following question: "Have the States of Europe any reason to dread the increasing ascendancy of Russia in the balance of power?"[69] Thanks to Brougham's initiative, the Society was soon discussing controversial topics like the King's prerogative to create peers, the statutory length of Parliament, the role of the Bishops in the House of Lords, pardons in criminal law administration, the propriety of repealing the Test Act, the value of colonies and alliances, the need for the East India Company, and the impressment of seamen. Just the year before, during its 1796-7 session, it had discussed traditional topics like the need for capital punishment and imprisonment for debt. The closest the Society came to debating current policy was to question the need of extending the crime of treason.

Brougham's radicalization of the Society was temporarily checked, however, by revolutionary activities in Ireland. Ever since 1783, the Society had permitted exchange membership with the Historical Society of Trinity College, Dublin, allowing members to attend one another's meetings. One of the Historical Society's members who had attended sessions of the Speculative

---

66. *The History of the Speculative Society, 1764-1904* (Constable, Edinburgh, 1905), p.10.
67. Holdsworth, *op. cit.*, vol.XIII, p.167.
68. *The History of the Speculative Society, op. cit.*, p.11.
69. *The History of the Speculative Society of Edinburgh from its Institution in 1764* (Speculative Society, Edinburgh, 1845), p.34.

Society was Thomas Addis Emmet, a leader of the United Irishmen who had transformed it into a rebellion, once Pitt's government had met Viceroy Fitz-William's promises of reform with repression. Predictably, the Speculative Society reacted thus:

> On November 20, 1798, "the Secretary (Mr Waugh) moved, and was seconded by Mr Henry Brougham, that as Thomas Addis Emmett has acknowledged himself a Member of the Executive Directory of the Irish Union, and has confessed himself privy to carrying on treasonable correspondence with France, his name should be erased from the List of the Speculative Society."[70]

The Tories, of course, moved to exploit Whig embarrassment over this development, but Brougham, who had became one of the Society's Principals, frustrated them. Alexander Maconochie, who had just retired from the Chair of Public Law at the University, had long been looking for a new audience for his conservative doctrine.[71] Maconochie had long ceased to give his theoretical history of man and nations when Brougham attended Edinburgh, making the Chair into a mere sinecure. Maconochie now told a colleague that he was going to spy on the Society for the University. The colleague, a Mr Fullarton, was instructed

> ... to take down the words of this night's debate, if they interfered with questions of modern politics, in order that he [Maconochie] might summon a general meeting of the Society, for the purpose of considering the propriety of resigning the privileges of the Society into the hands of the University, as such discussions being permitted were likely to produce in the walls of the University a political Society, perhaps a Jacobin Club.[72]

---

70. *The History of the Speculative Society, op. cit.,* p.8.
71. J. Lorimer, "The Story of the Chair of Public Law in the University of Edinburgh," *The Law Quarterly Review,* vol.4, p.150 ff.
72. *The History of the Speculative Society, op. cit.,* p.12.

Brougham immediately responded by moving that Maconochie had insulted the Society's honour, and had assumed an office in the Society inconsistent with membership.[73] Brougham prefaced the motion by recounting Maconochie's misdeeds at the University. The motion was not only carried but the Society also rescinded the rule against political debates. In fact, the Tory members were so intimidated by these developments that they either resigned from the Society or stopped attending its meetings. In their absence, the Society, under Brougham's leadership, discussed the value of parties in the promotion of free trade, Britain's role in Continental affairs, and the value of free trade in colonial development. While most members of the Society were subdued by the small audiences which considered these debates, a few were not:

> Brougham in particular, whose constitutional keenness made him scent the future quarry, gave his whole soul to this preparatory scene, and often astonished us by the vigour with which, even to half a dozen lads, he could abandon himself to his subject, and blaze as if he had been declaiming against Cicero in the Forum.[74]

While Edinburgh struggled to put the Speculative Society back together again, a process which would ultimately require a joint committee of the Town Council and the University's Senatus, Brougham enjoyed an unfettered intellectual life. When he was not debating contemporary politics before the Society's sessions, he was discussing wider aspects of current civilization in the City's mushrooming cultural organizations. The Academy of Physics had been formed in 1797, and Brougham used its meetings to discuss informally current ideas about such concepts as latent heat, light, colour, reflection, and refraction. The Academy's core, Brougham, Horner, and Jeffrey, went on to establish the Literary Society, an organization to investigate

---

73. *Ibid.*, p.12.
74. *Ibid.*, p.14.

nature and to discover "... the laws by which her phenomena are regulated, and the history of opinions concerning these laws."[75] Brougham's leadership of its discussions of science and the history of science convinced him that he was a budding Newton of the modern age, a natural philosopher prepared to resolve any conceptual or methodological problem. About 1800, Brougham helped found the Chemical Society whose proceedings were devoted to examining Priestley's and Black's latest discoveries, ideas which ran counter to Brougham's belief in spontaneous generation. This cultural development of Edinburgh culminated in the formation of the Friday Club, an informal dinner club whose meetings were intended as a relief from those of the Speculative and Academical Societies. It was after one of its meetings, where Brougham's famous rum punch had been served, at Bayle's Tavern in Shakespeare Square, that Playfair, Thomas Thomson, and Sydney Smith were almost arrested for trying to steal the bronze head of Galen over Gardiner the apothecary's door. Brougham, in typical fashion, not only suggested the prank but also alerted the watchmen.[76]

This incident was symptomatic of just how uninhibited Brougham had become in the wake of Scotland's collapsing system of government. With Henry Dundas's ostensible wishes at such a discount that Mr Smith, a town councillor for Edinburgh, voted as he saw fit on a proposal, an act of independence for which he lost his place,[77] Brougham let his new-found freedom degenerate into licence in all fields of endeavour. William Bryce illustrated Brougham's sense of novelty by suggesting that he could persuade the Literary Society of the impossibility of the Trinity by mathematical means, and by reporting how he, just like everyone else, had been chasing a French prostitute.[78] William Adam could well have had Brougham in mind when he complained thus about how

---

75. *The History of the Speculative Society, op. cit.*, p.12.
76. Harry A. Cockburn, "An Account of the Friday Club," in *The Book of the Old Edinburgh Club for the Year 1910* (Constable, Edinburgh, 1910), p.110.
77. Cockburn, *Memorials, op. cit.*, p.84.
78. Bryce's letter to Loch, dated November 6, 1798: Atkinson, *op. cit.*, vol.1, p.52.

Speculative Society debates had changed: "We were Ardent in Debate, and if private Business occurred we were eager there too. But the eagerness was without acrimony, and free from anything like the Spirit of Party. I think young minds engaging in this must lay the foundation of very unpleasant animosities which may endure for life ..."[79] Brougham was not restrained by such appraisals, however, he was too busy doing everything. Campbell described the visit of his secret society to the Hebrides on the "Mad Brig" thus:

> At Stornoway, Isle of Lewis, Brougham almost frightened to death the master of the hotel where they lodged by entering his bedroom during the night with loaded pistols, shooting a cat and pretending that he was a messenger from the infernal regions.[80]

Brougham even joined the Masons at the Fortrose Lodge there. His reckless abandon in everything even characterized his practice as a barrister. In the spring of 1800, Brougham passed the examinations in both Scots and Roman law, and was called to the Bar on June 10. While Campbell judged Brougham's behaviour as counsel as little more than taking liberties with weak Judges for court-appointed clients, he was just disagreeing on all controversial points in an environment where the authorities were most suspect. To Brougham, the Judges who had spent the last decade trying to give more definition to constructive treason could not even be trusted in determining the sex of stolen sheep, or what constituted half-boots. Despite what laymen thought, and common opinion held, Brougham believed that the first principles of everything, especially in the law, were in dispute. Campbell, when he heard of Brougham's tormenting Lord Eskgrove with such eccentricities in a case, agreed with Sir Thomas Lauder that he was simply insane. Campbell had forgotten what Cockburn had said about the Judge who presided

---

79. Adam's letter to Loch, dated November 24, 1798: *ibid.*, pp.58-59.
80. Campbell, *op. cit.*, vol.VIII, pp.234-5.

over the treason trials of 1793-4: "Liked passive lawyers who would let him determine result ... and consequently he hated the talent, the eloquence, the energy, and all the discomposing qualities of Brougham."[81]

Under the circumstances, however, Brougham's financial condition was better than expected. Brougham Hall only produced a few hundred pounds a year, and while his father lived a simple life, there was little left over for his fun-seeking son. The Faculty of Law at the University did appoint him Civil Law Examinator, which brought in some money for relatively little work. Brougham did not adjust well to the session's trials, however, despite his typical optimism at the beginning. When he was surprised by a guilty plea by his association in a sedition trial, he wrote to Loch, who had escaped to Lincoln's Inn in search of an English practice:

> All is practice and seeing and knowing ye court. I never go there that I don't wish you were by me that I might advise you most earnestly to consider and re-consider your London plan. For one thing, I am convinced that this bar is a better field than is generally thought ...[82]

In less than a year, however, Brougham was directing friends like John Richardson to look up Loch in London, only wishing that he too could join them. "The Law," he complained to Loch, "is more and more horrid every day - and the Parliament house is still more odious than the study part of the Law. Nothing but absolute necessity can keep me at it - I mean the total want of a substitute for it."[83]

In search of a substitute, he started researching a pamphlet on the colonial policy Britain should pursue in the West Indies as the European powers started reasserting their authority there. Brougham was disturbed by the anti-French bias with which

---

81. Cockburn, *Memorials, op. cit.,* p.106.
82. Letter to Loch, dated June 24, 1800: Atkinson, *op. cit.,* vol.1, pp.151-152.
83. Letter to Loch, dated April 6, 1801: *ibid.,* p.238.

Englishmen were trying to restore order in the islands that had been wrecked by black insurrections. He was "... astonished to see our government delay one moment in assisting the French, or any state that chuses to quell the Hispaniola Negroes; it is like refusing to help your neighbour (with whom you have an old quarrel) when his house is on fire and to windward of your own ..."[84] The people who wanted these islands to remain free, powderkegs which threatened the surrounding European colonies, were compared to those who wanted to continue the slave trade under the myth that it kept Africa contented.

Brougham was most disappointed when such views did not land an appointment in the army or a diplomatic post. "Altogether willing as I am to labour," he complained to Loch, "I see no chance of employment."[85] James Stephen's pamphlet on the West Indies, which Brougham was thinking of reviewing for the proposed *Edinburgh Review*,[86] finally forced him to write a two-volume study of the problem. Brougham totally disagreed with Stephen in *The Colonial Policy of Great Britain in the Present Crisis*. Britain should have supported the French expedition to re-establish authority at Santo Domingo, as its success was in the interest of all European colonial powers, and premature emancipation, as Stephen urged for the former slaves of Trinidad, would create difficulties for all.

When the volumes did little to improve Brougham's status, he joined Jeffrey, Horner, and Sydney Smith in founding the *Edinburgh Review*. There had been an earlier *Review* in Edinburgh to which Professor Robertson had contributed. Professor John Clive has described his grand-nephew's role at the new quarterly thus: "Brougham was a person of boundless ambition - brilliant, unpredictable, incredibly energetic - who regarded the *Edinburgh Review* from the very start as an instrument for his personal advancement and the dissemination of whatever political views

---

84. Letter to Loch, dated April 6, 1802: *ibid.*, p.320.
85. Letter to Loch, dated August 20, 1802: *ibid.*, p.345.
86. Letter to Loch, dated September 4, 1802: *ibid.*, vol.2, p.3.

he happened currently to espouse."[87] Actually, while Brougham did treat the journal as his own instrument, his reviews indicated a far wider interest than Clive indicated. Brougham still had visions that he might become a great explorer or scientist. His legal practice was just a matter of necessity, at best a basis for some kind of official appointment. Brougham explained his uncompromising ambition thus to Loch: "I rejoice at any event which keeps a man out of matrimony. I daily see men born for great things - turn domestic and leave not only the pleasures of freedom, but its views and prospects."[88] Brougham said that he enjoyed his long hours of freedom more "... than if I had a wife to go to bed with at that late hour."[89] After he had paid off his debts, and had saved up some money, he even hoped that Loch would run away with him to his castle in the sky.

In more realistic moments, Brougham struggled to make something of the law. He finally gained public notice with an impassioned defence of a client who had stolen money out of a letter, a capital crime under the Draconian criminal code. While the man went to the gallows, Brougham's reputation at the Bar improved. As usual, however, his anticipation of new business outstripped the market, and he was soon hoping that some charitable solicitor would find him some more clients. Only slated to give two appeals during the spring of 1802, he confessed to his friend Loch as to the probable result: "The worst will only be a return to Edinburgh to vent my Spleen on all manner of Books and make love to Mrs Gascoigne (the adorable Russian), or setting out for Germany with a clean shirt and a dollar ..."[90] While he was confident that he would rise near the top of society, he was determined "... not to sink to the muddy Bottom of Scots Law."[91]

His compulsive search for efficacy and position in society, and

---

87. John Clive, *Scotch Reviewers: Edinburgh Review, 1802-1815* (Faber, London, 1957), p.62.
88. Letter to Loch, dated November 7, 1802: Atkinson, *op. cit.*, vol.1, p.361.
89. *Ibid.*, p.364.
90. Letter to Loch, dated January 28, 1803: *ibid.*, vol.2, p.34.
91. *Ibid.*, p.35.

the bitterness which resulted when they were frustrated, characterized his articles in the *Review*. Fitting his selection as a Fellow of the Royal Society, he was its science and travel reviewer, with some interest in colonial and commercial policy. Brougham's reviews of various scientific works, while understandable, given the trouble he was having in finding a career, were particularly embarrassing. At a time when there were great discoveries in mathematics, astronomy, physics, chemistry, and biology, his assumption that there was little new to justify new theories and approaches were sadly deficient. Acting as if scientists like William Herschell, John Playfair, James Wood, Robert Woodhouse, Thomas Young, and Joseph Priestley were just another misguided majority of the Speculative Society, he dismissed their work with a reckless abandon that anyone would later regret. Brougham, in almost a child-like way, was using the anonymous prerogative of the reviewer to repudiate findings and ideas of a most distinguished group of men.

Perhaps, Brougham's worst review was on Herschell's work. Brougham dismissed his paper on asteroids thus: "It is to his conclusions alone that we object; and, with all possible deference, we hold ourselves as well qualified to judge of the truth of these, as if we had ourselves made or verified the observations upon which they are founded."[92] According to Brougham, astronomical optics had no need for Herschell's new terms and ideas. Brougham favoured treating planets and comets as part of one system, suggesting the name planetary comets for Herschell's finding. "Columbus, Cabral, Gama, and Cook," Brougham incredibly wrote in keeping with his static view of rhetoric and science, "left the honour of being attached to the regions which they had penetrated, to the imposters who succeeded them, or the princes and saints whom they served."[93] About Herschell's inference that solar spots had something to do with the earth's weather and grain production, Brougham offered

---

92. Art.XV, "Herschell on the New Planet", *Edinburgh Review,* vol.1, no.II, January 1803, p.428.
93. *Ibid.*, p.430.

this: "Since the publication of Gulliver's voyage to Lapata, nothing so ridiculous has ever been offered to the world."[94] The *Dictionary of National Biography*, in writing Herschell's life, was far too kind to this review when it said: "His proposal to designate the minor planets as 'asteroids' drew upon him a gratuitous attack, probably from Brougham, in the first (*sic*) number of the 'Edinburgh Review.'[95]

Brougham rejected James Wood's *The Elements of Optics* as a mere rehash of Newton which confused conjecture for experiment and induction. In addition, the work was said to lack a comprehensive view of optics which treated phenomena like rays in a scientific manner. In making this assessment, Brougham apparently overlooked the fact that Wood's volume was merely part of his scientific effort and should be judged in association with his *Elements of Algebra* and *Principles of Mechanics*, his volumes that formed part of Cambridge's course in mathematics. Thomas Young's attempt to defend the Bakerian theory of light met a similar fate in Brougham's hands. Young, a contemporary whose similar career at Edinburgh and the Royal Society had just resulted in his having been appointed professor of natural philosophy at the Royal Institution, was dismissed as a practitioner of "loose" science. In particular, Young's concern over his theory of the muscularity of the eye's crystalline lens was seen as the result of a scientific novice.[96] Brougham was equally condemning of Young's theory that light, a wave-like phenomenon, could be interfered with as it passed through a dense substance.[97] The *Dictionary of National Biography* was not guilty of overstatement when it condemned these reviews thus: "The vital importance of Young's work was, however, not understood, and the three memoirs met with severe and unjust criticisms at the hands of Henry Brougham in the 'Edinburgh

---

94. *Ibid.*, p.431.
95. *Dictionary of National Biography*, vol.9, p.724.
96. Art.XVII, "Bakerian Lecture on Light and Colours," *Edinburgh Review*, vol.1, no.II, January 1803, p.451.
97. Art.XVIII, "Young on Colours," *ibid.*, pp.457-60.

Review.'"[98] Brougham was hardly better in his treatment of the scientific efforts of Joseph Priestley and Izarn. The former, the famous "Gunpowder" Doctor whose support of the French Revolution was as celebrated as his discovery of oxygen, was belittled as a scientist, wanting allegedly in precision.[99] Instead of recounting Izarn's explanation of meteorites, Brougham advanced the quaint theory that they were caused by eruptions of the moon's volcanoes.[100]

In fact, the only scientists whom Brougham had a good word for were fellow Scots Joseph Black and John Playfair, the obscure William Hyde Woolaston, and chemist Charles Hatchett. Black's lectures on chemistry, which Brougham had attended as an undergraduate, drew this characteristic judgment: "An original genius is often to be found in all the departments of human excellence."[101] Brougham was particularly taken by the cool, fastidious way Black publicized his discoveries of latent heat and fixed air. Brougham sided completely with Playfair in his disputes with mathematicians like Robert Woodhouse over the use of new methods like imaginary numbers.[102] Again, the *Dictionary of National Biography* disputed the claim:

> Woodhouse is entitled to distinction in the history of mathematics in England for the important share he had during his earlier years as a teacher at Cambridge in bringing to the notice of his countrymen the developments in mathematical analysis which had taken place on the continent. He was the first in England to explain and advocate the notation and methods of the calculus.[103]

---

98. *Dictionary of National Biography*, vol.21, p.1311.
99. Art.VI, "Transactions of the Am. Phil. Society", *Edinburgh Review*, vol.2, no.IV, July 1803, p.348 ff.
100. Art.XII, "Izarn, Lithology Atmoshperique", *ibid.*, vol.3, no.VI, January 1804, pp.386-401.
101. Art.I, "Dr. Black's Lectures", *ibid.*, no.V, October 1803, p.5.
102. Art.XII, "Woodhouse on Imaginary Quantities", *ibid.*, vol.1, no.II, Jan. 1803, pp.407-12.
103. *Dictionary of National Biography*, vol.21, p.873.

As far as Playfair was concerned, however, Brougham took away with the right hand what he had given with the left, denying that his illustration of the efficacy of the earth's core had any validity. Again, it is instructive to compare Brougham's claim with that of the *Dictionary of National Biography*:

> ... but the work which will always be most prominently associated with his name is the *Illustrations of the Huttonian Theory of the Earth,* 8 vols., Edinburgh, 1802, on which he spent five years. This work is a model of purity of diction, simplicity of style, and clearness of explanation. It not only gave popularity to Hutton's theory, but helped to create the modern science of geology.[104]

Brougham saved his praise for William Woolaston's application of the Newtonian principle of reflection to a medium less rare than glass.[105] Hatchett's discovery of the element columbium was also noted with favour.

Some of Brougham's sharpest words were directed at the work of Henry Fuseli, the London artist who had just succeeded James Barry as the Royal Academy's professor of painting. Fuseli was a leading figure of London society who had visited Dr Johnson in prison while he was being held on a charge of sedition. About Fuseli's just-published lectures on painting, Brougham stated: "His performance is one great mass of shade, unbroken by a single gleam which might lead us of discover the objects upon which he is employed."[106] Brougham, who was becoming a painter himself, was most upset by how Fuseli described Rubens's use of the pallet. The *Dictionary of National Biography* characteristically has a higher opinion of Fuseli's efforts: "His lectures, especially the first three, which were published separately in 1801, show a wealth of learning and erudition unusual in an artist. His style, though often grandiose to

---

104. *Ibid.,* vol.15 p.1300
105. Art.VIII, "Woolaston on Prismatic Reflection", *Edinburgh Review,* vol.2, no.III, April 1803, p.98.
106. Art.XVI, "Fuseli's Lectures", *ibid.,* no.IV, p.461.

absurdity, was in the fashion of the time."[107]

Brougham had a field-day reviewing travel books, using ones he had already considered, and his own travels to tear apart the effort in question. For example, he used Baldwin's *Political Recollections Relative to Egypt* to mark the deficiencies of Oliver's *Travels in the Ottoman Empire, Egypt, and Persia,* and then attacked the former for his explanation of the plague, Egypt's geography, and the Porte's weakness.[108] In another book in the same area, Brougham made the startling claim that it was only the rewards of the slave market that induced some Africans to throw off the listlessness of the torrid climate. In reviewing Joseph Acerbi's survey of Scandinavia, Brougham took advantage of the visit that he and Charles Stuart had paid to the peninsula two years before.[109] Acerbi was found particularly wanting for not repeating Robertson's explanation of why such countries were so successful - their people were energetic and thrifty. Brougham appeared to go out of his way to curry favour with Scotland's secular and ecclesiastical leaders by praising what Swedish aristocrats and priests had achieved.[110] Domestic tyranny of an independent nation was preferred to enlightened foreign rule. Brougham was most upset by the stories and gossip Acerbi repeated, especially a silly story about the President of the Royal Society of London. (As usual, Brougham was taking out some insurance with the Society for his criticism of colleagues like Woodhouse and Young.) A travel book on America forced Brougham to note that its citizens were too prone to repeal taxes, and to copy other people. Nicolai Karamsin's account of his travels throughout Europe drew this response: "Such person will pass through the seat of warfare and revolution, with a notice of their own accommodation and fare at inns - of the spots where their emotions overpowered them, and the congenial spirits with

---

107. *Dictionary of National Biography,* vol.78, p.778.
108. Art.VI, "Political Recollections relative to Egypt", *Edinburgh Review,* vol.1, no.I, p.59 ff.
109. Letter to Loch, dated August 19, 799; Atkinson, *op. cit.,* vol.1, p.63.
110. Art.XXIV, "Acerbi's Travels", *Edinburgh Review,* vol.1, no.I, p.168 ff.

whom they enjoyed the luxurious feast of tears."[111] While in England, this Russian Rousseau had learned that convicts preferred to be hanged than transported to the colonies.

Such comments just reinforced Brougham's interests in colonies. In reviewing *The Crisis of the Sugar Colonies*, Stephen's four letters to the Chancellor of the Exchequer, Henry Addington, Brougham repeated many of the ideas of his *Colonial Policy*. To try to gain a diplomatic post, he called for a new policy towards Napoleon's France, especially in the Caribbean. In light of the successful expedition to put down the slave uprising at St Domingo, Brougham called for Britain to join in the First Consul's plans. "The negroes are truly the Jacobins of the West India island - they are the anarchists, the terrorists, the domestic enemy."[112] All colonial nations had an interest in the restoration of slavery in the area, the real interest of the French operation. "If the French yoke is re-established in the West Indies," he said, "we have the best possible reason for believing, that it will be harmless to our own empire - the clear interest of France to maintain it."[113] All Brougham could offer the negroes concerned was a cessation of the slave trade, and an improvement of their lot. He used this policy as a basis for calling upon the government to give general support to the balance of power in another review. Thanks to the check that it had given to revolutionary France, he concluded: "Let us hear no more, then, of the last century, as affording arguments against the balance of power."[114]

Certainly, the best evidence that Brougham gave of the influence that Professor Robertson had had in his intellectual development was supplied in the review of Dugald Stewart's life of the late Principal. About its bookish approach to the man, Brougham complained:

---

111. Art.V, "Karamsin's Travels", *ibid.*, vol.3, no.5, p.321.
112. Art.XXVII, "Crisis of the Sugar Colonies", *ibid.*, vol.1, no.I, October 1802, p.227.
113. *Ibid.*, p.229.
114. Art.IX, "Politique de tous les Cabinets de l'Europe", *Edinburgh Review*, vol.1, no.II, January 1803, p.352.

> The care with which Mr Stewart had avoided all descriptive anecdote, is indeed mortifying to the very natural curiosity inspired by a perusal of Robertson's works. We cannot avoid feeling some desire to extend our acquaintance with the man who has so often instructed, dazzled, enchanted us, by the profundity of his disquisitions, the brilliant majesty of his narration, the varied spells of his language.[115]

Brougham attributed the omission to Stewart's dread of offending surviving relatives, "... errors which often tend to throw upon the subject a little of the contempt that should be left entire for the authors."[116] Robertson, a benefactor of the whole world, deserved a more complete biography. Brougham particularly missed an account of the Professor's narrative, even although it was not all that valuable because it was too inductively oriented.

In Brougham's reviews of historical works, he tried to give the structure that he found wanting in Robertson's works. He attacked William Shepherd's life of Poggio Bracciolini as a laboured, pompous one which overrated the results of restorers of knowledge. "In this age," he advised, "the public would be more edified by dwelling upon the characters of a Washington, a Burke, or a Pitt, than a Poggio, or even a Lorenzo de Medicis."[117] The fact that Brougham was straining for his own political benefit with such views was illustrated when the University of Edinburgh gave Shepherd an LL. D. for the work, which had been translated into French, Italian, and German, in 1834.[118] Brougham admitted as much when he purchased Cornelius Henderson's portrait of Dr Shepherd a decade later, and placed it in Brougham Hall. Brougham denounced the abolition of specific payment - making permanent the Bank Restriction Act of 1797 - as a Jacobin expedient.[119] On the moral

115. Art.XXVI, "Life of Robertson", *ibid.*, vol.2, no.III, April 1803, pp.232-3.
116. *Ibid.*, p.233.
117. Art.III, "Shepherd's Life of Poggio", *ibid.*, p.53.
118. *Dictionary of National Biography*, vol.18, p.57.
119. Art.XI, "Guineas on Incumbrance", *Edinburgh Review*, vol.2, no.III, April 1803, p.101 ff.

duty of abstaining from meat, Brougham offered this bit of autobiographical jest: "Would it be more ridiculous in a righteous confectioner to preach the abolition of the slave trade, by uttering invectives against the use of sugar in tea, and practice his doctrines by conscientiously poisoning himself with sour punch, while he dealt out to the world every other species of saccharine preparation?"[120] About the tone of R.C. Dallas's history of the Maroons, Brougham advised:

> It would have been difficult, even for Robertson, to have sustained the complete propriety and decorum of his style, had he been called upon to narrate the actions of Cudjoe, Johnny, and Cuffy - at the Cockpits, Hellshire, Nanny, Derbiston Trash-house, Amity Hall, One-eye, or Putty-putty bottom.[121]

Brougham completed the preparation of his dossier for new employment in London by writing a stinging review of Josiah Walker's poem in defence of order. When Walker compared commanders like Lord Duncan, who put down a mutiny by displays of flogging, to Leonidas, Brougham asked sarcastically: "Who does not perceive the beauty and justness of all these comparisons?"[122]

Brougham did not get to London in the capacity he had hoped. These efforts did nothing to encourage Lord Hawkesbury to give him a diplomatic post. Andrew Clephane described the effect upon Brougham thus: "He, poor fellow, has been very ill of late, and whether it is that dissipation brings on disease, or which I rather think, that the disease takes that turn, he has been very unsettled."[123] Loch's visit to Edinburgh prompted Brougham to make the decision to move to London anyway, and he left without notice. Brougham wrote that he would remain in

---

120. Art.XIII, "Ritson on Abstinence from Animal Food", *ibid.*, p.132.
121. Art.VIII, "Dallas's History of the Maroons", *ibid.*, no.IV, July 1803, p.377.
122. Art.XII, "The Defence of Order", *ibid.*, p.428.
123. Clephane letter to Loch, dated March 14, 1803: Atkinson, *op. cit.*, vol.2, p.53.

the metropolis for five years,[124] a resolution made more firm because of the difficulties Dundas was experiencing. No sooner had Brougham settled in London, and joined Lincoln's Inn so that he could eat the necessary dinners to join the English Bar than he was off to the Continent on a secret mission of his own. He expressed confidence about its objective, to restore personally the balance of power in Europe, in a most Robertsonian way: "... I glory in the present state of the Nation, which is such as almost entirely to place its salvation and that of Europe beyond all danger from the weakness of its governors."[125] The mission's success would require all the wishes of a modern Columbus.

---

124. Letter to Loch, dated August 24, 1803: *ibid.*, p.78.
125. Letter to Loch, dated November 13, 1803: *ibid.*, p.92.

CHAPTER TWO

LONDON APPRENTICESHIP

Brougham was 25 years old when he arrived in London. He was merely a shell of the figure that its society would soon know. While he had gained the physical stature and appearance that was so characteristic of his political career - the tall, lean figure, with the rather strange, unexpressive features,[1] who could be such entertaining company, whether engaged in the social discourse of polite society or the antics of an all-male outing. He did not yet know who he really was, and what he wanted to do. He just knew that he wanted to get away from Edinburgh, and the practice of Scottish law. All that remained of his years there was the allowance that his father provided, the friendships he had developed at the University and on circuit, and his role at the *Edinburgh Review*. London was selected as a new abode because friends like Loch and Horner had sought out its resources. The metropolis could serve as a jumping-off spot for a variety of careers, perhaps an overseas posting in the diplomatic service, or as a professional traveller. Brougham had been in a most unsettled state ever since his younger brother Peter, a seaman on board the *Queen*, had been killed in July 1800 in a duel with its second mate at San Salvadore. In fact, it was Brougham's desire to bring Peter's killer to justice that got him so interested in Stephen's book on the sugar colonies in the first place. Plotting the course to his brother's killer, Brougham pored over the books on travel sent him to review. The impossible aim

---

1. Chester W. New, *The Life of Henry Brougham to 1830* (Clarendon Press, Oxford, 1961), p.190.

of such pursuits was illustrated by his letters to James Loch where he repeatedly called on him to run away with him. When Loch refused, Brougham came to London to be with him, joining Lincoln's Inn.

To improve his credentials for a diplomatic position during the peace with France, Brougham used his reviews in the *Edinburgh Review* to question the dire expedients that the government was contemplating if hostilities resumed. He noted the report that Charles Hatchett had written for the Privy Council, explaining the loss of value in circulating gold coin: the inflated value of specie was inducing subjects to dilute its content,[2] a most pointed reference to the effect of the Bank Restriction Act. Brougham took strong exception to Bishop Watson's alarming advice to the Ministry on how to meet the French challenge: the drafting of 17-year-olds into the militia was no answer to France's standing army. Watson's suggestion of conciliating Catholics and Nonconformists for support in the coming struggle by repealing civic disabilities was dismissed as gratuitous to the needs of the nation.[3] His advice to the Lords to pay off the national debt was seen as a financially irresponsible act which would just strengthen the upper classes at the Crown's expense. "There is little in this unspoken speech calculated either to edify or to rouse,"[4] he wrote. Brougham attacked anonymous surveys of France and Russia which contended that they had gained the mastery of Europe. The idea that the balance of power was dead drew this response from Brougham:

> ... like all those who assume the title of *plain matter of fact men*, he is perpetually under the influence of some vague hypothesis, rashly adopted from a limited range of observation, and confidently relied upon as a safe guide, from ignorance of the maxim, that, in political science, insulated

2. Art.XVII, "Hatchett on Gold Coin," *Edinburgh Review*, vol.3, no.VI, January 1804, pp.456-7.
3. Art.XIX, "Bishop Watson on the National Debt, Etc.," *ibid.*, p.472.
4. *Ibid.*, p.468.

facts can never lead to any solid or general conclusions.[5]

Brougham still favoured the resumption of French control at Santa Domingo. A new edition of William Morgan's pessimistic survey of the kingdom's condition drew this self-serving response: "His object is to prove, not that our expenses have increased, but that our government has been extravagant."[6]

To improve his political credentials for office, Brougham made most partisan reviews of works by Lords Lauderdale and Chatham. Lauderdale, an aristocratic leader of the Society of the Friends of the People which had been so embarrassed by the activities of the Corresponding Society, especially those of Margarot and Gerrald at its Edinburgh convention,[7] was an ideal target to attack for Tory approval. Once the Whigs had withdrawn from Parliament because of the political capital that the government had made out of the public alarm, Lauderdale devoted himself to safer concerns, the study of the sources of public wealth. No sooner had he published a book on the subject than Brougham made a political attack on it, offering sarcastically to "... Lord Lauderdale our unfeigned thanks for the zeal with which he has devoted his retirement to the cultivation of this great field of inquiry ..."[8] As for its content, however, Brougham was most constrained, stating that it was mostly either self-evident or false.

For example, Lauderdale made a false distinction between public and private wealth, creating "strawmen" subsequently to maintain the illusion. "His talents and rank, in the present instance," Brougham concluded most expediently, "we think greatly misapplied."[9] Brougham applied himself to the letters that Lord Chatham wrote to this nephew in most glowing terms:

---

5. Art.III, "Sketches on the Resources, Influence, and Projects of France and Russia," *ibid.*, vol.4. no.VII, April 1804, p.43. Italics Brougham's.
6. Art.V, "Morgan's Comparative View of Finances", *ibid.*, p.82.
7. Sir William Holdsworth, *A History of English Law* (Methuen, London, 1952, 16 vols.), vol.XIII, p.160 ff.
8. Art.VIII, "Lord Lauderdale on Public Wealth," *Edinburgh Review*, vol.4, no.VII, July 1804, p.343.
9. *Ibid.*, p.376.

> We challenge the admirers of Lord Chesterfield to produce a more winning, and at the same time a more judicious and ingenious defence of all that part of manners which is worthy of a reasonable being's regard, in the whole writings of their matter.[10]

Chatham, Brougham reminded potential Whig critics, did not let court life ruin his civic virtues and love of life: "In the minutest parts of conduct, as well as manners, the advices given in these Sketches are equally sedulous."[11]

Brougham even used James Loch to assist his campaign to find favour with Pitt's Government. In the *Review*, Loch gave a most critical accounting of Rev Tennant's *Indian Recreations*. Tennant, one of the King's Chaplains in India, was criticized for publishing a most ill-advised treatise under a most inappropriate title. Loch, anticipating another travel book about India, was most upset to find another defence of the East India Company. "The more the system of Indian monopoly is considered in its effects," he charged, "the more singularly mischievous it will appear."[12] The study was lacking in any originality, Loch explained, citing several examples of outright plagiarism. Tennant was charged with English prejudice and manifest error, especially about Indian castes. In calling for the Company's replacement by direct control of the Crown, following a policy of free trade between Britain and the sub-continent, Loch had introduced the subject so expansively that he almost sounded like the Brougham of old: "The fate of our American colonies seems to have frightened statesmen even from taking into consideration the policy of such a measure; and their timidity has been sedulously augmented by the influence of the exclusive trade."[13] Failure to effect such a policy risked the French seizing the colony because the British could not trust the loyalty and effectiveness of the Sepoy armies.

Brougham, when questioned by Charles Grant, who had just

---

10. Art.IX, "Lord Chatham's Letters to his Nephews," *ibid.*, p.384.
11. *Ibid.*
12. Art.V, "Dr Tennant's Indian Recreations," *ibid.*, p.309.
13. *Ibid.*, p.305.

been named Director of the Company, as to its authorship, made it quite clear that he was not the discontented, disappointed man responsible. Brougham did not try to dissuade Grant of the idea that it had been written by someone with a mischievous design against the Company, like a disgruntled employee or shareholder. Loch was living with his uncle William Adam, who was counsel for the Company, in East Sheen. Brougham made the most of a few errors that Loch had made about the castes: "Not that you have advanced an erroneous theory, far from it, but that you have committed to paper, and Jeffrey has allowed to be printed, a number of *plain blunders*."[14] When Loch did not immediately admit the errors of his ways, suspecting that Brougham's criticisms had something to do with the friendships that he was developing with William Wilberforce's Clapham Sect, the anti-slave trade group, Brougham replied: "But I wish you had only written on what concerned yourself; I mean the *Review*."[15] To drive home the point, Brougham reminded Loch of what had happened in Edinburgh five years before:

> If you are headstrongly bent on following your own idea, I only say that you will be the first to repent - that I trust you will learn by this lesson the reminder of what was begun (and I regret to see only begun) in the Speculative Society - that you can gain no credit by it, and perhaps the contrary.[16]

Brougham threatened Loch with losing the opportunity to publish further in the *Review* if he made a public dispute of the matter. When Loch continued to question Brougham's motive in it, he explained that the East India Company would be understandably angry if it knew from what quarter the attack had come.[17]

---

14. Brougham's letter to Loch, dated July 31, 1804: quoted from R.H.M.B. Atkinson and G.A. Jackson, eds., *Brougham and His Early Friends: Letters to James Loch, 1798-1809* (privately printed, London, 1908, 3 vols.), vol.II, p.143. Italics Brougham's.
15. Brougham's letter to Loch, dated August 3, 1804: *ibid.*, p.149.
16. *Ibid.*, p.151.
17. Brougham's letter to Loch, dated Sunday morning, *ibid.*, p.161.

To reassure Loch that he had not been responsible for any harmful disclosure, something that he must have done for Grant to get so agitated, Brougham disclosed the secret mission he was on for the government. To try to ingratiate himself with the Ministry, Brougham had organized a volunteer corps in Edinburgh, where he still maintained a residence. "But the government slighted its offer of service, and the corps was dissolved."[18] The Ministry was more interested in Brougham going to the Continent, disguised as an American, to see if the Emperor Napoleon could be assassinated. Brougham had certainly been biding his time at Lincoln's Inn, as Clephane noted to Loch: "It is my own private opinion that he will never practice at any Bar whatever."[19] When Brougham was not using its library to help prepare his reviews for the *Review*, he was sounding out government circles for such a secret mission. It was after this had been secured that he wrote so fatalistically to Loch during their dispute over his review:

> In you I take an interest which is of no recent standing and can only end with my life - I hope you know this and I believe the feeling to be mutual - I am often (I fear so very often that there may be truth in it) accused of coldness and hardness of heart and an unamiable want of feeling - To this I am reconciled by seeing the follies that fine feelings produce. But at any rate, I may desire you to believe, that when one of such a nature is melted, it must be by no common emotion, and that the sincerity of my attachment is the less to be questioned on this acco't.[20]

Having been appointed to stalk the French despot, Brougham travelled as a landscape painter with an American passport through Holland, Germany, Austria, and Italy in the hope of running into Napoleon or gaining an introduction to him.

---

18. *The Dictionary of National Biography*, vol.6, p.449.
19. Clephane's letter to Loch, dated December 27, 1803: Atkinson and Jackson, *op. cit.*, vol.II, p.111.
20. Brougham's letter to Loch, dated Sunday morning, *ibid.*, p.163.

Brougham even delayed for a week in a house with some French generals. "Nothing that I have seen, said or painted in favour of the sky and air here," he wrote to Loch from Italy, "appears half sufficient."[21] It was only after he had gone down and up Italy's "boot" that he finally gained Lucien Bonaparte's acquaintance. The Emperor's brother effected his release after he had been arrested on suspicion of carrying the plague. However, the introduction did not gain Brougham access to Napoleon whom he continued to stalk. Returning to Holland by way of Vienna, Brougham just missed Napoleon by a half-day. "I hope to overtake him tomorrow if possible,"[22] Brougham wrote to Loch on his way again to Frankfurt. The tour had been well worth its risks, expenses, and fatigues, he explained, provided that his mission had not been disclosed, and Pitt's government continued in office. Despite the notoriety that Brougham encountered in Holland because of his inquiry into colonial policy, and Napoleon's wariness, as he journeyed up the Rhine, Brougham tried to overtake him, disguising himself as well as possible. Posing as a Frenchman, he caught sight of the Emperor above Cologne, and avoided capture despite the elaborate security measures. "All this is not uninstructive," he wrote to Loch, "it shows the folly of such precautions as Bonaparte is taking - no one can take more."[23] May not an assassin, he asked rhetorically, be willing to pay the price for the accomplishment of such a deed. Henry's brother, James, wrote to Loch about the trip: "Everything has succeeded beyond any wish."[24] Once Henry returned safely from his dangerous mission, James added: "So it was a considerable relief to hear of his being out of the Imperial power of the Mighty Man."[25]

Brougham's purpose in the mission was not only to help rid Europe of Napoleon but also to assist passage of the abolition of the slave trade. Since settling in London, Brougham had

---

21. Brougham's letter to Loch, no date, *ibid.*, p.178.
22. Brougham's letter to Loch, dated September 14, 1804, *ibid.*, p.193.
23. Brougham's letter to Loch, dated September 22, 1804, *ibid.*, p.204.
24. James Brougham's letter to Loch, dated September 26, 1804, *ibid.*, p.209.
25. James Brougham's letter to Loch, dated October 27, 1804, *ibid.*, p.227.

become a member of Wilberforce's Clapham Sect, as his concern about Loch's treatment of the director, Grant indicated. Grant was a charter member of the Nonconformist group. Brougham's joining it, along with James Stephen and Zachary Macaulay, persuaded Wilberforce to try again to effect passage of the Abolition Bill. Brougham's *Colonial Policy* was circulated among Members before its second reading in the Commons, and Pitt spoke with him in mind as he successfully moved passage. The Bill failed in the Lords because there was not enough time to present the evidence to justify its passage. Actually, when the proposed measure was taken up to the Lords from the Commons, "... it was a member of the government, indeed the Secretary of State, Lord Hawkesbury, who opened the debate, not however as the Bill's official 'father' but as its firm opponent."[26] Hawkesbury, heir to the earldom of Liverpool, "... who was one day to bear a title taken from the greatest Slave Trade port,"[27] had proven more hostile to the previous abolition effort than the Prime Minister, Henry Addington. It was to ease passage of the new effort that Brougham undertook his mission for Hawkesbury, the new Home Secretary. He would be more sympathetic to abolition, apparently, if it coincided with the elimination of Napoleon, the destroyer of the peace. It was Hawkesbury who had negotiated the Treaty of Amiens with the French, and had staked his career upon its statesmanship. When it collapsed, Hawkesbury was willing to use almost any expedient to get even with the French despot.

While one does not know what use the Home Secretary made of Brougham's information about Napoleon's vulnerability, the mission paid off for the abolitionists, thanks largely to the way that Brougham hid the object of his anti-slave trade activities. To disarm the Whigs, he had taken advantage of his friendships with Loch and Horner to gain "... a footing in Holland House, where he soon became intimate. There he met Wilberforce, whose friendship and influence were to be of such assistance to him in

---

26. Sir Regionald Coupland, *Wilberforce* (Collins, London, 1945), pp.253-4.
27. *Ibid.*, pp.133-4.

the next few years ..."[28] Holland House was the centre of Whig society in Kensington where Lord Lauderdale was also so much in evidence. Given his past, and Brougham's own, it was only prudent for him to attack Lauderdale's views on public wealth. Brougham's motive for it, the favour he sought by it with the Tories in general and Hawkesbury in particular, was well in evidence when he was on his European mission. While he was so concerned about knowledge of it, especially if people might suspect what he was really up to, he was writing to Loch to learn what people at Holland House thought of his review of Lauderdale, as if there could be any doubt. Clephane, once James Brougham had paid a visit while he was recovering from sickness in the hospital, assured Loch that Brougham's slashing style had had the desired effect: "He tells me that all Lord Lauderdale's friends are wrath at Henry for cutting up his book so very unmercifully."[29] Under the circumstances, Clephane had to admit some sympathy for Lauderdale even though he too did not like him: "I have, however, a fellow-feeling with his Lordship, having equally lost my character as a sober, virtuous kirk-going young man."[30]

Brougham co-ordinated his trip to the Continent and his attack on Lauderdale with another slashing exposé of the slave trade. Just before Brougham left, Jeffrey had complained obligingly about his difficulties as editor of the *Review*: "I am in the greatest distress for MSS, and if it were not for my reliance on Brougham, I should have no hope of salvation."[31] Brougham kicked off his re-education of Hawkesbury on the slave trade with a review of M'Kinnen's tour of the West Indies. Brougham made much of the fact that M'Kinnen had not discussed conditions in St Domingo where the Negroes were apparently in the process of building a wild, uncivilized republic. The Treaty of Amiens had at least given the French the opportunity to try to re-establish their authority there. M'Kinnen did not understand that slavery

---

28. Atkinson and Jackson, *op. cit.*, vol.III, p.7.
29. Clephane's letter to Loch, dated October 25, 1804, *ibid.*, vol.II, p.220.
30. *Ibid.*, p.222.
31. Jeffrey's letter to Loch, dated June 21, 1804, *ibid.*, p.130.

was not based simply on threat and the possible use of force. "He seems indeed, like many others, to have expected nothing but one unvaried scene of flagellation and torture ..."[32] While slavery was a necessary evil, there was no reason to increase its numbers and justify its expansion, as M'Kinnen had. The slaves, Brougham charged, were worse off than the Africans. To confound any suspicion that this was special advice for ministerial ears, Brougham, in another review, said this about undue respect for the Royal Family: It "... did not prevent us from exposing what we conceive to be a bad and awkward compliment, paid at the expense of truth, with mean views and a dangerous tendency."[33]

Brougham, of course, continued to review scientific works in his customary cutting style. The work of Sir Benjamin Thompson, Count von Rumford, who determined that heat is motion, he dismissed with characteristic flourish: "Indeed, the confusion of ideas which pervades the whole of this explanation, is not only like, it is exactly the same with that which Swift has ridiculed in his picture of the Laputan projector, who wasted his life in extracting sun-beams from cucumbers, in order to preserve the rays for use during winter ..."[34] Rumford's most important work was the founding of the Royal Institution, and this paper was another published by the Royal Society. Brougham used another paper by Rumford to try to dissuade everyone that he was coming to terms with established ways and circles:

> There is an aristocracy, as it were, in the Count's manner of treating his adversaries, which we do not very well understand, and which is little suited to the republican constitution of the scientific world - the only region where we hope to see the column resist, for ages, all the attempts at giving it a Corinthian capital.[35]

---

32. Art.XIII, "M'Kinnen's Tour of the West Indies," *Edinburgh Review*, vol.4, no.VIII, July 1804, p.429.
33. Art.I, "Plans of National Improvement," *ibid.*, vol.5, no.IX, October 1804, p.22.
34. Art.XI, "Count Rumford on the Nature of Heat," *ibid.*, vol.4, no.VIII, July 1804, p.411.
35. Art.XII, "Count Rumford on a Phenomenon in the Glaciers," *ibid.*, p.417.

For good measure, Brougham levelled another most expedient attack upon the poor Dr Young. In the Bakerian Lecture of 1804, Young tried to clarify his ideas about the seeing of colour, a brilliant memoir with the concluding proposition that "radiant light consists of undulations of the luminiferous ether." Brougham said that he had assumed that his previous review had dissuaded Young from continuing his fruitless search into optics. The review concluded by reiterating the doubly insulting belief "... that the Society had remitted his effusions to the more appropriate audience of both sexes which throngs round the chairs of the Royal Institution."[36]

The purpose of this self-justifying smokescreen was manifested in the very next article in the *Review*. During Brougham's last days of Whig opposition to Scottish political ways, he wrote a most critical review of Josiah Walker's poem, "The Defence of Order." The poem was dismissed as a paean to ordinary people, used by the poet to gain immortality. Brougham found the comparisons of Nelson to a small diamond, Lord St Vincent to a bird tearing out a bull's eye, and Lord Cochrane to a sword-fish stabbing a whale, silly and trite. When Walker compared Lord Duncan to Leonidas, Brougham responded testily: "Who does not perceive the beauty and justness of all these comparisons?"[37] Adam Duncan was the admiral who had to deal with the Nore mutiny, and the threatened French invasion of Ireland. He put down the former by a vast personal display of flogging, and won the Battle of Yarmouth against the Dutch by using the most unorthodox tactics. For these deeds, he was made a baron, but his aunt complained to Henry Dundas that he had not been made an English earl.[38] Brougham found it now convenient to attack an Irish author who had the temerity to say similar things about Pitt's Government, especially its First Lord of the Admiralty:

In his native country, this author sees only a power, created

---

36. Art.VII, "Dr Young's Bakerian Lecture," *ibid.*, vol.5, no.IX, October 1804, p.97.
37. Art.XII, "The Defence of Order: A Poem," *ibid.*, vol.2, no.IV, July 1803, p.428.
38. *The Dictionary of National Biography*, vol.6, p.160.

> for the destruction of liberty, both at home and abroad; the enemy of happiness in foreign nations, and of all the comforts and rights of its own people; the universal fomenter of wars, and the oppressor of every thing like peaceful industry.[39]

About the expressed concern over the kingdom's mounting public debt, Brougham responded irritably: "In like manner, did Thomas Paine, by help of a numerical series, calculate, 10 years ago, the end of Great Britain."[40] Brougham concluded his account of what the government had done financially to save itself on this Tory note:

> The country was constantly threatened with an invasion, which the losses of our allies rendered every day more probable and which a gale, or a fog, or a calm, might render inevitable. The market price of gold exceeded the mint price so much, that a continual exportation of bullion was going on and specie became every day more scarce. An alarm among the country banks and private traders induced the Bank to contract its credits and supplies. A mutiny, un-exampled for magnitude, organization, and obstinacy, raged in the fleet, now deemed our only stay against the enemy's attacks; and a serious rebellion was breaking out in Ireland.[41]

While Brougham was gaining the ear of Pitt's Ministry by these efforts, he was losing the support of the Clapham Sect, especially Wilberforce. Wilberforce had been so grateful for the support that Brougham had given abolition of the slave trade in his *Colonial Policy* that he had been invited to join the Abolitionist "cabinet", but he was not prepared to accept this bald-faced support of the King's Cabinet. Wilberforce, in taking advantage of Brougham's offer to write for the *Review*, had observed all the niceties that had been demanded unsuccessfully from Loch, only to see

---

39. Art.VIII, "O'Connor's Present State of Great Britain," *ibid.*, vol.5, no.IX, October 1804, pp.104-5.
40. *Ibid.*, p.107.
41. *Ibid.*, p.112.

Brougham do as he pleased in its columns. Wilberforce had been most gentle with a defender of the trade, though he had complained in a letter to Stephen that "never surely was there so unconscionable a liar."[42] Brougham compounded his difficulties with Wilberforce by trying to write a most disarming but false account of his mission to the Continent which he developed in his memoirs. Brougham wrote to Wilberforce that he had followed the itinerary that the Abolitionist proposed, so as to give a cover story to his secret mission. Brougham fed him with information to support "... the Abolitionists' starry-eyed belief that once the Trade stopped, the Planters would soon raise their slaves into a kind of feudal vassalage."[43] To reinforce the cover story to disguise what he was trying to do by his trip up the Rhine, Brougham

> ... wrote enthusiastically from Holland too, that the Dutch had translated his book, were fast moving towards Abolition, and would move even quicker if they might please have their colonies back at once. Wilberforce sent the entire letter to Harrowby. For any other Foreign Secretary he would have copied out extracts, 'but to you in your *persona* capacity, I may be allowed to transmit papers of which you will show such parts to your *political* as it may be proper to lay before it.'[44]

At first, Wilberforce thought that Brougham, though a very clever young man, would see the Dutch get the better of him. Later, John Pollock, Wilberforce's latest biographer, tells us, he "... sometimes felt 'a little jealous' of Brougham's making our sacred cause of Abolition the ladder by which he climbs into political notoriety and eminence."[45]

---

42. Wilberforce's letter to Stephen, dated October 2, 1804, Bodleian Library, Oxford University, d. 16.32; quoted from John Pollack, *Wilberforce* (Constable, London, 1977), p.190.
43. *Ibid.*
44. *Ibid.* Italics Wilberforce's.
45. Wilberforce's letter to Harrowby, dated October 15, 1804, Harrowby MSDS, XII, f.193; quoted from *ibid.*, p.190.

While Wilberforce was prepared to make light of this fact in later life when the battle had been won, dismissing it as false delicacy,[46] he was not prepared to do so at the time. In fact, Brougham must have known that he had strained Wilberforce's credulity because he proceeded to write a stream of professional articles for the *Review*, once he had returned from the Continent, to try to hide his tracks. About Egerton's second edition of a study of European armies, Brougham had nothing but praise. Taking advantage of a trip that he and Loch had made down the coast to visit the headquarters of Sir John Moore, and to witness a parade,[47] Brougham was most sensitive to Egerton's criticism of British military leadership. As he had seen, the parade officer had as much to do with military combat as the quack with the practice of medicine. "The height to which this attention to dress is raised in some individuals," Brougham explained, "exceeds all bounds of belief."[48] In reviewing Venturi's study of light rays, Brougham found it to be such an addition to Newton that, with an eye towards Wilberforce, he hoped that Venturi would continue them because he favoured "... the further prosecution of studies far more dignified and delightful to a rational creature, than the intrigues of courts, or the vulgar turmoil of republican factions."[49] Brougham found Fontana's investigation of Maupertius's law helpful.[50] Talleyrand's study of colonies got this endorsement from Brougham: "Great as the resources of France are, if they were not wielded by such men as Talleyrand, she would soon cease to be the object of that watchful anxiety which, in the actual posture of officers, is the wisest part of wisdom."[51] Published papers by Turin's Academy on chemistry, mathematics, and electricity received high marks, though

---

46. *Ibid.*
47. Loch's letter to James Brougham, dated July 20, 1805, Atkinson and Jackson, *op. cit.*, vol.II, p.246. Brougham can be identified as Loch's companion on this junket by the fact that he was known as "the horse".
48. Art.XVI, "Caractere des Armées Européennes," *Edinburgh Review*, vol.5, no.X, January 1805, p.463.
49. Art.II, "Venturi, *Sopra i Colori*," *ibid.*, vol.6, no.XI, April 1805, p.43.
50. Art.V, "Fontana, *Sopra un Problema Euleriana*," *ibid.*, pp.50-6.
51. Art.VI, "Talleyrand, *Sur les Colonies etc*," *ibid.*, p.65.

Brougham did not have time to examine their content.[52] Work by the Italian Society of Verona got the same treatment.[53] In fact, Brougham could only bring himself to write a critical review of Toulongeon's study of credit. "His theory only differs from the old one," Brougham said, "in ascribing to paper money all the powers which were formerly attributed to the precious metals."[54]

Brougham's eight articles in the *Review*, the greatest number by far that he had contributed to any single issue, lacked the usual bite. He gave the impression of being greatly occupied, while, in fact, he was just going through the motions for this desired effect. The hundred pages of material were devoted to shorter articles in which he tried to give merely impressionistic coverage of material that he usually examined in depth. For example, in discussing the scientific papers published by Turin's Academy, he failed to mention the content of the ones on mathematics and electricity. The review of Fontana's article was a joint one of which Playfair wrote the greater part; the eight-page article on Italian science was a hotchpotch; the article on Henry IV's grand design for France was an attack on a "strawman" for traditional purposes:

> As often as the balance of power is mentioned, men recur to the chimerical project of Henry IV, and declaim upon the absurdity of attempting any similar arrangement, because the impracticability of what they term "the most perfect form of the system" is admitted.[55]

Brougham fell back into critical autobiography in reviewing Bory de St. Vincent's account of his voyage around Africa: "Our *sentimental* traveller appears to have derived much amusement from the *hunting of apes,* though even his redoubtable appetite shrunk from the flesh of those lovely creatures, from the

---

52. Art.VIII, "*Memoires de l'Academie de Turin,*" *ibid.*, pp.95-105.
53. Art.XIV, "San Martino, *Sopra it Carbone nei Pianti,*" *ibid.*, pp.170-182.
54. Art.X, "Toulongeon, *Sur l'Usage du Numéraire,*" *ibid.*, p.113.
55. Art.XIII, "Chrombrier, *Sur le Grand Dessein de Henri IV,*" *ibid.*, p.162.

conviction that a roasted ape must resemble a *roasted child*."[56] A similar sentiment marked his differences with Talleyrand over the cause of emigration: "The spirit of adventure, and the love of change, always tempt the first settlers."[57] The only continuity between these reviews and earlier ones was the complaint that Toulongeon had repeated Lauderdale's absurdity of confusing scarcity of goods for their value.

The reason for Brougham's retreat into the state of European science was obvious. While he had worked out an arrangement with Pitt's Ministry to end the slave trade under conditions satisfactory to Hawkesbury, and over the heads of the Clapham Sect, a more traditional political grievance seemed ripe for resolution. Lord Melville, the infamous Henry Dundas, had finally been exposed. As Treasurer of the Navy, a post that he had twice held, financial irregularities and monies unaccounted for had become so widely known that Parliament had to institute a commission of inquiry in 1802. When he was finally examined by it on November 5, 1804, he stonewalled it thus:

> I did not decline giving occasional accommodation from the funds in the treasurer's hands to other services not connected with my official situation as treasurer of the navy. If I had materials to make up such an account as you require, I could not do it without disclosing delicate and confidential transactions of government, which my duty to the public must have restrained me from revealing.[58]

Thanks to the activities of Melville's assistants, especially Mr Trotter, he was shown to have violated 25 Geo.III, c.31, an Act that he was responsible for the passage of, "... the object of which was to prevent the treasurer for the time being from appropriating any part of the money passing through his hands

---

56. Art.XI, "*Voyage de Bory de St Vincent,*" *ibid.*, p.128. Italics Brougham's.
57. Art.VI, "Talleyrand, *Sur les Colonies*, etc," *ibid.*, p.71.
58. *Cobbett's Parliamentary Debates*, vol.III, January to March 1805, Appendix, cols.1185-6.

to his own private use."[59] The commissioners' report was presented to Parliament on February 13, 1805, arriving like a bombshell for the opening of the Session.

Everyone except Wilberforce knew that parliamentary business, even the Abolition Bill, would take a backseat while Melville's political fate was being determined. Ostensibly, Brougham should have jumped at the opportunity to get even with Scotland's Tory tormentor. He had returned from the Continent in time to convert the *Review* into a veritable engine of Whig redress; yet, as we have seen, he did nothing. Professor New described the situation thus:

> During the years 1804 to 1807, from his moving to London to the passing of the Abolition Act, Brougham was giving thought to party politics. All his expression of opinion and his associations in his Edinburgh days has been liberal and in Scotland liberal meant to be aligned against the Tory rule of Henry Dundas. By every instinct of his youth and every political conviction of his manhood Brougham was at war with Dundas's system of government.[60]

Since Brougham did not lift a finger during the last campaign against Dundas, New's description must be seen as another example of his trying to make Brougham always consistent and enlightened. Actually, Brougham seemed too much at home with Pitt's government in general and Melville in particular when he came to London for one to be sure that his opposition to Tory rule was all it appeared to be. Had there been some kind of secret financial inducement from Dundas which helped determine

---

59. *The Dictionary of National Biography,* vol.6, p.189. *N.B.* This passage from Brougham's letter to John A. Murray, dated April 2, 1805: "If it is argued that had Lord Melville served the State with navy money on pressing emergencies, the answer is plain, he should have applied for a bill of indemnity ... I feel truly savage upon the whole affair, and only lament most sincerely, as every admirer of Pitt must do that he has become so long counted with such a dirty dog." *Life and Times of Henry Lord Brougham* (Harper, New York, 1891, 3 vols.), vol.I, pp.222-3.

60. New, *op. cit.,* p.32.

Brougham's ultra-liberal presidency of Edinburgh's Speculative Society? He certainly had more funds, and went more places than one would expect, given the money his father could provide, and what he got for his legal representations. Of course, without the actual accounts, one will never know. Brougham's concern about attacks on the East India Company, something that he rather lamely attributed to Grant, could have come from Melville. He too was a Director, and it was the lead that he took in Parliament in 1793 that secured its monopoly.[61]

There was an amazing two-month pause, from February to April, before the Commons acted upon the reports of the Commission. It was almost as if it waited until the April issue of the *Review* appeared before the Whigs and liberal Tories decided to move. When it appeared without anything on Melville's improprieties, something that a Whig constitutionalist should have had a field day with, Samuel Whitbread moved a series of resolutions condemning Melville's conduct. This feeble effort was undermined by the fact that the issue cut across party lines. Wilberforce, who had long been impressed by Brougham's attacks upon Melville, decided to do the deed, even if it sacrificed abolition of the slave trade for another Session. Melville was in favour of gradual termination. Wilberforce forced himself to say what Brougham should have said: "I must confess that it is impossible for me to leave the House this night without giving my vote in support of the Resolutions."[62] His effort was just enough to gain their approval. Melville resigned as First Lord. "Wilberforce was attacked afterwards for being Brutus to Pitt's Caesar."[63] John Pollock, Wilberforce's biographer, has rightly said that this made Brougham Cassius, but a most feeble one, it would seem.

In fact, there was a backlash in Melville's favour which finally forced the Commons to impeach him. On April 24, Peter Stuart, editor and publisher of *The Oracle*, inspired by someone sounding

---

61. *D.N.B.*, *op. cit.*, p.189.
62. Quoted from Pollock, *op. cit.*, p.192.
63. *Ibid.*, p.193.

much like Brougham, recklessly came to his defence:

> ... party rancour and popular clamour have at this time deprived our king and country of the great and powerful abilities of Lord Melville. In no period of our political history can be found such an instance of the strong effects of prejudice. With all our admiration of that spirit which arouses and animates the people in their expressions of indignation at the supposed malversations of an Individual - with all our regard for town and country meetings when properly directed in supporting the cause of independence, freedom, and public virtue - we cannot help again and again declaring, that Lord Melville has fallen a victim of confidence misplaced, and to indignation misapplied. He has been condemned without a trial.[64]

The next day, Lord Grey called the House's attention to this gross breach of privilege, moving that Stuart be called to the Bar to explain. In the debate, Robert Ward reminded the Commons that the article said that Melville had not benefited financially by his actions. "His most implacable enemies have not dared to charge him with such an act," Ward read to the House from the article. "Can as much be said of the fathers of some men?"[65] Stuart was ordered to appear before the Commons on April 26. When he did, Grey demanded an explanation of the article: "It was no discussion, it was mere invective, absolute and unqualified abuse, tending to vilify the proceedings, degrade the character, and insult the authority of parliament."[66]

Stuart feebly explained its appearance as the result of the "hasty composition of a newspaper,"[67] although the resolutions had been voted for over two weeks before the article had appeared. For the breach, Stuart was found guilty, and placed in the custody of the Serjeant at Arms. Stuart was released a

64. Cobbett, *op. cit.*, vol.4, cols.381-2.
65. *Ibid.*, col.396.
66. *Ibid.*, col.434.
67. *Ibid.*, col.440.

week later after he had been reprimanded by the House. Stuart was the elder brother of Daniel Stuart who had done so much to build up the *Morning Post.* He sold it in August 1803 for 25,000. While he was getting rid of it, he helped Peter at the *Oracle* in the preparation of its foreign news. The *Oracle* had been getting a secret service subsidy of 200 per year since the early days of the French Revolution, thanks to the connections of another brother, Charles, to Henry Dundas. About these Scots, Wilfred Hindle wrote, "there is a shadow of truth in the saying that the Stuarts avenged Flodden in Fleet Street."[68] About the character of the relation, he added: "His brother Charles had written to Henry Dundas, later Lord Melville in 1793: 'When I hear of the French casting *cannon,* I think nothing of that at all, provided you can only prevent them from casting *type.*'"[69] By the time the impeachment of Melville became a possibility, "the *Sun,* and the *Oracle* (which absorbed the *True Briton*) became the 'leading prints' of Pitt and his friends ..."[70] The Stuarts had been reduced to this base by the Whigs' effort to organize the press by raising money at Brookes' Club for the purchase of the *Morning Post, Morning Chronicle,* and *Morning Herald.* Holland House hoped through them to make political capital out of Melville's difficulties. Brougham had just the right connections with the Stuarts, especially Daniel, to stage a counterattack against a misguided Whig assault on Tory officialdom. More important, they would never suspect that he was the Tory defender of the due process of law.

This strange reversal of roles where Wilberforce was more interested in punishing Melville than attaining his long-sought Abolition Act, and Brougham wanted to protect his alleged Tory antagonist in order to gain approval of a ministerial termination of the slave trade goes a long way in explaining some political difficulties of the Session. For one thing, it shows why Pitt was unwilling to give governmental support to Wilberforce's plan to

---

68. Wilfrid Hindle, *Morning Post, 1772-1937* (Routledge, London, 1937), p.65.
69. *Ibid.,* p.85. Italics Stuart's.
70. Arthur Aspinall, *Politics and the Press* (Home & Van Thal, London, 1949), p.206.

carry repeal through the Lords on the strength of what had been achieved in the Commons the previous Session. "A more credible explanation," Roger Anstey wrote, "is that in 1805 Pitt was on the brink of making the abolition a policy and hence a government matter, but was fearful of dividing his followers by officially taking up Wilberforce's motion at that time."[71] Little wonder, as Coupland added, that Pitt was so shaken by the Commission's report on the Treasurer of the Navy: "It happened that Wilberforce was closeted with Pitt, discussing a Slave Trade question, when the first copy of it was delivered. 'I shall never forget,' he says, 'the way in which he seized it, and how eagerly he looked into the leaves without waiting even to cut them open."[72] Wilberforce, of course, should have remembered this the next day or so when he moved his Abolition Bill in the Commons. "General Gascoyne was at a loss to know whether the hon. gent. meant to introduce a bill, exactly similar to that of the last session. He might perhaps find, that the circumstances of the times had induced many of the members to change their opinion on the subject ..."[73] Wilberforce was surprised by this counterattack from a spokesman for Liverpool, but he made no adjustments in his campaign despite the lack of ministerial support. When Wilberforce persisted with the Bill's second reading, it was defeated by seven votes. While he knew that Dundas's votes had made the difference,[74] he did not understand why.

The Clapham Sect, and the Whigs, in accepting Brougham's challenge as to how to get things out of the Tories, compounded their difficulties by going after Melville. Right after Grey finished with the Stuart affront, Whitbread moved that the House appoint a select committee to investigate the charges brought against the former First Lord. Once adopted, it moved quickly, reporting that Melville should be called before the House to answer them. He

---

71. Roger Anstey, *The Atlantic Slave Trade and British Abolition, 1760-1810* (Macmillan, London, 1975), p.345, no.10.
72. Coupland, *op. cit.*, p.242.
73. Cobbett, *op. cit.*, vol.3, col.521.
74. Anstey, *op. cit.*, p.346.

appeared at the Bar on June 11, to answer his critics.[75] After his departure, Whitbread moved unsuccessfully that he be impeached. The House accepted Bond's amendment that he be the subject of a criminal prosecution. The trouble with such a prosecution was that it would be heard by the Lord Chief Justice, Lord Ellenborough (the former Edward Law) who had made his reputation defending Warren Hastings against another Whig-inspired prosecution. Ellenborough "... was a man of strong convictions and never hesitated to express and act on those convictions even though they ran counter to the policy of his party."[76] It was these attributes which bothered Pitt's administration most. Consequently, on June 25, Leycester moved in the Commons that it proceed against Melville by impeachment, and that the Attorney General stay the criminal proceedings. The motion passed. The next day, Whitbread went to the Lords with the Bill of Impeachment.

Brougham greeted these developments with a critical appraisal of Lauderdale's latest book in the *Review*. Acting as if nothing had happened since his last attack upon the Whig lord, and as if he were above the political battle, dealing with the eternal verities of political economy, Brougham introduced the new inquiry, which did not confuse scarcity and value, as the larger one had, thus: "The author may even deserve praise for adducing a new argument upon a topic already well considered; and the applause due to ingenuity would certainly be his, if real ingenuity could exist without solidity."[77] The negative judgment of Pitt's Act of Union, which Lauderdale saw as having such an adverse effect upon the British economy, was attributed to the Whigs' party spirit. Lauderdale contended that Union with Ireland had impaired free trade, forcing a quantity of Irish goods into the English market proportional to the interest on sums borrowed, and, consequently, threatening English manufacturing interests. "But in order to prove that the loan should be

75. *D.N.B., op. cit.*, p.186.
76. Holdsworth, *op. cit.*, vol.XIII, p.504.
77. Art.II, "Lord Lauderdaule's Hints to Manufacturers," *Edinburgh Review*, vol.6, no.XII, July 1805, p.283.

contracted in Dublin, rather than in London," Brougham explained, "Lord Lauderdale must begin by showing that the kind of stock in question abounds more in the former place than in the latter place."[78] London was where almost all loans were financed. Brougham attributed Lauderdale's "gross application of language" to local special interests:

> It is a pleading on behalf of the *monopoly* of English manufacturers; and seems to us to lead much more naturally to a system of restraining and prohibitory laws against importation from Ireland, than to any alteration in the practice of borrowing in this country for the service of the sister kingdom.[79]

This was indeed a good response to Whig suspicions that Brougham might be in the service of Indian monopolists and British masters through Lord Melville's secret dealings at the Admiralty.

Instead of the Whigs and Brougham engaging in such mutual suspicion and recrimination, he suggested that they devote their collective energies to the abolition of the slave trade. Nothing had been achieved by Wilberforce and the Whigs in trying to persuade Pitt even to end the foreign slave trade to the conquered territories in the West Indies. Meetings at Lansdowne House, the home of Brougham's friend Lord Henry Petty, and delegations to the Prime Minister had achieved nothing without Brougham's participation. As long ago as July 3, 1804, Pitt had promised Wilberforce to end the hated trade by royal proclamation. "The delay which intervened before this promise was redeemed, is the great blot in all Mr Pitt's treatment of this cause. "The Proclamation", Wilberforce's sons contended, "was promised week after week, and still causelessly delayed."[80] The cause of the delay, of course, was the threatened exposure of

78. *Ibid.*, p.286.
79. *Ibid.*, p.290. Italics Brougham's.
80. Robert Isaac Wilberforce and Samuel Wilberforce, *The Life of William Wilberforce* (Murray, London, 1838, 5 vols.), vol.III, p.184.

Melville which could reveal not only how Pitt gained power but also how Melville maintained it. The Prime Minister could not force Melville's qualms about ending the trade, either by proclamation or statute, while the Commission's final report was hanging over the former treasurer's head, without it smacking of the most self-serving blackmail. Only after the impeachment proceeding had been agreed to could Melville get a fair hearing, and abolition on all fronts could again go forward.

In the same issue of the *Review* as the Lauderdale article, Brougham called for just this. In reviewing a eulogy to slavery and the slave trade, he mounted a comprehensive argument against what a former landowner at St Domingo was trying to justify. Gone completely was his defence of French colonies in the West Indies, and of slavery itself out of a concern for the European balance of power. Under Napoleon, France had reached this condition: "An abhorrence of the *equality* worshipped in the earlier part of the revolution, gradually leads to adjuration of the *liberty* which used to be coupled with it."[81] Slavery, unlike the mockery which the English called liberty, the author charged, was the natural order of things, what the Africans wanted, what conditions there called for, and what slave owners saw as their interest. If the slave trade continued, Brougham responded, every colony in the West Indies would become another Negro republic like St. Domingo. He was most interested in repeating the explanations of those who benefited by the trade,[82] providing evidence which had been promised for over a year for Parliament to legislate its end. For example, he repeated the crazy claims of slavers about African barbarity, and familiar depravity. He concluded sarcastically:

> Yet the slave trade is a blessing to those poor Negroes! And the existence of the factories on the coast has no sort of influence on their lot! And it is quite indifferent to them

81. Art.VIII, "*Examen de l'Esclavage, Etc,*" *Edinburgh Review,* vol.6, no.XII, July 1805, p.327. Italics Brougham's.
82. For a different interpretation of this articles, see New, *op. cit.,* pp.28-9.

> whether they live at home, or are brought down this jaunt of pleasure to see a little of European manners.[83]

Parliament should rectify the situation by giving a pledge for "... total and immediate abolition of the slave trade."[84] While Brougham wanted the ultimate abolition of slavery, he only hoped for its amelioration for now. "The correction of the greatest evils in society generally increases, for the moment, the bad effects of the original error,"[85] he explained.

To emphasize the need of a co-ordinated approach to the problem, one which included Pitt's Ministry, Brougham published another short review of a scientific paper on statics, stating that De Langes's two approaches had to be integrated to determine "... the forces necessary to prevent the roofs of our houses from falling on our heads."[86] To show that his earlier scientific reviews had had a hidden political purpose, a kind of cover for what he had been trying to achieve behind the scenes, he explained, by a few pages of the most baffling calculations, that a combination of both formulas was required, as the previous reviews on the papers by Fontana and Euler had shown. To make sure that there was no misunderstanding, he complained that De Langes's work was mistitled, as it only applied to the statics of roofs, and not that of bridges and vaults! In another review of a Scandinavian tour, Brougham took exception to John Carr's endorsement of Gustavus III's autocratic ways, and his failure to appreciate any dramatic act, especially the assassination of his political idol. When Carr claimed that even Professor Aszeluis of Upsala only favoured a gradual ending of the slave trade, Brougham retorted:

> Indeed we are inclined to suspect a gross mistake, from the context of the author's account; for he adds, that the Professor "declared, in a very emphatic manner, his perfect conviction

---

83. Quoted from *ibid.*, p.29.
84. Art.VIII, *op. cit.*, p.350.
85. *Ibid.*, p.348.
86. Art.XI, "De Langes, *Statici per i Tetti*," *ibid.*, p.386.

> that a *violent emancipation* would only shock and endanger this great cause of humanity."[87]

Like Brougham, the Professor favoured gradual emancipation of the slaves, but immediate abolition of the trade.

While the Whigs paid no attention to Brougham's pleas, preferring to devote all their attention to Melville's impeachment, Viscount Castlereagh, who became Secretary of State for War and the Colonies when Sidmouth resigned, did what he could to effect the end of the trade. On August 15, 1805, Orders-in-Council were issued, preventing the introduction of slaves into territories ceded to the Crown - ie, Tobago, St. Lucia, Surinam, Demerara, Berbice, and Isequibo. The former Dutch colonies whose slave needs were supplied by the worst of the slave traders could only make up their slave losses through importation licences. Three days later, Nelson reported to the Admiralty that the French threat to the West Indies had been stymied. Castlereagh did what he could to try to mitigate some of the evils of slavery itself. He wrote to colonial governors about increasing the penalty for murdering a slave. Seaforth, the Governor of Barbados, wanted to make it a felony, whereas it was only now subject to a fine of 11 4s. Colonial legislatures were doing nothing to restrict the barbarous treatment that slaves were subjected to. Thanks to Brougham, the Crown was doing what it could to strengthen its regulations of the system. On September 13, Castlereagh ended the foreign slave trade to the territories ceded to the Crown.

While these things were happening, Brougham assumed that the Whigs would avoid unnecessary challenges to Pitt's weakened Ministry. Melville's difficulties should have been allowed to pass without serious dispute, permitting him to withdraw within a judicious interlude. Wilberforce made a big mistake in trying to exploit his troubles to gain passage of abolition of the trade. According to Brougham, the reaction of

---

87. Art.XII, "Carr's *Northern Tour*," *ibid.*, p.404. Italics Brougham's.

this failure would just redound to Melville's benefit,[88] and when he was proven wrong, he assisted the Stuarts to force Melville's prosecutions, a process that so threatened Pitt that he intervened so that the Lords would judge the former First Lord. To try to persuade the Whigs and the Clapham Sect of their impolicy in pursuing Melville, Brougham followed up his article in the *Oracle*, it seems, by an anonymous pamphlet on the impeachment, "An Exposure of the Prosecution of Lord Melville; in a letter to an intimate Acquaintance." As if he were writing Wilberforce, Brougham apparently explained:

> ... his Lordship may yet prove, as I apprehend it is open for him to do, that, although he actually diverted the money from one public service to the temporary use of another, yet he did so without any sort of personal consideration or personal benefit; and that, in doing so, he facilitated the service, promoted the interest and saved the purse, of the Nation.[89]

Brougham, it seems, explained away his previous concern over Melville's getting a bill of indemnity for those trifling sums he had used in the public service,[90] something that the Whigs' precipitate action had rendered unnecessary: "He did not come to Parliament for a bill of indemnity. If he had not felt confident in his rectitude, he would have done so."[91] About Melville's apparent lack of co-operation with the Commission, he added: "I confess to you, that his Lordship was over-scrupulously conscientious in the delivery of his evidence."[92] Public failure to understand Melville's innocence was attributed to incomplete reporting of parliamentary debates. The pamphlet concluded with a call for partisan restraint, just what should have happened when the Commissioners issued the Tenth Report back in

---

88. Brougham's letter to J.A. Murray, dated April 2, 1805: quoted in Brougham, *op. cit.*, vol.I, p.223.
89. As above, p.10.
90. Brougham's letter to Murray, Brougham, *op. cit.*, vol.I, pp.222-3.
91. Brougham (?), *op. cit.*, p.11.
92. *Ibid.*, p.16.

February.

Ministerial forces, especially Pitt's followers, were all in favour of restraint. The *Gentleman's Magazine*, in fact, had the audacity to print a summary of the pamphlet's content despite the fact that the action was *sub judice*. Risking contempt of the Lords, it underlined the pamphleteer's recommendation: "Further, while the question is at issue, and the trial on the point of taking place, we cannot go."[93] It is hard to imagine what else it could have done in Melville's defence. The Whigs and the Clapham Sect were hearing similar reports about Brougham's activities behind the scenes in favour of ending the trade, and the useless pursuit of the former First Lord, as we learn from Brougham's correspondence with Loch. The latter, who, because of his uncle, was in such a good position to learn of the East Indian Company's financial operations, something that Melville's agent Trotter had exploited while he was at the Admiralty, wrote to Brougham about such reports. Brougham, of course, denying everything, demanded an interview with the person "... from whom he heard the absurd and utterly groundless statement alluded."[94] Loch, especially because of Brougham's criticism of his review of Dr Tennant's work, knew just what he was up to, and capable of.

Brougham was not dissuaded by Loch's suspicions from continuing his effort to get Pitt to effect abolition. To show the Whigs that he cared little for aristocrats, he wrote a critical review of John Leslie's inquiry into the nature of heat. The recipient of the Rumford Medal was judged hardly better than its namesake. After Brougham had torn apart his method, he questioned Leslie's claim that radiation was conducted by the air, suggesting that it might be water. "It is by his discoveries in relation to the radiation of heat," the *Dictionary of National Biography* states, "first announced in this volume, that the name of Leslie is most widely known."[95] Brougham was on firmer

93. Entry 262, List of New Publications, *Gentleman's Magazine*, vol.70, (1805), Part II, p.936.
94. Brougham's letter to Loch, dated August 1805: Atkinson, *op. cit.*, vol.II, p.259.
95. *The Dictionary of National Biography*, vol.11, p.984.

ground when he said that these theories about the propagation of heat were not so important in themselves "... but because they enlarged our knowledge of the facts upon which a true system may hereafter be founded."[96] For Pitt's ears, Brougham wrote a most critical review of a biography of Frederic the Great whose opportunism would lead immediately to the crushing defeat at Austerlitz. "A truly great genius," Brougham announced with embarrassment, "will be the first to prescribe limits for its own exertions."[97] For the Prime Minister, a man who knew his own limits, and was capable of delegating authority, Brougham wrote a review of the official documents on the slave trade in the hope that its abolition would help restore the balance of power in Europe. He not only recounted what had been submitted to Parliament for the previous Session but also what Castlereagh had done as Secretary for the Colonies. "Our government has given a proof that it holds the traffic in abhorrence," he announced, "by abolishing the only branch which is under its power, without consulting the pretended rights of the West Indian body ..."[98] About what could be expected from such bodies to mitigate slavery's evils, Brougham discussed how they were treating the murder of a slave: "Here then is the answer of all those who refer us to the enlightened legislatures of the islands for the abolition of the slave trade, or the remedy of the glaring evils in the colonial system."[99]

As Brougham's plans for 1804 had been foiled by the Whigs and the Clapham Sect, he planned for the 1805 Session without allowing for the French. Napoleon's victories at Ulm and Austerlitz had more than compensated for Nelson's triumph at Trafalgar. While England was no longer threatened with invasion, Europe was Napoleon's. The whole experience had been too much for Pitt who collapsed and died. What Wilberforce had started in the Commons, the French completed with the Treaty

---

96. Art.IV, "Leslie's Inquiry into the Nature of Heat," *Edinburgh Review*, vol.7, no.XIII, October 1805, p.85.
97. Art.XV, "Thiebault, Memoirs de Frederic le Grand," *ibid.*, p.238.
98. Art.XVI, "Official Documents of the Slave Trade, Etc," *ibid.*, p.248.
99. *Ibid.*, p.246.

of Pressburg. Brougham tried to counter Pitt's departure as First Lord by making a belated, most self-serving appeal to the apparent heir, Hawkesbury, the ranking minister since Sidmouth had resigned the previous July. Brougham offered to Hawkesbury's father, Lord Liverpool, just the kind of review he had denied Lauderdale. About *A Treatise on the Coins of the Realm*, which the first Lord Liverpool had written as an invalid in semi-retirement, Brougham announced: "By the publication of this volume, Lord Liverpool has rendered an acceptable service to the student of political economy."[100] For those who thought that Brougham might be too soft on the poor old man, he retorted:

> But we have really found so few occasions on which lenity might be shown, and so much reason in general to commend, that we shall disregard our Author's peculiar claims to favour, and both indicate, without any scruple, the faults which present themselves, and specify very plainly the parts where we differ from him ...[101]

Brougham found no criticism of Liverpool's treatment of the issuance of coins, except this: "It seems to us eminently absurd to state the alteration of the nominal value of coins, already current, as a branch of prerogative."[102] Liverpool sought too strongly to show that gold coins had become the kingdom's measure of property, over-emphasizing the stability of gold bullion. Brougham recoiled over Liverpool's plan to reform the currency without including paper credit, and to legislate gold the measure of value. After a few more devastating criticisms - eg, the Mint should waive *all* profit in the making of coin - Brougham concluded on this note: "But, instead of wondering that Lord Liverpool has, in one or two particulars, been inattentive to the later improvements of the science, we should rather admire that this has occurred so rarely."[103]

---

100. Art.I, "Lord Liverpool on the Coin," *ibid.*, no.XIV, January 1806, p.265.
101. *Ibid.*, p.266.
102. *Ibid.*, p.268.
103. *Ibid.*, p.294.

The reason why Brougham could take such an opportunistic attitude towards this study was that Lord Lauderdale had made a most unwise rejoinder to Brougham's review of his inquiry into the nature and origin of public wealth. In reiterating his ideas about the differences between public wealth and private riches, falling into a series of paradoxes which made him mistake scarcity for value on occasion, he warned that "... it may induce those known to be concerned in the conduct of the *Edinburgh Review*, to consider what effect a succession of such Articles may have on their own characters, as well as upon that of their publication."[104] Lauderdale said that he had sought instruction from his readers by the study, and that he would have been disappointed if their approach had smelled of flattery. Lauderdale repeated his rationale in developing certain distinctions and concepts of works like Smith's *Wealth of Nations*. "To put the Reviewer out of conceit with his opinions," Lauderdale complained, "will probably be an arduous task."[105] He suspected that Brougham was incapable of even arguing a scientific question. Lauderdale maintained all his previous arguments - eg, the value of a nation's wealth could not be measured by internal exchange - and complained that Brougham had hardly considered his new ideas on augmenting wealth. His critic, Lauderdale concluded, was neither fair, impartial nor intelligent.

To Brougham, this ill-considered attack was like money in the bank, funds much more secure and generous, though, than any Melville could have provided, and he waited to reply at the most opportune moment. It came with the collapse of Pitt's Ministry, as the review of Liverpool's book indicated. His reply is one of the best he ever wrote, an engaging, point-by-point refutation of Lauderdale which left him seeking peace.[106] Brougham cast himself in the pamphlet as a bringer of bad news, introducing

---

104. "Observations by the Earl of Lauderdale on the Review of his Inquiry into the Nature and Origin of Public Wealth" (Constable, Edinburgh, 1804), p.6. It is interesting to note that the *D.N.B.*, for once, sided completely with Brougham in this dispute (vol.12, p.800).
105. *Ibid.*, p.25.
106. Horner's letter to J.A. Murray, dated May 26, 1806: quoted in New, *op. cit.*, p.36.

his prose with a verse from Pope's "January and May", ending in this couplet:

> Is this your love, ungrateful and unkind?
> This my reward, for having cured the blind?

Lauderdale was seen as a poor political philosopher or an enraged poet who would not be consoled when the world condemned his error. "Mr Hobbes, for instance," Brougham replied, "whose success in political philosophy was almost as signal as Lord Lauderdale's failure, thought there was no reason why he should not also discover the quadrature of the circle."[107] Hobbes, however, when his blunder was pointed out, mended his ways without undue breast-beating. Actually, Brougham considered Lauderdale's behaviour more like that of John Thelwall, the poet who complained bitterly when the *Review* did not consider him another Cicero or Pope. "Both have given their effusions to the world as the fruits of their retirement,"[108] Brougham added pointedly. "On one point the *Edinburgh Reviews* have, indeed, serious cause for alarm," he wrote sarcastically. "Both those egregious wizards have espied the fall of their journal."[109] Lauderdale's undue sensitivity was seen as a smokescreen for the concern he had developed because of past political animosities.

After this introduction, Brougham could have got away with almost any treatment of Lauderdale's inquiry. However, the reviewer provided a detailed refutation of the Whig lord's complaints. About the charge of personal malignity, Brougham replied that "... all the prepossession lay the other way, and that the favourable impression with which the Reviewer began his task, only yielded to the effects of a more careful perusal."[110] Lauderdale was shown to have been guilty of a want of truth and

---

107. "Thoughts suggested by Lord Lauderdale's Observations upon the Edinburgh Review" (Hurst, London, 1805), p.4.
108. *Ibid.*, p.10.
109. *Ibid.*, p.11.
110. *Ibid.*, p.16.

misquoting, rather than Brougham, as he had charged. In fact, Brougham retorted, "... the whole force of his argument depends on his peculiar manner of quoting."[111] Lauderdale totally destroyed himself by charging that Brougham had tried to ingratiate himself with the failing Prime Minister by means of his defence of the sinking fund: "It is hinted that the Reviewer's wish to recommend himself to Mr Pitt may have been the cause of his defending that minister's scheme from the attacks of - Lord Lauderdale."[112] Brougham had shown consistent support for this proposal, dating back to his attack on Bishop Watson's speech when Pitt was not in the government. In dealing with the specific differences over content, Brougham laced his argument with frequent contrasts between Lauderdale's behaviour and that of the true scholar, an obvious allusion to Liverpool. When Lord Lauderdale charged, for example, that the reviewer had misquoted him in his criticism of his handling of value in use, Brougham replied: "It is a kind of logic, indeed, more frequent in female or in juvenile disputation, than in the grave discussion of men 'retired from the battle of active life ...'"[113] Brougham was glad to see that Lauderdale was applying himself to the theories of politics rather than its practice during his retirement because it was easier to attack a measure than, say, *The Wealth of Nations*. Brougham concluded by thanking Lauderdale for the pointless attention, and by promising "... to repeat the same office upon any future occasion, when we may perceive symptoms of our assistance being required."[114]

Thanks to political developments, and Brougham's independent efforts, he was in an unprecedented position when the 1806 Session commenced. While officially no more than a mediocre Scots barrister, he was bound to be a leading voice in whatever Ministry followed Pitt's, despite the fact that he had not yet been called to the English Bar, and was not a Member of Parliament. It may well have been this prospect, with both the

---

111. *Ibid.*, p.22.
112. *Ibid.*
113. *Ibid.*, p.29.
114. *Ibid.*, p.91.

abolition of the trade, and the impeachment of Melville on the agenda, that persuaded Hawkesbury not to form a government. Brougham had prepared for his Prime Ministership under conditions, objectives, and sanctions that Hawkesbury could not have been happy with.

Consequently, George III sent for Charles Fox and Lord Grenville, the Whigs, to form an administration. It also included old Tories like Sidmouth and Lord Ellenborough, the Chief Justice of the King's Bench. Sir Samuel Romilly, the new Solicitor General, whom Brougham had met at the "King of Clubs",[115] a Whig club which included Smith and Horner among its membership, favoured Ellenborough's inclusion.[116] While it is easy to accept the conventional explanation, as was pointed out in the debates in Parliament, that the Chief Justice's presence in the Cabinet was a hypothetical threat to the rule of law,[117] it was an easy way to defuse the upcoming impeachment of Melville, something that Romilly might have gleaned from his conversations with Brougham while he awaited to attend the Lord Chancellor's Court in Lincoln's Inn. Ellenborough promised a most harsh judgment of the former First Lord, and, as Lord Campbell has said, the Chief Justice was willing to go to any length to gain a conviction. Everyone, especially the Whigs, was expecting Ellenborough to make amends. With Ellenborough a minister, however, his claims and rulings were just seen as partisan manoeuvrings. Except for the public display by the spectators, the trial itself was little more than a matter of course.[118] Romilly summed up the Commons' case against Melville in a way which made it seem that he had carried out the most controversial manipulations for reasons of state. The Lords found him innocent on all counts. Brougham had proven right about Melville after all.

---

115. New, *op. cit.*, pp.32-3.
116. Holdsworth, *op. cit.*, vol.XIII, p.176.
117. *Ibid.* For the discussions, see *Cobbett's Parliamentary Debates*, vol.6, cols.254-84, 286-341, and 502-3.
118. For an account, see "The Ceremonial of the Trial of Lord Melville," *Gentleman's Magazine*, vol.81, 1806, Part I, p.462 ff.

For the "All the Talents" government, Brougham prepared, in effect, the Address from the Throne. Pitt's Ministry had collapsed, Brougham complained, "... before the causes of our present calamities have been ascertained; before the nation has been able to determine, either the extent or the origin of its dangers."[119] The kingdom was in danger of invasion because England had been too willing to promote precipitate action that only contributed to its detriment. England had never really tried to mediate her differences with France, and now she was nearly at her mercy. The Third Grand Coalition, which Napoleon had crushed at Austerlitz, never had any clear idea of what its function was. "But above all," he charged, "though England furnishes the sinews of the war, and originates the whole operation, she is not allowed a single voice in directing or controlling it ..."[120] Brougham was most understanding of the reasons for this, "... things were not ripe for a new war."[121] He lashed out at Pitt's Ministry for the documents that it had laid before Parliament about the war:

> It was not enough then, that our fatal activity accomplished at last the subjugation of the continent; that our allies were by our exertions brought to utter discomfiture, we must hold them up to contempt after the struggle is over, by divulging secrets which the most limited discretion would have respected.[122]

Pitt's failure to recruit an army, and to improve its constitution had compounded Britain's threat of invasion. "The fate of the third coalition," Brougham wrote, "has in several ways augmented this danger; multiplying both the chances of the attempt being made, and increasing the probability of its success."[123] While the kingdom had been celebrating Nelson's

---

119. "An Inquiry into the State of the Nation ..." (Longman, London, 1806), p.3.
120. *Ibid.*, p.60.
121. *Ibid.*, p.84.
122. *Ibid.*, p.96.
123. *Ibid.*, p.127.

victory, making little of France's chances, Britain should have been sounding the alarm. France had become all-powerful. "Her ships of war may be captured," he explained, "but the commerce of France is safe."[124] A blockade of France would lead to the destruction of the colonies:

> ... if the produce of the French colonies is prevented from being exported, it must rot there, and the colonies must be ruined; the supplies of provisions must fail; the work of the plantations suspended; the Negroes revolt, and the whole be involved in ruin.[125]

Because America and Britain benefited by trade with the colonies, it was self-defeating to try to stop it. "The destruction of an enemy's trade is not to be desired," Brougham explained, "in order to annihilate his national wealth."[126] About abolition of the trade, he called on Fox's Government to see to "... the utter destruction of the grand evil that hourly endangers our existence in those rich settlements ..."[127] The Ministry should seek a moderate course, even with Napoleon. As for domestic policy, the new Administration should "... pursue these plans of moderate and salutary reform in the various branches of our national policy, without which no glory, no safety, not even the inheritance of a name will remain for England."[128]

Brougham's domination of the Ministry's policies and personnel choices was extraordinary for a man not yet thirty who had yet to be given a pocket borough. As for Lauderdale, "he was offered by Fox the post of governor-general of India, but subsequently withdrew his claims in consequence of the strong opposition of the court of directors to his appointment."[129] This must have been a joke that the defender of the Company tried

124. *Ibid.*, p.181.
125. *Ibid.*, pp.188-9.
126. *Ibid.*, p.196.
127. *Ibid.*, p.209.
128. *Ibid.*, p.219.
129. *The Dictionary of National Biography*, vol.12, p.800.

to play on the spokesman of the English monopolists. Viscount Strangford, another *bête noire* for Brougham about whom we shall hear more shortly, was sent off to France as minister-plenipotentiary *ad interim* to try to mediate the peace with Napoleon that Brougham wanted so dearly. Brougham himself was appointed secretary to a mission, headed by the renowned Admiral St Vincent, to Portugal to try to dissuade the French from invading the Iberian peninsula because of the risks involved. Unfortunately, unlike the poem "The Defense of Order" where St Vincent had torn out the bull's eye, Brougham saw another secret mission against Napoleon end in failure. Through his old Edinburgh associates though, he did get through the Holland House *inter sanctum* to Fox personally with whom he discussed ending the slave trade.

In the next issue of the *Review*, Brougham criticized Marcus Rainsford's account of developments at Saint Domingo for Fox's benefit. The Captain in the Third West Indian Regiment was seen as a defender of the trade who confused abolition for emancipation to the detriment of colonial policy. Conditions at St Domingo were seen in too favourable terms, as if it represented a model for the surrounding islands. "Such high colouring will certainly deceive nobody of ordinary sense,"[130] he wrote for Fox's benefit. This helped lead to the joint resolutions that Grenville and Fox introduced into the Houses of Parliament in June, calling for the trade's abolition. Brougham's pleasure in all this was captured in his correspondence with Loch. He was becoming a Fifeshire laird in the hope that it would help him to run independently for Parliament. Brougham even found the court session at Parliament House less trying than usual: "... I assure you it has not improved since I visited it last. However, Patience overcometh all things, even a long session."[131]

Brougham had prepared for everything but Fox's mortality.

---

130. Art.III, "Rainsford's Account of Hayti," *Edinburgh Review*, vol.8, no.XV, April 1806, p.51.
131. Brougham's letter to Loch, dated March 4, 1806: Atkinson, *op. cit.*, vol.II, pp.265-6.

When he died in August, his Ministry had little to show for itself except pointless negotiation with Napoleon, thanks to Brougham's influence. In fact, when the French emperor issued his Berlin decrees, trying to blockade trade with Britain, Grenville's Ministry responded with an Order in Council, dated January 7, 1807, "... establishing a blockade of France and all countries in Europe allied with or subject to her."[132] Brougham's alarm about French threats had panicked the Ministry to drastic action, now that Fox was gone, despite his prohibitions of military action against France's trade. Brougham had sought to minimize this backlash through his reviews in the *Review*, but to no avail. He dismissed Lemaistre's *Travels* "... as far as we can discern, to be one of the great multitude of English idlers whom every suspicion of hostilities pours over the face of the Continent, and who fortunately return, for the most part with as little inclination as talent, to become writers of travels."[133] Since Lemaistre's writing served no public purpose, Brougham urged him to hang up his pen. Brougham was equally concerned about Dutens's *Memoires d'un Voyageur*, but for a different reason, the inflated pretensions it gave to royal authority:

> All kings are immaculate, all courtiers pure and able, provided they do not quarrel with the ministry of the day; and all persons, of whatever rank, having large houses, full of good cheer, and open to parasites, are secure of the immortality which our author dispenses, and obtain a share of the same gift for their friends and guests.[134]

Dutens's life brought wit and learning into contempt.

With England getting caught up in war fever, Brougham tried to stay the disease by writing another Address from the Throne, in effect, for the 1807 Session of Parliament. In a review of Frederick Gentz's *Balance of Power in Europe*, Brougham tried to

---

132. Holdsworth, *op. cit.*, vol.XIII, p.177.
133. Art.II, "Lemaistre's *Travels*," *Edinburgh Review*, vol.8, no.XVI, July 1806, p.254.
134. Art.VIII, "Dutens - *Memoires d'un Voyageur*," *ibid.*, p.356.

secure a more moderate policy at home and abroad. The states of Europe were continuing expedient policies, in the name of the balance of power, for their own immediate advantage, a course which had proved so disastrous to the third coalition. Ideas like "partitioning system", which had seen to Poland's destruction, were being used to veil what was really going on. In such a crazy world, Brougham charged, not even the abolition of the slave trade was a sure thing: "Ancient usage, indeed, has made men talk of the slave *trade*, by which they mean repeated acts of robbery and murder, accompanied with unnecessary torture, for the purpose of gain."[135] On the Continent, especially in Germany, the war party was over-estimating Russia's potential in subduing France. "We cannot help remarking that some of the Germans appear rather too prone, without our author's exhortation, to wait for a saviour, like the Jews ..."[136] In all this panic, even intelligent people like Gentz were overstating France's strength, failing to account for the circumstances to which she owed her success. England, too, Brougham repeated, always adopted the line least calculated to assist the common cause. She had revived the ancient illusion of trying to conquer Germany by action in America. Small British forces were conquering strategic places all around the globe in the hope that these actions were somehow hurting Napoleon. Britain should devote all her resources to one grand army which could really make the difference some day. "Had such obvious considerations prevailed over the love of sugar islands, and our eternal activity in the line of small, secret expeditions," he concluded, "England would not now have been reduced to lament the decay of her influence in the counsels by which France must be opposed."[137]

In the face of such bitter invective, even the weakened Grenville Ministry could not have second thoughts about abolition. Just in case, however, Brougham being not the kind of

---

135. Art.I, "Gentz on the State of Europe," *ibid.*, vol.XVIII, January 1807, p.259. For a much more optimistic appraisal of abolition chances, see New, *op. cit.*, p.30. Italics Brougham's.
136. *Ibid.*, p.258.
137. *Ibid.*, pp.277-8.

man to take chances in such matters, he repeated the arguments. In a review of George Pinckard's book on Abercromby's expedition to the West Indies, he recounted new evidence that the doctor of the Royal College had found of the evils of slavery itself. Brougham added:

> Nor is it, we trust, necessary to multiply the proof, at this time of day, when the Legislature is on the eve of proceeding to the total destruction of the trade, upon the unexampled chain of evidence already before them - evidence which, we will venture to assert, renders this by far the clearest case of a union between justice and policy that occurs in the whole history of nations.[138]

While Wilberforce was savouring this moment of victory, and other members of the Clapham Sect were planning with Brougham new efforts of reform, Hawkesbury took advantage of the King's fear of any conciliation of the Catholics, beyond the immediate needs of prosecuting the war, to force Grenville's dismissal. The Opposition leader wrote to George III that the Prime Minister wanted a dissolution of Parliament to effect Catholic Emancipation. The King, thanks to Brougham, had heard far too much of abolitions and possible emancipations for his liking. In the event, Brougham was reduced to writing, with the help of Lord Holland and John Allen, a series of articles for the *Morning Chronicle*, which were widely reprinted, outlining what young politicians and George III risked by so behaving.[139]

In the ensuing General Election, Brougham staked his political career upon the Whigs winning at the polls. This activity was most out of character, given his stated opinion upon the subject, but Hawkesbury's dedicated opposition had driven Brougham to such dire expedients. Three years before, when he was complaining to Loch about his review of Tennant's book, he had

---

138. Art.III, "*Dr Pinckard on the West Indies,*" *ibid.*, p.315.

139. See the series, signed "Scaevola", starting April 8 and ending May 29. For more on this episode, see Aspinall, *op. cit.*, pp.284-91.

also objected to canvassing for Francis Burdett's cause in a by-election. In keeping with Brougham's support of Pitt's Ministry, he dismissed such electoral activity as raffish, except among the aristocrats of Holland House. "In others," Brougham added, "it is dirty work - fit for tools - not men."[140] In the face of Hawkesbury's reaction, Brougham jumped at Lord Holland's offer to direct the Whig campaign. New has explained:

> With a very limited assistance from others "in the course of 10 days", according to Lord Holland, "he filled every bookseller's shop with pamphlets, most London newspapers and all country ones without exception with paragraphs", and wrote and distributed to all the boroughs in the country handbills "adapted to the local interests of the candidates".[141]

Holland and Allen assisted Brougham in his electioneering operation.

Brougham's decision to join the Whigs was based upon Fox's death, and the growing recognition of Hawkesbury as the Tories' leader. The Whig leader's death left a void among the aristocratic ranks that Brougham hoped to fill. Hawkesbury, in agreeing to participate in a Ministry in place of the dismissed Whigs, left little question about the motivation of his action:

> He continued strongly to oppose the whole catholic emancipation movement, and in the same year he said that "a protestant government alone was consistent with the laws and constitution of the British empire", and declared the Test Act to be an indispensable guarantee to a protestant government.[142]

Brougham's review of a Quaker account of work among North American Indians, which had associated the most meritorious of

---

140. Brougham's letter to Loch, dated August 3, 1804: Atkinson and Jackson, *op. cit.*, vol.II, p.149.
141. New, *op. cit.*, pp.36-7.
142. *The Dictionary of National Biography*, vol.10, p.749.

the sects with distasteful but necessary reform, had helped trigger Hawkesbury's initiative. In contrasting their missionary work with the more conventional concern of effecting zealous conversions, Brougham wrote tellingly: "... it by no means followed that their growth in grace must be attended with a proportionate improvement in the arts of common life."[143] The Quakers were more effective in their instructions because, unlike many Americans, they did not own slaves.

After the General Election, Brougham's propaganda efforts for the Whigs were so successful that although still without a seat in Parliament, he made the Opposition's case against the Ministry's Orders in Council against Napoleon's Berlin Decrees. "In 1807 and 1808," Professor Aspinall has written, "Brougham made himself personally responsible for several pamphlets in which the government's home and foreign policy was vigorously attacked."[144] These pamphlets were apparently on the need of increasing the regular army, of granting Catholic Emancipation, of enforcing the prohibition against the trade, and of ending the totally counterproductive Orders in Council. Brougham reinforced their message by reviewing them favourably in the *Review*. Instead of trying to repair the plan of conscripting a 50,000-man army through taxes, and the use of substitutes, the "... government ought to raise an army perfectly adequate to the defence of the country whatever it may cost ..."[145] For Hawkesbury's benefit, Brougham said this about Catholic Emancipation: "There are some causes in which perseverance is sure to be rewarded with success ..."[146] For the West Indian planters who were finding no profitable market for their produce, Brougham advised: "The true remedy for the evil is only to be found in diminishing the growth of sugar. The abolition of the slave trade will gradually operate this in a great degree; both by

143. Art.XVI, "Civilization of the American Savages," *Edinburgh Review*, vol.7, no.XVI, July 1806, p.443.
144. Aspinall, *op. cit.*, p.291.
145. Art.XI, "Observations on the Means of Increasing the Regular Army," *Edinburgh Review*, vol.11, no.XXI, October 1807, p.175.
146. Art.VIII, "Pamphlets on the Catholic Question," *ibid.*, p.116.

forcing the planter to exact less work from his negroes, and by obliging him to provide more provision grounds for their use."[147] The Orders in Council, which Hawkesbury had effected contrary to Brougham's advice on the right of neutral nations, were seen as repugnant to the laws of nations, the kingdom's public law, and prudent policy. Brougham blamed these near-treasonable acts, which only helped Napoleon, upon party spirit:

> Is a great measure to be defended? Its friends never think what are its merits, but who are its opponents; and instead of justifying their conduct to the world, or to the people whose interests it affects, think they do enough, if they throw a sop to the barking animals who are attacking it.[148]

Brougham complemented these reviews with others which characterized the Ministry's activities in hardly more flattering terms. About the mercantilist policies it practised in places like New Holland in the name of free trade, he concluded: "So that the rules are all excellent, but every case is an exception; and the principles, even when acknowledged in the abstract, are frittered down absolutely to nothing in the application."[149] When a ministerial supporter called for a patriotic war against Napoleon, Brougham chided: "To hear such men as Mr Hunter talk of freeing Europe, and humbling France, one would really think that ships could sail by land, and take places among hills and woods."[150] As for war aims, Brougham added:

> ... we should once and for all give up every expectation of conquering France, or of seeing her exhausted by the war, or of enjoying the spectacle of a restoration of the old

147. Art.IX, "Sir W. Young and Others on West Indian Affairs," *ibid.*, p.163.
148. Art.XIV, "Examination of the late Orders in Council," *ibid.*, no.XXI, January 1808, p.486.
149. Art.V, "Turnbull's *Voyage Round the World*," *ibid.*, vol.9, no.XVIII, January 1807, p.337.
150. Art.XI, "Hunter's *Reasons for not making Peace*," *ibid.*, p.427.

> government by our fighting at sea, and our allies trying to themselves on shore, or of witnessing the political humiliation of that powerful and military people by any commercial difficulties whatever.[151]

When a West Indian planter called for freeing the people of Europe from French despotism, Brougham wrote bitterly: "They care no more about it, than they do about the African slave trade, or the traffic in crowns and princes carried on in the East Indies, or any other merely indifferent matter."[152] Wilberforce's pamphlet to his Yorkshire constituents on the slave trade gave Brougham an opportunity to discuss the remedies for such selfish action:

> To see this statute strictly executed; to watch over all the evasions which slave traders may attempt, and to pursue every hint which may be received of connivance on the part of colonial officers, or of new rulers at home, adverse to the abolition, will be the indispensable duty of those zealous and upright persons whose efforts have already triumphed over so many difficulties, and who have, in fact, only succeeded at last, because they found a government honestly favourable to their cause.[153]

In discussing pamphlets on the rights of neutrals during the bitter struggle between England and France, Brougham warned: "A war with America must not only raise the price of lumber and provisions, but increase incalculably the charges of freight and insurance."[154]

The result of this general attack upon the government, culminating in Brougham's review of his pamphlet, *Orders in Councils*, was that the Whigs were obliged not only to call for

---

151. *Ibid.*, p.432.
152. Art.XIII, "*Letter on Guiana*," *ibid.*, p.461.
153. Art.XIII, "Wilberforce *on the Abolition of the Slave Trade*," *ibid.*, no.XIX, p.205.
154. Art.I, "Randolph and Others on the Neutral Questions," ibid., vol.11, no.XXI, October 1807, p.29.

their revocation but also to hire Brougham to make their case at the Bar of the Commons. To be called to this Bar when he had not even been called to the Bar at Lincoln's Inn was indeed an honour. When the Commons had taken up the question at the beginning of the Session, the Whigs had been so ineffective in making the case against the Orders, in the face of the just declared American embargo, that he was given the task. Adapting the tactics of the recent election campaign, "Brougham urged on the merchants the method of mass petitions, as many names and as many petitions as possible."[155] He started examining witnesses at the Bar on March 18, and on April 1, he summarized the evidence thus obtained. About the petitions from London, Liverpool, and Manchester, praying for quashing the Orders, Brougham explained: "They are persuaded that if they delayed any longer seeking that redress which they now pray for, they would only have waited till instead of three petitions, a general clamour would have been raised all over the country ..."[156] He repeated his explanation for the cause of the difficulty:

> I think I can prove, sir, that we ourselves, blinded and alarmed by the empty menaces of the enemy, which we had often before experienced to be ineffectual, terrified by vain fears which he could not describe, and arguing from the very uncertainty of the darkness in which we were ... carried them triumphantly into execution by our all powerful navy ...[157]

Britain had invited the American embargo, and, consequently, the Orders in Council should be withdrawn. Brougham summed up his case in characteristic fashion:

> I do trust that this lesson which the wisdom of parliament, and let me add, of the country, shall have given to its ruler will be eternal, and frighten any rash projector from ever

---

155. New, *op. cit.*, p.42.
156. "The Speech of Henry Brougham before the House of Commons ..." (Ridgeway, London, 1808), pp.3-4.
157. *Ibid.*, p.25.

> again presuming to take for the subject of his wild experiments, the edifice of British commerce ...[158]

While Brougham's effort was widely applauded,[159] the Ministry rejected the petitions. In fact, Hawkesbury redoubled his efforts to frustrate Brougham. The following Session, he even improved upon his performance as counsel against a private bill to incorporate a metropolitan utility. When it threatened to pass on the bases of interested votes, he published the "Speeches of Henry Brougham ... in opposition to a Bill for .... the .... and Coke Company" to help secure its defeat.

When Brougham tried to capitalize upon his performance at the Commons, in a way which recalled his former ties with Pitt's Ministry, the government helped prevent it. On June 30, 1808, Brougham petitioned the Benchers at Lincoln's Inn, asking them to waive the customary number of keeping commons because of the special aspects of his case. He explained that he had "... performed all his exercises, attained the age of 21 years, and conformed himself in every respect to the Rules of this Society, except as to his full standing of five years ..."[160] Brougham wrote to Loch, asking him to get his uncle, the East India Company's counsel, to assist the petition. "... I fancy," Brougham wrote, "a special motion by your Uncle will be requisite."[161] Sir Vicary Gibbs, the Attorney General who had been so troubled by the prospect of prosecuting Melville, and Sir Thomas Plumer, the Solicitor General, who had defended the former First Lord during his impeachment, attended the Council of eight Benchers to make sure that Brougham's petition failed. When the Duke of Portland, the Ministry's nominal head, died, Spencer Perceval, the then Prime Minister, asked Lords Grenville and Grey to join a reconstructed one in the hope of isolating Brougham from his aristocratic supporters, but the effort failed. Perceval had been

158. *Ibid.*, p.83.
159. *Gentleman's Magazine*, vol.78, Part I, pp.442-3.
160. *The Records of the Honourable Society of Lincoln's Inn: The Black Books* (Lincoln's Inn, London, 1902, 5 vols.), vol.IV, p.113.
161. Brougham's letter to Loch, no date, Atkinson and Jackson, *op. cit.*, vol.II, p.251.

Pitt's Attorney General. Hawkesbury, who had become the second Earl of Liverpool when his father had died the previous December, took over the conduct of foreign policy.

Grey and Grenville had been sorely tempted by the offer because of Brougham's increasingly radical ways, but they had declined it due to fears of what he would do alone and unattended out of Parliament. Brougham's leadership of the press campaign against the Tory Ministry, claiming that it was undertaking wild experiments with the Constitution itself, was increasingly seen as a vindictive pursuit of political opponents. To get back at the Ministry, for example, Brougham attacked Sir Home Popham, the leader of a naval expedition to Rio de la Plata, so unmercifully in the *Morning Chronicle* when the Ministry rewarded him for acting without orders by appointing him captain of the fleet in the expedition against Copenhagen.[162] The perfunctory court martial of Popham, with his attempt to justify what he had done because Pitt's administration, the previous government, had favoured such an expedition, and the confidence that people like Lord Melville had in the mission,[163] recalled the means by which Hawkesbury had gained power from the Whigs. When the Ministry named Lord Strangford minister plenipotentiary to the Portuguese Court,[164] Brougham was beside himself. He had seen more than he wanted of this as secretary of the legation at Lisbon during his mission to Portugal. His attack on the appointment in the *Morning Chronicle* was so savage, claiming that Strangford's role in the departure of the Portuguese court had been encouraged by the Foreign Office, that he was angry when Loch identified him as the writer of the story in the *Citizen*. After Brougham had explained the special arrangements he had made to hide his identity in doing this most necessary task, he added: "And contrary to usual practice, *I plainly told you* that I was the author of the discussion in question - for the express purpose of preventing you from saying anything

162. Aspinall, *op. cit.*, p.291.

163. "Court-Martial of Sir Home Popham," *Gentleman's Magazine*, vol.77, Part I, 1807, p.262.

164. *London Gazette*, 1807, p.1748.

about it ..."[165] Once Holland House learned of the story's source, Brougham could not stop trying to justify himself, as Lord Holland was later to complain.[166]

When the expected briefs did not appear, especially after Brougham had been called to the Bar in November 1808,[167] his reviews became more acerbic and radical. What he had previously alluded to regarding the consequences of individual and collective licence, he increasingly spelled out. About John Barrow's biography of Lord Macartney, he said that it "... offers to our view an example above all praise, of a regular place-hunter, by no means wealthy, remaining in the last act of life devoted to his profession, altogether uncorrupted by half a century spent amidst the bribery of senates, the tricks of embassies, and the plunder of the East."[168] About Macartney's journal regarding his liberal administration in Ireland, Brougham added: "He wrote, it is true, before the royal conscience had been disturbed by the jesuitical arts of intriguing hypocrites ..."[169] About the ministerial excuse of the need for the Orders in Council, an act which reduced Britain to Napoleon's level, he wrote bitterly: "... this regret, which we have now seen expressed in declarations under the Sovereign's name, that we have so long abstained from deeds of violence, and struck so long to the wreck of public principle ..."[170] To try to hide that there were any partisan motives in these attacks, Brougham attacked the latest volume of Byron's poetry. In his *British Bards and Scotch Reviewers*, Byron dismissed the former Percy Smythe for teaching "the Lucian bard to copy Moore", and described him thus:

Hibernian Strangford, with thine eyes of blue,

---

165. Brougham's letter to Loch, dated Friday night, Atkinson and Jackson, *op. cit.*, vol.II, p.348. Italics Brougham's.
166. Quoted in Aspinall, *op. cit.*, p.291.
167. *The Records ...*, *op. cit.*, vol.IV, p.245.
168. Art.III, "Barrow's *Life of Lord Macartney*," *Edinburgh Review*, vol.11, no.XXII, January 1808, p.306.
169. *Ibid.*, p.310.
170. Art.XIV, "Examination ...", *ibid.*, p.498.

And boasted locks of red or auburn hue.[171]

Brougham found similar rhymes by this self-conscious youth completely wanting: "It is a plea available only to the defendant; no plaintiff can offer it as a supplementary ground of action."[172] Brougham concluded, however, that the reader must be content with these adolescent efforts "... for they are the last we shall ever have from him."[173] Brougham was hardly more charitable towards Whitbread's views, and actions by the Whigs on the situation in Spain.

The Whigs, of course, did everything they could to restrain Brougham's growing radicalism, as we learn from his correspondence with Loch. Gilbert Elliot, the second Lord Minto, had baited the hook by writing thus to Brougham's friend after the Commons' hearing of the petitions against the Orders in Council: "I shall be much obliged to you for Brougham's speeches when they are printed; is there any chance of his being brought into Parliament? It is really downright waste in these times of severity to confine his fine talents entirely to the Law."[174] During the summer of 1808, after Lincoln's Inn had turned down Brougham's petition, he visited the Duke of Bedford at Woburn Abbey for the purpose of finding a seat in Parliament. "By the way," Brougham wrote to Loch, "the party was very agreeable - only the journey there was not quite so much so - for the Hollands going about the same time, asked me to go with them which sort of family travelling is always a bore."[175] While Bedford wanted to make his acquaintance, Brougham found him almost incapable of speech when they met. About the talkative Duchess, Brougham added, "... she makes up for it."[176] Brougham found it even more difficult to get out of Woburn

---

171. *The Dictionary of National Biography*, vol.18, p.604.
172. Art.II, "Lord Bryon's *Poems*," *Edinburgh Review*, vol.11, no.XXII, January 1808, p.285.
173. *Ibid.*, p.289.
174. Elliot's letter to Loch, dated May 15, 1808, Atkinson and Jackson, *op. cit.*, vol.II, p.302.
175. Brougham's letter to Loch, dated July 30, 1808, *ibid.*, p.313.
176. *Ibid.*, p.314.

Abbey, having to wait in vain for two days for the Hollands to take him back to London.

Three weeks later when he was visiting Edinburgh, he gave Loch a good picture of his political situation as he sat down to write the famous "Don Cevallos" article. The previous April, Brougham had written his strongest condemnation of the Ministry yet, "Portuguese Emigration". About the books responsible for these reflections, Brougham wrote: "They neither influence the votes of senators, nor touch upon places and patronage, nor contribute to the change of the ministry, nor help the government to a triumph over its antagonists."[177] The volume by Ralph Rylance, Brougham continued, had proved that Canning, the Foreign Secretary, had deceived Parliament when he issued documents contending that Strangford had played a crucial role in the departure of the Portuguese court for Brazil:

> ... this government stands convicted of a base and unworthy attempt, either to falsify the statements of their agent, Lord Strangford, or to protect that noble Lord in giving to the world a delusive account of his conduct, for the purpose of arrogating to himself and his employers a credit which was due to neither.[178]

Three months later, he showed little more confidence in the Opposition when he concluded his critique of Whitbread's pamphlet thus: "... there is in Europe a fund both of power and of spirit, far more than sufficient to suppress the usurpations of France, if guided by better counsels, and husbanded in the mean time with economy and caution."[179]

"The last *E. Review* and some former ones," Brougham wrote to Loch, "have put the ministerial folks here out of all patience. They storm beyond bounds, and as I am accused of it, Jeffrey being no partisan, I have the whole brunt of it to bear now. Scott

---

177. Art.XIV, "Portugeze Emigration," *Edinburgh Review*, vol.12, no.XXIII, April 1808, p.246.
178. *Ibid.*, p.249.
179. Art.XI, "Mr Whitbread's *Letter on Spain*," *ibid.*, no.XXIV, July 1808, pp.447-8.

has refused to write any more on *this* precise ground - probably assisted by *Marmion*."[180] The Whigs were hardly happy with the situation either. "Lord Holland admitted in 1809 that the management of the Press had left much to be desired ..."[181] Professor Aspinall continued: "Brougham's name may have been omitted from the proposed list of managers because Lord Grenville disliked his politics ..."[182] As Brougham became more and more independent and radical in his press coverage, his Whig managers were increasingly left to their own devices, as we learn from Aspinall:

> Throughout 1808 and 1809 Brougham was writing for the *Morning Chronicle*, and his temporary absence from town in October 1809 gave Lord Holland some concern. "We shall be a little gravelled for paragraphs for some days," he confided to Lord Grenville. "Can you procure me any or give me sense for some. Hitherto the labour has fallen exclusively upon me."[183]

Brougham had made himself indispensable with the Whigs by setting "'... some *outcriesy* a-going' against the Tory Prime Minister. Brougham professed to find these activities extremely distasteful: it was 'dirty work, like most work of necessity.'"[184]

Brougham, in trying to develop some outcries against Liverpool's Ministry, made it appear that all aristocrats were potential collaborators with the victorious Napoleon. In "Don Pedro Cevallos *on the French Usurpation of Spain*", a joint article with Jeffrey to emphasize its nonpartisan character, Brougham lashed out at Ferdinand VII's former Secretary of State. Don Cevallos was seen as a self-serving architect of Spain's submissions and humiliations at the hands of the French who only recovered his

---

180. Brougham's letter to Loch, dated August 19, 1808, Atkinson and Jackson, *op. cit.*, vol.II, pp.319-20. Italics Brougham's.
181. Aspinall, *op. cit.*, p.293.
182. *Ibid.*
183. *Ibid.*, p.291.
184. Quoted by Aspinall from Atkinson and Jackson, *op. cit.*, vol.II, p.347. Italics Brougham's.

speech against the foreign invader when French armies were literally pouring into his country. Instead of aristocrats like Don Cevallos joining the popular effort of national liberation, Brougham continued, they were pursuing their own special interests:

> The resistance to France has been entirely begun and carried on by the people of Spain. Their Kings betrayed them - fled, and rushed, with the whole of their base courtiers, into the arms of the enemy. Their nobles followed; and it is painful to reflect, that some of the most distinguished of this body, after attending Ferdinand to Bayonne, returned in the train of Joseph, and only quitted his service when the universal insurrection of the common people drove him from his usurped throne.[185]

In the face of this mass treachery by those who had benefited under the former regime, he added: "Common sense requires an alteration in the political constitution of the monarchy, sufficiently radical to guard it against a recurrence of the late crisis."[186] Liberty would grow, thanks to British assistance; the tricks of the counter-revolutionary aristocrats were over. "But the *Spanish* revolution comes most opportunely," he said for the benefit of Burke's followers', "to turn the tide quite into the opposite channel; to awaken in the country all those feelings of liberty and patriotism which many had supposed were extinguished since the *French* revolution ..."[187]

While the Whig leadership chose to ignore Brougham's challenge, while the controversy over the Copenhagen expedition was developing, threatening a secession of half its members because of George Tierney's lack of leadership in the Commons, the Tories responded by establishing a new journal, the *Quarterly Review*. "It used to be said that the new journal was an unwilling result of the dangerous principles of a previous one, chiefly on the

---

185. Art.XIV, "Don Pedro Cevallos *on the French Usurpation of Spain*," *Edinburgh Review*, vol.13, no.XXV, October 1808, p.220.
186. *Ibid.*, p.221.
187. *Ibid.*, p.222. Italics Brougham's.

war, and on domestic reform."[188] Sir Walter Scott joined its ranks of writers. George Canning contributed the first article, "Affaires d'Espagne", which was directed at refuting Brougham's claims in the *Edinburgh Review*. Brougham was charged with seeing the invasion of Spain as an Englishman would:

> We do not suppose that a clear-sighted clergy, or the nobles, or the magistrates, ever felt, or now feel that enthusiastical affection for the person of Ferdinand VII ... His degradation was that specific violation of the national independence which became the universal signal of revolt.[189]

The Foreign Secretary was even more pointed in his criticism of Brougham's explanation of what had happened and his prophecy:

> It is predicted that the vigour of the *revolutionary* Juntas will procure for the nation, not indeed ultimate success and independence, but at least an honourable capitulation, a state of most dignified submission to France. And this example will be productive of marvellous good effects in this country, exciting us to effect that radical reform from the completion of which we were unhappily scared by Mr Pitt's reign of terror.[190]

The Spanish insurrection was becoming a crusade, like the Scottish one against the English invasion of the thirteenth century, Canning concluded. Jeffrey must have been looking at this article in the first issue when he wrote: "... if it were not for our offences, I should have no fear about its consequences."[191]

Brougham was responding, however, to another concern of Jeffrey's. In December, the *Review* editor had written to Horner: "I

---

188. Brougham's letter to Thomas Creevey, dated December 1808, in John Gore, ed, *Creevey's Life and Times: A Further Selection from the Correspondence of Thomas Creevey* (Murray, London, 1937), p.40.
189. Art.I, "*Affaires d'Espagne*," *Quarterly Review*, vol.1, February 1808, p.5.
190. *Ibid.*, pp.6-7. Italics Canning's.
191. Lord Cockburn, *Life of Lord Jeffrey* (Black, Edinburgh, 1852, 2 vols.), vol.I, p.193.

must say that a temperate, firm, and enlightened article on Spain, would, of all other things, be the most serviceable and restorative to us at this crisis."[192] In the April 1809 issue, Brougham tried to supply it. As the expedition against Copenhagen, something that he had dealt with in his own distinctive way in the previous issue, had "... probably ensured the subjugation of the North, and confirmed the alienation of the whole Continent from this country,"[193] the siege of Saragossa was confirming for the Iberian peninsula. Britain, instead, should have challenged Napoleon directly by sending an army to the Pyrenees to meet the French counter-offensive. Brougham dismissed Robert Vaughan's *Narrative of the Siege of Zaragoza* as just more ministerial propaganda to hide Britain's opportunism. The idea about a popular Spanish uprising, he said, was just a delusion. The Spanish Government had merely deceived everyone instead of mobilizing the country, and improving the people's condition:

> Such deceptions, practised by all the Juntas, might keep up the national spirit for a season, and render the talk of government more easy. But in a short time they were sure to be detected; and their effect must be to propagate alarm and distrust - alarm, greater than the occasion justified - distrust, equal to what the authors of the flattering statements deserved.[194]

Thanks to the Ministry's censorship and deception, the people knew hardly anything about military operations, and cared even less. "In the mean time," Brougham concluded, "our army is, as usual, locked up in a place where it cannot be of the smallest use."[195]

The impact of these hard-hitting reviews, often based upon Brougham's own pamphlets, was offset, at least temporarily, by the appearance of Byron's *English Bards and Scotch Reviewers*. Byron

---

192. Jeffrey's letter to Horner, dated December 29, 1808, *ibid.*
193. Art.XIII, "Expedition against Copenhagen," *Edinburgh Review*, vol.13, no.XXVI, January 1809, p.489.
194. Art.XVI, "Vaughan's Siege of Saragossa," *ibid.*, vol.14, no.XXVII, April 1809, p.250.
195. *Ibid.*, p.263.

built on couplets like this one from Pope:

> Such shameless Bards we have; and yet 'tis true,
> There are as made, abandon'd Criticks too.

About the result, the *Gentleman's Magazine* wrote:

> At length comes forth a poetical work that possesses not only the three avowedly grand recommendations of *time, place,* and *circumstance* - of such moment in all *worldly* matters; but, so far as regards Literature, the three no less important, though, alas! far less frequent recommendations of defying *enemies* - rendering the favourable sentiments of *friends* superfluous - and the quackery of *the trade* wholly unnecessary.[196]

In making an impassioned, patriotic plea in the great poetic tradition, Byron left bards like Strangford, and critics like Brougham to the world of party politics:

> For me, who thus unknown have dar'd to tell
> My Country what her sons should know too well,
> Zeal for her honour, no malignant rage,
> Has bade me spurn the follies of her age.
> No just applause her honoured name shall lose,
> As first in freedom, dearest to the Muse.
> Oh! would thy Bards but emulate the fame!
> And rise more worthy, Albion, of thy name!
> What Athens was in science, Rome in power,
> What Tyre appeared in her meridian hour,
> 'Tis thine at one, fair Albion, to have been,
> Earth's chief dictatress. Ocean's mighty queen:
> But Rome decay'd, and Athens strew'd the plain,
> And Tyre's proud piers lie shatter'd in the Main;
> Like these thy strength may sink in ruin hurl'd,

196. 37. "English Bards and Scotch Reviewers," *Gentleman's Magazine,* vol.79, 1809, Part I, p.246. Italics its.

And Britain fall, the Bulwark of the World.
But let me cease, and dread Cassandra's fate,
With warning ever scoff'd at, till too late;
To themes less lofty still my lay confine,
And urge thy Bards to gain a name like Thine.[197]

Brougham was able to reduce the impact of this attack by the mercurial artist by his review of science. Ever since Brougham had taken up pamphletering for the Whigs, and reviewing them favourably in the *Review*, he had tried to take politics out of what was going on in the laboratory. In four reviews of Davy's Bakerian lectures, he performed a constructive role for chemistry which rebounded to his advantage. In reviewing the 1806 lecture, Brougham said unrepentantly: "It is no small proof of Mr Davy's natural talents and strength of mind, that they have escaped unimpaired the enervating influence of the Royal Institution ..."[198] Davy was not only complimented for his experiments on the electrical properties of certain alkali metals but also urged to investigate the chemical reaction further. The next year, Brougham said that subsequent lectures had fulfilled his promise. Brougham answered Byron's patriotic plea with a most cosmopolitan appreciation of Davy's further experiments:

> The paper now before us contains fewer complete processes - fewer discoveries satisfactorily established than any of the former ones; - but it abounds in elaborate and ingenious experiments, the results of which, in their present state extremely interesting, are yet more so, as paving the way for further research, and scattering thickly the seeds of most important improvements in chemical science.[199]

Davy's experiments just corroborated what French chemists like Lavoisier and Gay-Lassac were postulating about combustion.

---

197. Quoted from *ibid.*, pp.248-9.
198. Art.VIII, "Davy's Bakerian Lecture," *Edinburgh Review*, vol.11, no.XXII, January 1808, p.390.
199. Art.XII, "Davy's Bakerian Lecture," *ibid.*, vol.14, no.XXVIII, July 1809, p.483.

Brougham explained:

> We then rather cite this passage, because persons, half informed on these subjects, and senseless enough (if, indeed, another word should not be used) to contaminate scientific inquiries with the vulgar feelings of political hostility, have of late been forward in extolling the discoveries of Mr Davy, not on account of their intrinsic value, but from some vague confused notion, that they overthrew the modern theory founded by the French chemists, and created, as it were, a sort of balance of invention in favour of England.[200]

Brougham was ashamed to mention such a disgusting topic, and only wished that Davy had made his discoveries three years earlier, before everything had become consumed in political controversy. "If the rulers of nations are resolved never to consult the interests of the species in abstaining from war," Brougham concluded, "surely they might contrive to conduct operations, which can only be excused from their necessity, in such a manner as to avoid unnecessary aggravations of the evil."[201]

Brougham, reassured that he was serving a higher authority than Byron's, renewed his attacks upon the Ministry's foreign policy in the hope of helping to create a crisis, unlike the controversy over the Copenhagen expedition, that the Whigs could not ignore. In reviewing James Jackson's account of Morocco, Brougham repeated how shabbily the government had treated its Emperor's friendly overtures.[202] In the same issue of the *Review*, he tried to revive interest in the idea of the balance of power in Europe by re-examining the history of the partitions of Poland.[203] In a column on foreign policy, Brougham expanded upon what he had said earlier in "*Pamphlets on West Indian Affairs.*" Lord Sheffield, after denying that trade had been hurt by the Order in Council, admitted the loss, blaming it upon the cessation of the slave trade.

---

200. *Ibid.*, p.489.
201. *Ibid.*, p.490.
202. Art.II, "Jackson's *Account of Morocco,*" *ibid.*, p.314.
203. Art.III, "Rulhiere - Anarchie de Pologne," *ibid.*, pp.388-406.

In reviewing another pamphlet, James Stephen's speech on Whitbread's motion about American overtures to end its embargo, Brougham said: "Mr Stephen understands the subject, and the science to which it belongs, too well, to contend, like Lord Sheffield, that the Orders in Council were in themselves of advantage."[204] The Orders in Council, in fact had been withdrawn, replaced by an embargo which hurt Britain and her allies more than the French. About Leckie's study of foreign policy, Brougham chided: "The expedition to Copenhagen is, according to him, the only right thing they ever did."[205] After reviewing the same policy himself, Brougham said this about Perceval's Government: "It adopted the only plan which could be entirely wrong, and was sure wholly to fail."[206] Brougham repeated the theme of the "Don Cevallos" article that conditions had to get worse before they could get better.

In the October 1809 issue, Brougham went all out to have a showdown with the government and Opposition. In reviewing the conduct of the war, he predicted a French victory in Spain and Portugal. "The whole vices of our policy towards foreign states," he wrote, "have been fatally exemplified in the management of the Spanish alliance; and the worst corruptions in the practice of our constitution have been displayed, with most pernicious effect, in the progress of this melancholy story."[207] In retracing the steps of Sir John Moore's army which led to its defeat, and his death, Brougham made much of the General's resolution to try to help the Spaniards, though the English had no business being there. "He was forced into this fatal step, contrary to his judgment and inclinations," Brougham explained, "by the remonstrances of the Spanish Government and English envoy ..."[208] As for what Britain could expect from current policies, he said: "We retain an unhealthy marsh in Estremadura, and keep a pestilential island in Holland, because the whole of the West Indies do not furnish a

---

204. Art.XI, "Lord Sheffield and Others on Foreign Affairs," *ibid.*, p.447.
205. *Ibid.*, p.455.
206. *Ibid.*, p.469.
207. Art. XIV, "The Conduct of the War," *ibid.*, vol.15, no.XXIX, October 1809, p.189.
208. *Ibid.*, p.223.

sufficient number of useless spots, where our army may be divided, and our hospitals filled."[209] As for what Britain could expect from the coming Session, Brougham added:

> It now remains to be seen, whether that Parliament, which stands in no need of representation - which is a fair representation of the people of England - which speaks the sentiments of the country - will be satisfied with this set off; and once more acquit the ministers of all blame for their recent mismanagement.[210]

If the government again escaped censure, it would show either that there was no blame or that it was inexpedient to declare it. Brougham developed his possible censure of the Opposition thus: "In the one case, the Parliament will show that it is not the representative of the country; in the other, we shall have a conclusive proof that the ministers of the crown are irremovable."[211]

With this challenge, the Whigs had no alternative but to find Brougham a seat in the Commons. With an abortive expedition on the parliamentary agenda, the one to the Scheldt, Brougham could be of use in trying to make the Whigs' case, and he would now have nobody but himself to blame if it failed. Consequently, once the public had absorbed the message of "The Conduct of the War", rather than have it rammed down its throat, as had been Brougham's earlier approach to gaining favour,[212] he was offered the seat for Camelford, a Cornish pocket borough in the nomination of the Duke of Bedford. It had been held by Lord Henry Petty, Brougham's childhood friend from Edinburgh, but he had been called up to the Lords upon the death of his father, the Marquis of Lansdowne. Brougham's only concern about this unexpected offer, having long suspected that his disagreements with Lauderdale were a barrier to Parliament, was whether he was

---

209. *Ibid.*, p.233.
210. *Ibid.*, p.234.
211. *Ibid.*, p.235.
212. For evidence of this, see Aspinall, *op. cit.*, p.292 ff.

sufficiently solvent to withstand its temptations. He sought advice from Lord Rosslyn, one of the heads of the mission to Portugal, and his father about the offer. While the latter was his customary, non-committal self about it, Rosslyn replied in terms so abhorrent to an independent Whig that he decided to accept: "If, however, you feel uncertain of your own powers of resistance, or likely to yield to the innumerable solicitations and temptations with which you will be assailed, I should think that every prudential consideration ought to deter you."[213] Brougham entered the Commons on February 5, 1810. Henry Brougham, Sr, conveniently died 12 days later at Brougham Hall.[214]

---

213. Quoted from Frances Hawes, *Henry Brougham* (Cape, London, 1957), pp.60-1.
214. *Gentleman's Magazine*, vol.80, 1810, Part I, p.386.

CHAPTER THREE

MEMBER OF PARLIAMENT

Brougham was bitterly disappointed by his experience in the Commons, but, as usual, when faced with adversity, he put it to good use. His problem was not the temptations of the Ministry, but the treachery of the Whigs who had gone to such trouble to get him there. Brougham thought that his selection for Camelford was an admission by them that the Ministry's expedition to the Scheldt, in the wake of its expeditions to Copenhagen and Spain, constituted grounds for censure. Certainly, his pamphlets on these subjects, and their favourable review in the *Edinburgh Review* represented the Opposition's leading claims against the King's Ministers. Lord Holland admitted as much when he recommended that Brougham follow Lord Henry Petty in the Cornish constituency. Brougham's reviews of Vaughan's *Siege of Saragossa,* and "The Conduct of the War" constituted the Whigs' complaints against a government which was on the verge of collapse. The Duke of Bedford recognized this when he approved Brougham's selection. During the next Session, Lord Grenville and Grey could not run away from the confrontation with Perceval's Ministry, as they had during the aftermath of the Copenhagen expedition. To do so would constitute the passing of the Whigs, and the opening of a more radical period, as Brougham had been predicting since his "Don Cevallos" review. Somehow, the Whigs had to accommodate the troublesome barrister without upsetting the government, a most difficult dilemma, given the expectations of the former, and the desperation of the latter.

Brougham, in anticipation of his election, devoted himself to becoming the Whigs' expert on the slave trade. Since Fox's death, they had needed a new parliamentary spokesman, a counterpart to the Tories' Wilberforce. In a *Review* article, Brougham traced the history of the African Institution in a most expansive way, recalling his pleas for a comprehensive, secular reform of government. The very name of the new institution, of which Brougham was a director, seemed a reminder of what the Royal Institution should constitute. The people who had started the African Institution, Brougham stated had not been taken in by Liverpool's counter-revolutionary stroke which had overthrown the Whig Ministry. Men like Wilberforce, Allen, Henry Thornton, William Smith, James Stephen, William Clarkson, and Zachary Macaulay were trying to undo the terrible evils done to Africa by the trade. "The Society", Brougham added, recalling the political and practical reforms which he had seen as necessary in discussing the activities of the Quakers, "also disclaims all schemes of religious mission ..."[1] The African Institution had the responsibility "... of watching over the strict execution of the abolition laws - those laws which daring speculators may attempt ..."[2] to circumvent. Brougham explained: "The Board has been actively employed in giving effect to the Abolition Act, by bringing to light evasions or violations of it by the arts of slave-merchants abroad, and their coadjutors in this country."[3] The Institution was also trying to improve the law, and to see that other countries adopted the most strict codes and enforcement. Brougham refrained from discussing the details of these functions for fear that they would assist felons, and offenders of the laws of nations. He did call upon those who knew of violations, or had suggestions for additional prohibitions to contact the Institution or the *Review*. About public action to assist the crusade, Brougham was hardly optimistic: "We confess, however, that, from such a government, little is to be expected."[4]

---

1. Art.XIV, "The African Institution," *Edinburgh Review*, vol.15, no.XXX, January 1810, p.495.
2. *Ibid.*, p.496.
3. *Ibid.*, p.501.
4. *Ibid.*

On this note, Brougham took his seat in the Commons, just as its inquiry into the Scheldt fiasco was getting into full swing. On January 23, the day that the Speaker, Abbot declared the seat at Camelford vacant,[5] the Opposition in Parliament moved amendments to the Speech from the Throne, calling for inquiries into the expedition. The Speech had justified it in these positive terms:

> An attack upon the naval armaments and establishments in the Scheldt, afforded at once the prospect of destroying a growing force, which was daily becoming more formidable to the Security of this Country, and of diverting the exertions of France from the important objects of reinforcing her armies on the Danube, and of controlling the spirit of resistance in the North of Germany.[6]

In the Commons, where the government was confronted by the call for an inquiry, Lord Castlereagh met Brougham's challenge head-on: "The Expedition to Copenhagen had given the Country the command of the Baltic, instead of being driven out of it."[7] The expedition to the Scheldt had been a *coup de main* which had been largely successful. "The loss both in Portugal and Walcheren," he added, "was greatly exaggerated."[8] While Brougham was involved in getting elected, the government was trying to divert the Whig challenge into manageable channels by claiming that censure should not precede investigation of the expedition. On January 27, Lord Porchester, a Whig leader in the Commons, got it to agree to an inquiry. A few days later, Castlereagh failed in trying to determine the composition of the investigation. On the very day that Brougham took his seat, the Commons named a secret committee, including William Wilberforce, to look into the matter. It also agreed to an Address to the Crown, calling for all the correspondence from the expedition's commanders, and the

---

5. *The Journals of the House of Commons*, vol.65, 1810, p.3.
6. *Gentleman's Magazine*, 1810, vol.80, Part I, p.65.
7. *Ibid.*, p.67.
8. *Ibid.*, p.68.

instructions that they had given their men. The Commons, as the Committee of the Whole, brought out the most damaging information against the government - ie, that it had not made the necessary consultations with the various specialists for the overall plan to have succeeded.[9]

The Crown, in answering the Address, showed that ministerial responsibility had broken down in explaining the expedition. The Earl of Chatham, its commander, and a member of the government, made a personal statement to the King, unknown to his colleagues, impugning the naval commander for its failure.[10] Parliament, as soon as it heard of Chatham's narrative, called for its investigation, charging that it constituted a constitutional abuse, justifying censure. Samuel Whitbread moved resolutions in the Commons, charging that Chatham had made a secret, unconstitutional communication with the Sovereign. Spencer Perceval, the First Lord of the Treasury, and Chancellor of the Exchequer, could not approve of Chatham's conduct, although he could not bring himself to say that it represented unconstitutional behaviour.

Brougham made his maiden speech upon Whitbread's resolutions, undoubtedly one of the most powerful first speeches ever heard in the Commons. While he claimed that he had not planned to speak, its content indicates otherwise. Brougham had been dying to make such remarks since his 1807 series in the *Chronicle*. He called on the House to focus its attention on the communication itself, ignoring what Chatham imputed to the services. His Narrative, Brougham charged, constituted unconstitutional behaviour. "It might be difficult," he admitted, "for him perhaps to point out any particular act of parliament making such conduct a violation of the constitution ..."[11] But the constitution was made up of more than just laws; it also included customs and conventions about collective responsibility of the Cabinet:

---

9. See, eg, "Inquiry into the Policy and Conduct of the Late Expedition to the Scheldt," *ibid.*, pp.260-6.
10. See "Copy of the Early of Chatham's Statement ...," Appendix, *Cobbett's Parliamentary Debate*, vol.16, cols.1105-15.
11. *Ibid.*, col.8**.

> ... he could confidentially appeal to any one of those sound and established principles of which the constitution is made up, or rather which form the constitution itself. Was it not necessary that the constitutional ministers of the crown should communicate with each other constitutionally and confidentially upon all public affairs? Was it not requisite that they should conduct the business of the government with united councils, and mutual advice and co-operation?[12]

Brougham mocked defence of Chatham simply because he was the son of the great Prime Minister: "He, it was, who had denounced the existence of 'that secret influence behind the throne, which was greater than the throne itself.'"[13] About efforts to mute the necessity of censuring the government, Brougham concluded: "He called upon the House therefore earnestly to fix their attention upon that conduct, and then decide whether they could pass over the present case without some marked declaration of their sense of its unconstitutional nature."[14]

Brougham's maiden effort did not receive the conventional niceties by the House because of the seriousness of its implications. If the Commons accepted his analysis, it would have to censure Perceval's Ministry, possibly leading to its resignation at a most difficult time. If this happened the Ministry had threatened that it would call for a dissolution of Parliament. The next speaker, a ministerial supporter named Bankes, consequently, denied the existence of the constitutional convention of ministerial responsibility. "The constitution, he must observe, was an old work ..."[15] indicating merely its legal basis. Lord Temple was surprised by such simplistic views, and James Stephen, the attempted apologist for Chatham because of who he was, explained that "he by no means called on the House not to proceed against the noble lord for the sake of his brother ..."[16] Only the Whig Adam gave

12. *Ibid.*
13. *Ibid.*
14. *Ibid.*, p.9**.
15. *Ibid.*, col.2***.
16. *Ibid.*, col.3***.

Brougham's effort its due:

> But Sir, the hon. gent. (Mr Bankes) says, in answer to the admirable speech of my learned friend (Mr Brougham) a speech which fulfilled that expectation of talent so truly formed of him, and which it gave me for many reasons, most peculiar pleasure to hear, that the cabinet is of modern date, and is therefore not part of the constitution.[17]

Adam concluded by mocking Bankes: "Surely, Sir, the hon. gent. cannot think that we are to be put down with a word, or to be diverted from our principle by a mere name ..."[18] Later, Canning moved an amendment to Whitbread's resolutions, charging that Chatham's conduct was highly reprehensible, and deserved censorship. Ultimately, the amended resolutions were passed, with Whitbread's support. When the Commons became unmanageable over what form the resolutions should take in being presented to his Majesty, Whitbread prevailed upon the House to have them withdrawn.

The Commons' handling of the expedition to the Scheldt was further eroded by the way that Sir Francis Burdett, the Radical Member for Westminster, chose to question their privileges. When the House was examining witnesses to the expedition, some of its testimony was taken in secret, and a printer, J. Dean, printed a notice complaining of the practice:

> The great anxiety manifested by the public at this critical period to become acquainted with the proceeding of the House of Commons, and to ascertain who were the authors and promoters of the late expedition to the Scheldt, together with the violent attacks made by Mr Windham on the newspaper reporters (whom he represents as "bankrupts, lottery office keepers, footman, and decayed tradesmen"), have stirred up the

17. *Ibid.*, col.3*****.
18. *Ibid.*

> public feeling, and excited universal attention.[19]

Yorke, the MP who was responsible for clearing the Strangers Gallery, of course, raised the notice as a breach of privilege. Ultimately, Dean was reprimanded for printing the notice for John Gale Jones, who was jailed at Newgate indefinitely at the pleasure of the House.

In anticipation of the House considering the Whigs' resolutions against the expedition,[20] Burdett, who had not attended the meetings over the notice, published in *Cobbett's Weekly Political Register* an address to his constituents, challenging the authority of the chamber under Brougham's view of the constitution:

> Either the House of Commons is authorized to dispense with the Laws of the Land; or it is not. If the Constitution be so delicate a texture, so weak a frame, so fragile a substance, that it is to be only spoken of in terms of admiration, and to be viewed merely as a piece of curious but unprofitable workmanship. If Magna Charta and all the wholesome Laws of England be a dead-letter: in that case, the affirmation of the proposition may be admitted; but, if the Constitution lives, and is applicable to its ends; namely, the happiness of the community, the perfect security of the life, liberty and property of each member and all members of the society; then the affirmative of the proposition can never be admitted ...[21]

As their forefathers had subdued the prerogative, they should limit undefined privilege. "We seek for justice," Burdett wrote, "and we need seek for *nothing new* ..."[22] The laws of England required no amendment. About Jones's imprisonment at Newgate, Burdett

---

19. *Ibid.*, vol.15, col.481.
20. See, eg, "A Notice of the Evidence given in the Committee of the House of Commons ... (Beckett & Porter, London, 1810), and "Expedition to the Scheldt. Thoughts on the Resolutions to be moved ... by Lord Porchester" (Beckett & Porter, London, 1810) for evidence to the length the Ministry was going to.
21. Quoted in *Cobbett's Parliamentary Debates*, vol.16, col.138.
22. *Ibid.* Italics Burdett's.

concluded: "Had the least doubt hung upon my mind of the illegality of the proceeding in the present case, it would have been altogether removed by the answers given to the reference made by me to the Great Luminaries of our Law and to the Laws themselves."[23] In "The Argument, etc," an accompanying paper, setting out the basis of Burdett's position, he provided a most ancient, common law view of the constitution.

With the powers of the Commons challenged, the House, with the Ministry's cooperation, devoted most of its attention to this gratuitous attack. Burdett had made this inevitable by unsuccessfully raising the alleged abuse of privilege two weeks earlier. "With regard to the privileges of that House," he said, in a pointed reference to constitutional "experts" like Brougham, "he knew there were persons who carried their fanciful notions of them to a very extraordinary length."[24] The Speaker, Abbott ruled that Burdett was out of order in calling the Commons the inferior branch of the legislature. Once Burdett published his breach of privilege, the House moved rapidly to commit him to prison. On the vote, Brougham voted against committal, and another MP, W.H. Lyttleton, expressed his sentiments when he said: "... the House would render a more grateful service to their constituents by rescinding the vote in favour of the Walcheren Expedition, than by provoking a contest respecting the existence of a privilege that was not attacked."[25] Burdett escalated the dispute by challenging the legality of the warrant for his arrest, resisting the Sergeant at Arms when he came to arrest him, and opening countersuits against the Speaker and Sergeant at Arms for false arrest and illegal entry. The House appointed a Select Committee to advise it on all these complicated legal questions.[26] The Commons got so worked up by these disputes that it not only would not receive petitions calling for Burdett's release from The Tower but also those calling for political relief for Roman Catholics.

---

23. *Ibid.*, col.141.
24. *Ibid.*, col.14****.
25. *Ibid.*, col.547.
26. For the first two reports from the Select Committee, see Appendix 13, *The Journals of the House of Commons*, vol.65, 1810, pp.732-4.

Throughout all this, Brougham continued to call for moderation, and a sense of proportion from the House, realizing that the Burdett affair constituted a red-herring, withdrawing the Commons' energies and constitutional concerns from more important matters. For example, when the House was considering Burdett's challenges to the Speaker for ordering his arrest, Brougham said:

> The House could never suffer in the estimation of the country, but through its own acts; and they could only bring themselves into contempt by waging a war, in which even success would be ruin; for what would their boasted privileges avail if they forfeited the confidence of the people.[27]

When the House took up the First Report from the Select Committee, and Francis Horner moved its re-committal "... with a view to move Resolutions, declaratory of the existence of the privileges to their utmost extent"[28] Brougham helped persuade the House to follow a more prudent course. He tried, with less success, to get the Prime Minister to distinguish petitions the House should receive. He said this about the differences between the ones calling for Roman Catholic relief, and for Burdett's release: "The former went to the whole constitution of the House: the latter only a part of its proceedings."[29]

Needless to say, by the time the Commons got round to really considering the expedition to the Scheldt, it had been so compromised by ministerial concession, and so complicated by radical diversion that it simply died. Lord Porchester's resolutions, detailing the failure step by step, culminating in a call for the Ministry's censure,[30] were so dragged out, thanks to Burdett's antics, that ministerial followers even tried to get it called a success. General Craufard moved this amendment to the proposed censure:

---

27. *Cobbett's Parliamentary Debates*, vol.17, col.176.
28. *Gentleman's Magazine*, vol.80, 1810, Part II, p.163.
29. *Cobbett's Parliamentary Debates*, vol.17, col.447.
30. *Ibid.*, vol.16, cols.78-9.

> The failure has been talked of as complete, which is entirely erroneous. An extent of sickness totally unexpected, and which those most experienced in that climate could not possibly calculate upon, alone occasioned the abandonment of a conquest, the permanent possession of which would have been cheaply purchased.[31]

Brougham was completely demoralized by the prospect: "... he could not satisfy his feelings even by voting for the original Resolutions, if the matter was to rest there."[32] The country's calamities, he charged, required looking to ulterior consideration "... which could alone afford the country justice for the past, and guard against similar delinquencies in the future."[33] In the final analysis, Portchester's resolutions were "... the salvation of ministers." Under the circumstances, the House approved of the retention of Walcheren which resulted in so much sickness and death, and of the conduct of Perceval's Ministry.

Brougham saved his real parliamentary thoughts for the *Review*. In reviewing George Rose's *Observations respecting the Public Expenditure and Influence of the Crown*, Brougham ridiculed the idea that its influence was declining. Rose, a ministerial supporter who was serving on the Burdett Select Committee, was portrayed as a self-serving apologist: "For *if* the influence of government really has *not* increased, how can those things be explained which are daily before our eyes, and which we only believe on the evidences of our senses?"[34] The Crown, Brougham responded, was the secret support which was maintaining the Ministry in Parliament. It was simply ludicrous to maintain that special inquiries were sustaining the constitution: "... instead of bringing the rulers of the country to account - to severe punishments for their misdeeds - the Parliament has actually voted them deserving praise for the worst

31. *Ibid.*, vol.253.
32. *Ibid.*, vol.421.
33. *Ibid.*
34. Art.VIII, "Rose *on the Influence of the Crown,*" *Edinburgh Review*, vol.16, no.XXXI, April 1810, p.188. Italics Brougham.

part of that misrule."[35] Rose, instead of tracing the abolition of a few obsolete posts, should have looked at the vast increase of public expenditure and indebtedness, and the new capability that it was giving the Crown to create positions and men's minds. Brougham cited the new creations in the colonies, the Bank of England and the East India Company. "How many men," he asked, "are Directors, who oppose government in Parliament or elsewhere?"[36] Placemen were still in the Commons. "This it is that enables the Crown to choose its own Ministers, without even a chance of the Parliament or the country controlling the appointments ..."[37] This influence directly affected how Members voted on the Walcheren division. Brougham explained the result:

> Had it not unfortunately been mixed up with other subjects, so successfully introduced by the ministers for the express purpose of distracting the public attention, we should in all likelihood have owed to that most eloquent event - that powerful display of the rhetoric of numbers - a complete change in the opinion of the people on the cause of reform, and a certain prospect of its being speedily victorious.[38]

To counter calls for radical reform by people like Burdett and Major Cartwright, Brougham called for gradual reform. He called for the elimination of placemen and judges, if they were attached to the Court, from the Commons. The Scottish franchise should be reformed, so that there could no longer be a corrupt traffic in votes. A person could have land in Scotland, and not the vote, and the reverse. While English and Irish county Members were almost equally divided on the Scheldt question "... only *five* Scotch county members voted against, while no less than *20* voted for, the expedition ..."[39] Brougham called for English copyholders to be given the franchise. The Septennial Act should be repealed:

---

35. *Ibid.*, p.204.
36. *Ibid.*, p.202.
37. *Ibid.*, p.204.
38. *Ibid.*, p.205.
39. *Ibid.*, p.208. Italics Brougham's.

> If triennial Parliaments were resorted to, it would follow, that the Crown, if it ever did threaten, could only hold out a threat of much smaller magnitude to intimidate the House of Commons, and that there would also be less danger of the threat being put in execution ...[40]

While there would, consequently, be fewer dissolutions of Parliament which assisted Crown interests, there would be more elections that suited popular opinion. Borough franchise reform would have to wait until quieter times when real interests and changes could be properly assessed.

In a private letter in 1810 to William Lamb, the future Lord Melbourne, Brougham explained why he opposed borough disenfranchisement. The letter was written while Brougham was living at the Albany, the residential chambers for "bachelor gentlemen", off Piccadilly, designed by Sir William Chambers. The letter was stolen for the government-backed press by one of Brougham's servants, and its contents became a matter of public concern during the passage of the Reform Act.

In another article in the same issue, Brougham considered a more pressing personal matter: how he could become a more effective defender of liberal causes in the Courts and Parliament. In reviewing a volume of Thomas Erskine's speeches, he made the most effective contribution to his career. In reviewing 12 of his pleas, Brougham said that Erskine's eloquence was comparable to Burke's. About the barrister's defence of Stockdale in a libel case, arising out of the House's impeachment of Warren Hastings, Brougham wrote for its benefit: "... no attempt was made to commit the printer or the author by the mere authority of the House of Commons; and Mr Fox himself was content to move an address for a prosecution in a court of common law."[41] About Erskine's summing up for the jury, Brougham said that it represented a model:

40. *Ibid.*, pp.209-10.
41. Art.V, "Erskine's *Speeches, ibid.*, p.109.

> ... for the solid and important purpose of interesting his hearers in the situation of Mr. Hastings, and of his defender, the author of the pamphlet - of leading the mind, to view the prisoner as an oppressed man, overwhelmed by the weight of parliamentary resentment, and ready to be crushed in the face of the country, by the very forms and solemnities of his trial ...[42]

Erskine succeeded in gaining Stockdale's acquittal, in the face of the monumental prejudice against Hastings, because he "... built on the matchless skill with which he could subdue the genius of the first rate orator to the uses of the most consummate advocate of the age."[43] The skills of such men, Brougham reminded his readers, were not out of date:

> We speak not from hearsay ... We speak, indeed, from notes that are still fresh and legible; for, turn, which way we will, we now see almost all the places of profit and trust in this island filled with persons, for whose elevation we should find it hard to account, if we did not look back to their apprenticeships in 1794 and 1795.[44]

Erskine's defence of the persecuted proved, however, that there was another, more honourable, way to success.

As long as Brougham followed Erskine's calling in the manner prescribed, he rarely went wrong. In fact, he immediately put it to use in finally mending the slave trade. When Parliament was confused about partisan affairs, Brougham had learned from the Melville impeachment, it was no time to tackle matters of conscience. With the Commons in total disarray over the Scheldt expedition, he decided to prepare things so that Parliament could act on the trade, once affairs had returned to normal. Brougham called for correspondence between the Foreign Secretary and foreign countries to learn why the Abolition Act had been so

---

42. *Ibid.*, p.110.
43. *Ibid.*, p.117.
44. *Ibid.*, pp.119-20.

ineffective.[45]

The Swedes, Portuguese, and Spaniards were supplying colonies with slaves, and were also carrying on an illicit trade with the West Indies. Upwards of 30,000 slaves were being transported a year. Brougham regretted that Americans had commenced an illicit trade, although he absolved their government from what was happening. Canning, the former Foreign Secretary who had resigned over the Walcheren fiasco, disputed Brougham's claim. The United States was less committed to ending the trade than the Portuguese. "But the hon. gent. had not read the correspondence with his usual accuracy,"[46] Canning charged. America opposed any agreement on the subject, and would complain over any unilateral legislation. "He had not been aware, till lately, that the illicit trade in slaves by British subjects had been carried on to so great an extent under the Swedish flag."[47] Brougham retorted that Canning had been too hard on America, and Wilberforce agreed. "It ought to be recollected that they had set us the example of abolition," Brougham explained, "a pretty strong proof that they were sincerely anxious for the success of the measure."[48] The motion was agreed to without opposition.

Brougham's star was rising so fast in the Commons that some Members tried to arrest it by embarrassing him for his modest views about parliamentary reform. Thomas Brand, who opposed Brougham's modern constitutional views, moved for a committee to examine the kingdom's representation, claiming that there would either be reform or a military dictatorship.[49] To try to draw Brougham out, he called for borough franchise reform, the area that the Member for Camelford was most reluctant to talk about. Brougham, while he supported Brand's motion, knowing that it was doomed to fail, would not fragment reformers further by elaborating his views.

Charles Williams Wynn, Lord Grenville's nephew, tried to get

---

45. *Cobbett's Parliamentary Debates*, vol.16, col.12******.
46. *Ibid.*, col.13******.
47. *Ibid.*
48. *Ibid.*, col.14******.
49. *The Times*, May 22, 1810, no.7,985, pp.2-3.

Brougham to support actively his Bribery Bill, but to no avail. Wynn even justified the measure in terms of what Brougham had said in the *Review*, and the procedure he used for ending the trade.[50] According to the bill, Members would have to take oaths upon entering the Commons that they had not given bribes. Brougham admitted that there was a need for the measure. "But he must observe that so little of the practices of bribery had been of late discovered because of the decency with which the thing was managed, and the experienced cunning of election agents."[51] Brougham would not be brought further into the matter because of the ferment caused by the unauthorized printing of his Melbourne letter on parliamentary reform which explained his ideas about borough disenfranchisement, elimination of placemen, Scottish reform, and bribery.[52] Brougham promised to bring forward his own measure on parliamentary reform, "... which would show that he was not open to the attacks which had been made upon him.[53]

Brougham circulated another letter, *Principles of Parliamentary Reform*, among friends and associates to show what he planned, once affairs had cooled down, and the servant who had passed it along to the *Satirist*, stating that it could be published, had been stopped. The paper claimed that the thief would get to the bottom of the St Alban's Street conspiracy, the Whig press operation that had opened in January 1810 to take over from the one that Brougham had had on Ryder Street:

> Our friend had promised to furnish us with numerous other documents, for he justly considers that there can be no moral impropriety in betraying the machinations of those who are sacrificing every honourable, every gentlemanly feeling at the shrine of ambition and avarice. Had he earlier known their

50. *Ibid.*, June 21, 1810, no.8,013, p.2.
51. *Ibid.*
52. For the full text of the April 28 letter in the Melbourne Papers; Royal Archives, Windsor Castle, see "Lord Brougham's letter on Reform," *ibid.*, October 10, 1831, no.14, 665, p.5.
53. *Ibid.*, June 21, 1810, no.8013, p.2.

> disposition and propensities he never would have attached himself to such an unprincipled ... party.[54]

Brougham obtained an injunction from Lord Eldon, the Lord Chancellor, against editor Charles Manners reprinting it,[55] claiming that it was a private, confidential letter. The *Satirist* responded by stating that the "conspiracy", thanks to its exposure, had been ended on June 13. "Their vexation and fury", it explained, "we are assured by an eye-witness, knew no bounds ..."[56]

June 13 was the day that Brougham planned to make his motion on the slave trade but, under the circumstances, he decided that delay was the better part of valour. "He was induced to do this," he told the House, "from having on that day received the mortifying information, that no less than six Slave Ships had been recently fitted out from one Port."[57] Very detailed information about it, he explained, would be necessary. Actually, Brougham seems to have put the extra time to good use. Like Erskine, he devised a speech to show that slave traders were as guilty of a felony as Stockdale had been innocent of one. There was also a difference between real murder, and ritual crime. In trying to remedy the former, and to avoid the latter, persons should be prepared for an occasional intemperate remark. As Britain's strength had called forth the unfortunate administration in India which Hastings had had to preside over, she could no longer plead that she did not have the capability to stop such infamous crimes as the slave trade. In reading over the speech, one feels increasingly as though Erskine had literally crawled into Brougham's skin as he delivered this impassioned plea.

In making the case for slave trading to be a felony, Brougham mentioned the American experience in such a way as to try to pacify Canning. While Americans were carrying on the most important trade in slaves, in open violation of federal laws, the

---

54. Quoted from A. Aspinall, *Politics and the Press, 1780-1850* (Home & Van Thal, London, 1949), pp.293-4.
55. *The Times*, June 3, 1810, no.7,999, p.3.
56. Quoted from Aspinall, *op. cit.*, p.294.
57. *The Times*, June 4, 1810, no.8,007, p.3.

national government was doing what it could to stop it. "But it is one thing to pass a law," Brougham said, "and another to carry it into execution, as we have ourselves found on this side of the water ..."[58] America should be offered naval assistance to help meet its obligations. About Britain's inability to effect the same, Brougham said: "Of this argument, I entertain very great suspicion, and for one plain reason, that it is on the single subject of the Abolition that I ever hear it used ..."[59] Harking back to Hastings's experience, he added: "Why, we never failed at all when the object was to obtain new colonies, and extend the Slave Trade!"[60] In anticipation of the decision before the Lords of Prize Appeal in the Privy Council, hearing the case of the *Amédie*, he justified the seizure of a ship engaged in the illicit trade, believing that a court could free the slaves, and confiscate the property. "I earnestly hope some persons connected with privateers and cruisers may soon try the question."[61]

Brougham was most effective in using the information that the African Institution, under Zachary Macaulay's leadership, had discovered about evasions of the Abolition Act. Concerning the six ships which had been remodelled after leaving port so that they could engage in the slave trade, operations sometimes commenced almost within sight of Westminster Palace, Brougham said that these perpetrators engaged "... in crimes of the deepest dye; in crimes always most iniquitous, even when not illegal; but which now are as contrary to law as they have ever been to honesty and justice."[62] He compared the difficulty of getting such crimes considered seriously by Parliament with the ease with which Lord Ellenborough could get trivial offences converted into capital felonies. "While you levy your pence," he said bitterly, "the wholesale dealers in blood and torture pocket their pounds, and laugh at your twopenny penalty."[63] As Brougham recounted the

---

58. *Speeches of Henry Lord Brougham* (Black, Edinburgh, 1838, 4 vols.), vol.II, p.23.
59. *Ibid.*, pp.24-5.
60. *Ibid.*, p.25.
61. *Ibid.*, p.30.
62. *Ibid.*, p.33.
63. *Ibid.*, p.37.

stealth, instruments, and calculations by which these "merchants" carried on their trade, the House got carried away by his eloquence, greeting each revelation of their criminality with "hear! hear!" Brougham concluded by calling for an Address to the Crown to stop subjects from such crime by Orders in Council.

Perceval concurred with Brougham's sentiments, but not with his means. As Brougham had been the most outspoken critic of the Crown, and its Orders in Council, the Prime Minister was not about to add fuel to his discontents. Perceval said that a general resolution would be more appropriate, something that Lord Holland would effect for the Lords. About Brougham's speech, William Smith found it especially cheering "... that so general an expression of concurrence was manifested in every invective which was bestowed on the Slave Trade, and upon those great criminals, who, under the false name of merchants, dared persist in those vicious practices."[64] Stephen also favoured a resolution, defending the Ministry's efforts against the trade. Canning favoured the Ministry's approach to the problem, defending his record as Foreign Secretary. Brougham denied that he meant to reflect badly upon the ministers, and "... had no objection whatever to separate the Resolution pledging the House, from the Address ..."[65] The House agreed unanimously to find a legislative solution to the problem during the next Session.[66]

During the 1810 Session of Parliament, the country had experienced the worst instability and insecurity of the French Wars. Local militias were rioting because of insufficient or no pay. In May, for example, the local militia at St Alban's went on a rampage for five days, demanding more money. When the sergeant stating its demands was arrested, he was rescued by his fellow troopers, but 19 of the rioters were arrested subsequently. The most refractory of them were tried, and upon conviction were sentenced to corporal punishment. The five ringleaders "... were sentenced to receive a 100 lashes each, and one was ordered 150: these

64. *Cobbett's Parliamentary Debates*, vol.17, col.677.
65. *Ibid.*, p.689.
66. *The Journals of the House of Commons*, vol.65, 1810, p.503.

sentences were put into execution."[67] This incident, when reported, apparently persuaded the Ministry to file an *ex officio* information for libel against William Cobbett for writing a story against flogging the previous July in the *Courier*. Cobbett had been stirred to action by how another riot by the militia had been suppressed and punished. Cobbett was particularly upset by the role played by the German Legion in both suppressing the Ely riot and inflicting the punishment. Cobbett, in his English fashion, continued to harp on the subject in his *Political Register*. His articles "... were addressed not to the understanding nor even to the feelings of the reader; but rather to those of the soldiery who suffered the infliction ..."[68]

Cobbett chose to defend himself, something characteristic of the man, but almost fatal in a court of law. Traditional institutions expect things to be done in traditional ways. The court was against Cobbett from the very beginning. He did not help matters by questioning the timing of the trial, and the role of the Germans in His Majesty's Forces. Cobbett tried to quote speeches from Parliament to show how respectable people had reacted to cruelty towards soldiers, but Lord Chief Justice Ellenborough prevented him from doing so, holding that the remarks were privileged. Unlike the *Courier's* printer and publisher, Cobbett tried to make a defence rather than surrender himself to the mercy of the court. Attorney General Sir Vicary Gibbs, in his summing up of the case against him for the jury, belittled what Cobbett had attempted "... for he has only made it the occasion for uttering new slanders against innocent and undefended persons ..."[69] Ellenborough agreed, stating that no responsible person was against temperate, reasonable pleas for change:

> I am sure that if such a discussion had been brought before a jury, you would no more have been inclined to construe it, than any judge in the situation which I unworthingly fill would be

---

67. "Local Militia," *The Times*, May 30, 1810, no.7992, p.2.
68. Brougham, *op. cit.*, vol.I, p.5.
69. *R.* v. *William Cobbett*, *The Times*, June 16, 1810, no.8009, p.4.

> to recommend you so to construe it, a libel.[70]

Cobbett had bad intentions, Ellenborough explained. "I do pronounce this to be a most infamous and seditious libel."[71] The jury immediately concurred, not even retiring from the box to reach its verdict. Cobbett was sentenced to two years' imprisonment.

While Brougham was celebrating his victory in the Commons over the slave trade, other journalists were exploiting Cobbett's sacrifice. In the *Review*, Brougham wrote a most self-serving review of the African Institution's annual report. About the parliamentary resolutions against the slave, he explained:

> The indignation which was so loudly expressed, indeed, in no very measured language, against the persons in question, by every one who took a part in the late debates, both in the House of Lords and Commons, but particularly in the latter, must afford to all friends of the cause, the best (evidence), that the time is at length arrived, when slave trading can no longer be tolerated ...[72]

For people who had doubts about seizing American slave ships, he added: "The slave trade, is not *juris gentium*; it is a traffic contrary to the law of nature, and cannot be sanctioned by the law of nations."[73] He, in Quaker-like fashion, recited the practical reforms that the Institution was effecting in Africa.

The Crown was preparing to prosecute Peter Finnerty for what he had written about Castlereagh's reaction to exposure of the Scheldt expedition. "The indictment, contrary to the usual custom, did not point out any particular parts of the paper, but embraced almost the entire."[74] Finnerty, in his history, tried to make out that the Crown's prosecution of him for libel was an integral part of the

---

70. *Ibid.*
71. *Ibid.*
72. Art.IX, "African Institution," *Edinburgh Review*, vol.16, no.XXXII, August 1810, p.439.
73. *Ibid.*, p.436.
74. *The Times*, July 11, 1810, no.8030, p.3.

fiasco, a claim which so outraged Ellenborough that he was unwilling to wait for possible facts to justify the libel. To state that a Secretary of State had abused his high office to gratify private malice was a dangerous untruth, and the Lord Chief Justice, having heard from Finnerty's counsel, was not willing to listen to the defendant himself. In fact, the Crown was going to such lengths to make sure that no editor tried to disgrace the government that another one, John Scott of the *Champion*, felt obliged to repeat Cobbett's concerns about flogging. Scott contributed a column on it to the *Stamford News*, published by John Drakard. "These researches of Mr Scott were soon afterwards copied into the *Examiner*, a London paper, then conducted by Messrs J. and J.L. Hunt ..."[75] The Attorney General filed an *ex officio* information against them for libel.

Brougham agreed to defend them in the belief that he could score a great victory over the law officers and the accommodating Ellenborough. For one thing, Cobbett had raised some most persuasive points during his trial. The editor of Brougham's speeches was engaging in characteristic exaggeration when he wrote about Cobbett's effort "... nothing could be more dull and unimpressive than his speech, nothing less clear and distinct than its reasoning, more feeble than its style, or more embarrassed and inefficient than its delivery."[76] Cobbett's mistake was in not hiring a barrister who could stand up to the Lord Chief Justice. To the charge that his complaints about flogging were undermining discipline in the army, Cobbett had replied: "What! is every man who puts on a red coat, to be from that moment deserted by all his world; and is no tongue or no pen, ever to stir in his defence?"[77] When he was prevented from actually reading from critical speeches, given in Parliament, he said:

---

75. *Speeches ..., op. cit.*, vol.I, p.7.
76. *Ibid.*, p.5.
77. *R.* v. *William Cobbett, The Times*, June 16, 1810, no.8009, p.3. For more on how Brougham learned from Cobbett in both his legal and newspaper careers, see T.H. Ford, "Brougham as a Barrister: Courtroom Dilemmas of a Notorious Radical" in *Custom, Courts and Appeal, Selected Papers of the 6th British Legal History Conference* (Frank Cass, London, 1985), p.110 ff.

> Well, then, it will suffice for me to say shortly, that there is no degree of cruelty, hardship, and oppression, which has not been charged to those who conducted the Walcheren expedition. When people speak against the ill treatment of our soldiers, the fair and natural presumption is, not that they want to overturn the government, but that they want these evils of which they complain to be remedied in future.[78]

Cobbett denied that evil motives were involved in his activities: "A man may be mistaken on a subject of which he complains, and yet may act without any of those bad intentions which have been imparted to me."[79]

Brougham, in a review of education pamphlets, showed that he understood the fear that editors like Cobbett instilled in the Establishment. These people, terrified of the prospect of radical reform, wanted to make sure that the poor received only the education they really needed. Whether they knew it or not, Brougham wrote, they were followers of Mandeville's, believing that unnecessary education would disrupt, even destroy, society. The poor, according to Mandeville's *Fable of the Bees*, should only be taught what would permit them to perform their function in society. Like Dr Bell, the author of one of the pamphlets under review, they did not want to teach the poor to write and do ciphers because of its potentially disruptive character on society. Brougham, in trying to persuade them to be less hysterical in their analysis of the problem, tried to show that the risks lay in too little, not too much, education. "The less a man reads, the more likely he is to be misled by plausible errors, or injured by unsound morality ..."[80] As for Cobbett's responsibility for the excesses in reporting current affairs, Brougham explained: "... the evils which are now not unfrequently occasioned by the daily press, are owing entirely to the ignorance of the community."[81] The remedy was to adopt

---

78. *Ibid.*
79. *Ibid.*
80. Art.III, "Education of the Poor," *Edinburgh Review*, vol.17, no.XXXIII, November 1810, p.64.
81. *Ibid.*

Joseph Lancaster's system of education by which its blessings "... may be extended to persons in the lower ranks of society, at a price within the reach of all but the poorest, and to them also, with a very moderate assistance from their happier brethren ..."[82]

Brougham also understood the frustration which the politically conscious people in Westminster and the City of London were experiencing because of their support of Burdett. The Member for Westminster, by his support of Jones, was just expressing what most electors felt, even though his protest was technically a violation of the House's privileges. Given the dimensions of the Scheldt fiasco, the House should have exercised restraint, as Brougham recommended. But Burdett made it difficult for the Commons to look the other way, with his threats on the Speaker, and challenges to the Sergeant at Arms, as the Ministry soon realized. Burdett had been, consequently, jailed for the remainder of the Session, and his counter suits against the Commons' officers, despite their popular support, promised to get nowhere in the courts, thanks to the care the House had shown in exercising its privileges. All the good people of the Metropolis had to show for their support of the liberties of Englishmen was a belated celebration for the Member on his release from the Tower. Brougham knew just how deep the anti-ministerial sentiments were running in the capital.

The Crown's case against the Hunts was heard in Westminster on February 22, 1811. The Attorney General, given his easy triumph in the first case, let the facts of their publication, "One Thousand Lashes!!", speak for itself. "Mr Cobbett having been convicted for this libel," Sir Vicary Gibbs declared, "the present publishers took up the subject."[83] He quoted several passages from the article in the *Examiner*, like this one:

> No, as the attorney general justly says, Buonaparte does not treat his refractory troops in this manner; there is not a man in his ranks whose back is seamed with the lacerating

---

82. *Ibid.*, p.58.
83. *R.* v. *Hunt and Another, The Times*, February 23, 1811, no.8228, p.3.

> cat-o-nine-tails; his soldiers have never yet been brought up to view one of their comrades stripped naked; his limbs tied with ropes to a triangular machine; his back torn to the bone by the merciless cutting whipcord, applied by persons who relieve each other at short intervals, that they may bring the full unexhausted strength of a man to the work of scourging.[84]

Gibbs thought that the mere mention of Napoleonic practice would be sufficient to justify the status quo without question.

Brougham, in defending the Hunts, retraced the history of Cobbett's prosecution in critical perspective, claiming that the present one was different. To justify criticism of the barbaric practice, he quoted from Sir Robert Wilson's "On the Means of Improving and Reorganizing the Military Force of this Empire," and had Wilson present in court to testify for the defence. Brougham distinguished what the Hunts had done from the actions of the more licentious press, particularly Cobbett's *Political Register*. In the process he gave the nub of Cobbett's own argument, a controlled analysis of a practice that even professionals complained about:

> They break the spirit, without amending the disposition; while the lash strips the back, despair writhes round the heart, and the miserable culprit, viewing himself as fallen below the rank of his fellow-species, can no longer attempt the recovery of his station in society.[85]

Brougham quoted similar sentiments from Brigadier Stewart. With respected professionals willing to express such views, Brougham reminded the jury that Englishmen had the right to talk about wars, expeditions, and taxes, even the abolition of the slave trade. "Is it rebellious," he asked, rephrasing one of Cobbett's more telling contentions about parliamentary debates, "to speak one's

---

84. Quoted from *Speeches ..., op. cit.*, vol.I, p.8.
85. *Ibid.*, p.28.

sentiments of the expeditions sent from this country?"[86] The Attorney General had forgotten to claim that no discontent with the practice had been perceived, Brougham continued, indicating that just one word, rather than the common experience of comrades, would be enough to spark a revolt. There was no malicious, seditious intent in condemning such practice, as long as Englishmen were still free. Ellenborough tried to save the prosecution by declaring, in no uncertain terms, that the article excited disaffection in the army, and helped alienate it from the society. The Westminster jury thought otherwise, bringing in a verdict of not guilty after deliberating for an hour and a half.

The decision, thanks to the *Chronicle's* assistance and approach of the result, just induced the Crown to try harder in the prosecution of the original libel in the *Stamford News*, and Brougham, puffed up by his victory, relaxed, a tendency that he displayed when causes no longer interested him. After the Ministry had survived the crucial vote on the Walcheren expedition, contrary to the verdict of public opinion, the Benchers of Lincoln's Inn became so upset that they "... passed a resolution, by which any person convicted of having ever written for the newspapers for hire, should be excluded from their body."[87] Brougham had not only written for them, but successfully defended the greatest use of press freedom in the King's Bench. There was nothing that the Benchers at Lincoln's Inn could do about it, as his subsequent call to the Bar and the repeal of the resolution indicated. Under the circumstances, the next trial of the libel action was, as far as Brougham was concerned, a cut-and-dried affair. Brougham tended to underestimate resistant opponents, believing his progress was synonymous with that of reason. He almost sounded like Cobbett with his irrelevant allusions, and constitutional proprieties.[88] The speech was anything but a model of Erskine's legal eloquence. The Crown denied directly what Brougham was trying to affirm - ie, the non-libellous character of the article had

---

86. *Ibid.*, p.44.
87. Louis Simond, *Journal of a Tour and Residence in Great Britain* (Constable, Edinburgh, 1815, 2 vols.), vol.I, p.67.
88. See the "Case of John Drakard" in *Speeches ..., op. cit.*, vol.I, pp.51-83.

already been determined. Counsel for the Attorney General showed that the *Examiner* article was a restrained abridgement of the Stamford one. "Can that be criminal in Lincolnshire," Brougham asked rhetorically, "which is innocent in Westminster?"[89] The Crown responded that this was a crude effort to overawe the jury. Baron Wood, presiding over the Lincoln Assizes, agreed, stating that "... the gentlemen he then addressed were not to be bound by the conduct of any other Jury ..."[90] It only took the Lincolnshire jury 10 minutes to register their independence, declaring that John Drakard had published a seditious libel.

Brougham's early defences in English courts were not all that successful. The few bright spots have been exaggerated in retrospect. Brougham lost another big case in the King's Bench two months later, a more embarrassing one. When he had been directing the Whigs' press campaign from the office on Ryder Street, he had written to John Allen about what kind of paragraphs writers should be supplying for the campaign:

> Different people should at their spare hours be reading Shakespeare and Swift, with a view to selecting passages suitable to the time, as, descriptions of base courtiers, particular characters of bad ministers, hits at bishops (if safe) etc. These passages may be published in a kind of series, as quotations communicated by Jenksberry, Castlerogue, etc, on whomever they apply to.[91]

Agents in Canterbury took this advice to heart, publishing a series of satires in the style of Juvenal at Mayor Powlet's expense. He took umbrage at the whole exercise, and asked the Attorney General to file an *ex officio* information against them for libel. They were found guilty.

Brougham was willing to go to the King's Bench to try to stay the conviction. He argued that the verdict was a complete

---

89. *R.* v. *Drakard, The Times,* March 18, 1811, no.8246, p.3.
90. *Ibid.*
91. Brougham's letter to Allen, dated April 8, 1807: quoted in Aspinall, *op. cit.,* Appendices, p.453.

miscarriage of justice. The defendants, he argued, had just been engaging in artistic pursuits, similar to Dr Johnson's. Lord Ellenborough was not convinced: "It is rather a liberal translation."[92] Brougham replied that only an unbalanced person would, unaided, think that expressions like "this haughty slave" applied only to the Mayor. Brougham continued in a most hilarious vein:

> But, my lords, there are other persons who fancy themselves alluded to in this publication (*The Whim*, nos.6 & 7), and who do not like to go before a Grand Jury and swear that the words *jackdaw* and *cur* mean them: these parties keep in the background, and urge Mr Poulet on, puff him up, with a grand idea that his official dignity is attacked, and so completely get the better of his good-nature ...[93]

The poem referred to a man of fashion, counsel said, and this could not mean the Mayor, a former auctioneer. The Attorney General reminded Ellenborough that Lawrence, one of the defendants, had been unwilling to swear that the person was not Poulet. Brougham said that the Mayor had been unable to swear that he was either always upright, or responsible. Ellenborough agreed, stating that no mayor could. Poulet should have only sought an indictment against the defendants rather than proceeding against them by information, Brougham replied. Sir Vicary Gibbs hoped "... that the extraordinary perseverance shown today will be of no avail."[94] It was, as Ellenborough made the rule of the trial absolute.

Brougham's independent ways in the Commons were hardly more successful. When the Whig leadership had not given him any responsibilities when he arrived in leading the Opposition to the Ministry, he increasingly settled for his own projects. With the closing of the St. Albans Street office, the process was completed, as Brougham's resolution on the slave trade indicated. In

---

92. *R.* v. *Rous, Kirby and Lawrence, The Times,* May 27, 1,811, no.8304, p.3.
93. *Ibid.,* Italics its.
94. *Ibid.*

preparation for more of the same for the 1811 parliamentary session, he published an article on parliamentary reform in the *Review*, the one the *Satirist* had published with such effect. The article did spell out what Brougham intended for the rotten boroughs and for constitutional change. "The people *has* increased in consequence, in power, and in political importance,"[95] he wrote. He attributed the cause of the change to the growth in intellect, a development upsetting the traditional balance between a society's governors, opposition, and its masses. As the people rose, they could either be accommodated into the existing power structure, as the Crown was trying to do through its increase of places, or it could become more representative:

> By the extension of the elective franchise, many of those who are most hostile to the existing system, because, under it, they are excluded from all share of power or political importance, will have a part assigned them, both more safe and more active than murmuring, or meditating vengeance against such a scheme of exclusion.[96]

As for the role of the Tories and Whigs in helping this inevitable process, unless Britain was to experience a revolution, he was not particularly hopeful. The Opposition was just complaining because there were not enough places to go round. With Parliament engrossed in a Regency crisis, following the final breakdown of George III, politicians were reminded that the people would only turn against the King "... when his throne is enveloped by treacherous advisers, with the hosts of corruption, and disguised, for their ends, in the borrowed colours of tyranny."[97]

Brougham, having hoisted his colours to the cause of popular reform, gave little encouragement to his Whig patrons and hosts. About being a Member for a pocket borough, at the disposal of the Dukes of Bedford, he said that it made one feel "... so as to be

---

95. Art.I, "Parliamentary Reform," *Edinburgh Review*, vol.17, no.XXXIV, February 1811, p.281. Italics Brougham's.
96. *Ibid.*, p.286.
97. *Ibid.*, p.289.

familiarly considered as a part of their rightful property."[98] About pocket boroughs, something he had attended to in his *Principals of Parliamentary Reform,* he said:

> ... though we admit them to be both contradictory to the general scheme of the constitution, and subversive of some of its important principles, we think they are to be regarded as flaws and irregularities brought on by time and the course of events, rather than as abuses introduced by the vices and corruption of men.[99]

While he was willing to see their gradual elimination, he wanted the immediate end of the Treasury borough, constituencies one generally found in Devon and Cornwall. They were just financial arrangements between attorneys who purchased the votes, and leading politicians, usually ministers, who found candidates to suit their interests at the expense of the country and constitution. "To say that both sorts of influence are derived from property," he explained, "and are therefore to be considered as identical, is a sophism scarcely more dignified or ingenious, than that which would confound the occupations of highwaymen and the honourable merchant ..."[100] This hardly sounded convincing, coming from a man whose most recent achievement was to make some "honourable" merchants felons. It sounded more like an expedient concession to his patron at Camelford, the Duke of Bedford. To end Treasury placemen, Brougham called for their peremptory exclusion from Parliament rather than fancy schemes to end bribery, like Mr Curwen's, which would only compound the problem in a self-deceiving way. "The matter was treated," Brougham complained, "as if they had been accused of occasionally drinking to excess, or of using certain profane expletives in their conversation ..."[101] The ministers took over the proposal and changed it, he explained, "... just as ancient husbands, who long

98. *Ibid.,* pp.268-9.
99. *Ibid.,* p.269.
100. *Ibid.,* p.272.
101. *Ibid.,* p.255.

for heirs, are often times not very curious in ascertaining the pedigree of their children."[102] To end the threat of tyranny, Brougham called for the retrenchment of public finances, and the devolution of political authority.

With Brougham in this state of mind, he gave the early Session, caused by the King's incapacity, a wide berth. He did not attend the inquiries into George III's physical state, and did not participate in the debates on the Regency resolutions. He did not even vote on them. This was the concern of scheming politicians. Brougham introduced the Slave Trade Felony Bill on March 5, 1811. "The House would recollect," he said in statesman-like style, "that he was talking of that which was robbery, torture, and murder, and they would not fail to punish such an offence with something at least the equal to the punishment imposed for stealing an oyster."[103] He was confident that "the trade was so much reduced, so far as they could be concerned, that a love of contraband alone could induce them to wish its continuance."[104] Joseph Marryatt supported the measure, although he disagreed with Brougham on the trade's extent. MP Barham continued in this vein, stating that the illicit trade, unless checked, would be worse than the original one. The measure made it a felony for a British subject to engage in the trade, subject to up to 10 years' transportation or five years' imprisonment upon conviction. It was passed without opposition. Brougham even acted as the Commons' agent in resolving the difference between the Houses over the act's effective date.

Brougham was apparently so angered by Marryatt's questioning his knowledge of the trade's extent that he attacked vigorously his effort to replace Spanish law by British justice in Trinidad. During May, the Commons had printed papers relating to Spanish treatment of slaves in their colonies.[105] They showed that while Spain permitted a harsh, almost unsupervised treatment of slaves, its free blacks did stand to lose rights by the introduction of British justice. At the end of May, moreover, the Commons printed papers

---

102. *Ibid.*, p.256.
103. *Cobbett's Parliamentary Debates*, vol.19, col.238.
104. *Ibid.*, col.237.
105. *See Miscellaneous Accounts and Papers*, 1810-1811, vol.XI, p.333 ff.

concerning Edward Huggins's savage treatment of slaves on the island of Nevis. One slave died from flogging. "A still severer torture was inflicted on one of them," J.W. Tobin wrote to the *St Christopher Gazette*, "by continued application of two cart-whips, to make him confess, what he persevered in declaring he was ignorant of ..."[106] Brougham, once he heard of these revelations, "... hoped the House would set its face against any alteration of the Spanish Law in Trinidad."[107] Marryatt's complaints about its judicial administration, especially a Judge hearing appeals from his own decisions, were dismissed as "... it was no more than what happened every day in the courts of this country."[108] Disgruntled suitors in equity, for example, could only appeal from the Lord Chancellor in Chancery to the Lord Chancellor in the Lords.

Brougham's inclinations against established ways of doing things were intensified by revelations that Arthur Hodge, a planter in the Virgin Islands, had carried on a private war of terror for years against his slaves.[109] It was only after he had killed many of them that depositions came forward which finally sent him to the gallows. Brougham, instead of seeing these events as isolated criminal acts, concluded that British institutions were not worthy of his confidence. British slavery was worse than that of the Spanish and Portuguese, and Perceval's Ministry was extending such despotism. When Sir Francis Burdett tried to get the Crown to institute a reduction in the use of flogging, Brougham asked angrily: "Why not, when it came nearer home, and among a gallant and manly race of beings?"[110] When Finnerty, who had been sentenced to the same term in prison as Drakard for libel, complained of his treatment at Lincoln Castle, Brougham saw new signs of oppression. Lincoln's gaoler, with the connivance of the magistrates, Brougham believed, was subjecting Finnerty to a

---

106. "Papers relating to the West Indies: Correspondence relating to Punishments ... in the Island of Nevis" (204); *ibid.*, p.358.
107. *The Times*, June 14, 1811, no.8320, p.3.
108. *Ibid.*
109. "Papers relating to the West Indies: ... The Trial and Execution of Arthur Hodge" (254); *Miscellaneous Accounts and Papers*, 1810-1811, vol.XI, pp.397-412.
110. *Cobbett's Parliamentary Debates*, vol.20, col.708.

harsher penalty than even the Judge had imposed. It amounted to solitary confinement. When the gaoler complained, demanding an inquiry into Finnerty's crimes while incarcerated, Brougham maintained that Finnerty's treatment constituted arbitrary justice: "He knew that Mr Drakard had been treated well; but this only placed in a stronger light the injustice done to Mr Finnerty."[111]

Brougham was becoming so out of sorts that he even turned his ire on Sir Robert Wilson, the professional witness who had been so helpful in the trial of the Hunts. When Burdett introduced his motion to the Prince Regent, praying for a gradual ending of flogging, he read a letter from Wilson, saying that "Drakard had, in fact, very much libelled the Russian nation, when he stated that they had copied the barbarity of our military punishments."[112] Brougham took umbrage at this remark at the expense of the imprisoned editor. Brougham, consequently, used the columns of the *Review* to get back at this opponent of flogging in reviewing his latest book:

> Sir R. Wilson is not content with bringing forward charges against Buonaparte, unsupported by evidence, and then leaving them until he can prove them; but he uses them as if they were already fully substantiated; and recurs to them, whenever he finds occasion, as if they were admitted on all hands.[113]

Regarding the book's composition, Brougham said that it was hardly written in the English language. As for the Russians' capability, he wrote that they were inferior "... to other nations in a supply of those men who can either improve the resources of the state, or draw forth into effective action the resources which it already possesses."[114] Brougham provided a similar review of a book on Spain for the same issue,[115] one which recalled his

---

111. *Ibid.*, col.775.
112. *The Times*, June 19, 811, no.8324, p.3.
113. Art.IX, "Sir Robert Wilson *on the Russian Army*," *Edinburgh Review*, vol.18, no.XXXV, May 1811, p.238.
114. *Ibid.*, p.248.
115. Art.V, "Jacob's *Travels in Spain*," *ibid.*, pp.123-52.

reservations about Spanish capacity, and the British Government's for reform.

When Brougham heard that seaman John Robinson had died, in irons and gagged, while undergoing punishment aboard ship, and the person responsible escaped without punishment, his rage knew no bounds. He called for the minutes and judgment of the court martial of the offender, alluding, in the same unfettered fashion that Wilson had engaged in to attack Napoleon, to the Navy's general oppression and cruelty. When Philip Yorke complained of the use of anonymous sources, Brougham explained that he had had to because navy officials would punish informers. "He should have the same apprehension," he explained, "were his own political friends in office."[116] Perceval responded that Brougham "... must entertain a strange notion of the effects of office, if he conceived that against the name of a person who gave information of a foul murder, gentlemen in office would set a black mark in their minds ..."[117] The Prime Minister added presciently: "The observation would be unfortunate, for the hon. and learned gent ..., if at any future time he should himself get into office, as it might be supposed to proceed from a conviction of what would be his own feelings under similar circumstances."[118] The former Attorney General, who had been so troubled by Brougham manoeuvrings for Lord Melville's benefit during Pitt's last days, would not let him have the minutes of the court martial.

Brougham responded by going on a rampage against the unfortunate Perceval which would only be ended by his assassination. In May, the Commons had passed a resolution establishing the convertibility of Bank notes and gold coin. There resulted a run on guineas, driving up their value. Prices were increasingly quoted in both currencies. In late June, Lord King announced to the Lords that his tenants would be required to pay their rents either in gold coin, or "... if they tendered Bank Notes, such notes would only be taken in payment at the rates of 16s. in

---

116. *Cobbett's Parliamentary Debates,* vol.20, col.1034.
117. *Ibid.*
118. *Ibid.,* cols.1034-5.

the pound ..."[119] A copy of this notice, stating that payment in paper currency must make up a 14s. rise in the price of an ounce of gold, helped force the Ministry to introduce the Gold Coin and Bank Note Bill to re-establish parity. When the measure was debated in the Commons, Lord King's individual way of dealing with depreciated paper currency became Brougham's model for resolving the crisis. John Calcraft triggered Brougham's response by this allusion: "He attributed Lord King's conduct to literary pride: for having written much, and finding it had no effect, he had determined on illustrating his own doctrines, and thus the Peer was merged with the Writer."[120] Brougham objected to making Bank notes legal tender, claiming that that was how the French Revolution got started. "He believed it was mere pretence to say that this Bill was occasioned by Lord King's intimation to his tenantry."[121] He too called for a system of two prices, one in coin and the other in paper, and concluded with a short history of money which recalled his review of Liverpool's treatise on gold coin. The proposed measure would defeat the Judges' opposition to the forced circulation of paper money, and Lord King's effort to distrain rent, Brougham charged.

When the Bill passed, despite his claim that it was defective in every regard,[122] he moved his own resolutions on the subject. They represented a censure of the Bank's directors, and provided for holders of Bank notes to receive what they wanted for them despite the unconstitutional legislation. Brougham, in making this most unusual motion, exchanged sneers with the Prime Minister. Perceval said mockingly that he did not think that the act would dispose people to give their property away. Brougham responded that he did not like to spoil jokes, but that the measure would accomplish just that. Perceval reminded Brougham that "... Swift had pronounced nothing to be more arbitrary, than for a man to make himself ridiculous, and then be angry at others for

---

119. *Gentleman's Magazine*, vol.81, 1811, Part II, p.67.
120. "Historical Chronicle," *ibid.*, p.161.
121. *Cobbett's Parliamentary Debates*, vol.20, col.923.
122. *Ibid.*, col.1014.

laughing."[123] Brougham's resolutions were defeated without a division.

He was not the kind of man to capitulate in the face of such opposition; he just redoubled his efforts. In the *Review*, he reviewed yet another report by the African Institution which showed that he was no longer so sanguine about the slave trade's end. After tracing the abolitionists' efforts, he wrote:

> They will even extend their enlightened and humane endeavours, to obtain the cooperation of other nations, in a measure so honourable to our own and will not rest satisfied, until the great continent, which the slave-trade had ravaged and benighted, shall be admitted to a fair chance of running with other countries the race of civility and improvement.[124]

Brougham veiled his disappointment over the current level of the trade by recounting the passage of the Abolition Act, and what Sir William Scott had accomplished by his decision in the *Amédie* case. The failure of Africa to revive was explained: "This is owing to the partial revival of the slave trade, and its baneful influence on the natives of Africa, as well as to the necessity imposed by it, upon the Directors ..."[125] Brougham quoted from an African official's letter about how the trade's revival was undoing all the good of abolition. In light of the Huggins and Hodge cases, Parliament was called upon to exercise general supervision over colonial treatment of slaves.

Although the St Alban's Street operation had been closed down for over a year by the Whig magnates because of the radical effect it was having on politics, Brougham tried increasingly to make up for the void. As soon as the Session ended, he apparently submitted columns to *The Times*, establishing a relation with reporter Thomas Barnes which would serve him so well in the future. About the slave trade, Brougham spelled out what he had

---

123. *Ibid.*, cols.1109-10.

124. Art.II, "Report of the African Institution," *Edinburgh Review*, vol.18, no.XXXVI, August 1811, p.305.

125. *Ibid.*, p.321.

only alluded to in the *Review*: "These documents prove, that the result of all we have hitherto done, is that the Slave-Trade, instead of being abolished, has only changed hands."[126] About Canning's gradual approach to getting other states to abolish it, he wrote:

> I never could comprehend the necessity of that overstrained delicacy with which we have treated our allies on this subject; nor why, in negotiating with them for the abolition of the Slave-Trade, the great principles of justice, humanity, and policy, are to be compromised.[127]

Brougham compared it to what the Chief Magistrate of the City had done in meeting the Gordon Riots. Britain should declare Spanish and Portuguese traders as *hostes humani generis*:

> ... let the Legislature declare, that from and after a certain day, all vessels under whatever flag they may be navigated, that are detected carrying on the Slave-Trade, shall be destroyed; the slaves re-landed; and the officers and crews set on shore, and left to the mercy of those whom they came to enslave.[128]

Brougham rejoiced at the prospect of Britain's power being used for man's freedom rather than his oppression and tyranny.

On September 27, 1811, Brougham apparently had another column published in *The Times*, a most important one for his future relations with his political patron, the Duke of Bedford, and his Whig associates. Brougham's interest in Joseph Lancaster's system of education had resulted in the formation of the Royal Lancastrian System the previous May. At the inaugural meeting, the Duke of

---

126. "Slave-Trade Felony Act," *The Times*, July 18, 1811, no.8375, p.2. While there are no records about who submitted anonymous letters and articles to the newspaper until 1846, the substance of an increasing number of them, basically after Barnes became editor in 1817, points to Brougham's hand. For the general survey of the relationship see Trowbridge H. Ford, "Political Coverage in *The Times*, 1811-41, the Role of Barnes and Brougham," *Bulletin of the Institute of Historical Research*, vol.LIX, no.139 (May 1986), pp.91-107.

127. *Ibid.*

128. *Ibid.*

Bedford had presided, and gave a most encouraging speech about what the Establishment thought of such projects, despite the religious questions it raised. Brougham was responsible for resolutions regarding the training of female students, and an annual subscription where individuals would pay between one to ten guineas for membership, a most controversial commitment in light of Brougham's struggle with the Administration over gold coin. Would subscribers in Bank notes now be expected to pay more? In the article, Brougham came down on the side of the Lancastrian approach to *all* education, signing the anonymous article, in characteristically *Review* fashion, as "A Friend of *Scriptural* Education". Brougham dismissed those who were calling for established religious schools, along the lines Dr Bell was advocating, as Church alarmists, like those fanatics who were responsible for the Gordon riots. "This party have tortured everything," he wrote, "into an apparition of danger."[129] The creation of more than one system of education would only be creating confusion: "The schools thus formed will become the rallying posts of religious party spirit."[130]

The position that Brougham had achieved in English society was well captured in Louis Simond's journal. During a tour of Great Britain during Brougham's time in Parliament, Simonds explained his role thus:

> One thing surprises me more and more every day; it is the great number of people in the opposition; that is, those who disapprove not only the present measures of ministers, which have not been of late either very wise or very successful, but the form and constitution of the government itself. It is stigmatized as vicious, corrupt, and in its decay, without hope or remedy but in general reform, and in fact a revolution.[131]

In case no one recognized who Simond had in mind as the leader

---

129. *Ibid.*, September 27, 1811, no.8410, p.2.
130. *Ibid.*
131. Simond, *op. cit.*, vol.I, p.36.

of public opinion, he singled out Brougham's review of the Huttonian theory about the earth's core to indicate just what a hostile critic could attempt. As for Brougham's general approach to reviewing, Simond said:

> One of the best articles begins in this manner, "Mr B is a good sort of man, who has not written a very bad book, on a very important subject," etc. Then, without any further notice of the book, the critic goes on with an essay of his own, on this same important subject; and it requires nothing less than the very great merit of the Essay on Female Education, to make good sort of readers forget this unwarrantable liberty taken with a man who had committed no literary offence.[132]

For further identification of the primary offender, the French traveller wrote: "The Edinburgh critics are decided Whigs of the Fox school ... The slave trade has found in them irreconcilable enemies. They recommend peace, - and reprobate paper money."[133]

With Brougham having reached such a manifest, revolutionary capacity that even foreigners could easily recognize his role, the Duke of Bedford decided that he could do without such a difficult, demanding piece of "... rightful property."[134] No sooner had Brougham been elected to Parliament than he cut off his relations with Whig society at Holland House because it might interfere with his public responsibilities.[135] Brougham apparently feared the restraining influence that the Whig ladies, especially Lady Holland, would have upon his radical tendencies. While their husbands had done everything they could to contain his ambitions, he still used them more than they liked, and they could not help suspecting that he was up to dangerous things behind their backs. Once the St Alban's Street establishment had been closed down, he ostensibly

---

132. *Ibid.*, vol.II, pp.24-5.
133. *Ibid.*, p.25.
134. "Parliamentary Reform," *op. cit.*, p.269.
135. For the conventional explanation for the break, see, eg, Frances Hawes, *Henry Brougham* (Cape, London, 1957), pp.78-9.

had little to do but attend the House and Whig society; yet, Brougham was often inventing excuses for being away.[136] The straw which broke the camel's back was apparently his undue politicization of the educational issue, setting off a furore like Brougham's dispute with Byron. The crucial comment appeared in the *Gentleman's Magazine*:

> The more important question regards the *generalizing* part of Mr Lancaster's plan, which embraces the children of all religious persuasions, and upon this question we have very serious doubts, and before these doubts are removed, we must see an able refutation of Dr Marsh's late Sermon at St Paul's.[137]

Under the circumstances, the Duke informed Brougham that he no longer could afford his services at Camelford, claiming that financial necessity forced him to do so. For Bedford to have done anything less would have smacked of, in Brougham's terms, his having run a Treasury borough all along.

While historians have invariably allowed Brougham to be the uncontested authority on the Duke,[138] so claiming because he never said a bad word about him, the explanation will not stand serious scrutiny. It is interesting to note the first gloss that Brougham gave to Holland of the dismissal:

> ... it gives me the most hearty satisfaction that it is owing to no difference whatever either of a personal or a political nature. The various reports and hints, *now* proved to be unfounded, which reached me both last session and the session before, I never took the trouble of inquiring into. I never gave them the smallest credit, and, had they been all true, I would have made

---

136. See, eg, his explanation to the Commons that he had to attend the House of Lords and Privy Council. (*The Times*, no.8,349, July 18, 1811, p.3). There is no record of Brougham's having anything to do with these courts at this time.

137. 101. "A Comparative View of the Plans of Education," *Gentleman's Magazine*, vol.81, 1811, Part II, p.343. Italics its.

138. See, eg, Arthur Aspinall, *Lord Brougham and the Whig Party* (Archon, Hamden, CT, 1972, reprinted), pp.26-7.

no change in my conduct.[139]

As for anything that the Duke could have written to him, one must remember that Brougham had found him almost inarticulate, the Duchess making up for his lack of words. The Duke was getting rid of him to satisfy others, proving that there had been something in all those reports. Brougham, for once, was telling the truth when he said that they had not made any difference.

As in all matters of historical controversy, actions speak louder than words. Brougham showed his true feelings about his dismissal for what he had done in the press, Parliament, and courts by pressing ahead in a manner most embarrassing to the Duke. In the next issue of the *Review*, he tried to answer his educational critics in a fashion which must have had Bedford squirming in his seat when he read it. Brougham discussed the formation of the Royal British System of Education, inspired by the activities of Lancaster, and the outgrowth of the Institution that the Duke had founded in December 1810. About the inaugural meeting the previous May, Brougham wrote that Bedford's speech from the presiding chair "... fulfilled the expectations of those who knew his Grace; and excited the liveliest admiration among such as believed the whole eloquence and sense of the country were to be looked for among the regular conductors of parliamentary content."[140] So that no one would miss how this leader of the Opposition treated his minions, Brougham quoted verbatim his resolutions on the recruitment of women, and payment of subscriptions, displaying his name as their source in great relief. After tracing the progress of Lancaster's movement, Brougham dealt thus with fair-weather benefactors: "Those who recollect the ferment which it at first excited among certain classes of feeble bigots and clerical jobbers, will easily believe that the events we have been dwelling upon could not but revive all the foolish alarms of the one, and the impotent spleen of the other."[141]

---

139. Quoted from *ibid.*, p.26. Italics Brougham's.
140. Art.I, "Education of the Poor," *Edinburgh Review*, vol.19, no.XXXVII, November 1811, p.13.
141. *Ibid.*, pp.21-2.

In case the Duke of Bedford missed the barbed character of these comments, Brougham made them more pointed. No sooner had the Duke informed Brougham that he could not afford his services than he took a leading role in financing the rebuilding of his Drury Lane Theatre. In 1810, a private act had been passed to remedy the results of a disastrous fire, but it had proved inadequate. A committee had been appointed to investigate the costs of renovating the site. It reported that nearly 400,000 would be required. "The claimant of the first rank was the Duke of Bedford, whose demand for rent amounted to 4,250. This sum his Grace had liberally consented to give up entirely, if the other creditors and claimants should agree to the arrangements proposed by the Committee."[142] The governing body, under the chairmanship of Brougham's radical competitor Samuel Whitbread, subsequently was informed of this condition: "The next claimants were the Patent Annuitants. This class had all priority in their claim to all but those of the Duke of Bedford for rent ..."[143] Bedford absolved himself of 12,000 in property claims in getting the project started,[144] hardly the kind of commitment of a person in financial distress. Bedford obtained 32,000 for the sale of the borough and its compliant electors. Brougham showed he understood the deception when he discussed public benevolence towards education: "Among these, we must give the first places to the Duke of Bedford and Lord Somerville (*sic*), the two earliest patrons whose kindness it has been the fortune of Mr Lancaster to experience."[145] About the December meeting which started the Royal Lancastrian System, he added: "The first and steady friends of the system, the Duke of Bedford and Lord Somerville, were nominated Presidents."[146] In effect, Brougham was trying to show that Bedford had forsaken social reform for Whitbread's more conventional projects.

Brougham gave the bibliophile Duke a most pessimistic appraisal of what Professor Marsh had to offer. In considering the

---

142. "Re-Building Drury-Lane Theatre," *The Times*, October 15, 1811, no.8,423, p.3.
143. *Ibid.*
144. *Gentleman's Magazine*, vol.81, 1811, Part II, p.478.
145. "Education of the Poor," *op. cit.*, p.3.
146. *Ibid.*, p.13.

sermon at St Paul's, he apologized thus:

> We must beg our readers not to be alarmed at the notion, that we are going to plunge into a religious controversy, for which we have neither the learning nor the gall! - nor let it be thought that we are disposed to treat irreverently anything which comes from the ministers of religion in the discharge of their holy office.[147]

The only difference between the systems of Dr Bell and Mr Lancaster, despite Marsh's superficial preferences, was the communities they would serve. Bell's would serve that of the national church, by law established, and to the benefit of its parochial clergy, while Lancaster proposed to serve society at large. Brougham quoted long passages from the sermon to illustrate the point. After professing the expected loyalties to the Church of England, he concluded bitterly: "Hence it is, that we view with more than common indignation the men whom we have now been occupied in exposing to the public, because in them we see at once the enemies of the Poor ..."[148]

No sooner did Brougham learn of why he had been rejected by the Duke than he apparently started looking for another patron. In a letter to *The Times*, "To Lord King," someone sounding much like Brougham made a special pleading for the vast landowner to continue his campaign against paper currency: "Defying clamour and popular prejudice, your Lordship has appealed to the laws of your own country; and I am convinced that the result will be, to bring back the nation to the only just measure of value, a metal circulation."[149] Lord King was advised to demand payment of 26, in one- or two-pound notes, from some city or London bank, going to the magistrates, if refused, to force sale of the banker's property for remuneration. If a magistrate refused to cooperate, or the bank paid Lord King Bank of England notes, he was further advised: "...

147. *Ibid.*, p.25.
148. *Ibid.*, p.41.
149. *The Times*, October 29, 1811, no.8435, p.3.

the next step will be, to bring an action on *assumpsit* in Westminster Hall, to recover payment of the same 26 1. due in one and two-pound notes."[150] The magistrates could also be asked for a writ of mandamus against the banker to pay in coin, and tenants could suffer ejectments if they did not pay up. The lord was cautioned to be on the lookout for failure in form in opening actions, difficulties presented by special juries, and limitations on decisions. Lord King was advised against taking any final appeal to the Lords because of what the Lord Chancellor, Eldon had said during passage of Stanhope's bill.

When this overture led nowhere, given the barrister's envisioned utopia, Brougham had to plan more realistically for the future. With no real electoral prospects, some Worcester reformers having apparently lost interest in his possible candidature,[151] he could merely do what he had planned in the hope that some popular constituency would turn up. For the coming Session, he had already prepared his speech for the Opposition benches, entitled "Campaigns of 1809". In the *Review*, he wrote a most critical analysis of the events leading up to the Walcheren fiasco, calling again for the Ministry's replacement.[152] Britain's failure to assist Austria around the time of the Battle of Aspern was seen as the critical mistake in stemming French expansionism. In reviewing three pamphlets on German aspects of the struggle, Brougham explained:

> We suggest, with great humility, that at a time when all Germany was in such a state as to render it possible for 1500 men to march safely across it, notwithstanding its occupation by French troops, the landing of an English army might have been materially inconvenient to the armies of France, and proved beneficial as a diversion in favour of their adversaries.[153]

---

150. *Ibid.*
151. For background to this offer, see Aspinall, *Lord Brougham ... , op. cit.*, p.27.
152. For a completely different interpretation, see New, *op. cit.*, p.56.
153. Art.VII, "Campaigns of 1809," *Edinburgh Review*, vol.18, no.XXXVI, August 1811, p.407.

Instead, Perceval's Ministry saw to it that "... armies were despatched to the greatest possible distances from the scene of action ..."[154] The force sent up the Scheldt was to wipe out the Walcheren fever, Brougham complained. The Cabinet, instead of riveting its attention on what Britain could do to help its allies in Central Europe, reinforced the expedition to Portugal, so that it could make a useless foray into Spain. The government lacked vision and energy for the successful termination of the war, preferring to use its resources to deceive public opinion by domestic diversions. Brougham concluded by calling for its ouster.

There were several possible issues that Brougham could exploit against the Crown, but he finally settled on the growing difficulties with America because of the revised Orders in Council. He had thought of using the revelations about barbarous treatment of slaves against the Ministry, but his airing of the subject showed more about his own difficulties than those of Perceval. In venting his rage against what Huggins and Hodge had done, he went through the various justifications for slavery, concluding, for the Duke's benefit, with biblical injunctions for it: "We really hope there is no intention of raising a religious cry, and making the 'crunch in danger' from the abolition."[155] No sooner were these views printed than Brougham thought better of them. Instead, harking back to his days at Ryder and St Alban's streets, he apparently turned out a pamphlet on the Orders in Council, "The Crisis of the Dispute with America". Brougham had rare praise in the *Review* for what the "Merchant of the Old School" had written: "This is a sensible and useful pamphlet, published by a very respectable merchant, who writes on a subject in which he treats of, and suffering severely under the evils of which he complains."[156]

In attacking policy towards America, he even had good words for Cobbett's opinions. While the ministers were winning over the Prince Regent, Brougham explained, the people were feeling the

---

154. *Ibid.*
155. Art.V, "West Indian Slavery," *ibid.*, vol.19, no.XXXVII, November 1811, p.135.
156. Art.II, "Disputes with America," *ibid.*, no.XXXVIII, February 1812, p.290.

evil effects of their policies, and were responding. Perceval's Ministry had made the blockade of France into a monopoly which only benefited British traders, recreating by licence the violations of international law that the amendments of April 1809 had tried to stop. Short of the Ministry seeing the destructiveness of the Orders in Council, Brougham could only find hope in the words of Sir William Scott in the Fox case:

> I have no hesitation in saying, that they would cease to be just if they ceased to be retaliatory, and they would cease to be retaliatory, from the moment the enemy retracts, in a sincere manner, those measures of his, which they were intended to retaliate.[157]

In the same issue, Brougham renewed his claims as the defender of the people's rights by reviewing another volume of Lord Erskine's speeches. After all, Brougham had given his parliamentary career a good start by reviewing the first volume. Maybe, he could now achieve real independence. In any case, it would help his legal career by reviewing a set of cases less geared to politically sensitive matters, especially *ex officio* informations for libel. As Brougham had concentrated upon the Stockdale case in showing how Erskine handled State Trials, he now stressed the Hadfield case, the attempted assassin of George III. About the postponement of the trial, Erskine said: "It is fit on that," giving the proper indulgences to the accused, "there should be a solemn pause before we rush to judgment ..."[158] The defendant's counsel, Brougham continued, showed that his client, like "... such persons, often reason with a subtlety which puts in the shade the ordinary conceptions of mankind."[159] Contrary to the opinion of Lord Chief Justice Hale, these persons were insane. Erskine, when he backed up this principle with telling evidence about the accused, completely converted the presiding Judge, Lord Kenyon, to the

---

157. Quoted from *ibid.*, p.306.
158. Art.IV, "*Speeches of Lord Erskine,*" *ibid.*, p.342.
159. *Ibid.*, p.343.

necessity of Hadfield avoiding the gallows. In recounting a seduction case for breach of contract, Brougham pronounced this *obiter dictum*:

> The proper degree of punishment is not meted out to guilt. Offences totally different in kind are called by one appellation, and visited with the same penalty; and juries are obliged to violate their oaths, in order to acquit, that they may avoid a greater evil, the undue conviction and consequent punishment, of the person accused. We trust that the Legislature will take this subject into its early consideration.[160]

At the conclusion, Brougham explained his interest in Erskine: "Had he not been the first in this path - had his powers been exerted in obsequiousness to the government, or in time-serving or timid submission to the court of justice, *we*, at least, should not have stepped aside to attempt the task of praising his eloquence."[161]

This effort, it seems, immediately paid off for Brougham. As part of the war effort that he most disapproved of, "fighting France on the islands around the globe," Britain forced the capitulation of the forces on the Isle de France. There was a significant contingent of British prisoners of war there, some of whom had become French turncoats. While, under the terms of the surrender, they could have gone to mainland France with the regular forces, they chose to return to England. No sooner did they arrive than the Crown appointed a special commission, under Judge Sir Archibald Macdonald, to inquire into their suspected treason. Twelve of these unfortunates were ultimately indicted, and brought to trial.[162] The defendants were unprepared to make a defence, being without funds. They appealed to the Lords of the Admiralty, thanks to Brougham's revelations in the House about its droits, for funds, but were refused. They had hoped that with the droits of the

160. *Ibid.*, p.352.
161. *Ibid.*, p.363. Italics Brougham's.
162. "High Treason," *The Times*, January 21, 1812, no.8505, p.3.

Admiralty so abundant that they were upsetting the constitution,[163] there would be something left for its dregs. The Secretary of State was no more responsive to their desperate straits. The special commission agreed to bring defensive witnesses to the court at its expense. Finally, the defendants were asked who they wanted to defend them, and they voted for solicitor James Harmer and barrister Brougham. "The assignments were made accordingly."[164]

During the trials, Brougham tried to get a Captain Willougby to give evidence "... that he was forced at the peril of his life to enter the service of the French at the Isle de France, and that one of his own crew was shot for refusing."[165] The defendant's affidavit, however, was denied. Willougby would not even come to testify on behalf of defendant William Cundell. During the cross-examination of the Crown's witnesses, Brougham said to the jury:

> ... the prisoner and 11 others, now indicated with him, had used the first moment they were allowed a free option, and preferred surrendering themselves to the British troops. After the capture of the island, he had given himself up voluntarily, as soon as he was able ...[166]

Brougham also introduced an excerpt from the *London Gazette Extraordinary* to show that the prisoners, under the terms of the capitulation, had been free to go to France. Cundell contended that his service under French colours had merely been a ploy. "It was given in evidence, however, that the prisoner not only wore the French uniform, but did duty as a French soldier; and that he had treated British officers, prisoners, with great contempt."[167] He was convicted of treason, but the jury did recommend mercy because

---

163. For Brougham's speech about the droits' unconstitutional character, see *Cobbett's Parliamentary Debates*, vol.21, col.241 fc.
164. "High Treason," *The Times*, February 4, 1812, no.8517, p.4.
165. *Ibid.*, February 11, 1812, no.8,523, p.2.
166. *Ibid.*
167. *Gentleman's Magazine*, vol.82, 1812, Part I, p.183.

he had returned. The next two defendants were convicted of treason without extenuating circumstances. Charles Bird was similarly convicted, but the jury "... strongly recommended mercy, on account of his having manifested much penitence at his conduct, and behaving humanely to his shipmates who were prisoners ..."[168] The next two defendants were convicted of capital crimes, but the jury had recommended mercy for one of them who, despite assisting the French, "... in attempting to escape, had one eye knocked out and one hand broken."[169] Irishman Samuel Macfarlane was also condemned after a witness testified that he was willing to die for Napoleon.

After another case had been heard, the Crown stopped prosecution of the other five. The Attorney General, Gibbs explained:

> ... he had most studiously concealed to that moment, from his Learned Friend who conducted the defence of the prisoners, the course he intended now to pursue, lest it should be imagined that he wished under any doubt of his ability to substantiate the charges which it was his duty to bring forward, or any intimation of a lenient intention ...[170]

Gibbs broke down into sobbing after he had stated that he thought the ends of justice would be served without convicting the remaining five of capital crimes. This was some concession from a prosecutor who, according to Brougham, thought he knew it all, and Gibbs went to great pains to try to show that he was not being soft. Brougham concurred with the decision, and complimented the Attorney General for the humane feelings that he had shown throughout the trials. Brougham, in asking for mercy for the convicted, said that it "... would to the end of their lives bind them with the liveliest gratitude for the mercy they should experience from a generous country, which thus, oblivious of their past errors,

---

168. *Ibid.*
169. *Ibid.*
170. *The Times*, February 15, 1812, no.8,526, p.4.

opened its arms to receive them ..."[171] All the convicted men fell on their knees, begging the commission to spare their lives.

Lord Chief Baron Macdonald, in pronouncing sentence, worked himself up to mete out the maximum penalty. The head of the Court of the Exchequer was a humane man, but not a particularly good Judge. As Attorney General, he had unsuccessfully prosecuted Stockdale, "... and Paine for seditious libels contained in his *Rights of Man*."[172] Macdonald had presided at the famous trials of Hardy, Horne Tooke, and Thelwall for high treason, but he was unwilling to go along with the doctrine of constructive treason that Sir John Scott, then Attorney General, felt obliged to advance against the accused. Gibbs had defended these radicals. Macdonald apparently felt that Gibbs had been too influenced by the defence in this case, pronouncing the traitor's death for all those convicted:

> ... to be drawn on a hurdle to the place of execution, where you shall be hanged by the necks, but not till you are dead; that you be severally taken down while yet alive, and your bowels be taken out and burnt before your faces; that your heads be then cut off, and your bodies cut in four quarters, to be at the King's disposal.[173]

Actually, this punishment was a fiction which the Home Office had long since moderated in practice.[174] Still, the Crown could have revived some of its more barbaric aspects. The prisoners merely suffered the indignity of being beheaded after they had been hanged to death.[175] Brougham, in helping save the other 54 from the worst rigours of the criminal law, had accomplished his biggest success at the Bar. For the effort, he was given a more respectable

---

171. *Ibid.*
172. Sir William Holdsworth, *A History of English Law* (Methuen, London, 1952, 14 vols.), vol.XIII, p.557.
173. *Gentleman's Magazine, op. cit.*, p.184.
174. 54 Geo.III, c.146 had reduced the actual execution of those guilty of high treason to hanging.
175. "Occurrences," *The New Annual Register*, 1812 (Stockdale, London, 1813), p.57.

brief calling for an order for mandamus in the King's Bench against the Justices of Suffolk for failing to administer the oath to a Dissenting Minister.

He was just as successful during the 1812 Session of Parliament, but his achievements were overshadowed by Perceval's assassination, and the war with America. As expected, he concentrated on the Crown's growth, thanks to the Orders in Council, and the droits of the Admiralty. Brougham looked for every opportunity to contend that the Ministry was resorting to dire expedients to purchase friends and influence for its failing policies, a course which drew him into ever more heated debate with the Prime Minister. As was Brougham's custom, he gave his own address to the House on the unconstitutional effect that the Ministry's naval and commercial policies were having upon the country. When this attack did not bring about Perceval's resignation, Brougham resumed it in such reckless terms that it backfired, a temporary setback which was completely eliminated by the commercial distress caused by the Orders in Council. Brougham's triumph, in gaining their repeal, was offset by Perceval's murder. Liverpool, the new Prime Minister, used it to justify repressive legislation against the Luddites. With its passage, Brougham gained a new avocation, defending the poor and oppressed, but, in the process, he lost his seat in the Commons.

Brougham previewed his attack on the droits by joining Creevey's opposition to Colonel M'Mahon's appointment as Paymaster of Widows' Pensions as the House was considering a motion for supply to the Prince Regent. Brougham's friend said that the appointment was contrary to reports on abolishing sinecures and places. Perceval objected to the motion, explaining that M'Mahon had resigned his seat in the Commons before accepting the post. "Did he think that if a barrister, for instance, had an opportunity of displaying great power, and extraordinary talents, combined with extensive judicial knowledge," the Prime Minister asked mockingly, "that all these should not be sufficient to recommend him to a public situation, because he was a member of parliament?"[176] Brougham was not put off by this, however, claiming that the appointment was an insult to Parliament. Perceval's assurance that M'Mahon knew that he was taking the sinecure subject to possible parliamentary elimination was seen as ministerial contempt for the intentions of the House. Brougham did think that Creevey's criticism of such appointments went too far in including the Masters in Chancery, a post to which Wilberforce had just been appointed. "He would be bold to say, indeed," Wilberforce told the House in a state of great agitation, "that no situation, no prospective, no actual reward, could influence him in his conduct as a member of parliament ..."[177] Only 11 Members supported Creevey's motion.

A fortnight later, Brougham moved his resolutions against the droits of the Admiralty with hardly more success. They were condemned as unconstitutional funds, not voted by Parliament, but at the government's disposal, which were so upsetting fundamental political relations. "One thing was certain," he charged, "that from whomsoever, or to whomsoever they came, they never went into the exchequer ..."[178] Brougham tried to show that they represented a secret reward fund in giving people like Sir Home Popham 20,000, a charge that Perceval rejected. "It was enough", Brougham continued, "if he had established a necessary tendency to corruption; but as the right hon. the Chancellor of the Exchequer seemed to challenge him for facts, he was by no means unwilling to produce them."[179] Perceval was not satisfied with the evidence that Brougham provided to show that the droits constituted an illegal fund, nor that the Copenhagen attack was stimulated by a desire for droits. The captors received nothing, the Prime Minister claimed. In fact, he was so incensed by Brougham's charges that he would not even go along with Tierney and supply information about them until Brougham's call for an investigation had been soundly defeated.

Frustrated by Parliament, Brougham took his complaints to *The*

---

176. *Cobbett's Parliamentary Debates*, vol.21, col.115.
177. *Ibid.*, col.121.
178. *Ibid.*, col.249.
179. *Ibid.*, col.255.

Times. In a letter, signed "Observator", Brougham apparently tried to provide what Perceval demanded in the way of evidence about captors benefiting from the droits. In the Copenhagen expedition, a Danish prize was seized, and was sold for 4,500. Sixty per cent of its value was given to prize agents by the Court of Admiralty, "... reserving the difference, as they reported, for droits of Admiralty."[180] The droits were diminished, the article concluded, by funds which went to the captors. Perceval immediately responded to Brougham's challenge:

> Those who correct the statements of others, should be accurate in their own; and I deny that that Court ever made any such award, and call upon OBSERVATOR to prove that it ever did make such an award, or even possessed any power so to do.[181]

Brougham decided to wage total war with Perceval's administration for its temerity. Two days later, he opposed a supplementary grant to the Prince Regent, claiming that he should have taken the necessary funds from the droits, as George II had done, and the establishment of a separate household for the Queen, unless a strict parliamentary inquiry showed that it was necessary.[182] Early in February, he moved for papers on the balance of trade between Britain and America over the past decade to show the adverse effects that the Orders in Council were having upon it. When the information did not come forward as quickly as Brougham wanted, he deliberately postponed another motion on the droits, complaining of the delay. When a ministerial spokesman explained that the returns were at the Bar of the House, only waiting to be presented, Brougham moved for an "... account of all the sums taken from the fund of Droits of the Admiralty, and repaid to the same during the last five years."[183] Perceval denied that an abuse had occurred, a claim that Brougham disputed. The Prime Minister responded by denying that the practice constituted

180. *The Times*, January 25, 1812, no.8,509, p.2.
181. *Ibid.*, January 27, 1812, no.8,510, p.2.
182. *Ibid.*, January 29, 1812, no.8,5112, p.2.
183. *Ibid.*, February 13, 1812, no.8,529, p.2.

illegal activity, but agreed to supply the information. A week later, when Alexander Baring complained to the licensing system that the Crown had adopted to ease the Continental blockade, Brougham jumped at the chance to gain more insight into how the Orders in Council were encouraging monopolistic practices in commercial circles. Perceval denied that the licences, which traders were willing to pay astronomical sums for, were either new or extraordinary.[184]

While Brougham was hoping that these efforts would pay off by his being invited to contest a popular constituency in the next election, he had not given up hope of finding another borough patron to replace the Duke. Early in the Session, several of Brougham's landowner neighbours in Westmorland and Cumberland had petitioned Parliament for the rebuilding of the bridge over the Eamont at Brougham Castle, and for building a road to connect Brougham with Penrith.[185] Before the last General Election, Brougham had sought to be adopted by the moderate Tory Lowthers in one of their Westmorland constituencies, but despite Wilberforce's assistance, the effort came to nothing.[186] Brougham hoped that a solid local achievement would appeal to the powerful Westmorland family. On February 21, Brougham reported to the House that the committee, headed by Sir James Graham and Mr Wallace, to see that the petition had complied with the standing orders relative to turnpike and bridge-building bills, supported the measure.[187] A few days later, Viscount Morpeth introduced the bill, and it was submitted to another committee, including Lord Lowther, but not Brougham. After the proposal had been amended in committee, Graham took it up to the Lords, and it passed Parliament without opposition. While the measure gave the county a more solid link with its richer neighbour, it did not help Brougham bridge his parliamentary isolation.

The unwillingness of the Lowther interest to let Brougham have any role in its representation affected, it seems, his handling of the

184. *Ibid.*, February 19, 1812, no.8,530, p.2.
185. *The Journals of the House of Commons*, vol.67, 1812, p.39.
186. For more on this, see New, *op. cit.*, p.34 ff.
187. *The Journals ..., op. cit.*, p.134.

droits. When he called again for an inquiry into them, he had another bitter exchange with the Prime Minister. After Brougham explained that he had obtained information about their distribution from a clergyman rather than *qui tam* informers, Perceval uttered a sarcastic cheer, an allusion to Brougham's hostility to church-related education. *The Times* report continued:

> Mr Brougham deprecated any idea of imparting the slightest blame to the clergy and if the interruption of the hon. Chancellor was intended to convey any such meaning, he begged now to observe, that a remark made on a man who was a disgraceful exception to his profession, could not, with any justice, be said to attribute reproach to the profession itself.[188]

Brougham then launched a most wide-ranging, critical analysis of the droits whose highlight was the implication that Sir William Scott himself had benefited from the uncontrolled distribution of the droits.

Perceval, who had obviously been primed for Brougham's renewed attack, made a most detailed refutation of his claims. The House, the Prime Minister said, would not appoint a committee to investigate the droits upon Brougham's representation alone. Perceval explained away his sarcastic interjection thus: "He thought that perhaps the interruption which he had given might have been the means of obtaining the explanation which he had made, and which rather softened down the expressions which he had originally made."[189] Scott, contrary to any false impressions that Americans may have had about his conduct at the Court of Admiralty, had received a small fee as counsel in an action before he became Judge, the Prime Minister further explained. In fact, his explanation was so satisfactory that Brougham's motion was defeated without a division.

Brougham, nearly desperate to find new parliamentary patrons, fired the last arrow in his quiver, the gratuitous illegality of the

---

188. *The Times*, February 26, 1212, no.8,536, p.2.
189. *Ibid.*

Orders in Council. They had been instituted to counter the Milan and Berlin decrees, and had been amended, thanks largely to Brougham's earlier attacks, to blockade French ports. This retaliation was only justified as long as the French persisted in the myth of having monopolized European trade by their own fiat. A revocation of the decrees would bring the trading monopoly that the English had established through the licensing system under the Orders in Council crashing to the ground. While the English practice was not justified by international law, they could maintain it under a scintilla of law as long as the French persisted in their pretences. For a year, however, there had been persistent rumours that the French had, indeed, revoked the decrees. In the meantime, Britain's trade had fallen to a snail's pace. On March 4, Brougham called for an inquiry into their effects after giving a most detailed speech about the law and practice of the Orders in Council. "Was this then, exclaimed Mr Brougham, the trade so much and fondly boasted of? Was this the mighty victory achieved over Buonaparte? Was this the way in which he was brought to bite the dust? Who were now the victims of this blocking system ...?"[190] After an increasingly bitter debate, the motion was defeated by a majority of 102 votes.

The state of the country, the lack of trade, and the distress of the working classes, guaranteed that the Ministry could not evade this issue. Brougham himself took a short vacation from Parliament, rushing off to the Yorkshire assizes to preach unsuccessfully *Gilbert* v. *Sir M.M. Sykes*, a Buonapartian wager case, and to defend unsuccessfully some rioters. As petitions calling for the withdrawal of the Orders in Council poured into Parliament, and reports of industrial disturbance mounted, Perceval's Ministry obstinately refused any change as if any concession constituted a justification of Brougham's calls for reform. "It was but a poor satisfaction that some inquiry should at length be agreed to," Brougham said back in London, in presenting petitions on the effects of the Orders in Council, "after the Right Hon. Gentleman's measures had reduced

---

190. *Ibid.*, March 4, 1812, no.8,542, p.2.

the House to the necessity of such inquiry."[191] The crucial event in Brougham's showdown with the government was the conditional resolution in Council that if the French had revoked their decrees, the Orders would indeed be withdrawn.[192] Hardly had the newspapers published the results of the meeting at Carlton House where it was agreed to that the Commons would investigate the effects of the Orders in Council. Because of the campaign that Brougham had directed against them from Liverpool, one much like the electoral campaign that he managed for the Whigs in 1807, he was given charge of the inquiry. The Orders in Council, he explained, were on trial.[193]

As the House was hearing witnesses whose evidence sounded the knell for the Orders, the government was using the industrial unrest to justify passage of emergency measures. As Perceval struggled to pass bills to prevent secret oaths, and to strengthen law enforcement, Brougham was elaborating the case of commercial distress due to the devastating effect of governmental arbitrariness. In fact, the Prime Minister was forced to try to portray the Whig opposition as opposed to any experiments to reduce the number of persons assassinated by the enraged masses,[194] a claim Brougham confidently denied. When James Stephen sarcastically jeered Brougham's accusation, he attributed it to jealousy over not being included in the complaint, and expressed sorrow to Perceval for being subjected to shouts and irrational behaviour by his own, official supporters. When Stephen explained that the Opposition was showing unusual discourtesy towards the government by objecting to its proposals so early, Brougham moved, when the House went into committee on the Orders in Council, that Stephen had put an illiberal question to a witness.[195] The House, of course, as in the past when it had had to consider his petty, rash moves, rejected the request, but Brougham, nonetheless, seemed to be winning the battle for its

191. *Ibid.*, April 18, 1812, no.8581, p.3.
192. Appendix, *The English Reports*, vol.XII (Green, Edinburgh, 1901), p.218 ff.
193. *The Times*, April 29, 1812, no.8,590, p.3.
194. *Ibid.*, May 6, 1812, no.8,596, p.2.
195. *Ibid.*, p.3.

allegiance and support.

This was graphically illustrated at a meeting for parliamentary reform, held by the Livery of London at the City of London Tavern. Brougham was the keynote speaker. After radicals like Whitbread and Burdett had spoken, Brougham presented his credentials for leading the struggle in most bold terms: "... he had never lent himself to the support of one political measure which had not for its object to operate against the overwhelming power of the Crown, and strengthen what remained of the liberties of the country."[196] As for people who were shocked by such appeals, Brougham added:

> But, after all, there were baser loves to be found in the world than the love of popularity. There were intrigues to be found more low and vile than intrigues with the people. He did not merely talk of the intrigues in the House of Commons, or of the political loves of the Minister, but he would ask them about intrigues at Court ...[197]

He concluded his speech on this note, to the crowd's great pleasure, and applause:

> The squeamish alarms of some men on the dangers of popular influence would soon lose their effect. The cause of Parliamentary Reform had survived the apostasy of its early friends; it had triumphed in principle in spite of the opposition of the powerful men of the last generation, and it would soon not only triumph but utterly sweep away the pay men of the present.[198]

The audience reciprocated with the following toast: "Mr Brougham and unshackled commerce of the country."[199]

Hardly had the cheers for this confident challenge to establish

---

196. "Parliamentary Reform," *ibid.*, May 11, 1812, no.8600, p.3.
197. *Ibid.*
198. *Ibid.*
199. *Ibid.*

authorities died than the Prime Minister was murdered in the Lobby of the House. Cobbett had described the meeting of the Commons thus: "Mr Brougham closed his examination of Mr Hamilton, and Mr Stephen was in the course of his cross-examination of the same witness, when at about a quarter past five o'clock the report of a pistol shot was heard in the House and Gallery ..."[200] Perceval had been shot in the heart by John Bellingham, a disgruntled, deranged trader, and died almost instantly in Stephen's arms. While the nation mourned Perceval's death, the Crown arranged to send Bellingham to the gallows in record time. The speed and charge of the prosecution was a complete denial of what Brougham had seen as so attractive in Erskine's defence of Hadfield, the best way for the Crown to show who was really responsible for destroying the Prime Minister, and his chief work. "Perceval had been one of the two principal authors of the Orders in Council."[201] Brougham met the challenge in characteristic fashion, refusing to postpone consideration of their repeal for even a day because of the threat of a new war with America. If the Crown could manifest such legal insensitivity in dealing with a poor unfortunate, Brougham was not interested in social conventions for the likes of Perceval.

Whatever parliamentary hopes Brougham had, once the government fell, and liberal Tories and the Whigs looked into the possibility of forming a new Administration, they were dashed by Liverpool's becoming First Lord of the Treasury. Whatever happened to the Orders in Council, the new Prime Minister already had enough grievances against Brougham to deny him any ministerial career, and he knew it. In fact, Brougham agreed to postpone presenting evidence from the Committee on their withdrawal while Liverpool's Government was renewing for fear that it would be lost. In moving their termination, Brougham was willing to withdraw his motion when Castlereagh said that he was willing to make some kind of suspension.[202] After Brougham got

---

200. *Cobbett's Parliamentary Debates,* vol.23, col.165.
201. New, *op. cit.,* p.63.
202. *The Times,* June 17, 1812, no.8,629, pp.1-3. This is the celebrated speech in which Brougham summarized the case against the Orders in Council.

into a flap with the government by charging that it had suppressed evidence on the depressed state of trade, something that he could not prove,[203] he was finally obliged to demand that something authoritative appear in the *London Gazette* about their revocation, or he would go ahead with his motion. "He knew the Ministers would give up", Brougham explained, "they had shown indeed, that they would give up anything except their places. (*Hear, hear, and general laughter.*)"[204] One day before Brougham's deadline, the Ministry did print a provisional withdrawal of the Orders in Council. It was conditional upon American endorsement of French withdrawal of the decrees being true. When hostilities with the United States were reported, Brougham explained: "If war should take place, it was referable, in his opinion, to the Declaration published by the late government in April."[205] At that time, the government, to try to offset Brougham's campaign, had called upon France to show its adherence to the decrees, so as to force America to repeal its Non-Intercourse Act with Britain.

In sum, Brougham knew that repeal of the Orders in Council had been such a bitter experience for Liverpool's Ministry that he could hardly expect to gain politically from it. He decided, consequently, to make more of his legal career. As the struggle over the Orders had strained his relations with the Saints, especially Wilberforce and Stephen, he became more friendly with the criminal law reformers he knew at the "King of Clubs", particularly Sir Samuel Romilly. It was through Romilly and James Mill that Brougham became a confidant of Jeremy Bentham, the mentor of all law reformers. In reviewing Romilly's observations on the Criminal Law of England in the *Review*, Brougham discovered a new cause.

The criminal law, he wrote, needed to be reformed completely. Its relaxation, which only commenced during the past 50 years,[206] should be placed on a systematic, statutory basis. The granting to

---

203. *Ibid.*, June 18, 1812, no.8,630. p.2.
204. *Ibid.*, June 20, 1812, no.8,632, p.2.
205. *Ibid.*, July 11, 1812, no.8,650, p.2.
206. Art.VII, "Sir Samuel Romilly *on English Criminal Law, Edinburgh Review,* vol.19, no.XXXVIII, February 1812, p.391.

judges of complete discretion in its enforcement would only make things worse, Brougham warned, making the punishment of crime dependent upon the ever-changing web of circumstances. "The only object," Brougham reminded his readers, "which lawgivers propose to themselves in public inflictions of punishment, is the effect which they may produce upon the spectators, and, through them, on the rest of the community."[207] Brougham discussed, with great effect, the total confusion that the criminal law produced in the minds of criminals and law enforcement officials alike. While Romilly had fought to remove the inconsistencies and anomalies from the criminal law, a most moderate course for which he had been condemned as a wild innovator, the situation called for a radical, across-the-board approach. Given this prospect, Brougham was deadly serious when he wrote thus to Creevey:

> As to being out of Parliament - don't laugh at me if I say I really should submit to such a fate with composure, indeed with cheerfulness. I am fond of my profession, which you'll say a queer taste; but I really so delight in it more and more every day. I see also how greatly I might rise in it by this means, and how infallibly I should command anything parliamentary that I might choose, after a few years. This is clear, and I might be as much of a *demagogue* as I thought fit to be - I mean, in a good sense - and these times require looking *outside* of Parliament, in my opinion, as much as any we have lived in.[208]

In preparation for this challenge, Brougham spent his last days in the House articulating the demands and needs of the people, in the face of growing repression by the government. He objected to increased taxes upon horses and leather to help pay for the war because of their effect upon the poor.[209] Not to be intimidated by Perceval's assassination, Brougham asked the new Chancellor of the Exchequer "... whether any attention was paid to the claims of

207. *Ibid.*, p.396.
208. Brougham's letter to Creevey, dated May 1812, in Sir Herbert Maxwell, ed, *The Creevey Papers* (Murray, London, 1904, 2 vols.), vol.I, p.156. Italics Brougham's.
209. *The Times*, June 27, 1812, no.8,638, p.2.

the Danish merchants whose property was seized in the capture of Copenhagen,"[210] something that Vansittart acknowledged. Brougham expressed hope that the rumour that the Nightly Watch Bill had been dropped was true, and when it proved baseless, he attacked the creation of superintending constables as another example of how the Crown created influence at the expense of respectable people, the constables. Brougham dismissed the Peace Preservation Bill, what the government had drafted on the basis of the report of the secret committee to look into industrial disturbance by the Luddites, as greatly compounding a simple problem.

Brougham then detailed what he would have told the committee if he had been called to testify before it, charging that its composition had been packed by the Ministry. Magistrates should not be given additional powers, he warned, because they tended to be alarmists. Spies and intimidation were becoming common practice in law enforcement. "These spies were the active agents of the magistrates, and the House should be guarded how they enlarged powers which might be used to such mischievous and oppressive purposes."[211] Amidst ministerial cries of "*question, question!*," he discussed how police had seized "dangerous papers" at a meeting to draft a petition against the Orders in Council. Spies were condemned, especially in light of their new respectability. About their effect on law enforcement, Brougham said:

> When it was considered, too, that these men were paid a very great price for their services, some of them 30s., others 40s., and some two guineas and a half a week, besides all their expenses, it was not to be wondered at that the Magistrates were strenuous supporters. Here was a view of part of the secret service money; and when waggons were travelling about the northern counties loaded with money to pay this host, was it nothing to have the disposal of it, - was it to be supposed that all this money passed through certain hands without some of

---

210. *Ibid.*, July 7, 1812, no.8,656, p.2.
211. *Ibid.*, July 14, 1812, no.8,652, p.3.

> it sticking to their fingers?[212]

Once this effort, like all his opposition to the Ministry's growing repression, failed, Brougham left the House, not to return for three years. He believed that his seat would end with the Session, and he had better things to do than to hold on to it until the bitter end, as if it were a kind of legislative sinecure. The people in the country, and in its gaols needed his legal services.[213] He would try to meet their needs as best he could, building up knowledge and experience which would make him a more effective leader than any parliamentary service could. After all, Brougham's greatest victories had been in 1808 and 1812 when he led the popular forces of reform against the established interests in Parliament. He needed neither party nor parliamentary colleagues to work the popular will upon his legislative masters, as he stated so effectively to a public dinner given to him at Liverpool on September 4.[214] All he needed was his own base of political support, and the authority to make it persuasive in legislative circles. It was in search of this that Brougham left the Commons in mid-July 1812.

---

212. *Ibid.*
213. For more on this, see his efforts, in cooperation with Romilly, to investigate conditions at Lincoln gaol; starting in *ibid.*, June 26, 1812, no.8637, p.2.
214. "Public Dinner to Mr Brougham," *The Leeds Mercury*, no.2,464, p.3.

CHAPTER FOUR

RADICAL BARRISTER

Brougham adopted a well-planned strategy for leading the nation's reform. In the columns of the *Edinburgh Review*, he laid out his credentials as a professional who had the proper remedy for the kingdom's ills, and a method for applying it. With Parliament having nearly another two years to run before there would be another General Election, Brougham outlined the way that his election in a populous borough, most likely Westminster, could neither be prevented by Treasury interests nor reactionary gentlemen. While the government tried to build up its parliamentary forces in the country, Brougham would build up a committee organization in a popular borough which would make his election irresistible. To enhance his vote-getting ability, Brougham stressed his professional capacity to serve the people's rights and needs in a systematic fashion, one which had a direct applicability to the legislative process. Reform required experts who could reorder society's institutions so that they would function more cheaply and efficiently. In order to do this, one had to know in detail how even the worst institutions operated so that their proper duties could be performed by reasonable agents. For reformers to reach this position under the unreformed constitution, which the Ministry was manipulating by means of money and alarms for its immediate purposes, they had to create a general climate of opinion favourable to change. The average subject had to be persuaded that his interests went hand-in-hand with those of the middle classes. In this way, Brougham thought, reformers could recapture an ancient constitution which had made few adaptations for their needs.

In the July 1812 issue of the *Review*, Brougham indicated the kind of constituency developments necessary if he were going to have a stable political base. In reviewing a pamphlet by William Roscoe, in response to Brougham's own on parliamentary reform which had been leaked to the press, and another one by J. Merritt in reply, Brougham outlined how one or two reformers in popular places could be returned in the looming General Election if they applied themselves. Bribery, travel expenses, election material, and costs at the hustings had made campaigns almost prohibitory except under the most controlled, planned conditions. Difficulties in many boroughs had been compounded by absentee voters in London who represented crucial swing votes in close contests:

> They become electioneering agents and agitators by trade - they are ever ready to stir up a contest and to profit by it - to sport with and prey upon the fears of sitting members, and the hopes of the candidate, or, as he is termed, (and it is an endearing appellation), the *third man* ...[1]

As long as these voters existed, Brougham explained, shortening the length of Parliaments would do no good. To help reduce expenses, he called for constant assemblage of voters at the hustings in various parts of constituencies, and for a cheaper, streamlined procedure for hearing contested elections by committee in the Commons. "At present," he complained, "the estimated expense of contesting Liverpool or Bristol, exceeds twelve thousand pounds; and the great Westminster contest, with the committee, is supposed to have cost about eight thousand ...[2] Unless a candidate had a committee to conduct his campaign with minimum expense, reasonable people would suspect his sanity. "A committee," Brougham explained, "entrusted with a subscription fund, can do things, not merely in safety, but with

1. Art.VIII, "Parliamentary Reform", *Edinburgh Review*, vol.20, no.XXXIX, July 1812, p.130. Italics Brougham's.
2. *Ibid.*, p.137.

credit, which would be looked upon as absolute meanness in a private individual ..."[3] To encourage potential committeemen to recreate what had been done in the 1807 election for Sir Francis Burdett in Middlesex, Brougham gave a most optimistic appraisal of what anti-ministerial candidates could achieve, given the sentiments of the press and the people.

In another review, Brougham emphasized the need to reform, in order to strengthen his qualifications as a candidate. After reporting that Secretary Zachary Macaulay had been succeeded by Mr Harrison of Queen's College, Brougham stressed the African Institution's continuing responsibility in suppressing the trade: "... a prodigious slave trade is still carried on by those famous allies of ours, the Portuguese and Spaniards. Cuba is daily extending her cultivation - the Brazils are more and more crowded with miserable victims."[4] To prevent deceptions that the *Amédie* case had exposed, Brougham urged the Americans to pass their own Slave Trade Felony Act. Brougham discussed the treatment of the Kroomen, an African tribe much abused by the administration in Sierra Leone, in personal terms: "Like the Swiss, the Scotch Highlanders, the Piedmontese and the Gallicians, they ramble from it only to love it the better, and to enable them to live, where alone they can be happy, at home."[5] To improve the slave system in British possessions, he repeated his call that no planter be given an important administrative position in the West Indies. Brougham concluded on this note:

> This retrospect gives us no feelings but those of pure satisfaction; because we verily believe, that we have in some small degree been useful to the great cause of humanity; and that Africa has been, in a manner, benefited by the progress of this journal.[6]

For new readers who were not aware of the *Review's* dedication

---

3. *Ibid.*, pp.140-1.
4. Art.V, "Sixth Report of the African Institution," *ibid.*, p.59.
5. *Ibid.*, p.70.
6. *Ibid.*, p.67.

to reform, Brougham provided a short introduction to the subject in another article. In reviewing another pamphlet by William Roscoe, "Considerations on the Causes, Objects and Consequences of the Present War", he tried to give substance to Hume's opinion that Britain had persisted in her wars too long. People had just become too used to their destructive ways. Peace, Brougham wrote, would end the need of loans, permitting the elimination of the worst of the customs and excise taxes. With the reduction and elimination of armed services, the income tax would be terminated, and property and assessed taxes would be reduced. The case for people was put in most rational, self-serving terms:

> We are known to be invincible - we have even been victorious - but we are mortal, and cannot destroy our antagonist. Then what shame is there in terminating a contest, in which we can no more conquer him, than he can subdue us?[7]

Brougham was even willing to see France continue to rule Spain as part of a general peace for Europe. Thanks to the revocation of the Orders in Council, reconciliation with America was seen as an accomplished fact. The people were coming to their senses about their power to dictate proper policy. "They will look forward", he predicted, "from conciliation with America - to a General Peace."[8]

To help achieve peace with the United States, Brougham volunteered his services as a negotiator to the Liverpool Government. Incredibly, Brougham thought that he could give substance to this claim made during one of the last debates on the Orders in Council: "... the country was governed as if his (Mr Brougham's) friends were in office, and Gentlemen opposite were breathing (what to them must be the greatest of conceivable miseries) the dark and gloomy atmosphere of opposition. (*Hear,*

7. Art.XII, "Of Peace," *ibid.*, p.231.
8. *Ibid.*, p.234.

hear.)"[9] The United States had declared war on Britain just five days before the Orders in Council had been withdrawn, and Brougham felt that he was best qualified to see to the restoration of peace. Liverpool's Government was prepared to do almost anything, even adopt Brougham's most advertised policy under humiliating circumstances, but it was not prepared to give him a post. It was one thing to be his legislative agent; it was quite another to be his Cabinet colleague or Crown employer. "The proposal came to nothing, the negotiations were not begun."[10]

Instead, Brougham was given the task of defending suspected Luddites under most challenging circumstances. During the spring of 1812, as industrial unrest, particularly the smashing of lace-frames, spread through Nottinghamshire, Lancashire and Cheshire, the Crown appointed special commissions to put down the violence while it passed measures to increase the penalties for the crimes complained of. The need for new legislation was shown at the trials Justice Bayley presided over at Nottingham during March. While Bayley did not hold out any hope of Parliament giving the rioters redress, he did admit this: "Frame-breaking is not a breach of the Ten Commandments, though it breaks down the barriers of peace and felicity, and as such, must be punished with the utmost rigour of the law."[11] Actually, Bayley was sufficiently lenient in punishment that Parliament felt impelled to increase the penalties for machine breaking, and giving oaths. At the same time, prosecutions and executions of rioters were going ahead in other cities, culminating in the special commission, under Baron Thomson and Justice Le Blanc, at York. The commission at Manchester was allegedly one of Perceval's last acts. "Whoever was responsible for the selection," the Hammonds have written, "made sure that the rioters in Lancashire should not meet with the leniency for which Mr Justice Bayley had been blamed elsewhere."[12] The only bright

---

9. *The Times*, June 20, 1812, no.8,632, p.2.
10. G.T. Garratt, *Lord Brougham* (Macmillan, London, 1935), p.53.
11. *The Times*, March 23, 1812, no.8,553, p.3.
12. J.L. and Barbara Hammond, *The Skilled Labourer, 1760-1832* (Longmans, London, 1919), pp.292-3.

spot in the prosecutions, characterized by suspected spies, working with unprincipled prosecutors, and cooperative Judges, with chilling results, was when Brougham helped save those charged with burning Burton's mill at Middleton from the gallows. Brougham persuaded juror Ewart, a merchant from Liverpool, that there was no evidence against the suspects.[13]

This failure pushed the man responsible, Manchester's Deputy Constable, Joseph Nadin, to new heights of vigorous law enforcement. Nadin had been consolidating Manchester's police for a decade - to the point where, if there was no crime to detect, he would make up for the absence. The breakthrough had come in 1805 when Nadin ended slackness among the night watchmen.[14] He had them spend their spare time trying to infiltrate suspected criminal groups so as to incite them to criminal action which would then be efficiently put down. Nadin's way in Manchester was based upon the many functions he had amassed, including control over the firemen and their engines. Food riots and the Luddites, especially when they decided to go underground, gave Nadin many opportunities for fixing crime, and settling scores. He met Brougham's setback by going after his followers in Manchester. When the followers of John Buckley, the second Winchester Secret Committee, started meeting to petition the Prince Regent and the Commons for redress, they were so infiltrated by Nadin's agents that they changed their place of meeting to avoid trouble. Nonetheless, at the second place, they were arrested, and charged "... for felony of administering or being present at the administration of the illegal oath to Samuel Fleming."[15]

"Now Samuel Fleming was an unemployed weaver, who acted under Nadin's charge, as one of the 'respectable sources' of the magistrates' information",[16] just the kind of individual who Brougham had complained about when he spoke against the

---

13. *Ibid.*, p.294 ff.
14. Arthur Redford, *The History of Local Government in Manchester* (Longmans, London, 1939, 2 vols.) vol.I, p.84 ff.
15. Hammonds, *op. cit.*, p.298.
16. *Ibid.*

Peace Preservation Bill. He complained about these "spies" in most self-justifying terms: "This was insulting a spy. These gentry had of late been raised to such extra-ordinary consequence, that to insult one of them was scarcely one degree removed from the crime of insulting a Magistrate."[17] With this farewell address to the Commons, it was hardly surprising that Major Cartwright, the famous Radical who had been so hounded for his support of the French Revolution, should have sought Brougham's services in defending "Manchester's 38". Brougham was assisted by James Scarlett, the future Lord Abinger, a most successful Whig barrister, and John Williams, another barrister who was to work with Brougham in several important cases in the future. Scarlett had a way of working his will with Judges, Brougham with juries, and Williams with witnesses.[18] The case was heard by a special commission, headed by Baron George Wood, a careful, demanding Judge, in August at Manchester.

The defence so demolished the Crown's case that if its results had been more widely communicated, the post-war counter-revolution, directed by Nadin from Manchester, and culminating in the Peterloo massacre, might never have happened. The press, especially *The Times*, was too persuaded, in light of Perceval's assassination, that a revolution was commencing to heed the advice of those who knew better, particularly when it came from the arrogant, radical Brougham. The authorities knew what they were up against, culling through the prisoner's letters in the desperate hope of finding incriminating evidence. The Whig barristers exposed everything, especially Fleming's serious blunders. He was shown to be Nadin's spy who was so interested in convicting the accused that his testimony was unbelievable. For example, to get John Knight, the leader of the Manchester reformers, Nadin had tried to have him situated in a prominent place in order for Fleming to be able to point him out. Unfortunately, Knight refused, and a turnkey

---

17. *The Times*, July 14, 1812, no.8,652, p.2.
18. Sir William Holdsworth, *A History of English Law* (Methuen, London, 1952, 14 vols.), vol.XIII, p.290.

of the prisoners was, consequently, in the spot. When Fleming pointed out the turnkey as one of those who had taken the oath, the court was amused, a rarity during these days of alarm caused by the disturbances and the secret reports that both Houses of Parliament had just issued. "The turnkey, it must be mentioned in Fleming's excuse, was sitting in the place into which Nadin had pertinaciously tried to force John Knight."[19]

Fleming also testified that William Washington, another ring leader, had given the oath. Actually, Washington could prove that he was elsewhere when the alleged event took place. Nadin himself, who had been called to the scene by Fleming right after the "crime", did not cover himself with glory either. It was shown that individuals, who should have been charged if Fleming was telling the truth, were allowed to escape, and to testify for the defence. The evidence could have also been better prepared by having the Bible present at the scene, the defence pointed out, rather than the documents for the Prince Regent and the House. Once Baron Wood indicated quite clearly that he believed the accused, the jury had no trouble in acquitting them, "... and the 'thirty eight bundles of Blue,' as Mr Lloyd of Stockport facetiously called them, were, to the deep and unconcealed regret of the Manchester authorities, allowed to return home instead of being transported across the seas."[20]

Brougham's achievement against the established system could not fail to impress his critics. William Roscoe, author of the radical critique of Brougham's ideas on parliamentary reform, apparently took the lead with reformers in Liverpool, especially his father, who had led the toasting of Brougham at the dinner, seeking to have him contest one of its seats. In September 1812, the Liverpool Ministry dissolved Parliament in order to take advantage of developments in Russia, Spain and America. Merchants throughout the country had been showering Brougham with gifts of thanks for his having ended the Orders in Council. "Of far more value than plate, cups, or blankets was

---

19. Hammonds, *op. cit.*, p.299.
20. *Ibid.*, p.300.

an invitation from a group of merchants in Liverpool to stand as their candidate in the approaching general election."[21] While accepting the offer would present some problems, particularly the impression of rushing into a popular constituency as a third man, Brougham had no other offers, and the contest presented a means of converting all the presents he was receiving into something which he could use. Despite the fact that the invitation came from a most unexpected quarter, as Liverpool had been the centre of the slave trade, Thomas Roscoe, merchant and banker, promised to provide the election committee with adequate resources and leadership for a successful result. Liverpool's sitting Members, Generals Tarleton and Gascoyne, were so weak that the committee decided to offer the voters a clean sweep by having Brougham run with Thomas Creevey, his friend, the local boy who had made it as a radical. Moreover, Brougham thought he had a valuable resource in the metropolis, *The Times*, to mobilize absentee voters if they were needed. Brougham, like all effective leaders, was not troubled by niceties of consistency when it came to winning. Anyway, the *Review*, in publishing a most favourable account of Brougham's campaign against the Orders in Council, gave his candidacy a good send-off: "To Mr Brougham, then, we think that the Commerce and Peace of England are indebted for their salvation in the day of their greatest peril ..."[22]

Brougham overestimated his chances at Liverpool. As usual, when he was in a tight place, he underestimated his opponents, and overlooked changed sentiments in crucial quarters. *The Times* was no longer supporting him. The way he had gone about ending the Orders in Council, especially his treatment of the assassinated Perceval, and his reaction to urban rioting had been too much for it, especially proprietor John Walter. Brougham imagined that it was willing to follow his campaign in Liverpool, as it had his ones against the slave trade, droits, paper currency,

---

21. Chester W. New, *The Life of Henry Brougham to 1830* (Clarendon Press, Oxford, 1961) p.69. N.B. how New sees, I believe erroneously, selection following as a matter of course from gratitude over repeal of the Orders in Council.
22. Art.XIII, "Orders in Council", *Edinburgh Review*, vol.20, no.XXXIX, July 1812, p.248.

and church-based education. He should have noticed that while the paper was giving big coverage to the special commissions in Nottingham, Cheshire, and Lancashire, it totally avoided any activities which reflected well on him. *The Times* was more interested in Brougham's excesses in seeking withdrawal of the Orders in Council, particularly his treatment of Robert M'Kerrell, another Liverpool merchant. It published correspondence between M'Kerrell and Brougham over how his testimony in their favour had been misused by him. When M'Kerrell failed to gain satisfaction from Brougham, he charged in its columns that "... it becomes a duty I owe to myself, to declare to the world, before whom I have been accused, that the whole of those calumnious assertions which have been the subject of my correspondence with Mr Brougham, are false and malevolent."[23] As long as Brougham was unwilling to explain his apparent leaking of distorted testimony for his own advantage, *The Times* was more interested in exposing his deficiencies than exploiting his potential. In fact, when the newspaper could have been reporting Brougham's triumph over Nadin's machinations at Manchester, it was giving a verbatim account of M'Kerrell's examination before the Committee of the Whole in order to embarrass the Whig barrister.[24]

While Brougham's arrival at Liverpool, and the activities of his election committee escaped *The Times*'s notice, he did what he could to make up for it. To catch the eye of absentee voters in London, he had an advertisement for the *Review* placed in the newspaper, emphasizing his contributions to the last issue. Brougham was portrayed as the friend of peace and commerce who was so committed to them that he was willing to restructure government in order to meet these interests.[25] To mobilize voters in the metropolis to Brougham's third candidacy at Liverpool, this advertisement appeared two days later:

---

23. "To the Editor of the Times," *The Times*, July 20, 1812, no.8,657, p.3.
24. *Ibid.*, August 31, 1812, no.8,693, p.3.
25. *Ibid.*, October 1, 1812, no.8,720, p.2.

> Liverpool election, - Mr Creevey respectfully informs those Liverpool independent freemen resident in London, Deptford, Chatham, Margate and Ramsgate, who are inclined to assist in preserving the honour of their native town, and the liberty, peace, and happiness of their country, by polling for Henry Brougham, Esq and Thomas Creevey, Esq, that he is commissioned to call them together previous to their conveyance to Liverpool, and that he will be happy in their attendance at the Globe Tavern, in Fleet-Street, London, on Monday next, the 5th instant, at 12 o'clock, to give in their names, that the Committee may be enabled to make arrangements for their comfortable journey.[26]

Brougham naively thought that such actions could make up for the paper's hostility to his candidacy.

Brougham also underestimated the Tories in Lancashire. Believing that opposition to him was based upon planters such as John Gladstone who selfishly supported the Orders in Council, he overlooked the hostility of local authorities, especially those involved in law enforcement. As Mr Lloyd indicated, Nadin and his followers had not forgotten about the city's "38", but had just redoubled their efforts to get the reformers. Gladstone indicated as much when he explained that the formation of a committee to oppose Brougham was not based upon his conduct as a barrister in the House: "It is because of his public conduct, and therefore, on public grounds only, that I have opposed him. It is on account of his political principles that I have held him a most unfit person to represent this great trading town."[27] When one realizes that this statement was made to an audience which included a deputation from Manchester, including the Borough-reeve, and that this city looked to Liverpool to represent its interests in Parliament, as long as it did not have its own seats, Gladstone's statement takes on new significance. Gladstone

---

26. *Ibid.*, October 3, 1812, no.8,722, p.2.
27. "Celebration of the Election of the Right Hon. George Canning," *ibid.*, October 31, 1812, no.8,746, p.2.

said this about Brougham's behaviour during the alarm over the Luddites: "In Parliament he has trampled upon those whom it was his duty to protect, and treated the well-grounded remonstrances of others with silent contempt."[28]

Here Gladstone meant people like M'Kerrell, and Huddersfield manufacturers, such as Mr Horsfall who had been murdered by Luddites the previous spring. In sum, the Lancashire establishment, threatened by the forces Brougham represented, organized to defend itself. No sooner did it hear of Brougham's nomination by the reformers than it asked George Canning to be its Member.

The Times, which had been ignoring developments in Liverpool, threw all its resources behind the former Foreign Secretary. It reported his Brougham-like acceptance of the invitation thus: "I have not words to express my sense of honour thus tendered to me. It is one which, unconnected as I am with the town of Liverpool, I certainly would never have presumed to think of soliciting ..."[29] The opening of Canning's campaign was, perhaps, bigger than Brougham's, although he had not been able to attend the festivities in front of Roscoe's bank because his carriage had broken down in Birmingham on his way from Devon.[30] The bank was Thomas Roscoe's, the chairman of Brougham's committee who also badly underestimated the Tory opposition.

Canning led the balloting from the beginning. It was a question of who would come in second, Brougham, Gascoyne, or Creevey. Tarleton, who had held the seat for 22 years, ran as an independent Tory. "He had once voted for the Catholic Question," he told the first meeting of the hustings, "and he did it because the times were altered. If he had lived in the times when those restrictions were imposed, he would have supported them."[31] While he did oppose the war, Tarleton explained, he had privately told his reasons to the murdered Perceval, a fact

---

28. *Ibid.*
29. *Ibid.*, October 4, 1812, no.8,723, p.2.
30. *Ibid.*, October 10, 1812, no.8,728, p.3.
31. *Ibid.*, October 12, 1812, no.8,729, p.3.

that Canning could corroborate. Gascoigne presented himself to the voters in a more bellicose vein, in his regimentals. His family, counting both sides, had represented Liverpool for 160 years, and this was no time for a change. He ran for re-election on the wartime platform of 1796. Brougham "... said, he for one thought it was time there was a change, and that a strict scrutiny was demanded."[32] Since all the candidates had high private characters, he added, the election should be a clean one where they were judged on their public merits. Creevey echoed these sentiments with an appeal to native feelings. He had been born in Liverpool, and wanted to represent it. He claimed that he had been doing just that since he had been in the House, but he was also seeking re-election in the pocket borough he held just to be safe. Canning ran on his record in office, and as a supporter of Liverpool's Ministry.

While the candidates discussed the issues, their organizations became so important in getting the vote out that Canning and Gascoyne joined forces to meet the reformers' challenge. Tarleton was irrelevant to the contest, attributing his lack of support to intrigues and whispers against him, and only continuing as a candidate to show how opinion had become polarized.[33] As the 3,000 eligible voters began casting their votes, prospects for the candidates became more tense, as *The Times* duly reported:

> Although no riots have taken place, it is painful to have to record the loss of two lives by accidents, which are to be ascribed to the bustle and tumult of the election. One person was killed by a stone; the other was engaged in a scuffle and being knocked down, a cart went over his head, and he never spoke more.[34]

The next day a journeyman tanner, working for Messrs Beckwith and Lafon, "... who, together with about 50 others, have paraded

32. *Ibid.*
33. *Ibid.*, October 15, 1812, no.8,732, p.3.
34. *Ibid.*, October 16, 1812, no.8,733, p.3.

the street together daily, in large new leather aprons, as emblematic of their trade, in Mr Canning's processions,"[35] was killed in a riot. Canning's committee increased the pressure on the Whig organization by printing, and circulating his speeches, an innovation which *The Times* appreciated:

> This is certainly an improvement on the old system of electioneering, and cannot fail to produce the most favourable effects; for when these speeches are read in families and social parties the ladies who are very zealous for Mr Canning, and to whom he never omits to pay court, always exert their influence with an increased energy and effect in his favour.[36]

Brougham had to settle for the old way, addressing any group he could find. During the eight days of polling, he gave 160 speeches.

Despite Brougham's almost superhuman effort, the Tories were starting to pull away. With well over 2,000 votes counted, the poll stood: Canning 1,361; Gascoyne 1,276; Brougham 1,105; and Creevey 1,055. There was talk that the Whigs would withdraw from the race. To continue the poll could be seen as merely vexatious, litigious and expensive. After all, Canning was maintaining that time was on the Tories' side: "... the time cannot be distant when the forces of my opponents will be exhausted."[37] Canning made this prediction particularly galling for Brougham by contending that the picture that he had painted of Liverpool during the hearings on the Orders in Council was partisan cant:

> I have found, Gentlemen, generally prevailing among you, not as by misrepresentation I have been taught to believe, a querulous impatience under the privations common to us all, and unhappily incident to a state of war such as that in which

35. *Ibid.*, October 17, 1812, no.8,734, p.3.
36. *Ibid.*, October 16, 1812, no.8,733, p.3.
37. *Ibid.*

> it is our misfortune to be engaged - not a disposition to separate the local and peculiar interests of Liverpool from those of the country at large, and to purchase a respite to yourselves at the expense of national interest and honour: No, Gentlemen, I have found here a lofty and determined spirit, patient under difficulties known to be unavoidable; and never looking to partial relief or benefit but connected with the general good.[38]

Brougham met the challenge head-on. By continuing the contest, "he pledged himself as a man of honour, that he was not actuated by such pitiful motives."[39] He then delivered a most damning speech against Pitt and his followers at Clayton Square. Peace, Brougham claimed, would win him the election. If the war with America continued another six months, its effects could be devastating. Brougham indicated that this, however, would probably happen since the government had issued Letters of Marque and Reprisals to privateers. "His opponents at this Election were the men who had supported the Ministers," Brougham explained, "whose measures brought us, into disrepute with the American Government, and they knew not how to get us out of it."[40] Canning and Gascoyne had supported Pitt too, a leader whom they considered immortal. "All that he considered him immortal for was, ruinous wars, bad policy, vicious measures, tyranny, and his apostasy from the cause of reform."[41] Brougham, feeling that he had nothing to lose, concluded: "Against us and against you stand those who call themselves the successors of that man."[42] Brougham said about himself that he had done nothing for the age "... to fear him or for posterity to curse him ..."[43]

Brougham's desperate gamble to win the election, despite the

---

38. *Ibid.*
39. *Ibid.*, October 19, 1812, no.8,735, p.3.
40. *Ibid.*
41. *Ibid.*
42. *Speeches of Henry Lord Brougham* (Black, Edinburgh, 1838, 4 vols.), vol.I, p.486.
43. *Ibid.*, p.487.

probable bribed voters that the Tories were holding in reserve, failed. He himself admitted as much when he said in his collected speeches that the address had been given on October 8,[44] the first day of polling. If Brougham had delivered this speech then, he, rather than Tarleton, would have been the fifth wheel to the election coach. *The Times* reported the speech on the 19th, clearly stating that it had been given on the 15th. When the speech was given, he had 1,132 votes. The final poll credited him with only 1,131.[45] The gamble had cost him a vote. Brougham, as usual, when faced with unexpected adversity, blamed it upon others: "... he was only a trustee to some very kind, affectionate and personal friends."[46] In explaining Creevey's announcement of their withdrawal from the contest, Brougham feebly said that his side could only supply another 100 votes: "... his friends having to fetch friends from a distance, he conceived that if he attempted any further continuation of the contest, it would be vexatious, and only harassing his opponents."[47] Brougham's rash speech had not lost the election; it had only ended it abruptly.

The Tory celebration of the victory indicated how deeply they had been mobilized by the reformers' anticipation of capturing the seat. When the sheriff announced that Canning and Gascoyne had been returned, the victory procession struck up "The Pilot that weathered the Storm". *The Times* explained: "This expression, which is so well known as the title and chorus of the celebrated song, written by Mr Canning for the anniversary of the birth-day of Mr Pitt, was exhibited in brilliant colours."[48] As an indication of just how committed the newspaper had been to Canning's election, it printed the important speeches that he had given at the hustings. It also reported that the poll in Liverpool, 2,438 votes, was the highest in history. At the formal celebration of the victory at the end of the month, Gladstone showed how committed he was to Canning by proposing that he be made the

---

44. See "Speech at the Liverpool Election," October 8, 1812: *ibid.*, pp.481-7.
45. *The Times*, October 20, 1812, no.8,736, p.3.
46. *Ibid.*
47. *Ibid.*
48. *Ibid.*

town's representative for life. Gladstone repeated his comprehensive opposition to Brougham's candidacy. Canning struck the same theme:

> These men talk of peace to a state of the world in which all those ties which compose the elements of society were weakened and almost run asunder by the desolating principles of our enemy. They talk of peace, as absurdly as if an inhabitant of a West Indian Island, amidst earthquakes and volcanoes, should talk of physical order and perpendicular position.[49]

"A deputation from Manchester, consisting of the Borough-reeve and other Gentlemen, were then introduced to the company."[50] A week later, there was a similar celebration in Manchester at which Canning committed himself to be its representative too.[51]

Brougham, characteristically, rushed back to Scotland to try to get elected from the Inverkeithing group of boroughs in Fife. In 1808, he had bought property there for just such a contingency, as he had explained to James Loch: "I become a fifeshire voter merely in the hope that it may be of some advantage to me on some future day."[52] The constituency lay just across the Firth of Forth from Edinburgh, and he was thinking of using it to strike some blow against Melville's sway in Scotland. The idea, of course, was even more improbable than reformers capturing Liverpool despite the hostility of the Twin Cities' corporations. The hopeless effort in Fife was more a testimony of his past commitments, and their repudiation than anything about the future. To the Tories' great delight, Brougham had just been carried away by the General Election.

---

49. "Celebration of the Election of the Right Hon. George Canning," *ibid.*, October 31, 1812, no.8,746, p.2.
50. *Ibid.*
51. *Ibid.*, November 6, 1812, no.8,751, p.3.
52. Brougham's letter to Loch, dated March 4, 1806, in R.H.M. Atkinson and G.A. Jackson, eds, *Brougham and His Early Friends* (printed, London, 1908, 3 vols.), vol.II, p.263.

Out of Parliament, Brougham devoted himself to his law practice, especially *ex officio* libel informations. The Hunts were in trouble again. The publishers of the *Examiner* were charged this time with libelling the Prince Regent. The *Morning Post* had printed a eulogy to him, and the Hunts responded that he was "... a violator of his word, a libertine over head and ears in debt and disgrace, a despiser of domestic ties, the companion of gamblers and demireps, a man who just closed half a century without one single claim on the gratitude of his country, or the respect of posterity."[53] With such an open-and-shut case available for ministerial interests, the Crown wanted to associate these sentiments with opposition politicians who defended the opponents of order, particularly the Luddites, and of the Prince Regent, especially the Princess of Wales. The case against the Hunts was to be heard in June 1812,[54] but was postponed for six months, apparently to exploit new revelations about rioters, and Princess Caroline.

While Brougham was awaiting this suit, he defended a divorce action in the Court of Exchequer Chamber. In Scotland, marriage was a contract which could be ended by the courts if adultery was proved, while in England this could only be done by an Act of Parliament. The action concerned the validity of a Scottish divorce in British law. Brougham's client was being sued for bigamy for remarrying, once his English marriage had been dissolved in Scotland. In arguing that a Scottish divorce, at worst, fell within the exceptions granted by the Marriage Act - ie, that an English marriage was not an indissoluble contract - Brougham explained:

> It was, indeed, absurd to suppose that the act of marriage could mean one thing in Scotland, and another in England, - could be dissolved in the former country, and indissoluble in the latter; that the mere circumstance of crossing a river could give a man all the rights of marriage, or all the

53. *R.* v. *John and Leigh Hunt, The Times,* December 10, 1812, no.8,780, p.1.
54. *Ibid.,* June 29, 1812, no.8,639, p.3.

> privileges of celibacy, - could, by a reflex operation, change what he had done in one country into something different in another.[55]

Lord Ellenborough, for the Court, postponed a decision until the end of term on this point, as well as those concerning whether or not a Scottish divorce could dissolve an English marriage, and collusion by the parties in obtaining such a divorce should not be considered by the Judges in reserved cases.

Ellenborough showed no such consideration for Brougham's clients when he tried to prevent the Solicitor General from getting a rule absolute in another case, *R.* v. *Bell and Harvey*. Brougham represented the defendants who were charged, in a criminal information, with challenging and posting Edward Parsons, a London merchant. During a business dispute in a coffee-house, Parsons became so incensed with Bell that he would have nothing more to do with him because he was no gentleman. The defence tried to quash the decision on a counter claim:

> The prosecutor's affidavit, said Mr Brougham, admitted that he complained of the defendant's conduct, and that he meant to administer to him a moderate rebuke for his unmercantile conduct; and neither his affidavit, nor that of his friend, negatived the conversation which was now sworn to have passed.[56]

The Solicitor General protested, and Lord Ellenborough agreed: "Really it is high time to put a stop to this spurious chivalry of the compting-house and the counter."[57] An aggrieved party, he explained, did not have to have an unblemished record to seek redress. The defendant not only had demanded an apology but also a duel. When Parsons declined the challenge, Bell posted a note in the coffee-house, calling him a coward. The original

---

55. *R.* v. *Lolley, ibid.*, November 17, 1812, no.8,759, p.2.
56. *R.* v. *Bell and Harvey, ibid.*, November 27, 1812, no.8,769, p.3.
57. *Ibid.*

conviction was allowed to stand.

Brougham fared little better in another divorce suit. He defended an officer in the Army against a charge of criminal conversation with the wife of a clerk at the Lisbon Packet-Office. His wife, long separated from him, committed adultery while living in Hoxton. Brougham was not satisfied with a token fine against his client because court costs would bankrupt him:

> ... he therefore addressed the jury, and besought them not to throw the defendant into gaol for the rest of his life, for being seduced by the arts of this most profligate woman to commit what was no injury to the plaintiff, for all the comfort which such a wife could afford he had lost long ago.[58]

Brougham even impeached the testimony of eyewitnesses as to the adultery. The Lord Chief Justice completely contradicted what Brougham said, in his address to the jury. The suit, Ellenborough explained, was to get the means for a parliamentary divorce. The jury agreed. At the same time, the Court of Exchequer Chamber decided the earlier divorce action, *R.* v. *Lolley*, "... the 12 Judges decided, that a divorce obtained in Scotland, could not be pleaded in the bar of an action for bigamy in England, where the marriage took place in the latter country."[59]

While the facts and law in these cases had presented Brougham with great difficulties in arguing them, he had not helped his case by what he had written in the *Review* about English administration. He reviewed two anonymous pamphlets on political reform which had the hallmarks of his propaganda efforts at Ryder and St Albans Streets. People were not to decide specific issues under political constitutions, but they should be consulted, he wrote. The House last Session, Brougham complained, discussed problems of urban centres not represented in Parliament, indicating just how removed Members had become from the people. Contrary to Pitt's management of the

58. *Chamberlaine* v. *Broomhead, ibid.*, December 9, 1812, no.8,779, p.3.
59. *Ibid.*, April 14, 1813, no.8,885, p.3.

constitution, the people should be allowed to meet frequently to discuss matters of concern. "To prevent or discourage popular meetings," Brougham explained, "might well answer the purpose of bad governors - if the taxing machine were not going on all the while, grinding the nation down."[60] About Members of Parliament who adhered to Burke's view of their function, he wrote:

> ... we dislike the sickly, foreign squeamishness, as much as we despise the slavish fears, which estrange popular men from an honest intercourse with the people, and prevent true patriots from leading on the strength of the country against its oppressors.[61]

Brougham reminded his readers that the last time he saw Fox, he was addressing a meeting in Palace Yard, Westminster, against Lord Melville's misadventure. Such speeches indirectly affected government policy. While the country still looked to Westminster for example and comfort, he concluded, "... the late elections have shown that the spirit of freedom is not confined to the Metropolis."[62]

The total effect of Brougham's activities was registered when the King's Bench finally heard the Crown's complaint against the Hunts. Unlike the first prosecution of the publishers of the *Examiner*, the Solicitor General, Sir William Garrow, had the offending article read to the jury for it to make its own effect. Brougham was charged with trying to prejudice the libel case by remarks he had made elsewhere, a reference to the article on "Rights and Duties of the People". Brougham responded that to prove libel, the author's motives had to be established, explaining:

> He is a retired, studious man, not far advanced in life, being

---

60. Art.VIII, "Rights and Duties of the People," *Edinburgh Review*, vol.20, no.XL, November 1812, p.415.
61. *Ibid.*, p.421.
62. *Ibid.*, p.425.

> now considerably under 30 years of age, with the habits of one who assorts with books rather than with men, and who delights to pursue his studies in that retirement which he has sought out.[63]

Brougham made the defence an even more personal matter by trying to read proof that the Prince Regent had come under the interest of foul flatterers, and by mentioning that the Hunts had been the object of another *ex officio* information. When Ellenborough prevented him from trying to justify the libel, he explained: "His object is not so much to attack the Court, as to expose the absurdity of the rhymes; their publication was his sole motive for writing."[64] Soon Brougham was justifying a most free reporting: "There is nothing to fear from open discussion, - from the press which enables us to speak as we think."[65] As in the Drakard case, Garrow said that the *Examiner* article spoke for itself, and the Lord Chief Justice agreed, saying that "if this were to be pronounced No Libel, there was an end of law ..."[66] The jury found the Hunts guilty as charged.

Surprisingly, Brougham also suffered a defeat on the parliamentary front. While there were all kinds of issues that the remaining radical Members of the House could have taken up in his absence, as a testament to his legacy, they chose the least important, most controversial matter. The unnecessary war with America was continuing, and the Portuguese could have been made to do something to help end the slave trade. Parliament could have intervened to improve the condition of slaves in the colonies, and of workers in the urban centres. The Commons had not really investigated conditions in Lincoln Gaol, where libeller James Finnerty had been incarcerated, nor the causes of delay in the Chancery and House of Lords. Instead, Whitbread and Creevey led an attack upon the Gold Coin Bill. In December, the Chancellor of the Exchequer introduced a bill to renew the

---

63. R. v. *John and Leigh Hunt*, *The Times*, December 20, 1812, no.8,780, p.2.
64. *Ibid.*
65. *Ibid.*
66. *Ibid.*, p.3.

previous act, making Bank notes interchangeable with guineas.[67] The radical opposition smacked completely of Brougham's campaign. In fact, when the Gold Coin Bill was scheduled to be read a third time, Whitbread moved Brougham's resolutions of the previous Session.[68] They were so unpopular and inopportune that they were easily defeated. Only one, charging that the statute would make real money disappear, even necessitated a division of the House. It almost seemed as though the opposition were trying to make it appear that Brougham's activities were irrelevant to its proceedings.

He was not dismayed by these developments, even though his career as a radical barrister was entering a most critical stage. Brougham's exposure of cotton spinner Bent, Nadin's informer within the so-called Secret Committee of Manchester, and Samuel Fleming, the Deputy Constable's *agent provocateur*, had upset the Crown's timetable in Yorkshire where General Maitland was doing the same thing with the police that Colonel Fletcher had been doing in Lancashire. In the summer of 1812, Taylor, Whitehead, McDonald, and Gosling had been sent to Huddersfield to get to the bottom of the violence, especially Mr Horsfall's murder. "These four men were acting under the orders of Mr Hay, and the magistrates of Manchester and of the Deputy-Constable, Nadin."[69] About the activities of McDonald and Gosling, *The Times* reported:

> ... two Bow-Street Officers have been in the neighbourhood of Huddersfield for nearly three weeks past, and that they had been *twisted in*, or in other words, had taken the oath of the Luddites. By this means they have learned the proceedings and ways of these infatuated persons, and have obtained the knowledge of the depot where their arms were concealed.[70]

---

67. *Cobbett's Parliamentary Debates*, vol.24, col.224.
68. *Gentleman's Magazine*, vol.82, 1812, Part II, p.643.
69. Frank Ongley Darvell, "The Luddite Disturbances and the Machinery of Order" (Ph.D. Thesis, University of London, 1932), p.571.
70. *The Times*, July 7, 1812, no.8,646, p.3. Italics its.

The information collected had led to the arrest of 50 ringleaders. "The actual murderer of Mr. Horsfall was discovered in a house about eight miles from Huddersfield ..."[71] The Secret Committees of Parliament were believed to have urged the extraordinary measures of the past Session upon the basis of this intelligence.

The Crown, for obvious reasons, immediately tried to scotch this most optimistic report. Out of the needs of criminal justice, it denied that it had solved Horsfall's murder: "The man is in custody at Huddersfield, on suspicion of being a deeply informed *Luddite*."[72] Once Brougham attacked the evidence upon which the emergency legislation was based, the Crown worked much more cautiously and carefully to gain convictions. In order to get indictments of the suspects in Horsfall's murder, the Crown offered a pardon to one of them in return for crucial evidence.[73] Even so, in light of what had happened at Manchester, the Crown was not happy with its solution to the crime: "Pretending to be interested in the Luddites and expressing a rash sympathy for their conspiracy, it was not difficult for McDonald to find someone who would talk as rashly as himself."[74] Crown lawyers were afraid that the story would break down under cross-examination.[75] To keep up the pressure for the prosecution, someone did the following to Joseph Mellor, a cloth dresser from Dungeon: "... a pistol was fired at him, the contents of which passed him, and lodged in the wall. Mr Mellor is one of the persons subpoenaed to appear at York, in the case of the late Mr. Horsfall's murder."[76]

The long-anticipated special commission at York was finally held in December 1812 under Baron Thomson and Justice Le Blanc, judges hardly prepared to see a repeat of the Manchester fiasco. Since these Judges were known for their moderating,

---

71. *Ibid.*
72. *Ibid.*, July 9, 1812, no.8,648, p.3. Italics its.
73. "The Murderers of Mr Horsfall," *ibid.*, October 30, 1812, no.8,745, p.3.
74. Darvall, *op. cit.*, p.574.
75. Henry Hobhouse's letter to Home Office, dated January 9, 1813, in Home Office file 42/132, Public Record Office, Chancery Lane, London.
76. *The Times*, January 5, 1813, no.8,802, p.3.

humane influences in their own courts, the Crown's case for extraordinary measures to meet industrial unrest was as much on trial as the prisoners in the dock. The court calendar concerned 59 defendants, ten of whom were indicted for administering illegal oaths, and the rest of whom were charged with Horsfall's murder, "... the attack on Mr Cartwright's mill at Rawfolds, stealing arms, and various burglaries, robberies, and riots."[77] Instead of relying upon the local prosecutor, as the Crown had done in Manchester, it called upon London's best barristers to make its case: James Parke, J. Topping, Holroyd, and John Richardson. It was only Topping's drinking, and early death, which prevented all these men from becoming High Court Judges.

The Crown led off with the cut-and-dried cases, the felony burglary at Samuel Moxon's house, and the murder of Mr Horsfall. The trial of Moxon's assailants hardly presented the special commission with any problems, as *The Times* reported: "They were all found guilty, and a more determined set of depredators never perhaps were before a British jury."[78] While the suspects in Horsfall's murder were first offenders, the Crown's case had been improved by one of them, Benjamin Walker, who turned state's evidence. He described how his fellow-workers at Wood's mill had plotted the murder in most incriminating terms: "... in a conversation about the attack on Mr Cartwright's mill, *Mellor* said there was no way to break the shears - but shoot the master."[79] George Mellor was the ringleader who procured the weapons, and gave the orders to kill the mill owner. "Witness and several others who were examined upon the trial proved, that the murder was well known amongst those *twisted in*, and an oath was taken not to reveal it."[80] The jury made short work of such a violent conspiracy, requiring only 25 minutes of deliberation to find the accused guilty as charged. The three culprits were sentenced to be hanged

---

77. *Ibid.*
78. "Special Commission," *ibid.*, January 8, 1813, no.8,805, p.3.
79. "Murderers of Mr Horsfall," *ibid.*, January 9, 1813, no.8,805, p.3. Italics its.
80. *Ibid.* Italics its.

48 hours later.

While these prisoners were waiting to go to the gallows, Brougham was given the responsibility of defending John Schofield, "... indicted for feloniously shooting at, or causing, aiding, and abetting some person to shoot at, with intent to murder John Hinchliffe."[81] He came from the same village as Schofield, Nether Thong in the West Riding, and "... had been in the habit of teaching the person to sing, and thereby became well acquainted with prisoner's voice."[82] Hinchliffe was positive that Schofield was one of the armed, masked men who had raided his house the previous July. Hinchliffe said that he had been lucky to escape with his life. He recalled an earlier meeting with Schofield where he had asked him if he were a Luddite. When Hinchliffe said that he was not, Schofield asked him if he would like to become one. Hinchliffe continued:

> Prisoner said they wanted a body of men for the liberty of Holmfirth and other places, that they might rise at once and overturn the government. Prisoner said he had been on that business in the morning, and was then going to a meeting; men were to be there from Manchester, and Delegates were to go to the House of Commons, and see what could be done; that a regiment of foot was *twisted in*, all but an old serjeant.[83]

The prosecution was apparently so taken by the implications of Hinchliffe's testimony that it permitted Schofield's alleged accomplice, the person who actually fired at the mill owner, to turn state's evidence in order to corroborate the story.

Brougham, in his cross-examination, tore the prosecution's case apart. He got the culprit, who had been given a pardon, to testify that Hinchliffe was a liar who falsely had taken out a warrant against Schofield. Hinchliffe was hardly a better witness than

---

81. "Special Commission," *ibid.*, January 11, 1813, no.8,806, p.3.
82. *Ibid.*
83. *Ibid.* Italics its.

Fleming when he contradicted himself several times about the persons who had attacked him. Brougham established that while Schofield had inquired in May about Hinchliffe's joining the Luddites, he could not have done what he was charged with. "An *alibi* was set up on behalf of the prisoner."[84] Actually, Schofield, once he had heard about the murder, fled to London because he was afraid that he would be implicated in it. Schofield was acquitted by the jury after a short deliberation. The Whig barrister had confounded the Crown's plans again. The *Leeds Mercury* was pleased with this result since it showed that there was no conspiracy to overthrow the government.

This time, however, the prosecution had an opportunity to beat a prudent retreat, and it did so. While the press and the populace were grabbing for details of the execution of Horsfall's murderers,[85] the Crown decided to minimize its losses. When the Grand Jury asked if it were going to consider any more true bills, Parke explained:

> My learned Friends and myself have examined the different causes which have not been presented to you; and, considering that many of these people have acted under the influence of other persons, we have, in the exercise of the discretion confided to us by the Crown, declined, at present, to present any other bills before you; and I hope this lenity will produce its proper effects, and that the persons on whom it is exercised, will prove themselves, by their future good conduct, deserving of it.[86]

Thanks to Brougham, the Crown decided to drop its case against over 30 of the "ringleaders" of the Luddites.

Even so, the Crown did not have smooth sailing with all those remaining whom it had chosen to prosecute. Joseph Brooke was found not guilty of burglary after the following trial:

---

84. *Ibid.* Italics its.
85. See, eg, "Execution of the Murderers of Mr Horsfall, at York," *ibid.*, January 12, 1812, no.8,807, p.3.
86. *Ibid.*, January 13, 1813, no.8,808, p.3.

> On the part of the prisoner was set up an *alibi*, which, together with the prosecutor's niece only discovering the features of the man's face, which she believed to be prisoner's, by the flash of the light occasioned by the man striking the stone floor with his sword, was left with the Jury by the learned Judge.[87]

The defence managed to save Zachary Baines from the oath-giving conviction that McDonald and Gosling had worked out with his relatives and associates at Halifax. Even two of those charged with the attack on Cartwright's mill, James Brook and John Hirst, were acquitted despite William Hall's testimony that they had been part of the murderous assault. Hall apparently "... was one of those deluded men connected with *Mellor* and *Thorpe*, who have been executed."[88] The defence established that Brook and Hirst were elsewhere at the time.

After three more prisoners were convicted of assaulting and robbing James Brooke of Sheepridge, Huddersfield, the Crown declared:

> The trials now closed; after which two prisoners, *David Moorhouse* and *John Smith* were arraigned upon an indictment for burglary; but Mr Parke said, he trusted that as the ringleaders of the deluded men were already executed, and several others were under convictions of capital felonies, they would see the error of their ways, and that by the punishment inflicted, and about to be inflicted on those convicted, the peace and tranquillity of the country would be restored.[89]

Moorhouse and Smith were then acquitted, and the other prisoners were released, either on bail or absolutely. Those convicted of giving an oath to McDonald were transported for seven years. Those convicted of the attack on Maxon's house,

---

87. "Special Commission," *ibid.*, January 14, 1813, no.8,809, p.3. Italics its.
88. *Ibid.* Italics its.
89. *Ibid.*, January 15, 1813, no.8,810, p.3. Italics its.

Cartwright's mill, and Brooke's house were executed at York Castle.[90]

Brougham, as usual, tried to make the most of these results for his own advantage. He had been writing to Lord Grey, trying to find a new seat in the Commons. Brougham had continuously tried to show that his services were indispensable to the Whigs in Parliament, a fact which would result in his being returned for another pocket borough. Instead of Brougham giving the Whig leader a candid explanation of what happened, an account which would have sounded much like what he had accomplished at Horsemonger Lane with the English prisoners from the Isle de France, he gave this prosaic account:

> There have been several acquittals since I last wrote, and several convictions; but as the *facts* were clearly proved of outrages, etc, the results of the trials were only interesting to the individuals, and could prove nothing more than whether *they* had or not a share in acts clearly proved to have been committed by somebody; therefore I need not trouble you further as to the details than to observe that considerably more were acquitted than we had expected.[91]

Instead of talking about the 30-odd who had escaped the Crown's clutches, Brougham stressed the need of more effective use of his services:

> Meantime a pretty severe example has been made by the judges here, for, three days ago, three of the four murderers of Horsfall were hung in front of York Castle; and 14 of the rioters will be executed to-morrow or next day. This is wholesale work with a vengeance![92]

---

90. "Executions of the Luddites at York," *ibid.*, January 19, 1813, no.8,813, p.3.
91. Brougham's letter to Lord Grey, dated January 12, 1813: quoted from Henry Brougham, *The Life and Times of Henry Brougham* (Harper, New York, 1871, 3 vols.), vol.II, p.63. Italics Brougham's.
92. *Ibid.*

Actually, no more rioters had been executed, but proven criminals.

The Crown, thanks to the continuing alarms sounded by officials, especially Manchester's police, exaggerated the threat of revolution, for its own reasons. To offset the unexpected reverses, the Ministry had the Prince Regent issue a proclamation, urging those who had committed Luddite crimes, but who had not yet been charged to come forward. If they did so before March first, they were promised a free pardon upon confessing their crimes, and promising to mend their ways.[93] Officials continued to believe that the stealing of weapons, and the committing of violence by subjects was "... induced by the artifices of wicked and designing men."[94] *The Times* agreed: "We are anxious that the Proclamation contained in last night's Gazette, should be understood by the infatuated people to whom it is addressed."[95]

When there was not even a trickle of people to magistrates and justices of the peace to confess, the Crown issued another Proclamation on February 2nd, exhorting subjects and the police to prevent a recurrence of the previous year's violence. *The Times* explained such action: "... after the late legal proceedings, which have informed the sufferers and the inflictors of violence, that though the law may linger, - though 'sentence against an evil work may not be executed speedily,' yet that justice will at last overtake the guilty, and avenge the innocent."[96] When there was still no exodus from the suspected massive criminal ranks, the Crown issued another Proclamation, promising a pardon for an accomplice of the person who sent threatening letters to a Worcester magistrate. In September, a person had threatened Thomas Biggs that farms would be burned if bread was not made cheaper, and in January, the same magistrate had been told that he would be killed if an innocent man was found guilty.[97] The

---

93. *London Gazette*, 1813, no.16,695, p.157.
94. Reprinted in *The Times*, January 20, 1813, no.8,814, p.2.
95. *Ibid.*, p.3.
96. *Ibid.*, February 3, 1813, no.8,826, p.3.
97. *The London Gazette*, 1813, no.16,705, p.378.

Stourbridge Association offered one hundred guineas "... to any person making such discovery as aforesaid ..."[98] The law enforcement establishment was developing an obsession about the political overtones of the record-levels of crime.

This sentiment was well in evidence when the Hunts were finally sentenced for libelling the Prince Regent. To mitigate punishment, Brougham prepared an affidavit for them, stating that "... they were actuated by no personal malice whatever, nor any love or purpose of slander; and that they are conscious of no motives which were not honourable, in writing and publishing the same."[99] Brougham tried to use what was lacking in English theory of punishment, a proper control of the role of circumstances in judging crime, to save the publishers from severe punishment. The Hunts were not rich, he said, and a long imprisonment would greatly injure their families. The Solicitor General, Sir William Garrow, called for the maximum punishment for such a gross libel despite Brougham's explanation: "Every thing that could be said in defence, extenuation, or apology, was, at considerable length, and with great ability, addressed to the proper tribunal, the Jury, who had found the defendants guilty."[100] Justice Le Blanc, who had just returned to London from the special commission at York, agreed: "... it behoved a Court entrusted with the criminal administration of the country, to protect the government of that country from those who acted upon such motives and opinions."[101] He sentenced the Hunts to two years' imprisonment, and fines of five hundred pounds, the same punishment that rabblerouser Cobbett had received for his article against flogging.

Brougham railed against such treatment in the *Review*. In an article on the trials of slave traders in Sierra Leone, he discussed judicial process for the benefit of all Judges: "It is not proper that, at a solemn trial, it should appear that the very person who is sitting in judgment on the prisoner, had, in the early stage of the

---

98. *Ibid.*, no.16,706, p.407.
99. *The Times*, February 4, 1813, no.8,827, p.3.
100. *Ibid.*
101. *Ibid.*

course, mixed himself up with the prosecutor, so far as to assist him in preparing his case."[102] Brougham explicitly corrected the writer of the pamphlet under review by stating that he, rather than Fox, had been responsible for the prosecutions in question because it was he who had gained passage of the Slave-Trade Felony Act. 51 Geo.III c.23, he explained to increase his own authority, was known as Mr. Brougham's Act. He then discussed the prosecution of Samuel Samo, who was not a British subject, in the West African colony: "... we cannot help regretting extremely, that the first proceeding under the new act should have been so irregular, and indeed so entirely contrary to law."[103] Samo's Judge had been too zealous, and his counsel too apologetic, Brougham explained, and Judge Robert Thorpe had only compounded matters by promising the unfortunate Negro a promise of a pardon. To reduce the prospect of similar judicial travesties, Brougham called for diplomatic efforts to end the Portuguese and Spanish slave trades. The British Government's apparent unwillingness to deal with the extended problem was detailed in several ways. This same government, Brougham reminded his readers, had demanded from the Danes surrender of their fleet, and had burnt Copenhagen when it was refused.

Brougham expanded upon the problems of British judicial administration by discussing the proposed creation of a Vice-Chancellor to assist Lord Eldon. The delay, costs, and want of due process in the Chancery, what a Commons committee had investigated without result the previous Session, had induced the Ministry to propose creation of the position. Romilly, the Chancery lawyer with whom Brougham was increasingly involved in litigating actions, opposed the measure, calling instead for the Lords to sit more often to hear appeals. Brougham, after noting the difficulty that the fellow reformer had had in being returned to Parliament,[104] indicated that this problem was just another illustration of where Romilly's

---

102. Art.III, "The Trials of the Slave-Traders," *Edinburgh Review,* vol.21, no.XLI, February 1813, p.76.
103. *Ibid.*, p.77.
104. Art.V, "Project of Creating a Vice-Chancellor," *ibid.*, p.103.

inclination for change was justified. The recent change in the Court of Session had increased rather than reduced appeals to the Lords. "The professed object of the new arrangement," Brougham wrote about the new bill, "is to give the Chancellor more time for attending to appeals in the House of Lords."[105] Brougham heaped invective upon Lord Redesdale's pamphlet calling for its passage: "... a person, might be promoted to the Seals, merely because he was capable of hearing Scots appeals, and taking his part in political and parliamentary business, although he had never in his life seen a Bill, or an answer in Equity."[106] The problem was Eldon's delays in Chancery, and the Chancellor should be given more time for Chancery business. Brougham wanted a Speaker of the House of Lords, other than the Keeper of the Seal, to conduct its sessions, possibly the Lord President of the Council. Also, it would be possible to separate the bankruptcy jurisdiction from the Great Seal, or, as Romilly suggested, to have extra sessions. The difficulty with a Vice-Chancellor, Brougham concluded, was that it would give Eldon, the champion of the status quo, more opportunities to prevent change.

While the Ministry's proposal was passing easily through Parliament, Creevey's difficulties only reminded Brougham of how limited his policy-making prospects were. The fellow-candidate at Liverpool, whose refusal to quit the constituency when Canning contested it, had proven so destructive of Brougham's chances that he tried to make up for it by pursuing a radical course in Parliament. Creevey, in presenting a petition against the continued monopoly of the East India Company, said this about Liverpool's newly appointed Inspector General of Taxes: "He designated the office of Mr Kirkpatrick as that of a common informer, and insinuated that he received a large annuity for undertaking to screw up persons' assessments to the extent of his own imagination."[107] To give

105. *Ibid.*, p.108.
106. *Ibid.*, p.113.
107. *Kirkpatrick* v. *Creevey*, *The Times*, April 2, 1813, no.8,875, p.2.

the complaint greater circulation and effect, Creevey had it reprinted in the *Liverpool Mercury*. By taking a broad view of a Member's privileges - ie, he could circulate what he had said in Parliament without fear of libel actions - Creevey hoped to act as Brougham's agent in the Commons for radical reform. Creevey's action was especially provocative to the Ministry because Brougham was consulting with him about its intervention in the Prince Regent's handling of his wife's and daughter's affairs. Liverpool's Government was afraid that Creevey would become the parliamentary mouthpiece of Brougham's efforts for the Princesses.

To reduce Creevey's potential to make trouble, the Crown instituted an *ex officio* information against him for libel. Park, the Attorney General for Lancaster, charged that Creevey, by printing the defamatory speech, was not protected by parliamentary privilege. "The Learned Counsel added that the libel went on to insult the memory of the late Mr Perceval; by asserting that he had given Mr Kirkpatrick this appointment, merely in consequence of having been his client."[108] Park cited *R.* v. *Lord Abingdon* as precedent against such use of parliamentary privilege. Brougham denied it. "He insisted, generally, that a Member of Parliament could not be held accountable for publishing a true report of what passed in Parliament."[109] Justice Le Blanc disputed the claim. Brougham explained that Creevey had been persuaded to contest the suit by other MPs for fear that a verdict against him would stifle dissent. *The Times* said this about Brougham's plea:

> He, then, in a very eloquent and ingenious speech, contended that there was nothing libellous in the publication; that matters reflecting in a much higher degree upon the characters of individuals had been published, as the speeches of Mr Burke, Mr Pitt, Mr Windham, and other eminent

---

108. *Ibid.*
109. *Ibid.*

> Parliamentary characters.[110]

Le Blanc said that the published speech vilified Kirkpatrick, libelling an official in the public trust. The jury agreed with the judge without hesitation, finding Creevey guilty of a gross libel.

Brougham was increasingly apprehensive because of the prosecution of the Hunts and Creevey despite his confident assurances to Lord Grey to the contrary.[111] Suspecting that the Crown had been reduced to getting its surrogates involved in the attacks on the Prince Regent and his government because Brougham had not given them a good opportunity for a successful libel action, he was more careful than ever about what he wrote for the press and the *Review*. To embarrass the Liverpool Ministry's prosecution of the war with America, Brougham apparently used the pen-name *Mercator* in letters to *The Times* to stress its difficulties, and favouritism. About the naval war in the Atlantic, Brougham, it seems, queried:

> Is it not lamentable to know, that six months after war had commenced with America, our Admiral on the coast of Brazil was under the necessity of taking a ship with such immense property as the *Bonne Citoyenne* has on board, to cruise for the protection of the trade, instead of her coming direct for England?[112]

The government was attacked for its delay in the prosecution of the war against the United States, and for understating British ship losses. The Ministry's expedient approach to trade with America, allowing its raw materials to enter the kingdom after payment of token duties, was similarly attacked: "And does Sir R. Peel, or any other of the class of weavers or spinners, wish it to be understood, that *national policy* is to be sacrificed to their

---

110. *Ibid.*

111. See, eg, Brougham's letter to Lord Grey, dated December 8, 1812: Brougham, *op. cit.*, vol.II, pp.59-60.

112. *The Times*, April 5, 1813, no.8,877, p.2.

local or partial interests?"[113]

Brougham's articles in the *Review* took on a more professional quality, quite probably induced by a fear that he would be prosecuted for libel if he held forth in customary fashion. About the growing dual system of education for the poor, Brougham suspected that even the Ministry opposed its inefficiency. State aid should only be used at first to assist Lancaster's comprehensive system, an impossibility if Bell's exclusionist principle in education was recognized. Brougham called upon England to adopt what the Board of Education in Ireland favoured, with the support of the Irish Church. "But grant, in any quarter of the globe," Brougham explained, "a reading people and a free press, - and the prejudices on which misrule supports itself will gradually and silently disappear."[114] In reviewing Eustaphieve's *The Resources of Russia*, Brougham defended the Ministry of All Talents' foreign policy in the face of the former Russian official's distortions and prejudices about its aims. Regarding the anticipated defeat of the selfish, bellicose Eastern power at the hands of the French, Brougham wrote: "We think it has been clearly proved, that Russia separated herself from this commons cause, by the pursuit of objects incompatible with it in every shape, and every sense."[115] While Napoleon was completing a new order for Europe, something that Britain would have to recognize, Brougham satisfied himself by reviewing books such as Eustace's *Tour in Italy*, a fitting reminder of what the French Emperor had accomplished since he had tried to see to his assassination. "This is one of the best books of travels that have appeared since we began our labours ..."[116] During the final stages of French consolidation of Europe, Brougham gave himself the responsibility of seeing that the government did everything it could to suppress the slave trade.[117]

---

113. *Ibid.*, April 6, 1813, no.8,878, p.2.
114. Art.IX, "Education of the Poor," *Edinburgh Review*, vol.21, no.XLI, February 1813, p.212.
115. Art.X, "Foreign Policy of England in 1806 and 1807," *ibid.*, p.250.
116. Art.VII, "Eustace's *Tour in Italy*," *ibid.*, no.XLII, July 1813, p.378.
117. Art.XI, "Seventh Report of the African Institution," *ibid.*, p.468.

Brougham showed this most patient approach to the government by dragging out Creevey's case. No sooner had the MP been convicted of libel than Brougham tried to enter a bill of exceptions to limit the verdict. "... but he was informed by the Learned Judge he could not do so in a criminal prosecution; and, besides, that he should have tendered it before he had taken the chance of the verdict being in his favour."[118] Brougham then moved for a new trial of Creevey in the King's Bench. Creevey had only had the speech published to correct misrepresentations of what had happened, Brougham explained. The proceedings of Parliament, like any court, were absolutely privileged, he added, and the Member and his counsel risked imprisonment by the Commons if they abused its privileges: "The general advantage to the country in having those proceedings made public, more than counterbalance the inconveniences to the private persons whose conduct may be the subject of such proceedings."[119] When the Lord Chief Justice denied that a Member could write what he wanted for his constituents, Creevey's counsel corrected him: "Mr Brougham said, that his argument was, that he might publish whatever he was justified in speaking in his place in the House."[120] Ellenborough still maintained that what had been published was a gross libel, and the other judges concurred. The motion was denied.

When it came time to sentence Creevey, Brougham persisted in trying to mitigate punishment by having him read an affidavit which repeated in great detail the defence's case, indicating that the King's Bench risked constitutional conflict with the Commons if it jailed the MP. Creevey said that he believed every word of his that had been printed in the *Liverpool Mercury*. Crown prosecutor Park explained the libel thus for Justice Grose: "The object of the publication was to create disaffection amongst his Majesty's subjects, and to introduce the Inspector General to the hatred of the people."[121] This view was more than offset by the

118. *The Times*, April 2, 1813, no.8,875, p.2.
119. *Ibid.*, May 8, 1813, no.8,906, p.3.
120. *Ibid.*
121. *Ibid.*, May 21, 1813, no.8,917, p.3.

delegation of Members whom Brougham had attend court to give substance to his threat that the Houses of Parliament would contest a harsh verdict. Under the circumstances, the King's Bench decided that prudence was the better part of valour, finding Creevey a paltry one hundred pounds. In light of what had happened to the Hunts, Drakard, and Cobbett for similar offences, Brougham's triumph was comparable to those he had achieved before the special commissions at Horsemonger Lane, Lancashire, and Yorkshire.

Brougham's courage in standing up to Ellenborough soon paid off in the House of Lords, where the Lord Chancellor, Lord Eldon, because of the creation of the Vice-Chancellor, began hearing appeals, especially from Scotland. Brougham's first appeal to the Lords' judicial committee was apparently *Brown et al.* v. *Smith et al.* where he worked with Park, Creevey's prosecutor, to recover the loss of the *Friendship* for some merchants. The ship had been involved in the famous slave trade from Liverpool while it was still legal. Soon after she had arrived at Africa, but before she had taken on any slaves, her crew mutinied, resolving to take her to any enemy port. The ship's boatswain secretly sailed her to the Barbadoes rather than to Cayenne where the mutiny's ringleaders were arrested, tried and executed. A government agent sold off the recovered cargo, but delayed the ship's sale until it became essentially worthless. The question before the court was whether this constituted a total loss for which the underwriters had to make reparations. When the merchants went to the Admiralty Court, Sir William Scott sided with them, but the Court of Session held that the underwriters only had to pay for the cargo.

Park's willingness to work with Brougham for the merchants was a shrewd exploitation of his rising reputation among the Bar. The previous year, Park and Brougham, along with Nicholas Tindal, the special pleader in whose office he had worked when he first came to London, had represented Mr. Baurain in a suit against Sir William Scott, Eldon's brother. "This was an action on the case, for unlawfully excommunicating the plaintiff."[122] Scott, as Vicar General and Official Principal of the Consistorial and Episcopal Court of Beiby, had appointed the plaintiff guardian *ad litem* in a suit before his court, and when he refused, Scott excommunicated him for contempt. "On appeal to Sir John Nicholl, as Dean of the Arches, that learned Judge held that Mr Baurain was compellable to become guardian *ad litem* to his son, and that the excommunication was regular."[123] Nicholl referred the case back to the Consistorial Court for action, and Baurain was excommunicated by his parish church. He appealed Nicholl's decision to the King's Bench, and Lord Ellenborough heard the case at *nisi prius*.

At the hearing, Scott's counsel, Solicitor General Garrow and Holroyd, pulled out all the stops to gain confirmation of the decision. They even had Nicholl testify that it was legal. Witnesses proved that Baurain, a practising attorney, knew of Scott's order making him guardian, and that he could have answered it with little time and trouble. The Lord Chief Justice agreed to let the matter go to the jury, although even he did not see anything unreasonable in what the Lord Chancellor's brother had done. Brougham denied that Scott had any authority to compel Baurain. Scott should have made one of his own officers guardian, as the equity courts did, or allowed a guardian to be appointed by the plaintiff in the suit, as the common law courts did. As precedent for these claims, Brougham cited *Boraine's Case*, 16 Vesey jun. 346, where his client had gone before the Chancellor in Chancery for a writ of *assailer*, to be directed to the Bishop of London, requiring him to absolve Baurain from excommunication.

"At present," Lord Eldon observed, in hearing the application, "I cannot see the principle, upon which, with regard to a son *forisfamiliated*, the father can be compelled to be guardian *ad*

---

122. *Baurain, Gent.* v. *Right .Hon. Sir W. Scott,* John Campbell, ed, *Report of Cases Determined at Nisi Prius* (Butterworth, London, 1811), vol.III, p.388.

123. *Ibid.*, p.389.

litem."[124] The Lord Chancellor admitted that Baurain could apply for the writ because he had been wrongly excommunicated, but refused to do so because he had not given Scott notice of his motion. In doing so, Eldon could not bring himself to mention his brother by name, however. Brougham was showing that he was not afraid to use helpful revelations and dicta, which were embarrassing to the powerful, for his clients. There was no one on the Bar who would have challenged Eldon in such a direct, official way. The jury in the case before Ellenborough awarded Baurain forty shillings in damages, due to Brougham's plea, observing that it did not want its award to be seen as casting the least reflection on Scott's reputation.

Brougham was counsel in *Brown* v. *Smith* even though it risked that the Liverpool merchants would suffer because of Baurain's verdict. Counsel for the underwriters contended that the assured were not entitled to abandon because the ship had not been lost, or if so, it had not been abandoned in time. "Here," Brougham responded, "the voyage was totally lost ..."[125] He stressed the peculiar circumstances in the case - ie, the owners had communicated their wish to abandon as soon as possible, and had not waived any of their rights. "The case of the assured rested entirely on the *dicta* of Buller and Mansfield."[126] Smith's representatives responded, reciting the judgments of other Judges in a way which they thought would require Eldon to find for their clients. They denied that the cases were applicable, but Eldon sided with Brougham, affirming Scott's ten-year-old decision of the Court of Admiralty.

Brougham apparently let this triumph before Eldon go to his head, and the Chancellor was not slow to take advantage of it. In the very next appeal that Eldon heard in the Lords, a most favourable decision by the King's Bench to a seaman for back pay was under review. As in the Drakard case, Brougham was more

---

124. *Ibid.*, n., p.391. N.B. how all the court reporters have got the name of the plaintiff against Scott wrong.
125. *Crown and Others* v. *Smith and Others*, *The English Reports* (Green, London, 1901), vol.III, House of Lords, p.727.
126. *Ibid.*,p.728.

interested in extolling another 10-year-old assumpsit verdict for wages lost during a Russian civil detention than in carefully arguing the case. The current case had originally been heard by the Common Pleas, and it had decided for owner Thomson of the *Aquilon*, judging that Emperor Paul had established an embargo which prevented Beale, the defendant, from rendering contractual service. Brougham got the King's Bench to overturn the decision on a writ of error. In a very long brief, he claimed that Beale, while under Russian detention, had been like a sick person. For those who might not be happy with the analogy, he offered this: "But there was no real distinction between the act of God and that of the king's enemies, as to this purpose."[127]

In light of Russia's titanic struggle with France, this allusion was hardly helpful to his cause. Brougham said that Eldon had already decided in a similar case that Russia's action did not constitute hostile capture. In fact, Brougham became so confused about what constituted an embargo that fellow counsel, F.L. Holt, an expert in maritime contracts and law, felt obliged to intervene to try to save the point. J. Gaselee, the model of J. Stareleigh in Dickens' *Pickwick Papers*, responded that Beale would have to show that the plaintiff had prevented him from performing service in order to gain compensation. Eldon, making sure of his ground, consulted the Judges about the status of the recovered wages. They held unanimously that they should go to Thomson, and the Chancellor went along with their opinion.

Brougham recovered nicely from this setback, however, by joining forces with Romilly in the successful prosecution of another case before the Lords. Brougham, as a rising barrister at *nisi prius*, and before the King's Bench, Common Pleas, and various assizes, was able to enlist the services of the leading Chancery lawyer in a most important suit. They represented a bondholder of the Bank of Scotland in his suit to reduce the cautionary bond he held on the ground of fraud, and that it was not properly executed. The cause had been remitted to the Court of Session as to its legality, and as to the admissibility of evidence

127. *Thomson* v. *Beale, ibid.*, p.710.

regarding fraud. The court decided against the appellants on both counts. "The fraud or undue concealment alleged by Appellants consisted in this, that at the time the Bank Company took the bond in question, they were aware of, or had strong reason to suspect, the misconduct and insolvency of Paterson,"[128] its agent at Thurso.

The Lords permitted evidence as to Paterson's machinations to be heard. Brougham and Romilly also contended that the bond had not been executed according to the requirements of two statutes. Romilly, for a precedent, made the most of one Maltby's problems with the Fishmongers' Company, a case which Eldon had heard in Chancery: "He had heard nothing further of that case, but concluded that the Fishmongers' Company had thought proper to acquiesce in the opinion intimated by the Chancellor on that occasion, and had refrained from attempting to enforce the bond."[129] When Lord Redesdale, a Law Lord hearing the case with the Chancellor, indicated that he doubted the appellants' case, Romilly redoubled his efforts:

> He had before stated the case too weakly for his client; for the appellants, by the improper concealment of the Bank, had become sureties not only for a debt incurred, but for a debt of which it was impossible they could have known the extent.[130]

Eldon found for Romilly's client, citing the Fishmongers' case: "He had since reconsidered the matter, and still retained his former opinion, and would act upon it judicially, if occasion offered."[131] Redesdale concurred, recalling a similar Irish precedent. The case was referred back to the Court of Session, calling upon it to allow the appellants to make their case against the Bank.

With this victory before the Lords, Brougham thought that he

128. *Smith* v. *Bank of Scotland, ibid.*, p.698.
129. *Ibid.*, p.700.
130. *Ibid.*, p.703.
131. *Ibid.*, p.705.

could effect a minor revolution in English law, using Scottish law as precedent and guide. When it suited his interests, or those of his clients, he was not above trying to legislate Scots law in the process. In the *Earl of Morton* v. *Stuart*, Brougham worked with William Adam to establish that the respondent had acquired by prescription the right to use roads passing through the Earl's property. When the case was first heard by Lord Meadowbank, he appointed Stuart to state in a condescendence the proof of the right. This was done, Stuart offering oral testimony to corroborate it. The Earl appealed the interlocutors that had been pronounced against him, claiming that the condescendence had not been precise enough. The Lord Ordinary agreed with Lord Meadowbank, and Morton took the case to the Lords. His counsel, Romilly and Francis Horner, argued that Stuart must prove title in himself as proprietor to the lands at Hillside, and the right of way across the Earl's land must have a precise object. Brougham responded: "It was not necessary here to set forth the particular uses, as the object of the action was to annihilate the servitude; and to this the mere allegation that the Respondent had a right of way was sufficient answer."[132] The Lord Chancellor was not satisfied, however. Eldon wanted to know precisely where these rights existed, and what their purposes were. "Unless the particulars were set forth, a variety of loose and improper evidence might be introduced."[133] The Lords remitted the case to the Court of Session, with findings about the inadequacy of Stuart's condescendence, pleadings, and evidence.

The Lords did not treat Brougham's view of a Scottish divorce any better. The question before the court was whether a Scottish court had jurisdiction to dissolve a marriage where one of the partners had committed adultery in England. In Scotland, adultery was a juridical offence, while in England marriage could only be dissolved by Act of Parliament. In 1802, Major Lindsay's wife was separated from him, and took up with another man. Her husband sued for divorce, charging that she had committed

---

132. *Earl of Morton* v. *Stuart, ibid.*, p.634.
133. *Ibid.*, p.636.

adultery at Bishop Auckland, near Durham. His wife denied that a Scottish court had jurisdiction in such a suit, so he opened a second suit for adulterous acts committed in Scotland. The wife's counsel, Romilly and Holyroyd, attacked the Scottish decisions in the husband's favour, denying that he had established domicile there, and that his wife's automatically followed his. The wife had established domicile at Durham, they contended. An English marriage could only be dissolved by Parliament.

William Adam and Brougham represented the Major, the respondent. The former said that the couple had been married by a Scottish chaplain in a Scottish regiment. Brougham reiterated the point, somewhat ineptly for Eldon, who still thought the case was one of English law:

> He would state the reasons why he thought that the question of indissolubility had no place here. The marriage was not celebrated in such a way as to make it a good English marriage; and it only became such, or rather the marriage was altogether constituted in Scotland, by the parties living there together, and being habit and repute man and wife.[134]

Brougham tried to distinguish the present case from Lolly's, contending that the Lindsay decision required recognizing foreign law. According to Scots law, the deed of separation was, like the marriage itself, revocable at the will of either party.

The Lords, especially Eldon, were perturbed by Brougham's claim that no Scottish lawyer questioned the power of their courts to dissolve English marriages. They were hardly more happy with Brougham's claim about Lindsay's right to revoke the deed. The allegations in the summons were very imprecise, they observed. "Here it must be taken," Eldon ruled, "that the parties were married abroad."[135] The Chancellor was less pleased with the second action, contending that it was opened to achieve a result if the first one failed. "The 12 Judges of England had lately

---

134. *Augusta M. Tovey* v. *Major M.E. Lindsay, ibid.*, p.646.
135. *Ibid.*, p.649.

unanimously decided, that an English marriage could not be any where dissolved except by act of the Legislature."[136] Regarding Lindsay's alleged Scottish domicile, Eldon declared: "Now, where the Court got that fact he did not know, for it certainly did not appear on the face of the papers produced."[137] The Chancellor called upon the Lords to return the cases to the Court of Session so that it could adjust its ideas about an English marriage to the Judges' new doctrine. Redesdale concurred, observing that it would be a dangerous precedent to permit a contract to be dissolved by law different from that under which it was formed. The five lay Lords who were sitting with the Law Lords while they heard the appeal, the conventional manner of maintaining a quorum in the Lords' judicial committee, agreed. For Brougham, it was such reversals which led to this observation: "'He strikes hard, sir, but he strikes wrong', said an attorney of Brougham."[138]

The Lords confounded Brougham's attempts at Scottish lawmaking by rejecting an appeal to block the sale of Craiglaw, a small estate in Perthshire, on the grounds that the contract was defective, and the seller incapacitated. While the Court of Session had already decided against the condescendence by Thomas Scotland's son to prove these claims, Romilly and Brougham still "... submitted, 1st, that the preponderance of the evidence, as to the imbecility and inadequacy of the price, was in favour of the appellant. 2nd, that the lesion under the clause of preemption was enormous, amounting to a forfeiture of the whole of Scotland's real property ..."[139] They also attacked the timing of the contract's completion, the fact that there was only one copy of the minute of sale, and the respondent's liberties with Scotland's papers after his death. The Lords made short work of such litigation for litigation's sake, however, finding for the respondent.

---

136. *Ibid.*
137. *Ibid.*, p.650.
138. Quoted from J.A. Lovat-Fraser, *Erskine* (Cambridge Univ. Press, Cambridge, 1932), p.112.
139. *Scotland* v. *Mercer, The English Reports, op. cit.*, vol.III, p.683.

In fact, Eldon was so irritated by such practice, especially by a barrister who was complaining about the Lords' arrears, and the Chancellor's despatch, that he punished Brougham's representation of wild appeals the very next time that he appeared before the judicial committee. Brougham and William Lyon Mackenzie represented the Duke of Hamilton in his opposition to the payment for the improvement of a manse. "The appellants insisted on the benefit of the statute 1663, cap.21, which they contended, clearly enacted, that after the manses had been put in sufficient repair, they should be upholden by the incumbent ministers."[140] Romilly, for the respondent, said that proceedings by the presbytery, and the Court of Session defeated the claim. Eldon agreed, in a most self-justifying way about this long-pending, apparently important case: "... it did not appear to him that this representation was well founded. The case did not necessarily involve any important general question of law as between the heritors and clergy of Scotland, but rested entirely on its own peculiar circumstances."[141] The Chancellor not only resisted Brougham's call to reinterpret the 1663 statute, but also awarded the respondent one hundred and fifty pounds from the heritors to help cover the costs of the experiment.

With judicial experiments in changing the law proving so expensive, Brougham looked to more effective means for law reform. He decided to review Dumont's 1811 edition of Bentham's *Theory of Punishments* for the *Review* before the collapse of Napoleon's empire ruined all interest in things French. In April 1804, Bentham's *Principles of Legislation* had received a most caustic review,[142] and Brougham now tried to explain away its justification of judicial discretion, fictions, and English common sense. Dumont, who had been originally seen as compounding Bentham's difficulties, was now pictured as revealing the philosopher's design, confirming "... the essential services rendered to the most important branch of legislation by this

---

140. *Duke of Hamilton* v. *Rev. J. Scott, ibid.*, p.741.
141. *Ibid.*, pp.742-3.
142. Art.I, "Bentham, *Principes de Legislation, par Dumont,*" *Edinburgh Review*, vol.4, no.VII, April 1804, pp.1-26.

promulgation of Mr Bentham's doctrines."[143] After outlining the theory, Brougham reviewed English practice with a vengeance, concluding:

> Those which are chiefly desirable, in the nature of punishment, are, that it should be *divisible* - *invariable*, or *certain* or *equal* - *commensurable* with others - *analogous* to the crime - *exemplary* - *economical* - *remissible*; that it should restrain the offender from doing harm - conduce to his *reformation* - yield a *profit*, in the ordinary sense of the word - be *simple* in its description - and so far popular as to shock none of the established feelings or prejudices of the community.[144]

Brougham took exception to some of Bentham's views on corporal punishment, believing that he overstated its use and effectiveness. Nonetheless, Bentham's effort was better than Montesquien's *Spirit of the Laws* and Becarria's incomplete ideas. While Bentham's approach did not constitute a science of punishment, Brougham concluded, it did permit "... that he who is possessed of the methods pointed out by the theory, is ready to apply them again and again to each new case presented for his consideration."[145]

Brougham backed up this comprehensive demand for law reform with an alarming appreciation of what the press could do to help. In reviewing John George's "A Treatise on the Offence of Libel", Brougham castigated his professional colleagues for taking a conventional view of the press's corruption and venality: "... we heartily wish that all lawyers had written and spoken a language as constitutional as he does through his volume."[146] The press, complained Brougham, was restricted in its operation because of the prevalence of servile opinions and ignorant views. While he promised a future review on the role of truth, juries,

---

143. Art.I, "Bentham's *Theory of Punishments, by Dumont,*" *ibid.*, vol.22, no.XLIII, October 1813, p.1.
144. *Ibid.*, p.8. Italics Brougham's.
145. *Ibid.*, p.31.
146. Art.V, "Abuses of the Press," *ibid.*, p.73.

and grand juries in libel trials, he harped on the public's ignorance of how the press and law of libel actually operated. The latter was much like the law against duelling; yet, the Crown could act in this most ambiguous area with near impunity because of the extension of party feelings against offensive libellers. Brougham illustrated the point by discussing the treatment of the Commissioners of Excise in the *Dictionary* and *Idler*:

> It is recorded by Mr Boswell, in the most entertaining, and not the least instructive books, that the Board laid a case before the Attorney General for his opinion: he deemed it libellous, but advised the "Honourable Commissioners" to take no further steps. Who then filled this office? - a courtier certainly, but a great and a wise man. It was Lord Mansfield.[147]

In case anyone missed the relevance of this discretion to how Creevey had been treated in the King's Bench, Brougham repeated some of Burke's libellous views of private individuals, a far worse offence. Brougham concluded by asserting that the press had not become more licentious, "... and that even the worst perversions of this great engine of improvement are not the growth of later days."[148]

In another review, Brougham belittled the capability of Britain's aristocracy for effecting change. In the process, Charles Kelsall was taken to task for his translation of Cicero's last two orations. An expert was needed, Brougham charged, for getting to the bottom of Cicero's difficulties in attacking Caius Verres. "They wrote, and published speeches pretty much as our modern orators sometimes speak pamphlets ..."[149] One had to cut through their vehemence, repetition, and deception since Roman orations were dramatic performances. "It seems Verres," Brougham explained, "had first flogged, and then crucified a

---

147. *Ibid.*, p.84.
148. *Ibid.*, p.88.
149. Art.VIII, "Kelsall's *Translations from Cicero*," *ibid.*, p.130.

Roman citizen."[150] Brougham reworked the oration to show the length to which Cicero had gone to defend Roman citizens from official violence, something that hardly appealed to aristocrats of any age. "Scarcely do any nobles look upon our exertions with a favourable eye," he added. "It is impossible, with all our endeavours, to attract their good will. As if disjointed by nature and species, so are they abhorrent of us in will and disposition."[151] English was not the language for rendering such difficulties intelligible, and the translation should not have been dedicated to Romilly, Brougham concluded.

Such a challenge to legal administration helped cause immediately an unexpected outcome in the King's Bench. The Lord Chief Justice, Lord Ellenborough, just the kind of noble whom Brougham thought most hostile to his efforts, decided for Sir Francis Burdett, his client, in an action to recover funds for services rendered at the hustings in Westminster during the General Election. The Attorney General, John Richardson argued that the tradesman was due to recover almost as a matter of course, and Lord Cochrane, the other elected candidate, had let his suit go by default.[152] In the case before the Exchequer, the court had ruled that Burdett, by taking his seat, had adopted the acts of his committee. Nonetheless, Brougham prevailed upon Ellenborough to non-suit the action because Burdett had been incapacitated from participating in the campaign. By November 1813, Thomas Plumer, who had unsuccessfully defended Burdett before the Lord Chief Baron, and was soon to become Vice-Chancellor, moved in the King's Bench for a new trial. Brougham argued successfully against the rule, however, claiming that Parliament envisioned the candidate as a suitor who actively sought the support of the voters, and that Burdett had done nothing to constitute such a role. The court agreed, discharging the rule, after stating that "it would be too much to attach a heavy expense on a person as a candidate, who had

---

150. *Ibid.*, p.137.
151. *Ibid.*, p.141.
152. *Morris* v. *Burdett, The Times,* July 17, 1813, no.8,965, p.3.

done no act directly or indirectly to make him one."[153]

In fact, with Brougham so combative towards the judicial establishment, his practice in the Lords before Lord Eldon took a turn for the better. In *Stewart* v. *Hall et al.*, Brougham teamed up with Charles Abbott in defending a shipyard which had made repairs on a ship whose owner had tried to put off paying the bill. Eldon, in upholding the decision of the Court of Session, tailor-made the facts of the case to fit the needs of the respondents. Since there was no great principle of law at stake, he explained, respondent Hall was awarded 60 pounds towards his expenses, in keeping with the decision in the *Duke of Hamilton* v. *Rev. J. Scott*, "... by this experiment on the part of the appellant."[154] Brougham was equally successful when he defended surgeon Macdonald in an action for excessive damages. "The Appellants had pleaded separately," Romilly and Nolan argued, "and the damages ought to have been apportioned."[155] They were upset that evidence of previous incidents by the appellant Macdonald had been admitted into the trial, and that there had been a judicial remit to the Lord Advocate to reconsider his status as a justice of the peace. While the Lord Chancellor did agree with these claims, remitting that part of the judgment which questioned Macdonald's continuance as a magistrate, he did not find the size and apportionment of the award for damages and fees excessive.

Brougham could hardly have been upset, except in a narrow professional sense, when he lost the appeal of the trustees of the Duke of Queensberry's estate to the House of Lords. The former Duke had been most liberal in giving away assets. To Brougham's intense displeasure, as we shall see shortly, he gave Lady Hamilton, Lord Nelson's mistress, a 500 annuity. Queensberry also granted a 97-year lease under his will in spite of a prohibition against alienation of estates. Brougham and Romilly argued unsuccessfully for the provision in the Court of

---

153. *Ibid.*, November 26, 1813, no.9,076, p.3.

154. *Stewart* v. *Hall, et al:* P. Dow, ed, *Reports of Cases upon Appeals and Writs of Error in the House of Lords* (Clarke, London, 1814, 6 vols.), vol.II, p.39.

155. *Macdonell and Others* v. *Macdonald, ibid.*, p.70.

Session, and they did no better in the Lords. Alienation, they claimed, only applied to the feudal right or property of the lands. Leases could be good for up to one hundred years, and prohibitions in entails must be crystal clear. The Lords disagreed, however, as Lord Redesdale explained: "He had been able to find no decision that a lease of this description could be supported in the face of such a restriction against alienation, without something special in its circumstances."[156] This decision not only quashed the lease, but also Lady Hamilton never got her annuity.[157]

Brougham and Romilly successfully defended the purchaser of St Andrew's Golf Club's right to use the course as he saw fit despite the claims of golfers who thought that the course would be ruined by the raising of rabbits. The golfers went to the Court of Sessions to stop the practice, and it, after ordering condescendances about the use and population of the animals, decided for the inhabitants. In the Lords, Brougham claimed that the townspeople had no standing for such an action, and that his client could only be restrained by a prohibition in Lord Kellie's will. "The game of golf," he said impishly, "was prohibited by the statute law of Scotland."[158]

The *Earl of Morton* v. *Stuart* case had been remitted to the Court of Session for less causes, he added confidently. Adam and Horner argued for the respondents that the statutes had fallen into disuse, the contract called for keeping up the course, and the will prohibited its being made less fit for golf. Eldon disagreed, stating that he did not understand why the Scottish court had restrained the owner. He was equally upset by the claim that all persons who chose to play golf here could object to the raising of rabbits. In fact, in reviewing the facts of the case, the Lord Chancellor could only envisage one material difference which would have made it more difficult: "If it were possible to feed black cattle there, he had before observed that, if these balls got

---

156. *Montgomery and Others* v. *Charteris, Earl of Wemyss, ibid.*, p.112.
157. *The Dictionary of National Biography* (Smith, Elder, London, 1908), vol.8, p.1037.
158. *Dempster and Others* v. *Cleghorn and Others*, Dow, *op. cit.*, vol.II, p.47.

into what they occasionally left behind them, they would be in a worse *scrape* than if they got into a rabbit scrape."[159] At no time since that of Augustus, Eldon added, had there been such a spirited contest between man and rabbit. The case was remitted to the Court of Session for the correction of errors and omissions.

In the *Review*, Brougham renewed his credentials for a seat in Parliament by his controversial views on international and domestic affairs. In commenting on "An Appeal to the Allies, and the English Nation, in behalf of Poland", an anonymous pamphlet which sounded much like Brougham's work for the Whigs, the writer called for diplomatic efforts to restore Poland:

> If a settlement of Europe is made upon the profligate scheme of each party taking as much as he can get by force or intrigue; if a few powerful states lay their heads together and despoil all the rest; if the interests and the feelings of the people go for nothing in the arrangement; who can expect that either the different cabinets will be ready at a moment's warning, to unite against anyone which may violate the arrangements thus foully made; or that popular feeling, which it wholly disregarded, will rise up to defend it?[160]

Brougham called for really looking at the cynical *real politik* that was going on behind the scenes rather than the impressions that politicians were trying to protect. He illustrated the point by explaining the riddle of what English judges did in theory as opposed to practice. "A distant view of an institution is deceitful;" he wrote, anticipating his review of Neild on prisons in the same issue - "we should see how they work in practice, before we decide their effects."[161] Poland was just like other nations, and its freedom must be restored if there was any hope for the concert of Europe.

In considering Neild's "State of Prisons in England, Scotland,

---

159. *Ibid.*, p.64. Italics Eldon's.
160. Art.III, "Appeal of the Poles," *Edinburgh Review*, vol.22, no.XLIV, January 1814, p.308.
161. *Ibid.*, p.326.

and Wales", Brougham took up the cause that the Gloucestershire magistrate had been trying to remedy, but with few results, for the past decade. As with international negotiations, prison life was different from what their whitewashed walls seemed to indicate. The justices of the peace, and the Crown were simply not giving prisons the oversight that law and justice required. The moral, educational, physical and spiritual needs of prisoners were, consequently, being neglected. "It would have been becoming the paternal care of the Ministers of the Crown, to have taken the lead in reforming this important and extensive department of the national police."[162] Since the Crown was unwilling to employ Neild to do the task, Brougham called upon Parliament to establish means of enforcing personal inspection and written reports, for which experience had clearly proved, particularly in town jails, that honour and conscience were too feeble obligations.

In the next issue of the *Review*, Brougham reiterated his claims for a seat even more boldly, and the reason for it is not difficult to discern. Lord Cochrane, the Member for Westminster, was being prosecuted for a Stock Market fraud, and if convicted, he would be expelled from the House, requiring a by-election there. Brougham, because of his defence of the Princess of Wales and Princess Charlotte, had long been seen as the heir-apparent to the eccentric Radical. Brougham's relation to the constituency had been well illustrated at a meeting of Westminster householders in Palace Yard the previous spring when the Radical, Wishart had proposed: "Her Royal Highness had, as he understood, been much benefited by the advise of a man whose legal knowledge was equal to his talents and his public virtues, and whose retirement from Parliament must be considered a great national loss. He alluded to Mr Brougham."[163] James Mill had been urging him to contest the seat, and *The Times* provided Brougham with excellent credentials for the Radical constituency because of the *Review's* sarcastic reception of Thomas Southey's "A Song

162. Art.VII, "Neild on Prisons," *ibid.*, p.399.
163. "Westminster Meeting," *The Times*, April 16, 1813, no.8,887, p.2.

of Triumph". In a leading article, the *Review* was portrayed as Brougham's political rag which had a set of radical doctrines for the world's ills, doctrine which had made too much of Napoleon and the French nation, and not enough of England. Brougham's schoolboy politics were dismissed thus:

> ... something more goes to the making of a statesman than a flippant style, a confident tone, or a string of threadbare sarcasms against men in power; but above all (and oh! more lamentable than all! they forget, that the fate of empires, the rise and fall of nations, man's true greatness and his wholesome liberty, depend not on one engine of power, however mighty, nor on the word of a single tyrant, however artful; but on the springs of action which pervade the minds of a whole people ...[164]

Brougham tried to show that Westminster voters and *Times* readers had something to gain from politicians like him. In the *Review*, he attacked parliamentary approval of Norway's forcible transfer to Sweden, Crown approval of the restored French colonial empire practising the slave trade, and government inability to protect the criminally insane. On the very day that Parliament voted the strongest address for freeing the African Negroes, he wrote, it agreed to the forcible transfer of Norway from Denmark to Sweden, "... so very discriminating is the philanthropy of this our age and nation!"[165] Britain had even threatened Norway with a blockade if it did not accept the terms of the transfer. People had a right to resist such action. Had ministers forgotten how they had reacted to the French invasion of Spain, Brougham asked. He compared the transfer to how slave traders attempted to justify the trade. "Surely some of the able advocates of the abolition in Parliament," he added sarcastically, "could scarcely have forgotten this circumstance,

---

164. *Edinburgh Review, ibid.*, April 7, 1814, no.9,189, p.3.
165. Art.IV, "Transference of Norway," *Edinburgh Review*, vol.23, no.XLV, April 1814, p.80.

when they so lately gave their support to the blockade ..."[166] Brougham was furious over the government's acquiescence to restoring the French slave trade for five years. "England had fully as good a right to make a stand for Africa as for Spain."[167] He called for the nation to express its opinion on the matter so that it could be redressed by the Congress of Vienna. Brougham also compared the Crown unfavourably with the Quakers in the treatment of the insane:

> For the aversion to inspect places of this sort is so great, and the temptation to neglect and oppress the insane so strong, both from the love of power and the improbability of detection, that we have no doubt of the existence of great abuses in the interior of many mad-houses. A great deal has been done for prisons; but the order of benevolence has been broken through by this preference; for the voice of misery may sooner come up from the dungeon, than the oppression of a mad man be healed by the hand of justice.[168]

To make himself more attractive to Westminster householders, Brougham agreed to household suffrage, fairer distribution of parliamentary representation, and annual parliaments, due to the proddings of Francis Place, the constituency's Radical organizer. Place even arranged for the propagation of Brougham's views on parliamentary reform when the press, especially *The Times*, failed to give adequate coverage to the Livery of London Parliamentary Reform dinner.[169] *The Times* had given this gathering a wide berth after Perceval's assassination. The Lord Chief Justice more than compensated for these moves, however, by his treatment of Lord Cochrane at the trial. Even *The Times*

---

166. *Ibid.*, p.102.
167. Art.VI, "Revival of the Slave Trade," *ibid.*, p.147.
168. Art.VIII, "Tuke's Account of the Retreat near York," *ibid.*, p.168. For those who find it hard to believe that Brougham wrote this review, N.B. what he said in the Neild article about the failure of the Crown to reform the prisons, "... the consideration of a subject on which other opportunities may soon enable us to enlarge" (*op. cit.*, p.399).
169. New, *op. cit.*, pp.158-9.

was willing to admit that Cochrane's only offence was to get caught in committing a widespread practice. He was, nonetheless, fined, imprisoned, and subjected to the pillory, treatment that Brougham had singled out for opprobrium in his review of Bentham's *Theory of Punishments*: "So the pillory (if such a disgrace to all criminal legislation may be mentioned on this occasion) is, according to the above arrangement, not a *corporal*, but either a *privative* or a *mixed* punishment."[170] By degrading Cochrane, Ellenborough assured his re-election at Westminster, denying Brougham the opportunity to institutionalize by Parliament what he was trying to achieve on a case-by-case basis in the King's Bench. In popularity contests, the victim of an abuse is always more attractive than the proponent of its reform. "It is certain, however," Holdsworth wrote, "that the severity of the sentence was generally condemned - it was, says Brougham, a sentence 'which at once secured Lord Cochrane's re-election for Westminster when the Commons expelled him upon his conviction, and abolished for ever the punishment of the pillory, in all but one excepted case - perjury'."[171]

Brougham, contrary to New,[172] had a most busy summer despite the setback at Westminster. He was not the type to do nothing. To think that he was uninvolved is just a confession that one has lost the thread of his activities. In fact, Brougham was involved in another important, totally unappreciated episode of his life. On May 30, the warring powers of Europe had signed the Definitive Treaty of Peace and Amity in Paris. After the government of Louis XVIII had expressed its agreement to the British Government on the barbarity of the slave trade, it stated that it approached the Congress of Vienna with the idea of its universal abolition, "... as it shall cease definitively, under any circumstances, on the part of the French Government, in the course of five years; and that, during the same period, no Slave Merchant shall import or sell Slaves, except in the Colonies of

170. Brougham, *op. cit.*, p.5, n. Italics Brougham's.
171. Holdsworth, *op. cit.*, vol.XIII, p.506.
172. New, *op. cit.*, p.160.

the State of which he is a Subject."[173] As soon as the abolitionists heard of the stipulation, they called a meeting of the Friends of Abolition of the Slave-Trade to map counter strategy.[174] With the Duke of Gloucester in the chair, Wilberforce called for quick, effective action to prevent the revival of the slave trade. England had been persuaded by Lords Grey and Grenville, he said, to abolish the trade, and he thought that France could be similarly persuaded if she were acquainted with its real character. "In this country, the Slave-Trade had lately received a deadly blow," Wilberforce added, "from a bill brought into Parliament by an hon. and learned friend near him (Mr Brougham), for placing it on the same footing as other felonies."[175] The group drew up a petition to be presented to Parliament, calling upon the government to force France to give up the trade.

While Brougham did not speak at the meeting, he did devote himself to its end in the columns of *The Times* and the *Review*. Just as the newspaper had changed to the government after Spencer Perceval's assassination because of the alarm over the Luddites, the threat of the revived slave trade obliged it to side again with Brougham. There was a column, signed "Alfred", and sounding exactly like Brougham on the subject, protesting the clause in the treaty permitting France to resume the slave trade. "Let the voice of the British nation once declare itself," he wrote, "and the African Slave Trade must universally cease."[176] In calling for a national protest like the one which ended the Orders in Council, Brougham ignored the parliamentary role that he had played in the earlier process. "Within a few weeks Parliament was deluged by 806 petitions signed by over 750,000 persons."[177] Up until then, the Whigs had been prepared to go along with the Ministry's explanation of the treaty. The Prime

---

173. "Definitive Treaty ...", in Clife Parry, ed, *The Consolidated Treaty Series, 1813-1815* (Oceana Publications, Dobbs Ferry, N.Y., 1969, 231 vols.), vol.69, p.194.
174. *The Times*, June 14, 1814, no.9,246, p.3.
175. "Abolition of Slave Trade," *ibid.*, June 18, 1814, no.9, 250, p.2.
176. *Ibid.*, June 24, 1814, no.9,255, p.2.
177. New, *op. cit.*, p.138.

Minister had told Lord Grenville that the ministers had every intention of ending the trade, and Castlereagh put down Whitbread's claim about the noncontroversial aspect of abolition by stating that the deposed Emperor had even been opposed to it. Lord Lansdowne, Brougham's friend and a Friend of Abolition of the Slave-Trade, was not put off by this, moving an Address, "... praying that the influence of government might be employed at the ensuing Congress to obtain the abolitions of the Slave Trade."[178] The Lords adopted the motion unanimously. In the Commons, however, despite the popular protest, the Ministry was given much more discretion in settling the matter. "Wilberforce was afraid of antagonizing the government and also feared that an attack would stimulate the Whigs and make the matter a party issue."[179]

Brougham went wild over Wilberforce's failure to make the case against the trade in the Commons, and forced the government to do in the international arena what they had been obliged to do domestically. As the campaign mounted, Castlereagh, an alarmist against greater freedom,[180] began to see the writing on the wall, as he wrote to his ambassador in Spain: "... the nation is bent upon this object. I believe there is hardly a village that has not met and petitioned upon it; both Houses of Parliament are pledged to press it; and the Ministers must make it the basis of their policy."[181] Brougham would make sure of that. The question was how far the Ministry would go to try to withstand it, and what it sacrificed in other areas to the principles of freedom.

Brougham gave decision-makers an idea of what they faced by his handling of abolition in *The Times*. When the newspaper failed to put it on the agenda for the Congress of Vienna, Brougham apparently reminded it of the fact: "I am even

---

178. *Gentleman's Magazine*, vol.84, 1814, Part 2, p.165.
179. New, *op. cit.*, p.137.
180. See, eg, his letter to Lord W. Bentinck, dated May 7, 1814, in Charles William Vane, ed, *Correspondence, Despatches, and other Papers, of Viscount Castlereagh* (Murray, London, 1853, 12 vols.), vol.X, p.18.
181. Castlereagh's letter to Sir H. Wellesley, dated August 1, 1814: *ibid.*, vol.X, p.73.

sanguine enough to suppose that the wrongs of Africa will not be pleaded in vain ..."[182] In fact, *The Times* was sufficiently embarrassed by the omission, and optimistic about the result that it allowed someone sounding exactly like Brougham to write a series on the evils of the slave trade for the Congress. In the first letter, Brougham appealed to the Sovereigns concerned to strike a blow for freedom, enlightenment, and prosperity around the globe.[183] Brougham then called for universal abolition in a manner which recalled passage of his felony act: "... why should man-stealing and the other atrocities in which the slave traders are either principals or accessories, in Africa, find a sanction in the abused name of commerce, which we should refuse to theft, or the felonious reception of stolen goods in this country?"[184] European ignorance of the subject was attributed to the long war, and press censorship. Brougham was, nonetheless, encouraged about abolition "... for it cannot be doubted that a paper like *The Times*, which so ably served the cause of the Bourbons and of Europe, is read with favour and confidence, in France and on the Continent at large."[185] In the third letter, Brougham described the means by which slaves were procured, relying upon Mungo Park's *Journal* for evidence to show that the European institution was far different from African vassalage. In the last "Juba" letter, Brougham recounted the terrible means by which Africans were handed over to the trade, a process culminating in a long trek to the slave magazines:

> ... but how is the *copple* or caravan of slaves, that proceeds from the interior to the coast, by a journey sometimes of three months' duration, to be victualled for its departure in a country pressed by famine? - and how is the food to be carried thither *across extensive deserts to purchase the starving inhabitants*?[186]

---

182. *The Times*, September 8, 1814, no.9,310, p.3.
183. "Duties of the General Congress," *ibid.*, September 16, 1814, no.9,317, p.2.
184. *Ibid.*, September 20, 1814, no.9,320, p.2.
185. *Ibid.*
186. *Ibid.*, October 4, 1814, no.9,332, p.2. Italics Brougham's.

Actually, *The Times* had seen enough of the information that Brougham had amassed from Park, a Privy Council report, and printed evidence of the Lords to stop the series, although Brougham was ready for more. As far as Thomas Barnes was concerned, the issue was no longer in doubt. Brougham finally expressed similar sentiments when he failed to have anything on the subject in the September 1814 issue of the *Review*, and a most superficial statement in November.[187] Brougham did promise more if it unfortunately proved necessary, however, and his later repetition of Park's description of the difficulties of a caravan could leave no doubt as to the source of the concern. Brougham satisfied himself with little more than taking Wilberforce to task for thinking that a pamphlet to Talleyrand, a cynical Machiavellian, could rectify the situation.

Actually, Brougham had more difficult matters at hand. The Princess of Wales, whom Brougham served as Attorney General, had finally left the country, and the status of her marriage to the Prince Regent would soon have to be decided, or run the risk of becoming, once again, the grist of party politics. Since this royal marriage has been given much consideration by historians,[188] there is no need to go into any detail about it now. While the politicians had switched their allegiances to the parties, due to the Regency crisis, and the investigations into the Princess's alleged adultery had achieved nothing, as her free access to Princess Charlotte, the heir to the Throne, indicated, royal relations were at a critical juncture, and Brougham, more than anyone else, knew it. The Ministry had to get up the initiative, something it was struggling for in anticipation of the Congress of Vienna, to tell the Prince Regent to treat the Princess as his consort, or to get a divorce. Either way, Brougham would get new duties and responsibilities.

In the *Review*, Brougham reviewed another pamphlet, "Some Inquiry into the Constitutional Character of the Queen Consort",

---

187. Art.VI, "Revival of the Slave-Trade," *Edinburgh Review*, vol.24, no.XLVII, November 1814, pp.106-33.

188. See, eg, New, *op. cit.*, p.79 ff.

an effort reminiscent of his efforts at Ryder and St Alban's Streets. The monograph was, Brougham explained:

> ... apparently the production of a lawyer, but certainly of one who has well studied the constitution of his country in its best school, and who combines a practical apprehension of legal questions with an enlarged and accurate knowledge of the history of our free government, and the common interests of prince and people.[189]

To show that he expected the highest state-manship in the handling of the Princess, he had repudiated the likes of Lord Nelson in such matters, in an earlier review.[190] The Princess was all but equal in rank to the Prince himself. "To hold any adulterous intercourse with the Queen-consort," Brougham warned, "is the highest crime known in the law, - belonging to the same description with the compassing the King's death."[191] She is a most important person whose issue the law must most closely guard the purity of. Brougham reminded Tory ministers, anticipating George III's death, that they were obliged to crown both the Prince and Princess: "It is necessary as a public recognition of that, for which alone the dignity of queen exists in the realm, the constitutional order of succession to the crown. She assumes the crown as a symbol of the right of her offspring to the monarchy ..."[192] If there were enmity between the Royal Couple, or doubt as to the issue's legitimacy, the double coronation was doubly necessary. In effect, Brougham called for the Ministry to prepare for the inevitable, unless it were prepared to shake the kingdom to its foundations by a divorce action, by instructing the Princess in her future role. If the ministers did not, Brougham concluded, "they involved the contemplation of the worst evils felt in political society - a civil war, and an incapable

---

189. Art.X, "Constitutional Character of the Queen Consort," *Edinburgh Review*, vol.23, no.XLVI, September 1814, p.441.
190. Art.VII, "Lord Nelson's Letters to Lady Hamilton," *ibid.*, p.406.
191. Brougham, *op. cit.*, p.445.
192. *Ibid.*, p.451.

ruler."[193] Brougham reiterated the need of the government to adopt a prudent course about the couple's marital relations in another review in the same issue, ruminating about Queen Marie Antoinette's thoughts at the Petit Trianon:

> What must have been the sensations of the late owner of this retreat, when she contrasted the voluptuous days which she had spent in its seductive seclusion, with the terrifying attitude of the temple, and the fetid dungeon of the Bictre? Evils are certainly heightened by contrast! And though a King is but a man, and a Queen a woman, yet the woes of Royalty must be attended with an anguish peculiar to themselves.[194]

Brougham was on very good grounds in thinking that the Ministry would have to adopt a most practical course regarding the Princess. When the Ministry was trying to keep her from seeing Princess Charlotte, a high point of the campaign was when George III heard that she had discussed the Mary Anne Clarke scandal in her daughter's presence. "He had laid down a rule that she should meet no one but her mother at these visits."[195] Mary Anne Clarke, the Duke of York's former mistress who used her favours for financial gain, went on to write a most censorious pamphlet about the Irish Chancellor of the Exchequer, William Fitzgerald. He asked the Attorney General to prosecute her *ex officio* for libel, and the case, in due course, was heard by the King's Bench, with Brougham representing the defendant. The pamphlet "... accused the prosecutor of seducing his friend's wife, procuring the husband to be sent to an unhealthy climate, and other matters (not fit to be mentioned in a newspaper)."[196] It seemed that there were some letters by Fitzgerald indicating that he was most desirous to get back at the defendant, and that he did so through false promises. Brougham's client wrote the pamphlet out of vexation, and disappointment, he explained.

---

193. *Ibid.*, p.468.
194. Art.XI, "Paris in 1802 and in 1814," *ibid.*, p.476.
195. New, *op. cit.*, p.87.
196. R. v. *Mary Ann Clarke*, *The Times*, February 8, 1814, p.3.

Crown prosecutors Scarlett and Park called for most severe penalties for the guilt to which she had readily admitted by allowing the indictment to proceed by default. Brougham explained why the court should be more merciful:

> This publication arose out of a long connexion between the parties, commencing with an acquaintance with the prosecutor's father; an intercourse, the learned counsel was not entitled to say, consisting in reciprocal obligations, for the favours seemed to be all on one side ...[197]

In passing sentence, Justice Le Blanc mentioned that "... the charges, if true, would render the prosecutor unfit for the situation he holds, or, indeed, for any other."[198] Under the circumstances, the court saw fit to send this infamous woman, caught red-handed in another crime dangerous to public order, for nine months to the King's Bench Prison. What could the Ministry expect of similar action against the Princess of Wales, a case fraught with many more difficulties, because of the full-time activities of her Attorney General?

Brougham made the dilemma clearer by an altercation with the Lord Chief Justice in the King's Bench. In *R.* v. *Geo. Houston*, a criminal information for libelling Christianity and established religion, which had gone to judgment by default, Brougham represented the defendant at the time of sentencing. In an effort to try to mitigate it, he introduced affidavits, and Ellenborough wanted to know how the author of *Ecce Homo*, an infidel tract, had sworn to their truth. "How could he be upon the New Testament?"[199] he asked testily. When Brougham tried to explain that a non-Christian could make an affidavit, the Lord Chief Justice retorted: "Are you prepared to suggest, Sir, what belief the defendant has, by which he may be sworn?"[200]

Brougham, never one to run away from a fight, as he indicated

---

197. *Ibid.*
198. *Ibid.*
199. *R.* v. *Geo. Houston, ibid.*, November 15, 1814, no.9,368, p.1.
200. *Ibid.*

in his letter to Lord Grey afterwards,[201] reminded the Judge that he was just doing his duty, and enjoined him not to mix him up with those causes it was his duty as an advocate to plead. Brougham, now under a full head of steam, attacked the judgment, denying that his client was the author of the infamous pamphlet, and the process by which he had been convicted, charging that he, with the Crown's help, had been made a scapegoat by the other persons involved. While Brougham made this tirade, Ellenborough was uncharacteristically silent. When Attorney General Garrow tried to explain for him, Brougham let forth again, stating that he was only doing his duty:

> ... but this I will say from my own observation of these canting times, that there are many better Christians as there are truer men, than those who go bawling out their faith in high places; that we may be sincere, though quiet - devout, though charitable - nay, that a man may look forward to benefit by his piety in the way of revision, though he has not the talent of turning it to present account by making godliness a great gain.[202]

While this did not much help his client, who was sentenced to Newgate for two years, and a 200 fine, it made a world of difference to the King's Bench and Ellenborough, as events later proved.

In this context, Brougham's big lesson for the Courts and Ministry came before Judge Joseph Burchall and a special jury at the Middlesex Sheriff's Office. During the past half-year, Sir Henry Mildmay had been having a most scandalous affair with his deceased wife's sister, the Countess of Roseberry. The adultery was so well established, and knowledge about it so widespread, despite the press's silence, that she allowed the original judgment in her husband's favour to go by default. In

---

201. Quoted in New, *op. cit.*, p.160. N.B. how New completely misrepresented newspaper coverage of the trial, thinking that they had ignored it, when, in fact, papers like *The Times* had given it unprecedented front-page coverage.

202. *The Times, op. cit.*, p.2.

Lord Roseberry's suit for damages at Middlesex, he called for 30,000 pounds, and Brougham represented Mildmay, his wife's seducer. The Attorney General, in making the Earl's case, went to extremes, indicating that Sir Henry lived a life of total lechery, "... one of multiplied incest."[203]

The case was certainly not without its shocking moments, particularly when the special jury learned that the Countess, who had been taken to Dalmeny Park in Scotland to get away from Mildmay, nightly excused herself after dinner to join her disguised lover in her bedroom. Garrow challenged the jurors to do their duty in Mildmay's case: "They would be addressed by a gentleman of great eloquence on the part of the defendant; but he defied that learned gentleman to remove him from his claim of exemplary damages."[204] The Attorney General even spoke of Mildmay's wearing the Countess's yellow garters as a sign of his triumph. There was no mention of the fact that Roseberry was so angry when he caught the couple in the act that he shot Mildmay in the arm. Garrow concluded his summation to the jury about the social import of its award thus: "They would answer that question well, or ill, by giving the whole of or less than the thirty thousand pounds damages claimed on this record."[205]

Brougham rose to the occasion. "The cause of morals generally is ill served," he complained, "as the justice of the particular case, by this confounding all distinctions, overleaping the bounds that separate different actions, shutting the eyes to various shades of impropriety and guilt, and by anticipating in slight cases the measures of reprehension due to the worst offences, at once over punishing the one, and defrauding the other of their just infliction."[206] While he would do no more as a lawyer in this clear-cut case of adultery than his instructions permitted, he would not allow his client to be portrayed as a classic seducer.

---

203. *The Earl of Roseberry* v. *Sir Henry St John Midmay, Bart, ibid.*, December 12, 1814, no.9,389, p.2.
204. *Ibid.*, p.3.
205. *Ibid.*
206. *Ibid.*

The Attorney General had drawn his picture from the details of far worse cases which had come before the courts. Brougham latched on to his calling the offence incest:

> He could not have described the case more vehemently, called down a graver reprehension, demanded an ampler retribution, if Sir H. Mildmay had stood before you a hoary letcher, jaded with a life of debauch, provoking to be the instrument of his lust the wife of his own friend, himself that friend's nearest relative, himself a husband, imposing upon his friend and relation an adulterous progeny ...[207]

In the wake of Lady Mildmay's death, it was only natural, given the close connection between the families, that their relation developed into a raging love, given Roseberry's almost criminal neglect of what was transpiring. Neither communal nor blood ties had been violated by their coming together. The jury had before it, Brougham concluded, "... the melancholy story of a mutual, sincere, ardent, devouring passion, overwhelming with misery two young and unfortunate persons whom accidental circumstances had placed within its reach."[208] The jury agreed completely that this was a most natural but illegal act, awarding the Earl only half of what he demanded.

The tonic effect that the Houston and Mildmay decisions had upon Brougham's legal career, especially in the King's Bench, was immediately apparent. Ten days after the former judgment, the court handled *R.* v. *W. Fraser*, a case much like the one against Mary Anne Clarke, in similar fashion, although Brougham did make this telling point against the King's Counsel who got the Crown to sue:

> There is no more pernicious, as well as vulgar error, than that there is or ought to be any other limit than the discretion of the judge who presides, or the good sense and good taste of

---

207. *Ibid.*
208. *Ibid.*

> the advocate, to that licence (he would choose to call it rather than liberty) of the bar, upon the lives, honour, and property of the community, and their safety from conspiracy, depend.[209]

After the Roseberry decision, the Lord Chief Justice fell all over himself in giving Brougham what he wanted in a breach of contract case. He wanted the action non-suited because there was no proof of the salary alleged. Ellenbrough was inclined to let the informal way that Brougham's client had tried to settle the dispute go to the jury, but counsel persisted. "Mr Brougham proposed, even now, to refer the compensation due from the defendant to the plaintiff to any barrister, with power for him to decide upon costs."[210] The Court agreed, referring the matter to Brougham's friend Nicolas Tindal.

In fact, things went so much Brougham's way there that John Campbell, fellow Whig, and recorder of cases at *nisi prius*, was forced to break his self-imposed silence about his activities by the following spring. In *Loweth* v. *Fothergill*, Brougham and Tindal teamed up to get Ellenborough to overturn Eldon's decision in *Beale* v. *Thompson*. The decision by the Lords, and the statute of limitations did not stand in the way of Ellenborough's awarding a seaman back wages: "I think this amounts to an acknowledgment, on which the law implies a promise. The defendant did not say that he had paid the wages, and on the contrary, he admitted that they were unpaid. He only expressed doubts on the law of the question, which had been finally decided against him."[211] Brougham and Tindal even got wages for a seaman while he had been in prison despite Parke's claims about *Beale* v. *Thompson* being a precedent. "The action is maintainable," the Lord Chief Justice explained, "on the ground that there was no severance of his services; and therefore, in contemplation of the law, he was working and labouring for the

---

209. R. v. *Fraser, ibid.*, November 25, 1814, no.9,377, p.2.
210. *Preston* v. *Butcher, ibid.*, December 22, 1814, no.9,398, p.3.
211. *Loweth* v. *Fothergill*, Campbell, *op. cit.*, vol.4, p.185.

defendant, from the commencement to the conclusion of the voyage."[212]

Brougham's efforts were just as successful at the Congress of Vienna. Because of the petition campaign, and what he had been doing in the press, Castlereagh became a vigorous opponent of resuming the slave trade. He got the King of Spain to limit the Spanish trade to Spanish territories and nationals. The Prince Regent of Portugal was induced to end the slave trade north of the equator, and determined to wipe it out south of the line. The culmination of this process was the Universal Declaration, signed at Vienna in February 1815, committing the eight signatories to abolition. In explaining their action, they put great emphasis on the campaign that had been raised for ending the trade as soon as possible, especially since the character and the details of its resumption had become better known.[213] As far as France was concerned, what Brougham had started, Napoleon finished. No sooner had he escaped from Elba, and resumed his regime than he, contrary to Castlereagh, abolished the trade by decree in an effort of gain international support. While it did not obtain this result, as the Battle of Waterloo graphically illustrated, the once-again restored Bourbon regime, for once, had the good sense to let it stay. As Castlereagh had learned that it was easier to work with Brougham than against him, a ministerial attitude which drove James Stephen to resign his seat in the Commons in protest, so had Talleyrand learned the risks of arousing Brougham's ire.

In domestic politics, his greatest contribution was settling the Roseberry divorce. During 1815, the barrister seemed to be biding his time, waiting for what he had done to sink in. For the government, the King could die at any time, bringing on the question of the coronation, and all it entailed. Once George III died, the Ministry would immediately have to decide what to do about the Princess and her Attorney General. The government seems to have left the matter to fate, neither seeking a showdown

---

212. *Delamainer* v. *Winteringhan*, *ibid.*, p.187.
213. "Declaration of the Eight Courts ...," Parry, *op. cit.*, p.474.

with the Regent's absent consort nor an accommodation with her restless counsel. The Whigs only risked more difficulty by leaving Brougham in this situation, especially when he seemed more effective in getting things done in the Courts, on the Continent, and, quite often, in Parliament than they did. Brougham knew that time was on his side. In the *Review*, he increasingly satisfied himself with less controversial subjects, like Davy's discovery of iodine, Carnot's republicanism, Brande's use of magnesia to shrink stones, and how Mungo Park actually died. Only this last review was a reminder of his political activities, with its account of the difficulties of a desert caravan of slaves.[214]

It was while Brougham was with the messe on the Northern Circuit that he learned that Roseberry was going to divorce his Countess, necessitating activities in the Consistory Court and Parliament which could do him much good. In such canting times, it was one thing to stand up for fairness and justice; quite another to engage in a course of conduct which might identify counsel with the adulteress. Brougham, consequently, left the circuit, returning to Brougham Hall, claiming that his life was in danger from a serious heart attack. It was during the French Revolution that Brougham had last sought his home's security, and for similar reasons. He had nothing to gain by being anywhere else. As his physician, Dr Baillie pointed out, he suffered from no bodily disease,[215] and one must be most careful about pleas of insanity. Professor New has been most vague about the matter, only stating that he had "a bee in his bonnet". While Brougham did prepare a review of Huber's study on bees, this hardly seems to be the subject about which he had developed an overly enthusiastic interest. Certainly, at no time in his career did he act more effectively, more prudently - more sanely.

Brougham apparently was the Countess' long-distance counsel as she went through the ordeals of a divorce judgment and act.

---

214. Art.XII, "Park's *Last Journey and Life*," *Edinburgh Review*, vol.24, no.XLVIII, February 1815, p.486.
215. New, *op. cit.*, p.161.

Of course, during the trial, there was someone there to repeat the argument he had made during the damage suit, but he was so insignificant that we shall not likely know his name. *The Times* described the proceeding thus: "The Counsel for Lady Roseberry admitted that it was impossible for them to offer any observations to resist the effect of this evidence, which they therefore left to the impartial consideration of the Court."[216] Once Sir William Scott had heard a repetition of all the sordid evidence, he granted a divorce, a decision which could only be effected by an Act of Parliament.

In its passage, the hand of a lawyer like Brougham seems more in evidence. The divorce bill was presented to the Lords by his friend, Lord Lansdowne. When the proposal was read a second time, Lord Roseberry had both the Attorney General and D.F. Jones, counsel who often worked with Brougham, representing him, while the Countess had none. As the *Journals of the House of Lords* tell us, this was all the more surprising since Lord Ellenborough, a most staunch defender of established ways, was presiding as Speaker by virtue of a former Commission. The Countess had nothing to worry about, because of some professional advice. When Lord Lauderdale objected to the Bill's special provisions, especially against the one prohibiting Mildmay's marriage to the Countess, Lord Grenville showed singular legal expertise: "Under the existing law, matters of this kind were left to the Ecclesiastical courts; and he understood that it was only under particular circumstances, and at particular times, that the object could be attained."[217] A sentence of nullity against such a marriage could only be obtained through considerable collusion and deception. Ellenborough, with Brougham nowhere in sight, had no trouble agreeing with the Whig leader, denying emphatically that the measure was "... a bill of pains and penalties against the wife",[218] as Lauderdale had charged prophetically. The bill, in permitting Roseberry to

---

216. *Earl of Roseberry* v. *Countess of Roseberry, The Times,* April 15, 1815, no.9,496, p.3.
217. *Hansard's Parliamentary Debates,* vol.31, col.562.
218. *Ibid.,* col.559.

remarry, did give the Countess alimony. Just to make sure that the deal was fair, as Eldon wished, the Commons increased her annuity by 200 pounds annually when it got the chance, a most unencouraging precedent for a Ministry desirous of punishing the Princess of Wales, and her political supporters, for similar conduct.

The Roseberry Divorce Act received the Royal Assent on June 28. The Whigs could no longer do without Brougham's services without risking his going over to the Tories. They probably planned to adopt him for one of the pocket boroughs, once the Session was over. On July 6, Whitbread, Grey's radical brother-in-law, most despondent over his role in the losing Drury-Lane venture which had denied Brougham his seat, slit his throat, and died. A few days later, William J.F. Poulett accepted the office of Steward of East Hendred in Berks., vacating thereby his Commons seat at Winchelsea.[219] Lord Darlington, the Whig patron of the constituency, agreed to Brougham's being the new Member. Despite the hopes and wishes of friend and foe, he had forced his way back into Parliament.

---

219. *Journals of the House of Commons,* 1815, vol.70, p.471.

CHAPTER FIVE

FROM WATERLOO TO PETERLOO

Brougham, contrary to conventional wisdom,[1] had another eventful summer in 1815. The activity had nothing to do with his election at Winchelsea since his return for Lord Darlington's pocket borough was a foregone conclusion. As in the summer of 1814, he was trying to influence the behaviour of government. Again, it was the French Government, only this time he was trying to effect change more through public opinion rather than through the good offices of the British Government. While the Roseberry divorce had been going through the Consistory Court and Parliament, Napoleon had escaped from Elba, and had returned to France to resume his tyrannical rule. Brougham had been a realist about French power as long as it seemed invincible, and he was willing to grant Napoleon a quiet retirement, once his well-established empire collapsed. After all, as Brougham well knew, the French emperor had withstood all attempts to unseat him for nearly a generation. A generous peace for a worthy adversary was one thing, but the treachery and betrayal which followed Napoleon's resumption of power were quite another. France was not only threatened by absolute chaos but also risked any hope of restoring a balance of power in Europe. If France persisted in Napoleon's crazy adventure, she might be carved up as part of the Holy Alliance's new order for Europe. It was essential, for Brougham, that Napoleon be crushed as soon as possible, and he was pleasantly surprised by the quickness with

1. See, eg, Chester W. New, *The Life of Henry Brougham to 1830* (Clarendon Press, Oxford, 1961) p.162.

which the Allies, under the Duke of Wellington, had done so at Waterloo on June 18. Brougham's task was to make sure that the restored monarchy prevailed.

He, as usual, set the scene for his effort in the pages of the *Review*. In analyzing critically Joseph Rey's *Adresse à l'Empereur*, and Benjamin Constant's *De la Responsabilité des Ministres*, he sided completely with the latter's view of the press as the palladium of society: "It is not only the grand source of hope for its advancement, but the only effectual security against its return to pristine wretchedness and barbarity."[2] The press was particularly important, he wrote suggestively, when systematic changes were required in society, as on the Continent in the wake of Napoleon's fall. Government by free discussion seemed unlikely when there was almost no protest when Louis XVIII eliminated the constitutional provision for a free press from the Charter. Constant, Brougham continued, had exposed the doctrine of passive resistance during the restoration, showing that France suffered "... from a tendency rather to venerate foolishly, than to complain without reason."[3] The result had been Napoleon's return to power. People should not venerate leaders, Brougham warned, explaining that "... for one evil which disobedience has brought upon mankind, there are tens of thousands to be traced to their slavish submission and acquiescence."[4] Francis Holt's strict ideas on the law of libel, Brougham added, just tended to legitimize such submissive behaviour by stressing that the magistrate was the servant of the law. This idea was a dangerous metaphor because officials were the servants of the people. The abuses of the press were minimized by more free discussion because "... it is undeniably certain, that the freedom of the press affords a complete remedy

---

2. Art.V, "Liberty of the Continental Press," *Edinburgh Review*, vol.25, no.XLIX, June 1815, p.112. New's ignoring this article in his text, when he cited it as one that Cockburn said Brougham wrote in an appendix, is baffling, especially since he had already debunked the idea that Brougham had been sick, the excuse now given for its note being his.
3. *Ibid.*, pp.117-8.
4. *Ibid.*, p.118.

for its own diseases ..."[5] Brougham repeated this sentiment in reviewing Sir N.W. Wraxall's scandalous *Historical Memoirs of my own Times* for the same issue.[6] However, Brougham concluded contemptuously, "according to English law, the greater the truth, the greater the libel."[7]

Brougham found a most effective vehicle for exploiting these ideas for the benefit of the restored regime of Louis XVIII in *The Times*. During the 1815 Session of Parliament, the stamp duties had been increased again, and the newspaper had led London's opposition to the measure. "Mr Vansittart went so far as to say that the increased taxes would be cheerfully paid, so anxious was the public for news."[8] *The Times* had considered the increase in the stamp and advertisement duties, and the pamphlet tax "obnoxious and prejudicial", and had called upon "the enlightened members of the Legislature" to defeat that part of the Chancellor's Budget. *The Times* had opposed the increases on principle, even if they gave it a news monopoly. Its willingness to confront the Ministry over the policy, and its public consequences were heightened when the restored Napoleon declared an embargo against *The Times*. The newspaper had long supported the cause of the Bourbons. Under the circumstances, Thomas Barnes felt obliged to hire Brougham to redress the situation. Brougham had advertised that he was ready for such a role in his review of Carnot's *Memorial* when he said that Europe looked to England as its Judge. He even made Carnot's translator, Goldsmith, sound like an identical convert to the Bourbon cause: "... the strenuous adviser of assassinating Buonaparte, from the moment that he lost his place of spy under him."[9]

No sooner had the captured Napoleon embarked for St Helena than "Probus" columns, apparently by Brougham, started

---

5. *Ibid.*, p.125.
6. Art.VIII, "Modern English History," *ibid.*, p.220.
7. Brougham, *op. cit.*, p.131.
8. A. Aspinall, *Politics and the Press* (Home & Van Thal, London, 1949), p.20.
9. Art.X, "M. Carnot's *Memorial*," *Edinburgh Review*, vol.24, no.XLVII, November 1814, p.188.

appearing in *The Times*. Napoleon ought to be punished by death, he wrote, rather than the French nation. The conspirators who made his return possible should suffer the same fate. All supporters of the deposed Emperor, especially Talleyrand, should be removed from office. Only by such actions could violence by the revolutionaries be stopped. "And if it be not eradicated in France," Brougham asked, "how is Europe ever to enjoy tranquillity?"[10] Conspirators like the Marets should be executed without mercy. "To save either of them from the gibbet," he added in typical English barrister style, "would be an act of equal folly and inhumanity."[11] Four days later, Brougham expanded upon what he wanted done to the deposed tyrant: "... I cannot but think, that the age will be for ever disgraced, and the cause of justice will endure a most fatal shock, if Napoleon Buonaparte be not brought to *solemn trial*, and to *public execution*."[12] Barring that, he fell back on his campaign against the slave trade for a proper punishment:

> If, however, the different powers of Europe, from motives of a weak and cowardly policy should be afraid to do justice upon this unparalleled villain, there is one place to which I should earnestly hope they would not refuse to send him. Let him be transported to Hayti; let him be put at the disposal of the countrymen of Toussaint; and I will venture to answer for it, that the blood of that just man will not long cry to Heaven unrevenged.[13]

To get readers to see Napoleon's acts as *malum in se*, answerable to the laws of nations, Brougham mentioned the fate of Captain Wright, the English officer who was allegedly murdered in a French prison.

In subsequent columns, Brougham expanded upon the need of executing Napoleon and the conspirators who brought him

---

10. *The Times*, July 22, 1815, no.9,580, p.3.
11. *Ibid.*
12. *Ibid.*, July 26, 1815, no.9583, p.2. Italics Brougham's.
13. *Ibid.*

back to power, of supporting the restored regime of Louis XVIII, and of *The Times* playing the role of the responsible opposition in French politics. The reasons for eliminating the deposed Emperor were put in these poignant terms in relation to Englishmen convicted of treason:

> I say, Sir, if Napoleon Buonaparte be not solemnly and publicly put to death, Colonel Despard was murdered, the self styled Admiral Parker, who headed the mutiny at the Nore, was murdered; in short, all the executions which have ever taken place in this or any other country for treason and rebellion, have been murders ...[14]

Napoleon's letter to the Prince Regent was denounced as an impertinence which should be met with summary justice. It was better to punish infamous leaders than the French nation which "... would create a sort of national Helotism in the civilized world; and would entirely destroy that balance of power, which is the best safeguard of civilisation."[15] Once the troublemakers had been shown exemplary punishments, Brougham would have full power given to the King's faithful servants: "... to them exclusively would be committed the care of the public revenue, or the public police, of the public instruction, and of the public defence."[16] The ravages of the past 25 years justified Brougham pursuing such a course in *The Times*. "Public opinion, in France", he explained, "has long ceased to follow anything but the actual display of force."[17]

Brougham started this series while he was in London, and apparently completed it at Brougham Hall. At least, that is where he wrote that he was going to Lord Grey in early August. It is interesting to note what he said about Napoleonic support in the same letter. "The accounts from France are quite dreadful, and the Duke and Duchess of Orleans, who were t'other day at

---

14. *Ibid.*, July 27, 1815, no.9,584, p.2.
15. *Ibid.*, August 3, 1815, no.9,590, p.2.
16. *Ibid.*
17. *Ibid.*, August 8, 1815, no.9,594, p.2.

Brocket Hall, gave, I understand, the most gloomy view of every thing."[18] Brougham's activities were not accounted for in his autobiography when he attributed his "sickness" to overwork, especially when he made the false claim that he did not contribute anything to the June 1815 issue of the *Review*.[19] Obviously, he was trying to cover up something. It certainly did not have anything to do with his activities as a barrister because he was not defending any cases, something, given his reputation, that he must have done by choice. He apparently used the excuse that he was taking a holiday at some coastal resort to return to Paris to view the scene first-hand. Brougham had visited Paris the previous summer to witness Napoleon's overthrow.

In a new series in *The Times*, entitled "Private Correspondence", he sought to correct the false impressions Englishmen had about French political sentiments. The Parisians were not for Napoleon but for the Bourbons. "They begin to consider what constitutes the real glory of a nation,"[20] he wrote, complementing what the French journals had to say on the subject. People who called for Napoleon's return were a small minority in the pay of conspirators like Labedoyere and Ney. The former had already been arrested, however, and the latter would not escape. In subsequent columns, Brougham harped on the importance of bringing these men to stern justice if France was going to return to the community of nations. He apparently helped provide the transcript of Labedoyere's trial, and witnessed his execution. While the French liked displays such as the Fete de St Louis, and Paris possessed an admirable police, they lacked much in the way of essential political organization. "Long, indeed, must it be, before France can possess such a body as our House of Commons."[21] Brougham urged the Opposition to press for freedom of the press, and for the retirement of expedient ministers like Talleyrand and Fouché. In fact, Brougham's articles

---

18. Brougham's letter to Grey, dated August 2, 1815: quoted from *The Life and Times of Henry Lord Brougham* (Harper, New York, 1871, 3 vols.), vol.II, p.221.
19. *Ibid.*, p.222.
20. *The Times*, August 12, 1815, no.9,593, p.3.
21. *Ibid.*, August 30, 1815, no.9,613, p.3.

became so popular that the French press extracted from them, and wondered who their author was. He was ultimately in a race against time to see Ney go before a firing squad before his identity became known. When the Court de Cassation ruled that only the House of Peers could Judge the French Marshal, Brougham returned to London in order to reduce the risks.

Apparently, he took over the running of the Printing House Square establishment upon his return. As leader after leader came out, calling continually for the execution of the ringleaders of Napoleon's return, and the exclusion from public service of those too closely associated with his regime, Brougham reserved himself for contributing the odd "Probus" column which would add to the legitimacy and support of the Bourbon regime. When he heard that the British Government was treating Napoleon as a king in exile, he exploded:

> Pray, Sir, let me ask at whose expense is this to be done? *Five hundred tons* of costly furniture are, it is said, to be despatched to St Helena. Who is to pay for this? Are the people of England to be taxed for such a purpose? Am I to pay a portion of my hard-earned income to indulge a monster, who I execrate and abhor, in luxuries and splendours, far beyond any to which my humble wishes ever ventured to aspire?[22]

Parliament was called upon to get to the bottom of such a waste of money. In another column, Brougham, it seems, challenged the supporters of Burke for not defending legitimate government in France: "Blind, indeed, must they be, who do not see, that the permanency of our own excellent constitution depends very mainly indeed on the final success or discomfiture of the French revolutionist."[23] France, like Britain, had an unwritten constitution, and Louis XVIII had to be permitted to re-establish it. Lawyers were seen as its guardian. Just before the next parliamentary Session, Brougham, in a column signed "M.B."

---

22. *Ibid.*, October 25, 1815, no.9,661, p.2. Italics Brougham's.
23. *Ibid.*, November 1, 1815, no.9,667, p.2.

(Maître Brougham apparently), was permitted to exploit this role in most reassuring terms: "England is, as France was before the revolution, a federation of divers political orders, of different corps, having each their common interests fixed and positive, their Constitutional rights, their privileges, franchises, and immunities."[24]

Thomas Barnes, in using Brougham to strike a middle course between editor Stoddard's ultra sentiments, and the Whigs' more radical ambitions towards France, tried to hide the fact as best he could. Once Brougham had returned from France, Barnes reported his activities while he had another reporter see that scores were settled with Marshal Ney. Brougham's presence at the colourful celebration of London's Lord Mayor's Day was prominently noted.[25] During Ney's trial, *The Times* gave most detailed coverage of the annual meeting of the British and Foreign School Society, especially Brougham's activities. His presence on the left of the chairman, the Duke of Bedford, was noted. Brougham's speech was fully reported. He mourned Whitbread's loss, calling upon the group to make sure that the blessings of peace were not lost. "For his own part, he should think those blessings but imperfectly restored, if they were not accompanied by a diminution of public burden ..."[26] Instead of prosecuting a religious war at home, something he feared would result from the rumoured Holy Alliance, he called for "... communicating knowledge and instruction to the minds of a people buried in ignorance and delusion."[27] Brougham did note, however, that Britain did have an opportunity to assist France in regaining responsible government. To make sure that people would not think that he was performing this role for *The Times*, it printed a most caustic review of General Pillet's account of Britain while a prisoner of war, concluding thus:

It was during this confinement, we presume, that he collected

24. *Ibid.*, January 27, 1816, no.9,742, p.2.
25. *Ibid.*, November 10, 1815, no.9,673, p.3.
26. *Ibid.*, November 27, 1815, no.9,689, p.3.
27. *Ibid.*

> the *materials* of this *excellent* work; and also found the leisure to put to paper several other curious observations, which he was desirous to have published in England, but the General, himself, gives us to understand, that these essays looked unluckily like lies, so barefaced and flagitious, that even Mr Brougham declined to notice them.[28]

Brougham's reviews for the *Review* were reserved, consciously so as to give the proper background for his efforts in *The Times*. As usual, the message sounded like a Speech from the Throne for a reform Administration. Regarding the restored Bourbons, he wrote, "... there never was a moment when the reasonable settlement of France was so important to itself, to its neighbours, and to posterity ..."[29] The present regime was a most fragile one, suffering from an unknown monarch, corrupted media, weak parties, and a restructured society, but it was the best hope for Europe and the French nation. "Seigniorial tyranny and ecclesiastical exaction had been entirely destroyed,"[30] he added. Louis XVIII, as a constitutional king, suffered from the fact that he had been restored to the throne by Allied arms, and he had to contend with democratic processes. As Napoleon had to contend with danger from without the country, Louis's problems, Brougham said hopefully, were wholly within. To avoid a recurrence of instability, he was advised to play an active part in restoring public order and confidence, something that seemed to be happening with the dismissals of Talleyrand and Fouché. Brougham warned against allowing the ultras, the counter-revolutionaries, to have their way. France was like England after the Glorious Revolution, and since she had re-established a reasonable constitution, should be allowed to sort out her own affairs. Brougham saved his most pressing concern, the destruction of France's military system and ideology, till the last, stating that she had to rid herself of them.

---

28. "Atrocious French Libel," *ibid.*, December 9, 1815, no.9,700, p.2. Italics its.
29. Art.XI, "France," *Edinburgh Review*, vol.24, no.L, October 1815, p.501.
30. *Ibid.*, p.506.

To make this message somewhat more palatable, Brougham had another review of Carnot's plight in the same issue. The reviewer was upset that only he, of Napoleon's restored ministers had been prescribed by Louis's decree of July 24. Unlike many of the others, Carnot neither knew nor assisted Napoleon's return to power. The regicide was made Minister of the Interior. "Does his acceptance of this office, and his discharge of its arduous duties," Brougham questioned, "constitute the ground of the decree against him?"[31] Brougham feared that the answer was yes, and that the Bourbon king only wanted to settle scores with the people who had destroyed his father rather than those who had ruined Europe. Carnot was a man of principle who had opposed all tyrannies. Instead of making one person suffer from a bill of attainder, Louis should have rooted out all the enemies of constitutional government. Brougham especially feared what effect such a partial approach to the restoration of stable government in France was having upon English politics. Liverpool's Ministry seemed to want to continue the nation on a war footing in case there was yet another coup. The people did not appear to care what the Ministry did. Civil liberty and constitutional government could be taken away, bit by bit, without any public protest. "Unless the whole fabric could be destroyed at once," he complained, "these men of cool sense see no real danger to the Constitution."[32]

In this frame of mind, Brougham developed his rationale against continuance of the income tax in a review of Walter Boyd's *Reflections on the Financial System of Great Britain*. Britain's war economy had to be given up because she could no longer afford it. The people had the right to be freed from every burden except those which were absolutely necessary. About the prospects of continuing emergency measures such as the property tax, he exclaimed:

Can any man pretend, that the people of England, would have

31. Art.VIII, "Carnot's *Defence*," *ibid.*, p.446.
32. *Ibid.*, pp.454-5.

> submitted to the income-tax, if they had not been told that it was for a season - and that beyond the moment of urgent necessity, no attempt would be made to enforce it?[33]

The income tax was portrayed as the instrument by which imprudent ministers could purchase what they wanted rather than what the nation needed. Brougham thought that it was so contrary to the constitution and individual security that its termination was a foregone conclusion. A general agenda for retrenchment, something that the Ministry was trying to put off by developing false threats, was promised in a subsequent issue.

Brougham's agenda for the new Session was completed by a call for a general registry of slaves. In reviewing the annual report of the African Institution, he hoped to pick up the matter where it had been left when Wilberforce's Bill to force a complete accounting of them had died the previous July. Stoppage of the illicit slave trade, he wrote, was essential if the slaves' condition was to be improved. Colonial legislatures had proved that they would do nothing for the Negroes, and the Crown had already established a partial register by Order in Council. Brougham explained the register's function thus, anticipating the role of many future Crown responsibilities:

> ... no one will be very anxious to have it recorded in his neighbourhood, and the fact also certified in England, that, during the last year, so many of his slaves died of blows or wounds; so many of overwork; and that there remain such and such a number, whose descriptions must be altered, in consequence of scars or mutilations.[34]

Such a record would have prevented Hodge, Brougham reminded *Review* readers, from doing what he liked with his slaves. The registry would cost some money, and require some administration, but it would define rights without risking the

---

33. Art.XIII, "British Finances," *ibid.*, p.548.
34. Art.II, "General Registry of Slaves," *ibid.*, p.338.

freeing of the slaves. The colonial legislatures, with their threats of non-compliance, were merely bluffing.

During the 1816 Session, Brougham became a complete politician in the modern sense of the term. After his defeat at Liverpool, he had been forced to concentrate upon his legal career, gearing his journalism to making the most politically out of his opportunities. Once returned to the Commons, he devoted himself completely to his political career, working as if he were the *de facto* leader of the Whig Opposition. Given the scope of the responsibilities, there was little time for his law practice. He not only had to become an expert on everything from agricultural distress to relations with Spain but also he had to take advantage of parliamentary procedure to achieve the results he wanted. He spoke over 200 times during the Session, calling for papers, questioning ministers, making motions, and debating in the House and in committee. He performed important work on at least three select committees. Brougham's journalism was geared completely to promoting the goals of these functions. His work with the *Review* trailed off to almost nothing, and he worked so closely with Barnes at *The Times* that it is rarely possible to distinguish his efforts from those of the editor. While one generally speaks of nineteenth-century politicians as part-time amateurs, this was rarely true of Brougham, particularly during the post-war years. He worked year round to promote liberty, prosperity, and limited government.

Brougham made his presence felt in Parliament immediately. Hardly had the Speech from the Throne been read, and ministerial spokesmen moved its adoption than he joined in. Vansittart, the Chancellor of the Exchequer, prompted the move thus:

> He had no difficulty in acknowledging that it was the intention of his Majesty's ministers to propose a renewal of the income tax, at 5 per cent. Upon the conviction that there was no mode of raising the necessary supplies less oppressive,

> or so economical. (*Cries of hear, from the opposition.*)[35]

Brougham received the largest coverage in *The Times* for supporting Brand's amendment, complaining about the government's failure to submit the actual peace treaties in time so that Parliament could give an informed evaluation of them. Fearing that Parliament would add harsh conditions to the settlement with France, Brougham took exception to the treaties that Britain had signed with the Iberian nations about the slave trade, fearing that she had agreed to *assiente* contracts with them. The thrust of his remarks was that the Crown had been far too soft with Spain's Ferdinand, whom he denounced as a contemptible tyrant, as well as his Foreign Minister, the notorious Don Cevallos. Brougham also hoped that Vansittart was not serious about maintaining the income tax, a challenge that the Chancellor met by stating that public burdens were not going to be reduced. Brougham responded: "There were laws that oppressed all classes of the community, which must be examined, and repealed."[36] The Corn and usury laws were examples and in addition "another subject, still more important, and to require consideration - the state of the poor laws."[37]

Brougham's reservation and challenge had the desired effect upon the Foreign Secretary. About the ideas of coercing Spanish officials, Castlereagh replied:

> He stood in his place to meet all attacks; but he deprecated the practice pursued by an hon. gentleman (Mr Brougham), of attacking foreign and independent sovereigns and states, in a place where they could not be defended. The noble lord was far from thinking with an honourable gentleman (Mr Brougham), that the address pledged the house of nothing.[38]

Castlereagh, at first, opposed Brougham's motion to postpone

---

35. *The Times*, February 2, 1816, no.9,747, p.3. Italics its.
36. *Ibid.*
37. *Ibid.*
38. *Ibid.*

consideration of the treaties, but he ultimately agreed. In the interim, Brougham moved without success an address to the Prince Regent, calling upon him to invoke British authority in Spanish affairs for the benefit of the late Regent and Cortes. Castlereagh took the bait, apparently not realizing the precedent it provided regarding France: "... foreign powers should not look upon the British legislature as arrogating a right to sit in judgment between them and their subjects, and as assuming a tone of dictation alike incompatible with their pride and their independence. *(Hear)*."[39] With Parliament so instructed about its role in foreign affairs, Brougham was happy to let the peace treaties come on. In fact, despite his hostile allusions about them,[40] he neither spoke nor voted against them. Brougham was very good at directing the Foreign Secretary.

Vansittart, not realizing what Brougham was trying to achieve through Castlereagh, decided to confront him squarely over the income tax. Early in the Session, when the House was in committee of supply, the Chancellor announced a continuation of the tax programme, stating that he proposed to raise six million pounds through the income tax. While the country was in temporary difficulty, it was not time for radical measures. Ponsonby, the Opposition leader, disagreed, and Brougham went through his agenda of tax changes needed for bringing the country out of depression. Vansittart was not interested in suspending the usury laws, repealing the wool export taxes, and equalizing the poor rate. Despite the support of *The Times*, the Chancellor thought that Brougham had adopted an unpopular position in supporting the end of the income tax, and wanted to make the most out of his embarrassment. Brougham spent the time presenting petitions against the income tax,[41] products of a campaign much like the one against the Orders in Council,

---

39. *Ibid.*, February 17, 1816, no.9,760, p.2. Italics its.
40. See, eg, *ibid.*, February 9, 1816, no.9,753, p.2. N.B. how Castlereagh reacted to the challenge: "... it was not to be endured that he should be thus questioned as to the manner in which foreign treaties might affect this country: this was really going too far."
41. *Ibid.*, February 23, 1816, no.9,765, p.2 and March 2, 1816, no.9,772, p.3.

contending that the government was just going through the motions by stating that it was interested in retrenchment. Brougham's apparent credibility in all this had been undermined by the Radicals' refusal to let him address a meeting of Westminster householders against it in Palace Yard. Brougham was undismayed, though, contending that the Ministry was rushing through the army estimates, and staying away from House meetings because it did not know what to do with the petitions against the income tax.

After Brougham had had a field day over the issue, attacking the government for wanting such a big budget for military fantasies, and for illegally disclosing individual returns, the Ministry decided finally to act. He forced the decision thus: "He (Mr Brougham) at present stood upon his own, for he had been accused of bringing forward charges night after night which could not possibly be immediately brought to issue, and with indulging in short-lived triumphs till he was silenced by a division."[42] Vansittart thought that he could force the issue by dismissing the protest as that of a small minority, activated by prejudice. The income tax, he said, after a long review of its history, was not just a war tax, and that he had made modifications in the rate to assist poor farmers. Brougham had banked everything on repeal, however, even using a pamphlet on the high prices of corn and labour as a pretext in the *Review* for demanding its end.[43] The review was too late for the vote, but it was not needed, as his confident conclusion of the debate indicated. Brougham countered Vansittart's claim that the tax was not a wartime measure by reading a section of the relevant act: "... the tax should continue during the war, and until April 4 next after the conclusion of peace, *and no longer*."[44] The Chancellor's proposal lost by a vote of 238 to 201. The Opposition went wild, and the humiliated ministers left the chamber, but later they thought better of leaving office.

---

42. *Ibid.*, March 14, 1816, no.9,782, p.2.
43. Art.VI, "Corn and Money," *Edinburgh Review*, vol.26, no.LI, February 1816, pp.135-56.
44. *The Times*, March 19, 1816, no.9,786, p.3. Italics its.

Repeal provided a positive impetus for taking Britain off a wartime basis. Ministers, despite Brougham's suspicions and doubts, did start economizing, and reform started being considered. He, as usual in such moments, let the triumph go to his head, and *The Times* compounded his error. He hoped to prove that the government had pressured the Excise Commission to dispense with penalties for smugglers for partisan advantage. *The Times*, hoping that further defeat would make the Ministry more tractable for reform, gave him free access to its columns to prove his case.[45] The Lords of the Treasury cooperated for their own advantage, postponing the supplying of accounts of seizures, and correspondence about them. The newspaper took advantage of the time to exploit Brougham's charges. While hoping that they were not true, it confessed "... that it does not augur well that so much *bashfulness* has been displayed by the parties immediately implicated, who seem resolute to postpone, to the latest possible moment, the documents on which alone they can be acquitted."[46]

When the documents were supplied, the case of John Abbott was stressed to show wasteful handling of corrupt practices for partisan advantage. When Brougham thought that the message had penetrated parliamentary circles, he moved a motion of censure against the Lords of the Treasury for how they used their discretion in a similar case, threatening a general vote of censure. Castlereagh was ready for Brougham this time, explaining that there was only one possible case of concern in an area where everyone was expecting the Treasury to ease the severity of the excise laws. "He really believed that the hon. gentleman would go to any lengths to have a temporary paltry triumph over the ministers."[47] The motion was badly defeated. Brougham saved some face, however, by soon showing that the Ministry would go to any lengths to try to save the income tax, calling for a circular letter from the Treasury, instructing surveyors of taxes

45. For the leaders concerned see *ibid.*, March 2, 1816, no.9,793, p.3; March 28, no.9,794, p.3; and April 2, 9,798, p.3.

46. *Ibid.*, March 27, 1816, p.3. Italics its.

47. *Ibid.*, April 3, 1816, no.9,799, p.3.

"... for full and complete copies of assessment of everyone's income."[48]

While the government did slowly retrench, recasting slightly the sources of its more limited revenue, it did at least think about reform, but not in the comprehensive terms Brougham wanted. His speech on agricultural distress, calling for the resumption of cash payments, poor law reform, and tithe adjustments, resulted in the select committee on the subject. The Ministry was willing to make conciliatory gestures in order to get its tough Aliens Bill, dictated by foreign policy, through Parliament. Brougham predicted that moves towards free trade "... would at least guard us against the great depression which may now be apprehended."[49] Brougham's Libel Bill, calling for the admission of truth in such actions, at least received a friendly hearing from the government, especially its Law Officers. The fact that all other evidence was admissible, Brougham explained, and that the Crown had stopped the use of *ex officio* informations before special juries called for law reform. "We had now arrived at quiet times", he said, "peculiarly fitted for a revision of this important chapter of the law."[50]

The Times, of course, gave Brougham complete access to its columns for the reform, declaring that freedom of the press was the "... ark and palladium of all our other liberties."[51] Brougham pushed for the Slave-Registry Bill, but it mattered little since Wilberforce was unwilling to force enactment. Slave uprisings in the West Indies, especially in the Barbados, which critics blamed unfairly upon the calls for the registry, clinched postponement. The Liberty of the Press Bill was given up for similar reasons, particularly because of the growing unrest that the Home Secretary, Lord Sidmouth seemed peculiarly inclined to exploit by Crown rewards. In fact, Brougham's most solid achievement of the Session was the appointment of a committee,

---

48. *Ibid.*, May 4, 1816, no.9,826, p.2.
49. "Speech on the Distressed State of Agriculture," in *Speeches of Henry Lord Brougham* (Black, Edinburgh, 1838, 4 vols.), vol.I, p.538.
50. *The Times*, May 9, 1816, no.9,830, p.2.
51. *Ibid.*, p.3.

dominated by liberals, to look into the education of the poor of the metropolis. The hope was that this would develop into an institutionalized way for eliminating ignorance, the root-cause of all social problems.

The problems of ignorance were becoming much more pressing because of social unrest, and law enforcement dominated by financial considerations. While the public was becoming increasingly concerned about the growing public disturbances in the Eastern Counties, and the Midland cities, H. Grey Bennet ultimately prevailed upon the Ministry to appoint a committee to investigate the police of the metropolis. Its reports were a revelation of how poorly paid, untrained, ill-disciplined police officers learned to survive, even thrive, in the urban wastelands. Brougham was extremely close to Bennet, having complete confidence in his ability to handle law enforcement. Bennet's reports showed the symbiotic but often highly anti-social relation that police were developing with criminals and publicans.

In fact, *The Times* was so impressed by the reports that it reprinted them. Their impact was dramatic upon Barnes, forcing him to assert his leadership over the paper a full year earlier than that stated by Derek Hudson in his biography of the former editor.[52] *The Times*'s elaboration of Brougham's complaints against the Lords of the Treasury for their handling of the Excise Commission shows that there was no basis to Hudson's claim that Brougham did not provide material for leaders before 1827. The testimony of people like the Middlesex magistrates about the police encouraging crime (until it became lucrative to suppress) convinced Barnes that he had to do something drastic. In the summer of 1816, he wrote to two leaders denouncing "blood-money" conspiracies in law enforcement. Barnes, knowing that something was terribly amiss at Bow Street, called for its quick exposure.[53] He was not pleased when the Home Office

52. Derek Hudson, *Thomas Barnes of The Times* (Cambridge Univ. Press, Cambridge, 1943), p.31.

53. *The Times*, July 18, 1816, no.9,890, p.2.

decided to take over the investigation from the magistrates.

To counter growing central control of law enforcement for what Barnes considered unconstitutional purposes, he decided to give more exposure to how it operated. Brougham apparently was made a roving reporter, a capacity that he could exploit by his attendance of the messe on the Northern Circuit, and his legal practice in London. Few would suspect that the barrister, suffering from a self-denying ordinance against employment in court, was, in fact, working as a correspondent. The work gave him a tremendous opportunity to take advantage of his retentive memory, critical abilities, and endless energy. His reporting had the added advantages of discussing cases *sub judice*, and in an explanatory fashion that no recognized court reporter would have the temerity to do.

Brougham's reporting, it seems,[54] first appeared in September 1816, covering the Lancaster Assizes where official pressure, particularly that of Manchester's Deputy Constable Nadin, seemed so effective in denying him legal work. After describing the stately spectacle of the Judges entrance into the palatial castle, Brougham mentioned what was scheduled to take place, especially the trial of a remarkable number of felonies which occurred in and around Manchester and Liverpool. The coverage was matter of fact until cases arose where the Bank of England appeared to be in collusion with the police in prosecuting forgery, and uttering actions.

These suits were recounted in larger than normal type. There was the case of Peter Montgomery who was sentenced to death for forgery on the basis of what an accomplice, working with the Bank's solicitor and Nadin, testified. Montgomery's snaring sounded like a typical Nadin job, and postponement of his arrest like another criminal operation - ie, the officer "... was delaying till he could obtain the means of conviction against similar offenders."[55] Crown Counsel Raine described the capture of an

---

54. For the conventional view of when this relation started and what it was, see Hudson, *op. cit.*, p.51.

55. "Lancashire Assizes," *The Times*, September 7, 1816, no.9,934, p.3.

utterer of forged money thus: "The prisoner was extremely cautious, but could not avoid the trap laid for him."[56] Another alleged utterer only escaped because she got caught up in a web against a more notorious offender. *The Times*'s account noted that the prisoners were not represented by counsel. Defendants "... are obliged, from poverty, to rely entirely on the Judge as their advocate, for stating the circumstances in their favour, and putting the most lenient interpretation to the jury of facts and expressions that admit of a doubtful meaning."[57]

The tonic effect of this account of the Assizes, whether transmitted by word of mouth, or other newspapers, was soon apparent. The very next day, Sarah Betley, the suspected utterer, escaped conviction when counsel Cross broke down the allegations of the Bank, Nadin, and his agents against the accused. In fact, Cross might have saved Montgomery if he had represented him, since he had exploded the story of Thomas Sutton, one of Nadin's agents: "... as he had not apprehended the prisoner at the time, and was not acquainted with her before, there was a doubt of his accuracy in identifying her person."[58] John Haslam, head constable of Rochdale who figured prominently in catching a notorious utterer, did not help the prosecution of Henry Cunliffe when he testified that he "... had received from the Bank many and liberal rewards; that he was better paid for detecting forgeries than for any other kind of police work; that he got handsome presents; that he would likely be rewarded liberally for the present prosecution ..."[59] Cross so convinced the jury of Cunliffe's good character, and probable innocent action, that he was acquitted. The presence of an aroused counsel in the defendants' corner, alerted by an enlightened public opinion, had converted the authorities' field day against "criminals" into a fiasco. Brougham, as counsel, given his reputation, could not have done so much for the prisoners.

When the next day's docket at the Assizes proved so routine

---

56. *Ibid.*
57. *Ibid.*
58. *Ibid.*, September 9, 1816, no.9,935, p.3.
59. *Ibid.*

that even Brougham dismissed it, declaring that the cases were devoid of "... any public interest whatever,"[60] Barnes made up for the deficiency in London, printing another excerpt from Bennet's committee on the police. This was the testimony of John Thomas B. Beaumont, a Middlesex magistrate. Beaumont was later to write a series on bills of sale in the *Law Times* which was published as a book. Here he took to task policemen, showing how they exploited poverty and ignorance in the City for their own advantage. Using the pub as a base, the officer worked with youths until they were suitable criminals to prosecute. "The thief-takers are thus interested in concealing and encouraging rising thieves until their crimes arrive at the highest growth,"[61] Beaumont testified. In order to end such a corrupt system, he called for comprehensive law reform, starting with a precise definition of substantive and procedural law. There was almost no interest in how to prevent crime, only in how to make it most rewarding. *The Times* highlighted his testimony by putting the most alarming aspects of his testimony in italics type.

In case readers were not getting the message, Brougham repeated it through two reviews in the September issue of the *Review*. To increase public support for candour in the discussion of political affairs, thereby establishing restraints against libel suits contrary to the public interest, he wrote:

> A minister of state who has committed, in the face of day, the greatest injustice or oppression, or whose incapacity has been testified by the most notorious blunders, may unblushingly avow his wrongs, or his incapacity, and punish whoever conscientiously and calmly states it to the country; or he may obtain the same end, by denying with still greater effrontery which is undubitable true, but what he knows must not be proved. The utmost readiness to prosecute, accordingly, has at different times been found, in persons conscious that the

60. *Ibid.*
61. "Police of the Metropolis," *ibid.*, September 9, 1816, no.9,936, p.2.

truth only has been proclaimed against them.[62]

While Brougham, in introducing his libel bill the previous Session, had stated that government had nothing to fear by the reform, he was now challenging Sidmouth to take him to court. In case the Home Secretary, who was busy trying to suppress urban unrest that the police, especially Nadin, were helping instigate, did not get the message, Brougham repeated it in a piece called "Dangers of the Constitution":

> Despotism is now grown old and weary. It has learnt how alone the people may safely be overcome: and its maxims, the result of long observation, are well worth our attention. One is, to change things without changing names - that something may be gained by surprise, and the vigilance of the enemy be evaded: - Another is, to be perpetually moving forwards, however slowly and silently: - A third, to choose the time when the attempt is the least expected. But the grand and ruling principle is to risk nothing - to go by steps - and never to move one foot until the other is safely planted.[63]

After an unprecedented delay, the Lancaster Assizes resumed, and Brougham was there to recount developments, especially those warranting public concern. Canning's action against rioters who tried to prevent his re-election at Liverpool drew his attention, especially when a police superintendent testified that he heard a troublemaker say: "There goes the Dock-police, the thieves, the robbers, let us murder them."[64] When the rioters were convicted, Brougham, tongue-in-cheek, said this about the court-appointed lawyer: "Mr Venables addressed the Jury for three of the prisoners, Murray, Cotterel, and Machale, but

---

62. Art.VI, "Liberty of the Press and its Abuses," *Edinburgh Review*, vol.36, no.LIII, September 1816, p.120. For more on this, see Trowbridge H. Ford, "Peterloo: The Legal Background," *Durham University Journal*, vol.LXXIV, no.2 (June 1982), p.218 ff.
63. Art.X, "Dangers of the Constitution," *ibid.*, p.252.
64. *The Times*, September 18, 1816, no.9,943, p.3.

adduced no tradictory evidence, or called any attestations to character."[65] In discussing a recovery action for damages against a debtor, Brougham editorialized thus about two other debtors languishing in Lancaster Gaol: "They have both been confined for nearly 20 weeks, and see as yet no prospect of a release, as their means are not increasing by their imprisonment."[66] In discussing *R.* v. *James Whelan and John Cummins*, a murder case, Brougham wrote:

> The principal witness was William Miller, at the head of the police in Liverpool, who stated the dispositions of Cummins, when he examined him, containing gross contradictions and falsehoods; but beyond presumption arising from this inconsistency, nothing appeared against the prisoners. The jury returned a verdict of *Not Guilty*.[67]

Brougham concluded his coverage of the Assizes with the case of Susannah Holroyd, an obvious madwoman who had poisoned her husband, son, and nursing infant after having had her fortune read, predicting these results. When she was sentenced to hang, Brougham noted sadly: "The prisoner, who had continued during the whole trial apparently insensible to her awful situation, and had even heard the word *guilty* without betraying any symptoms of emotion, seemed impressed with the solemn formalities and moving address that accompanied the delivery of her sentence."[68]

At the Assizes's conclusion, Brougham gave a devastating summary of its results. Despite the mitigating efforts by him and others, 31 prisoners had been convicted of capital crimes, and sentenced to death before Baron Wood, a Judge who had a good reputation as a lawyer.[69] Certain to be hanged were the two

---

65. *Ibid.*
66. *Ibid.*
67. *Ibid.* Italics its.
68. *Ibid.* Italics its.
69. Sir William Holdsworth, *A History of English Law* (Methuen, London, 1952, 14, vols.), vol.XIII, p.500 ff.

utterers, Montgomery and Boyd, whom Nadin and his associates had been instrumental in indicting and convicting. Four burglars of a house in Toxteth, convicted by an accomplice, were similarly doomed. During their trial, Brougham had remarked: "All the prisoners cross-examined this witness, as they had no counsel, but their questions tended to criminate themselves."[70] About 11 unfortunates convicted of highway robbery, Baron Wood warned them to prepare for death, "... as his Lordship was uncertain whether the sentence of any or all of them could be mitigated, but was afraid some examples must be made of the highest punishment known to the laws."[71] The token sentences that the Liverpool rioters received were contrasted with the terms of transportation that persons possessing forged Bank notes, and uttering counterfeit coin were given. The coverage of the trials concluded with a grisly account of the execution of Mrs Holroyd, a person more deserving humanitarian incarceration than the taunts of the mob at the hanging.

In preparation for the "blood-money" trials of Bow Street officers, Brougham positioned himself in the Old Bailey, covering the Crown's prosecution of James Turk for murder.[72] The report was by far the most extensive of any trial in this court in the paper's history. No sooner was Turk declared innocent than the paper reported that officer George Vaughan had been convicted by a Middlesex jury of conspiracy to commit household burglary. This Bow Street officer was given five years, and fined 80 for conniving with others in the crime "... that they might afterwards obtain the reward for their apprehension."[73] Vaughan carried a diary which indicated that he had long been involved in the trade. About such activity by police officers, prosecutor Turney declared: "... great in proportion was the guilt of those, who, for the sake of obtaining these rewards, should lay traps and throw temptations in the way of others, to induce them to commit

---

70. *The Times*, September 17, 1816, no.9,942, p.3.
71. *Ibid.*, September 24, 1816, no.9,948, p.3.
72. *Ibid.*, September 21, 1816, no.9,946, pp.2-3.
73. *Ibid.*, September 23, 1816, no.9,947, p.3.

crimes."[74] Vaughan supplied tools for the burglary, and knew of its location before it occurred. The next day, Vaughan appeared at the Old Bailey, charged with aiding and abetting another burglary. When the principal was only convicted of stealing, Vaughan's counsel tried to get his case dismissed, but Attorney General Garrow would not hear of it. Vaughan was found guilty.

On the next day three more policemen were charged with counterfeiting coin, and conspiring to involve others in a capital felony. One police officer, Brock, had already carried out a similar operation, and had plans for two more. The three Irish lads coerced into crime were only saved from the gallows by the intervention of their priest who obtained pardons for them from Sidmouth. Garrow again prosecuted the case vigorously, and Brougham gave him prominent coverage in *The Times*: "They had almost sacrificed the lives of the three poor Irishmen, comparatively innocent to themselves, to satisfy their own atrocious love of lucre."[75] The Attorney General said that conviction for such a heinous crime would be the proper way for the presiding Judge, Justice Burrough, scheduled to retire, to finish his career. Defence attorney Alley had only a procedural mitigation for the policemen's crimes, which the Judges overruled. Alley tried to make out their offences did not constitute high treason, what they were charged with, since they were only accessories to something less than plotting the King's murder. Burrough, in summing up for the jury, said that if it believed the principal witnesses, the accused "... were implicated in procuring the three Irishmen, getting them the implements, and setting them to work for the purpose of coining."[76] The presiding Judge admitted that the prisoners did not actually intend to utter the coins, constituting a crime whose punishment would have to be reserved for the Court of Exchequer Chamber. Brock and the others were found guilty.

---

74. *Ibid.*
75. *Ibid.*, September 26, 1816, no.9,950, p.3.
76. *Ibid.*

In providing this coverage for *The Times*, Brougham met the challenge that William Cobbett had presented in his weekly: "... I wish he was not a *lawyer*; and that he would convince us, by some overt act, that time had cured him of attachment to the principles of Fox, and has made him see, that *a radical reform of Parliament* is necessary to the restoration of our freedoms ..."[77] As a journalist, the Whig barrister had tried to show that a vigorous assertion of one's rights could restore the balance of Fox's beloved Whig constitution. Brougham had a challenge for Cobbett now: Was the rural radical a legitimate reformer, or did he agitate for absurd changes, like universal suffrage and annual parliaments, to foment counter-revolution? Barnes presented Cobbett with this dilemma in a November 1816 leader, recalling allegations that he had offered himself up as a government agent to get out of prison after his conviction for seditious libel in publishing the article against flogging.[78] *The Times* took the strongest exception to Cobbett's latest pamphlet, "Friends and Fellow-Countrymen", stating that he showed himself to be no friend of the distressed labourer by calling Members of Parliament "thieves and convicts". In alluding to the letters to officials that had been published, once Cobbett had been released from prison, the newspaper was challenging him to really show his colours or face the consequences. When the Radical agents Dyall and Preston reacted by calling for a meeting of the distressed of the metropolis, *The Times* responded: "... it would be a curious circumstance that the conversation of these obscure individuals at night over their beer, should lead to any disturbance, or what is still more unlikely, to any public benefit."[79]

Barnes and Brougham were surprised by events. Not only did the Radical meeting take place, but it soon led to the Spafield riots. The immediate purpose of the meeting was to frame petitions to the Prince Regent and Parliament for relief. *The Times*

---

77. *Cobbett's Weekly Political Register*, vol.XXX, no.9, col.271. Italics Cobbett's.
78. *The Times*, November 14, 1816, no.9,992, p.2.
79. *Ibid.*, November 15, 1816, no.9,993, p.2.

called its organizers the real enemies of the poor, "... the men who make sedition a trade, and grow rich by promoting the intoxication of the minds and bodies of their unfortunate customers."[80] While Barnes appealed to Lord Sidmouth to reduce the explosive tendency of the situation, the Home Secretary preferred to allow the police a free hand, refusing to have the Crown contest the appeal of Vaughan's conviction. The Exchequer Chamber was persuaded by Attorney Curwood that the crime was simply stealing, illegal gain in which Vaughan's accomplice was completely to blame, and prosecutor Bolland was willing to let it go at that.[81] Nowhere in sight was Attorney General Darrow who had described the original crime as a conspiracy. Ultimately, the court decided to quash the conviction, and Vaughan was given a pardon.

The message to the police was that the Crown and the courts would look the other way when it came to law enforcement involving the instigation of crime, and individual police officers raised their sights in order to manipulate an increase of rewards. When another meeting assembled at Spafields to receive the Prince Regent's answer, a party, completely prepared to start an insurrection, broke away from the assembly, and attacked an arms dealer, believing that the nation was ready for a violent revolution. Hardly a constable was in sight to keep order. The law enforcement establishment, starting with people at Bow Street and ending with spies like Oliver, Thistlewood and Castle was learning that if the distressed would not make trouble, they would be made to appear to.

Brougham, like most people, was confused by these developments, mistaking appearances for reality. At first, he tended to think that the problem was merely one of steering a course of practical reform through Parliament in order to avoid an arbitrary government or a more arbitrary mob, not appreciating the role that officials, especially policemen, were playing to help promote both alternatives. In the *Review*, he was

---

80. *Ibid.*
81. For an account of the hearing, see *ibid.*, November 18, 1816, no.9,995, p.3.

almost at a loss as to what to do during the coming Session. Though he had long supported Bentham on the abolition of usury laws, now was not the time to provide a long-term check on fraud, oppression, prodigality, and projects: "At present, the smallest movement may reach further than it is easy to calculate, or pleasant to conjecture."[82] Brougham could only bring himself to go along with Bentham on the abolition of law taxes, the most unjust tax of them all. They just spawned litigation, Brougham explained, for criminal purposes. In fact, Brougham was so convinced that things were in such delicate balance, that he reverted to his days at Edinburgh, at least in fancy. Reviewing a pamphlet on Columbus, a translation of a letter on his return from the New World made him recall what Dr Robertson had said about the explorer:

> ... he makes no mention of the source of the incidents, the most touching him personally in the course of his voyage, thus, he says nothing of the discontents and the mutiny of his crew; the alarm excited by the variation of the compass; the loss of his vessel by ship wreck in the West Indies, the desertion of Puson; the separation of the Pinto.[83]

Brougham would take a page from Columbus's memoirs when it came time to write his own.

The 1817 Session was far worse than Brougham bargained for. No sooner had the Prince Regent read the Speech from the Throne than a new alarm was raised, because his coach was attacked. It was thought that shots had been fired at it, a thing that Arthur Thistlewood and James Watson, Jr, suspects of the Spafields riots still at large, were believed capable of. It was just the previous week that the trial of Spafield rioters had occurred, with the acquittal of all of them, except John Cashman, of high treason.[84] The jury had been unpersuaded that these Spenceans,

---

82. Art.III, "Defence of Usury," *Edinburgh Review*, vol.27, no.LIV, December 1816, p.356.
83. Art.X, "Columbus", *ibid.*, p.503.
84. "Trial of the Rioters," *The Times*, January 21, 1817, no.10,050, pp.2-3.

especially James Watson, Sr, were collectively trying to effect a social revolution on the order of the Jacobins. The suspect of the new offence had a startling confession for the police in the affair: "The prisoner, being called upon for his defence, denied the charge; but said, he supposed somebody must be apprehended, and he had been selected for the reward."[85] Actually, he had called attention to himself by his loud, violent behaviour. When he was told that there would be no public reward for his conviction, he insisted that there would be a private one. The perpetrator of the "pop-gun" plot, an exaggerated stone-throwing incident in which a pane of glass was broken in the Prince Regent's carriage, was never caught, but the incident had the desired effect upon parliamentary affairs, with the ministers opting for the suspension of habeas corpus to meet the crisis.

Henry Brougham continued to believe that the greatest threats to the constitution were economic ones, especially the droits of the Admiralty, and the possible resumption of the income tax both of which could increase government favour through patronage. The creation of the Commons' secret committee to investigate the attack on the Prince Regent was treated as a matter of course, with only him having the temerity to name the composition of a most serious inquiry, when Brougham's prediction proved completely true, an objective explanation of the causes of unrest seemed unlikely. He likewise understood the role that Lord Cochrane and Burdett could play in the repressive process by their introduction of petitions, calling for annual parliaments and universal suffrage. "The men who made these statements", he said, "must know they were propagating delusions; and that truth and fact were against them."[86] When they persisted in wildly submitting petitions highly damning of Parliament, forcing Canning to get the Speaker to rule that only those petitions which had been read by Members could be introduced, Brougham was forced to intervene:

---

85. "Prince Regent", *ibid.*, January 27, 1817, no.10,057, p.3.
86. *Ibid.*, February 1, 1817, no.10,060, p.2.

> If, instead of shutting the doors of Parliament to the petitions of public meetings, if, instead of taking any severe methods preventing these meetings from assembling to petition, an attempt was made to convince them by sound reasoning and rational argument, much would be done to conciliate their minds, and to allay their irritation; much would be done to the cause of good order and constitutional liberty. (*Hear, hear, from all parts of the house.*)[87]

While Brougham concentrated his complaints on the splendours of the court, the police, especially Nadin's minions in Manchester, were filling the secret committees with such alarms that the government decided to arrest the Spencean troublemakers under Sidmouth's warrants. "Private information of a certain character having been received by his Lordship," *The Times* explained, "a Cabinet Council was summoned on Saturday, and the warrants were issued that evening ..."[88] Brougham could only complain thus of action which preempted Parliament: "If it was too early yet to form an opinion with regard to a spirit of disturbance, it was certainly too early to proceed to act upon it: yet, within the last 24 hours, there were certain practical considerations drawn against the conduct and spirit of the people ..."[89] He was particularly concerned with the conclusions being drawn about the activities of the Radicals Knight, Mitchell, Benbow and Ogden at Manchester's St Peter's Church. Their attempts to petition Parliament for redress, what had involved Brougham in an argument with Cochrane, were being portrayed as the portent of a general uprising. Soon rumour was connecting Arthur Thistlewood, its supplier of arms, with Colonel Despard's plot, the last treason conspiracy.

The government responded by introducing bills to tighten treason and sedition acts, and to prevent seditious meetings and habeas corpus. "The whole of these measures," Brougham

---

87. *Ibid.* Italics its.
88. *Ibid.*, February 12, 1817, no.10,069, p.2.
89. *Ibid.*, February 11, 1817, no.10,068, p.2.

complained, "appeared to have originated in a design to distract and divide their political opponents, as well as to divert attention of the country from the necessary redress of its grievances."[90] The proposals, nonetheless, were passed by overwhelming majorities. In fact, the Ministry was so confident of matters that it saw to the indictment of four Manchester radicals for high treason, and to the execution of Cashman, the leading troublemaker of the Spafield riots. Only *The Times* was keeping abreast of the source of the hanging: "... during the preceding evening bills were distributed with the following inscription: 'Remember, boys, that Cashman is to be murdered tomorrow! What has become of the conspirators!' - (meaning Vaughan, Brock, Pelham and others)."[91]

While the police, especially Bow Street Constable Nichols, tried, through provocative agents, to prove that Britain was in the throes of a revolution, Brougham raised the possibility of preventative measures. In March, he delivered another great speech on the depressed state of trade and manufacturers. Commercial policy, taxation, and foreign policy were blamed for the unprecedented depression. British production and trade had reached record levels at the end of the war, only to see the government continue wartime, adventuresome policies at the expense of the domestic market, he complained. The resulting unemployment and misery could not simply be suppressed. Stock Market activity, after the Ministry's call for the suspension of habeas corpus, he explained, went up, showing that either the Spenceans did not exist, or they represented no threat, a direct contradiction of the Prime Minister's explanation of the crisis.[92] While his motion was defeated by a comfortable majority, Brougham was not dissuaded from seeking practical remedies for Britain's condition. One day towards the end of March, he acted no less than a dozen times on the floor of the Commons, presenting petitions, making motions, asking questions, and

90. *Ibid.*, February 25, 1817, no.10,080, p.3.
91. "Execution of John Cashman," *ibid.*, March 13, 1817, no.10,094, p.4.
92. *Ibid.*, March 14, 1817, no.10,095, p.2.

moving amendments, to try to deflect government policy from a repressive course to a remedial one.[93] It was only after this policy had clearly failed, the government having gone to the extreme of preventing even philosophical discussion, that Brougham called for it to exercise its extraordinary powers with great caution.

Exposing the process by which law enforcement became the overriding political issue was *The Times's* first priority. It patiently recorded how false leads by constables like Nichols, because of tips by Manchester's police, spiralled into ever-increasing alarms which threatened to engulf the kingdom. By the end of March, the plans emerging from Manchester's St Peter's Church had resulted in mass arrests, based on the fear that the Midland cities were going to be attacked. There was a story that a rocket signal from the church would trigger armed assaults on the factories.[94] As Nadin's men were again rounding up Manchester radicals for conspiring allegedly to terrorize the Prince Regent by means of an armed procession 5,000-men strong, the police in other Midland cities were equally inventive, and prophylactic. The Spenceans, it seems, had created a whole network which threatened to have the distressed, particularly "The Blanketeers", march on the citadels of power in provocative fashion. A great catalyst in spreading the fantastic story had been the long-anticipated capture of the ubiquitous Thistlewood just when it was feared that he had escaped to America with the other trouble-makers, like Cobbett. By the time the plan had resulted in riots at Nottingham and Derby, instigated by provocative agents on the assumption that they were part of a general uprising, *The Times* asked: "Who could have led them on by the unfounded assurances of this nature?"[95] the *Leeds Mercury*, whose reports were reprinted by the London paper, identified the source as a man named Oliver who "... was, in truth, a spy, and that every step taken towards the execution of the project

93. *Ibid.*, March 29, 1817, no.10,108, p.2.
94. *Ibid.*, p.3.
95. *Ibid.*, June 17, 1817, no.10,175, p.3.

had been communicated to persons in authority, as the plot appears to have been known by some of the magistrates for several weeks past."[96]

Brougham, as in the past, was in court to expose these excesses when the time came, not as a barrister but as a reporter for *The Times*. Having made the most of the ineffectiveness of the Seditious Assembly Bill when it went through Commons, claiming that a group of radicals might "... meet in Westminster Hall, within a pistol shot of Parliament",[97] he detailed at great length what the Crown had done to separate prisoners indicted for treason because of the Spafield riots from spectators, and the trial from society. The incarceration of the prisoners, especially Thistlewood and James Watson, Sr, was described as if the inmates of the Tower were already on death row. When the King's Bench trial finally commenced in Westminster Hall, it was so well guarded that Sergeant Copley complained that his clients could not get a fair trial, obliging Ellenborough to have a dozen constables removed.[98] "The Court has warned," Brougham reported provocatively, "such as publish any part of the proceedings before it is concluded that they will incur the penalties of a contempt."[99] Brougham was not dissuaded, though, from repeating the testimony of the police officer who captured the Spencean Dr Watson, and his accomplice, the famous spy Castle. Because of a vigorous defence by a team of lawyers, Watson was acquitted. Castle, whose testimony had already resulted in the hanging of one man, and the transportation of another, Brougham complained, "... was brought, newly clothed, fed, and paid, into a Court of Justice, to swear a crime against a third accomplice, and that crime the greatest that is known in society, and leading to the most

96. "Horrible Plot of Spies and Informers to Encite Insurrection," *ibid.*, p.4.

97. *Ibid.*, April 1, 1817, no.10,110, p.2.

98. "The Trials for Treason," *ibid.*, June 10, 1817, no.10,169, p.3. For public recognition of Broughams role in protecting individual rights, see "Mansion-House Festivities," April 8, 1817, no.10,116, p.3.

99. *Ibid.*

dreadful punishment."[100] Brougham was appalled that the rights of Englishmen had been curtailed because of the leadership of such a troublemaker. Barnes underlined the message for his readers by publishing a most critical leader, and by reprinting a most damning article from the *Leeds Mercury*. "Nothing could equal the horror which was excited everywhere in London last night," he recorded, "when the narrative of this most disgusting transaction was reported."[101]

Brougham, who had taken an unprecedented seven-day leave from the Commons to cover the trial, was ready to spread the narrative throughout the country. Perhaps, to better hide his identity as the dutiful barrister who used his time in court to better advantage, he finally defended a case in one of the lower courts. For two years, Brougham had been reduced to arguing Scotch appeals without much success before the Law Lords.[102] In July, he represented Lieutenant Kent of the 21st Dragoons in an inquisition to assess damages for the criminal conversation that his wife had had with its Colonel. "The plaintiff could not have entertained the slightest suspicion that he was a person likely to form a deliberate plan of seduction,"[103] Brougham charged against the defendant. Colonel Sorell was godfather to one of Kent's children. He was even persuaded by the adulterer to return from the Cape to London to enhance his career, a cruel hoax that Sorell used to steal his wife. Brougham asked for ample damages in compensation, and the jury quickly agreed, awarding Kent 3,000. The defendant in the action at the Secondary's Court had permitted Brougham to gain an easy fee by allowing the case to go by default. This must have been some consolation when

---

100. *Ibid.*, June 17, 1817, no.10,175, p.3.
101. *Ibid.*
102. For Brougham's fruitless labours in the Lords, see *Sharpe* v. *Bickerdyke*, P. Dow, ed, *Reports of Cases ... in the House of Lords* (Clarke, London, 1814), vol.II, p.102 ff; *Davison* v. *Robertson, ibid.*, p.218 ff; *Newcastle Fire Insurance Co.* v. *Macmillan and Co., The English Reports, House of Lords* (Green, Edinburgh, 1901) vol.III, p.1057 ff; *Mucklow* v. *Attorney General, ibid.*, p.1069 ff; *Maxwell* v. *Gordon, ibid.*, p.1165 ff; *Steel* v. *Steel, ibid.*, p.1257 ff; *MacDowal* v. *Buchen, ibid.*, p.1275 ff; *Towart* v. *Sellars, ibid.*, p.1314 ff; and *Burdett* v. *Abbot*, and *Burdett* v. *Colman, ibid.*, p.1289 ff.
103. *Kent* v. *Sorell, The Times*, July 7, 1817, no.10,191, p.3.

he was obliged to argue unsuccessfully two days later in the Lords Sir Francis Burdett's most belated complaints against the speaker and the Sergeant-at-Arms for illegal trespass when they forcibly incarcerated him at the Tower in 1810.

Brougham set no such easy task for himself either when he decided to expose at the Summer Assizes the horrible plots that government-inspired spies had tried to instill among the distressed for its own purposes. Just when Henry Hunt was making much of Brougham's refusal to defend Dr Watson at a dinner celebrating his release from ministerial persecution,[104] the barrister was making so much of government contrivance against the Huddersfield rioters that he had to play the role of both reporter and concerned reader. In the wake of the spirited defence against the Crown before Baron Wood at the York Assizes, Brougham apparently commented:

> Of the 25 persons committed on charges connected with the late riots in the neighbourhood of Huddersfield, only eight were brought to trial and acquitted; against the greatest number no bill was found; two traversed; and *Thomas Riley*, one of the rioters, a tailor, stands charged under a warrant from Lord Sidmouth on suspicion of high treason. With the omission of the rioters, and those against whom no bill was found, the calendar was not numerous for such a county as York, in such a season of distress ...[105]

For those readers who were impatient to hear more about the encouraging results, Brougham wrote such a quick letter to the editor Barnes about the role of provocative agents in the affair that he had to be the person providing the coverage.[106] *The Times* repaid Hunt for his premature, ignorant swipe at Brougham by reprinting an article from the *Leeds Mercury*, celebrating the freed prisoners' triumphal return to Huddersfield.

---

104. *Ibid.*, August 1, 1817, no.10,213, p.3.
105. *Ibid.*, August 2, 1817, no.10,214, p.3. Italics its.
106. *Ibid.*, July 29, 1817, no.10,210, p.2.

The Crown's prosecutions, it explained, had been overturned by Baron Wood when he learned that critical depositions, which it had refused to supply, had not been taken under oath. The article indicated that the defence had much in reserve about the government's spy system if the Crown had persisted in the prosecutions.[107] Barnes's subsequent leaders stressed the disparities between what the government had been able to achieve through Green Bags of evidence in Parliament, and the trials at London and York.

Sidmouth had been badly beaten, and he knew it. He wrote confidentially to a Bolton magistrate, prosecuting "The Blanketeers", to drop charges, fearing that Brougham would simply inflame matters. The Home Secretary, with his contacts in the press, knew exactly what Brougham was doing in the courtroom, and at Printing House Square, and he wanted to cut his losses. The changes at the Lancaster Assizes had been dramatic. In April, *The Times* had noted, for example, the great contrast in the treatment of *R.* v. *William Abbott*, another incident involving rockthrowing at a carriage like the Prince Regent's. This time, though a reward had been offered, there were no witnesses forthcoming with wild stories about public unrest, and the Judge had no interest in exorbitant reprisals. The police were more interested in sending people such as Ann Lord to the gallows. In fact, John Ireland, who had been deputed by a constable to entrap her, bragged so much about soliciting persons to commit capital crimes that Baron Wood had to caution him to be more careful about his testimony.[108] While she had been sentenced to death, and another prisoner, her brother, was actually executed, the Home Secretary had been obliged to save her. At the September Assizes which heard the case of "The Blanketeers", the Crown, because of Sidmouth's initiative, was very weak. In dropping charges against them, prosecutor Topping explained to Barnes who thought that the government was resorting unnecessarily to the use of spies: "It cannot be the wish of any

---

107. *Ibid.*, August 5, 1817, no.10,216, p.3.
108. "Assize Report," *ibid.*, April 14, 1817, no.10,121, p.3.

government, and especially of our government, to punish unnecessarily."[109] The Crown was, it seems, satisfied that respectable people had seen to the restoration of order.

Brougham had better things to do than to be present at York. He was off to Paris again, to cover "The Black Pin" trial, a preview of what to expect in the trial of the "Pentridge rising" at the Derby Assizes in October 1817. The activities of the Princess of Wales were also a cause of concern. The Paris trial had all the earmarks of English treason trials, with police spies who could instantly remind readers of counterparts like Thistlewood and Oliver. The "plot" was obviously officially inspired in order to rebound to the benefit of the restored monarchy. In reporting the trial, he took liberties that he could never have taken in an English one: "Some English of distinction were present; and we particularly remarked Lord Holland and Mr Brougham."[110] In fact, he engaged in a bit of licence by repeating his presence in the next day's account. The accused, as at Lancaster, were all acquitted, and their counsel, despite warnings from the Judge, made most damning charges against the government and police in the affair.

Brougham did not restrict his licence to the courtroom, but, for once, even he was unwilling to talk about it. During the summer of 1816, he had run off to Geneva with Caroline Lamb, "Caro George", the wife of George Lamb. Brougham soon grew tired of her company, finding her utterly boring except in bed. In 1817, he was again seeking her company while in Paris. He also became involved in trying to sort out the money problems which Harriette Wilson was having with the Duke of Beaufort, her "common law" husband. While Dr Bourne postponed any serious affair Brougham had with her until after his marriage in 1819 to Mary Ann Spaulding,[111] this hardly seems in keeping with Brougham's temperament and style. He was a fun-loving bachelor who did not worry too much about the consequences

---

109. *Ibid.*, September 9, 1817, no.10,246, p.3.
110. "Private Correspondence," *ibid.*, October 6, 1817, no.10,269, p.2.
111. Kenneth Bourne, ed, *The Blackmailing of the Chancellor* (Lemon Tree Press, London, 1975), p.19 ff.

of his actions. Certainly, any affair he had while still unmarried was more in the interest of the kept-women to keep secret. While the Duke of Wellington, when threatened by Miss Wilson with blackmail, replied, "Publish and be damned", it is easy to imagine Brougham reacting similarly to any threat. After his marriage to Mrs Spaulding, however, a most unstable woman who provided him with a most unexpected heir, he became more sensitive to any threats, as we shall see. For critics of Brougham who like to make much of such things, they should remember that he at least preserved the letters for posterity, by which they can make their case. One can only wonder how many other friends of hers capitulated generously to her threats, and destroyed their letters.

Once back in England, Brougham had no time for such things, as the columns of *The Times* show. To hide his role, Barnes published criticism of his work in the *Review*. In the August 1817 issue, Brougham had a most innocuous review of a volume of Franklin's correspondence, and two hard-hitting reviews on West Indian and domestic affairs. The latter stressed how the Ministry was using unjustified alarm to sanction reaction. In a review of John Williamson's study of West Indian slavery, he showed how the doctor's description and analysis of slavery contradicted his own justifications of it. Brougham pictured the recent disturbance in the Barbados as just another pretext exploited for ministerial purposes and policies. "The most credulous alarmist has seen enough to make him doubt,"[112] he explained. In discussing internal administration, he was even more forthright: "We are convinced that real representation and frequent elections are the best means of securing good government."[113] The Spenceans were portrayed as a foolish irrelevancy. Sidmouth was seen as the head of the police who could well pay troublemakers like Thistlewood, and spies like Castle and Oliver to justify repression. These avowed government agents had been let off, Brougham complained, after they had instigated crime. The Prime

---

112. Art.IV, "Present State of Public Affairs," *Edinburgh Review*, vol.28, no.LVI, August 1817, p.348.
113. Art.XI, "Present State of Public Affairs," *ibid.*, p.522.

Minister's justification of informers and spies was denounced, citing Earl Fitzwilliam's change of heart over the suspension of habeas corpus, once he was informed of Oliver's activities in Yorkshire. "We must now call on all reflecting men," Brougham demanded, "to look at this system ..."[114] In the face of this indictment, however, Barnes could only imitate Stoddart's earlier criticism of Brougham finding fault with his inelegant praise of Dr Franklin.[115] When readers complained about the editor's narrow criticism, Barnes only obfuscated about another article in a harmless way,[116] indicating that Brougham himself may well have written the letters to the editor.

Brougham arrived back in England just in time to cover the "Pentridge uprising" at the Derby Assizes. Ever since the Crown had given up on "The Blanketeers", *The Times* had been gearing for this showdown with the government over the suspension of the Constitution for no apparent cause. When the indictment was presented to the grand jury against the prisoners for levying war against the King, and trying to depose him, the newspaper had a reporter on the scene to recount every detail.[117] For a fortnight, Barnes hammered away at the fantastic story that the Crown was attempting to prove against the 50 ringleaders. On October 16, *The Times* recounted the steps that Thomas Denman was taking to save Jeremiah Brandreth, William Turner, Isaac Ludlam, and George Weightman from the gallows. Counsel's argument was that they had tried to assemble a body of men under false pretences for the purposes of certain unknown parties and Oliver Denman tried to delineate responsibility between leaders and followers of the fiasco, drawing the line as to Weightman's guilt. In this, he was successful, and the Crown was willing to let the others plead guilty as charged, with the understanding that they would be spared the traitor's death. For this, Denman earned Brougham's enduring friendship and gratitude. Their close relationship would have some rocky

114. *Ibid,.* p.542.
115. "Edinburgh Review," *The Times,* September 25, 1817, no.10,268, p.2.
116. *Ibid.,* October 4, 1817, no.10,268, p.2.
117. "State Trials," *ibid.,* October 6, 1817, no.10,269, p.3.

moments, as when Brougham became Peel's "second Chancellor", but it never broke, as with so many others.

Brougham's efforts at Derby were no less prodigious than Denman's. He was *The Times* court reporter apparently, starting on October 21, as the "Trials for Treason" columns indicate. It is, indeed, bizarre that Hudson should single out this issue to mark Barnes's takeover, subjecting it to a most prosaic analysis. "It will be agreed that it lacks co-ordination and is badly balanced."[118] Actually, no such thing should be admitted. Instead of talking about layout in contemporary terms, and content in abstract ones, he should have tried to understand what Barnes was attempting - ie, to beat the government at its own game through Brougham's efforts. If one reads the column from Derby on that day, one soon discovers that it was explosive. Due to Brougham's credentials, he learned from Brandreth's jailer that he gained his leadership experience in the army, and by leading poor Luddites. The *Courier's* efforts to prejudice the trial for the prosecution, something that Denman had complained about to the Lord Chief Baron, was graphically illustrated. Instead of there being a sign on the walls of All Saint's Church, "Jurymen, remember Oliver!", as it reported, Brougham observed that seven signs had been seen there during the past week, calling for "Hang all Jacobins". To help safeguard such necessary reporting while the trials were *sub judice*, there were hints that the government was going to propose new restrictions on the press. *The Times* not only continued to report the trials but also introduced a special supplement on October 25 to keep readers abreast of all that had happened at Derby. There never had been anything like this in the paper's history. As in every case where Brougham had put his mind to stopping an indiscriminate, vindictive prosecution, dating back to the unfortunate turncoats at the Surrey Special Commission, the Crown cracked.

Brougham did not let up, however. While the jury had recommended mercy in Weightman's case, as Denman had pleaded, the Crown had not granted it, merely delaying his

---

118. Hudson, *op. cit.*, pp.31-2.

execution. Brougham covered the executions of the three ringleaders, and delved into the background of the "Southwingfield Rebellion", his name for the "Pentridge rising". As for Oliver's role in it, he mused: "It is not for us to solve this very important but most difficult question."[119] Brandreth, confronted with the prospect of the traitor's death, had lost all the inspired leadership which Denman had ascribed to him so eloquently during his trial. Surveying Southwingfield, a most deserted, peaceful place, Brougham could only explain the disturbances through the machinations of a Brandreth, inspired by the mysterious Oliver. Certainly, Brandreth himself did not help matters when he uttered just before his execution: "God be with you all and Lord Castlereagh."[120] Turner, about to suffer the traitor's death, blamed everything upon Oliver and the government. It finally capitulated, with the possible assistance by the tragic death of Princess Charlotte, commuting Weightman's sentence, and transporting him with the rest. Sidmouth had finally learned the torment and ordeal of trying to cross Brougham. The Home Secretary's naive days of relying upon the police for advice about what to do during these trying times were over.

Brougham, characteristically, began an attack. To close the gap with the Whig leadership, something he had experienced since the Spafield riots, he met with Lords Holland, Lauderdale, and Jersey, and George Tierney at Holland House to map strategy for the coming Session.[121] When the Law Officers, particularly the Attorney General, Shepherd, refused to follow Sidmouth's lead in letting up on the persecution, prosecuting William Hone of the *Talisman* for seditious libel on an *ex officio* information before a special jury in the King's Bench, Brougham and *The Times* were ready. This was just the type of vindictive, arbitrary action they abhorred, especially since Hone was saying nothing about the government and its "blood-hounds" whom many

---

119. *The Times*, October 31, 1817, no.10,291, p.2.
120. *Ibid.*, November 8, 1817, no.10,298, p.3.
121. *Ibid.*, December 1, 1817, no.10,316, p.2.

respectable people mistrusted. To help commit the King's Bench Justices and jury to do their duty in this scandalous prosecution, Brougham apparently wrote a eulogy for the retiring Master of the Rolls, Sir William Grant. Given the fact that it was written by a Lincoln's Inn barrister, and of Brougham's known respect and admiration for Grant and his office,[122] it is hard to imagine who else Barnes would have had write it. Grant "... has been in his great office upright, patient, learned, and decisive; for he held the scales of justice with so firm a hand, that not even a grain of political influence, or private feeling affected the balance."[123] The Master of the Rolls listened to all advocates in a dispute, Brougham reminded his readers. The King's Bench was subsequently on such good behaviour that Ellenborough was hardly in evidence. Brougham must have had this case particularly in mind when he discussed how the able *puisnes in banc* were able to restrain the Lord Chief Justice's impatience. After the Justices and the jury listened to Wetherell, Hone's counsel and acquitted him of the charge, the Attorney General sued him twice more with equally disastrous results, as *The Times* gleefully noted.

With the Crown itself totally humbled, Brougham, for once, did not let the triumph go to his head. In the *Review*, Brougham offered a well-veiled programme for criminal law reform. In an article on the identity of Junius, he discussed curiosity about the historical question precluding suspicion that he was interested in current ones. The possibility that Junius was Sir Philip Francis, Brougham explained, was not one that would interest philosophers concerned with utility, an obvious reference to Bentham's approach to social reform. Brougham, using a draft article prepared by Sir Samuel Romilly, reviewed Bentham's "Papers relative to Codification", and the success of the ploy is shown by the fact that it has been attributed to Romilly. The attribution to him overstated his role in the process, overlooking

---

122. Henry Lord Brougham, *Historical Sketches of Statesman Who Flourished in the Time of George III* (Lea & Blanchard, Phila., 1840, 2nd edn, 2 vols.) vol.I, p.76 ff.

123. *The Times*, December 16, 1817, no.10,320, p.3.

what he wrote in a codicil in his will about his writings on criminal law reform: "What I have written is not by any means in a state fit for publication, but I should be glad if some friend of mine would look over it ..."[124] Brougham had done exactly this in fact, taking the draft which sympathized with Bentham's complaints about English law, but not those about English Government, and their suggested cure, and converting it into a sound recommendation for codification due to Dumont's legislative activities at Geneva. The transformation resulted in Romilly's discovering that he had become, despite himself, a welcome promoter of the subject rather than the source of a well-deserved attack upon Bentham's "injudicious" activities.

The fact that this same pamphlet by Bentham was reviewed again by Brougham in the *Review*, long after Romilly committed suicide, also indicated that it was Brougham, whom Romilly even specifically called upon to give birth to his ideas. Brougham, in this article, compared and contrasted the role of public opinion, legislation, law, lawyers and Judges in common law and codified systems. Everything was somehow better under the latter. Brougham did admit that Bentham's style could be improved: "... it is to the graces of style which Mr Dumont has given him that he owes the reputation which he has acquired."[125]

During 1818, Brougham did everything he could to see that Bentham's ideals, despite his antipathy towards lawyers, were achieved. To end the suspension of habeas corpus, Brougham not only worked with those already detained to force its being quashed but also to block its renewal. In fact, he pushed so hard against the illegalities that the Ministry had committed under it that an act of indemnity had to be passed to protect ministers from prosecution. While seeking the end of provocative police, he sought preventive police through education and criminal law reform, bringing the famous Romilly into the process. As

---

124. "The Will of Sir Samuel Romilly," *ibid.*, December 25, 1818, no.10,552, p.3. For evidence of the transformation, read *Memoirs of the Life of Sir Samuel Romilly* (Murray, London, 1840, 2nd edn), vol.III, pp.315-35.

125. Art.X, "Bentham *On Codification*," *Edinburgh Review*, vol.29, no.LVII, November 1817, p.236.

chairman of the select committee on charities, Brougham plumbed for education to prevent crime. As a special correspondent for *The Times*, Brougham sought to get the new Parliament to reconsider the use of the death penalty, punishments in general, and prison discipline. To reduce the Bank of England's ability to exacerbate the process of criminal law reform, Brougham assisted an attempt to force it to disperse all its profits among its shareholders, a demand which, if successful, could have forced it to resume cash payments, to improve its bank notes, and to get out of the business of hounding counterfeiters and utterers.

In order to institutionalize this process within the new House of Commons, Brougham had challenged the Lowthers' monopoly in Westmorland by contesting one of the county's seats. By associating parliamentary developments with the closing stages of the election campaign, one which emphasized the magistrates' misuse of power for repressive interests, with the surprising results of the Northern Assizes, he had hoped to provide an example for similar challenges to established authority. Not only was he defeated, which forced him to be re-elected for Winchelsea, but the Whigs and reformers in general did not do well in the General Election. As a result, *The Times* became even more important in whipping up public opinion in order to demand reform. To assist these causes without fear of exposure, Brougham defended a few cases in court.

Brougham had no sooner represented James Gilchrist successfully in an action before the Sheriff's Court on Bedford Row, charging that the *Hampshire Telegraph* had libelled his client by stating that he had been transported for murdering in a duel,[126] than some Manchester prisoners, released by Sidmouth's warrant, presented themselves to the King's Bench, wondering if they faced any new charges under the suspension of habeas corpus. London Radicals, the Evanses, had most embarrassed a Bow Street inspector because of the role he had played with Magistrate Nathaniel Conent in having them arrested

126. "Law Report," *The Times*, January 17, 1818, no.10,357, p.3.

during the previous year's scare. The prisoners, brought especially to London by private expense, and primed by counsel, bearded Ellenborough. The result was an improvement upon Brougham's effort in the Houston case. When one prisoner, John Roberts, put the question of why he had been imprisoned to the Lord Chief Justice, he spluttered: "I charge against you? You must couch your application properly; I have no charge against you."[127] Ellenborough was forced to withdraw when the prisoners persisted in such questioning, and Justice Abbott finally explained: "... he had no doubt that they would not be again required to appear."[128] The prisoners were not put off by his advice, however, returning two days later, demanding either to be tried, or to be released from their recognizances. John Johnson explained that "... he wrote to Lord Sidmouth to consult with him how he was to act; but his Lordship declined an interview with him."[129] Ellenborough was again short for words, stating that he would not do so either. The prisoners would just have to continue to attend the court on a day-to-day basis as their recognizances called for. Attorney General Shepherd tried to smooth matters over by telling the court that the prisoners had been told before they left Manchester that their presence would not be required. This was not enough for the government, however; a few days later it announced termination of the habeas corpus suspension in order to avoid repetition of such embarrassing scenes.

No sooner had the Session opened than the Whigs tore into the Ministry for its appalling use of unprecedented power. Lord Althrop attacked the Attorney General for his vendetta against Hone. Romilly said that his parodies of the trials at Lancashire, Scotland, and Derby had been justified. They showed that the suspension of the Constitution had been unnecessary. Of course, the Law Officers tried to justify what had been done, and Castlereagh was obliged to intervene, stating that there was not

---

127. "Habeas Corpus Suspension", *ibid.*, January 24, 1818, no.10,362, p.3.
128. *Ibid.*
129. *Ibid.*, January 26, 1818, no.10,363, p.3.

one scintilla of evidence to prove that Oliver had been a government spy, a claim that Bennet said he could disprove. Brougham took this to mean that the Ministry was prepared to defend its record before an inquiry, and he anticipated the appointment of a most powerful select committee to look into the charges.[130] Castlereagh replied that he had no such thing in mind when he called for unanimous approval of the Speech which announced the restoration of habeas corpus. Brougham said that he was sorry to have misunderstood him, adding that the appointment of a committee which could have been dictated to by the likes of Nadin would have been a mockery anyway. Lord Folkestone, Brougham's close friend who had already charged that the Ministry had manipulated the courts similarly, raised the plight of those already detained. Brougham picked up the matter. "There was a case which would, he believed, shortly come under their notice, concerning the conduct of a certain Justice in London towards three individuals. (*hear*)".[131] The government defeated all parliamentary efforts to look into the matter.

In the Courts, however, the Crown adopted a more prudent course, one which led to Ellenborough's retirement. On the last day of January, the King's Bench heard the case which Brougham had alluded to. Joseph Mitchell asked the court for a rule discharging the recognizances that he had entered into under Sir Nathaniel Conant, declaring them illegal. "He had attended the Court with considerable trouble to himself and expense to his friends," Mitchell explained, "and fearing lest his recognizance might hereafter harass him, should some spy or police-officer falsely report his conduct ..."[132] Shepherd objected to the rule, denying that the recognizance had been illegally entered into. The rule was denied, but the Attorney General immediately moved to discharge all recognizances under the suspension. Shepherd said that he would have moved to quash them earlier if the

---

130. *Ibid.*, January 28, 1818, no.10,365, p.3.
131. *Ibid.*, January 30, 1818, no.10,367, p.2. Italics its.
132. *Ibid.*, February 2, 1818, no.10,369, p.3.

pleaders had not wished to express their legal objections. In scoring a legal point over Brougham, however, the Attorney General jeopardized the services of the Lord Chief Justice who thought that the war with the alleged rioters should be continued at all costs.

While the Ministry sought to maintain the status quo through party-directed activities in the Commons, it was continually rocked by new revelations. No sooner had the spy Thistlewood challenged the Home Secretary to a duel because of his failure to meet his demands for relief and redress, a red herring to divert public concern away from police abuses, than there was a new report of "blood-money" plots. Thistlewood's complaints, for which Sidmouth got the King's Bench to issue articles of peace against him,[133] had been intended to disarm allegations about spies' corruption of judicial process, and police treatment of prisoners in Manchester. John Johnson, one of the Manchester prisoners who had just been released from his recognizances, spoke at a fund-raising meeting at the Crown and Anchor about Nadin's role in his arrest, and transport to London in irons.[134] Philips, a member of parliament, presented a petition from Manchester, claiming that the city's law enforcement had degenerated into the worst police state. Despite the fact that the government had seen to the appointment of a most reliable secret committee to investigate the state of the nation, reformers were making the most of the claims. *The Times* wanted the secret committee to look into the process by which Manchester's magistrates had become the capricious agents of its police. "Mr Brougham hoped, that the petition from Manchester, containing so many very important facts, would be referred to it immediately."[135]

The reports from the secret committees were completely upstaged by Bennet's committee to investigate Newgate. In its inquiries, it discovered two prisoners on death row, due to a

---

133. *Ibid.*, February 9, 1818, no.10,375, p.9.
134. *Ibid.*, February 3, 1818, no.10,370, p.3.
135. *Ibid.*, February 10, 1818, no.10,376, p.2.

"blood-plot" reminiscent of the activities of Brock, Pelham and Powers. Alderman Wood, one of the committee, had heard how a police officer, Thomas Limbrick, conspired with a known thief to get two youths, Spicer and Kelly, to pass forged notes, a crime which almost invariably led to death.[136] Bennet's committee did what the Home Office should have been doing - ie, questioning the prisoners and their girlfriends about just who was responsible for the crimes. Just when Sidmouth hoped to be making the most of reassurances by the secret committees, he was having to deal with deputations from Bennet's committee to save the boys. It took two trips to get them reprieved. The Opposition in the Lords met Eldon's announcement of the secret committee "whitewashes" by asking what had really happened to Brock, Pelham and Powers. Parliament was told that they too had been pardoned, because of the precedent in Vaughan's case. Brougham's question about whether they would have been indicted for conspiracy was ignored.[137] The Ministry could hardly ignore the transcript of Thomas Linbrick's testimony which was printed in the next day's *Times*, especially since it had all the hallmarks of Brougham's pen. It called for the Bank to make better notes, and for parents to attend to the education of their children.

These revelations reduced Liverpool's Government to a comatose state, a kind of slumber which the bemused Canning would discuss in most poignant terms,[138] and from which the Deputy Constable of Manchester would awaken a year later. While the government fought off renewed attempts to investigate the riots, it was obliged to introduce an Indemnity Bill which confessed all. It asked for immunity from all acts occurring after the attack on the Prince Regent's coach. While Brougham did not take the lead in Parliament against the measure, *The Times* did outside.[139] Brougham finally spoke against the bill in mid-March despite his claim that the government would not listen to

---

136. "Blood-Money Plot," *ibid.*, February 24, 1818, no.10,388, p.3.
137. *Ibid.*, February 26, 1818, no.10,390, p.2.
138. For more on this, see J.E. Cookson, "Canning's Pantheon," *History*, vol.62, no.204, p.45 ff.
139. See its coverage throughout February 1818.

complaints. The petitions against the suspension of the Constitution, and how emergency measures were administered should have been investigated. About the Indemnity Bill, he explained:

> It was intended for the benefit of an informer and a spy, who, by obtaining the ear of the noble secretary of state, had made him his dupe, destroying the character and endangering the lives of innocent men. (The ministers) ... thought a plot necessary for their power; they made a plot, and they resolved to maintain their places, though they destroyed the liberties of their country.[140]

Liverpool's Government was so stung by these claims that it left the responsibility for improving the policing of the kingdom to Brougham, Bennet, and their followers. To improve preventive police, Brougham was permitted to renew his committee that had been looking into charity abuses, something that the alarms of the previous Session had stopped cold. "In 1818 the range of the committee was extended to the whole of England and Wales, and also to Scotland,"[141] a jurisdiction which must have caused Nadin and his friends concern. Soon periodicals such as the *Gentleman's Magazine* were noting that Brougham was involved with his usual gusto in cleaning out the Augean stable. In May, he not only called for the appointment of a commission to root out educational abuses but also for government assistance in the creation of a national system, efforts which finally resulted in a Crown appointed Education Commission. The Ministry gave similar free rein to Bennet, allowing him to do something about police rewards after two years of empty investigation. The Ministry, instead of living off opposition demands to functionless committees, was now trying to effect changes within reason. The limit was what the Lord Chancellor would accept. He would not think of eliminating parliamentary rewards, but only leaving

---

140. *The Times*, March 12, 1818, no.10,402, p.3.
141. New, *op. cit.*, p.213.

them a matter for judicial discretion.

Outside of Parliament, Brougham concentrated upon keeping Bennet's task in focus. When Henry was not in London, hearing evidence about how the government could better oblige charities to keep the spirit of their bequests, he was reporting for *The Times* on how it could better maintain police, and restrain the Bank. At the end of April, he appeared in the King's Bench, calling upon it to issue a mandamus against the Bank to divide its profits.[142] The suit was based upon the affidavit of a stockholder, claiming that the Governor and Company were not observing statutes. When Ellenborough asked Brougham how his deponent knew this, he said that he did not; he just believed that this was so. A minority of stockholders was entitled to a mandamus if it believed the Court of Proprietors had abused its powers. When the Lord Chief Justice demurred, stating this was a matter for Parliament, Brougham disagreed. It was an obligation on the Bank to show what the facts were. "If an alteration be necessary, Brougham said, harking back to the Ministry's difficulties, "the Bank should prevail upon the Legislature to grant them indemnity for having infringed the acts already passed, and permission for the future to accumulate capital."[143] Ellenborough, who was prepared to see anything Brougham complained of as a red flag, granted him a rule to show cause.

Sir Arthur Piggott appeared before the court a few days later, praying for a postponement of the mandamus rule. The Bank did not have time to answer Nathaniel Gundry's affidavit, the one Brougham had based his motion on. "Piggott observed that the motion was one of extreme novelty: the Bank of England had existed for 123 years and this was the first application of the kind ever made against it."[144] To put pressure on the Justices and the Bank to grant the writ, Brougham apparently covered the Lancaster Assizes for the *Leeds Mercury*, stressing the dreaded sacrifices made to maintain paper credit. Eight prisoners were

---

142. *The Times*, April 30, 1818, no.10,344, p.3.
143. *Ibid.*
144. *Ibid.*, May 2, 1818, no.10,346, p.3.

ultimately executed. In discussing the background, Brougham mentioned that one of the prisoners, William Oxenham, had recently been sentenced for the same offence, and Chief Baron Richards had seen to its commutation. Since it had not worked, Richards sent him to the gallows. Brougham called for change in the *Mercury* article that Barnes reprinted for London readers:

> ... since these executions have failed to produce the designed effect, some other mode of preventing the commission of his offence should be resorted to: and until the Directors of the Bank of England have satisfied the country that they have done all in their power to prevent the imitation of their notes, they must be considered as in some sort accessory to the death of the unhappy men who are on this account, from time to time, hurried off the stage of existence by a public execution.[145]

Piggott, the Bank's counsel, was able to stop Brougham's progress by getting the King's Bench to quash the rule *nisi* that Ellenborough had given for the mandamus. A trading corporation involved in pecuniary concerns, much less the Bank, had never to answer such process, Piggott argued. A mandamus was to give rights unjustly withheld, or to restore them to one from whom they had been wrongly taken. Ellenborough was induced to admit that Brougham's client had not done everything he could to get satisfaction. Brougham denied this, stating that the Bank had impeded his client: "He could only have a right to object to the dividend on the assumption that it was not the whole sum to which the proprietors were entitled ..."[146] Justice Bayley asked if Gundry should not have put the request to a vote at the stockholders' meeting, and Brougham said that he had demanded it in a letter. Ellenborough said that it was too late for the meeting, indicating that if it had been made in time there might have been some grounds for the mandamus. The affidavits

---

145. "Criminal Law," *ibid.*, May 4, 1818, no.10,347, p.3.
146. "Law Report," *ibid.*, May 26, 1818, no.10,366, p.3.

showed a surplus, Brougham replied. Ellenborough responded that they must show a divisible surplus and Justice Abbott said that Brougham was trying to get the Court to do what he had never tried. He was ultimately persuaded to seek redress from the Bank.

Brougham co-ordinated this with his campaign to gain a Westmorland seat from the Lowthers in the General Election. At the beginning of the Session, his brother James had visited the constituency, stopping at Kendall, to prepare his candidacy.[147] The violent reception his party received indicated just how ugly the campaign to wrest the county's independence from the Lowthers would be. Placards indicating the value of the Lowthers' sinecures were the ostensible cause of the riot. Brougham blamed Lonsdale's ale for the disturbance. Towards the end of February, Brougham was the guest of honour at a meeting at the City of London Tavern. MP Curwen introduced the candidate by stating that the Lowthers had favoured the ministers who favoured everything Brougham opposed, especially the income tax. Brougham expanded upon the subject, stating that the Lowthers "... were the guardians of the execrable system which employed spies to excite treason."[148] After a month's canvassing in the county and metropolis to gain support, he finally visited Westmorland, "... in a manner that must strike dread in to the breast of the venal, and inspire the best hopes of the county,"[149] the friendly *Carlisle Journal* reported. Friends drew his carriage from Heron Syke to Ambleside, a distance of about 30 miles, Brougham addressing crowds along the way. He contrasted what the King, government, and Lowthers had been able to achieve for justice, with what their agents had been able to exploit in the name of Jacobinism:

> ... not the tribe of unknown or secret agents who surround our local chief magistrate; half avowed, and perhaps authorized

---

147. *Times* reprint of *Carlisle Journal* article, February 4, 1818, no.10,371, p.3.
148. *Ibid.*, February 23, 1818, no.10,387, p.3.
149. *Ibid.*, March 31, 1818, no.10,318 (*sic*), p.3.

> one day, disavowed and denied the next, whose proceedings it would be a degradation to watch, and whose existence we should be unconscious of but for the inconvenience that even such creatures may now and then occasion.[150]

It was to dramatize the importance of the county contest that Brougham covered the senseless hangings at the Lancaster Assizes. His canvassing around Westmorland was conducted as if he were a kind of Assize Judge whose election could change the criminal code.

Hardly had Brougham renewed his campaign against the Bank by getting Gundry to publish his challenge against its officials in *The Times* than the Crown dissolved Parliament. Brougham's election campaign was equally unsuccessful. His attempt to recruit Lord Morpeth to help in his campaign against the Lowthers failed when Morpeth refused to contest the Cumberland seats with MP Curwen.[151] In Westmorland, a favourable prognosis, as in the Liverpool election, proved unjustified. Brougham fell behind in the polling, due partly to the activities of sailors or carpenters, brought in from Liverpool by stage coaches, to intimidate Brougham's supporters. Two hundred special constables were enlisted by the Lowthers to help in their campaign. Brougham's campaign concentrated on whether the county was their pocket borough or a popular constituency. Once he fell well behind in the voting, he blamed the result on police interference as follows: "From what he had seen today, he knew him to be an officer from Bow-street, who had come down to head the bludgeon-men (*immense howling and confusion.*)"[152] His voters had been disenfranchised because they had not been given land assessment, Brougham complained bitterly. In the wake of the Lowthers' victory, he organized an independent voters' association to help insure victory at the next General Election. During the interim, Brougham had been

150. *Ibid.*
151. *Ibid.*, June 30, 1818, no.10,396, p.3.
152. *Ibid.*, July 7, 1818, no.10,402, p.3. Italics its.

re-elected by Lord Darlington's pocket borough, Winchelsea.

With the new Parliament hardly different from the last one, as far as the prospects for reform were concerned, he and *The Times* redoubled their efforts to induce new Members to effect it. Coming back from the Westmorland election, he covered the York and Durham Assizes. Each time, he recounted how the Judges and barristers entered the city, and attended divine services. For their benefit, Brougham wrote about the Archbishop's sermon: "... men in course of a long train of reasoning are apt to lose sight of the principles from which they set out."[153] As with the Lord Chief Baron at the Lancaster Assizes, Brougham noted that Justice Bayley had sentenced 15 men to be hanged for current crimes because remission of past offences had not remedied behaviour. In explaining the process which resulted in one unfortunate going to the gallows, Brougham wrote: "There is an infatuation in crime which facilitates detection ..."[154] These concerns were developed when the Assizes reached Durham. Brougham approved of the Bishop's sermon in which he said that ethics must not be based upon political wisdom. About the plight of an utterer, he wrote characteristically: "All the usual apparatus of police-man, constable, and Bank-agent from London, was put in action, and the miserable woman was convicted."[155]

Brougham, back in the metropolis, attended the Royal inspection of the British and Foreign School Society. The joint interest in the project by the Duke of Kent and Prince Leopold, comrades in arms against Napoleon, was seen as an encouraging sign for peace and progress. "We are glad when we see the most distinguished characters in the country," Brougham said, "countenance and support those plans and institutions which are calculated to do more towards the repression or diminution of crime and misery, than any laws which it is in the power of the legislature to enact."[156] He hoped that Parliament would

---

153. "Northern Assizes," *ibid.*, July 23, 1816, p.3.
154. *Ibid.*
155. "Durham Assizes," *ibid.*, August 3, 1818, no.10,425, p.3.
156. *Ibid.*, August 5, 1818, no.10,427, p.3.

continue his campaign to see that the rich did not steal the patrimony of the poor. "Funds, destined to education, had been shamefully diverted to luxurious enjoyment, by persons already in possession of wealth ..."[157] To strengthen Establishment support for a permanent commission to oversee educational reform, Brougham moved a resolution thanking the Duke for his efforts, and urging the Royal Family's continued support.

In the *Review*, he worked to persuade the less exalted, especially new Members of Parliament, of the need for comprehensive measures to reform the kingdom's management. For those reassured by the Lowthers' triumph in the recent election that all was well, he wrote "State of Parties", a root-and-branch refutation of the idea that conventional, aristocratic politics would do. Britain had to have educational and criminal law reform whether the party leaders liked it or not. He deplored the failure of Radicals like Hunt and Cartwright to join the process due to delusions such as annual parliaments and universal suffrage.[158] Peel's departure as Chief Secretary for Ireland was seen as a hopeful sign that even the Ministry had recognized that change was necessary. In an earlier review, Brougham had attacked him for being such a cautious reformer in policing Ireland that he had sacrificed its substance for empty forms, like the Dublin Castle-directed Constabulary.[159] Brougham, thinking that argument over criminal law and police reform had been exhausted, pushed in another review for prison reform. Britain should adopt a system of prison discipline which protected the innocent, and treated convicts with some hope of their reformation.

To get the leaderless Parliament behind his educational reforms, he wrote an open letter to Romilly, the Chancery barrister who would be most sensitive to his arguments. Brougham traced the background of the Crown Commission, protesting that Sidmouth was using the opportunity to simply

---

157. *Ibid.*
158. New, *op. cit.*, p.189.
159. Art.III, "Irish Affairs," *Edinburgh Review*, vol.29, no.LVII, November 1817, p.126 ff.

reward the party faithful. Brougham was also upset by the reduced ambulatory capacity of the Commission, because of the larger quorum that the Lords imposed on its proceedings. The Ministry also established six honorary Commissioners to supervise the stipendiary ones. Brougham was most concerned about the voluntary character given their inquiries because of the protests by Eldon, Ellenborough and Sidmouth. They had called compulsory findings unconstitutional and unprecedented, false claims which Romilly had heard so often when he called for criminal law reform. "The objects of the Bill were as materially limited," Brougham added, "as the powers of the Commissioners had been crippled."[160] They could neither inquire into the state of education in charity institutions nor abuses unrelated to education. Charities with special visitors, and governors had been exempted from investigation.

Brougham illustrated his complaints against such exceptions. The idea that the Chancery would be a remedy for such abuses was groundless, as Romilly well knew. Brougham could only hope that the commissioners' capacity to expose wrong would force trustees of charities to make matters right. "It is with great pain that I now feel myself compelled by a sense of duty, to state the disappointment of the expectations ..."[161] The commission's posts have been filled by its enemies, Brougham concluded, the Ministry thereby compounding its corruption of the measure.

Brougham went on to explain ministerial motives for undermining reforms in most revealing terms, for both friends and foes of abuses:

> ... they may be deterred from fearlessly joining in the exposure of it by the clamours of those who are interested in its concealment, or the alarms of men easily disquieted, willing to believe that there is safety in supporting whatever exists, ready to fancy that there is danger wherever there is

---

160. Henry Brougham, "A Letter to Sir Samuel Romilly ... upon the Abuse of Charities" (London 1818), p.13.
161. *Ibid.*, p.33.

> movement, and to forget that in the neighbourhood of mischief repose is perilous.[162]

This was true in every case, and only Parliament could force the Ministry to mend its ways. "The season has happily passed away," he wrote confidently, "when the country could be frightened out of a necessary attention to the mismanagement of its affairs ..."[163] Brougham devoutly hoped that Parliament would not be diverted from doing justice for the poor during the coming Session by "... the still more dangerous intrigues of men directly interested in the continuance of abuse."[164] The Education Commission should be restored to its original design despite the protests and machinations of its enemies, especially the public schools and universities. This would lead to the reform of the Poor Laws whose administration had injured the character of the poor. Their reform would result in an immediate reduction in the numbers of poor. "Upon the justice of this course," he concluded, "there can exist no difference of opinion."[165] Brougham reserved further steps for a later stage of inquiry.

As Brougham was using Romilly's good name as a Chancery barrister to enhance the chances of educational reform, he used the columns of *The Times* to expand his views on criminal law reform. Romilly and other Whig barristers who favoured reform had to gain a better appreciation of systematic change, and of the need for Bentham in their plans. Brougham apparently made the case in yet another *Times* series, on capital punishment. In discussing punishment, he used Beccaria, Blackstone, and Montesquieu to show that its proper aim should be deterrence. Hanging was a fast, efficient way for dealing with murder. Britain's code which prescribed death for a multitude of crimes, and then allowed a most discretionary use of remission was a system of mere quackery. In another column, on the Lancaster Assizes which Brougham covered to see how the Crown handled

---

162. *Ibid.*, p.45.
163. *Ibid.*, p.46.
164. *Ibid.*
165. *Ibid.*, p.66.

capital convictions, he was amazed that no one was executed, especially a rapist: "It is remarked as new and extraordinary that none should be left in Lancaster for execution."[166] In fact, things were so quiet that Brougham could only revert back to his struggle with the Lowthers while in Kendal: "We observed *Brougham Street* in a conspicuous part of the town. The confidence of Mr Brougham's friends is very great."[167]

Back in the metropolis he could only compare the treatment of vicious murderers to that of William West, an innocent young man who was sent to the gallows because the Bank did not allow him to plead guilty to the possession of forged notes. "He was the dupe of others who were extensively engaged in the practice, and who have on this occasion eluded justice."[168] Brougham wanted to know the principles upon which the Bank sought death, and its remission:

> Is there a reflecting mind that can contemplate the present condition, and possible fate, of these unhappy persons, without feelings of painful solicitude, without fearfully anticipating the recurrence of those scenes, when fresh victims shall be sacrificed to the mistaken policy of men ...[169]

Brougham called for Parliament to end immediately this most anomalous situation.

During September, *The Times* turned its columns over completely to Brougham's aims. It published excerpts from his letter to Romilly. While it strongly supported his demands for the commission's strengthening, the pamphlet "... will prompt the Commission now appointed to act with vigour in order to remove suspicion and avoid reproach, though we do not know that it will convince the doubtful that its author ought to have been a member of that commission ..."[170] When the *Morning*

---

166. *The Times*, August 28, 1818, no.10,447, p.3.
167. *Ibid.*, August 20, 1818, no.10,440, p.2. Italics its.
168. "Capital Punishments," *ibid.*, September 2, 1818, no.10,451, p.3.
169. *Ibid.*
170. "A Letter to Sir Samuel Romilly, M.P.," *ibid.*, September 10, 1818, no.10,458, p.3.

Chronicle expressed similar reservations about Brougham, however, Barnes ran to his defence. When there was a meeting of the Bank's shareholders, *The Times* was there to see that it measured up to statutory requirements, and the demands of public opinion. Shareholder R. Jackson asked Director Dorrien how the Bank was going to treat criminal matters, and what it was doing about the alarming number of forgery cases. A committee of directors, he was told, were to handle prosecutions, rewards, and pleas for mercy, while a commission had just been appointed to seek remedies. "He doubted not that they were deeply impressed with the consciousness, that the life of a fellow-creature hung on every hour of their deliberations. (*Hear, hear.*)"[171] When shareholders argued about the role of small Bank notes in the crisis, the Governor said that the Directors were not opposed to the resumption of cash payments if Parliament so desired. In fact, Barnes's coverage was so geared to Brougham's interests that he had to publish a belated letter critical of Brougham's "State of Parties" in the *Review* in order to cover himself.[172]

Things looked so good for reform during the next Session that *The Times* took up the question of prison discipline, publishing first reports about it, and then Brougham's apparent letter on it. Then disaster struck: Lady Romilly fell critically ill, dying on October 29. Stephen Dumont had come over to Cowes to help in Romilly's education as a systematic law reformer, only to witness his wife's tragic death. Romilly had desperately feared this, arranging his will, as best he could, against his own insanity. Within four days, the poor man had been reduced to a crazed, wild animal, slitting his throat on November 2. Brougham, of course, was crushed by this turn of events. Fearing that Dumont would reveal what Romilly was involved in when he killed himself, Brougham wrote a letter to him at the inquest asking him to restrict his testimony. Brougham was then living at St James Square, and could not leave his room. "It was of the

---

171. "Bank of England," *ibid.*, September 18, 1818, no.10,465, p.3. Italics its.
172. *Ibid.*, September 22, 1818, no.10,468, p.3.

utmost and pressing importance," the letter said, "that he should communicate with Mr Dumont before the inquest should be proceeded in."[173] Dumont was excused to see Brougham, but he was not questioned about the meetings when he returned to the inquest. Romilly's will was more informative about the matter, as *The Times* duly reported. John Whishaw was named Romilly's executor. "He has left, besides, some fragments, or materials, as he expresses it, on the criminal laws, which will, no doubt, one day see the light."[174] If Whishaw could not see to their publication, Romilly wanted the matter left to Brougham's judgment, "... of whom he speaks in high terms."[175]

Brougham tried to effect Romilly's aims. When London's Common Council debated petitioning Parliament to revise the criminal code, he was most appreciative of the process, writing into *The Times*: "Such recapitulations of facts and reasons, from time to time, form a genuine British mode of ultimately bringing about those improvements, which the more cultivated sense and increasing experience of society discover to be desirable."[176] Brougham attacked the arguments of Councillor Jacks, an opponent of the petition, as if he personified all reactions which had frustrated Romilly. Jacks opposed innovation in the law, its mitigation for private stealing, and questioning the Judges in such matters. Once Brougham had answered these quibbles, he added, with a flourish, for his departed friend: "... but, to say the truth, the all powerful demonstration of circumstances is at present so irresistible, it would only be 'gilding refined gold' *at this time*, to dwell longer upon the subject."[177]

Despite this claim, enough was never enough for Brougham when it came to legislative change. The very next day, Barnes printed a letter from a "former under-sheriff", agreeing totally with Brougham's sentiments about capital punishment. Years of watching prisoners on death row had produced the following

---

173. "Sir Samuel Romilly," *ibid.*, November 4, 1818, no.10,505, p.3.
174. *Ibid.*, December 23, 1818, no.10,550, p.3.
175. *Ibid.*
176. "Capital Punishments," *ibid.*, December 28, 1818, no.10,554, p.3.
177. *Ibid.* Italics its.

effect in him: "I mean the fact of the comparatively little effect produced by the apprehension of death upon me in general."[178] In fact, Brougham was so convinced that the matter was settled for the coming Session that he concentrated, it seems, upon improving the chances of prison reform, writing yet another series for the newspaper.[179]

The 1819 Session was a strange anti-climax. While the Ministry gave such wide support to the Opposition's demands that Peel was obliged to complain, Brougham was not inclined to make the most of the opportunity.[180] When George Ponsonby died, and the Whigs finally had to find a replacement, they elected George Tierney as leader. Despite the claims of Whigs like Mackintosh, and historians like New that Brougham would be the real leader, he behaved like a Private Member, out of anger at being passed over, something that the ministers were quick to notice. When he asked Castlereagh if the Charity Commission would be strengthened, something that he had plumbed for in the latest issue of the *Review* by his analysis of Fellenberg's system in Switzerland,[181] he was surprised to hear that the Ministry would do so. When it came time to issue a new writ for Romilly's seat, something that promised rhetorical fireworks, given Brougham's support of the Corporation of London's petition for law reform,[182] he was silent. "The selection of Mr Brougham for this painful duty led to an opinion," Barnes noted sadly in *The Times*, "that the motion would be attended with a eulogy on the deceased from his friend."[183] Brougham was apparently the author of a new series in the paper on the Insolvent Debtor's Bill. He took exception to the idea that the City was totally correct when it called for revision of the criminal

---

178. *Ibid.*, December 29, 1818, no.10,555, p.3.
179. See issues of January 11, and 29, 1819, for example.
180. For a more detailed examination of the Session, see Trowbridge H. Ford, "Peterloo: The Legal Background," *Durham University Journal*, vol.LXXIV, no.2, pp.220-4.
181. Art.VII, "Mr Fellenberg's Establishments at Hofwy," *Edinburgh Review*, vol.31, no.LXI, December 1818, pp.150-65.
182. *The Times*, February 2, 1819, no.10,586, p.2.
183. *Ibid.*, February 6, 1819, no.10,590, p.3.

law.[184] Its suggestions for debtors would add to their miseries ten-fold. When Brougham wrote another letter, defending Lord Redesdale's role in the current administration, the Attorney General found a place for him on the select committee looking into the matter. Brougham had already been appointed to the inquiry into the Windsor establishment because of Castlereagh.

Barnes was increasingly alarmed by Brougham's independence. He had rebelled because of Lord Grey's calling upon the Whigs to complete Romilly's task of criminal law reform at the Newcastle Fox Dinner at Dodworth's Queen's Head Inn just before the new Session. This was just the kind of party stealing of issues under false pretences, and at the expense of his leadership which made him despair of politics. Barnes knew it, allowing Brougham free access to his columns in the hope that he would be pacified. When it did not seem to work, *The Times*'s editor hoped that he could embarrass and induce him to resume his usual role. In discussing the possible resumption of cash payments by the Bank, he said that Brougham, though "... accomplished in the knowledge of general politics, has never taken any prominent part on the subject of the Bank restriction bill."[185] Barnes was reacting to Calcraft's unsuccessful effort to get him added to the secret committee on the Bank in hardly a fair way. Barnes tried to make up for it by encouraging Brougham to pare down the Windsor establishment. He was ecstatic when the committee docked the equerries of their pensions, stating that big things come from such small decisions. When Wilberforce gave Romilly's eulogy, Barnes hoped that this would force Brougham to honour his dead friend's legacy: "We sincerely wish Mr Wilberforce success in the new cause of philanthropy upon which he seems disposed to enter."[186]

Brougham ignored these inducements and pressures. When Canning attacked the report on the Windsor establishment for not going far enough, Brougham almost sounded like

---

184. "On the Insolvent Debtors' Bill," Letter I, *ibid.*, February 22, 1819, no.10,603, p.3.
185. *Ibid.*, February 9, 1819, no.10,592, p.3.
186. *Ibid.*, February 10, 1819, no.10,593, p.3.

Castlereagh, defending the 1816 Budget. The committee had saved several thousand pounds, not several hundred, as he had alleged. With Brougham's position clear, the Whigs finally decided to move ahead with criminal law reform, and Castlereagh appointed him to a rival committee on the state of the prisons. Lord Lansdowne and Alderman Wood had prepared the ground for law reform, calling for returns from Sidmouth about crime, convictions, executions, and the prison population. When the Whigs got the committee established over ministerial opposition, they appointed Brougham to it in the hope that he would change his mind. He had other ideas, however. He tried to revive his campaign for a seat at Westmorland, telling a dinner at the City of London Tavern:

> ... he was a friend of religious liberty - that he was a friend of reform of all abuses - that he was a friend of all means of retrenching the expenditure - that he was a friend of those reformations which every day's experience proved to be necessary in the legislative and judicial authority ...[187]

Brougham reminded his audience that he had been a Member of the Walcheren and Indemnity Parliaments. "Those two Parliaments," he said, "had passed away."[188]

On April Fool's Day, Brougham married Mrs Spaulding, the former Mary Ann Eden. He had been seeing her for well over a year, and, as Dr Bourne has written, the marriage had "... a whiff of the shotgun about it."[189] Mrs Spalding was a handsome woman, but her charms did not interfere with Brougham's public career, at least not after awhile.

While Brougham was attending to her, and assisting his special projects, especially strengthening the Charity

---

187. "Dinner of the Friends of the Independence of Westmorland," *ibid.*, March 15, 1819, no.10,621, p.3.
188. *Ibid.*
189. Bourne, *op. cit.*, p.22.

Commission,[190] the police establishment staged a counterattack. When Mackintosh's committee on criminal law started its inquiries, Nadin's people in Manchester had long been engaged in exploiting Hunt's activities there, ones so reminiscent of the acts in London which resulted in the repressive legislation of 1817. Hunt applied to the Boroughreeve and the constables for permission to hold a meeting to petition Parliament for Corn Law reform. When Hunt's people refused to stand when "God Save the King" was played at a performance at Manchester's Theatre, causing a riot, "the Boroughreeve and constables were all at the Theatre, and looked on without interfering."[191] Before the instigators of the riot could be discovered with the help of a fifty-guineas reward, Hunt planned another visit to the theatre, forcing it to close. While Hunt stayed in the area, helping to induce all kinds of activities and rumours, the Crown prosecuted Blanketeers J. Johnston, S. Drummond, and J. Bagueley for seditious conspiracy to change the Constitution by force. They were sentenced to two years' imprisonment by the Chester Assizes through the testimony of Manchester special constable John Lloyd who had been following their activities since the fateful march.

Mackintosh's committee, in looking into reform of the criminal laws, only exacerbated the process by carrying on its inquiries without the Judges' assistance. The committee justified its course by considering it improper to ask them to criticize laws that they were obliged to enforce. While the Judges could understand this restriction, magistrates, such as those in Manchester, felt that the criminal law system was collapsing, making them amenable to almost any demand from the police. Ellenborough's resignation the previous fall had not helped, moreover, giving the impression that the Lord Chief Justice was dissatisfied with recent developments in the Ministry's law enforcement policies. The Regent, in whose name much of it was carried on, had

---

190. Art.XII, "Education Committee and Abuse of Charities," *Edinburgh Review*, vol.31, no.LXII, March 1819, pp.497-549.

191. "Hunt in Manchester," *The Times*, January 26, 1819, no.10,580, p.3.

considered his departure as the greatest public calamity.[192] Brougham was completely bemused by developments, intrigued that Castlereagh now favoured the Charitable Foundations Bill that the Lords had gutted in 1818:

> ... he was indeed surprised that all the clauses which had been indignantly rejected, were now restored to the measure now brought before the legislature (*hear*); and besides, had the singular facility of coming recommended to the House by ministers, and of enjoying their patronage.[193]

By the Session's end, Brougham was having little to do with the Commons, although this was not the common impression. While he had only been paired in favour of Tierney's motion on the state of the nation, and had not supported Burdett's motion that the House take up the representation of the people in 1820, the press had reported that affairs were so confused on occasions that he and John Lambton, another Radical, had been seen on the ministerial benches, while Castlereagh and some ministers had joined the opposition. In this most confused context, Mackintosh reported to the House about the inquiry into the criminal law. "The frequent occurrence of the unexpected threat of Death in a criminal code," the report explained, "tends to rob that punishment of all its terrors, and to enervate the general authority of the government and the Laws."[194] In light of the excessive use of hanging for forgery, the committee called for reform. It called for the elimination of the death penalty for those crimes that Romilly had found particularly barbaric. In explaining its recommendations to the Commons, Brougham must have found this statement about the inquiry by Mackintosh especially galling: "I have never, indeed, met with a body of gentlemen

---

192. Regent's letter to Ellenborough, dated October 18, 1818, in A. Aspinall, ed, *The Letters of George IV* (Cambridge University Press, Cambridge, 1939, 3 vols.), vol.II, p.259.
193. *The Times*, June 15, 1819, no.10,700, p.3. Italics its.
194. "Report from the Select Committee on Criminal Laws," *Reports from Committees, 1819*, vol.VIII, p.8.

more decidedly superior to every thing like party feeling or influence."[195] The Whig leadership, after having taken up the issue, had decided, after all, to leave it to the legal experts in the House.

Without Brougham in the forefront of legal reform, the police decided to stage a counterattack, hoping to set off a backlash which would save the established system. The Bow-Street police had hoped to create a backlash at Smithfield in July with Hunt, as had happened at Spafields. Intervention by the knowledgeable Alderman Wood prevented the Radical meeting which put such a high priority on law reform from degenerating into a police-directed riot.[196] With all City expedients exhausted, Nadin himself had to assume direction of the campaign. With Brougham content to give his usual coverage of the Yorkshire and Durham Assizes for the mitigation of capital punishment,[197] Barnes struggled on to prevent a conflagration at Manchester. When General Byng offered a reward for the arrest of rioters, the editor chided: "Blood-money has now had pernicious consequences, and a reward to a witness for the conviction of a prisoner might not be at all times favourable to the cause of truth."[198] Hunt's triumphal return to Manchester had been compared to the provocative actions of Jack Cade and Brandreth. By the time that Hunt went down to the New Bailey with Joseph Johnson, his host who had complained without success to Sidmouth about Nadin's misuse of rewards in 1816, to challenge his alleged arrest, *The Times*'s reporter on the scene began to fear for the worst, "... though in my opinion nothing of the kind is like to occur unless there be some interference of the Magistracy, which is partly expected, in order to put a stop to the proceedings of the meeting."[199]

Reporter John Tyas proved so accurate about developments that Nadin had him arrested with the speakers at St Peter's Field

---

195. *Parliamentary Debates*, 1st ser., vol.40, col.1520.
196. "Smithfield Reform Meeting," *The Times*, July 22, 1819, no.10,732, pp.2-3.
197. See his series, concluding with the one, dated August 15, from Durham.
198. *Ibid.*, August 11, 1819, no.10,749, p.2.
199. *Ibid.*, August 17, 1819, no.10,736, p.2.

on August 16 to facilitate the suppression of the crowd. In the same issue in which Brougham expanded upon George Crabbe's moral portraits of the condemned,[200] because of the results of the Durham Assizes, Tyas exposed the full criminality of Nadin's activity at Peterloo, putting the lie to the later claim that the Riot Act had been read. From the speakers' stand, Tyas reported: "Mr Nadin, the chief police officer at Manchester, then came forward and said, 'I will arrest you; I have got informations upon oath against you,' or something to that effect."[201] This had been the basis of Hunt's threatened arrest earlier, and showed that the Deputy Constable had been holding it in reserve all along. Nadin refused later to show them the warrants for their arrest, stating "... that he had information upon oath against them which was quite sufficient for him."[202] With Brougham reduced to expressing his self-pity about how Parliament treated his current activities, "... just as the reading of an obnoxious bill is postponed for six months,"[203] Deputy Constable Nadin settled scores for the reverses he had experienced at Lancashire, Derbyshire and Yorkshire. The infamous Six Acts would be Nadin's reward, but Brougham would have the last word.

---

200. "Durham Assizes," *ibid.*, August 19, 1819, no.10,738, p.3.
201. *Ibid.*, p.2.
202. *Ibid.*
203. *Ibid.*, p.3.

CHAPTER SIX

REVISIONARY-INTEREST POLITICS

Brougham, while caught unawares by Manchester's Peterloo, was quick to respond to the challenge. Hardly had he been informed by *The Times* of what had happened than he apparently rushed to the Midland city to assist the infirm Tyas who had been arrested with speaker Hunt, for reporting events, corroborating his assessment thus:

> The magistrates and the local authorities have incurred an awful responsibility; and their conduct, which is loudly praised by one portion of their fellow-citizens, and as loudly condemned by another must become the subject of solemn examination and impartial decision. The effect which their late proceedings may produce on English liberty and English constitution is incalculable.[1]

Brougham found the magistrates' explanation of having read the Riot Act away from the crowd before it had even assembled, totally unacceptable. At best, the magistrates had just acted so as to entrap the crowd. "It is a frightful defence to make for the magistrates," Brougham wrote, drawing upon all his experience as a barrister, "that they were impelled by the depositions of the timid or the passionate to act against their own better judgment

---

1. "Manchester", *The Times*, August 23, 1819, no.10,705, p.2. For readers uneasy about these attributions, N.B. what *Times* Archivist Gordon Phillips wrote: "... one thing you can be sure of and that is that these items are *unidentifiable* - by us or anyone else. Our archives are strong from c.1847 onwards but before then, not so." (Letter to author, dated August 9, 1982). Italics his.

and the evidence of their own senses ..."[2] Nadin's anonymous affidavits were equated with the constables' batons in the bloody routing of the crowd. Brougham wondered out loud if this was a trap set for Hunt, so that he could be convicted of high treason. If that was the plan, it was certainly fortunate that the Deputy Constable saved him from the City's Yeomanry, so that he could stand trial. A few days later, Brougham apparently tracked down special constable Murray who reported that he would have finished off the crowd if he had had his way.

As the authorities started prosecution of the crowd's leaders, Brougham reminded readers:

> Whatever opinions may be entertained concerning the mischievous insanity of Hunt and his compeers, when agitating the country by their intemperate nonsense, it should be recalled that they are now prisoners, and that the preservation of the laws of England is of more value to society than the punishment of these individuals by an apparent deviation of justice.[3]

As for Nadin's potential under the circumstances, Brougham had no doubts: "... would men who beat their prisoners, with the evident design of rendering a trial unnecessary, hesitate about twisting a phrase or adding an expression to procure a conviction?"[4] In the next column, he rejected the claim that the Riot Act had even been read, explaining that the magistrates had simply relied upon Nadin's "depositions". When Sidmouth said that his inquiries into the affair had proven satisfactory, having the Prince Regent issue a message approving what Manchester's authorities had done, Barnes replied in a leader: "The informants of Ministers, however, it may be remarked, were the official

---

2. *Ibid.*
3. *Ibid.*, August 25, 1819, no.10,707, p.2. For how this coverage effected Manchester's supporters, see Trowbridge H. Ford, "The Constitutional Association: Private Prosecutions in Reaction to Peterloo," *The Journal of Legal History*, vol.7, no.3 (December 1986), pp.293-314.
4. *Ibid.*

personages whose conduct is the subject of discussion."[5] This critical reporting of what had happened at Peterloo helped induce the Law Officers to decline to prosecute the leaders for treason, forcing Manchester's authorities to make this their care against them in court and Parliament. Because of these developments, *The Times* earned the Home Secretary's ire, who threatened to file a criminal information against it for reprinting on the same day Burdett's letter condemning Peterloo.[6]

Despite this threat, and John Walter's advice that Barnes consult the moderate Peter Fraser before he rush into print, the editor persevered in his campaign against Liverpool's Government. Brougham, his best reporter, contrary to reports that he was indisposed at Brougham Hall, attended the Westmorland Assizes as part of a campaign to get the North of England to redress the evils of the South. Taking Rev. Christopher Bird's sermon on law and order for his theme, Brougham lectured readers on the need for education to prevent crime:

> It is worthy of remark, that of the multitudes who are deluded and agitated by visionary and impracticable theories, and who seem prepared to seek redress for their grievances through scenes of confusion and bloodshed, by far the greater number are men whose early education was entirely neglected ...[7]

To be specific, Brougham congratulated the efforts of MPs like himself who, contrary to party spirit, had sought its establishment. For troublemakers like Hunt who stirred up the passions and dispositions of evil men, there was no alternative but to send them to prison by due process of law. Whatever had happened at Peterloo, Brougham was not sorry to see Hunt's agitation ended.

Brougham covered the Lancaster Assizes, backing up John Ross's reporting for *The Times*. Brougham again got the cue for

---

5. *Ibid.*, August 26, 1819, no.10,708, p.2.
6. Derek Hudson, *Thomas Barnes of THE TIMES* (Cambridge University Press, Cambridge, 1943), pp.37-9.
7. "Westmorland Assizes," *The Times*, September 2, 1819; no.10,714, p.3.

his reporting from the sermon by the High Sheriff's Chaplain, Rev. Houghton. He stood for everything reactionary in law enforcement: "In order to repel this evil, the laws ought to be enforced with a vigour that might on other occasions be considered rigorous severity, and religious instruction ought to be provided for children employed in the manufactories."[8] Rather than devoting more space to such destructive eloquence, Hunt's unexpected presence in court was stressed. In light of what had happened at Peterloo, Brougham felt "... it a duty to give every public appearance of Mr Hunt a degree of attention which could never otherwise belong to him."[9] While "Orator" Hunt tried to get the grand jury to find true bills against officials involved in the massacre something that Baron Wood would not consider, Brougham concentrated upon the impact that events in the crowded courtroom could have upon public opinion. As Hunt tried to get relatives of the magistrates removed from the grand jury, Brougham described the crowd:

> We observed several women in attendance who had been sabred, and trampled down by the Manchester Yeomanry. One of them held a infant in her arms, the same which she had preserved on that occasion at the hazard of her life. A boy exhibited a deep and lasting laceration on his head inflicted by a sabre.[10]

The court preliminaries went according to expectations, except no true bill was found against Joseph Johnson, and all the cases relating to Peterloo were traversed to the next Assizes. Under the circumstances, Brougham concentrated on Nadin's failure to get lesser criminals. For example, Lucy Wilson's innocence of uttering forged Bank notes was explained thus: "Mr Nadin and all of them had combined against her. Mr Nadin had offered 50 for her life."[11]

---

8. "Lancashire Assizes," *ibid.*, September 6, 1819, no.10,717, p.2.
9. *Ibid.*
10. *Ibid.*, September 7, 1819, no.10,718, p.3.
11. *Ibid.*

Brougham returned to Westmorland to await the results of the inquests and trials around Manchester to have their effect upon public opinion. To increase pressure upon Liverpool's Government during the next Session, he revived his campaign in the county against the Lowthers, denying rumours that he was about to resign his seat. "The independence of the north," he explained to a dinner at Kendal's King's Arms Inn, "was now too hardy a plant to dread any storm that might blow ..."[12] Such dinners were urged to increase legal resistance to threats against the Constitution. About Peterloo, he declared:

> All he could say was, that after a careful consideration of every thing that had been published on both sides, and a good deal of private correspondence with persons of very different political opinions, and who by no means agreed in their views of the transactions in question, he found himself at a loss to conjecture upon what the defence of those proceedings was to be rested.[13]

A parliamentary inquiry was called for.

Brougham refrained from giving a final judgment on Peterloo after six weeks' study, although the Ministry had had the Regent endorse what the officials had done after an inquiry lasting only six hours. While the meeting had been a legal one, Brougham said, he refrained from declaring the magistrates guilty, "... though there was no evidence at all for them."[14] Common decency called for expressions of regret over the City's Address to the Regent, condemning what had happened, even if the acts were necessary. Here Brougham was referring to what the Commons Hall had adopted over the protests of London's Aldermen and what Sidmouth had had the Regent reject out of hand. Once Brougham drew an invidious comparison between the Manchester Yeomanry and those of the North, the dinner

---

12. "Dinner of Mr Brougham's Friends," *ibid.*, October 5, 1819, no.10,742, p.3.
13. *Ibid.*
14. *Ibid.*

broke out into a series of wild toasts to Brougham, his new wife, and mother. He responded by calling attention to what the *Carlisle Journal, Kendal Chronicle,* and *Whitehaven Gazette* were doing to keep the public informed, about assaults on the Constitution, intimating that there were "... new and dangerous invasions of it daily practised."[15]

To minimize this effect, at least as far as *The Times* was concerned, Brougham backed up its coverage of the trials and inquests around Manchester. When reporter Ross had trouble recounting the inquest on William Dalton, one of those killed at Peterloo, Brougham apparently reported the proceedings which the Coroner, Milne wanted to keep from the press, especially Barnes's paper. Milne denied that he was postponing the proceedings in order to find a verdict of accidental death. Brougham also attended the trial of the Yeomanry's trumpeter, Edward Meagher, charged with shooting two men who had followed him home after he had been recognized by a crowd. Brougham described how he and Ross sought entry to the controversial trial at the New Bailey: "The object we had in view, and the name of the paper to which we send our reports, we seldom found an insufficient passport into the Courts of Justice; we did not venture to proffer it here."[16] After having gained entry, they reported the evidence against the notorious trumpeter. Brougham, it seems, also went to Oldham to assist Attorney James Harmer in the inquest on James Lees before the Coroner, Ferrand. "I was most happy at Mr ....'s arrival,"[17] Harmer wrote for the benefit of *Times* readers. Brougham's presence had the desired effect on the authorities. While Dalton's death was attributed to unknown causes, and the jury found Meagher justified in the shootings, Ferrand was so panicked by the coverage of his inquest that he postponed it until after the Special Session of Parliament to deal with Peterloo, an act that Harmer denounced as a high misdemeanour.

---

15. *Ibid.*
16. "New Bailey," *ibid.*, October 6, 1819, no.10,743, p.3.
17. "Mr Harmer," *ibid.*, October 8, 1819, no.10,745, p.3.

Brougham decided to take the case against the Ministry to the country. As he had indicated in a letter to Lord Grey, while he was engaged in setting up county requisitions on Peterloo, "in these counties we have the grand advantage of a *clear stage* and no Hunt, etc."[18] The Cumberland meeting took place on October 13 at the Wigton hustings, as the *Carlisle Patriot* reported. With the High Sheriff in the chair, the county worthies called for the adoption of resolutions to Parliament to rectify the situation. After the MPs Curwen and Graham had spoken, and the resolutions had been agreed to, Brougham addressed the assembly: "He trusted that as the meeting had been firm this day, so they would always be temperate: that each would inculcate upon his neighbour the necessity and wisdom of paying strict obedience to the laws, that the enemies of the constitution might be deprived of all pretence for encroachment upon it."[19]

A few days later, there was a similar meeting in Yorkshire, and as soon as the Ministry heard that Lord Fitzwilliam had attended it, he was dismissed as Lord Lieutenant of the West Riding. Barnes denounced the dismissal as provocative: "Lord Fitzwilliam's part in the meeting also, where he acted with men of equal rank, or almost equal rank, with himself, was as little prominent as could be conceived."[20] Brougham followed up the Cumberland meeting with one in his home county. Before a crowd of 4,000 people at Stricklandgate, a part of Kendal, a petition was adopted, calling upon the Regent to institute an inquiry into Peterloo. Mr Thomson called upon the Lowthers, with Brougham's assistance, to take the resolutions to London, an act of revenge by the county's independent voters. Brougham was delighted with the task. After reviewing recent events, culminating in the Lord Lieutenant's sacking, he demanded: "What, my Lord Fitzwilliam, preaching up rebellion!"[21] About ministerial manipulation of the Crown during the coming

---

18. Brougham's letter to Earl Grey, dated September 18, 1819, in *The Life and Times of Henry Lord Brougham* (Harper, New York, 1871, 3 vols.), vol.II, p.264. Italics his.
19. "Cumberland County Meetings," *The Times*, October 19, 1819, no.10,754, p.3.
20. *Ibid.*, October 23, 1819, no.10,758, p.2.
21. "Westmorland County Meeting," *ibid.*, October 26, 1819, no.10,760, p.3.

Session, in response to loyalty petitions from reactionary bodies, he added: "... like slaves, they beg his Royal Highness to recommend restricting measures; and, like fawning sycophants, they assure him they will cheerfully submit to them."[22] Despite this initiative, the Tories stymied it by the time Parliament assembled. Manchester's authorities had been obliged, however, to justify what they had done at St Peter's Field, a case so weak that Nadin had apparently invented an assassination attempt against himself to strengthen it. *The Times* and the radical press exploited the damaging revolutions.

Brougham spoke against the Address from the Throne for the Special Session which did not specifically mention Peterloo. Tierney's amendment, calling for an inquiry into it, was supported. Brougham answered the questioning of what Manchester's magistrates had done about the meeting by citing the requisitions that the county meetings around the country had adopted: "The legality was spoken of with similar caution at Cumberland and Westmorland. All that was said was, that it was *prima facie* legal, and that an inquiry should be made whether it was legal or not."[23] Illegal means had been used to disperse the meeting, and MPs, like C.W. Wynn, who defended it, were attacked with the greatest sarcasm. Rather than pass the proposed six measures that Manchester's authorities were demanding, Brougham urged the vigorous enforcement of law already on the statute books, especially that against the licence of the press: "In some of those writings assassination had been inculcated, forgery defended, and almost every act which violates allegiance encouraged."[24] The Whigs' amendment was defeated, but they had managed to enlist 150 votes against the government's suspension of the constitution.

When Castlereagh, the leader of the House, moved passage of the Ministry's Six Bills Brougham put it on notice that he would contest it every step of the way. About the proposed

---

22. *Ibid.*
23. *Ibid.*, November 25, 1819, no.10,785, p.3. Italics its.
24. *Ibid.*

restriction on seditious meetings, he wondered if they would prevent meetings like those he had organized in the North, or the ones Canning was addressing. The measure, if made permanent, could interfere with parliamentary elections, he suggested ominously. Until facts justifying such acts were presented to Parliament, a critical allusion to the documents Nadin had put together for its information, Brougham vowed to fight them *in toto*.[25] When Castlereagh moved that the House go into committee on supply, Brougham opposed it as a matter of principle, contending that redress should be granted first. He wanted a delay on the proposals so that the country could have time to decide if it wanted a new constitution. The House had not been forced to take such precipitate action during the 1795 crisis. Brougham threatened a day-to-day fight against the proposals, but to no avail, as the Speaker left the Chair. The Stamp Bill was condemned by him as unnecessary.

Brougham wound up the Opposition's effort against the Seditious Meeting's Prevention Bill on the second reading, denying that it represented any kind of compromise. Brougham, in fact, was carried away, comparing the resolutions that had been adopted at meetings like the one in St Peter's Field with the House's resolutions on the currency. To make amends, he made a most damaging concession: "He was very far, indeed, from thinking that there was no ground for alarm: for seven or eight months his opinion had been, that there was ground for apprehension."[26] Alarm did not justify the present legislation, however, especially since the measure would suppress meetings more easily in small parishes than large ones. Brougham wondered if the development of manufacturing was causing the country to lose interest in liberty. Despite the losing effort, he was greeted by loud and continuous cheering when he sat down exhausted. When Castlereagh introduced the Seditious Libels Bill, Brougham was back on his feet, opposing even its introduction. "The Bill was then read a first time, Mr Brougham being the only

---

25. *Ibid.*, November 30, 1819, no.10,789, p.3.
26. *Ibid.*, December 3, 1819, no.10,792, p.3.

person who called out 'No' against it."[27]

The next day, in *The Times*, there appeared another one of his inimitable letters, it seems, against the press gagging act: "Permit me, through the medium of your journal (there can be no better) to direct the attention of the public to that monstrous production, which is called 'A bill for the more effectual prevention and punishment of blasphemous and seditious libels'."[28] Brougham wondered if the public knew that offending gentlemen reporters of politics, and editors printing their accounts, upon a second conviction "... should be liable to *banishment for life*, or to *transportation among felons for seven years*, and for breach of either, to death?"[29] The disjunctive character of the proposed bill, dealing with any blasphemous or seditious libel, caused Brougham alarm. The lack of a time limitation for committing an offence, and the fact that it could concern different libels also worried him. Brougham was sure that Barnes's opposition to it would prevail: "You, Sir, will do that with ample ability and weight; but if assistance should be necessary, depend upon it you will not want supporters."[30]

While Barnes and Brougham laboured hard to prevent passage of the Six Acts, they did not prevail. The libel bill passed despite this protest by *The Times*: "In what state of mind must those men be - for we would not tax their nature with habitual barbarity - who could think of disgracing our statute-books with such a law!"[31] The government did remove the Attorney General's power to postpone trials, something that Brougham had proposed in his 1816 bill. The *ex post facto* character of the second offence was removed from the measure, and its penalty was transportation for a term of seven years rather than for life. Brougham was not upset by measures like the Seizure of Arms, and the Training Prevention Bills, although he did protest in the *Edinburgh Review* for popular effect against the

---

27. *Ibid.*, December 4, 1819, no.10,793, p.3.
28. *Ibid.*, December 6, 1819, no.10,794, p.3.
29. *Ibid.*, Italics its.
30. *Ibid.*
31. *Ibid.*, December 16, 1819, no.10,803, p.2.

ministerially-contrived alarm. The provisions of the Seditious Meetings Bill were essentially what he wanted since they would prevent large public meetings which could be manipulated by agitators like Hunt, and the police. "My fear is that, if matters are left to themselves," Brougham wrote to Lord Grey, "we shall have a green bag, which is worse than Hunt."[32] With George III's death imminent, as Brougham indicated by his decision of the effect of a dissolution upon the Seditious Meetings Act's provisions,[33] he thought that he had helped trap Liverpool's Ministry. A General Election was expected to turn out the ministers responsible for the Six Acts.

With the government on the defensive, Brougham was prepared to resume his legal career. He defended Lord Ranelagh before the King's Bench on a charge of trying to provoke a duel with John Adolphus, a fellow barrister. A year before, Adolphus had defended some of the Lord's servants in an action he had brought against them. The day after the trial, Adolphus, who had acted as a public defender in the case, was visited by Ranelagh in his chambers, calling him a liar, coward and a scoundrel. Adolphus responded to this challenge with his action. Brougham, in representing Ranelagh, questioned Adolphus so as to show that he had only been doing his duty as a barrister in the previous suit. It seemed as if Brougham was identifying Ranelagh with the authorities at Peterloo, suitors who had been provoked into doing understandable, but nonetheless, illegal actions. Adolphus was questioned by Brougham about what he had said in court during the previous hearing about Ranelagh's character, and his case. Adolphus admitted that he had charged that the Lord had instituted a laughable, ungentlemanly action, one which reflected badly on his counsel. Ranelagh, he said, should have sought legal redress for his treatment in court rather than a duel. "Mr Brougham acknowledged that there was no defence to the indictment, even if the threats had been used. This unpleasant

---

32. Brougham's letter to Earl Grey, dated September 19, 1819, in Brougham, *op., cit.*, vol.II, p.264.
33. *The Times*, November 30, 1819, no.10,789, p.3.

affair had taken place in consequence of Lord Ranelagh having mistaken the expressions as having been applied to him."[34] Ranelagh was convicted.

No sooner had word reached London that George III had died than Brougham opened his campaign against the government in anticipation of a General Election. This advertisement was placed in *The Times* for Westmorland's independent voters:

> The approaching dissolution of Parliament affords another opportunity to you of assisting your independence, and to me of redeeming my solemn pledge, never to desert you in this noble struggle. This event is on every account, except the melancholy occasion of it, a subject of sincere congratulation - it offers an almost certain prospect of our endeavours being crowned with that success which can alone terminate our exertions in this cause; and it restores to us, in their ancient extent, those constitutional rights which the late statute has suspended.
>
> As soon as Parliament is dissolved, I shall be among you, to meet our adversaries, whoever they may be, and to render an account of my public conduct since we last met. In the meantime I trust every one will be at his post, and preparing to strike a last and effectual blow.[35]

When the Lowthers reacted to the advertisement by contending in their own advertisement that it was a cruel exploitation of the King's death for partisan advantage, Brougham responded with another: "Had I not seen Colonel Lowther's advertisement, I should have thought it quite impossible, that a person capable of reading could have applied to the King's death what I had most distinctly and exclusively said of the dissolution of Parliament."[36] While Brougham had been saddened by King George's death, he was not going to parade his melancholy over

---

34. R. v. *Lord Ranelagh, ibid.*, December 24, 1819, no.10,810, p.4.
35. "To the Independent Freeholders of the County of Westmorland," *ibid.*, February 1, 1820, no.10,843, p.2.
36. *Ibid.*, February 3, 1820, no.10,845, p.2.

it for electioneering purposes.

Once Parliament assembled, everything seemed to fall into place for Brougham and the Whigs. The King's Address from the Throne intimated that the dissolution was imminent. Brougham thought it was unprecedented for the House to be asked about its propriety. He felt obliged to raise two questions about it. "In the first place, he supposed it had been well considered, to what a degree of inconvenience the public would be subjected by a general election, all over the country, in the very middle of the assizes."[37] The House was reminded that in 1818 the Assizes had been postponed so that they would not interfere with the General Election. "The moment parliament was dissolved," he continued, "the moment a new parliament was called, that bill, which a few weeks ago they were told was essentially necessary to prevent meetings throughout the country became, in effect, a nullity."[38]

Brougham so stressed the Ministry's inconsistency about the state of the country, something that the new King was forcing on it so that he would have a government more amenable to his plans for divorcing Queen Caroline, that Canning felt obliged to intervene. Brougham, he said, was the one who had started the alarm over the new Parliament, reminding the House of his complaints in appeals to Westmorland's voters in *The Times*. Brougham denied the claim. "Now he had, in fact, said twice over, so far from complaining, he actually rejoiced in the measure ..."[39] While the Whigs had been able to learn that the Ministry, despite its postponement of the Civil List Bill had made ample provision for the new Queen, they continued to try to make political capital out of her treatment, so much so that Brougham felt obliged to join in. He told the House not to overlook her slights in not being mentioned in the Liturgy, and addresses: "... she who was wedded wife of a King regnant, was *eo ipso*, Queen-consort, and that her claim to that title was as indisputable as that of the King himself."[40] For ministers interested in seeking

37. *Ibid.*, February 19, 1820, no.10,859, p.3.
38. *Ibid.*
39. *Ibid.*
40. *Ibid.*, February 22, 1820, no.10,861, p.3.

a royal divorce, he warned: "... he was totally unacquainted with any grounds of suspicion."[41]

With the Ministry in a most uncomfortable position, Brougham opened his election campaign with a dinner at the City of London Tavern. Resolutions were carried for his candidacy, contending that Lord Lonsdale had violated the understanding agreed to after the last election of only seeking a place for one of his sons. Lord and Colonel Lowther held the Westmorland seats, and Mr Lowther sat for Cumberland. Brougham promised a concerted assault on Lowther power in both counties. Everyone who had a 40-shilling freehold had a right to vote, he claimed, and the Lowthers were losing control of traditional strongholds like Whitehaven. "It was because he wished to see this yoke thrown off by their beloved native county that he had entered the lists against those who held it in political thraldom."[42] Colonel Lowther's claim that Brougham had shown disrespect towards the deceased monarch was denied. While George III had been a good man in private life, Brougham explained, his public life left something to be desired, especially his policy towards abolition, the Whigs, and Catholic Emancipation. Brougham did not raise interest in a dissolution by publishing his address to electors on the day after the King's demise; everyone in the Commons was preparing for the impending election by sending out their own election material. Brougham claimed that ministers were particularly melancholy because of George's death because the dissolution meant that they would be out of Parliament. "What a fuss had been made," he explained, "about the indelicacy of such a proceeding! What cant had been uttered about the sacred reverence due to the memory of so excellent a King!"[43] Brougham, working himself up to a climax, said that the new King had been raised on the proper principles, and had eminent talents for a chief of state. Continuous effort was promised until a Reform Ministry was imposed upon a constitutional king.

---

41. *Ibid.*
42. "Meeting of Mr Brougham's Friends," *ibid.*, February 21, 1820, no.10,860, p.3.
43. *Ibid.*

Brougham was so confident that events were working against the Ministry that he remained in London, taking legal work which served his purposes. He and Denman teamed up to defend London's Sheriff Parkins and several members of the Livery in a criminal action for disturbing the election on Lord Mayor's Day, September 29. As Brougham had tried to do in Parliament, the Liverymen had attempted to have a Common Hall consider grievances, especially the repression instigated by Peterloo, before it elected Mayor Atkins's successor. The defendants had been singularly unsuccessful in getting Atkins to have such a meeting about their complaints. When he and the Aldermen retired to prevent consideration of critical resolutions, Sheriff Parkins allowed Liverymen, led by Alderman Robert Waitham to continue with their complaints, a process which the minority converted into a new riot. It then took the majority to court, contending that it had engaged in illegal activity.

Once Denman had gone through the evidence and precedents of the dispute, Brougham argued for quashing the rule for it: "It appeared to him at the outset, that if the Court were to listen to applications of this nature, it would be to open a very wide door for cases and arguments of so edifying a description ..."[44] Such cases would make the Courts of Westminster appeal bodies for minorities at Common Halls. "In such circumstances," Brougham said, reverting to his disputes with the Bank, "the Court would, as had been said by a lamented friend of his (Sir A. Pigott), in a case not quite similar to the present, appear among the other novelties of the day, a Court destined to new uses."[45] Brougham argued sharply with the Judges that the Liverymen had a right to do what they had done, contrary to any narrow reading of the City's Charter: "There were certain rights inherent in all public bodies, not only in common law, but in common sense."[46] With the Court on the verge of finding for the defendants, Abbott postponed the decision because Justice Holroyd had to leave. The

44. R. v. *Parkins and Others, ibid.*, February 11, 1820, no.10,852, p.3.
45. *Ibid.*
46. *Ibid.*

next day, the postponement was continued despite Liveryman Henry Hunt's protests.

With the Ministry confronted by an election in which its prospects were not good, elements in the police establishment decided that a new alarm was needed to redress the situation. The plan was tailor-made to suit Brougham's apprehensions and contempt: one for Spenceans to assassinate the King's ministers. With Nadin and his agents completely engrossed with the Manchester prosecutions, these London troublemakers, so infiltrated by the Bow Street police and the Home Office, would have to suffice. Thistlewood, their leader, had excellent credentials for the task. He had tried to trap important Spenceans after the Spafield riots, challenged Sidmouth to a duel in 1819 in order to still complaints about police abuses, and tried to create other Peterloos before the Special Session. George Edwards, another Home Office spy, contacted J.T. Brunt, a hopeless Spencean plotter, about the plan to kill the ministers. Robert Adams, who infiltrated the conspiracy for the Crown, testified thus before the Special Commission trying the plotters: "He had seen nothing of Edwards since. He was employed to carry a sword, as being expert at it. He was not sufficiently near to have killed the man in the loft with the sword."[47] Thomas Monument, who turned state's evidence against his brother, overheard Brunt explain to him: "The King's death had made some alterations in our plans."[48] Thomas Dwyer, another government agent, volunteered to Arthur Thistlewood, the mad Spencean who had been released from Horsham Gaol for sending his challenge to Sidmouth, nearly 30 Irishmen to do the job. The circumstances of Dwyer's offer were all the more alarming, as he testified long after the event: "They did not know me, and I did not know them, yet I was let into their secrets on the morning of February 23."[49] Even Lord Harrowby, the Lord President of the Council at whose house the slaughter was to take place, had known of

---

47. "Supplement to the Times," *ibid.*, April 24, 1820, no.10,915, p.2.
48. *Ibid.*
49. *Ibid.*

the plan since the previous day. "The preparations went on," Harrowby told the court, "as if the parties were to dine together ..."[50]

The government's outplanning the plotters was even more in evidence during their suppression. While Thistlewood was preparing "his" men in a loft on Cato Street, off Edgeware Road, law enforcement officials were amassing more than enough forces to deal with the situation. According to the conspirators, there would be no parliamentary inquiry for the ministers whom Thistlewood held responsible for Peterloo, but Green Bags for the severed heads of Sidmouth and Castlereagh! Thistlewood was going as far as he could to settle scores with Manchester's Yeomanry, having the plotters sharpening their swords in preparation for Harrowby's dinner.

Force and determination were all on the other side. While Constable Birnie, from Bow Street, was leading a patrol of a dozen men to the rendezvous, Captain Fitzclarence set out from the barracks with a detachment of Coldstream Guards. When the detachment reached Cato Street, the Captain ordered his men to fix bayonets. "Almost immediately afterwards they heard the report of a pistol: they were instantly commanded to advance in double quick time ..."[51] This report sounded like a signal, if we are to believe accounts by Birnie's party. The policemen went straight to the loft, securing the only approach to it, a ladder. Once inside the loft, the policemen confronted Thistlewood's party. There was a tense standoff until an altercation developed, and someone ran Officer Smithers through with a sabre. Thistlewood was blamed for the deed, and he never denied the charge. But then he was quite mad, too, looking for a niche in history even if he had to mount the gallows to attain it. It is interesting that Adams, the plotter who turned state's evidence, went out of his way to give the infamous Edwards an alibi for the deed, and not a very good one at that, though by then no one

50. *Ibid.*

51. "Horrible Conspiracy and Murder!" *Gentleman's Magazine*, vol.90, 1820, Part I, p.168*.

suspected him. "While this deed was doing," the *Gentleman's Magazine* reported, "the lights were extinguished, and a desperate struggle ensued, in which many of the officers were severely wounded."[52]

While one can make allowances for dramatic reporting under such circumstances, the press, because of official inflated reports, went wild over the Cato Street conspiracy, much to the delight of the ministers. What was portrayed as a struggle between David and Goliath, where the villains had all the advantages, was more like a situation where one needed an official programme to know what was really happening. Once the smoke cleared, according to the report, a man jumped up from beside the dead Smithers, and exclaimed: "I hope you will make a difference between the innocent and the guilty. Don't hurt me, and I'll tell you how it happened."[53] An earlier incident sounded like something from a movie of the Keystone Kops: "Captain Fitzclarence being first, was attacked by another of the gang, who pointed a pistol which flashed in the pan: the soldiers took him likewise, to whom he said: 'Don't kill me, and I'll tell you all about it'."[54] Another incident sounded like the "blood-money" conspiracies that the Bow Street patrol was famous for: "Five more were then secured, one of who declared he was led into it that afternoon, and was innocent."[55] Then there was the miraculous escape by Thistlewood from the loft, and the frantic effort by police to find them. Edwards made the task easier by turning himself in, and directed the officers to Thistlewood, only for the spy to disappear again. The bloodshed was nowhere near what first reports claimed. Outside of the poor Smithers, Officer Surman received a superficial scalp wound. Serjeant Legger's serious wound to the arm, caused by preventing a colleague from being shot turned out to have been merely a torn sleeve, the ball travelling up his arm harmlessly. The Cato Street conspirators were even failures as ordnance men.

---

52. *Ibid.*, p.166*.
53. *Ibid.*, p.168*.
54. *Ibid.*
55. *Ibid.*

The desired effect of the alarm was manifested in the election returns. The spirit of the country was well represented by the crowd when the police brought in Thistlewood. As he was being taken to Bow Street, people followed along chanting "Hang the villain! hang the assassin!"[56] Under the circumstances, the Whigs and Brougham thought that prudence was the better part of valour, although he did discuss the need of a long-term solution in the *Review*. They did not raise the matter in Parliament during the last few days before the dissolution.

While the possibility of another government-managed crisis seemed an ideal issue for his struggle in Westmorland against the Lowthers' thraldom, he thought better of it, much to Barnes's anger and chagrin. Whoever caused the Cato Street conspiracy, a spirited attack on the establishment would lose him the Westmorland seat, and sacrifice his place at Winchelsea. Lord Darlington would not have tolerated a free-swinging campaign against the Lowthers from his placeman. Without a seat in Parliament, Brougham could hardly have expected to remain the Queen's chief legal advisor. He was soon to become her Attorney General. Consequently, he fought a most pedestrian campaign for the county seat, as the columns of *The Times* duly noted. Brougham started out with a narrow lead over Lord and Colonel Lowther,[57] but he soon fell behind, just when the trial of the conspirators commenced. While Brougham blamed his waning upon Lowther bribery, Westmorland conservatism seemed a more likely explanation. At the end, he trailed the second-ranked Colonel by 63 votes.

Back in the Commons, Brougham saved all his resources for the coming struggle against George IV over his divorce. When Alderman Wood, who was trying to ingratiate himself into the Queen's service, raised the possibility that Edwards had arranged the conspiracy, Brougham would have nothing to do with it, much to the chagrin of the liberal *Leeds Mercury*. The prospect of the evasive spy at the Bar to answer questions from the Whigs

---

56. *Ibid.*, p.167*.
57. "Westmorland Election," *The Times*, March 21, 1820, no.10,886, p.3.

as to his whereabouts and actions on the fatal day was just too much for Brougham. "Why, good God!" he exploded, "was all this mere play? Was it a matter to be treated with laughter and ridicule? When hand-grenades were to be taken to the houses of Cabinet Ministers, then the act became high treason! Then most lost their heads for it!"[58] Men like Thistlewood made the employment of spies necessary, Brougham explained, possibly harking back to when he too had worked for Harrowby's colleagues in messy but vital projects. "He confessed that he was not disposed to join the common clamour and vulgar outcry against spies, seeing that frequently they were proper and necessary instruments."[59] When Wood raised the matter again, Brougham defended the use of spies so much, explaining that even the Old Whigs had used them, that Barnes was obliged to protest. In fact, *The Times* claimed that a Middlesex grand jury had found a true bill against Edwards for harbouring Thistlewood after the attack on the loft, but nothing came of *The Times*'s effort to get him tried for treason.

While Brougham was turning a blind eye to the use of spies in cases of peculiar emergency, he did defend a victim of a particularly vicious libel, a good trial-run for the case against the Queen. During the 1818 Middlesex election, Henry Hunt wrote a letter, stating that Thomas Cleary, a supporter of Major Cartwright, one of the candidates, was "... a kept man-mistress, who had not a shilling but what he obtained by his own prostitution."[60] The letter was published by the *New Times*, the morning daily that D. John Stoddart had established when he left *The Times*. Brougham prosecuted the libel action, calling for exemplary damages, for the barrister of the Inner Temple, and Scarlett defended the editor, claiming that the suit had been engineered for political purposes. Brougham denied the charge emphatically: "If it was a libel, it was a libel barbed with a charge that made it sink deeper, and stick longer, than any ordinary

58. *Ibid.*, May 3, 1820, no.10,923, p.2.
59. *Ibid.*
60. *Cleary* v. *Stoddart, ibid.*, April 51, 1820, no.10,908, p.3.

libel. The dart was envenomed with the most atrocious gall."[61] Scarlett tried to defend "Dr Slop", as Stoddart was now known, contending that the claim was relatively harmless, and Lord Chief Justice Abbott showed some sympathy for the effort. Brougham would not hear of it, however, and the jury found for Cleary, awarding him 100 pounds. The case did not augur well for the Crown in its dispute with the Queen because it showed Brougham to be at the top of his abilities and power.

Queen Caroline did not leave the government any choice in its treatment of her. Despite the stories of scandal, dating back to the Delicate Investigation of 1806, she decided to return to England to assume her rightful place, now that George III had died. The Tories, especially the Lord Chancellor, had undermined the first charges of adultery by dismissing them as Whig propaganda, and burning the evidence that they were based upon. As the Prince Regent freed himself from the Whigs, Brougham took the Princess in tow because of the restrictions that the Prince placed on Princess Charlotte's visits to her. Brougham forged a permanent link not only with the Princess but also *The Times* by exposing the injustice and perversity to which they had been subjected. The Princess of Wales was portrayed by Brougham as a guiltless mother who had been denied access to her only child for political expediency. Public support of the Princess's position obliged the government to avoid further consideration of the Royal marriage despite the Prince Regent's desires for a divorce. In 1814, the Princess of Wales had followed Canning's advice and moved to the Continent settling down in Italy, something Brougham feared would be used against her if there were a divorce trial.

Princess Charlotte's death in 1817 forced Liverpool's Ministry to reconsider the Princess of Wales's conduct, appointing an inquiry under John Leach, Chester's Chief Justice. "He was an eager supporter of the Prince's project to get a divorce, managed the Milan commission which was sent out to get evidence against the Princess, and hinted that the Prince was not properly

---

61. *Ibid.*

supported in this project by his ministers."[62] Brougham's own fears about the Princess's conduct had been increased by his own inquiries about her while on his trips to the Continent, and his brother James's own investigation in March 1819.

Despite most suspicious circumstances about Queen Caroline's sexual conduct, all was not lost, and both the Ministry and Brougham knew it. While James's letters left no doubt that everyone and everything indicated that she and Bartolomeo Pergami, her chief officer, were lovers,[63] there was little evidence that would sustain a legal divorce. A criminal proceeding, like high treason, provided all kinds of jurisdictional problems since the actions complained of had to have been committed in the kingdom. Of course, if the government was forced to take unprecedented action, like a secret committee to vouch for an extraordinary divorce bill, it could work, but it would require the Opposition, especially Brougham, washing their hands of the whole affair. To precipitate a showdown on the question, George IV prevailed upon the government to drop a reference to the Queen in the Liturgy, an illegal act which soon brought her running to the kingdom to establish her rights and dignity. The government, as James Brougham had done, had misinterpreted her willingness to accept a settlement without becoming Queen, as a confession of guilt, and a plea of *nolo contendere*. Everyone was unprepared for her letter to the Prime Minister, complaining of the omission, and her departure for the metropolis. It was with great haste that Lord Hutchinson and Brougham set out from London to intercept her. Hutchinson was a Whig whose friendly relations with the Queen, it was thought, would help facilitate a compromise. On April 20, Eldon thought that the Ministry had made the Queen's Law Officers more amenable to compromise by his announcing that they could sit inside the Bar of the Chancery, next to the King's Counsel,[64] something that

---

62. Sir William Holdsworth, *A History of English Law* (Methuen, London, 1952, 14 vols.), vol.XIII, p.665.
63. Chester W. New, *The Life of Henry Brougham to 1820* (Clarendon Press, Oxford, 1961), pp.228-9.
64. *Gentleman's Magazine*, vol.90, 1820, Part I, p.366.

Brougham had longed for.

At St Omer, where they intercepted Queen Caroline, she confounded all her critics. She had already sent letters to various officials, complaining of past treatment, and demanding better in future. On June 4, Brougham was introduced to her while she was taking her morning coffee. "In spite of his carefully arranged agreement with Lord Liverpool, Brougham decided to reverse the roles and have Lord Hutchinson present to the Queen the memorandum of April 15."[65] In the process, he informed her that the government was willing to give her 50,000 pounds per annum, provided that she would neither assume the style of a queen consort nor live in Britain. *The Times* described her Attorney General's role thus:

> Mr Brougham, whose opinion was asked, is said neither to have recommended the adoption nor the rejection of the proposals. His remark was, that her Majesty was the best Judge of the real state of her case, and that it was for her to decide what was best and most consistent with that knowledge.[66]

The Queen rejected the terms indignantly, leaving almost immediately for England, via Calais. Brougham stayed behind with Hutchinson, trying to pick up the pieces. When the Queen reached Dover, she was not only met by approving crowds but also by a message from the King, informing her that the Houses of Parliament were going to investigate her criminal activity. The Leaders of both Houses presented them with sealed Green Bags of evidence as if this were yet another conspiracy against the Crown. Brougham remained silent over Castlereagh's action, but "... he took it for granted that the noble lord and his colleagues were prepared to set places upon the event of the proceeding."[67]

The next day, while the Lords were balloting on their secret

---

65. New, *op. cit.*, p.239.
66. "The Queen," *The Times*, June 6, 1820, no.10,952, p.3.
67. "Message from the King," *ibid.*, June 7, 1820, no.10,953, p.2.

committee to consider the contents of their Green Bag, Brougham called upon the King's Bench to make a decision on the criminal information that the Crown had instituted against the Liverymen of the City Corporation. The outcome of this case was critical to the Queen's cause as the Liverymen were her most prominent supporters. A verdict against them would have had a chilling effect upon opponents of the King's plan up and down the country. "The main question upon which their Lordships would have to decide was whether, upon the day appointed by charter for the election of the Lord Mayor, it was or was not," Brougham stated confidently, "competent to the Livery to enter upon the consideration of other business."[68]

For the Livery to so act was a matter of course, as far as he was concerned, just as was the Princess becoming Queen upon George III's death: the arrangement was in *eo ipso*. When Justice Bayley remarked on the possible inconvenience of such proceedings, Brougham said that the Common Council had done so 10 times since 1769. The duty of all to attend election meetings guaranteed that the minority would not divert public business by such a practice. Brougham "... concluded by commenting upon the impropriety of granting a criminal information in a case where nothing like corrupt intention had been proved."[69] Sir John Copley, who had been holding the case over Brougham's head as a sword of Damocles,[70] was prevented by the Court from saying that the prosecutors were right in seeking a criminal information against the practice. While the Justices admitted that the Liverymen were acting illegally, the Crown was wrong to try to end the harmless practice this way, thereby acquitting them.

With this decision, the Common Council went wild in its defence of the Queen. It got up an address to welcome her arrival in the kingdom. It said that the Corporation approached "... your

---

68. *R.* v. *Waithman, Parkins, Hunt and Others, ibid.*, June 9, 1820, no.10,955, p.3.
69. *Ibid.*
70. N.B. that when this trial was postponed on the same day in the King's Bench because of the Solicitor General's absence Eldon announced to the Chancery that Brougham and Denman were on their way to becoming King's Counsels: *ibid.*, April 21, 1820, no.10,913, p.3.

Majesty with sincere expressions of loyalty, attachment, and regard."[71] Regret was shown for her fortunes since she had left Britain, especially since George III's death. If there was an inquiry into her past conduct, the Address continued, "... we trust such investigation will be conducted in an open and impartial manner."[72] The Corporation, with the Lord Mayor leading, paid a visit to Portman Square to deliver the address to the Queen's temporary residence, Lady Anne Hamilton's home. Because of Brougham's defence, the City had become the bastion upon which the Queen hoped to convert the country to the justice of her cause.

Brougham concentrated upon converting the Commons to her cause. The King's message was answered by one from the Queen: "... she learns with still greater astonishment that there is an intention of proposing that these should be referred to a select committee."[73] After 14 years of secret, partial inquiry into the charges, it was time for a responsible one, Brougham said: "In the face of the Sovereign, the parliament, and the country, she solemnly protests against the formation of a secret tribunal to examine documents, privately prepared by her adversaries, as a proceeding unknown to the law of the land and a flagrant violation of all the principles of justice."[74] Despite his pleas against acts prejudicing her case, Castlereagh, like Liverpool, moved immediately for the appointment of a secret committee to consider the contents of the Green Bag, but unlike the Lords, the government did not actually name one. The ministers were somewhat uneasy about the real mood of the House. When Brougham and Denman persuaded the Queen to make an initiative to settle the dispute, the Ministry was forced to enter into negotiations despite Castlereagh's objections to them.

Brougham used the time to strengthen impressions that the Queen was being punished without due process. After negotiations had almost broken down again, Wilberforce revived

---

71. "The City Address to the Queen," *ibid.*, June 16, 1820, no.10,961, p.3.
72. *Ibid.*
73. "Message from the Queen," *ibid.*, June 8, 1820, no.10,954, p.2.
74. *Ibid.*

them with a plea that the Queen concede the vital points, pointing out to Brougham that he "... must concur with him in thinking that her Majesty's true dignity and real honour could never be better promoted or supported than by preventing that fatal inquiry which it was the object of his motion to render unnecessary."[75] Brougham brushed aside the proposed compromise claiming that Queen Caroline had obtained recognition of much of what she wanted, and wanted and feared little more. There was no contradiction between his duty as an MP and the Queen's Attorney General, "... a duty which every professional man owed to the client whom he was selected to serve."[76] While Castlereagh was driven to fury by Brougham's contention that there was nothing partisan in his defence of the Queen, the House adopted Wilberforce's compromise. In the subsequent negotiation, the Queen gave proof to Brougham's claim that she was acting for herself, dismissing the call for sacrifice as a violation of elementary principles of justice. Brougham's stature was raised all the higher by this frustration of injustice, as *The Times* duly reported. The spectators outside the Portman Street residence were only dissuaded by him personally from pulling the carriage which carried the Queen's Law Officers to his Hill Street residence. The crowd had only been restrained by hearing from Brougham that the Queen had not surrendered her rights.[77]

The next day, Brougham assured that the Queen's petition against the secret inquiry was presented to the Lords. To exploit Eldon's role in the "Delicate Investigation," he was asked to present it, but declined the embarrassing task on a technicality. The Whig Lords so hounded the Lord Chancellor for this dereliction of duty that he promised never to do it again. Lord Dacre, who did it instead, called upon the House to hear Brougham on her behalf. The *ex parte* proceedings, he said, should be delayed for six weeks so that the Queen could get the

---

75. *Ibid.*, June 23, 1820, no.10,967, p.2.
76. *Ibid.*
77. "Parliamentary Deputation to the Queen," *ibid.*, June 26, 1820, no.10,969, p.2.

necessary witnesses to refute the Crown's "wretches", "... he begged pardon of their lordships for his warmth; he meant of those person, whose evidence had been thrown into the sealed bag."[78] While the Lords denied the motion, the government thought better of the matter, Castlereagh announcing to the Commons that in the interest of justice, there would be an open inquiry into the Queen's alleged adultery. The Leader of the House stated that he had been moved to this compromise by her plea for justice. Brougham was most gratified by the move: "there was at length an end of that species of inquiry which it was the tendency of the message, and of the bag, to cause to be instituted against the illustrious person to whom their contents applied."[79]

The Times attributed the introduction of the Bill of Pains and Penalties to what he had done in the Lords.[80] While the secret committee of the Lords continued its inquiry until completion, with Brougham and Denman demonstrating against the proceeding, the government had been reduced to moving against the Queen by an unprecedented bill whose second reading was delayed so that she could have time to prepare her defence. Brougham had helped cause the delay by protesting the measure's introduction into the Lords at the Bar of the House, complaining about the anomalous condition in which it put Queen Caroline: "A bill of divorce, not founded upon any evidence of adultery - a bill of pains and penalties, not founded upon any previous proceedings, either in the courts of common or civil law."[81]

Brougham used the delay to increase his legal efficacy for the coming trial. On the Northern Circuit, every opportunity was exploited for the Queen's benefit, and duly reported in *The Times*. To highlight the Ministry's treatment of Queen Caroline in the Liturgy, Brougham noted her conspicuous absence at the opening of the York Assizes: "The names of all the Princes of the Royal Family, including Prince Leopold, and, we believe, the names of

---

78. *Ibid.*, June 27, 1820, no.10,970, p.1.
79. *Ibid.*
80. *Ibid.*, p.3.
81. *Ibid.*, July 6, 1820, no.10,979, p.2.

all the Privy Council are included in the Commission."[82] The next day, he reported about his role in *Smithson* v. *Taylor* on the civil side at *nisi prius*: "It was very manifest that there existed an extreme degree of curiosity to hear Mr Brougham address a jury on any subject."[83] His client's opponents, a preacher and his flock, were made to appear as scrupulous in moral matters as the King and his religious advisors in the suit against the Queen. Brougham gloried in his triumph over the hypocrites. In another action, *Tootal and Another* v. *Dickinson and Others,* he was particularly pleased with a verdict against Richard Oastler, the famous Tory radical. Oastler, a bankrupt oil dealer, was portrayed by Brougham as an operator who used his corrupt conscience and knowledge of the law, as did George IV himself, to try to victimize honest subjects. About his attempt to confound the large trover action, defended by the famous Scarlett, Brougham exclaimed: "Mr Oastler knew as well the legal meaning of it as if he had done it in his attorney's office ..."[84] In forcing Oastler to testify against himself, it almost seemed as if Brougham had cornered a substitute for the King's agent.

After a week of such well-publicized triumphs, despite the loss of two simple recovery causes to Scarlett, Brougham found the Archbishop's sermon at Yorkminster, based on a theme from *Ecclesiastes,* most reassuring: "religion alone can secure temporal happiness as well as eternal salvation."[85] The contrast to the Queen's repose, based upon obedience to God's Commandments, was highlighted in another Brougham article about the Ministry's lack of confidence.

> The Mayor of York received this morning a letter from Lord Sidmouth, enclosing a letter from York, which informed the noble lord that 200 stand of arms were concealed in a certain house in York. The Mayor instantly issued a warrant to seize them. The officers found 200 toy-guns, bought two years since,

---

82. "York Assizes," July 20, 1820, no.10,990, p.3.
83. *Ibid.,* July 21, 1820, no.10,991, p.3.
84. "Yorkshire Assizes," *ibid.,* July 25, 1820, no.10,994, p.3.
85. *Ibid.,* July 26, 1820, no.10,995, p.3.

price 11d. each.[86]

In fact, Brougham was so confident that he, as usual, let it go to his head. In subsequent cases at York, his mock trials of the Queen's dispute became too obvious. In *Roe, dem. Raine* v. *Bustin*, Brougham was unable to overturn Raine's will because of insanity. "This was one of those actions which arose from the disputes in the bosom of families," he explained to the jury, "and they were reduced to find their way through a mass of conflicting testimony."[87] Actually, Scarlett got Raine's family to testify about his competence when he made the will, and got the verdict. "Mr Brougham," faced with a similar result in *Hill* v. *Wells*, "at length surrendered."[88] In *Hill* v. *Wear*, Brougham went to the greatest length to prove that his plaintiff was not a rogue in a slander action. "For the mighty sum of 5 guineas, then," he asked sarcastically, "was this most respectable man, in good business, and with a virtuous family, to throw away his character, his reputation, and his good conscience."[89] The jury, in keeping with the evidence, decided that, indeed, this was so. In a bankruptcy action, Brougham attacked a Colonel Beaumont as if he were George IV, and lost the case. When he tried to explain that he was only acting according to his instructions, Justice Bayley interjected that he disagreed with the tactic. Actually, Brougham only won those cases where his opponents acted as if they were prosecuting the Queen. Scarlett, the barrister whose services had not been considered necessary to Queen Caroline's defence, lost *Boardly* v. *Fawkes* when he tried to prejudice a trespass action by impugning the sexual conduct of the plaintiff and her daughter, because they had had bastards. Brougham got Milner, a tailor, 40s. by this plea: "The jury would show by their verdict whether a man then rejoicing in his strength was to tyrannize over his weaker brother in this land of liberty and law."[90]

---

86. "A Radical Magazine in York," *ibid.*
87. "Yorkshire Assizes," *ibid.*, July 29, no.10,998, p.3.
88. *Ibid.*
89. *Ibid.*, July 31, 1830, no.10,999, p.3.
90. *Ibid.*

Brougham's impatience in all this, wanting to get on with the trial in the Lords, was manifest in *The Times*'s coverage of the Assizes. One day, when there was little to report of his exploits, there was a letter to the editor by a barrister on circuit who sounded exactly like Brougham. It attacked the Milan Commission, contending that it was an extraordinary, illegal investigation which gave the lie to the Ministry's claim that it was treating the Queen like any subject. Drawing on his practice before French courts, he said that the government could have had a competent, foreign tribunal examine the witnesses that it was not relying on. The Ministry had compounded the lack of substantiated testimony by denying the Queen a list of her accusers, contending that this was permissible because she was not being tried for treason. "But can any honourable or high minded woman," the writer asked, "consider it for a moment in this light? Is the character of the Queen or her throne of less consequence to us, or to her, than her head?"[91] The depositions of the Queen's accusers were dismissed as suspect. To offset their effect, he urged the use of private certificates, a French procedure, for the rapid amassing of evidence supportive of Queen Caroline's case.

Brougham stayed at Lambton Hall during the Durham Assizes, repaying the favour by successfully prosecuting an assault on one of Lambton's supporters in an election, and by defending Lambton himself in a suit by the Corporation of Newcastle when the Circuit moved to Northumberland. Richardson, a youth, had a tooth knocked out by a clergyman named Le Mesurier when he shouted "Lambton for ever!" during the recent election when the hustings went by his church at Haughton. Brougham got him 10 pounds in damages for his injury.[92] In fact, when the Cumberland promoters of freeing the county from Lowther interest gathered for a public dinner at Rosley, the toasts ultimately turned to the absent barrister from the next county. Graham, the MP for St Ives, like Francis Herries

---

91. "The Milan Commission," *ibid.*, July 28, 1820, no.10,997, p.3.
92. "Durham Assizes," *ibid.*, August 8, 1820, no.11,006, p.3.

in the novel *Judith Paris* of the Hugh Walpole series, proposed: "The health of Mr Brougham, and the independence of Westmorland."[93] The assembly immediately broke out into cries of "The Queen! The Queen!" Brougham missed a similar meeting at Gateshead because of exhaustion from defending Lambton's interest before the assizes. Beaumont, one of the county's MPs, proposed Brougham's health in his absence. While Brougham had been unable in the case to exempt Lambton's corn from a toll when it was transported over the Tyne Bridge, he delivered an address of over five hours in length, wonderful practice for what was soon expected of him in the Lords. About the trial, he wrote:

> This cause, though the least interesting that can well be imagined, yet crowded the Court throughout the whole day as much as if it had been murder or crim. con. Many had come from a great distance, and several ladies had taken their seats in the Court at seven in the morning. The reason was, that the Queen's Attorney General was known to be engaged in it.[94]

No sooner did Brougham return to London than the case against the Queen came before the Lords. The Duke of Leinster, after presenting a petition from Sheriff Parkins of the City against proceeding against the Queen, was heavily defeated when he tried to stop the trial. Shortly thereafter, Brougham asked to be heard against the Bill of Pains and Penalties, and delivered a masterful argument against it. The measure was dismissed as a private act, *ex post facto* in nature, and based upon rumour and innuendo which the Ministry had cultivated. "Here nothing is or has been proved," he said contemptuously; "and is it because calumnies have been bruited and gossiped about - because such a jealous watch has been kept upon the Queen abroad, that we are to think they are to have more force than conduct less

---

93. "Cumberland Independence," *ibid.*, August 10, 1820, no.11,008, p.3.
94. *Mayor and Corporation of Newcastle* v. *Lambton*, "Northumberland Assizes," *ibid.*, August 15, 1820, no.111,012, p.3.

equivocal at home?"[95] Brougham warned the Lords of precipitating the country into a grave constitutional crisis the outcome of which it could not foresee. Barnes not only printed his speech in extra-large type but also wrote this about it: "Mr Brougham addressed their Lordships against the Bill in a speech distinguished alike for fervid eloquence, powerful reasoning, intense thought, and glowing language, every word of which will be eagerly read, and long remembered by the country."[96] *The Times*'s leader noted particularly the sensitive way in which the Queen's Attorney General handled her wounded feelings.

The next day, Denman tried to get the Lords to drop the Bill. "They had heard from his learned friend (Mr Brougham) a powerful and convincing argument on the evil tendency of bills inflicting penalties, and on their utter repugnance to every principle of justice,"[97] the Queen's Solicitor General explained. The Attorney General, Sir Robert Gifford, was not persuaded, stating that Queen Caroline's relation with Bergami constituted adulterous conduct. "His opening speech was not a success, but his reply was an able summing up of the evidence against her."[98] Brougham replied that the Ministry had not answered the defence's claim that it did not have a case against the Queen, as its offer of concessions showed. The Bill was unnecessary and inexpedient. The measure, nonetheless, passed its first reading with a majority of well over a hundred votes.

On August 21, once Gifford had finished his charge, the Crown started presenting its evidence against the Queen. The first witness, Theodore Majocchi, put the worst interpretation possible upon Caroline's personal life on the Continent, something that only a personal servant of long standing could effectively do. When the Queen saw him advance towards the witness box, she raised her veil to get a good look at him, moved towards him, and cried out his name, only to rush out of the chamber. Her performance was effective among the Lords who,

---

95. *Ibid.*, August 18, 1820, no.11,015, p.1.
96. *Ibid.*, p.3.
97. *Ibid.*, August 19, 1820, no.11,016, p.2.
98. Holdsworth, *op.cit.*, vol.XIII, p.664.

whatever they thought about marriage and conjugal fidelity, detested breaches of the master-servant relationship. Majocchi lived up to what Brougham had predicted in his letter to Barnes on the Milan Commission, testifying with shocking certainty about the Queen's adulterous conduct, while, at the same time, showing an amazing ignorance about routine, obvious matters. Majocchi sounded like a witness with a mission, with his frequent responses of "*non posso ricordormi*" ("I cannot remember") and "*non mi ricordo*" ("I have no recollection").

Brougham sat back, listening to the Crown's chief witness spin his tale of lies and innuendo. To maximize the impact of Majocchi's testimony, Brougham prevailed upon Eldon to separate and remove witnesses from the chamber so that they could not concoct more persuasive stories by hearing sworn testimony from others. Later in the day, when the Commons decided to adjourn for four weeks while the trial went ahead, Brougham showed just how confident he was about its result when he rejected a call to prorogue Parliament, whatever the Queen's guilt:

> A witness - the chief witness - the witness to whose testimony they had been looking forward. The witness who was to prove almost the whole case; this witness had been examined - not cross-examined, for his examination in chief was not yet over - and was this a moment to stop the proceedings in the House of Lords?[99]

That night, while the Queen gave added emphasis to Majocchi's affronts by having herself bled, her counsel planned her defence so that the Commons would never have to consider the merits of the proceeding. In case anyone misinterpreted Queen Caroline's reaction to seeing Majocchi in the witness box, as historian New has done,[100] Barnes wrote a letter in anticipation of Brougham's cross-examination of the Crown's leading witness:

---

99. *The Times*, August 22, 1820, no.11,018, p.3.
100. New, *op. cit.*, p.250.

"On the contrary the Queen knew that he was one of the original promoters of the plot: on his coming into the House of Lords, therefore, she was seized with a kind of hysterical affection at the sight of a man who had shown such ingratitude for her liberality and kindness."[101] When the cross-examination began, Brougham showed that he was in charge, allowing the Crown's interpreter Marchese Nicolas Spinetto to remain rather than be replaced by his own, Beneditto Cohen. Earlier, Brougham had expressed concern about the reliability of courtroom translations. Now he was willing to allow the Marchese to explain the meaning of Majocchi's almost constant mental lapses about crucial details, such as where courtiers William Austin and Dr Holland were when the Queen was committing open adultery. "The constant repetition of the witness answer *'Querto non mi ricordo'* (I don't remember) occasioned some laughter."[102] Brougham obliged Majocchi to deny that in one particularly suspicious situation, he was in an exclusive position to monitor her adultery. Counsel kept punching away at all the other witnesses there must have been, but who had, strangely not come forward to corroborate Majocchi's disgusting story. About "Signor Non Ricordo's" performance, Barnes wrote:

> This creature, who affected in his first examination to detail a series of events and circumstances of a criminatory nature which had taken place in the course of three years, could, when put upon his cross-examination, absolutely know nothing, or almost nothing, by which his own assertions were exposed.[103]

Short of a surprise witness who could reclaim the case by truth or stealth, the Crown's task was hopeless, and it knew it. Barnes had a field-day over its difficulties: "To say that the Queen or the Queen's Counsel had not known for many months that Majochi

101. *The Times,* August 22, 1820, no.11,018, p.3.
102. *Ibid.,* August 23, 1820, no.11,019, p.2.
103. *Ibid.,* p.3.

(*sic*) was in training against her is the foulest and most absurd calumnies.'"[104] To compound Majocchi's difficulties, *The Times* printed a letter to the Queen's counsel, complaining that he had not been properly sworn by a priest before he testified.[105] The Earl of Darlington, Brougham's patron at Winchelsea, did his part by calling on the House to print the minutes of evidence from day to day. "The evidence given in support of the bill, on the first day, had made, he confessed, a very strong impression on his mind; but the cross-examination which took place yesterday had, on the contrary, tended very much to diminish that impression."[106] The motion's failure was compounded by Majocchi's first response to the resumed cross-examination - "*non mi ricordo.*' While the House waded through his claims, and those of Gaetano Paturzo and Vincenzo Garguilo, Barnes continued his pursuit of Majocchi, receiving a letter from John March which stated that while the Queen's servant had been living with Adam Hyatt in Gloucester, he had said consistently that she was an "excellent, a good woman." Not only did *The Times* print the letter but also it turned it over to the Queen's Counsel, forcing Majocchi's re-examination. The story was, indeed, true, but Majocchi was much more reluctant to testify about whether he had been prodded to give evidence against the Queen.

When the Ministry declined to give up this most embarrassing case, Barnes turned *The Times* over completely to the Queen's counsel. To get the Judges to take a more active role in ending the proceedings, "Common Sense" wrote in from Lincoln's Inn, describing how an attorney had been committed by a Judge for doing what the Crown was doing with the Queen's servants: "Yet, Justice Best and all the other learned Judges are perfectly silent on the present occasion, although it is as clear as the light that the whole power of the King's advisers has been applied to the arrangement and production of the most pitiful and nauseous

---

104. *Ibid.* During the trial, Majocchi's name was spelt this way, and Bergami was called Pergami.
105. "To Messrs Brougham and Denman," *ibid.*
106. *Ibid.*, August 24, 1820, no.11,020, p.2.

story that ever soiled the records of a Court ..."[107] About the Crown's previous examinations of Paturzo to make his testimony more persuasive, Brougham explained: "Good God! can those things be, and not excite disgust?"[108] A few days later, Brougham was apparently again in its columns, as "John Bull" protesting the scandalous, pointless proceedings: "If Ministers had been in possession of evidence to support their charge of adultery, why, in God's name, enter into that of a thousand acts, when the proof of one would have sufficiently answered their purpose?"[109] Barnes's leaders, of course, were daily indictments of the Crown's criminal activity in continuing the scandal.

Perhaps, the funniest parody of Brougham's confrontation with Majocchi was "A Match for Signor Non-Ricordo", a song sung to the tune of "Monsieur Nong-tong-paw". These are its better verses:

> ... Don't fancy I'm afraid of Brougham,
> I well know every sleeping room:
> At Naples, Venice, Genoa, d'Este,
> At Tunis, Zavouor, and the rest:
>
> And when I saw a naked man,
> And met him, I directly ran.
> In summer, winter, spring and fall,
> I perfectly remember all.
>
> ... By the same means I fall and rise:
> Chas'd by the Queen for telling lies,
> I day and night since then have swore
> To please the King by telling more.
>
> I've fairly earn'd my bread to-day,
> And now have nothing else to say;
> But you'll agree, though no great catch,
> *Non-mi-ricordo's* met his match.[110]

---

107. *Ibid.*, August 25, 1820, no.11,021, p.3.
108. *Ibid.*
109. *Ibid.*, August 31, 1820, no.11,026, p.3.
110. *Ibid.*, September 2, 1820, no.11,028, p.3.

By the time the defence had finished its cross-examination of the witnesses, plumbing even the soiled bed-linen for tell-tale evidence, the Crown's case was finished, and the Prime Minister knew it. Brougham wanted to wind up the case immediately, but Liverpool called for a four-week adjournment. Actually, he wanted time in the hope of finding the one conclusive witness whom Brougham was always calling for. After all, the prosecution had worked on the assumption that there must be one credible witness of the Queen's adultery, the possibility of which had always put Queen Caroline's counsel in a cold sweat. Brougham retired to Brougham Hall with his ailing wife to renew himself for the case's resumption. In the interim, the *Traveller* ran a series of articles, which Barnes reprinted, showing just how little headway the Crown had made with its claims. Short of a miracle, the Ministry was just postponing its humiliation.

When the Lords resumed the hearing on October 3, Brougham opened for the defence. About the leading witness, all he could state was "... that one sentence, appeared to comprise the entire practical result, all the wisdom and all the experience which he had accumulated in the study of his art ..."[111] The evidence had disproved the charge. To illustrate how Gifford had been influenced by Majocchi's lies and exaggeration, Brougham told the Lords:

> They would recollect that the Attorney-General stated he had evidence to prove that the Queen and Bergami were for a considerable time locked up together in a room at Messina in the night, and that the sound of kisses were heard from within: it now turned out, that only voices were heard, and of whom the witness could not say![112]

About his day-long performance, Barnes wrote: "The history of the Queen's long persecution, and the several epochs of it, were

---

111. *Ibid.*, October 4, 1820, no.11,055, p.2.
112. *Ibid.*, p.1.

affectingly detailed by Mr Brougham."[113]

During the second day, Brougham went on the offensive, comparing what the Ministry was trying to do to Queen Caroline with what was the police system's stock in trade: "Suppose the trial of a highway-robbery: their lordships well knew that the account given of the transaction by a Bow-Street officer, perhaps panting for his reward, would not be deemed sufficient."[114] The anxious fabrication of evidence, in the hope of finally finding something, had totally defeated itself. "Save the country - save yourselves," Brougham appealed. *The Times* gave the Ministry's effort the same evaluation: "For, as to convicting the Queen upon such evidence, it is not such as would supply a bench of justices with a pretext for levying a fine upon a poacher."[115]

While the other counsel were giving speeches, and examining defence witnesses, Brougham supervised the process to see that nothing which served the Queen's interest was missed. When the Solicitor General, Sir John Copley, tried to prevent Lady Charlotte Lindsay from being asked why she quit the Queen's employ, Brougham, with Dr Lushington's help, prevailed. The Lord Chancellor, who was increasingly upset about the position the Judges were being put in by the case, permitted the question without asking them. Copley had opposed the question because it was merely rumoured that she had resigned because of Queen Caroline's adultery. "I never myself observed any impropriety to induce me to resign,"[116] she explained. The Queen's lady-in-waiting quit because of the vicious rumours, and the penny-pinching treatment of her mistress. The testimony proved the accuracy of Brougham's complaint that the Crown, with the Judges' acquiescence, was willing to do almost anything to prove its "more pitiful and nauseous story."[117] The Law Lords, Lord Eldon and Lord Redesdale did not look any better when they agreed with Lord Donoughmore's answer to Brougham's

113. *Ibid.*, p.3.
114. *Ibid.*, October 5, 1820, no.11,056, p.2.
115. *Ibid.*
116. *Ibid.*, October 7, 1820, no.11,058, p.1.
117. "Common Sense," *ibid.*, August 25, 1820, no.11,021, p.3.

objection to a question he had asked Lt Flynn, only to have Donoughmore, when he heard his own question repeated, state that "... if I put the question in this shape, it ought to be objected to by counsel."[118] When Donoughmore tried to ask the leading question yet again, Eldon was obliged to stop him.

Once Lord Carnarvon heard that Rastelli, an agent of the Milan Commission, had been found guilty of bribery, he called for dropping the Bill. Brougham questioned Vilmarcati about his role in the process, forcing the Judges to determine the propriety of questions about bribery. While they gave a most convoluted, indecisive answer, the Attorney General permitted the question anyway. Its answer showed that Vilmarcati had tried to bribe the Queen's servants. The House appointed a secret committee to investigate Rastelli's bribery mission. When Brougham failed to get the Lords to accept some Austrian accounts of the Queen's esteem, he blurted out this explanation: "He was not here in a court of justice."[119] While the sides were summing up their cases, Brougham interrupted Gifford's address, to tell the House that he had just received Baron Ompteda's letters, calling upon Queen Caroline's servants to betray her. The Baron was the Regent's Hanoverian envoy to the Vatican. The letters were printed in *The Times* while the Lords were debating the Bill's second reading, and it only passed by a majority of 28 votes. After Liverpool's Ministry merely compounded the problem by dropping the Bill's divorce clause, reducing the majority in the Lords to nine votes on the third reading, the proposal was dropped.

While the Queen's supporters were celebrating the victory, Brougham moved quickly to stop the government from disarming the crisis by giving her a grant of money, and proroguing Parliament. On the day of the scheduled prorogation, Brougham communicated to the Speaker that the Queen had a message for the House, and it met early to consider it. While Denman was reading it, informing the Commons that she would refuse any

---

118. *Ibid.*, October 11, 1820, no.11,061, p.2.
119. *Ibid.*, October 24, 1820, no.11,072, p.2.

offers from the Crown, preferring to throw herself upon its mercy, Black Rod's Deputy Usher arrived, informing the House to attend the Lords to hear the King's message.[120] While the Opposition cried that he should withdraw, the Speaker suspended the meeting, and went to the Lords with some of the ministers. Once the prorogation was ordered, the Queen's representatives waited in vain for the Speaker to return to the Commons to complete her business. In this way, Parliament failed to deal with Brougham's demands on the government for resolving the crisis, giving Queen Caroline all the constitutional rights of a queen consort.

A few days later, *The Times* published a letter from Keppel Craven, the Queen's Vice Chamberlain, elaborating on what Parliament had to do, once the Bill of Pains and Penalties died: "The justice and wisdom of the Legislature at that period, beyond all doubt, have restored her to the full enjoyment of those rights which the constitution has vested in the Queen-Consort."[121] To force the King to dismiss the Ministry for failing to do so, the Queen arranged a procession and service at St Paul's to demonstrate her plight,[122] hoping that similar events throughout the country, because of Barnes's coverage in *The Times*, would accomplish George IV's humiliation.

Brougham tested the sentiments of the Courts on the King's prerogatives to see if a legal confrontation with the Crown over the Queen's status had any prospect of success, concluding that it did not. When some Somerset farmers were brought up before the King's Bench for sentencing, convicted during the Summer Assizes of riotous assembly in trying to stop the tax surveyor from assessing them with surcharges on farming stock,[123] Brougham tried to minimize what they had done. The case sounded like an assembly against the King, with the farmers gathering with effigies against the tax-gatherers and assessors. Brougham made much of the taxes the accused had already paid,

---

120. *Ibid.*, November 24, 1820, no.11,160, p.2.
121. *Ibid.*, November 27, 1820, no.11,101, p.3.
122. "Procession of Her Majesty to St Paul's," *ibid.*, November 30, 1820, no.11,105, p.2.
123. *R.* v. *T. Middlecomb and Others*, *ibid.*, November 24, 1820, no.11,160, p.3.

and the expenses they incurred coming up to London for sentencing: "That circumstance, he was persuaded, would have due weight with their lordships in awarding punishment, if they did award any, especially when they considered the pains and penalties which the defendants had already suffered."[124] The Lord Chief Justice, in light of what London's Liverymen had been able to do with their precedents, was not about to let such behaviour constitute a precedent for the mitigation of punishment. The prisoners, unlike the Queen, had not experienced any suffering. When Brougham demurred, Abbott said that their penalties did not justify what they had done. Copley agreed, stating that the riot "... was encouraged by two churchwardens and the high constable of the hundred,"[125] one of Brougham's clients. He received two months in jail, and a 100-pound fine, while Brougham's other clients were given fines.

The decision that the Queen was unequal to the King served as a good guide when Daniel O'Connell inquired about being appointed the Queen's Irish Attorney General. Ten days earlier, the Irish leader had suggested the possibility to Thomas Spring Rice, explaining that "the Penal Laws do not exclude a Catholic from being Attorney-General to the Queen ..."[126] Alexander Wood told O'Connell that he would have to apply to Brougham for the appointment because he was completely in charge of such things. Two days after the decision in the King's Bench, Brougham wrote to O'Connell that he would only make such an appointment if there was a precedent for it.[127] While O'Connell was unable to find any, he was willing to force a recognition of the right with a suit financed out of his own pocket. He thought that he could get mandamus in the Chancery for the appointment. Brougham was not willing to risk it in Eldon's own

---

124. *Ibid.*
125. *Ibid.*
126. O'Connell's letter to T. Spring Rice, dated November 16, 1820, in Maurice R. O'Connell, ed, *The Correspondence of Daniel O'Connell* (Irish Univ. Press, Shannon, 1972, 2 vols.), vol.II, p.288.
127. Brougham's letter to O'Connell, dated November 25, 1820, *ibid.*, p.293.

court, however, explaining much later that he had decided, after consulting Denman, "... that the right in question is not sufficiently established."[128]

Brougham hoped to exploit in Parliament the Queen's plight, and the need for educating the poor so that the Ministry would be forced to recognize his interests. Barnes threw *The Times* behind his educational measures to provide primary education for the poor, and to improve the administration of educational endowments.[129] At the annual Fox dinner, Jeffrey helped the cause by proposing a toast: "The health of Henry Brougham, and success to the diffusion of knowledge throughout every rank of the people."[130] Brougham chaired the annual meeting of the Educational Clothing Society, stressing the need for some kind of educational measure.

The King's Speech to Parliament was a direct challenge to Brougham, however, calling upon the Commons to make new arrangements for the Queen. While Tierney objected to the obscurity of the appeal, something that Castlereagh denied, Brougham moved the next day to have Queen Caroline's name restored to the Liturgy. When the Leader of the House dismissed a Whig motion to this effect as party politics, Brougham called for restoring the Queen's rights completely, a move Castlereagh countered by calling on the House to go into committee on her financial needs. Brougham responded with a message from the Queen: "... she is apprehensive that such a provision may be unaccompanied by the possession of her rights and privileges in the ample measure, wherein former Queens Consort, her Royal predecessors, have been wont in times past to enjoy them."[131] When this fear proved true, with the Ministry offering her 50,000 pounds *per annum*, and its supporters wanting her to get less because of her alleged adultery, Brougham was reduced to threatening libel actions against her detractors. Holme Sumner,

128. Brougham's letter to O'Connell, dated May 8, 1821, *ibid.*, p.322.
129. See leader on January 5, 1821, and "Mr Brougham's Educational Bill," *The Times*, January 8, 1821, no.11,138, p.3.
130. "Anniversary of Mr Fox's Birthday," *ibid.*, January 17, 1821, no.11,146, p.3.
131. *Ibid.*, February 1, 1821, no.11,159, p.2.

Brougham's biggest protagonist in the House, responded by telling a Surrey meeting that the Queen was an adulteress, and had evil advisors.[132] The core of the Queen's detractors was Dr Stoddart's constitutional Association which the *New Times* had helped organize to deal with the cities of Peterloo.

Brougham met the challenge by instituting a criminal information against Rev. Richard Blacow for what he said about Queen Caroline in a service at St Mark's, Liverpool the previous November. In the sermon, Blacow made allegations about her advisers, what the Constitutional Association had organized against being said of respectable people: "They have elevated the goddess of Lust on the pedestal of shame ..."[133] The good reverend went on to say that the Queen had committed adultery on land and sea "... to gratify to the fill her impure desires, and even polluting the holy sepulchre itself with her presence, to which she was carried in mock majesty, astride upon an ass."[134] In getting a rule for the prosecution at the King's Bench, Brougham had been encouraged by the prosecution Scarlett had opened against the *John Bull* for what it had printed against the Queen and Lady Caroline Wrottesley, an action, he complained, with an eye on the Constitutional Association, that should have been instituted by the Attorney General.[135] The previous December, Brougham had shown that he was not above using libel actions for similar purposes, opening yet another suit for the unfortunate Thomas Cleary. This time, Cobbett had libelled the radical barrister and was fined 40s. for it.[136]

Brougham's parliamentary efforts against the King and his Ministers for their actions against the Queen were unsuccessful. In supporting Lord Tavistock's motion, censuring the Ministry for the Bill of Pains and Penalties, Brougham adopted the mantle of the Judge, but to no avail: "... if, instead of an advocate, I had been sitting as a Judge, at another tribunal, I should have been

---

132. "Meeting of the County of Surrey", *ibid.*, February 3, 18221, no.11,161, p.3.
133. *Ibid.*, February 5, 1821, no.11,162, p.3.
134. *Ibid.*
135. *Ibid.*
136. *Cleary* v. *Cobbett, ibid.*, December 5, and 6, 1820, nos.11,109 and 11,110, p.3.

found among the number of those men who, laying their hands upon their hearts, conscientiously pronounced her Majesty 'Not Guilty'."[137] Brougham's brief to have the Queen's name restored to the Liturgy, the basis of a motion to this effect, similarly failed.[138] On the educational front, Brougham's efforts were also set back with the unexpected death of Dr James Lindsay, the minister of the Presbyterian meeting-house on Monkwell Street. Lindsay was a dissenting minister who had been trying to get the Dissenters to back Brougham's educational bill, and he was at a meeting for this purpose at the trust library of Dr William's, in Red Cross Street, when he died. "Dr Lindsay," *The Times* reported in his obituary, "had delivered his opinions on the subject with extraordinary zeal, energy, and clearness. He sat down in full health, and expired without a groan."[139] Barnes even wrote a leader to rally the survivors behind Brougham's bill,[140] but they refused.

With the Queen reduced to writing a letter to the Prime Minister, asking that the King "... allow her to be publicly prayed for by the Clergy of the Established Church - a privilege which has been enjoyed by all her predecessors since the Reformation,"[141] Brougham absented himself from fruitless parliamentary disputes with the Ministry. He concentrated upon bringing the Queen's enemies to justice through the pen and gown, saving his appearance in the Commons for assisting these efforts. At York, Brougham limited damages against the *Leeds Intelligence* to one-hundredth of what Scarlett called for, in calling a Huddersfield merchant irreligious and a brutal husband after voting for a Loyal address to the King during the recent dispute. Brougham worked with Barnes to see that the editor and publisher of *John Bull* were sent to Newgate for calling Queen Caroline the most abandoned of her sex. "..... God!" a *Times* leader

---

137. *Ibid.*, February 7, 1821, no.11,164, p.3.
138. "Exclusion of Her Majesty from the Liturgy is historically and legally considered, by a Barrister," *ibid.*, February 14, 1821, no.11,170, p.3.
139. "Funeral of the Rev. Dr Lindsay," *ibid.*, February 24, 1821, no.11,179, p.3.
140. *Ibid.*
141. *Ibid.*, March 22, 1821, no.11,200, p.3.

exclaimed, "What has the Queen done since the trial to call forth these fresh aggressions?"[142] Brougham defeated James Park's effort to quash the rule *nisi* against Rev. Blacow, a subscriber to the infamous Constitutional Association, because the Queen had not entered an affidavit, denying the libels. The Queen was no ordinary subject, Brougham explained. "She stood (still according to Lord Coke's authority) precisely in the same situation with the King himself."[143] Brougham later used Coke's *obiter dictum* before the Privy Council to establish the Queen's right to attend George IV's coronation.

Brougham, who had recently been given the freedom of the City of London for his legal exploits,[144] argued for the right on the basis of uniform practice since Anglo-Saxon times. When married kings had been crowned, he explained, their queens consort had invariably been crowned too.[145] Gifford, the Attorney General, denied that the right could be established by usage. The coronation of the Queen depended upon the King's will. The Privy Council agreed with the Crown's argument. The Queen was not persuaded by its decision on the basis of Brougham's argument, however, and she tried to crash the ceremony at the Abbey, thanks to Barnes's encouragement in *The Times*.[146]

The difficulties the Queen was causing were avoided because Brougham was forced to occupy himself at his London residence, 5 Hill Street, off Berkeley Square, where his infant daughter, Eleanor Sarah, was dying. He was especially fond of children, being able to play with them on their own terms, and his failure to produce a healthy heir was the greatest disappointment of his life. The *John Bull* had helped earn Brougham's enmity by referring to her as "Mrs Brougham's seven-months child." When

---

142. *Ibid.*, May 15, 1821, no.11,246, p.3.
143. *R.* v. *Rev. Richard Blacow, ibid.*, May 26, 1821, no.11,256, p.3.
144. "Court of Common Council," *ibid.*, June 4, 1821, no.11,263, p.3.
145. "The Queen's Right To Be Crowned," *ibid.*, July 6, 1821, no.11,291, p.3. and July 7, 1821, no.11,292, p.2.
146. See leaders, starting July 17, the day Barnes reprinted Brougham's plea: "Substance of the Argument before the Privy Council ..." (no.11,300, p.3).

she died on July 30, he went to York for the assizes, prosecuting a contested will, an assault action, a libel case,[147] and an action to recover a debt.[148] While Brougham split the decisions, they hardly added to his reputation since they were suits engineered by greedy plaintiffs, and grasping attorneys.

During this time, the Queen developed an inflammation of the bowel, and died. When the truth of her death was finally established, Brougham and Denman left the Circuit for London to make arrangements for an official party to accompany her body back to her native Hanover. In the process, Brougham made the most of the family inscription over the tomb of the House of Brunswick, assisted by the Crown's intervention to keep down public displays in her favour, and *The Times* delighted in pointing out every misstep:

> Here envy, persecution, and complaining cease.
> *Hic finis invidise, persecutionis, et querelae.*[149]

The procession, in leaving the metropolis, entered the City despite the Ministry's precautions and soldiers' shots, to the delight of her most loyal supporters. Barnes duly reported its more successful arrangements at Dover to prevent similar outbursts when she left England's shores for the last time. Brougham did not accompany the body to its final resting place.

Back in York, Brougham immediately resumed his work on the Northern Circuit. While Queen Caroline's ordeal was finally over, Brougham was out to prove that her antagonists, especially the Constitutional Association, would suffer similarly if they did not change their ways. Rejoining the assizes at Carlisle, Brougham won three cases in quick succession against Scarlett. In defending an action for false imprisonment, England's foremost barrister was reduced to this, something that Brougham might well have asked in earlier days when he had the weaker

147. *Merryweather* v. *Brumfitt, ibid.,* August 9, 1821, no.11,320, p.3.
148. *Hudson* v. *Roberts, ibid.,* August 10, 1821, no.11,321, p.xxx.
149. *Ibid.,* August 13, 1821, no.11,323, p.2.

side of a dispute: "What motive could Mr Forster have, a respectable man and a banker, to send a man who is no voter to gaol?"[150] Mr Forster, nonetheless, lost ten guineas for his trouble. Brougham won a libel action against a potential prosecutor for sheep stealing who was too liberal in his use of "sheepstealer" in making his way to the Association for Prosecuting Felons.[151] Sarah Thompson was awarded an unexpected 100 guineas out of her breach of promise suit to marry, against Mr Blamire, despite Scarlett's claim that it was just another suit engineered by a grasping attorney. Brougham agreed to settle another breach of marriage case for 200 pounds and obtained 40 shillings for a plaintiff in an open case of criminal conversation. About the actions, he wrote for *The Times*:

> Scarcely had the abrupt termination of the breach of promise in one court became known, when the *crim. con.* was announced for the other. The ladies at the same time were cruelly dragged out from the other court, though an opposing torrent of the rougher sex rushing in with unbounded curiosity.[152]

Another breach of marriage suit that Brougham was defending was non-suited, and he was able to get a fishing dispute settled out of court.

These triumphs, like the ones before the Queen's trial, provided the proper background to Brougham's prosecution of Rev. Blacow before the Lancaster Assizes in September. Of course, the trial was an open-and-shut case, as the preacher's libel of the Queen was obvious. What is interesting about the prosecution, what one does not glean from reading his address from his *Speeches*, is the exchange between Blacow and Brougham during cross-examination. The preacher tried to associate counsel with the people who opened the prosecution against him: "My

---

150. *Crowby* v. *Forster, ibid.*, September 5, 1821, no.11,343, p.3.
151. *Lamb* v. *Dafton, ibid.*
152. "Summer Assizes," *ibid.*, September 8, 1821, no.11,346, p.3.

Lord, I wish to show the spirit of the party in Liverpool with whom Mr Brougham is connected."[153] When Justice Holroyd dismissed the claim as irrelevant, obliging Blacow to read his sermon, he explained: "But Mr Brougham was the first to disturb her ashes. Her counsel were determined to carry their vindictive feelings beyond the tomb."[154] Over the Judge's rulings, Blacow claimed that Denman's argument had justified what he had said. After dragging in what Hone and Richard Carlile had done to mitigate his offence, Blacow attacked the City's Common Council: "They were as ready to cast off the Queen when she should have answered their purposes as that old crazy headed goat, Lord Erskine, to cast off his concubine."[155] Ultimately, Holroyd restored order in the court, and Blacow, after the jury deliberated for quarter of an hour, was found guilty. He was later sentenced to six months' imprisonment, and fined 100 pounds. Brougham made much of Blacow's behaviour under cross-examination when this occurred: "The Court had heard the libel read, but they had not heard the defence made by Mr. Blacow at his trial; and certainly, in this country, there never had been exhibited a scene more disgraceful to the character of a clergyman."[156] Still, Blacow only served three months.

By this time, Brougham had more important business. Since the previous spring, he had been most concerned about the activities of the Constitutional Association, and its London leadership, the Bridge-Street Committee. In the Commons, he had complained most bitterly about the circulars they were sending magistrates, which called upon them to see to the prosecution of radical troublemakers like Richard Carlile. Actually, the radical publicist, his wife and sister had long since been imprisoned, and the Association's continuing efforts against his shop in Fleet Street, especially when the *New Times* printed an advertisement to promote its illegal activities, were private prosecutions of a most gratuitous nature. In trying to promote prosecutions for

153. *R.* v. *Blacow, ibid.*, September 17, 1821, no.11,353, p.3.
154. *Ibid.*
155. *Ibid.*
156. *Ibid.*, November 27, 1821, no.11,414, p.3.

seditious libel, they were usurping the powers of the Attorney General, Brougham said, an opinion which gained Scarlett's assent.[157]

Consequently, when the Bridge-Street Committee saw to the prosecution of Daniel Ridgeway for printing something of Carlile's which a Westminster jury had not found libellous, Brougham jumped to his defence. Bolstered by the birth of a second daughter, Eleanor Louise, and the collapse of the Association's prosecutions of Thomas Dolby for publicizing Nadin's expresses at Peterloo, Brougham attacked the prosecution of Ridgway as the worst injustice. Thomas Nadin, the infamous Joe's son, had persuaded bookseller Ridgway to order a copy of Carlile's pamphlet, denying the existence of the British constitution. About the activities of the Bridge-Street Committee in the affair, Brougham appealed to the jury, one he believed had been picked by the Association's Charles Hurray: "I call upon you to rescue this victim from the fangs and grips of harpies and leeches."[158] When Ridgway was convicted, Brougham wanted a bill of exceptions against the verdict, but settled for a rule to set it aside. "Nadin, my Lord," Brougham explained for the Lord Chief Justice's benefit, "he is son to the Manchester thief-taker, so called."[159]

The Times had run a series of leaders on how "blood-money" induced corrupt police to fabricate evidence for private prosecutions, like those of the Bridge-Street Committee, and the Bank. The King's Bench was obviously sensitive about such charges. The rule was quashed, however, because the conflicting affidavits favoured the prosecution. In the wake of this victory, the Bridge-Street Committee overplayed its hand, and Brougham got a second prosecution against the jailed Ridgway for perjury quashed because of more attorney misconduct, traversing the case from one Assize to another to confound the defence,[160] and then

---

157. *The Parliamentary Debates*, n.s., vol.V, col.1050.
158. *R. v. Ridgway*, *ibid.*, September 24, 1821, no.11,359, p.3.
159. *Ibid.*, November 13, 1821, no.11,402, p.3.
160. For the conclusion of this battle, see *ibid.*, November 28, 1821, no.1821, no.11,728, p.3.

using a writ of certiorari aggressively. The tempest-in-a-teapot reminded the King's Bench of the lengths that the Constitutional Association had gone to in the City to pursue Dolby for what he had printed about Nadin's depositions in the *Parliamentary Register*. Under the circumstances, the Deputy Constable decided to retire.

In the meantime, the Bridge-Street group had lost a direct confrontation with Brougham and *The Times*. Dr Stoddart's group had been inclined to sue the newspaper because of comments about it in the October 28th issue, but *The Times* stopped the effort with an exposé of its former editor.[161] The Bridge-Street Committee settled for K.B. Lewis's suing the newspaper on six counts of libel when it reprinted the *Hampshire Telegraph's* coverage of his client's trial. Lewis took strong exception to Serjeant Onslow's saying that he was no attorney during the trial. The Solicitor General, Copley, in taking up the case, as part of government policy on newspaper reporting of police trials, explained what the sometime Coroner of Westminster, who had been involved in the Dolby fiasco, hoped to achieve by the prosecution: "A correct publication of proceedings in court of justice was not only (the learned counsel said) a matter of much interest, but of great real benefit to the community at large; but nothing could be more cruel, more unjust, and, he might say, more illegal, than to publish statements of counsel, such statements were not established by evidence."[162] John Manning, Lewis's attorney, submitted a copy of his admission as an attorney to the King's Bench in 1813.

Fortunately, for *The Times*, defence counsel showed that there was more to the matter than met the eye. Scarlett established that he had no certificates of practice in the court since 1816. "Mr Brougham said that there was not even evidence of the plaintiff having acted as an attorney."[163] As a result, the action was non-suited. Barnes was ecstatic over the defeat of the Ministry's

---

161. "Dr Stoddard," *ibid.*, December 19, 1821, no.11,433, p.2, and December 21, 1821, no.11,434, pp.2-3.
162. *Lewis* v. *The Times*, *ibid.*, January 10, 1822, no.11,451, p.3.
163. *Ibid.*

policy for the Association's benefit:

> Whether we acted unfairly by Mr. Lewis, we know not; but it will be seen that we adopt the same course against ourselves, for we publish the trial of yesterday, which also went off upon a technicality, and of which therefore there remain little but the Solicitor General's speech against us - *valent quontum valed,* we say.[164]

Copley failed to get a new trial by contending that the Lord Chief Justice had been too demanding of evidence.

With Stoddart's vigilante group on the verge of collapse, Brougham decided to go all-out in his defence of the *Durham Chronicle* against a charge of libelling the City's clergy when the Queen's death was announced. At York in March, Brougham had stolen a page from the Constitutional association's unsuccessful prosecution of Thomas Dolby, seeing that *R.* v. *Brook,* an indictment against the *Yorkshire Gazette,* stood over until the next assize because only one coroner had been present to fill up the special jury. Besides, on an 11-count criminal indictment for forging a bill of exchange, and knowingly uttering it, prosecuted by Scarlett, Brougham saw to the complete exoneration of John Balme, a most respected resident of Somerset, and a result which was universally acclaimed.

The *Chronicle's* editor, John Ambrose Williams, had had an article in his paper, singling out Durham's clergy for not joining in the ceremonies occasioned by Queen Caroline's death, and Scarlett had been hired to prosecute the action. Brougham felt particularly sensitive about the Queen's legacy, as his letter to *The Times* defending Alderman Wood showed. Despite the fact that Queen Caroline left the Alderman no money in her will, Brougham wrote, she still "... sincerely respected him even to the last moment of her life."[165] Brougham could be no less generous towards the *Durham Chronicle's* editor, trying to quash the rule

---

164. *Ibid.,* p.2.
165. "Mr Alderman Wood," *ibid.,* October 2, 1821, no.11,366, p.3.

Scarlett had obtained against him because the name of its real prosecutor was unknown to the law.[166] When this effort to expose Stoddart failed, and the case was finally heard (after a busy parliamentary Session where Brougham disputed everything from the Ministry's handling of the Queen's funeral to agricultural distress), counsel felt even more obliged to defend the editor since he had printed a story which said that Brougham had rejected a silk gown unless Denman was offered one too.[167] Brougham also was encouraged by his defence of *Jones* v. *Stephens*, a libel action in the Exchequer where its practices were even in dispute. Stephens had written a pamphlet, charging that Jones was no attorney, and that the Court had assisted in his conniving. While Brougham was not able to get the Exchequer Justices to adopt the King's Bench view of what constituted attorneys, being greatly hindered in trying to justify the charges, he got his client off with a 50-pound fine.[168] Jones had called for 1,000 pounds in damages.

On the Northern Circuit at the Yorkshire Assizes during 1822, Brougham tried by implication to make light of what Williams had written about the Durham clergy when he prosecuted the *Yorkshire Gazette* for what it had printed about editor Hargrove of the *York Herald*. The action's purpose was to get back at the *Yorkshire Gazette* for a libel suit which it had won against Hargrove's paper. Editor Hargrove objected to a letter in the *Gazette*, complaining of how the *Herald* covered the suits resulting from Peterloo.[169] The jury went along with the defence counsel and the Chief Justice, finding that freedom of the press took precedence over any misconduct in publishing the letter. Abbott explained that Hargrove in publishing his views of controversial matters, laid himself open to such attacks, an opinion which Brougham hoped would apply when the Assizes took up the Durham libel case. An earlier successful prosecution of a recovery action against the *Leeds Gazette* for materials supplied, over the

---

166. *R.* v. *John Ambrose Williams, ibid.*, January 26, 1822, no.11,464, p.2.
167. For the story reprinted in *The Times*, see *ibid.*, no.11,538, p.4.
168. *Jones* v. *Stephens, ibid.*, May 29, 1822, no.11,570, p.3.
169. *R.* v. *Brook and Others, ibid.*, July 29, 1822, no.11,623, p.3.

claims of Scarlett and Chief Justice Abbott, had also strengthened Brougham's hand in the Williams case.

As counsel tried to establish during cross-examination of witnesses in the case against Editor Williams, the clergy, by not pealing the bells when the Queen died, had broadcast its seditious antipathy towards her. "It is your duty," Brougham declared to the jury, "to proclaim that light must continue to visit every recess of that hierarchy, and that by that light its abuses must be corrected."[170] Scarlett was portrayed as the Bishop of Durham's Attorney General in prosecuting the case, a role which sounded uncomfortably similar to that of the Bridge-Street Committee. Brougham, in his charge of the jury, said more about the Established Church than he was willing to acknowledge later in his *Speeches*; "Let its members therefore, above all let us, as well for religion as for civil policy, set ourselves to destroy vermin which breeds in that corruption, and which stink, and sting the hand that would drive them away."[171]

When Williams was found guilty of libel, Brougham decided to have his charge to the jury reprinted in *The Times* without the most offensive passages.[172] Barnes, in a leader, explained that the revised version was due to technical considerations, "... a more correct report of Mr Brougham's speech than could be hastily inserted on the close of the proceedings."[173] Brougham then sought to arrest judgment because the verdict was so inconsistent to the charges, an effort which resulted in the prosecution of Williams being dropped.[174] The verdict favouring Williams heralded the demise of the Constitutional Association. Brougham's routine losses on the Circuit - a breach of promise case to Serjeant Cross, and a trover action to Scarlett - were more than compensated by this achievement. It was 14 years to the day since Brougham had been called to the Bar, and he had climbed

---

170. *R.* v. *Williams, ibid.*, August 9, 1822, no.11,631, p.3.
171. *Ibid.*
172. "Mr Brougham's Speech at Durham," *ibid.*, September 25, 1822, no.11,674, p.3.
173. *Ibid.*, p.2.
174. *R.* v. *Williams, ibid.*, November 22, 1822, no.11,723, p.3.

to the top of his profession.[175]

Brougham's position at the Bar was dramatically illustrated during the next of the summer assizes. At Newcastle, he teamed up with Scarlett to get *Bell* v. *Hill*, a slander action, non-suited. It was Brougham's persistent cross-examination of the prosecution's chief witness, who claimed that Hill's anonymous letter had ruined the plaintiff's prospective marriage, which forced this fatal admission. "I did say it was a woman's hand, it was so small. I won't swear that I did not a month after I saw it and at a public leader's meeting, say it was a woman's hand."[176] At Carlisle Brougham not only turned the tables on Scarlett but also got sweet revenge against the Lowthers in the process. Lord Lonsdale, a charter member of the Constitutional Association, had Scarlett prosecute some people for fixing up Workington harbour on the Derwent, claiming that it had injured the rights of his manor. The special jury, despite Scarlett's warnings about the danger of legal novelties, still found for Brougham's defendants in this most spiteful of cases. As usual, the accounts in *The Times* made the most of Brougham's efforts. About the opening of the Cumberland assizes, for example, it wrote: "The Court was exceedingly crowded in all parts in consequence of an expectation that Mr Brougham was to lead in some of the causes."[177] After he saw to the mitigation of punishment in two exercise suits, a leading article called for the repeal of laws which made such crimes, "... imbittering the lower order, of the nation against its most active authorities."[178]

---

175. For a very different assessment of Brougham as a Northern Circuit barrister, once he was no longer the Queen's Attorney General see Robert Stewart, *Henry Brougham, 1778-1868. His Public Career* (The Bodley Head, London, 1985), p.160 ff.
176. "Summer Assizes," *The Times*, August 13, 1822, no.11,636, p.3.
177. Earl of Lonsdale v. *Nelson and Others, ibid.*, August 19, 1822, no.11,641, p.3.
178. *Ibid.*, p.2.

CHAPTER SEVEN

CROWN'S CHIEF COUNSEL

Brougham was prepared to take immediate advantage of the death of Queen Caroline. While her sudden end had prematurely removed her status as an issue in British politics, Brougham knew that this would ultimately happen, like the end of the alarm system that Nadin and the Bow Street police had established with the Home Secretary, Lord Sidmouth. The dream-like quality of the post-war world, with its threats of treason, and crushing taxes, would have to give way to a return to normality. Whatever Liverpool's Government did with the Whig challenge, it would have to find places for liberal Tories like Peel, and more useful employment for Canning. These ministers were capable of effecting reforms, provided that they were shown how. Brougham set about explaining just that.

The problem was to show that there was a way of dealing with questions such as law reform, prisons, police, economic policy, international relations, and colonial policy other than the way Sidmouth, Ellenborough, and Eldon advocated. In order to overthrow the status quo, one had to show, in a controlled, step-by-step way, how the destructive aspects of current policy could be eliminated. It would do no good, for example, to recommend a complete change of the law and legal system, as Bentham had done. Such efforts just encouraged arch conservatives to make extravagant plans under the current system. More limited objectives, such as what the Select Committee on the Criminal Law in 1819 had sought, were little better since they alienated just the very people who would have to effect them. It simply would not do to want to effect changes in domestic and international policy without the support and co-operation of ministers, administrators, and Judges. What was required was a revolution in government, and Brougham knew that this meant re-educating officials about law and policy.

In anticipation of Peel's rejoining Liverpool's Ministry, Brougham provided a general approach to all reform. Taking English conveyancing as his subject, Brougham, in typical fashion, acted as if he were reviewing Edward Sudgen's pamphlet, "A Series of Letters to a Man of Property, on the Sale, Purchase, Lease, Settlement, and Devise of Estates", and Bentham's 1817 "Papers relative to Codification." Actually, Brougham, as usual, wrote almost nothing about what he was ostensibly reviewing, using them rather as convenient points for a *via media*. Brougham introduced, in this deceptive, disarming way, the crucial topic:

> When the public mind is occupied by questions of great political importance, and whilst the discussions relating to the criminal laws, and the education of the poor, are yet unsettled, it is perhaps not politic to introduce a question respecting the enactment of new laws; and one, at the same time, which is so entirely stripped of all moral and political interest, that it is not probable the discussion of it will call forth supporters such as Sir Samuel Romilly, Mr Brougham, or Sir James Macintosh.[1]

---

1. Art.XI, "English Conveyancing," *Edinburgh Review*, vol.35, no.LXIX, March 1821, p.190. While New had not attributed this article to Brougham (*op. cit.*, appendix, p.439), subsequent ones show that it must have been his. New's analysis, especially for the 1820s, is most suspect because he relies too much upon the attributions supplied by others, long after the fact, and upon the gross output by Brougham, in terms of pages, rather than a comprehensive reading of the periodical, trying to figure out what it was trying to do, and what the contributions of individual writers might have been. New claimed that Brougham wrote articles 4, 9 and 12, claiming that they amounted to 83 pages, as the Brougham Manuscript Lists maintained. Actually, these articles only total 80 pages. It seems more likely that Brougham wrote articles 9, 11 and 12, the one on conveyancing, another on "Three Months near Rome," and another on his education bills, articles totalling 83 pages. To attribute the conveyancing article to C.H. Bellenden Ker, as *The Wellesly Index* has done, is totally unconvincing.

Of course, Brougham felt that the continuous support he was giving his education bills in the *Edinburgh Review*[2] would satisfy readers that he was not responsible for yet this article too. Bentham's approach, while good for reforming the criminal law, he wrote, citing his review of his theory of punishment as proof, "... no such change with regard to the laws of property would be productive of a beneficial result."[3] Bentham's plan for the law of property could only be established by force because it was neither understandable nor known. These established laws called for the reforming spirit of a Bacon or a Hale: "*a pruning and grafting of the law, not a ploughing up and planting it again.*"[4] The situation required the conservative proclivities of barristers, like a Blackstone.

Brougham then outlined how property was transferred, by deed, record, or devise. Fines and recovery actions, fictitious suits, had developed in the courts to get round the paralysing effect of entails, a procedure which the Chancery had expanded to trusts. A cheaper, quicker, more reliable process was needed. Brougham recommended that Parliament establish a process of enroling deeds in a general register, something that opponents of the slave trade had recommended for the colonies to help preserve their human resources. About piecemeal efforts to remove the problem of conveyancing, harking back to Romilly's 1819 concerns about codification efforts, Brougham added for the Ministry's benefit:

> Some one, at the suggestion of a busy constituent, brings into the House of Commons a bill to remedy some existing defect in the law. This, in general, is framed without much care, and

---

2. For Brougham's articles justifying them, *see* Art.VII, "Mr Ellenberg's *Establishments at Hofwyl,*" vol.31, no.LXI, December 1818, pp.150-65; art.XII, "Education Committee, and Abuse of Charities," *ibid.*, no.LXII, March 1819, pp.497-549; art.XIII, "Establishment at Hofwyl," *ibid.*, vol.342, no.LXIV, October 1819, pp.488-507; art.XI, "The New Plan of Education for England," *ibid.*, vol.34, no.LXVII, August 1820, pp.214-54; and art.XII, "Education Bill," *ibid.*, vol.35, no. LXIX, March 1821, pp.214-57.
3. "*English Conveyancing,*" *op. cit.*, p.195.
4. *Ibid.*, p.198. Italics Brougham's.

> with very little knowledge of the subject; the fate of the bill is, either that it excites no interest at all, or perhaps some clause is added, not always improving the consistency of the whole; and, in the House of Lords, it is either thrown out entirely, (and, whilst its defects are exposed and ridiculed by the learned Lord who presides there, the necessity of the remedy is not infrequently admitted); or if it should pass this ordeal, it rarely escapes some addition or rider, by which its inconsistency or insufficiency is rendered more glaring.[5]

A note explained that this was exactly what had happened when Parliament threatened to enrol memorials of grants of annuities.

Proper law reform required that the bills should be prepared by the Law Officers in consultation with the Judges. They were already law-makers, he wrote, casting aside the 1819 Committee's reluctance to use their advice because it would require them to criticize what they were required to enforce. In discussing the complicated system of leases and releases, which required stamping, Brougham showed that this was a much larger cause of concern because without controlled law reform, it allowed persons engaged in such expensive, cumbersome practices to prevent it. "The principal cause why a general enclosure bill did not pass the House of Lords," Brougham explained, "was, the loss which would be occasioned to the clerks and officers of Parliament, who reaped large sums, in the way of fees, upon private bills."[6] A general register of deeds, something that Lord Kenyon had prepared a bill for, should be tried, Brougham concluded, because registers had been found to work in Middlesex and Yorkshire.

In the next issue, as Peel's appointment to the Home Office drew closer, Brougham provided an article on the reduction of capital punishment in the *Review* for his benefit, one so successful in execution that historians have attributed it to his best-known

5. *Ibid.*, p.206.
6. *Ibid.*, p.208. For how this effort affected Peel see Trowbridge H. Ford, "English Criminal Law Reform: from Peterloo to Peel," *Durham University Journal*, vol.LXXVI, no.2 (June 1984), p.213 ff.

critic, William Hazlitt. The wayward essayist was equally unfair in his portrayal of Brougham, and Barnes of *The Times* because of how they had treated his brother-in-law, the infamous Dr Stoddart. Hazlitt, in his portraits for *The Spirit of the Age*, passed the Whig barrister and politician off as just another Scottish bore. Brougham simply practised Scottish oratory: "... it sees no visions but its own set purpose, its own *data*, and its own dogmas."[7] As for his effectiveness, Hazlitt added:

> In so many details (which he himself goes through with unwearied and unshrinking resolution) the spirit of the question is lost to others who have not the same voluntary power of attention or the same interest in hearing that he has in speaking; the original impulse that urged him forward is forgotten in so wide a field, in so interminable a career.[8]

Hazlitt treated Brougham as if he were unable to learn by experience, as if he would treat Peel in the same way after Peterloo that he had treated Castlereagh, Sidmouth, and Eldon before. Of course, Brougham was working with potentially a vastly different set of ministers, and Hazlitt knew it, preferring to see him hopelessly lost in trying to induce people to change policies who "... are not *calculated into* contempt or indignation on abstract grounds."[9] Brougham was counting on Peel to be shamed into making reasonable reforms when it was clearly shown that they were necessary, and could be effected without risking chaos.

Brougham tried to persuade the Ministry to legislate a vast reduction of capital punishment. In dismissing the arguments by proponents of Paley's penology, Brougham engaged in just what Hazlitt thought he was incapable of: "To treat men as brute beasts in our speculations, is to encourage ourselves to treat them as such in our practice; and that is the way to make them what we

7. William Hazlitt, *The Spirit of the Age* (World Classics, Oxford University Press, 1904), p.199. Italics Hazlitt's.
8. *Ibid.*, p.202.
9. *Ibid.* Italics Hazlitt's.

pretend to believe they are."[10] In considering the complacency of some towards capital punishment, although the times, and the needs of society had changed, Brougham sounded much like Romilly in teaching Hazlitt a lesson: "We see the same names (some of them great and grave ones too) opposed successively to the Abolition of the Slave-Trade, to the concession of the Catholic Claims, and to the Amelioration of the Penal Laws, - on the same stale plea of guarding against innovation and theories."[11] The recommendations of the Report of the Select Committee on the Criminal Law were reviewed to rekindle interest in law reform despite Peterloo, and the infamous Six Acts. Brougham denounced the idea that severity of the law often added to its efficiency, illustrating his argument by the empty exchange Lord Granville had had with Eldon over ending executions for stealing five shillings from a shop. To assist ministerial support for a limited repeal of the capital statutes, Brougham examined how the Waltham Black Act, and the statute against injuring Westminster Bridge had become the basis for the harsh penal code. "We here see," Brougham wrote for the benefit of a prudent Home Secretary, "an example of the effects of this miscellaneous style of legislating."[12] For good measure, to assist Brougham's effort with the Ministry, editor Jeffrey added Sydney Smith's article on the need to reform the prisons to the *Review* issue.

Brougham had a piece on the nomination of Scottish juries in the next issue of the *Review*. While it was ostensibly on Bentham's "The Element of the Art of Packing", Brougham admitted in characteristic style that this was just a stratagem for his getting a sympathetic hearing by law reformers: "We must confess that we have no intention of saying anything of Mr Bentham or his book on the present occasion; and that we have borrowed the title of it merely as a peg on which to hang a discussion of a

---

10. Art.IV, "Capital Punishment," *Edinburgh Review*, vol.35, no.LXX, July 1821, p.318. N.B. that this article is just the number of pages that he is said to have contributed to this issue.
11. *Ibid.*, pp.320-1.
12. *Ibid.*, p.338.

more local and domestic nature."[13] The way the Scottish judicial system functioned, especially jury selection, was his pressing concern. Proper judicial process required Judges whose discretion was reduced to a minimum by rules and laws, courts whose officers were free, as far as possible, of executive and administrative responsibilities, juries whose deliberations and decisions were of constant significance, and proceedings which were subject to constant publicity. While the Scottish system possessed some admirable aspects, Brougham continued somewhat inaccurately, it gave the Crown and Judges too much power. The Attorney General was too free to prosecute offences, and the Bench too free to declare new crimes. Since grand juries were unknown to Scotland, Brougham favoured Kennedy's bill to end the Judge's selection of juries, especially since their promotion rested with the Crown, and to establish the peremptory challenge of jurors. The reviewer explained that the measure's objectives were in harmony with the achievement of judicial independence.

> It is for this very reason, that every one who understands the right application of the principle, that old institutions are not to be rashly touched, must be friendly to the success of this simple and yet renovating measure. By adopting it, everything else may stand. The good that remains cannot possibly be hurt, and what is bad or doubtful must be corrected and improved.[14]

When Robert Peel was appointed Home Secretary in January 1822, and showed immediate sympathy towards Brougham's approach by assisting passage of Kennedy's bill, the barrister

---

13. Art.IX, "Nomination of Scottish Juries," *ibid.*, vol.36, no.LXXI, October 1821, p.174. For Brougham's authorship of this article, N.B. what he said in the next article on the same subject, one that New claimed was his, about this one: "Our statements, upon that occasion, were so full and so minute, that there can be no need for resuming them." (*Ibid.*, vol.38, no.LXXV, February 1823, p.226). The claim by *The Wellesley Index* that these were done by Henry Cockburn, overlooked the fact that he later wrote two of his own to refute their claims and conclusions.

14. *Ibid.*, p.219.

directed his attention towards re-educating the Law Officers. While Brougham did not place much confidence in Attorney General Gifford, Eldon's close friend who had prosecuted Dr Watson, Thistlewood, the Queen and the "Pentridge rising,"[15] he had high hopes for Copley, the Solicitor General. Gifford was bound to be raised to the Bench soon, and Copley would have to resume the responsibility of instituting *ex officio* informations against the press. Brougham took as his text Lord Liverpool's pamphlet on the degraded state of the political press, contending that irresponsible elements justified libel prosecutions. Brougham went through government policy towards inflammatory publications, stressing the leniency it showed towards them before and after Peterloo. "It was strongly suspected, from circumstances which afterwards came to light," Brougham concluded, "that some of the government spies were connected with the worst of the publications in question ..."[16] While the Ministry had used them to help justify the Six Acts, reactionaries followed their example by libelling the Queen, and forming the Constitutional Association. About how its vigilantes pursued Carlile, Dolby and Ridgway, Brougham reminded Copley: "Alas, an informer has only to purchase any old book with a libellous passage in it ..."[17] In the face of the government's expedient approach to such unjust, private prosecutions, liberal groups were obliged to protect themselves. Such a competition of private prosecutions threatened a constitutional crisis if the Lords became involved since the upper house would be the court of last resort and members like Lord Lonsdale had provided the backbone of the Constitutional Association. The prudent thing for the Ministry to do would be to take exclusive control of criminal prosecution, and to reduce reliance upon *ex officio* informations for libel to an absolute minimum, Brougham concluded.

In the next issue of the *Review*, he let the Crown know just

---

15. Sir William Holdsworth, *A History of English Law* (Methuen, London, 1952, 14 vols.), no.XIII, p.664.
16. Art.IV, "Constitutional Association," *Edinburgh Review*, vol.37, no.LXXIII, June 1822, p.112.
17. *Ibid.*, p.116.

what it risked if it continued to let the Bridge-Street people have their way. In preparation for Williams' sentencing for libelling Durham's clergy, Brougham prepared a revised version of his charge, leaving out his bitterest condemnation of the clergy. "The report of Mr Brougham's speech bears the marks of having been, in great part at least carefully revised," he explained, "a precaution, perhaps, necessary for a professional man defending publications respecting the Church and its members ..."[18] In reviewing the case, Brougham said enough about the people who caused the attack that Dr Phillpotts, the Bishop of Durham, was made to sound like Rev. Blacow in his condemnation of the Queen, leaving little doubt about what would happen to such people if the Crown continued to offer its facilities to such interests. If anyone thought Brougham was bluffing, he wrote this in a footnote about his defence of the Durham publisher: "It is criminative, contemptuous, and defying."[19] Under the circumstances, the Crown adopted a more prudent course towards *ex officio* informations already instituted,[20] and initiated a review of what should be its policy towards all informations in future.

When Castlereagh committed suicide in late summer 1822, Brougham moved immediately to force Canning, his replacement at the Foreign Office, to join the reforming of Liverpool's Government. Fearful that Canning would just observe the reactionary policy-making of the Lord Chancellor, as he had with Sidmouth and Castlereagh after the war, Brougham attacked him as a defender of the status quo in the *Review*.[21] Brougham, in reviewing Canning's collected speeches, denied the new Foreign Secretary's claim that the government could do nothing about conditions, recalling his predecessor's feeble plea that England could do nothing about Spain and Portugal's treatment of the slave trade. The City of Liverpool needed a reformer, not a

---

18. Art.IV, "Durham Case - Clerical Abuses," *ibid.*, no.LXXIV, November 1822, p.358.
19. *Ibid.*, no.58.
20. G.T. Garratt, *Lord Brougham* (Macmillan, London, 1935), p.165.
21. Art.V, "Mr Canning, *and Reform*," *Edinburgh Review*, vol.37, no.LXXIV, November 1822, pp.379-407.

proclaimer of patience, as Canning had stated. The people needed to be given more power, parliamentary reform had to be effected, Brougham continued, if the government was going to deal with the host of abuses which existed. New political power, Brougham contended, would see the country dealing with questions such as the Draconian criminal code, and the failure to suppress the slave trade rather than Canning's *laissez-faire* approach to conditions.[22] Canning was being challenged to drop the observer role which characterized the operation of his Pantheon,[23] or face the political oblivion of a follower of the Lord Chancellor. On the eve of the opening of the next Session, Brougham reminded Canning again of what was expected of him, in a review of Henry Grattan's speeches:

> He strenuously supported all the measures of reform, whether economical or Parliamentary, both in the Irish and English House of Commons; and though he agreed with those who, alarmed by the French Revolution, approved of the war both in 1793 and 1815, yet he never suffered his views of foreign affairs for an instant to abate his hostility towards the baneful corruption of our internal administration.[24]

Brougham showed by his own behaviour that he too was capable of change. Starting in 1822, he adopted a very different approach towards politics, with his behaviour in the Commons. Instead of coming in with a programme for an alternative government, probably based upon an anonymous pamphlet written specifically for an article in the *Review*, he took each issue separately, and in the least contentious way. After he had given his answer to the Address, speeches on the country's distress, as he had the previous Session, he withdrew from the political scene to let his

---

22. *Ibid.*, p.406.
23. For an account of how Canning had been reduced to a ministerial scribbler by the post-war alarms, see J.E. Cookson, "Canning's Pantheon," *History*, vol.62, no.204, pp.45 ff.
24. Art.III, "Grattan's *Speeches*," *Edinburgh Review*, vol.38, no.LXXV, February 1823, pp.77-8.

advice take effect.

While New is convinced that Brougham was again ill, requiring his absence from Parliament,[25] research and writing for *The Times* about the activities of the Bridge-Street committee seem more likely reasons. There was nothing Brougham could do in the Commons to assist police, prison, and criminal law reform. Without parliamentary pressure, Peel had been willing to see to the appointment of committees to inquire into police and prison conditions, something which forced Macintosh, who had seen almost no results from the 1819 Report on the Criminal Law, to intervene. Up to now, all the criminal law reformers could show for their confidence in the new Home Secretary was the defence's right to peremptory challenges in the Scottish Juries Act, something to which Brougham had seen, to Peel's "infinite credit". In June, Macintosh called upon the House to commit itself during the next Session to a comprehensive review of law enforcement with the idea of radical reform.[26] While Gifford reacted to the motion in predictable fashion, Peel committed himself to a bill to improve prison discipline, and some experiments in preventive police, once the select committee had reported. "God forbid that he should mean to countenance a system of espionage," Peel said for Brougham's benefit, "but a vigorous preventive police, consistent with the free principles of our free constitution ..."[27] was certainly desirable. While the Home Secretary regretted the blanket character of Macintosh's indictment, he promised a constructive attitude towards proposals in 1823.

While this commitment seemed good enough for Brougham since he did not speak on the motion, Macintosh pushed the matter to a vote, explaining that its passage would put the country on notice that change was envisaged by the House. "They would thus invite persons of knowledge and experience to lay their sentiments upon the subject before parliament."[28] The

---

25. New, *op. cit.*, pp.263-4.
26. *The Parliamentary Debates*, vol.VII, n.s., col.791.
27. *Ibid.*, cols.803-4.
28. *Ibid.*, col.804.

motion passed over the government's objection, with Brougham voting with the majority. During the next year, events showed the emptiness of Macintosh's approach. Nothing happened, although there were the expected petitions asking for reform of law enforcement.

Finally, towards the end of May 1823, after Brougham had done nothing to make good the pledge, Macintosh came forward, asking for the approval of resolutions which would bring the demands for criminal law reform up to date. Peel agreed with much of what Macintosh requested, although he objected to his citing foreign authorities to justify the changes. The Home Secretary thought that Macintosh did not sufficiently appreciate the need of capital punishment for some crimes against property, although he did say that he favoured the repeal of the most notorious of the capital statutes, such as those for cutting down trees, killing or wounding animals, and impersonating Greenwich pensioners.[29] In the ensuing debate, while the reformers, except for Brougham, said the expected things about Peel's proposal, Scarlett said that they had misunderstood him, and that the Home Secretary had been converted to Romilly's principle. Macintosh reacted thus to the idea: "The conduct of his majesty's ministers upon this subject reminded him of an expression of a friend of his, with respect to another person, that he was a great friend to general principles, but had an exception for every particular case."[30] The House sided with Peel, however, rejecting each one of Macintosh's resolutions.

Events proved Peel to be a man of his word, as Scarlett had suggested. During the next Session, Parliament repealed capital punishment for over a hundred crimes, as the Home Secretary suggested, without so much as a dissenting voice. Thomas Denman, it seems, made note of the fact in the *Review* in exactly the same terms that the busy Brougham would have if he had had the time. Using Dumont's *Traite des Preuves Judiciaires* as another peg upon which to base another discussion of law

---

29. *Ibid.*, vol.IX, col.426.
30. *Ibid.*, vol.431.

reform, Denman applauded the English manner in which Peel was proceeding. Bentham's naturalistic approach to criminal procedure was repudiated for a more traditional one to law reform. As Bacon had suggested, existent rules had to be improved rather than imposing a completely new system. Denman illustrated the need by discussing rules which helped defeat justice, but without any of the gratuitous contempt for English procedure which had so angered Bentham's critics. "The exclusion of testimony, the most fatal bar to justice," Denman explained, "is by no means peculiar to the law of England."[31] Contrary to Paley's assurance that all those who were executed because of faulty procedure died in service to the nation, Denman called upon the Home Secretary to see to its rectification. As a precedent for such action, Denman cited what Peel had just done about capital felonies, noting that he had done in a single Session what the Whigs had been unable to do since Romilly first raised the matter in 1809.

Brougham helped ensure that Peel kept his promise to Macintosh by the way Brougham handled Canning during the 1823 Session. Brougham, happy to see such liberal Tories join the Ministry, and yet fearful that they would purchase reforms in some areas by agreeing to reactionary ones in others, adopted a new policy towards the Speech from the Throne. Instead of moving the customary amendment to it, as he had in every previous Session, he supported the government's foreign policy both in the New World and the Old. Instead of joining the Holy Alliance against liberal regimes around the world, the government had committed itself to a policy of tolerance, and non-intervention. Brougham promised his co-operation with what Canning was doing, stating that he would not quarrel with any servants of the Crown who "... in performing his duty to his country, to freedom and to the world, speak a language that is truly British, pursue a policy that is truly free."[32] Brougham was

---

31. Art.VIII, "Law of Evidence - Criminal Procedure - Publicity," *Edinburgh Review*, vol 40, no.LXXIX, March 1824, p.177.
32. Quoted from New, *op. cit.*, p.269.

only afraid that conservative opposition to Canning's policies, both in Parliament, and the Cabinet, would oblige him to adopt reactionary policies at home.

When the Foreign Secretary charged Lord Folkestone, one of Brougham's most faithful followers, with "truckling" on an issue, he, most calculatingly, attacked Canning for doing the same on Catholic Emancipation. Brougham, feigning anger as though he were representing some client in a courtroom, charged the Foreign Secretary with truckling to the Lord Chancellor:

> If at that critical moment he who had said on the last night that he would not truckle to a noble lord, but who then had exhibited a specimen, the most incredible specimen, of monstrous truckling for the purpose of obtaining office, that the whole history of political tergiversation could furnish ...[33]

Canning, sensitive to charges that Wellington had procured some restraining commitment from him in joining the Ministry, was immediately on his feet, protesting: "I rise to say that that is false!"[34] The Speaker tried without success to get Canning to retract the charge, and Brougham merely used the opportunity to amplify the Foreign Secretary's subordination to the Chancellor. Brougham forced out of Canning a commitment to maintain a liberal course under conditions which he would find difficult to overlook. The House was most irritated with Canning because he had violated its rules to establish his integrity.

With Eldon so isolated that even Peel had not tried to defend him during Brougham's attack on Canning, Brougham started closing the door on the Chancellor. Brougham set the scene by having an article in the May 1823 issue of the *Review*, showing that Eldon had allowed the Chancery to deteriorate into a sorry state, and calling upon him to reform it. In July, Brougham expanded his attack by claiming in the Commons that Eldon, not

---

33. *The Parliamentary Debates*, vol.VIII, n.s., col.1079.
34. *Ibid.*, Art.XII, "The Court of Chancery," *Edinburgh Review*, vol.39, no.LXXVII, October 1823, p.248.

Liverpool, was for all intents and purposes, the Prime Minister. By October, when no progress had been noted, Brougham wrote another article in the same periodical on the Chancellor, based upon a convenient, anonymous pamphlet about Eldon's performance on the Woolsack. The Chancellor's plodding pace in dealing with cases was seen as the height of irresponsibility:

> The continuance of Lord Eldon's dynasty, which has endured for nearly a quarter of a century, and has considerably exceeded the average length of the reigns of the Kings of England since the Conquest, has afforded an unlimited opportunity for the formation or perfection of a system.[35]

The only way that this could occur, how the demands for reform by such MPs as Taylor and Williams could be effected, would be to have the committee of inquiry, which had been most reluctantly appointed, consult expert witnesses about institutional changes. True professionals would advise changes such as separation of the Chancellor's judicial and political functions, and removal of the bankruptcy jurisdiction from the Chancery. When the Ministry preempted Brougham's promise of another article on the Lords' jurisdiction by making Gifford a peer and appointing him Deputy Speaker,[36] his review was overtaken by the event, denouncing the appointment of a Speaker without a peerage: "... the wit of man never invented any thing more inconvenient, and indeed absurd, than a speaker not a member of the House over which he presides."[37] The problem of the Chancellorship would not be resolved by creating new offices, Brougham wrote, but by making the Chancery more efficient, a most pointed reminder about Eldon's reactionary sentiments about the need of judicial reform. Brougham's advice about new offices proved correct when Gifford died prematurely in 1826. By then, the Chancery business was in shambles.

---

35. *Ibid.*, p.250.
36. Holdsworth, *op. cit.*, vol.XIII, p.664.
37. Art.VII, "Court of Chancery," *Edinburgh Review*, vol.39, no.LXXVIII, January 1824, p.445.

Because of Brougham's long-range, controlled approach to reform which put a premium on policy changes, and statutes rather than the more traditional one of simply scoring points against the government in the Commons, he had much more time for his rapidly expanding legal practice. His stature at the Bar was captured by his directing the team which sought to have Lord Portsmouth declared insane by the Lunacy Commission during February 1823. During the three-week hearing at London's Freemasons' Hall, which *The Times* gave front-page coverage to, Brougham examined the most persuasive witnesses as to the peer's insanity. Dr Ludlow, his personal physician who had known him for more than 20 years, testified that he was "... a person quite unable to guide himself."[38] A long-time servant described how the Lord had twisted the leg of a bed-ridden servant, suspected of feigning a fracture: "... I heard it snap."[39] Brougham had another servant testify that Portsmouth had a schoolboy lashed 80 times for nothing. When Lady Portsmouth, better known as Mrs Adler because of the affair she was having in closest proximity to the "King of Hampshire", was reported as having consigned her husband to a dung cart, *The Times* gave it special prominence. This experience helped cause Brougham to have the greatest sensitivity towards the problems of the insane, especially after they had been committed to madhouses, and came under the jurisdiction of the Chancery. On the last day of February 1823, the jury declared Portsmouth to be insane.

While Brougham was winning this case, Serjeant Hullock was appointed a Baron of the Court of Exchequer, giving Brougham the lead of the Northern Circuit. The promotion was intended to reduce Brougham's chances of making trouble at Westminster and in the North. By increasing his responsibilities on Circuit, while denying him the services of more senior colleagues as junior counsel, the petition guaranteed that his representation would be most expensive unless he acted alone. In effect the promotion tended to divide the business between Brougham and

---

38. *The Times*, February 12, 1823, no.11,793, p.3.
39. *Ibid.*, February 13, 1823, no.11,794, p.3.

the leading K.C., especially Scarlett. It was intended to reduce Brougham into another Hullock. "Mr Brougham is thus compelled, in justice to himself," Barnes explained in *The Times*, "and in the duty of securing by his exertions, his independence of character, to leave the House of Commons, at a moment when his eloquence is adding fresh dignity and force to the cause of civil liberty."[40] The leader complained that because of Eldon's antipathy, Brougham had not been made King's Counsel, as his standing in legal practice, and his performance on the Queen's behalf justified. The *Leeds Mercury* printed a similarly favourable portrait of Brougham as a parliamentarian in its May 21st issue, especially of his ability to attack the propositions of others, particularly Peel's.

This new difficulty was much in evidence at the Yorkshire Lent Assizes when Brougham first appeared as leader, defending *Higgins* v. *Reid*, an insurance recovery action, however, Scarlett got the verdict despite the crowd's involuntary burst of applause at one point in appreciation of Brougham's losing effort. He celebrated his elevation at the Lancaster Assizes by getting some rioters at Ashton-under-Lyne, marking Peterloo's anniversary in a most seditious way, released on their recognizances, once they had pleaded guilty. Brougham, in getting the court to accept what the parties had agreed to, explained their behaviour most freely to the presiding Judge: "They acted under the influence of their feeling, my Lord. If I had been in their situation, I do not know but I should have done the same."[41]

Once the Spring Assizes were over, Brougham was back in London, combining parliamentary and legal activities in ways that suited his interests. He set up the famous April 17th attack on Canning by complaining, to the House's great pleasure, about the government's reaction to French intervention in Spain, once the relevant correspondence had been made public: "He believed from all he had seen, that the conduct of the French Government

---

40. *Ibid.*, March 1, 1823, no.11,808, p.3.
41. *R.* v. *Charles Walker and Others*, *ibid.*, April 12, 1823, no.11,844, p.4.

had been most perfidious."[42] Once the Foreign Secretary had called Brougham a liar, he played an important part in the House's inquiry into the conduct of Dublin's High Sheriff, showing that the operation of Ireland's judiciary indeed called for the passage of Catholic Emancipation, something Canning was suspected of being too opportunistic about.

As Brougham's legal business had expanded because of his handling of adultery cases, it now increased in lunatic cases because of his handling of the Portsmouth dispute. In *Poppleton* v. *Simpson,* he moved successfully for a new trial in an ejectment action for the heir at law because the devisee had unjustly benefitted by the will of an insane person. Brougham failed, however, in the defence of *Leach* v. *Veitch*, an action brought by a lunatic because of his treatment under a doctor's care.[43] In *R.* v. *Noel*, Brougham and Copley failed to have an action thrown out of court because the plaintiff, magistrate Matthew Wilson, had obliged the defendant to write letters calling for a duel, a defence that the King's Bench would not hear of. When the same was heard at York, Brougham lost it, and a few others to Scarlett when he compared the conciliatory plaintiff to the discredited Majocchin. Recognition and increased authority usually brought out the worst in Brougham until new situations and circumstances forced him to adjust his behaviour.

Brougham could not have been too upset by these setbacks in court because his plan for enlisting Canning's services for reform was going ahead. While the House was sitting as a Committee of the Whole to examine the complaints against the Sheriff of Dublin, the *Dublin Evening Mail* published some of the more shocking evidence about how he operated, contrary to its order. John Williams MP moved to have its printer called to the Bar for a breach of privilege,[44] something which was in the Ministry's interest. Brougham intervened, however, stating that the Commons should not move to punish defenceless persons

42. *Ibid.*, April 15, 1823, no.11,846, p.4.
43. *Ibid.*, May 14, 1823, no.11,871, p.3.
44. *Ibid.*, May 15, 1823, no.11,872, p.2.

when more powerful ones were more deserving of it, citing how he had called upon the House to treat a similar dispute the previous July. Punishing innocent violations of House orders, Brougham complained, could only be motivated by party spirit. Once another MP had offered further explanation of the newspaper's behaviour, Canning allowed the matter to drop, although he disagreed with Brougham's apology.

The next day, while the House was debating Fowell Buxton's motion for emancipation, Brougham prevailed upon the Foreign Secretary to admit the ultimate justification of the freeing of the slaves through this argument about slaveowners: "Motives of interest would not, therefore, be safely trusted as a guarantee for humanity."[45] In case Canning had any reservations about where Brougham was leading him, the barrister intervened in the questioning of another witness before the Dublin Sheriff's inquiry to show that he was not motivated by any party spirit. When Jones, a Whig MP, had asked the magistrate, Henry Sirr how he ordered committals, Brougham was incensed at how the questioner tried to lead the witness to the conclusion that the Law Officers ordered him, "... assuming a fact, and putting into witness's mouth what he did not say."[46]

As the parliamentary Session drew to a close, Brougham was most busily occupied in court, initiating prosecutions,[47] trying to change verdicts,[48] and defending clients.[49] In *Shaw* v. *Williams*, he brought forth the full powers of his invective in defending a rich man, charged with seduction. The prosecution was torn apart, showing that the plaintiff had openly pursued the defendant, only to be stopped by her father when she was visibly pregnant.[50] It took the prosecution three years to open the damage suit, Brougham complained. If the jury must give the

---

45. *Ibid.*, May 16, 1823, no.11,873, p.2.
46. *Ibid.*, May 24, 1823, no.11,880, p.1.
47. See, eg, *In the Matter of Clark, Isaacson, and Brooks, ibid.*, June 14, 1823, no.11,898, Supplement, p.3.
48. See, eg, *R.* v. *Triebner, ibid.*, June 2, 1823, no.11,887, p.3.
49. See, eg, *R.* v. *Maria Glenn, ibid.*, June 4, 1823, no.11,889, p.4.
50. *Ibid.*, June 21, 1823, no.11,904, p.3.

plaintiff something for the loss, let it be of the basest coin. The jury agreed, awarding 40 shillings.

As was sometimes the case, Brougham let the victory go to his head, and the next time he faced the barrister, Phillips in the King's Bench, he was more interested in scoring points than in getting justice for his client. In *Wood* v. *Wainright*, the defendant had been charged with assaulting the plaintiff, once he had heard that he had called him a most damnable character. Wainright knocked Wood from his horse, causing his head to bleed. Brougham admitted that his client had done wrong, and should pay something. The call for the mitigation of damages was, however, completely defeated by his claim that Wood had already jilted a lady for 2,000 pounds through breach of promise to marry.[51] Once the humorously-put charge was shown to be not only false but also irrelevant, the jury docked Brougham's client for the full hundred pounds that the prosecution had asked for. Brougham fared no better before the Judicial Committee of the Privy Council in pressing Lord Douglas's claim to carry the Imperial Crown of Scotland in royal processions. In contesting the Duke of Hamilton's right to perform this privilege, Brougham got into a dispute with one of the presiding Judges, Lord Redesdale, about the status of Scotland under the Act of Union, and whether or not the King could be crowned in Scotland, issues reminiscent of his claims about the Queen's coronation. In July, the Privy Council decided in Hamilton's favour.[52]

Once free of legislative concerns, when the Session ended, Brougham had more time to better prepare his cases on the Northern Circuit, and his increased application showed in the results. At York, Brougham helped get difficult defamation, libel, and seduction suits settled with most modest damages, and he won *Frith* v. *Blacklock*, a debt-recovery suit over a contested will. In the libel action, Brougham was so successful in his cross-examination, getting a witness to admit that the plaintiff might indeed be called Sir Robert Numskull, that he abandoned

---

51. *Ibid.*, July 4, 1823, no.11,915, p.3.
52. *Ibid.*, July 10, 1823, no.11,920, p.3.

justification of what the defendant had said for a plea of reduced damages.[53] At Durham, Brougham saw *Kilburne* v. *Kilburne* go to arbitration, as he had moved, and at Newcastle Assizes, he was pitted against Scarlett in three assault actions. Brougham lost *Dickson* v. *Hodson* when Scarlett showed that the attorney responsible for the prosecution had opened no less than three suits.[54] Scarlett, however, saw Brougham's plaintiff in another action receive significant damages after he tried to play down the consequences of the assault. Brougham reciprocated by trying to make too much of a witness's past crime in another assault action, a liberty which resulted in Scarlett's client receiving 30 pounds in damages.[55]

At the Lancaster Assizes, Brougham recovered beautifully by getting *R.* v. *Hinton*, a drunken squabble between friends which had been blown up into a case of attempted murder, dropped. Brougham, during cross-examination of the victim,[56] showed the danger of not having a public prosecutor to stop such prosecutions. In other actions, Brougham, when he was not working with Scarlett, had so much the better of the argument that he was reduced to dire expedients. In *R.* v. *Blackhurst*, Scarlett was willing to see the restoration of the pillory to punish the defendant, an attorney charged with compounding offences under the game laws. Brougham had him released on his own recognizances, once he pleaded guilty to one of the mildest charges in the 57-count indictment.[57]

Brougham's practice before the full King's Bench during 1823 had been even more successful, experience which makes one doubt the claims by Horner, Tindal, and Campbell about Brougham as a barrister, especially about his presenting an argument *in banc*.[58] Horner, for example, claimed that Brougham's arguments there lacked the "precision and clearness

53. *Earshaw* v. *Charlton*, *ibid.*, July 28, 1823, no.11,935, p.3.
54. *Ibid.*, August 4, 1823, no.11,944, p.3.
55. *Walton* v. *Watson*, *ibid.*, August 5, 1823, no.11,942, p.3.
56. *Ibid.*, August 18, 1823, no.11,953, pp.2-3.
57. *Ibid.*, August 20, 1823, no.11,955, p.3.
58. Holdsworth, *op. cit.*, vol.XII, pp.198-9.

in the details, symmetry in the putting of them together, an air of finish and unity in the whole ..."[59] Actually, Horner would have been on better grounds if he had said this about Brougham's efforts in the *Review* concerning the Lord Advocate, efforts intended to oblige Peel to take up criminal law reform, and whose overstatements Henry Cockburn was struggling to correct in the same journal.[60] Before the Lord Chief Justice's court, Brougham won all the cases he wanted to, except for getting the King's Bench to issue a writ of *procedendo* against the Bridge-Street Committee for its forgery prosecution of Daniel Ridgway.[61] The King's Bench experience was most rewarding to Brougham as it reinforced his convictions that Parliament's Private Bill procedure was a veritable Augean stable which required drastic reform. In *Taylor* v. *Higgins*, Brougham's client, an engineer, was entitled to remuneration for the preparation of an incorrect map for a Private Bill even when it had failed to pass.[62] It was the solicitor's responsibility to see that all was in order for parliamentary passage, and on petition he should have seen to its correction. In *Holmes* v. *Higgins*, Brougham saw to it that a surveyor who spent his own money in preparing material in support of a railway bill, before the commencement of the partnership, was not rewarded.[63] Frederick Pollock argued vainly for the award which had been given by an arbitrator for the York Assizes. Brougham even triumphed over his future nemesis, John Campbell, in *Laing* v. *Barclay*, an award which the biographer of the Lord Chancellors argued unsuccessfully against. It seems that it was experience such as this which later led Campbell to write so negatively about Brougham's performance

---

59. Quoted from *ibid.*, p.198, no.8.
60. See, eg, Art.V, "Office of Lord Advocate of Scotland," *Edinburgh Review*, vol.39, no.LXXVIII, January 1824, pp.363-92.
61. For documentation of Brougham's triumphs, see the first volume of a new publication, *The Law Journal, 1823* (Paget, Chancery Lane, London), pp.5, 20, 31-2, 47, 53 and 153.
62. 1LJ20. For a fuller account of this side of Brougham's career, see Trowbridge H. Ford, "Henry Brougham and the Reform of Private Bill Legislation," *Parliaments, Estates and Representation*, vol.4, no.2 (December 1984), pp.169-186.
63. 1LJ48.

as a barrister, to Pollock's benefit.[64]

Once the Northern Circuit was over, Brougham did what he could to keep up the pressure on the liberal Tories, especially Peel, to continue reform. In a leader in *The Times*, he apparently recounted the difficulties suitors were experiencing in Chancery for the Home Secretary's benefit: "Our firm opinion is, that no inconsiderable portion of the next session of Parliament and very much of public attention out of Parliament, will be directed to the Chancellor ..."[65] Romilly's failure to do anything about Eldon's sway in Chancery was explained by the fact that the court's barrister feared that if he made an enemy of the Lord Chancellor, the court would simply stop. "The kind of vengeance that would have been inflicted has been evinced," the article added, "in the case of another lawyer. Mr Brougham resisted the detestable bill of pains and penalties."[66] To show Peel that reform was practical, Brougham allowed a dinner to be given in his honour at Glasgow later in September at which he extolled Scotland's improvement during the past 30 years, because of efforts by people like himself.[67] To give immediate substance to English possibilities, Brougham wrote to Dr George Birkbeck about the need of establishing a mechanics' institute in the metropolis along the lines of the one in Glasgow, a recommendation which, with the assistance of *The Times*, almost immediately became reality.[68] For once, Brougham did not overplay his role in directing change, refusing to serve, as did Denman, on a committee to find a site for a statue of Lord Erskine.

During the fall, Brougham immersed himself so totally in two cases that the rest of his practice suffered. One of Gifford's last actions as Attorney General had been to prosecute *The Sunday Times* on a *ex officio* information for libel after it wrote that the King was insane. After its printer and publisher had been found

---

64. Holdsworth, *op. cit.*, vol.XIII, pp.198-9.
65. *The Times*, September 13, 1823, no.11,976, p.2.
66. *Ibid.*
67. *Ibid.*, September 16, 1823, no.11,978, p.2.
68. *Ibid.*, November 13, 1823, no.12,028, p.3.

guilty, Brougham and Denman argued *in banc* before the King's Bench that they should be granted a new trial because the Lord Chief Justice had misdirected the jury.[69] In making a defence reminiscent of the one in Creevey's case, they contended that the claim, since it was not based upon malice, was reasonable under the circumstances. Abbott should have instructed the jury to find them guilty only if they had a wilful motive. Once the Judges upheld his direction to the jury, Brougham mounted such a protest in *The Times* that they never went to prison,[70] and Copley, Gifford's successor, never instituted another *ex-officio* information for libel. Brougham explained the change thus to the Newspaper Press Benevolent Association in July 1839:

> It certainly was not owing to the Press itself, he said, that no ground for prosecution was afforded. If his noble friend had chosen to pursue a different line of conduct to that which he had taken up, there was not a day during the time that he was Attorney-General in which he might not have filed an *ex officio* information.[71]

Brougham was more directly successful in arguing the Peruvian Loan case, *Kinder* v. *Everett*. As insurrections against Spanish authority in the New World succeeded, creditors of the governments became very worried about how their funds on deposit in English banks were spent. In 1823, parties were so concerned about how the funds of the Peruvian Government were dispensed that they obtained an injunction from the Chancellor against it, relief which was dissolved in July.[72] When the bankers holding the funds refused to do as the contractor of the loan directed, he had taken them to court. Brougham explained the action by the defendants before Eldon thus: "Perhaps they thought, that in the multitude of counsellors there

---

69. *R.* v. *Harvey and Chapman*, 2LJ4.
70. See the coverage in *The Times*, starting with the leader on November 1, 1823, no.12,017, p.2.
71. Sir Theodore Martin, *A Life of Lord Lyndhurst* (Murray, London, 1883), p.205.
72. *The Times*, July 5, 1823, no.11,916, p.3.

was safety, and that in the Court of Chancery there was a comfort (a laugh) but that Court no longer laid on them its friendly restriction."[73] Copley, the Solicitor General, tried to make light of the defeat in Chancery by explaining that the defendants had favoured the injunction's dissolution because it had not been brought by the right parties. Brougham's claim that the country was just experiencing civil strife, and that the bank should honour business as usual was brushed aside as an argument contrary to Britain's national interest. The money in question, Copley charged, had been used to support an insurrection against Spain, a government with which Britain had friendly relations. The funds were being withheld from their contractor out of legitimate interest for the welfare of the subscribers and their agents. Brougham responded by stating that the plaintiff was just a regular depositor, entitled to the free use of the monies. His Majesty's Government had withdrawn its envoys from Lima, Brougham reminded the jury. Abbot, for the King's Bench, ruled that Kinder was fully entitled to the deposit in his name, but the right to the account in the name of the "State of Peru" was left for the jury's determination. It found for Brougham's client. Barnes hailed the decision in a leader as obliging the Spanish Government to recognize the independence of the South American states.

To make sure that the government stopped suppressing information and reasonable comment about controversial matters, *The Times*, apparently under Brougham's direction, made a spirited defence of police reporting, and a dogged attack on *ex-officio* informations for libel, especially at the behest of the Bridge-Street group. The demand for greater liberty was so pervasive that the Attorney General tried to use the claim to set aside the verdict in the Peruvian Loan case, but to no avail.[74] In December, when a coroner tried to prevent full reporting of criminal proceedings, a practice which might have covered up a murder, the *Leeds Intelligencer* exposed what was happening,

---

73. *Ibid.*, December 22, 1823, no.12,062, p.3.
74. *Ibid.*, January 27, 1824, no.12,094, p.3.

and *The Times* joined the fray, reprinting the article on the "Publicity of Trials". This confrontation between the press and courts would result in *Duncan* v. *Thwaites*, and *Duncan* v. *Trend*, cases in which Brougham would play a big role.

In the wake of *R.* v. *Harvey and Chapman*, *The Times* was so concerned about Justice Best's ruling in the case, which it considered a dictum that the Judge was holding over the press *in terrorem*, that it made an all-out effort to defeat the Crown's prosecution of John Hunt for libel, by publishing "The Vision of Judgment", an *ex officio* information that Mr J.B. Sharp's Bridge-Street association wanted.[75] While Scarlett hammered away for the defence about the pointlessness of the prosecution, requiring the Lord Chief Justice to read the alleged libel to the court, and *The Times* reported it fully in a most challenging way, Brougham repeated in a leader his complaint about Abbott's charge to the jury in such cases. To disturb the King's mind was not necessarily libel,[76] Brougham explained. Justice Best's dictum was an obvious absurdity which suited the fancies of the Bridge-Street group, who had enlisted the Law Officers into its service. While Hunt was found guilty, the defence had made such a fuss over his fate that he was released by the court, once Scarlett had assured it about his future behaviour. Brougham was so involved in these disputes that he failed to prosecute properly a damage suit resulting from criminal conversation.[77]

The 1824 Session of Parliament could have proved critical for Brougham and the liberal Tories, because their growing co-operation in reform could have been exposed. Instead, the Irish provided an unexpected diversion which allowed it to continue. After all, backbenchers of both parties were getting restive as to where their leaders were taking them. Lord Holland captured this uncertainty when he wrote these verses about the Whig leader for Miss Fox:

---

75. *R.* v. *Hunt, ibid.*, January 16, 1824, no.12,085, pp.2-3.
76. *Ibid.*, January 17, 1824, no.12,086, p.2.
77. *Lodge* v. *Hurrell, ibid.*, January 14, 1824, no.12,083, p.3.

There's a wild man the world doth roam,
A giant wit. - They call him *Brougham,*
And well me thinks they may.
He deals, whene'er he speaks or acts
With friends and foes and laws and facts
In such a *sweeping* way.[78]

In January, O'Connell, despite his irritation at not being appointed the Queen's Irish Attorney General, wrote to Brougham to take advantage of his capacity for the Catholic Association. "He outlined some plans. 'We are indeed desirous to conduct the cause in the manner which should meet the approbation of our *sincere* friends in the House, amongst whom *on every account* you hold the first place.'"[79] Whatever tactics the Catholics adopted, their demands for Emancipation, the elimination of Orangemen from juries, and the reform of the Irish Church were bound to inflame Tory opinion.

To give Brougham the power to decide when this reaction would take place was, indeed, to strengthen his hand, and he made the most of it. After he had set the stage by writing to people like Lambton that the Whigs had nothing to fear by action in support of Irish measures, he completely destroyed any confidence in the process when it was convenient to do so. On May 31, when Brougham returned to London from the Spring Assizes, where he had forced Scarlett to capitulate in *Greaves* v. *Beaumont*, a defamation action, Brougham finally presented the Catholic Association's petition, calling for the reforms in most caustic terms. A week earlier, *The Times* had printed the correspondence between the Irish and Whig leaders, in which Brougham wrote that "... I feel most strongly the necessity of restoring to the Catholics the full benefits of the Constitution."[80] Barnes also provided an alarming leader, with a shopping list of Catholic demands.

---

78. Quoted from New, *op. cit.*, p.273. Italics Holland's.
79. Quoted from *ibid.*, p.273.
80. *The Times*, May 24, 1824, no.12,346, p.2.

With parliamentary opinion fixed on this diversion, domestic reform could continue, as Brougham intimated in his answer to the Speech from the Throne. The plight of suitors in Chancery was raised for ministerial action. Three weeks later, John Williams called for a committee to investigate the delays and expenses in Eldon's court.[81] Peel, after contending that everything was fine within the Lord Chancellor's domain, dumbfounded the House when he said:

> It was quite impossible for him to deny, upon a review of all that had been said as to the constitution, the proceedings, and delays of the court of chancery, that the time was now come when the whole of these matters should be thoroughly inquired into.[82]

A royal commission, under the Chancellor's direction would be appointed to look into the matter. When Brougham complained of the possibility of a whitewash under such an arrangement, although urging Williams to withdraw his motion to see what developed, Canning was most eager to reassure the House that there would be no truckling to the Chancellor:

> Even if any disposition existed to trifle with so important a subject, hon. gentlemen must be aware, that no government, in the present enlightened state of the age, could, after consenting to institute an inquiry, conduct it in such a manner as to prevent it from arriving at a salutary and beneficial result.[83]

With these ministerial assurances, Brougham had little to do with Parliament except for his concerns about the treatment of the slaves in the West Indies, and, of course, the subjects of Ireland. It was during one of his rather infrequent visits to the House in

---

81. *The Parliamentary Debates*, n.s., vol.X, col.372.
82. *Ibid.*, col.410.
83. *Ibid.*, col.429.

June that he was attacked by Robert Gourlay in the Lobby. Brougham was thought to have betrayed him in taking up the plight of missionary Smith in the Demerara insurrection. "It is hardly necessary," Barnes wrote in *The Times*, "to add, that Mr Brougham is totally unconscious of the alleged desertion, and that Gourlay labours under a complete and melancholy delusion."[84] Peel concurred when Brougham said that the person for whom he had once presented a petition was deranged. "The blows appeared to be inflicted with a small switch," Brougham explained, "and he at the same time heard the voice of a person, as if muttering something."[85] Gourlay, an astonished House was told, had lately been contesting a suit in Chancery against the Duke of Somerset about a tenure of a farm, but without much success. After Gourlay's arrest, he was held at the House's pleasure. Once the Session ended, the matter was turned over to the Bow Street magistrates, and they sent him to the House of Correction.

Once free from these parliamentary duties, Brougham allowed himself a most litigious existence in London, and on circuit. He even found time to prosecute William Cobbett's complaints against the Kensington Turnpike Trust for overcharging, but without success. Brougham did have time too for more important cases, such as *In Re Clement*, where he worked with Scarlett to prevent the *Observer* from being fined for publishing the trial of the Cato Street conspirators, Thistlewood and Ings, before it was completed. Of course, there was the usual complement of seduction and criminal conversation cases with their hefty settlements. In *Laing* v. *Delamere*, Brougham got the rich defendant off for 2,000 pounds damages in a case of criminal conversation in which Scarlett had asked for exemplary ones.[86] At the Spring Assizes at Lancaster, Brougham won *Bell* v. *Sutcliffe*, a breach of promise to marry case, involving another wealthy man. The jury awarded Brougham's client, Matilda Bell,

---

84. *The Times*, June 12, 1824, no.12,363, Supplement, p.3.
85. *Ibid.*, p.4.
86. *Ibid.*, January 30, 1824, no.12,097, p.3.

400 pounds in damages.[87] The most interesting aspect of the cases on the Northern Circuit was the falsely reported death of Scarlett, who had recently beaten Brougham in *Rist* v. *Maxon*, a debt-recovery action in the King's Bench. When the York Assizes heard a similar case, prosecuted by Brougham, Scarlett made a point during the examination of witnesses of establishing that the report of his death had been premature.[88]

Certainly, the case arousing the greatest human interest was *Dick* v. *Fletcher*, another breach of promise case, tried in the King's Bench by a battery of distinguished lawyers. Brougham and Thomas Wilde, another future Lord Chancellor, represented the plaintiff, while Scarlett, Gurney, and Chitty defended the action. The case should not have come to trial because Scarlett was obliged to explain its postponement thus: "Mr Fletcher now offers all the reparation in his power; and, as that reparation has been accepted by my learned friend, I gladly leave the case in his hands."[89] Mr Fletcher had been obliged to renege on a promise to marry Eliza Dick because of family pressure, and offered Brougham a most fulsome apology for his failure. While this last-minute settlement prevented court disclosure of correspondence between the parties, which might well have resulted in more litigation if published, *The Times* risked publishing it,[90] and public comment about it, once the Rev. Fletcher fell foul of religious authorities on other grounds.

The most interesting case was *Dowling* v. *Hicks*, an action by the editor of the *Observer* against the proprietor of *The Times* for false arrest. The dispute had been an outgrowth of Brougham's visit to Scotland the previous summer. No sooner did the *Morning Chronicle* hear of his plans to go to Glasgow from Edinburgh than its editor sent three reporters, including Dowling, to report his speech about Scotland's steady and inexorable improvement to the metropolis. The paper thought that it had a scoop, Attorney General Copley explained for the prosecution,

87. *Ibid.*, March 23, 1824, no.12,141, p.3.
88. *Whitacker* v. *Mallinson*, *ibid.*, April 1, 1824, no.12,301, p.3.
89. *Ibid.*, April 15, 1824, no.12,313, p.3.
90. "The Rev. Alexander Fletcher," *ibid.*, October 30, 1824, no.12,476, pp.2-3.

because "the proprietors of no other newspaper had sent reporters to Glasgow ..."[91] Little did the *Morning Chronicle* realize that Barnes had called upon Brougham to report his own speech, and when the package containing his report disappeared in Carlisle, Hicks took out a deposition, charging that Dowling did "feloniously steal, take, and carry away a paper parcel directed to the editor of *The Times*, containing a report of what had transpired at a dinner given by the citizens of Glasgow to Henry Brougham and Thomas Denman ..."[92]

Once Dowling had been arrested in Birmingham, and taken to Carlisle, the case against him collapsed, and he quickly opened a counter suit, charging *The Times* with pursuing him in an irrational, malicious manner. Vincent George Dowling had long been the recipient of secret service money, and the reporter of reactionary causes in Sidmouth's interests. Scarlett called for the action to be dropped as Hicks was only acting upon information given him by the clerks of the coach house where the report disappeared. At first, Abbott rejected the idea, holding that the magistrates were agents of the person seeking the warrant. After Brougham cross-examined the arresting officer, George Ruthven of the Bow Street police, showing that there had been nothing vindictive in Dowling's being taken to Carlisle, however, the Lord Chief Justice granted the defence's motion for non-suiting the action. The other two reporters involved did not attend the hearing, leaving the observer to surmise that the Bridge-Street group had been behind the effort to injure *The Times*.

Brougham won another important case for *The Times* the following July. As part of his campaign to assist the poor's physical and mental needs, an outgrowth of his inquiry into charities, Barnes directed a barrage of criticism against the Mendicity Society, especially the financial dealings of its secretary, Mr Bodkin. He decided that he would no longer put up with its charges against him, due to the proddings of the Bridge-Street gang, and took *The Times* to court, calling for a hefty

---

91. *Dowling* v. *Hicks, ibid.*, May 1, 1824, no.12,327, p.3.
92. *Ibid.*

1,000 pound damages. Attorney General Copley was conspicuously absent in both the indictment and prosecution of the case. The prosecution was a normal civil case for libel rather than an *ex officio* information, as Brougham had long recommended to the Crown. In the courtroom, Scarlett pulled the prosecution's case apart, and Brougham concentrated upon writing it up for *The Times* so that Stoddart's group would have nothing further to complain of in court.[93] Instead of receiving punishing damages, the plaintiff received 30 shillings damages, and 30 shillings for costs from the jury.

Earlier in the month, the *Real John Bull*, the vigilante group's own propaganda organ, received a fatal setback when the Bishop of Exeter took it to court for libelling him.[94] Brougham, in prosecuting the criminal information, claimed that there was no substance in its claim that the Bishop vindictively pursued a bachelor clergyman for a sexual liberty, while he, in fact, lived openly in sin with a courtesan. Brougham and Pollock explained that the action against the clergyman concerned matters of religious doctrine, and that the Bishop only prosecuted because he had no alternative. The defendants let the verdict go by default, pleading that they had printed a retraction. Under the circumstances, the prosecution pleaded for leniency, and they were only fined 10 pounds, but were obliged to put up considerable security for future good behaviour. In finally routing Dr Stoddart's private prosecutors, Brougham could afford to show mercy.

Brougham had much more chequered success in cases free from political overtones, but even here, they might have helped persuade the Attorney General to avoid unnecessary aggravation by not prosecuting *ex-officio* informations defended by the likes of Brougham and Scarlett. In *Holmes* v. *Collett*, they teamed up to obtain 500 pounds for the plaintiff in a case of criminal conversation. Copley denied that the defendant had committed

---

93. *Bodkin* v. *The Proprietors of "The Times" Journal, ibid.*, July 17, 1824, no.12,392, pp.2-3.

94. *R., on the Prosecution of the Bishop of Exeter* v. *Pavey and Rowland, ibid.*, July 7, 1824, no.12,384, p.3.

adultery with Holmes's wife, but Brougham, through his examination of Charlotte Bingham, established the seduction.[95] He showed less success against Scarlett, losing a debt-recovery action at the York Assizes,[96] another one in the King's Bench,[97] and a nuisance suit in the same court.[98] Perhaps Brougham's most embarrassing defeat at Scarlett's hands was when he ruined the prosecution of the assault action against the *Morning Chronicle* by obliging Parkins, the former Sheriff of the City, to say ridiculous things under cross-examination.[99] Brougham could find consolation, however, in the fact that no one had been able to handle the zealous official. Parkins had fatally exposed the financial ruin of the Bridge-Street group, sending one of its agents, Oxton, to jail in the process, after a sound thrashing. Brougham did get *Banks* v. *Clement*, a libel action against the same newspaper for what it had written about the plaintiff's lace factory, non-suited, and a similar action, *Davis* v. *Grattan*, discharged after he presented a letter from the editor, and Brougham made an open apology in court. Then there was a host of cases which Brougham won concerning sexual liberties of various kinds. He obtained 1,000 pounds from Lord Brudenell for debauching a wife, a liaison which Scarlett unsuccessfully dismissed as no loss.[100] *Irving* v. *Greenwood*, a breach of promise case, netted Brougham's client 300 pounds and costs. The end of July saw Brougham prosecute most successfully two cases of criminal conversation, one in the King's Bench,[101] and the other at the Secondaries Office.[102] The Sheriff's Court, Red Lion Square, had been the scene of another Brougham victory, *Baring* v. *Webster*, a hearing to assess damages for the seduction of Henry Baring's wife. The MP was awarded 1,000 pounds despite Denman's claim that his client was not in a position to pay heavy

---

95. *Ibid.*, April 16, 1824, no.12,314, p.3.
96. *Steer* v. *Unwin, ibid.*, March 29, 1824, no.12,298, p.3.
97. *Whitesides* v. *Weston, ibid.*, April 27, 1824, no.12,323, p.3.
98. *R.* v. *Champion, ibid.*, April 29, 1824, no.12,325, p.3.
99. *Swift* v. *Thwaites, ibid.*, April 30, 1824, no.12,326, pp.2-3.
100. *Johnstone* v. *Lord Brudenell, ibid.*, June 24, 1824, no.12,373, p.3.
101. *Peter* v. *Hancock, ibid.*, July 30, 1824, no.12,404, pp.2-3.
102. *Erskine* v. *Murray, ibid.*, July 24, 1824, no.12,399, pp.2-3.

damages.

Just before the Summer Assizes opened, Brougham prosecuted Colonel Bradley's claim of false imprisonment against a former commander in the King's Bench, claiming that his superior, being an officer on half-pay, was not capable of command. Even if he were, Brougham added, he had had Bradley held an unreasonable time. The jury, despite Abbott's *dicta* in favour of Bradley's military superior, agreed, awarding him 100 pounds in damages. Not satisfied with the award, Brougham, in November, argued for a new trial, and prevailed, although Copley opposed the motion for a special case. Brougham contended that Bradley suffered total false imprisonment under Colonel Arthur, "... that no man who is not amenable to military law is capable of military command."[103] Despite this eloquent plea that all the King's subjects were subject to the rule of law, the jury held that Bradley's imprisonment was proper, and that he had been adequately compensated for being held too long. The following summer, Brougham called for yet another trial of the case on the basis that the Lord Chief Justice had left to military witnesses the powers of half-pay officers, what he should have decided as a matter of law. The Lord Chief Justice disagreed, denying the motion.

With Brougham so busy, and political and legal matters going well, he had neither much time nor interest in the *Review*. When a barrister wrote a pamphlet unfavourable to conditions in Spain, however, Brougham wrote a review condemning its substance and source. The fact that a professional man would openly side against the people was duly noted.[104] The pamphlet's appearance in Britain could only be attributed to assistance by the government. In future, people would have to judge work in the public arena by the liberality of its opinions, Brougham concluded, rather than the professional status of the author.

To show his own liberality, he added an article on how

---

103. *Bradley* v. *Arthur*, *ibid.*, November 13, 1824, no.12,497, p.2.

104. Art.III, "Quin's *Visit to Spain*," *Edinburgh Review*, vol.40, no.LXXIX, March 1824, pp.66-7.

missionary John Smith had been treated in the wake of the insurrection in Demerara in anticipation of a parliamentary debate on the subject. West Indian alarms had characteristically clouded real questions about slavery. The 1823 instructions by the home government against the use of the lash had not solved the problem. In fact, they had helped promote the insurrection since the slaves were led to believe that there was an emancipation order which was being withheld. The failure to instruct the slaves had merely been savagely exploited during the suppression of the insurrection, and its aftermath. About the unnecessary court martial of the pacifist missionary, Brougham complained: "... hearsay of the most vague and indefinite description is constantly allowed ..."[105] About the death sentence it handed down, the reviewer asked indignantly: "How, then, can a white be guilty of a capital offence for being the accessary to a crime, which, if done by himself as principal, could only have been a misdemeanour?"[106] Smith had died because of harsh prison conditions despite the Crown's reprieve. Brougham agreed with his widow's verdict that he had died because of false accusations, cruel prosecution, and long imprisonment. His Majesty's Government was urged to do all in its powers to remedy the evils of slavery. "If it cannot exist together with Christianity," Brougham reminded the readers, "then is it indeed condemned to swift destruction!"[107]

As the next Session approached, Brougham did have time to prepare *Review* readers about the need of public education at home, and of improving the condition of slaves in the colonies. Liverpool's ministers were put on notice that Toryism was not sufficient for meeting these challenges: "An affection of courtly principles is becoming more prevalent than formerly, among certain politicians who used to be satisfied with supporting bad measures because they were in place ..."[108] Tory principles, when followed by French aristocrats, had led to the destruction

105. Art.X, "West India Missions - Insurrection in Demerara," *ibid.*, p.256.
106. *Ibid.*, p.268.
107. *Ibid.*, p.270.
108. Art.I, "*High Tory Principles,*" *ibid.*, no.LXXXI, October 1824, p.30.

of their constitution, and Louis XVI's execution, Brougham wrote. Public education, in both primary and scientific areas, had to be increased, and little additional financing could be expected by charity reform.[109] Cheap books, libraries, and Mechanics' Institutions, like the one Dr Birkbeck had established in the metropolis, all had a role to play, and concerned subjects should not allow the movement to suffer from political attack. What Glasgow had started through the establishment of Anderson College, the medical college, was starting to have a national impact.

About the slaves' plight, Brougham demanded that both the Crown and Parliament had to intervene in a situation which had become intolerable. "The risks of Negro rebellion have always been greatly exaggerated ...,"[110] he explained. Just as in the case of domestic alarms, positive improvement by public authority was the only remedy for the slaves' condition. The Crown should expand the Order in Council to prohibit the use of the whip to all the conquered West Indian colonies, and Parliament should see to its exclusion elsewhere. Brougham mocked pleas that Britain was helpless in the face of the infamous trade, something that Canning had espoused when he was first Foreign Secretary.

Conditions were becoming intolerable for junior counsel too on the Northern Circuit because of the Crown's unwillingness to offer Brougham a patent of precedence, something that he had tried to resolve yet again when Hullock went to the Court of Exchequer by writing directly to Eldon. Brougham wrote "... of the injurious effects occasioned to others by my want of standing ..."[111] The Chancellor was quite content to turn down the request, however, blaming the rejection quite feebly upon the King's antipathy. As a result, Scarlett, who was a King's Counsel, and Brougham received a disproportionate share of the business which Assize Judges were not able to alleviate by dealing directly with the senior barristers.

---

109. Art.V, "*Scientific Education of the People,*" *ibid.*, pp.96-122.
110. Art.X, "*Abolition of the Slave Trade - and of Slavery,*" *ibid.*, p.216.
111. Letter to Eldon, dated February 25, 1823, *The Life and Time of Henry Lord Brougham* (Harper, New York, 1871, 3 vols.), vol.II, p.349.

At York, Scarlett had the better of the confrontation, winning a recovery action,[112] a suit for patent infringement,[113] trespass action,[114] a suit for blocking the Tyne,[115] and an action for injury against a coach company.[116] Brougham won assault action *Booth* v. *Barehead,* breach of promise case *Molloy* v. *Swallow,* and *Hardy* v. *Dewsnap,* a libel suit. The strain that their arguments were having upon the Judges was well illustrated when Justice Bayley got into a dispute with Brougham for not having settled the breach of promise case out of court, an action that Scarlett attributed to an artful woman.[117] Bayley just made matters worse when he claimed that the jury would find that the plaintiff was not entitled to great damages, an interruption which so angered Brougham that he reduced the Judge to silence. The jury awarded the plaintiff two hundred pounds. The shoe was on opposing counsel's foot when Scarlett prosecuted the libel action against a person for what he signed during a drunken brawl. During cross-examination, however, Brougham induced the leading witness to admit: "Somebody said at the time that Dewsnap, if asked, would sign his own death-warrant."[118] As the Assizes moved north, into territory where Brougham had better contacts and clients, he got the better of his confrontations with Scarlett, but the relation turned again when the Assizes got to Lancaster. Back in London, Brougham put pressure on Eldon to appoint him King's Council by openly contradicting in *The Times* his explanation of why it could not be made.[119]

Brougham continued to press the government to recognize him, and the interests he represented. Peel was criticized in *The Times* for not obliging the Recorder of London to make timely reports about those on "Death Row" at Newgate so the prerogative of mercy could be exercised expeditiously: "Whatever

---

112. *Scaife* v. *Jackson, The Times,* August 5, 1824, no.12,409, p.3.
113. *Sykes* v. *Sykes, ibid.,* August 10, 1824, no.12,413, p.3.
114. *White* v. *Arnitt, ibid.,* August 11, 1824, no.12,414, p.3.
115. *R.* v. *Russell, ibid.,* August 14, 1824, no.12,417, pp.2-3.
116. *Williams* v. *Clegge, ibid.,* August 16, 1824, no.12,418, p.3.
117. *Ibid.,* August 9, 1824, no.12,412, p.2.
118. *Ibid.,* August 14, 1824, no.12,417, p.3.
119. "Mr Brougham," *ibid.,* November 12, 1824, no.12,496, p.2.

might have been the defects of Lord Sidmouth, those who have occasion to transact business at the Home-Office soon discover, that in point of urbanity and facility of access his successor suffers much in comparison with him."[120] Brougham made so much of the Crown's prosecution of the Portuguese ambassador for how he tried to dispose of duty-free wine that even the Lord Chief Baron was obliged to compliment him. After arguing *R.* v. *Thornton* twice, only to lose both actions, Macdonald admitted that "... every thing which it was possible for knowledge and talent to do had been done by the learned gentleman ..."[121]

Brougham closed the year by defending *Foote* v. *Hayne*, a case of breach of promise to marry which would mushroom into more legal business. Miss Foote, a promising actress, had twice been jilted out of marriage first by a Colonel Berkeley, and then by a Mr Hayne. The Colonel had lived with her for five years, producing two bastards, and when Hayne proposed successfully, the Colonel ruined it by telling him of her past. Brougham argued for mitigation of damages under the circumstances, and largely succeeded. Copley had called for 10,000 pounds in damages,[122] but the jury only gave her 3,000.[123] Barnes later printed Berkeley's letters in order to calm public feeling against him and Hayne.[124]

In 1825, Brougham's biggest case was *Duncan* v. *Trend*, a prosecution against the *Morning Advertiser* for printing an account of a hearing for indecent assault at Bow Street Magistrates Court. For a few years, there had been a growing dispute, prompted by Bow Street magistrate Sir Robert Birnie, as to whether or not court reporting which defamed parties could be prosecuted for libel, something that the Constitutional Association had wanted. Andrew Duncan had prosecuted the *Morning Herald* the previous October for reporting his sexual assault on a minor, and once the Lord Chief Justice held that police reports which were libellous

---

120. *Ibid.*, October 20, 1824, no.12,476, p.2.
121. *Ibid.*, November 27, 1824, no.12,509, p.3.
122. *Gentleman's Magazine*, vol.94, 1824, Part II, p.638.
123. *Foote* v. *Hayne*, *The Times*, December 22, 1824, no.12,530, p.1.
124. *Ibid.*, December 24, 1824, no.12,532, p.2.

were not legal, the jury convicted the paper's printer and publisher.[125] Duncan then proceeded to prosecute the *Morning Advertiser* with every confidence of winning.

Brougham, in defending the paper, made much of the fact that its account of the trial had not made it clear that he was also the plaintiff in this action. There was also, Brougham said, a presumption that the report was legal until Abbott made his decision: "Until then, at least, the law must be considered as unsettled, and it is not surprising that parties, strongly feeling the utility and policy of such reports, should not scruple to publish them."[126] In fact, the point had not been decided because Abbott's earlier decision had been appealed to the Lords. The Lord Chief Justice, however, made light of the distinction, stating that "it was scarcely contended on the part of the defendants, that the plaintiff was not entitled to a verdict ..."[127] The special jury, perhaps swayed by what a witness admitted under Brougham's examination, ie, justification might be argued if there was another Duncan prosecution, found for the *Morning Advertiser*. *The Times*, sounding very much like Brougham as leader writer, praised the press victory, explaining its significance thus:

> By the searching and sagacious press, the prosecutor and the witness will be forced to tell the truth - by it the magistrate will be compelled to impartiality and to patience - by it the names of witnesses are promulgated, and his own name and person are brought into notice, that his friends, if he be falsely accused, may have time and opportunity to save him.[128]

During the Session, Brougham concentrated again on diverting Parliament's attention from what was going on, so that the liberal ministers could continue legal, police, and judicial reform,

---

125. The case of *Duncan* v. *Thwaites* was disposed of on November 29 when Abbott handed down his ruling.
126. *Duncan* v. *Trend, ibid.*, January 15, 1825, no.12,551, p.3.
127. *Ibid.*
128. *Ibid.*, January 17, 1825, no.12,552, p.2.

especially of the Chancery, without undue difficulty. As he had done a decade earlier, he opposed the Speech from the Throne, calling for the suppression of O'Connell's Catholic Association. Brougham challenged the Ministry to put the Association out of business by meeting its demands. Catholic Emancipation, he explained, would not force Eldon to resign despite his fanciful claims. As for the government's proposed changes in the navigation laws, and the silk duties, he claimed that it was doing just what he had recommended for years. Canning, of course, responded in kind. As for Brougham's claim that the Ministry was doing his bidding in fiscal policy, he said sarcastically: "Having in the course of his parliamentary life, proposed and supported almost every species and degree of innovation ... it was not easy for ministers to do anything ... without borrowing, or seeming to borrow, something from the honourable gentleman ..."[129] Brougham's contention that Catholic Emancipation was simply a matter of effecting a political consensus was dismissed with contempt. The Foreign Secretary assured the House that he would follow his own conscience when it came to the repeal of the Penal Laws. Behind this smokescreen, though, Brougham had persuaded liberal Tories like Peel and Huskisson to pursue a middle course on industrial policy, one between Eldon's total opposition to combinations, and Bentham's unrestricted right to combine.

Brougham was 46 when his influence among liberal Tories in Liverpool's Administration was at its height. While he possessed a profile, mannerisms, and mode of expression which delighted caricaturists, especially at *Blackwood's Magazine* and later *Punch*, he was not an unattractive figure, as his portraits in the National Portrait Gallery by James Lonsdale and Sir Thomas Lawrence show. Brougham was not yet in the habit of emphasizing his physical peculiarities by wearing a black "choker" and plaid trousers which were characterized in cartoons, and the Gambardella portrait at Lincoln's Inn. In the contemporary portraits by Lonsdale and Lawrence, we see Brougham looking

---

129. *The Parliamentary Debates*, n.s., vol.XII, co.72 fc.

almost directly at the painter, a pose which minimizes the sinister or silly aspect of his famous, twitching nose.

The man's faculties, his eyes, mouth, nose, ears and intelligence, seem to be fixed to deal with the outside world in most effective fashion, as the pointing finger in the Lonsdale picture shows so tellingly during an episode of the Queen's trial. Brougham's expression in the Lawrence portrait indicates a man who is still deeply responsive to the stimuli and demands of the world in an attractive enough manner for the viewer to want to know more about him. There is little evidence of the twisted expression of later portraits, with the cynical, down-turned corners of the mouth, and the rather abstract stare of the eyes outside the canvas and beyond the beholder. In 1825, Brougham appears a man of the world, totally consumed by its opportunities, and delights. For aspiring whig politicians like James Graham, Brougham's parliamentary performances, by precept and example, had become the model for other reformers and his approach was the most valued of all. John Cam Hobhouse captured the same image in another medium when he described Brougham's chairing a meeting of the Sublime Society of Beefsteaks, in his memoirs:

> ... Brougham sang us a song in French, "The Pipe of Tobacco". He was in high force. He told us he always gets up every morning at seven, let him go to bed when he will, and that he is a good sleeper. He is a most extraordinary man.[130]

In January 1825, Brougham began to feel the costs of some of his past pleasures in life. After he had successfully prosecuted *Mackintyre* v. *Layard*, a false imprisonment case during the trial of which he was able to score more points at Eldon's expense,[131] he was obliged to defend Edmund Kean, the famous actor, in a damage suit for criminal conversation with the wife of one of the

---

130. Quoted from New, *op. cit.*, p.282.
131. N.B. what he said about where the King's Bench could meet after term: "My Lord, there is the Court of Chancery in Westminster Hall vacant. (A laugh)." (*The Times*, January 24, 1825, no.12,558, p.3.).

City's aldermen. Kean had taken advantage of Mrs Cox from Westmorland during his dealings with her husband in the operation of the Drury Lane Theatre. When the King's Bench fined the actor 800 pounds for his liberties, *The Times* went wild in its denunciations of him for continuing his stage performances as if nothing had happened, an editorial campaign in which Brougham not only participated but also had an interest. Kean, like Brougham, was a friend of courtesan Harriette Wilson whose memoirs publisher Joseph Stockdale was supplying to eager London readers at the rate of 17,000 copies per week.

The previous July, Miss Wilson had written to Brougham from Paris about the possibility of including him in her *Sketches of Character in High Life* unless he met her demands. When he did not respond to her liking, she wrote again, explaining that his "... flaming love letters etc. would certainly add to the value & interest of the book ..."[132] Brougham's defence of Kean seems likely to have been part of the price for his not being included among the exploits of other thinly-disguised worthies, such as the Duke of Wellington, Marquis Graham, and Lord Robert Manners. Brougham apparently compensated himself for the indignity by not only railing against Kean's sins in *The Times* but also prosecuting successfully *Reynolds* v. *Welch*, a breach of contract suit in which Kean failed to persuade the jury, on the basis of Miss Wilson's letter, that his posing for an engraving of himself as Sir Giles Overreach, had only been conditionally agreed to.[133]

Despite Brougham's diversion at *The Times*, the scandal associated with the publication of the *Memoirs of Miss Harriette Wilson*, unlike Tory criticism of what Peel and Canning were accomplishing at Whitehall, would not go away. As Stockdale serialised her account of life in high society, he experienced mounting legal, financial, and copyright problems, and Brougham was pressed into his service under most humiliating

---

132. Miss Wilson's letter to Brougham, dated July 15, 1825: quoted from Kenneth Bourne, ed, *The Blackmailing of the Chancellor* (Lemon Tree Press, London, 1975), p.26.

133. *The Times*, February 16, 1825, no.12,578, p.3.

circumstances. In June, Stockdale himself defended a libel action caused by publication of Miss Wilson's claim that her sister, another prostitute, had been proposed to by a respectable person, a falsehood which cost Stockdale 300 pounds.[134] In November, Brougham was obliged to come into the King's Bench, and call for the award to be set aside because it had been excessive, arguing that the plaintiff's claim that he was already married was not supported by the evidence. Brougham told the Lord Chief Justice, when asked, that he should have so directed the jury to make sure that it did not award excessive damages. Justice Bayley added, however, that no evidence had been introduced about the claim, and the matter was dropped.[135]

In early December, Serjeant Wilde got the Common Pleas to drop *Poplett* v. *Stockdale*, a recovery action for printing part of the infamous memoirs. After he had contended that the sum desired was unreasonable, and not properly demanded, Wilde denounced the work as "... a robbery, by means of the press, of the reputation of individuals, for the purpose of effecting another robbery of their purses."[136] No sooner had Lord Chief Justice Best heard that the work was the history of a prostitute than he non-suited the action, only regretting that he did not preside over a criminal court so that he could take appropriate action against its authors, At the Court of Requests, Stockdale lost yet another action, one where he had refused to make good on an imperfect copy of the memoirs supplied to a King Street bookseller.[137]

It was against a background of such embarrassing, scandalous circumstances that Brougham was obliged to prosecute *Stockdale* v. *Onwhyn*, a suit against another publisher for "... having pirated and published a copy of that work (*The Memoirs of Harriette Wilson*), to the great detriment and injury of the property which the plaintiff had its copyright."[138] Brougham went into great detail about the law and facts of the case. "For that the work

134. *Blore* v. *Stockdale, ibid.*, July 2, 1825, no.12,695, pp.3-4.
135. *Ibid.*, November 14, 1825, no.12,810, p.3.
136. *Ibid.*, December 2, 1825, no.12,826, p.3.
137. *Harris* v. *Stockdale, ibid.*
138. *Ibid.*, January 12, 1826, no.12,862, p.3.

published by the defendant was as gross a piracy as had ever been attempted," he explained, "was shown by the very frontispiece which he had had the audacity to prefix to it."[139] Brougham cautioned the jury against what Scarlett might have to say about the case, and corrected Abbott when he said that the work had already been judged libellous. Blore's action, the earlier suit, had concerned another volume, Brougham replied. Scarlett, of course, made much of the decision in the Common Pleas, and had Poplett testify that Stockdale had used the same defence in his case. While Brougham had Stockdale testify that Wilde's plea in his case had been his own idea, Abbott non-suited the action, explaining that "... the law cannot recognize as property the history of the low amours of a notorious courtesan."[140]

A fortnight later, Brougham moved for a new trial, contending that one could be indicted for stealing a licentious book. Lord Chamberlain Talbot's issuance of an injunction to protect the licentious play *Polly* from piracy was cited as a precedent. The Lord Chief Justice denied such a work was entitled to damages, explaining:

> Can any lawyer plead he has a right to publish such a work as this, when the act of issuing every copy to the world is an offence against the law, for which he may be punished by the law? No, every lawyer, and every man of sense must say at once, that no such right exists.[141]

Justice Bayley, who had clearly had his fill of Brougham's confrontations with Scarlett in court, said, obviously with tongue in cheek, that Brougham might seek relief in Chancery for suppression of such a publication. Motion for a new trial was denied.

While most barristers would have been crushed by these

139. *Ibid.*
140. *Ibid.*
141. *Ibid.*, January 28, 1826, no.12,876, p.3.

events, ones which any man of means would have been willing to spend sums far greater than the amounts Kenneth Bourne has mentioned to avoid for what Harriette Wilson was trying to extort from Brougham,[142] he went about his business as if he did not have a care on his mind. Despite the appeal in the Thwaites case, and Copley's motion for a new trial in the Trend case, Brougham, assisted by columns in *The Times*, presented the government with such a challenge on the issue of court reporting that the King's Bench decided prudently to agree to a *stet processus* in the new action.[143] By letting the decision stand, Britain was assured that accurate reporting of criminal cases, no matter how scandalous their testimony, was privileged. While Brougham did not take the *Onwhyn* case to Chancery, he did defend *Abernethy* v. *Hutchinson* before Lord Eldon. This was an action for an injunction against the defendant for publishing in the *Lancet* Dr Abernethy's lectures to students at St Bartholomew's Hospital, which was prosecuted by Solicitor General Charles Wetherell. While Horne presented the case's background to the court, Brougham took over the defence as soon as he arrived, explaining that "... it would probably be convenient to Mr Brougham if he were heard before his leaders."[144] He denied the prosecution's claim that Abernethy had an equitable remedy for lost property as a mere *obiter dictum* by Ellenborough in *Debos* v. *Beresford*:

> But if a man has property in his picture (S.G.'s example), he has a stronger property in his face; that may be fairly called *personal property* (a laugh); but if I speak in public, and a man takes a copy of my face, and that copy, unluckily for me, happens to be very accurate (for some people do not like their faces to be accurately drawn), I may regret that the likeness is good, but should I be justified in asking this Court to issue an injunction to restrain the picture shops from exhibiting it?

---

142. Bourne, *op. cit.*, p.26 ff.
143. *Duncan* v. *Trend*, *The Times*, June 16, 1825, no.12,681, p.3.
144. *Ibid.*, June 11, 1825, no.12,677, p.3.

> (A loud laugh, probably from supposing that an allusion was here made to a caricature of Mr Brougham in the picture-shops of London, in the dress of an old broom-woman.)[145]

Eldon, nonetheless, granted the injunction. Brougham could not have been too upset, however, since he had just received a large fee in *Swift* v. *City of London*,[146] the first of several damage suits that he prosecuted for the building of the new Fleet Market.

Brougham's confrontations with Scarlett, particularly during the Spring Assizes, were especially galling. Before they began, Brougham won *Steadman* v. *Mayop*, a damage suit for breach of promise in the King's Bench, getting the better of both the argument and the repartee. Scarlett, consequently, went all out at the Lancaster Assizes, winning an ejectment action,[147] and a damage suit for seduction, in which he reduced Brougham to this lame argument: "He really thought, that if this was treated as a fit subject for damages, there was not a milkmaid, barmaid, housemaid, chambermaid, or dressmaker in the country, who would not forthwith bring her sweetheart into court."[148] The shoe was on the other foot at York, however, when Justice Bayley was obliged to interject in another seduction suit, after Brougham had established during cross-examination that the female plaintiff had deliberately met the defendant for sexual intercourse: "She, from her age and from her conduct, seemed much more likely to have been the seducer than the seduced."[149] Brougham managed to get the better of Scarlett in the other cases they represented at York, and they did team up to defeat *Doe. Dem. Birtwhistle* v. *Vardill*, an ejectment action over a contested will. Brougham was conveniently locked in such disputes when the Catholic Emancipation Bill was introduced into the Commons. Leadership of the Northern Circuit was not only a professional boon but also a parliamentary excuse for avoiding unnecessary

---

145. *Ibid.* Italics its.
146. *Ibid.*, June 10, 1825, no.12,676, p.4.
147. *Finney* v. *Roylance*, *ibid.*, March 15, 1825, no.12,601, p.3.
148. *Sutcliffe* v. *Taylor*, *ibid.*, March 19, 1825,n o.12,605, p.3.
149. *Metcalfe* v. *Webster*, *ibid.*, March 25, 1825, no.12,610, p.3.

partisan debate.

Back in London, Brougham seemed more interested in scoring points against Scarlett in the King's Bench than in Parliament for O'Connell. In an action for debt, Brougham defended a husband whose wife had run off with another man.[150] Scarlett claimed that the husband's immoral living had forced her to do so, but Brougham provided a letter from the woman which proved her to be a common prostitute. The action was duly non-suited. In an action for criminal conversation, when the Lord Chief Justice proved too favourable to Scarlett's case, Brougham not only corrected Abbott with conviction but also got his client off with a shilling damages.[151] Scarlett was criticized for a weak prosecution of the case.

By this time, the Commons was becoming so impatient to hear Brougham's views on Catholic Emancipation that he got into a dispute with Thomas Plunkett about what he was planning to say about it. When Brougham was finally permitted to say that he wanted Emancipation now, it had lost most of its sting, except for the ideologues on the backbenches, as *The Times* duly reported: "The Hon. Member was at length suffered to speak, and the discourse, frank, animated, and energetic, well repaid the toil of forcing a way for it through such obstructions."[152] Until the Roman Catholic Relief Bill died in the Lords, Brougham was more in evidence in court than the Commons.[153]

Brougham concentrated his limited parliamentary activities upon improving Private Bill procedure, a non-partisan endeavour which grew out of his concern over the management of madhouses, and would not risk his influence with the liberal ministers. In February 1825 he complained about voting in committees, citing what had happened to the Highgate Chapel Bill. Members who had never considered it in committee,

---

150. *Walton* v. *Green, ibid.*, April 14, 1825, no.12,627, pp.2-3.
151. *Lord Lismore* v. *Bingham, ibid.*, April 19, 1825, no.12,631, p.3.
152. *Ibid.*, April 27, 1825, no.12,638, p.4.
153. For cases Brougham was involved in, see *Cooper* v. *Price, Westroy* v. *Egan, Cobbett* v. *Parkins, R.* v. *Perry, Waldo* v. *Martin, R.* v. *Sweet, Hall* v. *Vivian, Lord Harborough* v. *Graham, R.* v. *Sunday Herald,* and *R.* v. *The John Bull.*

Brougham said, voted it down, substituting their own self-serving measure in its place. "The good sense of the house fortunately prevailed at last," he added, "and the bill was rejected."[154] Private Bill committees were unlimited in size, composed of locally interested Members, and those Members the one in charge of the measure chose to name, "... and there was no means of requiring committee members to attend throughout the proceedings."[155] In March, Brougham made such a fuss over the Liverpool and Manchester Railway Bill's receiving a fair hearing in committee that he involved the House in its oversight. Due particularly to Brougham's complaints, the House appointed a select committee to investigate the problem, but unfortunately, without him on the committee, it minimized the problem. Brougham tried to make up for the deficiency by getting *The Times* to print leaders on the need of reform in light of the manifest corruption of the Chairman of Committees James Brogden, Sir William Congreve and John Bent in the creation of the Arigna Iron and Coal Company. About the result, one expert has written:

> The timorous attempts at reform of private bill committees in 1825-6, produced a reduction in the theoretical maximum size of opposed bill committees to 120, but local representatives, based on revised county lists of Members, were carefully preserved and no means were found for compelling attendance at committee proceedings.[156]

While subsequent practice did eliminate Members, on the spur of the moment, from trying to determine their results, the comprehensive reform of Private Bill procedure would have to wait until 1837, when Brougham started the process in the Lords.

In the *Review*, Brougham kept up the pressure on the Chancery Commission to come up with some really dramatic plans for the

---

154. *The Times*, February 24, 1825, no.12,585, p.2.
155. D.L. Rydz, *The Parliamentary Agents: A History* (Royal Historical Society, London, 1979), p.93.
156. *Ibid.*, p.94.

reform of Eldon's court. As he had done when the movement for criminal law reform was flagging before and after Peterloo, Brougham reviewed an old pamphlet on court reform, M. A. Taylor's 1821 speech on the delays in Chancery and the Lords. "Nobody can have forgotten, by what slow and painful steps the late revered Sir S. Romilly advanced towards a very limited amendment of the penal laws,"[157] Brougham reminded the readers. Just when reformers were about to give up hope of criminal law reform, Peel, the Home Secretary acted so dramatically, repealing capital statutes, institutionalizing the role of the courts in the exercise of the prerogative of mercy, extending the benefit of clergy to all kinds of felonies, and improving prison conditions.

Taylor's efforts in the Commons, not to forget those by John Williams, had apparently fallen on deaf ears when Peel intervened most effectively once again. After Brougham recounted the debate which had led to the appointment of the Chancery Commission, he repeated the claim that he had been most anxious to make at the beginning: "It is curious to observe by what slow degrees, and after how many struggles and difficulties, every public grievance is redressed in this country."[158] As he had done in Parliament, he criticized Eldon's heading the commission, particularly after 25 years of wasted opportunity. The commission was so weighted in favour of the status quo that Brougham despaired that Commissioners Lushington and Smith could make any practical suggestions. After outlining all the changes which could be made to make the Chancellor more effective, Brougham added this personal note about his lunacy jurisdiction: "The public will not easily forget the number of days stiff and hard expended upon the case of my

---

157. Art.VI, "Court of Chancery," *Edinburgh Review*, vol.41, no.LXXXII, January 1825, p.411. While *The Wellesley Index* has attributed this article to John Williams, and he could have written it, it seems much more likely to have been done by brougham, given its expression of ideas so characteristically his, and the convenient ignoring of efforts he himself had made for Chancery reform, especially in earlier issues of the *Review*.

158. *Ibid*., p.410.

Lord Portsmouth, in which was to be decided - whether he was competent?"[159] The article concluded with a most pessimistic analysis of Eldon's caseload in Chancery. The Chancellor had stopped hearing appeals in the Lords.

In other articles in the *Review*, Brougham kept up the pressure on Canning to do more for improving the condition of the slaves in the colonies despite the Demerara insurrection. Fearful that Colonial Secretary Bathurst's dispatches had become dead letters in the wake of slaveowner alarm, Brougham used a pamphlet by James Stephen to reiterate all his complaints about the legal status of slaves, criminal procedure in the West Indies, and religious instruction for slaves there. "If we wish to keep the Colonies," he warned, "we must take prompt and effectual measures for raising the condition of the slaves."[160] *Review* readers were reminded that conditions at Haiti proved that emancipation could work. For subjects at home, he stressed what he was doing for public education in the primary schools, at the mechanics' institutions, and for the middle-class children at university. The partisanship of his critics, the alarmists against public efforts, was contrasted with the practical way in which he was attempting to achieve reform. To prove that he was achieving success, Brougham took the liberty of having reprinted his inaugural address as Lord Rector of the University of Glasgow.[161] Brougham had been elected over Sir Walter Scott thanks to Sir James Macintosh's tie-breaking vote.

His installation was the culmination of a triumphal tour of his native Scotland. In the spring of 1825, Brougham was the honoured guest at a dinner in Edinburgh, chaired by his childhood friend Henry Cockburn. About Brougham's upbringing at the "Athens of the North", Cockburn said proudly: "It was in this town that he had formed his earliest, and there were many who thought, his dearest friends ..."[162] Brougham used the opportunity to advertise Scotland's cultural advantages over

159. *Ibid.*, p.420.
160. Art.IX, "The West Indies," *ibid.*, p.487.
161. Art.VIII, Mr Brougham's *Inaugural Discourse, ibid.*, pp.241-54.
162. "Dinner to Mr Brougham at Edinburgh," *The Times*, April 9, 1825, no.12,623, p.2.

England, especially for the benefit of the new university that he was trying to establish in London. The dinner, an acknowledgement of how conditions had improved, was seen as the proudest day of his life. Cockburn admitted as much when he granted him the City's freedom, while the mere mention of Brougham's name 20 years before would have brought inquiries from the police. Brougham felt particularly nostalgic because of the festivities, making light of the prosecution of Queen Caroline, and proposing a toast for his departed friend Horner. The strength of the opposition to the government was the object of several more toasts. When the dinner started to break up at around one a.m., Brougham tried to keep the festivities going, saying that he was used to staying up until four in the morning at Edinburgh. While Barnes in a leader in *The Times* discounted Brougham's contrast between Scottish and English education, he still wrote that "... a system which has trained such a mind must do honour to any country."[163]

Brougham was on his best behaviour when he arrived at Glasgow for the installation as Lord Rector. Not only had he narrowly been elected over Scotland's other most distinguished son but also the negotiations for a London University had entered a most sensitive stage. Dissenter and secularist alike had to be persuaded that they could put their children in the charge of such a man. Brougham had to show that he could create a university which could help meet a man's practical needs without jeopardizing his salvation. Basic educational needs would be provided in an environment which would stress man's opportunities in this world and the next. "The cultivation of science has never really promoted turbulence or unbelief," he explained for the dissenters, "but its progress is the forerunner of liberality and enlightened toleration."[164] Of course, in true professorial style, Brougham stressed the oratorical arts for a discriminating audience. It was not the diction of an author that

163. *Ibid.*

164. "Installation of Mr Brougham at Glasgow University," *ibid.*, April 12, 1825, no.12,625, p.3.

counted, he said, but his message. While the speech sounds rather hackneyed by today's standards, it was quite good for an overworked barrister and politician who had grand dreams for educating a nearly illiterate society. It was one of those times where a little classic dullness was called for.

Back in London, Brougham arranged a number of conferences between the two groups interested in a university, and by the end of April, the dissenters had agreed to join, thanks to his lightening the way. In February, Thomas Campbell wrote to Brougham about establishing a metropolitan university, a letter he later had published in *The Times*.[165] It called for 2,000 people to provide funds for a London University, employing 30 teachers, and charging students fees, along the lines of the University of Glasgow. Campbell wanted an organizing committee established to investigate the matter, and was pleased to hear that Brougham was interested. *The Times* sounded very much like Brougham was leader writer when, after the usual explanations, it dismissed Campbell's suggestion as a crude offer, based upon ignorance.

The problem was to get the Dissenters, particularly Rev. F.A. Cox's Baptists, to agree to a secular university. After consultations between the two groups in Brougham's chambers in Lincoln's Inn Fields during April, a Bill was introduced into the Commons to establish a secular, non-degree-giving metropolitan university. An abstract of the measure was printed in *The Times* to give the middle classes an idea of the kind of institution they should seek.[166] Two days later, a private meeting was held to interest the well-to-do in the project, resulting in the appointment of a committee to look into its feasibility.

Before it reported, Brougham won a nice action in the Lord Mayor's Court, *Swift* v. *City of London*, a suit which showed that the establishment consistently underestimated the needs, contributions, and potential of the labouring classes. A surveyor named Montagu had valued Swift's trading business without

---

165. "Proposal of a Metropolitan University," *ibid.*, February 9, 1825, no.12,572, p.4.
166. "London University," *ibid.*, June 2, 18925, no.12,670, p.3.

considering what loss and inconvenience he would experience by moving it to make way for the Fleet Market.[167] On July 2, the Lord Mayor was in the chair when there was a meeting for establishing the University. Brougham not only spoke effectively and amusingly for its creation but also spent much of the summer, writing "begging letters" to friends and acquaintances to become shareholders.

Before Brougham went off for the Summer Assizes, he won three more important cases in the King's Bench. In *Dibdin* v. *Morris*, a stage-manager of the Haymarket Theatre was awarded 20 pounds more than the defendant offered, once a prosecution witness established that he had prepared a play for which he had not been paid. Scarlett maintained that his contract for services with the theatre recompensed him sufficiently for the work. Brougham denied the claim, adding that the contract had not been duly stamped. This resulted in an argument with Abbott which Brougham won. "I should be sorry," the Lord Chief Justice lamely explained, "if I were obliged to know all the acts of Parliament that ever were passed."[168] Brougham got a conspiracy charge against an informer on the operation of gambling houses dropped because of lack of evidence. Brougham teemed up with Scarlett to force an apology and 50 pounds out of the *Quarterly Review* for libelling Buckingham's *Travels in Palestine* in a review, a result which drew Abbott's approval.[169] Defence counsel Park had argued unsuccessfully that the review did not fall under the libel laws.

On the Northern Circuit during the summer of 1825, Brougham was so loaded down with business that the court system only kept functioning because of the tireless efforts he made to meet his responsibilities. At the York Assizes, Brougham arrived just in time to postpone the first case on the order paper, as *The Times* explained: "The plaintiff's attorney had only been

---

167. *Swift* v. *City of London, ibid.*, June 10, 1825, no.12,676, p.4.

168. *Dibdin* v. *Morris, ibid.*, June 24, 1825, no.12,688, p.3.

169. *R.* v. *Grant and Hollingbery, ibid.*, July 8, 1825, no.12,700, p.2. For Brougham's pursuit of the extortionists, see the related case, *R.* v. *Hollingbery and Others, ibid.*, June 21, 1825, no.12,685, p.3.

able to get to York by pursuing a very roundabout road. He had taken a seat (the only one left) in the dicky of the Diligence which runs between Whitby and Scarborough, and from Scarborough had got to York."[170] When the biggest case finally came on, a libel action which Brougham and Scarlett won, the defence tried to make much of the fact that they previously represented the defendant, until Serjeant Hullock had been called to the Bench. Justice Bayley dismissed the objection thus:

> A man did not pass his life in courts of justice, without desiring that particular counsel were generally selected for particular cases, and that suitors were, upon all occasions, anxious to intrust their causes to the greatest talent that could be had. It might be from a motive of this kind, that it happened that Mr Scarlett and Mr Brougham had been selected to conduct this case, as the two counsel of the most eminent talent on the circuit.[171]

They then split the decision in the Bradford Market Case with Brougham establishing that householders could not only sell goods in their own houses but also maintain separate shops.

In fact, their stature was so high that they sometimes tried to usurp the Judges' function in a manner reminiscent of some of Ellenborough's abuses.[172] *The Times* was obliged, consequently, to discredit rumours that Justice Bayley was going to quit the circuit because of their liberties, once it had been reported that neither Scarlett nor Brougham had worn wigs in court to publicize the difficulties caused by not making him King's Counsel.[173] The leader explained away the rumour rather lamely:

> The Judge and one of the leaders differed once or twice on a matter of legal nicety, and had in consequence some

170. *Bell* v. Hill, ibid., July 21, 1825, no.12,711, p.3.
171. *Ibid.*, July 25, 1825, no.12,714, p.3.
172. See, eg, *Wasling* v. *Gooddey*, *ibid.*, July 26, 1825, no.12,715, p.3.
173. *Ibid.*, August 1, 1825, no.12,720, p.3.

> contention: and to this was owing the expression of the learned Judge's intention to desist from doing the Northern Circuit.[174]

The culprit appears to have been Brougham when he successfully prosecuted *Harrison* v. *Brooke* in an assault action. The load was becoming almost too much for him.

This was vividly shown in another lunacy case which he defended because of the successful results in the *Portsmouth* and *Williams* cases. Brougham was retained by Rev. Edward Frank before a lunacy commission, headed by Chief Commissioner Phillimore. The hearing was delayed an hour in opening because of Brougham's Assize duties. "Mr Brougham arrived express from York, being specially retained for Mr Frank."[175] Brougham could only stay for five days of the eight-day hearing, addressing the jury before leaving. "To constitute insanity," he argued, "a man must be what the law termed *non compos*."[176] Brougham admitted that Frank lived a most immoral life of drinking, gambling, and whoring, but claimed that he was still competent. Frank's case was distinguished from Portsmouth's where the defendant had had to sleep with his wife and her paramour. After Brougham returned to the Northern Circuit, Spence completed Frank's defence, but Solicitor General Wetherell, for the prosecution, had the better of the argument. Frank was declared to have been insane for the past nine years. Brougham had thought that, by putting in an appearance, he would prevail, but the illusion, as in some other cases,[177] had not prevailed.

Back at the Lancaster Assizes, Brougham won a most impressive seduction suit. About the plaintiff, *The Times* reported: "She was a stout brawny woman, apparently about 40 years old, and more like an antidote than an incentive to passion."[178]

---

174. *Ibid.*, August 4, 1825, no.12,723, p.2.
175. "Commission of Lunacy," *ibid.*, August 2, 1825, no.12,721, p.3.
176. *Ibid.*, August 8, 1825, no.12,725, p.2.
177. See, eg, *Wheatley* v. *Gibson*, a libel action against the Cumberland Packet at the Carlisle Assizes: *ibid.*, August 12, 1825, no.12,730, p.3.
178. *Fox* v. *Wilkinson*, *ibid.*, August 22, 1825, no.12,738, p.3.

Nonetheless, Brougham argued in court that she had been hoodwinked into sleeping with the defendant after he had promised to marry her, a contention which had the courtroom tittering. Williams, the defendant's counsel who was upset by Brougham's courtroom informality, made light of the woman's claim, that she "... had yielded with breathless haste to the solicitations of the defendant; and of the father, who night after night had all but solicited the debauching of his daughter."[179] Williams made a point of Brougham's failure to mention Miss Nelly Fox's age. The jury still awarded her 50 pounds for her injury.

Back in London, Brougham divided his time between court appearances and educational activities. Despite his strenuous search for shareholders, and looking into the purchase of a site and the building of the university, things were not going well. The fund-raising campaign had flagged, and the Evangelicals of the Church of England were increasingly upset about the idea of a secular university. In the *Review*, he had justified the proposed university on the basis of Scottish experience.[180] In the next issue, he tried to reassure people such as Wilberforce that they had nothing to fear from the cultivation of knowledge. The demands of science were not antithetical to religion, Brougham reassured them. In the February 1826 issue, he repeated the university's justification, stating that it was neither a threat to established religion nor to public morality. Young men, by living at home, would be able to avoid London's temptations. The university, in fact, would provide them with an opportunity to mix with respectable female society. The Oxford and Cambridge model of the university suffered from past abuses of much wealth and privilege in the alleged pursuit of knowledge. "We abhor intellectual perpetuities,"[181] Brougham explained. By then, another general meeting had agreed to a deed of settlement, and a Council had been appointed. It was devoid

179. *Ibid.*
180. Art.III, "New University in London," *Edinburgh Review*, vol.42, no.LXXXIV, August 1825, pp.346-67.
181. Art.III, "The London University," *ibid.*, vol.43, no.LXXXVI, February 1826, p.307.

of religious representation because the Church had passed a rule against clergymen serving on it, a ruling which helped promote the foundation of Kings' College in London.

In court, Brougham continued to record impressive verdicts, although he did have to experience another humiliation because of Harriette Wilson. In a case of fraudulent purchase, the barrister restricted his client's loss to a 250 pound fine for selling a pub for 1,600 pounds, with the expectation of making 200 pounds per month.[182] The *Two Spies* actually brought in only 75 pounds per month. Brougham tried to minimize the loss by bringing in witnesses who testified that they had offered similar terms for the rest of the 14-year lease, indicating, at worst, that the pub was a good speculative purchase. In a criminal conversation case, Brougham assured that his client was awarded 500 pounds when a first cousin of his wife took advantage of her sexually by means of secret messages, written in lemon juice.[183] In *R.* v. *Adlard,* Brougham persuaded the King's Bench that the defendant was not liable to serve as constable in the parish where he carried on his printing business. The case had first been heard by Abbott at *nisi prius* at the Guildhall, and he had decided for the Crown, with Brougham contending that he was only liable to a fine. When the Court *en banc* heard the appeal, it decided that "... it did not follow that he should perform personal duties when he required no personal protection."[184] Adlard was not domiciled in St. Bartholomew the Great, in the City. A fortnight earlier, however, the same Court had thrown out Brougham's motion to set aside the award in *Blore* v. *Stockdale* because it was excessive.

Brougham finished the year, nonetheless, on a positive note, winning an important damage case before Abbot at the Guildhall. An officer in the Royal Navy sued his superior for unlawful treatment, a charge which the Attorney General, defending the case, treated as a contradiction in terms. Brougham replied that

---

182. *Pearson* v. *Wheeler, The Times,* October 31, 1825, no.12,798, p.3.
183. *Gould* v. *Tanner, ibid.,* November 5, 1825, no.12,803, p.3.
184. *Ibid.,* November 28, 1825, no.12,822, p.3.

Captain Hunn of the *Tweed* was a violent, capricious man, and provided witnesses to prove the charge. He summed up his charge:

> ... by imploring the jury to show by their verdict that sailors had rights as well as others, and to sustain the discipline and character of the navy by proving that, although just authority must be sustained, redress would always follow when grievous wrong was committed.[185]

The speech produced such a sensation within the courtroom that the audience started to applaud when he sat down, but it subsided when the Court threatened to intervene. Lt. Hannaford was awarded 250 pounds for his injury, an unprecedented award. In fact, the Duke of Bedford was so impressed by the result that he had Brougham try to reverse his suit before Abbott for the collection of tolls from one who sold vegetables outside the Covent-Garden Market, but the non-suit was sustained when it was shown that the Duke had altered the royal grant for financial advantage. There was a limit to what even Brougham could do.

When Brougham was not involved in the legal problems which Harriette Wilson was causing, he helped promote the legal reform which Peel was effecting. To get the Home Secretary to take an even broader view of reform, Brougham wrote a review, "Lord Suffield *on* the Game-Laws".[186] The Norfolk peer was in favour of criminal law; yet, he was an adamant defender of the game laws as constituted. Brougham surveyed his argument and prejudices for the status quo, suggesting that the game laws had to be changed to reduce the inducements and penalties for poaching. Brougham's diagnosis was an object lesson in how to get conservatives to be reformers despite themselves. When Peel, after consulting the Law Officers and the Judges, introduced legislation to consolidate the larceny laws, Brougham went out

---

185. *Hannaford* v. *Hunn, ibid.*, December 24, 1825, no.12,846, p.3.
186. Art.XII, "Lord Suffield *on* the Game-Laws," *Edinburgh Review*, vol.43, no.LXXXV, November 1825, pp.248-62.

of his way to compliment him most generously in *The Times*:

> Sir Samuel Romilly's was a theory for the diminution of crime by the mitigation of penalties; Mr Peel's is a simplification of statutes, for shortening process, cutting away useless forms, and rendering the amended law easy and intelligible to its administrators. This is something like that work of King Edgar of which Lord Bacon speaks in his offer of "A Digest to be made of the Laws of England", cited by Mr Peel.[187]

Because William Lamb's bill to provide counsel in all felony cases had not passed muster with the Attorney General and the Judges, Peel very cautiously opposed its passage in terms which Brougham most appreciated: "On both sides authorities might be adduced, the weight and respectability of which no one could doubt, and which placed the mind of anyone who examined them, as Lord Bacon said, in *confluentiis aquarum*."[188] Under the confused circumstances, the Home Secretary declined to recommend passage. Brougham, in fact, while he favoured passage of the measure, in principle, admitted that it would make trials more contentious, which caused him to urge the House to act with caution. The proposal was easily defeated, because it would have reduced Peel's responsibilities in criminal law administration.

For Copley's benefit, Brougham wrote an article on the creation of a public prosecutor to make the Law Officers more conscious of their public responsibilities. "We have formerly had occasion to observe upon the extraordinary powers vested by the Law of Scotland in the Lord Advocate," Brougham wrote, recalling the article which had proved so productive in getting Peel on the road to reform, "powers wholly repugnant to the

---

187. *The Times*, March 11, 1826, no.12,912, p.3.
188. *Ibid.*, April 25, 1826, no.12,950, p.2.

genius of our free constitution ..."[189] The established system of prosecution, based upon public vigilance, needed amendment. Even Bacon, Brougham wrote, recognized that Britain's ancient institutions were not perfect. Infamous felons used the private procedure to walk away from court. "Could this scandal possibly have happened," he asked "had there been an officer of the law answerable for its due execution?"[190] Neither the severity of the law nor the existence of private associations, such as the Society for the Prosecution of Felons, could justify the absence of a public prosecutor who worked with the grand jury to see that justice was done. The defunct Constitutional Association, Brougham painfully reminded Copley, would never have existed if such an office had existed. The strength of Brougham's appeal was shown in *Rowe* v. *Brenton,* a case where the Attorney General was obliged to become involved as a matter of public policy in the settlement of a civil dispute concerning mines on Crown land, and one in which Brougham made the intervention absolute by contesting the motion unsuccessfully by affidavit.[191] He had the amazing capacity to keep track of a wide variety of aims, nurturing along these interests despite the confusion, and myriad of detail.

Brougham even had time for keeping up with Canning's handling of the slaves. In December 1825, there had been a meeting of the Anti-Slavery Society at which Brougham spoke. He called for putting pressure on Parliament about the slaves' plight as a first step towards emancipation.[192] Without such steps, there would be no improvement of their condition for the foreseeable future. Brougham had increased pressure for such a

---

189. Art.XI, "*Office of Public Prosecutor,*" *The Edinburgh Review,* vol.42, no.LXXXIV, August 1825, p.401. *The Wellesley Index* claim that Henry Cockburn wrote this article is unconvincing because of the way it refers to the previous ones on the nomination of Scottish juries, and its referring to Stoddart's group for private prosecutions of seditious libels, the Constitution Association, which Brougham is known to have written about in the *Review.*
190. *Ibid.,* p.406.
191. *Rowe* v. *Brenton, Law Journal, 1827* (Paget, Chancery Lane, London), King's Bench, pp.137-8.
192. "Anti-Slavery Society," *The Times,* December 22, 1825, no.12,844, p.3.

move by a discussion of the latest developments at Barbados in the *Review*. Neither the Crown nor Parliament had been able to do anything about the colony's denial of religious instruction to the slaves. "In none of the islands has the great, and safe, and obvious improvement been carried, of making the Negro's evidence admissible in the courts of justice."[193] Passage of Brougham's bill was called for to permit it, and to prevent things such as whipping.

Early in the Session, Brougham had asked Canning what the colonies were doing to assist manumission, and reforms which would have enabled Negroes to be treated more like other subjects. Not satisfied with the Foreign Secretary's assurances, particularly because of James Stephen's pamphlet on the subject, which Brougham also reviewed,[194] he pressed so for evidence and answers from Canning that there was finally a showdown in the Commons in May. In the subsequent exchanges, and analysis of the evidence, Brougham was shown to be right in his contention that hardly anything had been done by the colonial legislatures, despite the 1823 instructions from the Colonial Office.[195] Canning had deceived himself and the kingdom about the state of affairs, something that he would have to make up for to Brougham.

While matters were so progressing with the Ministry's liberal Tories, Brougham kept pressuring Eldon to retire. After Brougham had kept readers of the *Review* abreast of developments in the Chancery, once the Commission reported, he took advantage of *The Times* to make known his complaints: "The anomaly of suffering the Lord Chancellor to be one of the members of the Commission, appears from the following fact, - that his own Report is presented to him in open court, by certain other members of the Commission."[196] The problem with the Court, the report stated, repeating almost verbatim what the

---

193. Art.X, "Outrage at Barbadoes," *Edinburgh Review*, vol.42, no.LXXXIV, August 1825, p.494.
194. Art.VIII, "Colonial Slavery," *ibid.*, vol.43, no.LXXXVI, February 1826, pp.406-41.
195. New, *op. cit.*, pp.302-3.
196. "Report of the Chancery," *The Times*, March 22, 1826, no.12,918, p.3.

House inquiry had found wrong with the Private Bill system, was not its organization and rules, but "... the carelessness of some parties, the obstinacy or knavery of others, or the inattention or ignorance of agents."[197] Brougham had nothing but contempt for such an explanation: "That the Court is not answerable for all or any part of the criminality here imputed to those who practise within its precincts, or appeal to its judgments, is what we cannot conceive."[198] For the delay caused by Chancery, rules which Eldon had permitted to develop during his long tenure there, the report could only recommend more officials and working longer hours.

In May, Brougham had called for limiting appeals to the Chancery, and for getting rid of its bankruptcy jurisdiction to ease the backlog of equity cases in its courts. "That he does anything more than trot about from one to another," Brougham wrote sarcastically about the Lord Chancellor, "is really the surprising part of it ..."[199] In August, Redesdale's minority report was reviewed for *Times* readers. Apparently, Brougham thought that Redesdale's complaints about the length of conveyances and pleadings were to the point, but he complained about the Lord not having advocated them as a commissioner.[200] It seemed as if Redesdale had decided that the Court's faults were beyond cure, and had printed a mildly critical report so that opponents of change could take a stand against it during the next Session.[201] Apparently Brougham countered with a series of articles in *The Times*, examining the evidence witnesses had given to the Commission, and what reforms they had recommended.[202]

In court, once freed from Stockdale's problems with Onwhyn for pirating Miss Wilson's memoirs, Brougham's practice steadily improved. At the Spring Assizes, he obliged a malicious injury

---

197. *Ibid.*
198. *Ibid.*
199. *Ibid.*, May 24, 1826, no.12,975, p.2.
200. "The Court of Chancery," *ibid.*, August 31, 1826, no.13,060, p.3.
201. *Ibid.*
202. See the series, starting with the September 14th issue.

suit against an attorney to be non-suited,[203] obtained 50 pounds for a woman in a breach of promise suit,[204] and won a replevin action for cattle, setting aside a will because the person who made it was insane at the time.[205] In losing actions, about the customs of grinding corn in the Soke of Wakefield, a case involving a question of whether or not there was a monopoly of the business, where he did establish that the plaintiff could not interdict the building of other mills within it, he made political capital out of fines imposed for violating rights in a related case before Lord Eldon:

> ... he (Mr Brougham) cared not what might have been paid by a man with a mill-stone of Chancery hanging over his head: a poor man might as well be crushed between the upper and nether mill-stones of the Soke-mills, as engage in a law-suit with their wealthy proprietors.[206]

Also York, the son of a journeyman file-maker received 15 pounds for assault and false imprisonment when Brougham established that he had had to leave work because of sickness, rather than malingering. He would have received more, Justice Bayley chided counsel, if the arresting constable had also been prosecuted. Brougham lost a libel action, though he limited the award by effectively making fun of the plaintiff's canvassing, and agreed to the paying of 300 pounds in damages in a suit involving a coach driver, guilty of gross negligence in an accident.[207]

Back in London, Brougham was pursuing a most successful legal practice when Lord Liverpool had the King dissolve Parliament. It had already been agreed that Brougham would stand again for Westmorland because of the closeness of the last contest. Once again, his opponents were Lord and Colonel

---

203. *Craven* v. *Rushworth*, "Spring Assizes," *ibid.*, March 23, 1826, no.12,922, p.3.
204. *Harland* v. *Hepworth*, *ibid.*, March 25, 1826, no.12,924, p.2.
205. *Smith* v. *Wilson*, *ibid.*, March 27, 1826, no.12,925, p.3.
206. *Dodsworth* v. *Ingham*, *ibid.*, March 30, 1826, no.12,928, p.3.
207. *Forster* v. *Pearson*, *ibid.*, April 5, 1826, no.12,933, p.3.

Lowther. During the campaign, Brougham's supporters, particularly James Graham, contrasted how Lord Lonsdale monopolized the county's representation with its handling in Northumberland. Brougham so divided his time between the demands of the constituency and Parliament during its closing days, contesting the Ministry's feeble Chancery Bill, and moving resolutions for improving the slaves' condition, that his health nearly broke down. The Lowthers contested the election by claiming that the Ministry had adopted the measures of "Henry Sky-blue". For electors interested in his success, they warned: "We shall soon be inundated with Polish corn and French manufacturers, and our ships may not be unloaded in our ports, whilst the Pope and Jesuits *erect behind the throne* a power greater than the throne itself."[208] In the face of such hysteria, Brougham did his poorest yet, losing by more than 700 votes.[209] The Lowthers apparently spent 50,000 pounds in winning the election, and Brougham's supporters provided 9,000 pounds. He and Lord Howick were returned for Lord Darlington's pocket-borough at Winchelsea.

Joining the Summer Assizes at York, Brougham became involved in hearing a few cases before the Wakefield case, a conspiracy indictment against a family for arranging the marriage of the rich heiress, Ellen Turner, to Edward Gibben Wakefield without her father's consent. After Scarlett totally outclassed Brougham in a simple recovery action, he managed to win *Platt* v. *Platt*, a case his constant opponent dismissed without success as a "triumphery ale-house assault", and to prevail upon a special jury to find that the inhabitants of Sawley were not obliged to maintain a popular road. When the recognizances against co-conspirator William Wakefield were called at Lancaster Castle, he was no where to be found. "It is confidently asserted," *The Times* reported, "that William Wakefield left Lancaster in female attire, and in the company of two ladies."[210] While Justice Park

208. *Ibid.*, June 15, 1826, no.12,994, p.2. Italics its.
209. See the coverage, starting June 26th.
210. "Flight of W. Wakefield from His Bail," *ibid.*, August 23, 1826, no.13,053, p.2.

hoped the absence would be explained by the congestion in the streets, Wakefield's attorney stated that he would not appear. When Brougham as leader of the circuit moved for a bench warrant for his arrest, Park refused, asking him to get one from the King's Bench to apply to the whole kingdom. Ultimately, Brougham defeated Scarlett's attempt to have the trial moved to the King's Bench because the Wakefields could not get a fair trial at Lancaster. In winning a writ of *procedendo,* Brougham explained:

> With regard to the prejudice excited in the minds of a Lancaster jury, the same reason would operate against a jury of every county in the kingdom, as every newspaper had written on the subject, and unless the deaf and blind were selected, it would be impossible to find anyone ignorant of the subject.[211]

This most important case was awaiting trial in February 1827 when Lord Liverpool suffered a stroke, ending the longest Ministry in British history.

Brougham had prepared for this eventuality by subjecting the Report of the Chancery Commission to the most critical scrutiny in *The Times*. About a minority report, he wrote: "There is a great deal of good sense in all that Lord Redesdale says respecting the absurd length of modern conveyances and pleadings."[212] The Law Lord, as a Commissioner, should have seen that his complaints were made part of the official report rather than saving them for a pamphlet. Sensing that this ploy indicated that the opponents of Chancery reform were going to take a stand against it during the next Session, Brougham went through the Commission's report to marshall every bit of evidence to defeat it.

Shadwell, for example, had testified that the elimination of the bankruptcy jurisdiction would improve Chancery practice "... as

---

211. *Ibid.*, February 12, 1827, no.13,200, p.3.
212. "The Court of Chancery," *ibid.*, August 31, 1826, no.13,060, p.3.

often and almost pertinently as the Italian courtier used to say, *non mi ricordo.*"[213] About Henry Bickersteth's explanation of delay, Brougham wrote, "the whole of his evidence is extremely creditable to the character as well as to the talents of the gentleman by whom it is given."[214] Basil Montagu disclosed the Commission's abuses, detailing that the bankruptcy jurisdiction was the worst in the kingdom.[215] After Brougham had gone through the devastating testimony of the Chancery attorneys against its officials, especially the Six Clerks, he concluded about the Commissioners' Report:

> All, however, that they think fit to do is to recommend some insignificant alterations in the practice of the London examiners' offices, and some regulations respecting the expenses of the country commissioners, which fall so far short of the evil, that they can hardly be felt in the way of relief.[216]

In another article, Brougham wrote about the evidence of a troublesome but helpful attorney: "Mr Lowe seems to be a kind of Cobbett in his way, and to think that talking big, and always about himself, is the way to ensure respect."[217] Once the Six Clerks had pitifully testified for maintaining the status quo in the Chancery, Brougham concluded his series by predicting that changing the Chancellor would be the first order of business in 1827.

When Brougham was not telling tales on Eldon in the Chancery, he was making news in court himself. He won several important libel cases, an interesting one being *Buckingham* v. *Bankes* where an author of travel books was awarded 400 pounds for what a review said about his work.[218] When Brougham lost another case, it seemed that his legal adversary was willing to

---

213. *Ibid.*, October 7, 1826, no.13,085, p.3. Italics its.
214. *Ibid.*
215. *Ibid.*, October 11, 1826, no.13,088, p.2.
216. *Ibid.*, October 27, 1826, no.13,102, p.3.
217. *Ibid.*, December 20, 1826, no.13,154, p.4.
218. *Buckingham* v. *Bankes*, *ibid.*, October 20, 1826, no.13,096, p.3.

settle for an apology, given his reputation with juries, but the continued effort by Brougham's client to justify himself cost him 100 pounds.[219] In *R.* v. *Shackell*, Brougham teamed up with Scarlett to obtain a guilty verdict of libel against the editor of the *John Bull* for printing that Lord Arundel had discharged a servant for not changing his religion. Brougham represented Lord de Palmella, a Portuguese official, in a suit against the Portuguese Government for having charged him with having absconded with funds, obtaining a most favourable result, and winning ultimately two convictions.

Certainly, Brougham's greatest court triumphs were his defences of the *Sunday Monitor*, and the *Examiner* when they printed stories, calling Nicholas Bochsa, a Fellow of the Royal Academy of Music, a robber, forger and bigamist. When the Justices of the King's Bench permitted the plaintiff to proceed by indictment, a mode of proceeding which prevented the newspapermen from justifying what had been published, Brougham thoroughly applied himself. Lord Chief Justice Abbott's suggestion that criminatory information about Bochsa should have been privately communicated to its directors was dismissed with contempt, as something worthy of the Constitutional Association. In fact, Brougham prevailed upon Barnes to print an excerpt from the *French Moniteur*, showing that Bochsa had indeed been sentenced by the Paris Court of Assize to 12 years' imprisonment at hard labour for forgery, having signed Wellington's signature to a bond.[220] *The Times* made such a fuss about Bochsa's record that the verdicts against the other papers came to nothing.

When the new Session opened, Brougham was at his peak. Having once again articulated his liberal policies when Parliament had assembled in November, calling for Catholic Emancipation and retrenchment on taxes in most eloquent terms,[221] he was positioned to play a role in any Ministry.

---

219. *Jones* v. *Hanbury*, *ibid.*, October 12, 1826, no.13,089, pp.2-3.
220. "M. Bochsa," *ibid.*, December 6, 1826, no.13,142, p.3.
221. *Ibid.*, November 22, 1826, no.13,123, p.2.

Brougham's credentials to effect reform were increased when Lord Chief Justice Best of the Common Pleas adopted his position on libel in his charge in *Stockley* v. *Clement*. Malice had to be proved in establishing that libel had been committed in publishing derogatory material about a person, setting the stage for legislation against the presumption of malice in libel actions. The need for constitutional reform was graphically illustrated when Lord Eldon handed down his decision in *Lucena* v. *Crawford*, a dispute of such long standing, *The Times* reported, that counsel no longer remembered which side they represented.[222] Chancellor Eldon's ability to stop embarrassing discussion about delay in the Chancery would not last much longer. Liverpool's seizure ended Eldon's tenure of the Woolsack, leaving the way clear for Brougham's rise in government.

---

222. *Ibid.*, January 16, 1827, no.13,177, pp.2-3.

CHAPTER EIGHT

KINGMAKER

Brougham and *The Times* moved immediately to institutionalize liberal politics when Lord Liverpool's paralysis was announced. While the Ministry had been increasingly adopting policies that Whigs such as Brougham favoured, the Tory backbenchers slowed the pace of reform, and provided some legislation of a reactionary nature. The task was to force a restructuring of party politics, to start a process whereby Tories and Whigs of a liberal bent would reorganize under a unified leadership. There was certainly a pressing agenda for such a party. The Corn Law, parliamentary reform, Catholic Emancipation, currency reform, legal consolidation, Chancery reform, and improvement of the slaves' condition in the colonies, to name just the most important areas, all demanded extensive legislative attention. The problem was to oblige party leaders to throw off the political inertia of the past 15 years. Liverpool was dead, for all practical purposes. A process had to be devised by which leading politicians would no longer organize, and operate in conventional terms. Just as Lord Grey, and Tierney had to be persuaded to work ever more closely with Liberals such as Canning until there was no longer any need to keep separate party existences, so Peel had to be induced to see that there was no longer any reason to isolate himself from people such as Brougham and Barnes. This development would itself make radical parliamentary reform less necessary because it would rid the Commons of Members who blindly supported the Crown while effecting private measures which assisted themselves and some of their constituents.

While the ministers tried to act as if Liverpool's incapacity was temporary, *The Times* did everything it could to disabuse its readers of the idea. Barnes, taking advantage of the tax relief granted in 1825,[1] used the paper's increased size to show that dramatic events were happening. Day-after-day, exploiting the six-column layout, *The Times* dramatized the leadership crisis, and the need for extensive reform. With such demands on reporting, and on editorial comment, parliamentary affairs were increasingly given front-page coverage. The inside page was crammed with leaders about what needed to be done, often written apparently by Brougham. Hardly had Liverpool's political demise sunk into readers' minds than Brougham renewed the call for law reform. With an eye on the Home Secretary, and the Chancery Report, he said that legal practitioners could not be expected to effect legal reform. About his deceased friend of the Chancery Bar, Brougham wrote: "Sir Samuel Romilly, it is well known, proposed to himself as the dearest object of his ambition, a recasting of the whole code of our criminal law."[2] Erskine had been correspondingly only interested in equity reform. Only Peel had been able to cut through such parochialism, and Brougham urged him to take up the law of libel, once he finally got his consolidation of larceny law through Parliament. Because of the way the Home Secretary exercised the Crown's mercy in capital felonies, Brougham was increasingly irritated with prospective jurors of the Old Bailey who refused to serve because they were opposed to capital punishment. When the expected Chancery bill, based upon the recommendations of Eldon's commission, was presented to the Commons, *The Times* subjected it to a withering dismissal.

Brougham was also going from triumph to triumph in court. When Denman dismissed the claim against the City, as Corporation Counsel, for premises taken in the building of the Fleet Market, calling for only nominal compensation, Brougham defended printer Richard Taylor's interests with great ability. He showed that he would have to provide a steam press at a new

---

1. *The Times*, July 13, 1825, no.12,704, p.2.
2. *Ibid.*, February 24, 1827, no.13,211, p.2.

establishment, another printer had received 15,000 pounds compensation, and Taylor had underestimated his loss.[3] Through the cross-examination of the City's witnesses, Brougham proved his case. The jury awarded Taylor nearly 8,500 pounds. Brougham defeated Campbell in *Edis* v. *Bury*, a recovery action in the King's Bench where the defence pleaded unsuccessfully that it did not owe the money because it had signed a bill of exchange rather than a promissory note.[4] Scarlett was humiliated in a criminal conversation and seduction case, one he said he was honoured to prosecute, when Brougham reduced the damages to one shilling by showing that the plaintiff drove away his wife so that he could consort with prostitutes.[5]

The best evidence of Brougham's infuriating success was provided by "Dandy" Raikes. Brougham defended proprietor Richards of the *Age*, a Sunday newspaper, against Raikes's libel action. The said libels concerned stories about why Raikes could not bring his daughters out in society, and a characterization of him in the *Liar*. Scarlett, in prosecuting the case, said that it was time for a jury to teach such an editor a lesson as Raikes was "a gentleman of great respectability."[6] Brougham said that the latter story did not refer to Raikes, and he objected to Scarlett associating placards based upon it with his client. Scarlett was completely taken aback by Brougham's challenge because the editor had just let another libel action, *Hughes* v. *Richards*, go by default, resulting in a 150-pound verdict for the plaintiff. This action was a different case, Brougham explained. "It was quite absurd to say that Mr Raikes's character was likely to suffer, or had suffered," he said, "or his feelings had been lacerated by these publications."[7] The statement that Raikes was not fit for genteel society was brushed aside as something no industrious man would object to. Brougham, taking note for the future, said this in justification of a fake obituary notice for "Dandy": "The

3. *Ibid.*, January 25, 1827, no.13,185, p.3.
4. *Ibid.*, February 19, 1827, no.13,206, p.3.
5. *Sir Jacob Astley* v. *Thomas Garth*, *ibid.*, February 20, 1827, no.13,207, pp.3-4.
6. *Raikes* v. *Richards*, *ibid.*, February 21, 1827, no.13,208, p.3.
7. *Ibid.*

advantage of this practice was, that the person thus prematurely killed, heard all that good of himself during his life-time, which under other circumstances, would have been kept for his executors and administrators." (*Continued laughter.*)[8] While the Lord Chief Justice instructed the jury that to call a man a liar was the greatest moral censure, it could only award him 40 shillings for his loss.

During March 1827, negotiations about a new Ministry were reaching a critical stage. Sir Robert Wilson, Brougham's old friend, from the campaign against flogging, was consulting with Canning about the Whigs joining a new Ministry, and the busy barrister was constantly advising him what the liberal Whigs expected from such an arrangement. While Brougham was preparing to prosecute the Wakefields at the Lancaster Assizes, he wrote to Wilson, explaining to him the difficulties that Canning faced if he formed a totally Tory Administration. An arrangement with co-operating Whigs had to be made. "For my own part," Brougham wrote, "I will only say that I am ready to back him in whatever way he himself would seem most effectual."[9] When this proposal was suggested to Canning through Lord Erskine, who was acting as Wilson's intermediary, Brougham was asked to explain further his reasons and aims in supporting the liberal Tories. A few days later, while at York, Brougham wrote again, describing how things had developed since he had charged the Foreign Secretary with "truckling to Eldon":

> C.[anning] had, I own, made me angry or (to speak more properly) vexed, and hurt me by what I thought yielding to the Chancellor in 1822; but all I have since seen of him, including his indignation when I attacked him (in a moment of anger) had satisfied me he is disposed to act a high, manly, and honourable part, and to secure to himself permanent

---

8. *Ibid.*
9. Brougham's letter to Wilson, dated March 18, 1827: quoted from Chester W. New, *The Life of Henry Brougham to 1830* (Clarendon Press, Oxford, 1961), p.309.

> power by risking temporary loss of place ...[10]

Brougham had ambitions of achieving a similar rapprochement with Peel. In February, when the Home Secretary had presented to the Commons several bills to consolidate the criminal code, Brougham used Copley's weak Chancery Bill, introduced a few days later, as a basis for attacking Eldon, hoping that it would force Peel to choose between the ultra Tories and reform. While they were disputing the Chancellor's performance, Brougham gave a "... pledge that he would undertake a revisal of the law of property, the source of most of the difficulties, and of much of the delay, in Chancery proceedings."[11] In harking back to the problems of conveyancing, what had convinced Peel to take up reform at the Home Office, Brougham hoped to force him, as it had Canning, to repudiate his ultra colleagues. The same sentiment was indicated in Brougham's letter to Wilson of March 28 when he discussed Peel's potential: "... for we may think him an ordinary man, and far inferior to C.[anning]: yet we respect him, and value the victories he had gained over his prejudices, and I hope good things from his pushing those victories still further."[12] As for Brougham's own capacity in a liberal Ministry, he would support it on the front bench only. He was far too busy in court to think of office.

At London and Lancaster, Brougham gave graphic illustration to his claim of disinterest in office. Hardly had Raikes received his paltry verdict that he charged into Brooks's Club to insult Brougham deliberately for what he had said in court about him, hoping to instigate a duel with him.[13] Brougham accepted the challenge, and there would have been a duel if it had not been for the efforts of Thomas Spring Rice. Meanwhile Brougham, still stung by the idea that it was because of his efforts that Gourlay

---

10. Brougham's letter to Wilson, dated March 26, 1827: quoted from Edward J. Stapleton, ed, *Some Official Correspondence of George Canning* (Longmans, London, 1887, 2 vols.), vol.II, p.300.
11. *Gentleman's Magazine*, 1827, vol.97, Part I, p.257.
12. Brougham's letter to Wilson, dated March 26, 1827: Stapleton, *op. cit.*, vol.II, p.301.
13. New, *op. cit.*, pp.318-9.

was languishing in gaol, was getting second thoughts about the meeting. Spring Rice convinced officer Dunlop of Bow Street to arrest Brougham. Once Spring Rice and Lord Sefton had bailed Brougham, his having been bound over to keep the peace, the Lord Chief Justice issued an order against his leaving the country, to prevent a duel in France. The Whig leader was far too important to national politics to be snuffed out over a matter of professional pride by a dandy who had been incited by his Tory colleagues to a fatal confrontation. Even Scarlett, Raikes's counsel, confessed to *The Times* that Brougham had only been doing his job in his defence of Richard Richards.[14] Raikes immediately apologized to Brougham for the insult to avoid exclusion from the club.

At the Spring Assizes at Lancaster, Baron Hullock heard the case against the Wakefields for conspiring to arrange the marriage between Miss Turner and Edward Gibbon Wakefield. Scarlett, in defending the young man after having failed to move the venue to York, stood by the Scottish marriage that they had arranged under false pretences, vows which prevented her from testifying against her husband. Brougham, for the prosecution, objected to the rule, stating that the defendants had criminally conspired to obtain her wealth and silence, a view which the presiding Judge found persuasive despite Scarlett's objection, under the circumstances.[15] Other witnesses established that the Wakefields had contrived a complicated plot to oblige the schoolgirl to marry the penniless Wakefield, believing that only he could save her rich father from bankruptcy. Scarlett contended that Miss Turner had been happy throughout about the affair. Hullock had been persuaded that the Wakefields had engaged in a hoax before their defence was even attempted. The jury convicted them on all counts of conspiracy except the use of force in carrying out their designs.

The next day, Miss Turner's husband, and his brother, William Wakefield, pleaded guilty to her abduction. Brougham then saw

---

14. *The Times*, March 12, 1827, no.13,224, p.2.
15. *R.* v. *The Wakefields*, March 26, 1827, no.13,236, p.3.

to the resolution of a libel dispute between the *York Herald* and *Leeds Mercury*, to the reduction of an insecure claim in a ship-repair case to the non-suiting of a trover action, to a reduced award in another libel action by claiming plaintiff's counsel usurped the Judge's function, to the failure of the nuisance indictment against the inhabitants of the West Riding to maintain the Sutter Back Bridge, and to the giving of a substantial award to Lord Doune in a damage suit against a canal company, all cases where Brougham gave battle with Scarlett.

Brougham was in a most confident mood as he set off from Lancaster to Brougham Hall to plan the final steps of the liberal union with the Canningites. Yet, he was not so involved that he ignored writing about a great disaster, the explosion of a coastal trader, for *Times* readers, an article whose intimate details showed that he was providing coverage for Barnes's paper. Just as Brougham set off for Penrith, there was a terrible rumbling and shaking of the countryside. People first thought it was an earthquake. "The four horses of one of the northern coaches, then about to proceed to its destination," he reported, "stood fast and trembled excessively, and one of the leaders fell down with every appearance of terror ..."[16] The explosion produced this effect: "Near the Sheep Fells (a range of hilly moorland) in Westmorland, about 28 miles from this place, the shock was very violently experienced, and the windows of Brougham Hall, the residence of Mr Brougham, were shattered. Considerable damage was also done at Kendal and Lowther Castles ..."[17]

Brougham travelled west to Peel Castle, the site of the explosion. There he learned that the *Commerce*, a dogger vessel travelling from Lancaster to Liverpool, had caught fire and blown up after it had taken on 10 tons of gunpowder at Blackborough Mills. The tiers of the ship had been flooded to prevent disaster, but the water did not prevent the cotton cargo, also on board, from catching fire. The crew scuttled the ship in the hope of preventing the explosion, but without success. The unfortunate

---

16. "Explosion of the Commerce Trader," *ibid.*, March 28, 1827, no.13,238, p.3.
17. *Ibid.*

ship seemed lifted by her knees out of the water, he reported, and then blew up momentarily, with a terrific explosion. While much damage was done, no one was killed.

Three weeks later, the *Leeds Mercury* was in a similarly expansive mood when it examined Brougham's career as a barrister, an assessment which should finally lay to rest any doubt about his professional abilities. Editor Edward Baines had had his differences with counsel over the years, so the evaluation cannot be just written off as that of an uncritical admirer. The article was an extract from a letter by a person who had just seen Brougham in action at the Yorkshire Lent Assizes for the first time. The writer felt enriched by 1,000 pounds because of the experience.

Brougham was then described in court, and followed through a cause. While he had a most singular face, he was, nonetheless, a most undignified unattractive person until he acted professionally. Brougham's combat with Scarlett was then described in an insignificant case where he learned about the facts of the matter from his junior while he addressed the jury in his Scottish twang, incessantly twitching his cheek and nose. The writer found Brougham's oratory near perfect in defending his losing cause, a most effective mixture of body mannerisms, good nature, sound reasoning and light moments that almost transformed the court into something else.

When the shoe was on the other foot with Scarlett - a will's case where Brougham demonstrated the knavery of his clients - the writer concluded: "In short, this was the highest oratorical achievement it has fallen to my lot to hear, and it was of course successful, though it certainly was not one of his greatest efforts."[18] Brougham, in sum, was a first-rate genius, and a man of great learning, a fitting vindicator of liberty and justice. While Baines had previously printed a series on the kingdom's leading politicians, this tribute to Brougham stood by itself, and was not followed by ones dedicated to other barristers.

At Brougham Hall, once the broken glass had been swept up,

---

18. "A Portrait," *Leeds Mercury*, April 21, 1827, no.3,232, p.3.

and the panes replaced, Brougham was back to business as usual, writing a letter to *The Times*, it seems, announcing the demise of the Whig Party. There was no one left in Fox's party, he complained, to stand up to the abuses of the prerogative if the King wanted to behave like an oriental despot. Of course, the Tories were hopeless "... because the will of the Prince is their law."[19] For the true followers of Fox, those who favoured liberal politics, he proposed a compromising opposition to take advantage of the policy differences among ministers, who were not all alike. Short of such a coalition by liberals, Brougham could only foresee "the desultory efforts of individuals, how truly soever deserving the name of Whig, can have no other effect than that of exposing the Constitution to fresh inroads from the prerogative ..."[20]

While this hyperbole was far from the truth, it did have the desired effect upon Canning. Actually, Liverpool's Ministry, during its dying days, had behaved anything but like a Tory one. When complaints about the way private business of Parliament had been carried on were not stilled by resolutions altering the composition of select committees hearing bills, a process initiated by Brougham when he took up the cause of the Liverpool and Manchester Railway, the Commons not only deprived James Brogden, the Chairman of the Committee of Ways and Means, of his office, but also appointed a committee to look into the operation of the Arigna Mining Company. MPs such as Brogden, Sir William Congreve, and John Bent had pocketed part of the sale price of the company as directors. During the debate on the Address for the Special Session, Brougham had raised Brogden's reappointment under the circumstances thus: "He alluded to the report that a certain proposition might be expected to be made to the house, savouring of anything rather than necessity, and entirely opposed to the just feelings and expectations of the people of this country."[21] Once this helped spark a dispute

---

19. "To the Editor of *The Times*," *ibid*., March 29, 1827, no.13,239, p.3.
20. *Ibid*.
21. *Ibid*., November 22, 1826, no.13,123, p.2.

between Waithman and Brogden about the latter's role in the Arigna affair, Canning had been obliged to see to Sir Alexander Grant's appointment as Chairman of the Committee of Ways and Means *pro tempore*. While Brougham made light of the inquiry, recalling what he had said about the Irish lad in Canada who wanted to be tried by his brother,[22] its report was more than even *The Times* had bargained for.[23] Congreve was ruled to have engaged in fraud, and Brogden and Bent had treated it in such a cavalier way that they had failed the public.

With such a judgment by a committee composed of liberals such as Althorp, Warburton, Waithman, Robert Grant, Ashley, and George Lamb, willing to serve the public interest despite party differences, Canning moved to make good on his pledge to be Prime Minister.[24] When the Tory ministers resigned *en masse*, Canning's chances completely rested with what Brougham could work out with the Whigs. Lansdowne, the Whig leader in the Lords whose co-operation was so essential for the creation of a coalition, soon caused the negotiations to break down by pushing the Whig party's claim to a government with a more Catholic flavour to still O'Connell's last complaint against the Penal Laws. Brougham took a back seat in Whig consultations, apparently treating *Times* readers to doggerel like this at the Home Secretary's expense to force Peel to join the new Ministry:

> That the law I reform, as far as I may,
> Without adding one title, or taking away;
> But, by clipping with scissors, and pasting with gum,
> Contrive good old Jeremy Bentham to hum.[25]

Once Brougham learned that his Whig colleagues were playing into the hands of the ultra Tories, and the prerogative, he took

---

22. *Ibid.*, December 6, 1826, no.13,142, p.3.
23. *Ibid.*, April 4, 1827, no.13,244, p.3.
24. "Report from the Select Committee on the Arigna Mining Company:" *Reports from Committees*, 1826-7, vol.III, pp.37-68.
25. "Soliloquy of a Decorous and Very Pure Statesman," *The Times*, March 31, 1827, no.13,241, p.3.

up matters, writing to Althorp about their selfish stupidity. He told a group of them at a meeting at Brooks's Club the same thing in no uncertain terms. "When he sat down," Professor New wrote, "the coalition was saved."[26]

Brougham was ecstatic about his success, closing finally, he wrote to his friend Thomas Creevey, "... the door for ever on Eldon and Co."[27] He was, nonetheless, somewhat hard on Lansdowne due to the breakdown of negotiations. His life-long friend had been placed in a most awkward position by Grey's refusal to consider the possibility of coalition, and Lansdowne had to aggregate demands by a group of politicians who had had little impact on British policy for a generation. It was far easier to deal with the party rank-in-file who had gone for so long without, and did not stand to gain so much, than with Brougham, who would get more than his share whoever ran the government. That very month, he had had the King's Bench uphold the verdict he had achieved at the previous Spring Assizes in *Wilson* v. *Smith*, a contested will suit.[28] Brougham and Scarlett then teamed up to win *Harnett* v. *Thwaites*, a libel action against the *Morning Herald* for printing a police report which damaged an attorney. The defence pleaded that the editor had not been motivated by malice in printing an erroneous address about him, but the jury awarded him 100 pounds.[29] Brougham even had time to write another article on Chancery reform, criticizing what Copley, the new Master of the Rolls, was proposing to do about Eldon and Co.[30] In fact, Brougham was so much in evidence that *The Times* tried to quash the rumour that he was to take over after Canning resigned.[31]

When the new Ministry appeared in Parliament, Brougham, along with Tierney, Burdett, Calcraft, Newport, Stanley, Spring Rice, Sir Robert Wilson, and Fowell Buxton, took unaccustomed

---

26. New, *op. cit.*, p.312.
27. Brougham's letter to Creevey, dated April 21, 1827: quoted from *ibid.*, p.312.
28. *The Times*, April 5, 1827, no.13,244, pp.2-3.
29. *Ibid.*, April 26, 1827, no.13,263, p.3.
30. "The Chancery Bill," *ibid.*, April 16, 1827, no.13,254, p.3.
31. *Ibid.*, April 25, 1827, no.13,262, p.2.

places on the ministerial front benches, and Peel moved to the lower benches. W.S. Bourne became the new Home Secretary. Lansdowne received a Cabinet post, and Brougham's rival, Scarlett, became the Attorney General. Peel advertised that he was not about to join any government which treated Catholic Emancipation as an open question. His former Under Secretary for the Home Department, George Dawson, used a question about Whig ministerial appointments to charge Brougham with seeking office himself through most unprincipled manoeuvres. Brougham replied: "He had never dreamt of taking office under the present arrangements."[32] He politicized things more by seconding Dawson's question for answers about Whig appointments. When Dawson learned that there would be five Whigs in the Cabinet, he denounced that coalition "... as the basest, most unnatural, and unprecedented that had ever taken place."[33] Dawson blamed the press, especially *The Times,* for making Canning's Ministry possible.

Brougham compounded Peel's difficulties by making fun of him in Barnes's columns in the hope that he could induce him to forsake colleagues such as Eldon, Westmorland, Dundas, and Wellington. In "The Late Resignations", there was this bit of doggerel:

> Mr Peel, Mr Peel!
> Very soon you must feel
> That the reign of exclusion is past;
> Then to Oxford repair,
> Leave your bigotry there,
> And in politics a new coat.[34]

In an unaccompanying article, Peel was urged to change his mind. "It becomes you to pause and listen to the honest admonitions of one not now for the first time your correspondent

---

32. *Ibid.,* May 2, 1827, no.13,268, p.2.
33. *Gentleman's Magazine,* 1827, vol.97,Part I, p.450.
34. *The Times,* May 10, 1827, no.13,275, p.3.

..."[35] As for Brougham's message, he wrote: "You have mistaken the character and resources both of Mr Canning and of his enemies, and you have not discerned the spirit of the country."[36] Protestant Tories simply could not run the kingdom. Peel should seek repentance, and rejoin Canning.

In making this appeal, Brougham misjudged Peel's character, and the political adaptability of Tories such as the Duke. Moreover Brougham underestimated Canning's mortality, showing greater sensitivity to the state of the market than to that of his leader. When Waithman wanted to have a parliamentary inquiry into the Cornwall and Devon Mining Company, Brougham prevailed upon the House to drop it because it involved no misuse of Parliament, and the courts were seeing that justice was being done, citing his role in the prosecution of *Moore* v. *Hamond*. This was hardly reassuring experience, however, because the King's Bench had non-suited the recovery action because the transactions complained of had not been done according to the settlement deed.[37] Brougham even downplayed, of all things, his complaints about Lord Charles Somerset's administration of the Cape, something he had previously harped on. Brougham concentrated his efforts upon the Penryn Disenfranchisement Bill, engaging in cross-examination which allowed him to go after the Ministry's enemies rather than run the risk of alienating its friends. Brougham obviously enjoyed questioning John Stanbury, a general electioneering agent for the constituency whose effort had landed him in jail: "Come, answer; you need not be afraid for you know you are in Newgate already? (Roars of laughter)."[38] Despite Scarlett's complaint that the examination was wasting time, it continued, to the delight of the House.

Brougham's pressing problem was to get an annulment of the Wakefield marriage through Parliament, especially since Eldon presented a petition from young Wakefield against it. The bill

---

35. "To Mr Peel," *ibid.*, p.3.
36. *Ibid.*
37. *Ibid.*, May 1, 1827, no.13,267, p.3.
38. *Ibid.*, May 19, 1827, no.13,283, p.2.

declared that the *de facto* marriage should be null and void.[39] Two days later, in presenting Wakefield's petition against Brougham's, Eldon declared: "The petitioner stated, that the most material allegations of the petition of William Turner were untrue."[40] The statement of the ex-Chancellor (Capley, as Lord Lyndhurst, had replaced him on the Woolsack), panicked even the bill's sponsors to doubt its validity, but Brougham had already cleared the way for passage. One of the first honours of the Canning Ministry had been to raise Lord Chief Justice Abbott to the peerage. "Public justice," the new Lord Tenterden exclaimed, "demanded that they should pass the bill."[41] The only possible hitch in its passage concerned the hearing of witnesses when the bill was to be read a second time. Wakefield, stealing a page from the Roseberry divorce bill, called upon the House to hear him, hoping that his pleas of love and admiration for his wife would more than offset her claims that he had carried her off like a modern Helen. Brougham responded in kind, having his brother William, who was working with him out of the office at 8 Old Square, Lincoln's Inn Field, childhood friend Adam, and Sergeant Cross representing the teenage bride.[42] Wakefield was completely dumbfounded by the battery of legal talent at her disposal, and the bill was passed without difficulty.

In fact, the proceeding made Eldon look so bad that Peel was obliged to introduce the bill into the Commons, going out of his way, at Brougham's expense, to say that the marriage was legal, but the law should be changed to prevent a recurrence. The leader in *The Times*, sounding much like Brougham, and discussing Peel as a statesman, had stung the Tory leader to action. D.W. Harvey tried to compound Brougham's "difficulties" by presenting another petition from Gourley, complaining about his incarceration for his attack upon the barrister. This obliged Peel to explain that Gourlay was not being held for the attack, but for his letters to the Speaker, and his failure to give sureties

---

39. *Journals of the House of Lords*, 1827, vol.59, p.308.
40. *The Parliamentary Debates*, n.s., vol.XII, col.876.
41. *Ibid.*, col.883.
42. *Journals of the House of Lords*, 1827, vol.59, p.351 ff.

for his future good behaviour.[43] In sum, this was another legal case that Campbell overlooked when he wrote his malicious characterization of Brougham as a barrister.

Brougham had been biding his time in court, pleading mostly for the mitigation of punishment. For example, in a case of 20 cotton spinners, convicted of riot and assault against fellow workers in a strike, Brougham, while opposed to their actions, said that the men had now made a proper apology for what they had done. "The misguided men had come to a proper sense of their duty, and he submitted that a lenient punishment would answer the ends of justice."[44] While Scarlett was opposed to any mitigation of punishment, the court sentenced the leaders to around a year each, at hard labour, at Lancaster Gaol. Brougham and Denman went all out to have Cooke, an attorney of eminence, declared innocent of a manifest conspiracy to issue a fraudulent commission of bankruptcy.[45]

Brougham's patience paid off, as the Canning Ministry finally saw to his becoming the equivalent of King's Counsel, through a patent of precedence in the common law courts. It was more than a symbolic gesture when he arrived at the King's Bench, for the morning session on June 6, in a silk gown, and took his seat within the bar, "... bowing to Lord Tenterden and the gentlemen of the bar."[46] Later that day, at the opening of the parliamentary meeting in the Commons, Peel presented the Turner annulment bill. A fortnight later, at a Liverpool dinner in Brougham's honour for being successfully retained by the Corporation in its opposition to paying poor rates on the newly constructed Liverpool Docks, Brougham explained the effects of his promotion, stating that it would not lead to an increase of 5,000 pounds in retainers as rumoured. He would lose money, in fact, by being K.C. because it allowed six juniors to be promoted also. Unlike Scarlett's lead of the Northern Circuit, Brougham explained, he would find himself in a most competitive situation.

---

43. *The Times*, June 7, 1827, no.13,299, p.2.
44. *Ibid.*, May 26, 1827, no.13,289, p.5.
45. *R.* v. *Cooke, Ramsden, and Others, ibid.*, June 4, 1827, no.13,296, pp.4-5.
46. *Ibid.*, June 7, 1827, no.13,299, p.3.

While it is possible that this claim provided some of the basis of the contention that Brougham lost out to barristers such as Frederick Pollock, and his income suffered, it is not true. If it were, leading members of the Bar would have been reduced to penury. Brougham would soon be making nearly 10,000 pounds a year in his legal practice.

Brougham celebrated his advancement by winning two cases in the Common Pleas, a court known for the near monopoly that its Serjeants had of its practice. The defendants, in two libel actions, had reported that two Indians, concerned with the publication of *The English Gentleman*, had experienced severe condemnation for their mode of operation at a trial at the Court of Requests, Leicester Square. On the basis apparently of a statement at the trial, repeated by one of their reporters, the defendants had printed: "Our gentlemen may pride themselves in not paying their tailors; but the *English Gentleman* alone can boast of not paying its reporters."[47] Brougham argued that the remark had never been made by the Judge. Even more important was Brougham's thinking in wanting to revamp the system of local courts, as he explained:

> The Court of Requests was one of that description in which trifling demands were heard and decided, and which, from the no great celebrity of the persons who attended it, was not one of those which were so fortunate as to be regularly reported.[48]

For making up the fictitious report, the defendants were given moderate fines.

The controversial role that Brougham had played in effecting the coalition with the Canningites was the main order of business when the shareholders of the Haytian Mining Company gathered for their annual meeting at Finsbury Circus, Moorfields. Mr Hay, realizing how Brougham had exploited stock speculation by

---

47. *L.J. Pouchee* v. *Grant and Young, ibid.*, June 8, 1827, no.13,300, p.4.
48. *Ibid.*, p.3.

certain influential Tories to help break up their coalition with Canning's followers, tried to make political capital out of his financial dealings in company formation. Brougham was criticized for letting his name go out as a potential director, an effort to use Brogden's disgrace to his detriment. Hay "... considered the Company as great a bubble as ever was introduced."[49] Lord Nugent, who was in the chair, called him to order, but Hay persisted in his motion, claiming that Brougham's behaviour was dishonourable, and a public deception. Once Hay's motion had been seconded, Mr Smith MP ran to Brougham's defence, stating that there was nothing dishonourable in what he had done. "He took 20 shares, and regarded the deposit he paid," Smith explained, "as a subscription."[50] Nugent too ridiculed the idea that Brougham had time to be actively engaged in the company's affairs, advancing his own speculative interests. When Hay's resolution had been defeated, he responded bitterly: "Our ancestors, he said, had been plundered by priests and monks (laughter), and now we were to be plundered by priests and lawyers (laughter)."[51]

Brougham showed in court the next day his contempt for wild charges about his conduct. In the King's Bench, he prosecuted Richard Downing Richards for libelling Lord Glengall in the *Age*, only to turn around, and defend the same editor for charging that Mr Easthope took advantage of inside information about Chilean bonds to make a killing in the Stock Market.[52] While the defence failed, Brougham was showing that he was willing to defend detractors, such as Hay, as far as the law would allow. Brougham was willing to prosecute them if other people felt injured by their activities, or he would even represent such people if they wished. It was simply a question of what clients wanted, and they would have to suffer the consequences of the verdicts. This was vividly shown when Brougham prosecuted Sir John Soane's complaint against the *Quarterly*. The celebrated architect thought that the

---

49. "Haytian Mining Company," *ibid.*, June 11, 1827, no.13,302, p.3.
50. *Ibid.*
51. *Ibid.*
52. *Ibid.*, June 12, 1827, no.13,303, p.3.

periodical had defamed him when it called his renovation of Westminster Hall a Boeotian work of art.[53] Scarlett answered that the comment was a legitimate exercise of freedom of the press, and not motived by malice. The jury agreed, and Barnes, with whom Brougham had such close ties that he constituted a second editor, had a favourable leader on the verdict in *The Times*.

When Brougham received his patent of precedence in Chancery, he seemingly let it go to his head, overarguing an appeal before the Judicial Committee of the Privy Council. The case concerned what the East India Company could do, and whether its actions were answerable to the Supreme Court of Madras. When its counsel argued that it had a most broad authority, Brougham cited a proclamation by Lord Clive in 1801 as evidence to the contrary, denouncing the appellant's claim as monstrous doctrine. This epithet induced Sir John Leach, who had replaced Copley as Master of the Rolls, to caution Brougham to moderate his pleas. Leach was not the kind of Judge he was apt to listen to, as we learn from Holdsworth: "He was an eager supporter of the Prince's project to get a divorce, managed the Milan commission which was sent out to get evidence against the Princess, and hinted that the Prince was not properly supported in this project by his ministers."[54] Brougham reacted thus to the advice: "He then contended at considerable length, and with much force, that private property did not, and ought not to pass to the conqueror ..."[55] The Judicial Committee found for the appellant, the East India Company.

In parliamentary affairs, Brougham continued to ridicule Peel for Canning's benefit. At the Liverpool dinner, he said this about the former Home Secretary's rash resignation: "He hoped that he (Mr Peel) would live long enough to come back to office, improved by being out of office ..."[56] In *The Times*, there was a

53. *Soane* v. *Knight*, *ibid.*, June 13, 1827, no.13,304, p.3.
54. Sir William Holdsworth, *A History of English Law* (Methuen, London, 1952, 14 vols.), vol.XIII, p.665.
55. *East India Company* v. *Syed Alli and Others*, *ibid.*, June 25, 1827, no.13,314, p.3.
56. "Dinner for Mr Brougham at Liverpool," *The Times*, June 20, 1827, no.13,310, p.3.

series of articles criticizing Peel, in the writing of which Brougham must have participated. For example, one leader concluded a comparison of Peel to Sidmouth on this note: "To talk of such a person as a statesman! or a chief! is merely an idle abuse of words ..."[57] Brougham, bolstered by a letter from Wilberforce about his anticipated role in improving the slaves' condition,[58] tried to prepare a political environment in which Canning's results would make Peel rule his resignation. In June, Brougham presented a petition, calling for legislating the reforms for the West Indies that he had been continually justifying in articles in the *Review*. In the June issue, he discussed the plight of their mulattoes.[59] To steel the Prime Minister for enactment of such a programme, he discussed his role as Foreign Secretary in the ending of the slave trade, concluding in most glowing terms: "That odious traffic no longer existed by law. (Hear, hear)."[60]

In July, Brougham won a libel action which he must have felt particularly pleased about. In defending *Wright* v. *Whiting and Another*, he used the same argument which Scarlett, the prosecutor, had used so effectively in the Soane case. The case concerned a review that had appeared in *Atlas* about *Alma Mater*, an exposé of sexual liberties at Cambridge by a Trinity man. "Had the notorious Harriette Wilson been still qualified to carry on her infamous trade," the review said, "she would not have betrayed the names and conversations of her paramours."[61] Scarlett denounced the review as a personal attack upon the author of *Alma Mater*, deprecating the comparison between it and Miss Wilson's work. Brougham said that if the plaintiff won, there would be a spate of exposés. The author had violated personal confidences in publishing the material, and did not deserve the law's protection, a sentiment which drew Tenterden's

---

57. *Ibid.*, June 6, 1827, no.13,298, p.2.
58. New, *op. cit.*, p.303.
59. Art.IX, "West Indian Mulattoes," *Edinburgh Review*, vol.46, no.XCI, June 1827, pp.218-24.
60. *The Times*, June 13, 1827, no.13,304, p.2.
61. *Wright* v. *Whiting and Another, ibid.*, July 11, 1827, no.13,328, p.5.

approbation: "The man who thinks fit to apply the appellation of bear and beast to others, is not entitled to any very great compensation in damages for publications upon himself."[62] The jury gave him nothing.

A few days later, Brougham struck another blow for freedom of the press in court cases by his defence of *Scott and Wife* v. *Clement*, a libel action in the Common Pleas. The defendant published affidavits in the Wellesley case, a custody battle of the most scandalous proportions, imputing various crimes to Susannah Scott. She, of course, sued, and her counsel, Serjeant Bosanquet, said that if the charges were untrue, hardly any sum would be adequate to compensate her injury. Brougham, during cross-examination of the plaintiff, established that some of the charges were true. She was a "professional lady" who had obviously committed adultery. Lord Chief Justice Best was shocked by the content, and the practice of such reports. "He was of opinion that it was injurious to the best interests of society to publish those proceedings."[63] His daughters were not even allowed to read the accounts in the *Morning Chronicle* and the *Observer*. Despite such direction, the jury found that the libel did not impute perjury, and Mrs Scott had committed adultery. For the untrue charge of theft, the jury awarded her a farthing in damages, and 40 shillings in costs. Brougham was not satisfied with the proceedings, however, complaining apparently in *The Times*:

> It is said to be illegal to publish proceedings not yet terminated. Where is the law that makes it so? In what reign was it passed: And, thank GOD, the opinion of Judges does not yet *make* the law in this country.[64]

On the Northern Circuit, Brougham showed the emptiness of his claim about being King's Counsel reducing his case load. He had

---

62. *Ibid.*
63. *Ibid.*, July 14, 1827, no.13,331, p.3.
64. *Ibid.*, p.2.

as many cases as ever, and more favourable verdicts, while Cross, a new King's Serjeant, had assumed Scarlett's prized place in the court below the Judges, and Pollock and Williams, new King's Counsels, were in Brougham's old place across the table, relegating him to the seat to the right of the Clerk of the Court, Brougham was constantly occupied. At York, he was involved in defending an assault action, and prosecuting a counter suit over the same altercation. Brougham's client gained 200 pounds less one farthing, for his trouble. Brougham had previously won a hefty damage suit, Pollock giving up the case as soon as it was stated, only to see himself lose an even bigger one. In a trover action, Brougham obtained for his client over 600 pounds until it was discovered that the most important item, the vats, had never been removed, causing the dispute to be settled for nominal damages.[65] *Balme* v. *Hutton*, another trover action, obtained nearly 1,000 for his plaintiff. In an assault and battery, when the plaintiff refused Brougham's offer of 25 pounds, and took the case to trial, the jury only awarded him five pounds.[66]

Most of the other cases in Brougham's busy schedule led to a successful result. When the Assizes reached Durham, Brougham prosecuted a libel action for the house steward of Lord Darlington, Brougham's patron in which an associate had circulated wild rumours about the steward. During the presentation of evidence, it was established that the defendant had tried to use the information for a cash payment. The jury awarded Brougham's client 50 pounds in damages.[67] In *Feuster* v. *Bell*, a trespass action of dubious validity, Justice Bayley was upset when the jury awarded Brougham's plaintiff one shilling in damages. One serious case that Brougham lost on the Assize was *Eaton* v. *Trotter*, an assault and battery case which cost the defendant 60 pounds. Brougham's biggest victory was at Carlisle when he induced the jury to find for his client in a case of contested wills which the Chancery had ordered the Assizes to

65. *Assignees of Wm. Tute* v. *James and John Tute, ibid.*, August 9, 1827, no.13,353, p.3.
66. *Shaw* v. *Walshaw, ibid.*, August 13, 1827, no.13,356, p.3.
67. *Barnes* v. *Hodgson, ibid.*, August 16, 1827, no.13,359, p.3.

try, a decision which John Williams had warned would cost his client nearly 4,000 pounds.[68] At Lancaster, Brougham trounced Pollock in *Bewley* v. *Butterworth*, a mean recovery action by a penniless illiterate against an accommodating agent, and a titanic struggle with Scarlett, on special retainer, over whether a canal company was lost the Mersey's operation.

The only real loss that Brougham experienced during the summer was Canning. He died early in the morning of August 8. Brougham was particularly unprepared for the event because he was in the midst of educating Lord Lansdowne, the new Home Secretary, of the necessity of drastic law reform. Peel's unwillingness to serve with Canning made it inevitable for a whig to serve.

Brougham may well have been prodded to increase the effort because of an embarrassing incident in his own household. On June 27, his coachman, William Nelson, was arrested for assaulting officer Ballard when he tried to stop him from ignoring the redirection of traffic around the Admiralty caused by a soiree that the Duke of Clarence was having. When Brougham heard about the arrest he went down to the Marlborough Street Court to arrange for his release. Of course, the coachman and his associates maintained that he had done nothing wrong, making out that he had misunderstood the officer's directions, and contending that the lash from the whip which struck him had been intended for the horse. Finally, Nelson had been willing to apologize to the officer for what he had done, but Brougham would not hear of an out of court settlement. During the trial at the Westminster Sessions, it was established that Nelson had replied thus to Ballard's intervention: "Damn you, I'll teach you to stop my horses."[69] Barrister Law, who represented Nelson, tried to mitigate punishment by having the footman, and another coachman testify that the whipping was accidental. The jury convicted Nelson of assault, and the magistrate fined him 10 pounds.

---

68. *Skaife* v. *Skaife*, *ibid.*, August 27, 1827, no.13,368, p.4.
69. *R.* v. *Nelson*, *ibid.*, July 23, 1827, no.13,338, p.3.

It was on this personal note that Brougham set off for the Assizes, and he was particularly sensitive to the failure of the courts to render justice without special intervention. The failure of the prosecution of George Clarkson at York revolted him, as he duly reported for *Times'* readers. Clarkson was charged with murdering two bastard infants by poisoning. About one prosecution, Brougham apparently wrote: "There were several counts in the indictment, some of them stated the child's name to be James, and others called him George."[70] The Crown spent much of its time questioning witnesses about whether the deceased had been properly baptized, and what his name actually was, issues that Serjeant Jones duly exploited to the accused's advantage. As a result, the jury acquitted Clarkson, and the second case was dropped because there was even greater doubt about the victim's name, and baptism.

For Brougham, this was the last straw. He must have written a leader in *The Times,* because he had personally witnessed the trial. "A variety of incidents have occurred to make us acquainted with the present miserable state of our criminal law."[71] The Clarkson verdicts recalled the case of the man who decapitated a child, only to escape the gallows because there also had been doubt about the deceased's real name. Then there was a case of a coachman whose recklessness resulted in a terrible accident where one person was killed, and several injured; yet, the culprit was acquitted even of manslaughter. Of course, Brougham repeated the facts in the Clarkson cases in his most sarcastic fashion. The greatest absurdities passed for the due process of law, and it was almost a matter of random chance whether the greatest villains walked out of court scot-free, or the tenderest innocents went to the gallows. Brougham concluded:

> We expect nothing from professional lawyers in this case: they are in general sufficiently occupied in administering the laws as they find them written, without turning their attention to

---

70. *R.* v. *Geo. Clarkson, ibid.,* August 6, 1827, no.13,350, p.3.
71. *Ibid.,* August 7, 1827, no.13,351, p.2.

> the improvement of them; but it were greatly to be wished that some statesman, of a really capacious mind and strong intellect, would dedicate his time and talents to the improvement of the criminal code of the realm.[72]

While this plea had been intended for Lansdowne, Canning's death led to a change of Ministry. The new government was that of Lord Goderich's, the former Frederick Robinson whose career had so paralleled Canning's. The problem in its formation was that George IV put such a premium on J.C. Herries being made Chancellor of the Exchequer. Herries had been implicated in the scandal which brought Brogden crashing down, and when he was removed as Chairman of the House's Committees, Herries was given the position of Chairman of the Whole House.[73] Brougham was not opposed to Herries being made minister if he received suitable compensation. The very creation of Canning's Ministry had required him to look the other way when it came to some official appointments. Brougham intended to keep Herries on a short leash, as he indicated in this letter to the Duke of Devonshire:

> We cannot certainly have this *stockjobber* crammed down our throats, if he does not fully and frankly and immediately clear himself by disclosing how he got his wealth, whether by marriage, lottery ticket, highway robbery, cheating at cards, horse-racing at Doncaster, or any other legitimate mode of amassing wealth.[74]

The *quid pro quo* was a suitable stand-in for Brougham at the Home Office. When Lansdowne agreed to stay on in the Ministry, Brougham wrote a most appreciative, informative letter to his new Under-Secretary, Thomas Spring Rice, who was so concerned

---

72. *Ibid.*
73. For details about the changes Brogden's scandal effected, see *Journals of the House of Commons*, 1827, vol.82, pp.1-52.
74. Brougham's letter to the Duke of Devonshire, dated August 26, 1827: quoted from G.T. Garratt, *Lord Brougham* (Macmillan, London, 1935), p.203. Italics Brougham's.

about his welfare:

> I have some half-dozen reforms in our law and policy well matured, for I must avail myself in the House to do permanent good; viz. all the weight of being out of place (both weight with King and country) and the favour of the old Tory opposition, who I do not think will attack me rashly.[75]

Brougham began consulting first from Brougham Hall and later in London, with Bentham about systematic law reform, taking advantage of what he had written on the subject over the years. While the radical octogenarian was at first somewhat cool to the suggestion, he became ecstatic when he realized that Brougham was deadly serious about it:

> I could this moment catch you in my arms, toss you up into the air, and as you fell into them again, cover you with kisses. - It shall have - aye that it shall, the dear little fellow - some nice sweet pap of my own making - three sorts of it - 1. IV Evidence: 2. Judicial Establishment. 3. Codification Proposal: - all to be sucked in, in the order of the numbers: all sent to No. 8 - Old Square Lincoln's Inn this very blessed day, with an intimation that they should be *immediately forwarded...*[76]

Bentham anticipated great things from Brougham during the coming Session, lending forever his *The Note* on law reform, predicting that Brougham's promises about law reform would triumph over Elden's inclinations or else. If not, Bentham predicted that he would "gobble up Brougham, all at mouthful, screaming and sputtering notwithstanding."[77]

When Brougham was not consulting with Lansdowne and

---

75. Brougham's letter to Spring Rice, dated September 4, 1827: quoted from Arthur Aspinall, *Lord Brougham and the Whig Party* (Archon, Hamden, Conn., 1972 rep.), p.159.
76. *Ibid.*, f.5, Bentham's letter to Brougham, dated September 24, 1827: Brougham Papers: University College Library, London, no.26,002, f. 1. Italics Brougham's.
77. *Ibid.*

Bentham about legal reform, he was busier than ever in court. At Liverpool, the Corporation retained him again to prosecute its case against the Irwell and Mersey Canal Navigation Company for hurting river traffic by removing water from the river for its canal. In fact, people in Liverpool became so desirous of having him represent the city in the Commons that they often asked him, a request that he only turned down for fear of being charged with spurning Westmorland's advances. While Brougham lost the verdict, it did not slow his number of briefs. In a malpractice suit against a surgeon, *Meaches* v. *Taylor,* he established that he had bandaged injuries too tightly, resulting in 50 pounds compensation for Brougham's plaintiff. Brougham established that the curate of Crook, near Kendall, debauched a young woman after he had promised to marry her, a wrong for which the jury awarded her 70 pounds.[78]

Perhaps, Brougham's most interesting case was the defence of *Blacklow* v. *Farebrother and Others,* a prosecution of the late Sheriff of Middlesex and his officers for false arrest. Scarlett explained the case: "His client was a responsible attorney, whose object in bringing the action was not damages, but to punish the two officers for the misconduct."[79] Brougham responded thus about the case of mistaken identity: "... the jury would hear that he was over and over again accosted by the name of Pearson, and that he suffered himself to be so addressed, without taking any pains to undeceive the officers until he got a copy of the warrant ..."[80] Once Brougham's witnesses established just this statement, Scarlett said that the defence had just compounded its offence. The jury did not agree, however, and acquitted the Sheriff and only fined the officers 10 pounds each. Brougham was not capable of the impossible, however, as the South Devon Insurance Company learned when it hoped that he would save it from having to pay up on its policies for losses at sea.

Brougham did not do so well when the King's Bench was

---

78. *Sandford* v. *Richardson, ibid.*
79. *Ibid.,* October 20, 1827, no.13,415, p.3.
80. *Ibid.*

sitting *en banco*, but then he rarely did. This time he did even more poorly because some of his actions paid off political debts. In *Berry* v. *Sempronius*, he failed to get a new trial in a false arrest case by contending that averment of arrest was immaterial, and that the giving of bail bond amounted to the same thing, a claim which drew this response from Scarlett: "To pronounce that an arrest was made in this case would be to let in questions of constructive and implied restraint until they would become refined, even to metaphysical nicety."[81] In *The Duke of Devonshire* v. *Lodge*, Brougham teamed up with Scarlett and Tindal to persuade the court that the grouse was a bird of warren, but the case was non-suited. The defence in the trespass action relied upon *Manwood's Forest Law*, and *Barrington's* case which only listed the hare, coney, pheasant, and partridge as such creatures. "But both those authorities referred to 1 *Inst.* 233," Brougham argued, "where Lord Coke described those beasts and fowls by way of instance and example only ..."[82] Williams pointed out for the accused that *Manwood's* work came first, and was the authority. Brougham failed to arrest judgment in a case concerning the right to hold an ancient market when it was shown that there was precedent for not pleading the exception.[83] In sum, his only triumph *en banc* during 1829 was *Bloxam* v. *Elsee* where he was able to get a new trial in a patent suit because the patentee had withheld important particulars about his paper-making machine. Brougham and Scarlett successfully argued "... that where the Crown is deceived in a grant, that grant is void."[84]

At *nisi prius*, however, Brougham continued to obtain most favourable results. When Scarlett resorted to character assassination to gain conviction in a conspiracy to give goods on credit under false pretences, the defence had the charges dropped: "Mr Brougham hoped the Attorney-General would not

---

81. *The Law Journal*, 1827 (Paget, Chancery Lane, London), Court of King's Bench, pp.215-7.
82. *Ibid.*, p.319.
83. *Moseley* v. *Walker*, *ibid.*, pp.358-63.
84. *Ibid.*, p.110.

think of going on with such a case."[85] Brougham won a libel case in which a fellow employee wrote to his employer, stating that the plaintiff had had sexual intercourse with the butler, an injury which Denman greatly mitigated by showing that it had not prevented her from getting another good position. Jodrell, the President of the Athenaeum was prevented from stifling a recovery action by a carpenter for work done there by Brougham's discounting the claim that he was incapable of incurring debts for it. In *R.* v. *Crook and Others*, a conspiracy case, Brougham helped all the accused to be acquitted, except for one, and the jury even recommended leniency here. Brougham defended a damage suit by a farmer against the leader of a hunt for what it did to his crops in trying to take a stag, a liberty which cost Captain Grantley Berkeley a hundred pounds. When a Hindu failed to answer a jury summons in a capital felony, instituted by the Postmaster General, because of conscientious objections, Brougham obtained his release after a fortnight sentence in jail.[86] In the fashion of the *Atlas* case against *Alma Mater*, Brougham had quashed a libel case that a distinguished Latin scholar instituted against a periodical for dismissing his speech as silly when he called the dead Canning no sincere supporter of Catholics.[87] *Bishop* v. *Chambre*, a recovery action of ancient vintage against a Cambridge student while still a minor, failed when Brougham told the jury this: "He was sure that they would not approve of tradesmen lending money to students in the Universities, when all their necessary bills were paid to their tutors."[88] Brougham did end up the year on a sour note, though, seeing the rich award in a suit against Covent Garden overturned because the singer broke his contract, and the management did not waive the breach.[89]

Things were turning decidedly sour on the political front too. As Lord Althorp warmed to the idea of the coalition between the

---

85. *R.* v. *Trevett, Dunne, and Others, The Times*, October 29, 1827, no.13,422, p.3.
86. *Ibid.*, November 27, 1827, no.13,447, p.5.
87. *French* v. *Young, ibid.*, November 28, 1827, no.13,448, p.3.
88. *Bishop* v. *Chambre, ibid.*, December 10, 1827, no.13,458, p.2.
89. *Sinclair* v. *Kemble, ibid.*, December 11, 1827, no.13,459, pp.2-3.

Whigs and Canningites, a development which promised a showdown with Herries, the Tories took fright, possibly through what Peel was learning from Bentham about Brougham's plans for law reform. Althorp, as chairman of the Finance Committee, promised to institutionalize the process against the Chancellor of the Exchequer which had brought Brogden down. Althorp had played a big role in the Arigna inquiry. Under the circumstances, Herries resigned, and Huskisson followed suit. Brougham provided the diversion from the resignations, however, by becoming enthusiastic about what Admiral Codrington had achieved against the Turks in the Battle of Navarino. "I am for seeing the Turk out of Europe," he wrote to Wilson, "even if Russia is to have Turkey (the Greeks the Morea of course). It brings them only more within the power to England and France."[90] By January, the King, who had already prevented Holland from becoming Foreign Secretary to effect a liberal foreign policy had had enough, turning Goderich out, and calling upon Wellington to form a more reliable government.

Brougham, as usual, in such circumstances, did not understand what was happening. Apparently, he had this Christmas message for the scheming Tory leaders in *The Times*:

> A meeting of Lord Eldon, Westmorland, Melville, Mr Peel, and even Sir J. Beckett, is said to have been held at Lord Eldon's house on Thursday. The resolutions proposed to be taken there are of course concealed. We may add, that this worthy conclave may save themselves the trouble of putting themselves in readiness: nobody is likely to send for them.[91]

Brougham, instead of turning his sarcastic invective against Herries's financial improprieties, turned it on Lord Lonsdale, at his birthday celebration. While at Brougham Hall for the holidays, Brougham mocked the following statement by Chairman E.W. Hasell in support of Lonsdale against Tories such

---

90. Brougham's letter to Wilson: quoted from Aspinall, *op. cit.*, p.161.
91. *The Times*, December 21, 1827, no.13,468, p.3.

as Canning:

> Men are placed at the head of affairs in whom he had no confidence; he therefore hoped the day was not far distant when the late trustworthy Ministers of the country would be called back to office, power, and emolument.[92]

When Brougham realized that the Tories had been proven right about forming a government, he acted as if he had known it all along. "To Brougham and to the Whigs generally, the inglorious collapse of Goderich and the Coalition came neither as a shock nor as a disappointment,"[93] Professor Aspinall wrote. Actually, Brougham's rage knew almost no bounds, but he was not about to act as if Peel had proven him wrong about Tory prospects. When the Session opened, Brougham acted as though it were business as usual, giving notice of a motion on the state of the law, and its administration. About the Speech from the Throne, he said: "He looked not to the members of the Administration, but to their measures; and if these were good, the Administration should have - not a reluctant or tardy support - but as hearty, as sincere, and as active a support as if he were sitting at the other side of the house.[94] This was obviously a sad consolation for a law reformer who had seen Bentham wax so enthusiastically about the Session's prospects just four months earlier.

Once Brougham was prepared for the business at hand, his great speech on law reform, he turned on the liberal Tories, especially Huskisson, saving his bitterest comments, it seems, for the columns of *The Times*. Huskisson's joining the Duke's Government was just his latest treachery. As "Algernon", he attacked Huskisson for resigning after Herries, and Goderich for leaving the fate of the Ministry up to the King. Wellington was charged with treachery for not passing along the King's request that certain Whigs remain, particularly Lansdowne. He, of course,

---

92. "Meeting at the New Crown Inn, Penrith," *ibid.*, January 5, 1828, no.13,481, p.3.
93. Aspinall, *op. cit.*, pp.164-5.
94. *The Times*, January 30, 1828, no.13,502, p.3.

would have turned down the request, but it was not communicated, the writer charged, in order to forge a reunion between the Canningites and Tories. A few days later, Barnes printed another letter, sounding much like Brougham, which charged Huskisson with deserting to Canning's enemies, and conspiring to bring Wellington to power. For such efforts, however, Huskisson was not given much better a fate than Brougham had predicted for Peel: "How long you may enjoy the place you have so dearly purchased, I known not, - possibly not long."[95]

To compensate for the consequences of Huskisson's treachery, Brougham treated the Commons to an all-night session, devoted to his complaints about the law. In seeking from a hostile Ministry yet another inquiry after the Crown had only just agreed to investigate the abuses in equity, Brougham was asking almost the impossible from Members, but he still succeeded. The House was as eager to hear what he had to say as he was to tell it.

As for Taylor's attempt to establish equality between the courts of common law and equity, Brougham remarked: "There was, however, no other way to produce an equality of business, but by really throwing open the courts, removing the monopolies, and leaving it to men's own discretion to select as they pleased."[96] The strength of the Bench should be increased by allowing barristers with standing to take bail cases. "Those who advise an increase of the Judges beyond their present numbers," Brougham told the House, "were not innovators."[97] Judges should neither be selected for their political principles nor simply advanced up the ranks. The Welsh circuits should be consolidated into two jurisdictions, the Privy Council reorganized, and the magistrates reformed. Procedure should be made cheaper and more expeditious, allowing, if possible, one court to settle all questions in a dispute. "Fourthly," Brougham said, "he would not place the *onus* of proof on the party who had

---

95. "To the Right Hon. William Huskisson," *ibid.*, February 18, 1828, no.13,518, p.2.
96. *Ibid.*, February 8, 1828, no.13,510, p.1.
97. *Ibid.*

a fair presumption of right ..."[98] Just as obsolete proceedings should be ended, he favoured increasing use of declaratory suits to speed judicial process.

To be more specific, Brougham recommended this change in equity: "He would propose, as another improvement, to take away from the Court of Chancery its jurisdiction in trusts, mortgages, etc, by extending the statute of uses."[99] The Chancery would have to be reduced to its original jurisdiction of account, idiots, infants, and long trusts. To increase the capacity of the King's Bench to conduct equity cases, Masters and arbitrators, with the proper training and experience, should be appointed. Brougham, to disabuse people of the idea that he was interested in these reforms for his own benefit, explained: "There were very few persons who made more money by the law than he did. Few persons shared more largely in the benefits which resulted from its abuses."[100] The average amount involved in a dispute was about 30 pounds; yet, the costs of an action were around 100 pounds. On the Assizes, as at Lancaster, the costs were less, but they still were more than the amounts concerned.

To expedite trials, Brougham called for new rules to bring on the issue, particularly in cases of insolvency. Sir Nicholas Tindal, the new Solicitor General, was complimented for what he had taught Brougham about courtroom practice. To convince Members that he was serious when he said that he benefitted by the abuses, he questioned a plea he had used in defeating some recovery suits: "Why should a man be allowed to plead infancy under the general issue?"[101] The inconsistency was that a defendant would plead that he had not made a promise to pay, but then he would admit it, excusing himself for being a minor. "Perjury," Brougham added, "was encouraged by the vagueness and indistinctness of modern pleading ..."[102] Actions should not fail because they did not meet the requirements of mere judicial

98. *Ibid.*
99. *Ibid.*
100. *Ibid.*
101. *Ibid.*
102. *Ibid.*

administration, as with failure to comply with the stamp acts. Brougham wanted a greater reliance upon juries, permitting their use in equity cases. His Herculean speech was concluded by moving for a commission to investigate the common law courts.

Tindal responded by moving that its consideration be postponed for a fortnight so that the House could have time to digest its content. Peel was less in doubt as to how to deal with Brougham's proposals. This was a far cry from the reforms that he had suggested in the past, starting with the alteration of the law of real property. As Brougham had written to radical Francis Place, who had been so effective in persuading the 1824 inquiry to get rid of the laws against combinations, he was proposing a "... commission to inquire into the state of the law preparatory to a reform with a view to the formation of a code ..."[103] Peel was not about to do this, so he was eager to note his differences and reservations. He said that there was no need for more Judges on the common law courts, and disputed what Brougham said about the Puisne Judges being promoted. Abbott and Thomson were cited as examples of good Judges who came up through the ranks. The Home Secretary did agree with Brougham's suggestion that Judges should serve on a fixed term, subject to mandatory retirement. Peel took exception to the idea that there was anything wrong with the magistrates. The Judicial Committee of the Privy Council was not as bad as Brougham indicated, although Peel did call for legislation to regularize its operation. He called upon Brougham to recast his motion into draft resolutions because it, "... if submitted in its present shape, would only obstruct his object."[104] To make his reservations crystal clear to Brougham, Peel concluded: "He would meanwhile turn the measures projected in his mind, and consult with those whose habits and station rendered their opinion more valuable: he alluded to the Lord Chief Justice, and His Majesty's Attorney-General."[105]

---

103. Place's letter dated January 18, 1828: quoted from Aspinall, *op. cit.*, p.166.
104. *The Times*, February 8, 1828, no.13,510, p.3.
105. *Ibid.*

By this time the House actually voted for Brougham's commission on the common law courts, the government had indicated that it wanted to continue a more prudent course in law enforcement and court reform than he envisioned. Rather than a vast restructuring of the legal system, and its functioning, Peel called for a select committee in the Commons on the police, a course which called on the Crown to take more effective steps in combating crime. Brougham admitted as much the next day when he renewed his call for court reform, a plea which again involved him in a dispute with Edward Sugden about its need, especially regarding the Chancery. While Peel was willing to have an inquiry, he was not willing to let Brougham set its approach by naming the members of the commission, as he suggested to the House: "He knew some individuals peculiarly qualified for such an investigation, who were utterly free from all party bias, and felt personally anxious to enter upon this good work."[106] In fact, Peel appointed two commissions, a second one on the reform of the law of real property to show Brougham the need of caution in such matters, recalling his plea for the reform of conveyancing. The Home Secretary named only the most practical men to the commissions. Peel even tried to get Henry Hobhouse, Sidmouth's Under-Secretary at the Home Office, and Sir John Richardson, the master of the art of pleading which Brougham so condemned, to serve on the Common Law Court Commission.

Brougham was disappointed, but not daunted by not being named to the commissions. His practice in these same courts increased as the parliamentary session progressed. While he failed to get a new trial in *Hall* v. *Longman*, charging the Lord Chief Baron of the Exchequer with misdirection of the jury in the libel case,[107] Brougham won the verdict in a recovery action against a lady of high society who was becoming the object of increasing litigation because she could not keep track of what she

---

106. *Ibid.*, March 1, 1828, no.13,529, p.3.
107. *Ibid.*, January 28, 1828, no.13,500, p.3.

had contracted for.[108] At the Exchequer, Brougham also defended successfully *R.* v. *Rawson and Others*, establishing that a Rochdale bank had the right to appropriate a large sum of money to discharge a debt rather than place it at the credit of the Crown. In another case in the King's Bench, one of negligent driving by a wagon driver which Brougham was defending, the jury could not decide whether the accident had been preventable or unavoidable. When the foreman announced the deadlock to the Lord Chief Justice, requesting a copy of *Selwyn's Nisi Prius Law*, Tenterden refused the request, much to his dismay. In desperation, he asked how the division was to be resolved, and Brougham set about explaining how it could be done, only to draw this rejoinder from the Judge: "Mr Brougham, we must hear nothing about it."[109] In the end, the jury awarded Scarlett's plaintiff one farthing. In a libel action against the editor of *The Lancet*, Brougham limited the damages to five pounds for his charges that the editor of the *London Medical and Physical Journal* suppressed and fabricated cases in its reporting.[110] Scarlett's charges that the publication was motivated by malice, and that Brougham's defence was malicious did not impress the jury. They teamed up to prosecute a perjury case against the agent of a Member of Parliament, but failed to convict, as *The Times* duly reported:

> Mr Brougham submitted, that as defendant and Mr Spence went to Dover's house on the same day, and for the same purpose, the defendant had sworn falsely, when he stated that he did not go with Mr Spence. Suppose the passage had been so narrow that two persons could not get in abreast, but that one immediately followed the other; would not that be entering the house together?[111]

This did not prevent them, however, from convicting three

108. *Hall* v. *Lady Gresley*, *ibid.*, February 5, 1828, no.13,507, p.3.
109. *Burrows* v. *Unwin*, *ibid.*, February 19, 1828, no.13,519, p.4.
110. *M'Leod* v. *Wakley*, *ibid.*
111. *R.* v. *Blandy*, *ibid.*, February 25, 1828, no.13,524, p.3.

defendants the next day of a conspiracy to defraud the creditors of one of them.[112]

Brougham's busy court schedule did not prevent him from playing a crucial role in partisan politics, the repeal of the Test and Corporation Acts. Unlike what he had done a decade before - speak about everything, and anything - he saved his contributions for the appropriate moment. When Lord John Russell moved for a committee to consider the repressive legislation, a necessary preliminary to its repeal, Brougham wound up the debate thus:

> If the law shall be denied, and there be any still found to repeat the assertion, that there is no grievance, I answer him by pointing to 1,700 petitions, attesting the contrary, and I ardently confide in the justice and liberality of the house when it disposes of those petitions (Cheers).[113]

The committee was appointed by the narrowest of margins, and Parliament repealed this long-outstanding grievance of Dissenters, thanks in part because of Brougham's continuing assistance. No sooner had Russell's committee been appointed than a person wrote to *The Times*, calling upon Brougham to see that the University of London appointed a clergyman as professor of divinity to still complaints about the lack of religious instruction. His lectures could be optional, and Dissenters could get religious instruction at home. Rev. Mr Burder raised the very same matter at a meeting of the university's proprietors, an Establishment solution to the problem which drew Brougham's response: "The great difficulty in the case was, that no two sects could be found to agree in their definition of what Christianity was."[114] Religion was, consequently, better left as a private matter since it was an area where no compromise was possible. Brougham's opinion was persuasive enough that competitor

---

112. *R.* v. *Thomas Rees and Others*, *ibid.*, February 26, 1828, no.13,525, p.4.
113. *Ibid.*, February 27, 1828, no.13,526, p.3.
114. "The University of London," *ibid.*, February 28, 1828, no.13,527, p.1.

King's College, London followed suit, much to the pain of High Anglicans.

During March 1828, Brougham went from triumph to triumph before Tenterden who was sitting at *nisi prius*. In an assault case against a ship's captain, Brougham helped win a verdict of 50 pounds for his client.[115] Scarlett's perjury case, *R.* v. *Joseph Hudson*, was thrown out of court when Brougham showed that the indictment upon which it was based had been misdescribed.[116] In *R.* v. *Samuel Sutton and Others*, a most complicated conspiracy case against employees of the East India Company, Brougham managed to save Captain Prescott from conviction by having witnesses stress his good character, and by persuading the jury that he alone had not had guilty knowledge of the conspiracy. Scarlett and Brougham teamed up to obtain average compensation for a ship damaged by the defendant's negligence.[117] Perhaps, these victories had been helped by the fact that Brougham had won an important case before the King's Bench *en banco* the previous month. *Golding* v. *Fener* concerned the custom relating to the number of members of select vestries. Scarlett wanted the King's Bench to overturn the verdict on the basis that allowing for an indefinite number was inherently unreasonable. Brougham, who had been made Master of the Walks by the Benchers of Lincoln's Inn,[118] moved successfully to quash the rule for a new trial by arguing by analogy with the custom of other immemorial bodies, the Inns of Court: "... the benchers of these societies are a legal body there can be no doubt, and they bear a strong analogy to a select vestry."[119]

On the Spring Assizes, Brougham finally laid to rest any doubt about his being the kingdom's foremost trial lawyer. At Lancaster, he won a nice verdict for his client in *Houghton* v.

---

115. *Grimall* v. *Heaviside, ibid.*, March 3, 1828, no.13,530, p.3.
116. *Ibid.*, March 4, 1828, no.13,531, p.4.
117. *Dale and Others* v. *Nelson and Others, ibid.*, March 8, 1828, no.13,535, p.3.
118. *The Records of the Honourable Society of Lincoln's Inn: The Black Books* (Lincoln's Inn, London, 1902, 5 vols.), vol.IV, p.174.
119. *Golding* v. *Fener, The Law Journal*, 1828 (Paget, Chancery Lane), Court of King's Bench, pp.180-1.

Scott. While the barrister, Williams contended that the plaintiff's daughter was an artful woman who slept around, and called for trifling damages, Brougham won the father 20 pounds. Brougham had earlier triumphed in two recovery cases, one for money paid by a family for services to be rendered while emigrating to America, and the other for insurance money when a ship burned, a claim where the jury differed from Baron Hullock on its validity and extent. In the main case, one of attempted murder during a dispute over game, Brougham behaved as no prosecutor had before. While he allowed the indictment of four men on the same charge to be dropped, provided that they pleaded guilty to the misdemeanour of being out at night, with intent to kill game, he went all out to gain a conviction of James Ashton for the shooting of Lord Sefton's gamekeeper at Farbok. When the Ashton party had been stopped by Peter Lucas for the possession of illegal game, the defendant hit one of the game-keeper's party over the head, setting off a struggle in which Lucas was nearly killed. About his not testifying for the prosecution, Brougham explained: "He has never been well since; and, though now in Lancaster, was not well enough to appear as a witness to-day. There was no gun carried by witness's party: they carried sticks."[120] Justice Bayley summed up the case by stating that if the jury was satisfied that the party on the Coppey Wood estate was trying to resist arrest when the shot was fired, it should convict. The jury, after five minutes' deliberation, did so, and Bayley held out no possibility of the culprit escaping the gallows.

The next day, Brougham was back in court not only to utterly defeat Serjeant Cross's prosecution of *Ackers* v. *Heaton*, a debauching case, but also to preempt the Crown's role in the exercise of mercy in the Ashton case. Brougham asked the court to consider a petition on Sefton's behalf, recommending mercy. "The grounds on which he presumed to make the recommendation were, that it was clear that the wound had not been inflicted by the hand of the prisoner, and also, that it was obvious that the gun of the prisoner had not been fired in the

---

120. *R.* v. *James Ashton, The Times*, March 18, 1828, no.13,543, p.4.

affray."[121] While Bayley was uncertain of the plea's effect, Ashton escaped the gallows.

At the York Crown Court, Brougham achieved more notable victories before the same Judge. In a recovery action against the South Devon Insurance Company, Brougham contended that it should have to pay for the rest of the loss when the brig *Gratitude* sank, half of which had been paid for by another insurance company.[122] The company argued that the loss was partly caused by the rotting of hides on board, a natural occurrence rather than a matter of unseaworthiness. Once Justice Bayley sided with Brougham, the jury agreed, awarding his client nearly 1,000 pounds.

Earlier Brougham had induced Bayley to non-suit a case about the custom of a Knaresborough under-steward in preparing the surrender of copyhold estates, and to see that an owner of a cottage was properly compensated for water damage. In *Jefferson* v. *Hardy*, a recovery action by an agent for a parliamentary candidate at Pontefract during the 1827 General Election, Brougham destroyed the claim by this cross-examination of an agent of the successful candidate who said he had carried on work of great anxiety and incessant fatigue:

> Mr Brougham - Well, now, did he do anything else then, but drink to Mr Hardy's honour and glory? - Yes, a good deal.
>
> Did he praise him by eating? - I can't say.
>
> Did he magnify him by dancing? Did he dance before him? (Loud laughter). - I think he did.
>
> What was he paid for head-money? - I don't understand.
>
> Oh, you don't understand. What was paid for votes? Do you understand that? - Yes, I understand that.
>
> Well, how many voters in Pontefract might there be, who

---

121. *Ibid.*, March 20, 1828, no.13,545, p.3.
122. *Park and Others* v. *Mudge*, *ibid.*, March 29, 1828, no.13,553, p.3.

> were not paid for their votes? Where there 10 righteous men to save the city? - There might be 10. (Loud laughter).[123]

Not only did the jury not give the plaintiff any more money, stating that he had already been given too much, but also *The Times* printed an unprecedented second report of the case, probably Brougham's own.[124] The power of Brougham in court was best illustrated when a tyrannical officer called upon him, of all people, to see to the mitigation of damages after he had almost seen to the forcible drowning of one of his soldiers during a punishment exercise.

The scene was now set for the two most important cases of the circuit, a libel action, and a cause concerning the custom of grinding corn in the Soke Mill of Wakefield. The *Leeds Mercury* announced that Scarlett had been given special retainers to defend the libel action, and to prosecute the Soke cause.[125] Brougham was retained on the other side of both actions. About his chances, the *Billing's Liverpool Advertiser* wrote:

> He has had a considerably larger share of business than any counsel, and has in a great majority of instances been retained for the plaintiff. His success in obtaining verdicts was also distinguished, and many of his speeches were masterly specimens of organization, replete with varied information, enlarged views, wit, and satire, and well calculated to advance the interests of his clients.[126]

This was all the more remarkable, the article added, because there had been little in the cases to excite his powers. Under the circumstances, Scarlett prudently decided to leave the more explosive case, defence of Mrs Beaumont's libels, to John Williams. No counsel on the Circuit wanted to take the heat of too many of Brougham's actions.

---

123. *Ibid.*
124. *Ibid.*, April 7, 1828, no.13,560, p.3.
125. "Sir James Scarlett," reprinted in *ibid.*
126. "Mr Brougham," reprinted in *ibid.*

Whatever the calculations of Brougham's opponents, they made no difference in the courtroom. Mrs Beaumont had to pay 1,700 pounds for the libels on her former steward Horsington, and the jury declared that the Soke Mills at Wakefield had no monopoly of the grinding of corn. Brougham, through the examination of witnesses, and the introduction of telling written testimony, showed that Mrs. Beaumont's charges that Horsington had compounded his fraud and speculation against her by bastarding a child by a daughter of one of her tenants were totally malicious.[127] Scarlett explained that the Soke case concerned "... whether there existed a custom within the manor of Wakefield, which bound all persons resident within the manor to have their corn ground in the soke-mill."[128] While he had no doubt about it, Brougham did, and expressed it in a most embarrassing way:

> He said that he felt glad to see his learned friend (Sir James Scarlett) once more amongst them, for never did a case require more the aid and support of his great talents and learning as an advocate and a lawyer than the present ...[129]

While Brougham could conceive a custom where inhabitants were bound to have the corn they grew for their own consumption ground in the manor, the idea that they acquiesced in a total monopoly was dismissed with contempt: "He had heard of a birthright being sold for a mess of pottage, but the plaintiffs would have them here believe that the defendants had given up their birthright, and did not even stipulate for a single spoonful of pottage."[130] The jury, after long deliberation, also dismissed the idea.

Back in London, Brougham kept up such a busy political and legal life that his literary efforts in the *Review*, as they had been ever since the departure of Liverpool from the political scene,

---

127. *Horsington* v. *Beaumont and Wife, ibid.*, April 7, 1828, no.13,560, p.3.
128. *Dodsworth and Others* v. *Ingham, ibid.*, April 11, 1828, no.13,564, p.3.
129. *Ibid.*
130. *Ibid.*

were mostly accounts of what he was intimately involved in.[131] To keep pressure on Lansdowne to prevent the Tories in the Lords from gutting the Test and Corporations Acts repeal, Brougham had Barnes publish a letter to him in *The Times*, complaining about the reason why Quakers' affirmations did not make them eligible to serve on juries.[132] When the Commons was debating Taylor's motion for improving the equity courts, Brougham corrected Peel when he said that Shadwell's testimony before the Chancery Commission had indicated that it would take three angels to get through its business: "Three angels, he said, could not get through it. (A laugh)."[133] When the Lords' amendments to the repeal of the Test and Corporations Act returned to the Commons, Brougham complained about the changes, but to no avail. For his efforts, he was toasted as an enemy of all religious tests when the repealers celebrated their victory at Freemasons Tavern in June.

At the annual meeting of the Anti-Slavery Society, he called upon its members to exert themselves most vigorously to stamp it out, so that Wilberforce could live to see its end.[134] Brougham also wound up the debate on Burdett's motion, calling for repeal of the last penalties of the Penal Laws. While Tories had made much of the persons who opposed Catholic Emancipation, Brougham retorted: "The question rested, however, not upon authority, but upon reason and evidence."[135] The motion carried by a narrow six votes, creating a most serious challenge to the Duke's Government.

Just as Brougham had come to recognize that there was more to Peel, for good or ill, than he had previously imagined, he had grudgingly come to recognize the same about Wellington, especially after he had sent the Canningites packing over

131. See, eg, Art.VI, "State of Parties," *Edinburgh Review*, vol.46, no.XCII, October 1827, pp.415-32, and Art.V, "Wakefield case," *ibid.*, vol.47, no.XCIII, January 1828, pp.100-18.
132. "To Mr Brougham," *The Times*, April 14, 1828, no.13,566, p.3.
133. *Ibid.*, April 25, 1828, no.13,576, p.2.
134. "Anti-Slavery Society," *ibid.*, May 5, 1828, no.13,584, p.3.
135. *Ibid.*, May 13, 1828, no.13,591, p.3.

parliamentary reform. With Barnes's help, Brougham came to a more accurate view of why Goderich's coalition had been replaced by the Duke's Government. While Huskisson's resignation, and Godrich's weakness had played into the hands of the Tories, Wellington had made sure that liberal Whigs such as Lansdowne did not serve in his government. Moreover, the Duke pounced upon a misunderstanding about constituency disenfranchisement to force the withdrawal of Huskisson and his followers. Huskisson, far from being the kingmaker that Brougham himself had become, was a pawn in the hands of the Duke. Wellington was a political leader capable of political re-education, however. Once Brougham learned of Wellington's capacity, Barnes explained away Brougham's departure for Brougham Hall, "... the cause has been the *positive order* of his medical advisers to suspend the course of his labours for a week or 10 days."[136] The reason why Brougham had not left sooner was because he had helped argue Mr Long Wellesley's appeal to the Lords to overturn the Chancellor's order to prevent Miss Long from returning the reprobate's children.[137] In a losing cause, Brougham provided his critics with an embarrassing plea, made deliberately to provide an excuse for his disappearance: "The gist of the learned counsel's object appeared to show that the jurisdiction in this instance claimed by the Chancery was never in existence; that it was tyrannical in its operation, and iniquitous in its principle ..."[138]

Brougham went to Westmorland, it seems, to use the information that he had gained as one of the House's conferences on Catholic Emancipation with the Lords to outline a government programme for its passage. The theory was to persuade Tories that concession was essential under the circumstances, provided, of course, that it was not made to appear that the government was capitulating to O'Connell's illegal Catholic Association. *The Times* vastly increased its coverage of Irish conditions, with

136. *Ibid.*, July 12, 1828, no.13,643, p.3. Italics its.
137. *Wellesley* v. *Wellesley* (1828), 4 ER 1078.
138. "The Wellesley Cause," *The Times*, May 22, 1828, no.13,599, p.2.

Brougham apparently providing a regular synopsis from the Irish press. It was only by leaving London that he could find the time the subject required. By the time Brougham showed up for the Yorkshire Assizes, the fruit of his work started to appear in *The Times* in articles about precedents for the contested election at Clare, and its effect upon Ireland.[139] Once the circuit was over, Brougham returned to Brougham Hall to continue the project, missing thereby the opening of the University of London.

As far as the Prime Minister was concerned, the culmination of this process was the bitter open letter to him, seemingly by Brougham, that Barnes published in October. It attacked the feigned omniscience and omnipotence of his government. About the political manoeuvres which led to Wellington's Ministry, the writer queried: "If any one should feel dubious as to the integrity of your cabinet, are you not assured by the presence of Herries?"[140] As for the Duke's remedial political education, Brougham wrote sarcastically that he would leave it to traitors Hunt and Cobbett who were again on the scene. "Is Ireland to be calmed", Brougham asked, recalling the Duke's reaction to the Battle of Navarino, "is Russia to be arrested by your single arm?"[141] Peel was dismissed as an administrator capable of legislative compilations rather than a maker of policy. Peel's real constituency was the universities, such as Trinity College, Dublin which had finally awakened from its slumber to speak out on the Irish question in an insane way. "Lay aside your horn - look for one hour," Brougham entreated the Duke, "and read the Irish newspapers."[142] Wellington was urged to beat a retreat not only in Ireland but also in Downing Street.

At the Summer Assizes, Brougham won more than his share of cases. At York, he induced the presiding Judge to non-suit a trover action against his client because the statute of frauds prohibited the recovery of a stack of hay after the title to the

---

139. See, eg, "Clare Election," *ibid.*, July 22, 1828, no.13,651, p.3.
140. "To His Grace The Duke of Wellington," *ibid.*, October 21, 1828, no.13,729, p.3.
141. *Ibid.*
142. *Ibid.*

property had passed hands.[143] After recording another verdict in his favour in a petty trespass action, he obtained for a surgeon ample compensation for assault and false imprisonment by a constable and a neighbour. Brougham won the case by establishing that the neighbour arranged the seizure by entreating the constable thus: "Take him to the lobby; he is a d--d rogue like his father."[144] The only big case was *Murgatroyd* v. *Murgatroyd* a seduction cause where Brougham gained his client 300 pounds for the injury when Alexander tried through discredited witnesses to implicate her in other crimes. In *Hardistry* v. *Nunn,* Brougham prevailed upon the jury to dismiss a slander action against his client for words said against an attorney in the heat of passion.

While Brougham did lose a simple recovery action for the loss of a horse, due to his client's negligence, he more than recovered it by the way he handled a case over a contested will. After the plaintiff had tried to upset the defendant's claim, Brougham left it at that: "For his own part, he felt the evidence to be so irresistible, that without calling one of the witnesses with whom he was provided, he should rely upon the verdict of the jury."[145] Brougham won a similar big case at Carlisle. The damage, trespass and wills cases on the rest of the circuit were of mixed results, and the only one which fired Brougham's imagination was *Duckworth* v. *Johnson,* a refusal to marry case. About Miss Duckworth's motive to sue, Brougham opined: "What it was that had at length made her a plaintiff instead of a wife, and induced her to seek a lawyer rather than a lover, they were left to conjecture as they could ..."[146] Brougham and Scarlett also fought a case at Carlisle to a standstill, one about whether certain stations for loading coal in the Tyne blocked navigation.

Back in London after the holidays, Brougham seemed more concerned about persuading the Duke's Government to pursue a liberal course, particularly about Ireland, than in swaying juries

143. *Eshelby* v. *Baines, ibid.,* July 24, 1828, no.13,653, p.3.
144. *May* v. *Booker and Moody, ibid.,* July 28, 1828, no.13,656, p.3.
145. *Doe, Dem. Hirst* v. *Hirst and Others, ibid.,* August 4, 1828, no.13,662, p.3.
146. *Ibid.,* August 30, 1828, no.13,685, p.4.

for clients. While he did help win *The East India Company* v. *Lewis*, a vindictive prosecution to recover an enormous sum on the basis of an administrative oversight,[147] he did appear to be hoping to achieve the impossible in other cases, oblivious of telling facts. In the case concerning the Duke of Saxe-Gotha's disputed will, Brougham made light of the mass of evidence about his obvious insanity,[148] and once the case was non-suited, he went to excessive lengths to try to revive it. He also went to great trouble in *Smith and Another* v. *Jones*, a prosecution of a jailer for negligence in keeping a prisoner. It almost seemed as if jurors were stand-ins for Wellington and Peel, ignorant officials who had to be persuaded that there was another realm of experience that they had to answer to. Brougham saw a perjury case non-suited because of an oversight in the indictment.[149] In the final settlement of *Rowey* v. *Brenton*, the Attorney General so overplayed Brougham's light treatment of the accession rolls in determining the rights of the Crown in mine leases, which drew a rebuke from Tenterden,[150] that the extent of the loss was somewhat lost on the court. There was little doubt about the pipe-dream character of the prosecution of the banker Sir Peter Pole for a fabulous sum on the basis of the flimsiest evidence, the omission of entries in the publisher Longman's passbooks. Even the successful defence of John Wilks, the vestry-clerk of the parish of St Luke's, Old Street, was more the work of Scarlett than Brougham.[151] He largely showed that the plaintiffs were trying to blame him for their mistakes in paying bills, and to mix him up in the frauds of others.

Brougham's appetite for the courtroom was renewed by Lord Strangford's libels of Canning. When an article said that this

---

147. *Ibid.*, October 22, 1828, no.13,730, p.4.

148. *Baron von Lindenau* v. *Desborough*, *ibid.*, pp.3-4. Also see the unsuccessful effort to get a new trial before the King's Bench *in banco*, *The Law Journal*, 1829 (Paget, Chancery Lane), Court of King's Bench, pp.42-8. For other cases in which Brougham showed similar blind persistence, see *Churchill and Another, Assignees, etc.* v. *Day*, pp.78-9, and *Crossley* v. *Beverly*, pp.127-30.

149. *R.* v. *Small*, *The Times*, November 4, 1828, no.13,741, p.3.

150. *Ibid.*, November 20, 1828, no.13,755, p.3.

151. *Whitmore and Another* v. *John Wilks*, *ibid.*, October 25, 1828, no.13,733, p.3.

reviler was not to be believed, and Strangford went to court to get a criminal information against the author, Brougham charged into the King's Bench to frustrate the effort. He set out to prove that Strangford was indeed a reviler, but the Attorney General tried to justify some of his deceptions in his diplomatic correspondence, an effort which caused Justice Bayley to say that he preferred the truth. The Attorney General, as he had in *Rowe* v. *Brenton,* went overboard, trying to prove that the article in *The Times* which the *Sun* article was based on was also libellous. While the King's Bench denied that Brougham had justified the article, it held that Strangford had not brought his charge within the rule which justified a criminal information and the case was dropped. Brougham's renewed interest in court cases was shown in a damage suit, brought by the publisher Murray, against a pirated edition of Byron's work. To mitigate damages, Brougham said that his client had lost 75 pounds in publishing the work, and was willing to give up his ability to publish if only nominal damages were awarded. "The offensive matter in the original poems having been omitted in these 'Beauties'", Brougham explained, "the work did not sell well."[152] Murray got one shilling in damages.

Brougham's mind was more concerned with what responsible officials were recommending to the government, and what it was prepared to effect. To help prime the Common Law Commission to recommend extensive changes, he apparently reviewed for *The Times* an anonymous pamphlet on the reforms he wanted. While Brougham did not know what the Commission was proposing, little could be expected, he said, of one composed of lawyers. "Not one moment of the precious hours devoted to public justice ought to be wasted in inquiring whether the parties to the suit have given themselves a true description,"[153] he added, repeating his disgust at the murder trials which had so failed at York. "Prolixity and repetition in pleading ought to be

---

152. *Murray* v. *Limbird, ibid.,* December 10, 1828, no.13,772, p.3.
153. "Legal Reforms," *ibid.,* October 8, 1828,n o.13,718, p.3.

stigmatized as the worst species of legal jobbing."[154] The way a Judge summed up a case could just compound the injustice. On the matter of court reform, Brougham wanted the superior courts of Common Law to be returned to the *nisi prius* practice of ancient times. Concerning preventive police, Brougham and Barnes encouraged Peel to do more than just appoint inquiries. Before the Session opened, *The Times* debunked the idea that a preventive police would be a repressive instrument in England: "A State police would, in truth, be without an object here, where conspiracy against the State itself would be the wildest of all chimeras."[155]

The Speech from the Throne was all that Brougham desired from the Duke. Instead of standing pat, Wellington showed that he had indeed been reading papers about Irish conditions. "The state of Ireland has been the object of His Majesty's continued solicitude,"[156] the Lords' Commissioners told Parliament. While the government wanted to see to the suppression of the Catholic Association, it was willing to consider the ending of Catholic disabilities, provided that it did not jeopardize the existence of the Church of Ireland. The Speech, of course, caused Peel all kinds of difficulties. He had wanted to resign, but the Duke said that it would just compound his difficulties. Peel concluded his speech by saying that he would "... do all he could to fulfil the solemn injunctions of His Majesty, to consider this question involving so deeply the best interests of the country, the tranquillity and concord of the United Kingdom. He considered it his duty to leave nothing untried to contribute to a deliberate and dispassionate consideration of this question, with a view to a final settlement. (Cheers)."[157]

Brougham was immediately on his feet to complete Peel's conversion to Catholic Emancipation. Despite the Home Secretary's habitual antipathy to granting Catholics rights that other subjects possessed, circumstances required the new policy.

---

154. *Ibid.*
155. *Ibid.*, January 2, 1829, no.13,784, p.2.
156. "Parliamentary Intelligence," *ibid.*, February 6, 1829, no.13,822, p.1.
157. *Ibid.*, p.3.

Even Protestant Members for Ireland favoured the change, Brougham said. "He believed that no man living would take upon himself to answer for the possibility of putting down the Catholic Association by any means but one, and that was by concession."[158] Once Peel introduced the penal legislation against O'Connell's group, it disbanded as Brougham had recommended. In fact, the Session was more concerned with what ultra Tories such as the Duke of Newcastle and Lord Kenyon would say in response to Wellington's betrayal of the Protestants than any question about Repeal not passing. Lord Winchelsea became so furious over what the Ministry had done to placate liberal Whigs like Brougham on Ireland that he withdrew from the King's College fund, the closest thing he could do to get back at its competitor, the University of London. *The Times* was so appreciative of what Peel had done that it backed him completely when he sought re-election for Oxford University as a matter of principle. Under the circumstances, it would have been better if Barnes had not done so, as Peel was soundly beaten by the ultra Tories of the more undistinguished colleges.

While Peel was finding a safe seat, Brougham had a most impressive run of court performances. Brougham started by obtaining for his client a shilling in a libel case where a newspaper had published an account of a trial in which a witness had said that he had committed criminal intercourse with her, once Denman established that the plaintiff may have tried to tamper with the witness,[159] Brougham more than made up for it by a defence of his own. In *Pilford* v. *Becke*, a seduction suit in the Common Pleas where Serjeant Wilde tried to make out that Pilford's marriage had all been bliss until the defendant came along, Brougham showed that the plaintiff's wife had been so brazen in trying to get evidence against the defendant that it seemed contrived: "Was it not, he would ask, with a view of affording evidence to enable an action to be brought, and a divorce to be obtained, with damages, if they could get them

---

158. *Ibid.*
159. *Vessey* v. *Pike*, January 20, 1829, no.13,807, p.4.

from Captain Becke?"[160] The Chief Justice was impressed by the argument, explaining that he thought that he had heard everything in such cases, "... but never did he witness so extraordinary one as the present."[161] The damages were, consequently, limited to 100 pounds. In *R.* v. *Jones,* a long-standing criminal information initiated by a magistrate, Brougham obliged the case to be dropped because it was just an empty gesture. In a compensation case, Brougham obtained for Mrs. Margaret Price 4,000 pounds for two pieces of property on Chandos Street. They would have fetched even more if it had not been suspected, because of the testimony, that one of them was a whorehouse. In *R.* v. *Samuel Horrox,* Brougham, who had gained conviction, spoke in aggravation of the penalty because Horrox's libellous letter against a firm had cost the company 500 pounds through loss of reputation.[162] Horrox was sentenced to two months in the house of correction. A 10,000 recovery action against Lord Cochrane was non-suited, once Brougham showed the Court of Exchequer that the plaintiff did not have that kind of money to lend.[163] In the King's Bench, Brougham won a libel action against the *Morning Herald.* Brougham finally did lose a recovery action, one which Tenterden even admitted was "... a very clear case."[164]

On the Spring Assizes, leading up to the famous Martin case, Brougham was even more impressive. In another recovery action, he was so convincing about the defendant's having no right to the goods in question that Alderson agreed to arbitration. The defendant, it seemed, had conspired with the assignees of an insolvent partnership to bilk its resources. "Their plan had been to run into the market and purchase goods upon credit," Brougham explained, "and immediately to sell at a great loss for ready money."[165] Alderson, once he had capitulated, feebly

---

160. *Ibid.,* January 23, 1829, no.13,810, p.4.
161. *Ibid.*
162. *Ibid.,* February 7, 1829, no.13,823, p.4.
163. *Dean* v. *Lord Cochrane, ibid.,* February 24, 1829, no.13,846, p.4.
164. *Russell and Others* v. *Avery, ibid.,* February 28, 1829, no.13,850, p.4.
165. *Moult and Others* v. *Anderton, ibid.,* March 16, 1829, no.13,863, p.6.

contended that he would have refuted all of Brougham's dishonourable imputations if the trial had been allowed to continue, to which Brougham replied that he had only been following instructions. In *R.* v. *Hyde*, Brougham successfully prosecuted Liverpool's surveyor of assessed taxes for trying to take sexual liberties with the wife of a ratepayer in return for tax concessions. On the witness stand, the injured lady testified: "In the lobby he said to me, 'Come, give me a kiss, and I'll tell you what windows there are.'"[166] While the presiding Judge made light of the offence, the jury convicted the surveyor, and he was subsequently fined 20 pounds. Brougham followed this up by winning another case reminiscent of the Wakefield one. The defendants were charged with conspiring to arrange a marriage with a rich young woman contrary to the banns stipulations of the Marriage Act. About how the conspiring parties arranged the deceit, Brougham said: "In that register, the parties contracting the marriage were described as being of the parish of Manchester, as plainly as written, or rather as printed, words could make it."[167] While Pollock tried to underplay what had been done, the jury believed Brougham's explanation of the crime. He only permitted the defendants to escape from felony charges for arranging the marriage with Miss Hickson because it had not been consummated, permitting an annulment. Brougham only lost minor disputes at Lancaster.

The culmination of the Assizes was the trial of Martin for burning down York Minster. While the report of the fire was first dismissed as a hoax, it was soon discovered to be all too true. About the damage, *The Times* reported: "The roof of the choir quite gone, the wood work on each side consumed, the matchless organ entirely destroyed, many monuments broken, and the communion plate melted."[168] As to the fire's origin, the *Leeds Mercury* reported a few days later: "the infatuated wretch appears to be another Ravaillac or Erostatus, and looks something like

166. *Ibid.*, March 23, 1829, no.13,869, p.6.
167. *R.* v. *Thomas Baxter, and Others*, *ibid.*, March 24, 1829, no.13,870, p.3.
168. "Destruction of the Interior of York Minster," *ibid.*, February 5, 1829, no.13,821, p.3.

a religious enthusiast of the lowest order."[169] If true, that a Catholic fanatic had done the 100,000 pounds damage, the result could jeopardize passage of Catholic Emancipation. Fortunately, the culprit was caught, and turned out to be the brother of John Martin, England's foremost Protestant painter since William Blake. About John Martin's purpose, his biographer wrote: "To him mankind were puny creatures set in an overwhelming universe, and God appeared only in his inanimate works, the high mountains and illimitable plains, and, by a curious irony, in the stupendous work of man himself."[170] Martin's crazy brother, Jonathan, worked himself into such a state about the condition of the clergy that as a kind of anti-Christ, he set fire to York Minster. The fact that he was a militant Protestant completely backfired on the ultra Tories in their opposition to Catholic relief, as *The Times* duly noted in discussing the Bishops: "As to the *furiates*, they deserve here, and will obtain there where they speak, but little notice. They would probably, if left to themselves, propagate *their* faith as JONATHAN MARTIN has endeavoured to propagate *his*."[171]

Under the circumstances, the Crown treated Martin as if he were another Bellingham, Spencer Perceval's assassin. About his return to York from Hexham where he had been apprehended, *The Times* reported: "Owing to the very irritated state of the public mind, it was deemed prudent that he should be brought to this city at an hour when its inhabitants should be taking their repose."[172] While the Crown wanted to save him from vigilante justice, it seemed quite prepared to have him meet Bellingham's fate. Alderson, for the Crown, even compared the building's destruction to the Prime Minister's assassination, recording the punishment meted out for such crimes. Brougham, who had been retained by Martin, objected to the practice, and Baron Hullock obliged the prosecution to leave out the verdicts for similar

---

169. "Fire at York Minster," reprinted in *ibid.*, February 7, 1829, no.13,823, p.4.
170. Thomas Balston, *John Martin, 1789-1854* (Bibliographical Society, London, 1934), p.383.
171. *The Times*, April 5, 1829, n.13,879, p.5. Italics its.
172. *Ibid.*, February 11, 1829, no.13,826, p.4.

crimes. While the Crown was willing to portray Martin's crime as calculated destruction of the highest order, Brougham argued that Martin was hopelessly insane, despite protests by his client. Instead of being an agent for the return of Napoleon's son, as Alderson wanted to make out, Brougham showed through cross-examination of the Crown's witnesses that the facts were far different. For example, the surgeon, Champney, who testified that Martin was rational, was forced to admit that he knew nothing of insane asylums where Martin had been incarcerated several times. When Brougham examined defence witnesses who gave telling evidence of the accused's insanity. To prove Martin's irrational obsession, he even took the stand, and gave a monomaniacal account of what had happened, concluding thus: "Suddenly he heard a voice which told him it was his duty to destroy the cathedral on account of the misconduct of the clergy."[173] Martin was declared not guilty by reason of insanity, and committed to Bedlam under 40 Geo.III c.94 for his own protection. Later, the same day at *nisi prius*, Brougham won two profitable recovery actions, and later during the Assizes, he saw that another most oppressive one, *Wood* v. *Norton*, was non-suited because of insufficient stamps. In fact, the *Leeds Mercury* devoted its April 11 coverage of the Assize just to Brougham's efforts to show that its assessment of his abilities had not been overstated.

Back in London, Brougham kept up the pressure for reform, apparently writing yet another column for *The Times* on the inadequacy of Eldon's policies, especially towards Ireland:

> ... it becomes a question whether a larger quantum of human misery has, during the last five-and-thirty years, been entailed on the people of this country by the noble and learned lord's doubts upon all parts, in the court of Chancery, or by the uniform absence of all doubts in his mind on this great question, in the Cabinet and in the House of Lords.[174]

---

173. "Trial of Martin for Burning of York Minster," *ibid.*, April 2, 1829, p.3.
174. "Lord Eldon," *ibid.*, April 3, 1829, no.13,887, p.5.

Once Peel introduced his Metropolitan Police Bill, Brougham was apparently back in *The Times*, wanting more in the way of reform from the Common Law Commission because of the inquiry's expense. Instead of encouraging disputes, he wrote, "I look upon the means of successfully restraining the spirit of litigation ..."[175] The amends and moneys involved in cases should be tendered into court to check disputes. Once Brougham had studied its report, he gave *Times* readers a completely favourable appraisal of what the Commission recommended.[176] On the Chancellor of the Exchequer's motion that the Commons go into Committee of Supply, Brougham said as much in the House, asking if the government was prepared to effect the Commission's recommendations. "He thought that they had limited the field over which they had a right to go; but still, as far as the report went, he could not conceive any thing much more complete."[177] Peel complimented Brougham for his characterization of the profession's reaction to it, and when pressed by him, the Home Secretary said that he was willing to have the Commission look into the law of arrest. In fact, once Brougham complained about Lyndhurst's Chancery Bill,[178] calling for returns on how the Great Seal performed in commission, as opposed to when Lords Thurlow and Loughborough sat on the Woolsack, Peel withdrew the bill for improvements.

There was also a question of whose Home Secretary Peel was when O'Connell finally tried to take his seat in the House. While the minister had apparently paved the way by quashing any objection among their ranks, although the Catholic Relief Bill only removed the disability against persons being so elected after its passage, Mr Speaker said that O'Connell must withdraw because he was not prepared to administer the particular oath which O'Connell was prepared to take. O'Connell, he explained, had been elected for County Clare long before the relief act had been passed. Brougham was immediately on his feet, stating that

175. "Courts of Common Law," *ibid.*, April 19, 1829, no.13,891, p.3.
176. "Report of the Common Law Commissioners," *ibid.*, April 21, 1829, no.13,894, p.3.
177. *Ibid.*, May 5, 1829, no.13,906, p.1.
178. "New Chancery Bill," *ibid.*, May 23, 1829, no.13,922, p.5.

O'Connell "... had a right to state his reasons for adopting the course which he appeared to have done."[179] As for the Speaker's ruling, he added: "But it is of great importance that no opinion of any individual member, whether in the chair or out of it, should bind this house."[180] After stating the precedents under which a Member had been heard in such circumstances, Brougham moved: "That the hon. member for Clare be called back, and heard at the table. (Hear, hear.)"[181] All Peel could do was to move a postponement of hearing O'Connell, preferably at the Bar, because Brougham had not given notice of his motion. A few days later, the House heard the merits of the case, with O'Connell at the Bar with counsel, and decided that he had to undergo another election if he were not prepared to take the old oath. Brougham argued that the relief act was "... retrospective as far as prohibitions were concerned, and prospective with regard to oaths and declarations ..."[182] While the House was not prepared to give O'Connell the benefit of the doubt, he was prepared to undertake another campaign because of the consideration the House had given him.

The ultra Tories were enraged by this turn of events. While they toyed with the idea of contesting O'Connell's re-election, they soon gave it up as a hopeless cause. Instead they decided to attack those who made Catholic Emancipation possible. Editor Alexander of the *Morning Journal* had initiated such a course when he attacked the *Courier* for supporting Canning's coalition.[183] The former paper had merged with Stoddart's *The New Times*, the mouthpiece of the abortive Constitutional Association. The ultra Tories were beside themselves over what Brougham had been able to achieve with Wellington, Peel, and Lyndhurst. Since Attorney General Wetherell had resigned because of his opposition to Catholic Emancipation, and Solicitor General Tindal had been appointed the Chief Justice of Common

---

179. "Mr O'Connell," *ibid.*, May 16, 1829, no.13,916, p.3.
180. *Ibid.*
181. *Ibid.*
182. *Ibid.*, May 19, 1829, no.13,918, p.1.
183. A. Aspinall, *Politics and the Press* (Home & Van Thal, London, 1949), p.218.

Pleas, the Law Officers needed to be appointed. There was no difficulty in renaming Scarlett Attorney General. The problem was who was to be the new Solicitor General, and there was also a question as to whether or not the ailing Master of the Rolls, Sir John Leach, would continue. Brougham had hoped to get this position when he had been appointed in 1827, and would not settle for being named Chief Baron of the Exchequer as a consolation.[184] Now Lyndhurst was thinking of making him the new Solicitor General to restrict his influence on the government. In his consultations with Lyndhurst, Brougham continued to press his claim to be Master of the Rolls, explaining that Sir Edward Sugden could be Solicitor General. When the ultra Tories heard about the negotiation, probably through Wetherell, they went wild. On May 30, the *Morning Journal*, after reporting Lyndhurst's conversation with Brougham about the appointments, added: "The reasons which led to this promotion are really so natural, that we beg leave to explain them, as Sterne would have done, by the mouths of his inimitable *Uncle Toby* and *Corporal Trim*."[185] In the alluded to exchange, Trim duly indicated that he could become General if he could muster sufficient bribes.

As soon as Lyndhurst learned of the libel, he instructed Scarlett to prosecute. Actually, the libel more applied to Brougham as chief briber, but he did not take such things seriously. The Ministry could not tolerate the idea that Brougham was buying a position in it. He just confounded his enemies by getting more recognition. Lincoln's Inn had promoted him to be the Society's Keeper of the Black Book. At the first prize day for the graduates of the new University of London, Lord Grey, who was in the chair, said that its progress had been far beyond the expectations of its founders, "but when speaking of the establishment of the University of London, he might more properly, perhaps, make use of the singular number and say, its founder, because, when he spoke of the origin of the institution,

---

184. New, *op. cit.*, p.316.
185. *R.* v. *John Fisher and Others*, *The Times*, June 30, 1829, no.13,953, p.6.

all eyes were necessarily directed to one man."[186] *The Times* report continued: "Very loud and prolonged applause followed this allusion to Mr Brougham, who had entered the room while the noble earl was in the midst of his address."[187]

The *Morning Journal* went crazy over such reports. It also charged the *Courier* with being a government newspaper because of its defending the Chancellor against the libel. About *The Times*'s role, Alexander wrote: "This conduct is disgraceful to the Press. It is enough to sanction a censorship and induce an arbitrary or military minister to place a gag on public opinion, and extinguish the most valuable liberties of the English."[188] When the Prime Minister did not impose censorship, the *Morning Journal* stole Brougham's strategy, having a communication in kind from ultra Tory John Little Crosbie, the Duke of Cumberland's chaplain, published:

> The libel was contained in a letter addressed to the Duke of Wellington, in which the writer, among other things, says: "I hereby publicly arraign your Highness of the grossest treachery to the country, or else the most arrant cowardice, or if you please, treachery, cowardice, and artifice united."[189]

Unlike what had happened to Brougham and Barnes under similar circumstances, the Law Officers took the officers of the *Morning Journal* to court for libelling the Duke.

While the Crown was busy bringing the libellers to heel, Brougham concentrated upon expanding its reformist inclinations. The Report of the Real Property Commission was greeted with a favourable column in *The Times*. As with the common law one, the reader was left in little doubt about its origin: "Mr. Brougham's forcible and well-directed exertions on the same

---

186. "University of London," *ibid.*, July 10, 1829, no.13,962, p.5.
187. *Ibid.*
188. Quoted from Aspinall, *op. cit.*, p.218.
189. *Gentleman's Magazine*, 1829, vol.99, Part II, p.556.

subject are well known."[190] In trying to hide the article's paternity, the writer mentioned an article that H. Bellenden Ker had written on the subject in 1818 for the *Edinburgh Review*. While there was no such article, the strength of the suggestion is shown in *The Wellesley Index* which attributed the later article on conveyancing to Ker. Brougham's article in *The Times* stressed the scope of the problem:

> ... there is no civilized state in the world where the laws relating to the enjoyment, succession, and alienation of property, are more obscure and uncertain, more burdensome in their operation, or more directly tending to inflict upon the community the evils of expense and litigation, and to thwart the administration of justice.[191]

While the Judges had tried to make the law more in tune with the needs of the nation, their outlook and restrictions had forced the problem to be taken out of their hands. In the dispute about who should draft legislative reform, Brougham sided completely with what reformers like Ker proposed over that of codifiers like Benthan, a shift which soon would have him calling in the *Globe* for a debate on the proper approach.

In the courtroom, Brougham had his usual busy schedule. While he did fail to win a libel action against the Society for the Protection of Trade because he could not establish that it was responsible for the circular which damaged his client,[192] he defended a similar action, *Goodchild* v. *Jackson*, well enough that his client only had to pay plaintiff's costs. In a notorious case of criminal conversation where the offending defendant had been obliged by his irate wife to go down on his knees, and acknowledge his adultery, Brougham restricted what the well-to-do apothecary had to pay in damages to 400 pounds. Long Wellesley, the infamous adulterer who was known for

---

190. "First Report of the Law of Real Property," *The Times*, August 5, 1829, no.13,984, p.3.
191. *Ibid.*
192. *Humphrey* v. *Miller*, *ibid.*, July 15, 1829, no.13,966, p.3.

having recommended a life of promiscuity to his infant children until they had been taken away from him, failed to get a conviction in *R.* v. *Susanah York*, a perjury suit Brougham helped prosecute for the purpose of obtaining a rehearing of the Chancery decision.[193] It is hard to imagine a client with whom Brougham sympathized less. Mr Wellesley personified all that was wrong with the legal system - endless, expensive adjudication whose results were contrary to nature. His retainers were the ones Brougham especially had in mind when he said that he could do without them in his great speech the year before on law reform. Brougham achieved good results in defending two damage suits, restricting the fine to 40 shillings for his client's using "Harvey's Fish Sauce" label without authority, and limiting the recovery to the absolute minimum the prosecution wanted for the loss of extensive woollen goods.[194]

As usual, the more exciting cases were on the Northern Circuit. Brougham's exposure of a dreadful trover action, where a husband was trying to recover his deceased, estranged wife's clothes, was so convincing that the presiding Judge tried to get the prosecution to stop it, but when this failed, he still obtained a verdict for the defendants.[195] In losing a breach of promise case, Brougham helped reduce damages by showing that the plaintiff had been blessed by escaping union with his client. The most interesting case at York was *Doe, Dem. Turnbull* v. *Shepherd and Watson*, an ejectment action that Scarlett had been specially retained to prosecute.[196] The plaintiff was a surgeon who was noted for getting deathbed bequests. The Attorney General made light of the stories questioning his latest patient's will: "That will was now in court, and was ready to be produced, if the calumny should be repeated that day."[197] Brougham, before a large audience, including the Archbishop, did more than repeat the calumny; he established it to be nothing less than the truth.

193. *Ibid.*, July 25, 1829, no.13,975, p.3.
194. *Yeates and Another* v. *Dexter, ibid.*, July 31, 1829, no.13,980, p.3.
195. *Tate* v. *Linton and Wife, ibid.*, August 8, 1829, no.13,987, p.3.
196. *Ibid.*, August 17, 1829, no.13,994, p.3.
197. *Ibid*

During the cross-examination of conveyancer Samuel Dales, who had prepared the will, Brougham induced him to admit that he was a patient of the good Doctor, and that he had made out the will without ever having seen the testator. "'It was a good thing they could not strike me off the rolls,' he continued, 'because I was not an attorney.' (A laugh.)"[198] A witness to the will, William Young, testified that he did not see the testator, Stephenson, sign it while he was in the dying man's room. After Scarlett intervened, reminding the witness that he was under oath, Brougham obliged him to explain how the surgeon had managed the scene: "'When I saw Dr Turnbull, as if putting the pen into Stephenson's hand, my wife had gone. That was after we had all signed.'"[199] Another witness, Thomas Hodgson, completely corroborated what Young had said, stating that Turnbull was guilty of a "villainous and iniquitous transaction." Justice Bayley asked Scarlett if there was any point in going further, and he replied not, adding that he still had witnesses to show that the testator knew that he had left his property to Turnbull. "Mr Brougham - 'And I am prepared with evidence to show exactly the reverse.'"[200] The case was non-suited because the plaintiff had failed to show that the will had been properly executed.

On the rest of the circuit, Brougham was not so successful. At Durham, in defending an assault suit, he overplayed his role: "For his own part, he scarcely knew whether he ought to call witnesses, since the effect would only be to reduce the damages from a shilling to a farthing ..."[201] When Brougham called witnesses, the jury found for the plaintiff, awarding him 10 pounds. At Carlisle, Brougham sought valiantly to establish that the sister of a notorious bankrupt did not know what she was getting into when she executed a money bond for his benefit.[202] While Brougham stated that she was merely a witness to the

198. *Ibid.*
199. *Ibid.*
200. *Ibid.*
201. *Lax* v. *Barnes, ibid.*, August 21, 1829, no.13,998, p.3.
202. *Palliser* v. *Crosse, ibid.*, August 31, 1829, no.14,006, pp.3-4.

transaction, the jury said she would have to pay back the money advanced by the half-pay officer. At Lancaster, Brougham decided on a more prudent course in a similar suit involving a bankrupt's estate, consenting, as prosecutor Pollock explained, "... to make a variety of admissions which would considerably curtail the evidence, and conduce to an early decision of the cause."[203] In the end, the plaintiff was awarded 40,000 pounds, and the defendant was given leave to move for a non-suit before the King's Bench *en banc* on the grounds which the defence had argued barred it.

Brougham's concern about property was much more geared towards preventing it from becoming the object of such court cases. He had been eagerly awaiting to discuss further the report of the Real Property Commission, and was pleasantly surprised by what it recommended for improving inheritance laws. The root of all problems, he said, was that inheritance could never lineally ascend when there was no legal heir:

> This rule may be traced to the same fruitful source from which most of the inconveniences of the system of real property law have sprung, the feudal system, and the absurdity of applying to existing interests and regulations of a local or peculiar nature, and which, whatever may have been their worth (if they possessed any) in their origin, are wholly unsuited to the habits of modern society.[204]

The report proposed to get rid of the absurdity of a father not inheriting from his son, of escheats to the Crown, and of the exclusion of half-brothers. Brougham was not so happy with what the Commission proposed to do about other vestiges of ancient law, especially dower and courtesy, preferring rather to see that the possessor should have "... always a complete power

---

203. *Dobson, Assigne* v. *Rathbone & Co., ibid.*, September 7, 1829, no.14,012, p.4. For cases where Brougham got better results, see *Jones* v. *Potter, Hodgson* v. *Ridehalgh,* and *Walker* v. *Lyon.*

204. "Report of the Law of Real Property," *ibid.*, September 8, 1829, no.14,013, p.3.

of disposition over his estate."[205] The recommendations about dower and courtesy were quoted to illustrate the point that the Commission should recommend laws for the benefit of society rather than make proposals which fitted the wishes and feelings of those immediately concerned.

Brougham was able to exploit both approaches to the reform of the law of real property. Because of the professional contact he had developed with Colonel Berkeley in dealing with Miss Foote's marital difficulties, he was given the task of making good the Colonel's claim to a barony by tenure, subject to a writ of summons to the Lords. Berkeley's family had anciently been given Berkeley Hernesse in Gloucestershire, "... a personal dignity conferred by writ, and as such it would have descended to the heirs of the body possessed of such dignity."[206] The title had long since died out, but Brougham was trying to establish the claim for the descendant of the general heir who had lost it during the reign of Henry V, and whose estate had been vested in the Crown. Colonel Berkeley was presently, Brougham argued, "... seized of the castle, lands, and tenements, constituting the barony."[207] The Colonel was just trying to do what John Fitz Alan had done in reclaiming the Earldom of Arundel, Brougham concluded. Berkeley's petition had been given to Wetherell as Attorney General, and he had had it referred to the Lords' Committee of Privileges, where it remained for years.

Brougham found what the Real Property Commission recommended about fine and recoveries actions more promising for the rest of society. After he had described in *The Times*, how these expensive and obtuse actions had developed, he agreed completely, as usual, with what Bellenden Ker had recommended to the Commissioners for their improvement. Fortunately for

---

205. *Ibid.*
206. "Berkeley Barony, By Tenure," *ibid.*, September 29, 1829, no.14,031, p.3. As to its authorship, note this introduction: "The grounds on which the claim is made are detailed at great length, in a case ably drawn up by Mr Fonblanque and Mr Brougham; and as they are novel and curious - an application of such a nature not having been made for 160 years - we subjoin an abstract of them."
207. *Ibid.*

Brougham, they went along with Ker's advice, urging their abolition. To bar entails, they proposed common conveyance, and the establishment of standing commissions in each county to assure alienation by married women of their estates. "In these suggestions the Commissioners have endeavoured," Brougham apparently concluded, "while they abolish the inconveniences and cost which have been so abundantly occasioned by fines and recoveries, to preserve the benefits which have resulted from their use."[208]

Back in the King's Bench, Brougham won an important case against Scarlett for a fellow Member of Parliament. The suit was for the recovery of an 8,000 pound note which Frederick Hodgson had given to a nefarious bankrupt as down payment for Pitt's Place, a country residence near Epsom in Surrey, as Scarlett explained to the jury: "He, to his misfortune, had been on terms of great intimacy with Mr Rowland Stephenson."[209] Hodgson's note had been endorsed over to the plaintiff, and he was now in court to collect. It was unnecessary to go further into the matter, his counsel stated, although "... Mr Brougham, who appeared for Mr Hodgson, might do so if he pleased."[210] Plaintiff Murray, Brougham explained, received the note after it was due, "... and that therefore the instrument was, as between Rowland Stephenson and Mr Hodgson, nothing more than waste paper."[211] The deal had fallen through because Stephenson could not provide proper title to the property. The note, consequently, was a dead letter, the court held, and no one could collect for it.

Brougham, after he had ably defended a libel case which the *News* had suffered for copying a police report from the *Morning Journal*,[212] was given the unenviable task of prosecuting another Member of Parliament, Lord Melbourne in an adultery suit with Lady Brandon. While there was little doubt about the case, Lord

---

208. "Report of the Law of Real Property," *ibid.*, October 3, 1829, no.14,035, p.4.
209. *Murray* v. *Hodgson, ibid.*, October 23, 1829, no.14,052, p.3.
210. *Ibid.*
211. *Ibid.*
212. *Wilks* v. *Phipps, ibid.*, November 2, 1829, no.14,060, p.3.

Brandon's prosecution of the former Chief Secretary for Ireland seemed more geared to exploding the impression that he had been cuckolded in the affair than to gain damages. Barrister Gurney, in stating the case to the jury, and Brougham, in examining witnesses for the prosecution, were far from proving the charge, much to Tenterden's exasperation. Brougham examined a milliner who said that he knew a woman who lived on Northumberland Street who turned out to be Lady Brandon, a revelation to which the Lord Chief Justice responded: "Pray call somebody who will prove something for the purpose. (A laugh)."[213] After another witness shed no light on the alleged adultery, Brougham questioned a hackney driver, Henry Hall, who spoke of picking up two men on Grosvenor Place, and driving them around the West End. He had taken one of them to near where Lady Brandon was living, waited until one a.m. when he returned. Hall then had taken the man to a residence in Whitehall. "It was Lord Melbourne's House,"[214] Hall explained. After one more similar attempt to establish the case, Tenterden non-suited the action. When Scarlett, who was representing Melbourne, tried to explain that his client had had nothing to do with the case, the presiding Judge agreed sarcastically. While the case had not pleased Tenterden, it had certainly helped make the cynical Melbourne more dependent on Brougham, as we shall see.

Melbourne was not the only aristocrat to be beholden to Brougham. In *The Times*, apparently Brougham wrote another letter to the Prime Minister. Instead of the writer sounding like a bitter protagonist, as he had just a year before, he sounded like a Sovereign, writing to his first minister. After Brougham had described the kingdom's current economic difficulties, and their possible causes, he concluded: "... all that the Legislature can do, or is in fact required to be done, is, that a wider field for our exertions should be afforded."[215] Free trade had to be

---

213. *Lord Brandon* v. *Lord Melbourne, ibid.*, November 4, 1829, no.14,062, p.4.
214. *Ibid.*
215. "To His Grace The Duke of Wellington," *ibid.*, November 9, 1829, no.14,066, p.3.

established in the Far East, including China, and something had to be done about the East India Company's monopoly. Parliament had to investigate the 1813 measure which reduced India's sovereignty to an empty shell. "Numberless and immense as your claims are to the gratitude of your country," Brougham concluded, 'you would find the removal of these restrictions an additional title to it ..."[216]

As the parliamentary session approached, Brougham had leaders in *The Times* to keep pressure on the Home Secretary, Lord Chancellor, and Law Officers to enact reasonable law reforms. It was a matter of striking a balance between wild codifiers, such as Bentham, and practitioners who wanted to change nothing. "General principles," Brougham apparently wrote, "can never provide for all the incidents and varieties of particular cases."[217] In a modern society, there would have to be a place for individual precedents to elaborate an effective code, whatever first principles were legislated. "There seems to be a wish extending itself in this country," he warned, "to cry up the Code Napoleon as something incomparably more perfect - and perfect on the side of brevity and perspicuity - than the system of English law."[218] Excerpts were printed from a pamphlet by Byles to show the reality of French courtroom experience. "The doctrines and decisions of French law are as voluminous as those of the law of England," the article concluded, "or more so, and the reference to cases of precedents more common in their courts than in ours."[219]

In the courtroom, Brougham was establishing precedents which augured well for the Crown's showdown with the *Morning Journal* for its libels on the Duke's Government. In a court of compensation, Brougham restored the original award for the compulsory purchase of *The Key*, the notorious hotel on Chandos Street, by Crown Commissioners. Campbell had induced the King's Bench to overturn the first award because of its

---

216. *Ibid.*
217. *Ibid.*, December 5, 1829, no.14,089, p.2.
218. *Ibid.*
219. *Ibid.*

informality, and Brougham had moved for a new trial. Scarlett, in defending the case, tried to dilute the award by stressing the hotel's reputation. For example, when James Elms, an architect, was asked about its character, he replied: "The character of this house is very well known. It is first-rate in its way. (A laugh.)"[220] Scarlett went on in this vein, trying to make out that the owner, an aged woman, would only suffer injury if she had to take up residence as one of the house's ladies. Brougham showed that the Crown had operated under a bias, not agreeing to the higher compensation its witnesses had recommended. The jury awarded the original 4,000 pounds. Brougham followed up this decision by obliging the King's Bench to drop *R.* v. *Taylor*, a libel action which Campbell was most anxious to prosecute, and by obliging Scarlett to apologize objectly for any inconvenience caused by a cut-and-dried libel.[221]

A lunacy commission hearing provided Brougham with the ideal stage to setting the scene for the *Morning Journal's* libels against the government. Wetherell argued that Edward Davies was insane, in a way which reminded Brougham of how he had tried to make the case against Queen Caroline. When Wetherell tried to impugn Davies's rationality because of the fact that he had purchased shares in the University of London, it turned out to be the London Institution, a revelation, Brougham said, which cut short Wetherell's wit.[222] Then the defence exploited the fact that the solicitor, Hobler, the prosecution's chief witness against Davies, had been used in an *ex parte* fashion. Wetherell tried to limit his testimony to points which only assisted its case, but Brougham forced a full testimony from him. When William Davison tried to imply that Davies was strange because he did not keep change in his pockets, Brougham responded: "Then I ought to be considered insane, for I have not a six pence change in my pocket right now."[223] The prosecution later admitted that its witnesses had cut corners in the treatment of Davies's alleged

---

220. "Court of Compensations," *ibid.*, November 9, 1829,n o.14,066, p.4.
221. *R.* v. *Thwaites and Another, ibid.*, November 28, 1829, no.14,083, p.3.
222. "Commission of Lunacy," *ibid.*, December 15, 1829, no.14,097, p.3.
223. *Ibid.*, December 18, 1829, no.14,100, p.3.

insanity. On December 24, after the King's Bench handed down its first decision in the *Morning Journal's* cases, Brougham was roasting Wetherell, its chief counsel, for his handling of the Davies case. In a brilliant five-and-a-half-hour summation, to which *The Times* gave front-page coverage, Brougham contrasted proper inquiry into a person's alleged insanity with what the ultra Tory had done. "Sir C. Wetherell," he said, "even turned the alleged conversations of Mr Davies into ridicule ..."[224] In response to this Christmas Eve present, Wetherell was reduced to dire predictions: "If Mr Davies were acquitted by this jury, and were to take the life of his mother, or any other person, could the jury find him guilty on the ground of his having a sound exercise of his understanding?"[225] The jury declared Davies sane.

The case provided insight into just how much money Brougham was making. The lunacy commission cost about 5,000 pounds. "Mr Brougham's fee, it is stated, was 300 guineas, and 30 guineas for each day's attendance after the first."[226] All told, for the 11-day hearing, he received 600 guineas. This was nearly 50 per cent more than Wetherell was paid. The listing of the other costs was a continual reminder of Chancery abuses. Wright, the prosecution's junior counsel, made 210 pounds. The three commissioners received five guineas per day for their efforts, and each juror received a guinea. Each witness, upon showing a copy of his subpoena, had been paid similarly. While the Davies case was particularly remunerative for Brougham, he must have been making 1,000 pounds per month, considering his rents from Brougham Hall, his royalties from his pamphlets, and articles for Barnes, and the *Review*. Brougham, was indeed the primary beneficiary of the lack of law reform, but not for want of trying to reduce fees.

Brougham was little involved in the settlement of the libels against the Duke's Government, something for which he blamed

224. *Ibid.*, December 24, 1829, no.14,105, p.1.
225. *Ibid.*, December 26, 1829, no.14,108, p.3.
226. *Ibid.*

Scarlett. During the preliminary hearings, the Law Officers Scarlett and Sugden did everything. When it came time to examine witnesses as to who the *Morning Journal* had been referring to, Brougham only examined the first witness, the Chief Justice of the Common Pleas. The *Gentleman's Magazine* described the process thus: "Lord Chief Justice Tindal, Lord Bexley, the Master of the Rolls, Baron Vaughan, Lord Holland, Mr Courtenay, and several other gentleman, gave it as their belief, that the words of the libel applied to the Lord Chancellor."[227] The editor, printer, and proprietor of the *Morning Journal* were found guilty not only of this charge but also of libelling the King and the House of Commons. The next day, Alexander, the editor, and Marsden and Isaacson, the proprietors, were found guilty of libelling the Duke in the July 30th issue. In a related case, the editor of *Atlas*, a Sunday paper, was convicted of libelling Lyndhurst when he published a story, claiming that Lyndhurst was selling ecclesiastical livings.[228]

With Wellington's Government so desirous of effecting Brougham's policies, his patron, Lord Darlington, decided to join the Tory ranks. While Brougham did not mind joining the Duke on practical grounds, Brougham certainly did object on matters of party and principle. To cross the floor to join Peel was not something he could do, especially after his 1827 letter to the Home Secretary to accomplish just the reverse. Also, Brougham as a Tory would lose all influence with liberal Whigs, just when they needed him most. George Tierney, the Whig leader, was on his last legs, dying in January 1830. The way was clear for Brougham to finally gain the leadership officially that he had so long exercised. Fortunately, the Duke of Devonshire, Tierney's patron, was persuaded of the possibility of Brougham's deserting the Whig ranks, and offered him the seat for Knaresborough.[229] Brougham, after a two-day delay to give the impression that his defection was a serious possibility, graciously accepted. For him,

227. *Gentleman's Magazine*, 1829, vol.99, Part II, p.556.
228. *R.* v. *Bell, ibid.*, p.556.
229. Aspinall, *op. cit., Lord Brougham ...*, p.172.

the Duke's Government would not survive the death of George IV.

As the Session assembled, Brougham's only concern was the Chancery. To keep pressure on the property commission, he kept calling in *The Times* for a general register of property. To push Lyndhurst to effect Chancery reforms, he reviewed Long Wellesley's pamphlet, critical of the Chancery. While Wellesley could have made a telling commentary against it by just describing what had happened to him, he charged the court with being corrupt. Brougham, most sensitive to the charge because of what the *Morning Journal* had written, totally denied this. The Chancellor had exercised a most questionable jurisdiction in the Wellesley case, Brougham wrote. The Chancery needed a complete re-ordering of its structure and process, especially the taking of evidence. Affidavits had to be replaced by oral testimony. Wellesley, because he could not expose his critics, should never have written the pamphlet, although he did have some interesting comments about how the court swallowed up 20,000 pounds in hearing his disputes. "The whole of this money has gone into the hands of the lawyers," Brougham wrote, "so that it is no wonder that the law should be indisposed to let so profitable a cause out of court in a hurry."[230] The review concluded with an eye on the future, stating that although Lord Eldon had handled Wellesley's disputes badly, Lyndhurst, despite all the difficulties of the Chancery, had tried to give him justice.

Brougham's analysis of what to expect from the 1830 parliamentary session proved completely correct. The Speech from the Throne indicated agreement with everything that he wanted in the way of law and economic reforms. In fact, it was so solicitous of Brougham in the expansion of trade, and in looking into the East India Company's monopoly that he was placed in a quandary about not supporting it, especially since his old mentor moved the House's Answer. "... Lord Darlington, who, finding now, as he expressed it, 'a Tory Administration

---

230. "A View of the Court of Chancery," *The Times*, January 9, 1830, no.14,119, p.3.

acting on Whig principles,'" Barnes explained "has deserted the opposition benches, and carried 'Whig principles' to the other side of the house."[231] Brougham stayed with the Whigs, but had been reduced to complaining about the vagueness of the proposed remedies.[232] Peel exhausted this expedient by proposing an inquiry into the Company's charter, and by moving quickly to effect reforms proposed by the Common Law Commission. In fact, Brougham was even brought into the process, suggesting to the Lord Advocate how similar reforms could be effected in Scotland.

On the strength of this, Brougham made another important speech on law reform, calling for the creation of local courts to ease the congestion in the Superior Courts of Law and Equity, especially in the King's Bench. Here Brougham was taking advantage of what Parliament was proposing for Scotland's sheriff's courts, and the Court of Session, and applying them to a new English institution. In proposing a court which would do away with trial by jury in some cases, Brougham distinguished his efforts from those of Bentham, although he was generous in his practice of the law reformer's efforts.[233] When Parliament was considering Peel's latest digest of the law, that dealing with forgery, Brougham wound up the debate, calling for an abolition of capital punishment for the offence, and when the amendment passed, Peel turned the measure over to Brougham and his followers to assure its passage.[234] In sum, Brougham was increasingly seen as the Home Secretary's Minister of Justice.

This function was largely based upon what Brougham was doing in *The Times*, and in the Commons. In Barnes's columns, Brougham continued to contrast what was being proposed for the Common Law Courts, with those in equity. When Ker wrote a pamphlet, addressed to Peel, calling for a general registry of real property, Brougham explained: "The topic is an insulated one, and may be disposed of by itself. If a registry is adopted,

---

231. *Ibid.*, February 5, 1830, no.14,142, p.3.
232. *Ibid.*
233. *Ibid.*, April 30, 1830, no.14,214, p.2.
234. *Ibid.*, June 8, 1830, no.14,247, p.3.

the way will be cleared for many other recommendations of the commissioners ..."[235] When Lyndhurst finally introduced his equity measures, essentially calling for more officials to meet its backlog, *The Times* reacted in a dismissive manner: "We look upon this speech, however, as only the prelude to other and more important reforms."[236] About the new orders, the Master of the Rolls's new hours, and the proposed new Vice-Chancellor, it explained: "... there is a glaring and very ominous distinction between the proposed Chancery reforms and those making under Mr Peel's auspices."[237] *The Times* kept printing columns about what the Common Law Commission was proposing, almost matters of course,[238] and ones hostile to what the Chancellor was trying to effect in Chancery.[239]

The conflict over law reform (the differences between the Home Secretary and the Chancellor) ultimately became the crucial issue between ultra Tories and Brougham. Wetherell and his followers became so incensed over what Peel was doing for the Whigs that they tried to defeat his programme. They tried to postpone the Administration of Justice Bill until after the Session's end. D.W. Harvey, in explaining their opposition to changes in the number of Welsh Judges, added bitterly: "... the hon. and learned member for Knaresborough [Brougham] had introduced a measure, apparently with the sanction of His Majesty's Government, which would have the effect of establishing local courts, and giving birth to 50 Judges."[240] The MP, Fergusson had made the charge necessary when he explained the new role of the sheriff's courts in Scotland under the Court of Session Bill: "They were, in fact, to them what the hon. and learned member of Knaresborough's proposed local jurisdiction, would be to the people of this country, the means

---

235. "A General Registry," *ibid.*, March 9, 1830, no.14,169, p.3.
236. *Ibid.*, March 24, 1830, no.14,182, p.6.
237. "Chancery Reform," *ibid.*, April 3, 1830, no.14,191, p.7.
238. "The Common Law Report," *ibid.*, April 12, 23, and 28, 1830,n os.14,198, 14,208, and 14,212, pp.3, 5, and 3.
239. "Court of Chancery," *ibid.*, June 21, 1830, no.14,258, p.3.
240. *Ibid.*, June 25, 1830, no.14,262, p.1.

of affording cheap and prompt law to the less wealthy."[241] The Lord Advocate had underlined Brougham's role in the process by stating to the House "... that he would be always ready to receive any suggestion in writing for the further improvement of the Scottish law."[242] The Radicals had already had enough of Brougham's successes in law reform with Bentham issuing his open challenge in the *Globe* for a war of pamphlets as to the proper approach.

The courtroom provided a forum to increase Brougham's stature. While he did not participate in as many cases as usual because of his growing commitments to *The Times* and the *Review*, he made his appearances count. Campbell had tried to force a new trial in *Fisher* v. *Clement*, the last of the cases growing out of *The Memoirs of Harriette Wilson*, and something that Brougham clearly wanted to see the end of. Fisher's verdict for libel damages in the Common Pleas had ultimately been set aside by the King's Bench on a writ of error, and a new trial in July 1828 at the Guildhall had resulted in a verdict for the defendant. The appellant, a former attorney of Lyme Regis, sought a new trial on the ground that Tenterden had misdirected the jury about the effect of doggerel lines between Miss Wilson and Stockdale which had been printed in *Bell's Life in London*. Brougham had contended that "... their object was not to reassert the truth of the imputations against the plaintiff's character, but rather to expose and hold up to public odium the writer and publisher of the *Memoirs*."[243] Campbell complained that the Lord Chief Justice stressed this too much in his charge, and not the effect that they had had upon the previous verdicts against them. He would not agree to the *stet processus* as Attorney General urged, demanding that the rule be made absolute for a new trial. In the rehearing, Brougham said that "... there was no instance where the Court had been called on to say that a publication was libellous which a jury had pronounced to be not libellous."[244] The King's Bench

---

241. *Ibid.*, June 19, 1830, no.14,257, p.1.
242. *Ibid.*
243. *Fisher* v. *Clement, ibid.*, January 30, 1830, no.14,137, p.5.
244. *Ibid.*

accepted the argument, discharging the rule.

With this weight off Brougham's shoulders, he might have been tempted to let his legal career take a backseat to his political aims, restricting his courtroom performances to cases he had to defend. For example, when Miss Hickson was indicted at the Salford Quarter Sessions for her role in the arranged marriage by others, he went to the King's Bench, rather than to his re-election at Knaresborough, to get a writ of certiorari to transfer it to the Assizes so it could be quashed.[245] However, the solicitors at Lancaster and York had decided to boycott his services because of his commitment to reducing fees, forcing Brougham to undertake the unprecedented task of finding his own clients and witnesses by handbill and advertisements. They had been persuaded that Peel's reforms would benefit London's legal practitioners, so they decided to get Brougham. They figured that Justice Park who postponed the special jury trials, giving Brougham time to get other attorneys and to find witnesses for his causes such in the fashion of the placard carrying attorneys. Despite the inconvenience caused by the delay of the special jury cases, Brougham had his share of the business, thanks to his influence with outside interests like the Society of Apothecaries. Years later Brougham still felt obliged to describe the most unusual challenge to the Law Amendment Society because it thought that only Lyndhurst had acted as a solicitor. The process was so exhausting, though, that he had to take Justice Parke's carriage back to Brougham's lodgings at the end of the Lancaster Assizes. The high point of the ordeal was when the *Leeds Mercury* featured Brougham's efforts in winning a title dispute after six years of effort and at a cost of 6,000. Brougham had had no discretion in defending *Critchley* v. *Dorke*, a bitter false imprisonment case in which he saved his demanding client, who was in court, 60. While the barrister did lose cases on the Assizes, he did protect the interests of Wakefield's poor shop-keepers from unscrupulous competition, and the deed of settlement of a bankrupt, Bent-Mill cotton-spinner, which

245. *R.* v. *Elizabeth Hickson, ibid.*, February 4, 1830, no.14,141, p.3.

benefitted his wife, though the court refused to hear her interested testimony on the matter. The truly amazing aspects about his performance were that he had been so successful with so little help, an achievement which renewed Northern Liberals' commitment to reform, and he needed to have received his usual fees no matter what the result.

Back in London, when Campbell sued the Society for the Diffusion of Useful Knowledge for libelling Burton's brewers in its publication, *The Art of Brewing*, Brougham defended it instead of writing another article about its wares for the *Review*. When the case came on, he persuaded the plaintiff to drop it by explaining how the authors had come to the conclusion that Burton brewers made beer illegally. The only way the authors could see the process working was by the introduction of an illegal ingredient, such a gypsum, overlooking the action caused by the compounds in Burton's famous water. His clients, Brougham explained, were wrong, and promised to make the necessary corrections in the next edition. "Very well," Tenterden said, "the lovers of Burton ale may now drink it without fear." Brougham replied: "If they drink it in moderation (a laugh.)"[246] There was no chance of such a settlement in three damage cases which he defended, one of which involved a New Bond Street auctioneer for maliciously suing out a bankruptcy commission against an army officer.[247] Brougham was similarly over his head when he claimed that he would win an ejectment action by showing that a testator was insane when he willed his property to its occupiers.[248]

These defeats just put Brougham in the proper frame of mind for more challenging cases. *Rowlands* v. *Gargrave,* a recovery action against another attorney for jewellery his wife had bought, brought out the best in him. "The learned counsel said he was at a loss to conceive on what ground the action was defended."[249] Proof was given that the articles had been

---

246. *R.* v. *Baldwin and Another, ibid.,* May 11, 1830, no.14,233, p.3.
247. *Roper* v. *Phillips, ibid.,* April 21, 1830, no.14,206, pp.2-3.
248. *Doe, Ex. Dem. Grindall* v. *Stuart Grindall, ibid.,* April 21, 1830, no.14,206, pp.2-3.
249. *Ibid.,* April 23, 1830, no.14,208, p.3.

supplied by the Coventry Street jeweller. Scarlett blamed the prosecution upon the woman's imprudence, explaining that the attorney resisted payment out of fear that she would ruin him. While Tenterden ruled that a spouse was liable for payment of goods in keeping with the wife's estate and degree, he added: "Gentlemen, there is no proof that husband ever had possession of any of the plate, or even saw it, much less did he see the trinkets, which were never worn by the wife in his presence."[250] Brougham's summary of the evidence was so telling, however, that the jury did not require him to make a summing up. After a few minutes' deliberation, they awarded his client, the jeweller, the full amount, nearly 170 pounds.

Brougham enjoyed prosecuting an assault and false imprisonment case even more. During the Davies sanity hearing, one of the doctors for the prosecution was Dr. Burrows, one who had cut corners, and Brougham did later admit that he might have been unfairly treated during the hearing.[251] Dr Burrows overreacted to his critics, however, by having Freeman Anderdon, an eccentric, arrested as a lunatic without proper authorization. Dr Burrows signed a certificate for his arrest without seeing him, admitting that he had acted upon the information of others. The doctor, for acting contrary to the law, was fined 500 pounds. Brougham, because of his handling of insanity cases, was getting such a reputation that later in the year, when another doctor ran into trouble with the Metropolitan Commissioners of Lunacy for the same offence, he had the barrister represent him to mitigate damages.[252]

Brougham had also taken charge of handling the affairs of the University of London. The problem of its having no religious affiliation had broken down into squabbling between some of the professors and the Warden, Leonard Horner. Various professors had taken it upon themselves to give lectures pertaining to religion, often having them published. This practice resulted in

---

250. *Ibid.*
251. "The Late Commission on Mr Davies," *ibid.*, April 1, 1830, no.14,189, p.3.
252. *R.* v. *Jones, ibid.*, November 4, 1830, no.14,375, p.4.

Horner's trying to stop them, and soon the parties were exchanging letters in the press justifying themselves. At the February meeting of the proprietors to hear the Council's report, Brougham made it quite clear that the Council was handling the matter, and that it would not sanction administrative interference in academic freedom. When Alderman Fearon and Colonel Jones called for prohibition, Brougham answered: "On the principle of interference with the proceedings of the professors out of doors, he would beg to add, that as long as the council did not interfere, there could be no responsibility ..."[253] for termination. When the problem persisted, and Brougham could not attend another proprietors' meeting because he was delayed at the House to take the oath of allegiance to the new King, it was postponed until he could come. At the resumed meeting, he showed that he would not permit any meddling in his domain. When Althorp proposed an inquiry into the disputes between the Council, faculty, and Warden, Brougham would not hear of an independent inquiry of how the Council operated issuing this warning: "But they must not go on as they had done; they must have their hands strengthened; and be they who they might, who in future should attempt to trifle with them, he would tell them that in four and twenty hours they would be turned out of the institution. (Cheers.)"[254] While some of the proprietors complained of Brougham's imperious manner, he prevailed. There was no inquiry into the Council's Government of the University.

The Duke's Government had no such immunity in Parliament. Brougham had completely primed the Commons to defeat Lyndhurst's Chancery bills, culminating in this call in *The Times*: "... before a new Judge is appointed, in my opinion, a review of the law as administered in the Court of Chancery should take place."[255] Consequently, when Peel moved the second reading

253. "London University," *ibid.*, February 25, 1830, no.14,150, p.3.
254. *Ibid.*, July 5, 1830, no.14,270, p.3.
255. Quoted from Bell's "Thoughts on the proposed Alteration in the Court of Chancery" for added effect: "Court of Chancery," *ibid.*, June 21, 1830, no.14,258, p.3.

of Lyndhurst's bill, Robert Grant, the MP who had been so effective in delving to the bottom of the Arigna scandal, called for its postponement. The Home Secretary tried to persevere, citing what Brougham had said in favour of the appointment of another Vice-Chancellor. Brougham responded by saying that many things had happened since he had said that. For those who had not been reading Barnes's columns, he added: "There had been no changes in the essential part of the court, in what was the very stink of delay, the very storehouse of abuses."[256] Lyndhurst, he charged, apparently wanted another Judge so that he could do nothing but enjoy the privileges and powers of the Woolsack. Peel persisted in getting the order of the day calling for the Bill's second reading agreed to, prevailing by a narrow margin. Brougham then moved what Grant had wanted, and the House agreed. The Commons would consider Lyndhurst's bill on June 28, and Brougham got it to adjourn until then.

By the time the House reconvened, matters had drastically changed. George IV had died on June 26. During the debate on William IV's Message to Parliament, Peel announced arrangements about legislative requirements so that a new election could be held as soon as possible, which had ultra Tories suspecting that a deal had been struck with Brougham's Whigs. Lyndhurst's bills were dropped. Brougham was not prepared to support the Duke's Ministry any longer, however, Wellington, in his opinion, had only retained office because of King George's favour, and now that he was dead, the Duke's power was ended. Brougham had given a preview of his new aims in severely criticizing the Lord Steward, one of Wellington's cronies, for not informing the House immediately of the King's death.[257] In answer to Peel's proposal about what measures could be passed, Brougham retorted: "The day of force had gone by, and that he who would rule this country by royal favour, or by military power, might be hurled down from his height."[258] The ministers

---

256. *Ibid.*, June 26, 1830, no.14,263, p.2.
257. *Ibid.*, June 26, 1830, no.14,263, p.3.
258. *Ibid.*, June 28, 1830, no.14,264, p.2.

were merely the dead King's flatterers. Peel, understandably, could not believe his ears, but when Brougham persisted with charges about fawning parasites, the Home Secretary angrily denied it. "He had a perfect right to attack Ministers," Peel explained, "but he had no right to accuse them of being flatterers, who were as independent as he was. (Hear, hear.)"[259] When Brougham refused to retract anything, Peel apologized for what he, Brougham, had said. Brougham would only admit that he might have become a little hotter than usual.

While most people forgot about the incident, Brougham did not. He was deadly serious about the break, even if he was most insulting and unfair in explaining it. Wellington had not stayed in power because George IV supported him. He had remained in power because Brougham was willing to support him after the dismissal of the liberal Tories. Committed to Brougham's programme, Wellington had been able to convince the other Tories to go along with enough of what had to be done, especially the repeal of the Test and Corporation Acts, and Catholic Emancipation. The ultra Tories had been reduced to carping statements and futile efforts, such as trying to defeat court reform. If Brougham had not laboured with the Ministry, it would have collapsed. The King's favour was just a convenient myth by this time by which Brougham justified what he was doing. The Ministry could have been shown for what it was if it had chosen to continue before, denying liberal policies at home and abroad as circumstances dictated. Curiously, however, once Brougham made the challenge, Wellington's Government did everything it could to make the myth reality, and the Ministry did not have a monopoly on such practice, as we shall see. This phenomenon says much about what Brougham was capable of, both for good and ill. He was no ordinary politician.

In a pamphlet, not one Bentham had called for, Brougham portrayed the Ministry as the Duke's creature, totally unsuited for the country's needs. "The moment is one requiring all the resources of civil wisdom and experience in the acts of

---

259. *Ibid.*, July 1, 1830, no.14,267, p.3.

government; but it is, at the same time," Brougham wrote, with an eye on the growing constitutional crisis in France under Charles X, "one in which a familiarity with the Art of War is absolutely of no use."[260] Brougham, in explaining the failure of persons like himself to find a place in the Ministry, put equal emphasis upon the King's preferences, and those of ministerial flatterers. To remedy the situation, he added:

> ... if Mr Brougham, *in himself a mighty host*, were to unmask the battery which may now *at length* be supposed to be ready charged, and to await the slow, the very reluctant match - if *they* were to hold up the government and their measures to the wonder of the country, how could so baseless a fabric continue to exist even for a short period ...[261]

In unmasking the Ministry, Brougham called upon the new King and country to do their duty towards ministers who would assist repressive ministers like the Duke de Polignac in their policies. To give the greatest impact to these views, he harked back to the days before he had entered Parliament, giving a most approving review of his own pamphlet in the *Review*.[262]

The pamphlet had an electric effect upon the respectable people in England's unenfranchised towns, especially in the West Riding of Yorkshire where the sitting Members, Lord Milton and John Marshall, were not running again. The West Riding had been kept informed by Baines's *Leeds Mercury* of Brougham's battles with the judicial and parliamentary establishments. While Lord Morpeth was willing to stand, most likely candidates were unwilling to do so because of the costs of running in such a populous constituency. Brougham's candidacy was bruited, but rejected because he was not a Yorkshireman.[263] Finally, because

---

260. "The Country without a Government; or Plain Questions upon the Unhappy State of the Present Administration" (Ridgway, London, 1830), p.2.
261. *Ibid.*, pp.9-10. Italics his.
262. Art.XII, "The Ministry, and the State of Parties," *Edinburgh Review*, vol.51, no.CII, July 1830, pp.478-95.
263. "Yorkshire Election," *The Times*, July 21, 1830, no.14,284, p.3.

of the pamphlet and review, a committee in Leeds, headed by such stalwarts as Edward Baines, William Tottle, and George Rawson, invited Brougham to stand for the same seat. Leeds had been denied representation the previous February when the Commons threw out Lord John Russell's most modest reform measure despite Brougham's eloquence on its behalf.

In accepting the offer, Brougham said that he was running on a programme of commercial and parliamentary reform. His aims for the latter included enfranchising the big towns, and giving the vote to home occupiers. Because of these unprecedented aims Mittons wrote to Brougham to underline the unique character of his selection. Brougham moderated his opposition to the Ministry thus: "I feel great gratitude to some members of the present government for some measures which they have carried through."[264] The Duke's weak Administration had made Members such as himself more effective. The campaign was unusually short and easy for Brougham, with his continuing his appearances on the Northern Circuit up until almost the polling days. After a two-day poll in early August 1830, he was returned second behind Morpeth out of a field of five candidates, four seats being the complement for Yorkshire. With 1,295 votes, he trailed Morpeth by nearly 200 votes. Never had a candidate, who was neither from Yorkshire nor owned property in it, had an easier, cheaper time being returned. His success was confirmation of the role he had played at the recent Assizes, one which permitted people to establish their rights, and secure their interests despite the lack of political representation.

In the courtroom, Brougham was suffering unusual losses. It almost seemed as if he was choosing to be on the losing side of disputes for political effect. Before he left London, he defended a libel action against the *Liverpool Mercury*, making light of what had been printed, and complaining that it should have been heard at Liverpool. When he called no witnesses for the paper, it was fined 50 pounds. While he did win *Kirby* v. *May*, a recovery action for fraudulent concealment of a bankrupt's

264. *Ibid.*, July 30, 1830, no.14,292, p.3.

property, he saw the plaintiff awarded the full amount in another recovery action where attorneys, his clients, had not shown due care in investing the plaintiff's money in a mortgage.[265] At York, while the election was in progress but the disputes with the Northern Circuit's solicitors were still continuing, Brougham went a bit overboard in defending a damage suit against a surgeon who had not taken proper care of a person who had had an epileptic fit, attributing the evidence against him to professional jealousy. For this political licence in *Standcliffe* v. *Chorley and Another*, the jury awarded 150 pounds damages, heavy ones under the circumstances.

Once the votes had been registered in the election, Brougham went from triumph to triumph at Durham, Carlisle, and Lancaster. His most satisfying case must have been *R.* v. *Williamson* at Carlisle, an assault case he so successfully prosecuted that the defendant's attorney was so terrorized by his client's fist during the hearing that he took refuge under Brougham's silk gown and wig. His most sensitive prosecution was in a failure to marry case where he said this about the woman's plight: "She had arrived at that time of life which with females was a critical one, as they were not subsequently to meet with many offers of marriage, and her feelings had been greatly outraged."[266] The jury awarded his client 100 pounds in damage, and 40 shillings in costs. On the same day, Brougham obtained for another woman 300 pounds in damages after she explained to the jury how she had been seduced.[267] While a barrister cannot totally determine the verdicts in his cases, he can take hopeless cases to unexpected results when they serve his interests. Brougham had done just this before the Yorkshire election, but had not compromised his clients' rights in the process.

Whatever the country thought about Brougham's Yorkshire activities, Barnes was angered by them because he had turned

---

265. *Taylor* v. *Street and Others, ibid.*, July 24, 1830, no.14,287, p.3.
266. *Hall* v. *Grandy, ibid.*, August 30, 1830, no.14,318, p.6.
267. *Goodier* v. *Travis, ibid.*

against the Duke. At an election-day dinner for Brougham and Morpeth, the barrister became more candid about what he thought about the government: "Mr Brougham charged his Majesty's present Ministers, and particularly the Duke of Wellington, with wishing well to the Polignac Administration!"[268] *The Times* said, in no uncertain terms, that this was untrue, repeating Brougham's strange idea that if the Duke allowed Charles X political asylum, this validated his claim. Brougham was unaware of this attack, however, sending this message from Carlisle when he was unable to attend a dinner for the triumph of constitutional freedom in France at Free-masons' Tavern, London: "From the inroads of Royal prerogative there is now little to fear; especially if the representation of the people shall be established upon a more extensive foundation - the best security both for the liberty of the subject, and for the stability of the Throne."[269] Barnes was furious when he saw Brougham's review of his own pamphlet in the *Review*:

> ... it consists of the wailings of some disappointed suitor for place, whose occasional misgivings, between his mortification at defeat, and his not quite abandoned hope of possible promotion, give a whimpering vacillating tone to the composition, which excites at once our laughter and compassion.[270]

Brougham's remedy for the current malaise, a coalition of Whigs and ultra Tories, was dismissed as trash. "The whole article is a mere exposition of personal and party motives," Barnes concluded, "for why the present Ministry should be dismissed."[271]

Once Brougham learned of his newspaper patron's unprecedented ire, he wrote another pamphlet to justify himself.

---

268. *Ibid.*, August 17, 1830, no.14,307, p.2.
269. Letter dated August 16, 1830: printed in *ibid.*, August 19, 1830, no.14,309, p.3.
270. *Ibid.*, August 21, 1830, no.14,311, p.2.
271. *Ibid.*

The Duke of Wellington had just compounded his own difficulties, Brougham wrote, by the dissolution of Parliament. "Boundless indignation was displayed against Mr Brougham," he continued, "when he warned the government against counting upon this resource."[272] Instead of picking up nearly 100 favourable supporters, as the Duke's advisers had promised, they lost 20 seats despite claims to the contrary. "'So reckoned Prince Jules de Polignac,' said he, 'and where is he?'"[273] asked Brougham, quoting from his earlier pamphlet. After naming the new hostile Members in England and Ireland to the Ministry, and stating that returned Whigs and ultra Tories would be most disciplined in their opposition, he threw down the gauntlet to the Duke by discussing the significance of his own election: "For a Ministry to permit their most prominent adversary in the House of Commons to be thus elected, almost unanimously, by 1,200,000 people of all descriptions, must be allowed to be the very depth of discomfiture and disgrace."[274] One of the election's lessons was that the aristocracy had been taught its inability to control events. The Duke should have learned the dangers of supporting reactionary governments, and opposing popular government. "It is time for the Duke to foresee the coming tide which may lead on to fortune or utterly overwhelm him, according as he tries to ride or to stem it."[275] William IV, Brougham added, would be courting disaster if he gave his undivided support to a Ministry which carried on as if nothing had to be changed. Under the circumstances, the government would probably propose some form of limited parliamentary reform to retain favour. After a most critical examination of the capacities of individual ministers, Brougham concluded by calling upon the King to install "... a government which has some chance of being firm at home, and respected abroad!"[276]

Before Brougham could even publish a favourable review of

---

272. "The Result of the General Election, etc," (Brettell, London, 1830), p.6.
273. *Ibid.*
274. *Ibid.*, pp.20-1.
275. *Ibid.*, p.28.
276. *Ibid.*, p.38.

the pamphlet in the *Review*,[277] Barnes let *Times* readers know what he thought of it. In a long article, he disputed Brougham's analysis of the overall change in Parliament's political complexion. For all the seats that could be shown to have fallen into the hands of the Opposition, there were other seats which could be shown to have gone the other way. "The lesson to be drawn from it," Barnes complained about the pamphlet, "and other Whig elections, both by the people and by Ministers, are put with edifying malice."[278] Brougham was even wrong about how parliamentary majorities were obtained when the parties were divided, and poorly disciplined: "Is it not quite unfair to demand of such a reasoner, whether he has always valued a motion in Parliament by the majority which supported or opposed it?"[279]

Brougham just redoubled his attack in the face of such criticism, especially when it seemed that Tories who had helped his candidacy in Yorkshire were beginning to have second thoughts. At a dinner for the Members at Sheffield, Brougham indicated that he was not satisfied to go along with Morpeth's liberal principles, possibly supporting the Duke's Government, as *The Times* duly reported: "He entered into a long and eloquent speech, in which he advocated the cause of Parliamentary reform, and passed some high encomiums on the conduct of ancient families of the county in the revolution of 1688, and from that period to the present."[280] At another dinner at Leeds, the seat of his successful candidacy, he repeated what the election meant: "... it was to that town in particular that the country was indebted for the practical reformation of Parliament which Yorkshire had accomplished without asking the leave of the House of Commons."[281] About Brougham's mandate, he said that "... he

---

277. Art.XIII, "The General Election and the Ministry," *Edinburgh Review*, vol.52, no.CIII, October 1830, pp.261-79.
278. *The Times*, September 23, 1830, no.14,339, p.2.
279. *Ibid.*
280. "Dinner to Mr Brougham and Lord Morpeth at Sheffield," *ibid.*, September 30, 1830, no.14,346, p.3.
281. "Public Dinner at Leeds," *ibid.*, October 1, 1830, no.14,347, p.3.

would leave in no other man's hands the great cause of Parliamentary reform."[282] His programme, calling for enfranchising the new cities, ending absentee voting, and breaking up Scotland's nomination system, was elaborated upon. Macaulay had encouraged Brougham in these efforts.

The Ministry, encouraged by *The Times's* continuing hostility to Brougham's programme,[283] decided to challenge him by stirring up fears of rebellion just before the next Session. To show its disdain for public opinion, it cancelled the King's traditional visit to the City on Lord Mayor's Day on the grounds of national security. While the revolutionary spirit had spread to Belgium, and agricultural unrest was appearing in Kent, the Duke's Government decided to adopt a most reactionary stance in the Speech from the Throne. There was nothing in it about parliamentary reform, only putting down sedition was stressed, and the government was most supportive of Holland in suppressing the Belgium uprising. When Lord Grey, the Whig Leader, questioned Wellington about the former, the Prime Minister dismissed the subject, stating that parliamentary representation was near perfect. The Duke's hyperbole had obviously been conditioned by who the Whig Leader in the Lords was, just the person whom Brougham had made such a point of in his pamphlets as being the politician the new King would not only consult but also make a minister out of concern for Brougham's mandate. Wellington decided to close the door on such political options.

In the Commons, Brougham proved him wrong. Once the House had reconvened, and the Speaker had resumed the Chair, after the second reading of the Clandestine Outlawry Bill, Brougham told Members what had to be redressed before Parliament would deal with the King's requirements. Brougham's plan for parliamentary reform, he explained, had been confused by rumour and distortion, an allusion to what *The Times* had

---

282. *Ibid.*
283. *Ibid.*, October 15, 1830, no.14,358, p.2.

assisted.[284] "His proposition would be founded in the sacred principle of rational public freedom, as established by our ancestors, - he was not for revolution, but restoration; and it was his object to repair, not to pull down, the temple of the constitution. (Cheers.)"[285]

Members would be consulted during the next two weeks so that a plan with the widest support could be worked out. Once Lord Trimston moved the House's Answer to the Speech, and debate on it ensued, Brougham spoke, explaining that the Ministry's proposals were totally unacceptable, especially its policy towards Belgium.

While the Answer was approved, the first critical votes concerned the civil list, the bellwether Brougham had identified in his latest pamphlet, of how the Ministry would fare.[286] Sir Henry Parnell had given notice of moving an inquiry into the matter. Brougham said the question was of great importance to the monarchy, "... and he hailed with satisfaction the notice that had been given of a determination to take the sense of the House of Commons, as to the propriety; of adopting the moderate course of referring the question of the civil list to the consideration of a select committee. (Hear, hear.)"[287] He had prepared for the showdown by waiting on the Lord Major, Aldermen and Commons of the City a few days before, a challenge of momentous proportions to the Crown. On November 15, the first motion came on, and it carried without one word of dispute between Peel and Brougham over its necessity. Parnell's amendment for an inquiry then passed by 29 votes. Brougham had indicated that he was going to continue moving amendments to the Ministry's proposals on the civil list until the inquiry was agreed to. In fact, the House was acting with such speed that he was not prepared for the immediate naming of the committee, but he bowed in the face of overwhelming pressure. Brougham postponed his motion on parliamentary reform, which he thought

284. See esp., "To Henry Brougham, Esq, MP," *ibid.*, October 23, 1830, no.14,366, p.3.

285. *Ibid.*, November 3, 1830, no.14,374, p.4.

286. "The Result ...," *op. cit.*, pp.31-2.

287. *The Times*, November 13, 1830, no.14,383, p.2.

represented the final showdown with the government, until the 25th, but it proved unnecessary. The Duke's Ministry resigned in the face of certain defeat.

The King asked Grey to form a government, something even Barnes said was inevitable, once the Duke came down against reform. While Brougham would have liked to have been the Master of the Rolls, retaining his seat in the Commons, the idea was impossible on several grounds. The only other position that Brougham bruited he wanted was the Woolsack, the post the abused Lyndhurst tried to keep, with *The Times*'s encouragement. Once Grey had persuaded the Chancellor to retire, Brougham was offered the Great Seal, and he accepted it ultimately because of advice that many people offered that only he could hold it. Bentham, of all people, even became enthusiastic over the prospect of Brougham on the Woolsack. If he had not taken office, others said, there would have been no Reform Government. He had become the kingdom's leading subject. On November 22, Brougham first appeared in the Lords as Lord Chancellor. About the appointment, a smitten Barnes wrote:

> The new Lord Chancellor stands more peculiarly bound before the world, not only to Parliamentary reform, but to execute on a broad and mighty scale, a plan of reform in the jurisprudence of the empire, of which, when he shall overcome the difficulty, we shall be the first to ascribe to him the full and abundant honour. But the first and last subject of solicitude for the new Ministers must be, that they accede to office by *capitulation* with the people - they *must redress our grievances*, or be forever ruined.[288]

The next day, after hearing appeals to the Lords, he was raised to the peerage as Baron Brougham and Vaux, entering a new world of power and responsibility, thus completing a volume of his life.

---

288. *Ibid.*, November 22, 1830, no.14,390, p.2. Italics his.

INDEX